THE WHISTLER
AT THE PLOUGH

Alexander Somerville

Edited with an Introduction by
K.D.M.Snell

LONDON
THE MERLIN PRESS

AUGUSTUS KELLEY
FAIRFIELD N.J. USA

This book was first published in 1852
by James Ainsworth
Reprinted in 1989 by
The Merlin Press Ltd.,
10 Malden Road
London NW5 3HR
England
and Augustus Kelley Inc
300 Fairfield Road,
Fairfield NJ 07006
Introduction © K.D.M.Snell 1989
Printed in England by
Antony Rowe Ltd.,
Bumpers Farm
Chippenham, Wilts.
Merlin Press ISBN 085036 384 5
Augustus Kelley ISBN 0 678 0808 2

British Library Cataloguing in Publication Data
Somerville, Alexander, 1811 – 1885
  The whistler at the plough.
1. Great Britain. Rural regions. Poor persons. Social
  conditions, history
  I. Title   II. Snell, K.D.M. (Keith D M)
  305.5'69'0941

  ISBN 0-85036-304-5

    Library of Congress Cataloging-in-Publication Data
Somerville, Alexander, 1811 – 1885.
  [Whistler at the plough. Selections]
  The whistler at the plough: containing travels, statistics, and
descriptions of scenery and agricultural customs in most parts of
England/Alexander Somerville: edited with an introduction by
K.D.M. Snell.
  p.   cm.
  Reprint. Originally published: Manchester: J. Ainsworth, 1852
– "Letters from Ireland and Free trade and the League, a
biographic history, are not included in this reprint edition" –
T. p. verso.
  Includes bibliographical references.
  ISBN 0-678-08082-8
  1. Great Britain—Rural conditions.   I. Snell, K. D. M.
II. Title.
HN385.S72725   1989
307.72'0941 — dc20   89-15532

INTRODUCTION

K.D.M. Snell

ALEXANDER SOMERVILLE, subsequently known as "The Whistler at the Plough", was born in 1811, the eleventh child of a family living in a one-roomed, tiled hovel in Oldhamstocks, East Lothian. The hovel was windowless, except for a single pane of glass, owned and treasured by his farm labouring father, who moved it with him every time he changed his residence. His father was born in Nether-aichlin-Sky, Perthshire, and his mother came from Ayton in Berwickshire — both were from very poor labouring familes. Alexander himself worked in his youth as a farm helper, ploughboy, sawyer, limekiln labourer, stone breaker, sheep shearer, itinerant harvester, drainer, quarryman, and dock labourer. This was not the most usual or auspicious start to the career of a "man of letters" — a man whose voluminous writings included the forceful, deeply humane and imaginative *The Whistler at the Plough*, here reprinted for the first time since its original publication in 1852.

He was also the author of one of the most readable of nineteenth-century working-class autobiographies, *The Autobiography of a Working Man* (1848).[1] In this he gives some account of his childhood. "I came into the family at a time when I could have been very well spared," he wrote, referring to the famine prices of 1811–13 and the poverty in which he grew up. His mother engaged in heavy agricultural work. His schooling had to be delayed because his parents could not find adequate clothing for him, other than the rags he normally wore. He was accordingly mistreated by the other children at school, many of them from a "better" background than himself, on account of his raggedness.

His introduction to history — he was to write a history of the British Legion and the 1835–7 war in Spain, and a history of free trade and the Anti-Corn Law League[2] — began when he befriended an old blind shepherd, who held imaginary conversations with Elizabethan courtiers. At a young age he began his miscellany of employments in agriculture and other labouring work, the experience of which probably contributed much to the empathy and sympathy for the labouring poor manifest in his agricultural writings later. The early pages of his *Autobiography* are indeed an excellent source for working conditions in this region of Scotland at the time. On harvest migration, he wrote that "To us who went from Lothian to the Merse, the higher wages was always the ruling cause of our migration, and no amount of work . . . deterred us."[3]

But it was a hard time for men of his class, with many facing unemployment, and much political agitation on the part of those who felt that political reform might enhance their miserable living standards. He seems himself to have joined in some of the activity in Edinburgh in support of reform. Many entered the army as an alternative. Somerville, after failing to find employment as a librarian (he was considered socially too inferior for such a job), and being unsuccessful in trying to attract subscriptions for a newspaper, himself joined the Scots Greys.

In doing this, he set in train the tragic and brutal course of events which made him celebrated among the public, and which was to have a major influence on his later development. The harrowing story is told in considerable detail in his *Autobiography*. He first served in Brighton, and was then marched to Birmingham, through the rural areas affected by the "Captain Swing" unrest of 1830–1.[4] Birmingham at this time was regarded as a danger to the political establishment, a hotbed of radical reformist ideas, one of the main venues for Reform riots, on the eve of the Reform Act. The Scots Greys were ordered to sharpen their swords in preparation to deal with potential trouble. It was of course only a decade or so since the Peterloo Massacre.

Somerville wrote a letter to the editor of the *Weekly Dispatch*, saying that while the Scots Greys could be relied upon to put down disorderly conduct which threatened property, they should never be ordered to lift up arms against the liberties of the country and peaceful demonstrations of the people.[5] The inexperienced officer in charge, Major Wyndham, saw fit to take this as a libel on the regiment. Accordingly, Somerville was then charged at an informal and very hastily convened "court martial" with a trumped up offence regarding his reluctance to ride an impossibly refractory horse. He was sentenced to a military flogging of two hundred lashes. He refused to grovel before Major Wyndham in the anticipated manner, refused to accept rum from the other soldiers before the flogging, and bore the flogging in silence in front of the regiment on parade. The relentlessly detailed pages which tell of it in the *Autobiography* provide one of the most harrowing episodes in nineteenth-century literature, an enduring castigation of the army at this time. "I put my tongue between my teeth, held it there. and bit it almost in two pieces. What with the blood from my tongue, and my lips, which I had also bitten, and the blood from my lungs, or some other internal part ruptured by the writhing agony, I was almost choked, and became black in the face ... Only fifty had been inflicted, and the time since they began was like a long period of life: I felt as if I had lived all the time of my real life in pain and torture, and that the time when existence had pleasure in it was a dream, long, long gone by."[6] Finally, after a hundred lashes, he was taken down in case he died—and in the hospital afterwards said, "This shall be heard of, yet; I shall make it as public over England as newspapers can make it."[7]

His case became front-page news, discussed in Parliament, referred to the King; the incident was officially investigated by a Court of Enquiry, the regiment's officers execrated whenever they appeared in public by indignant crowds. There were a number of large popular demonstrations against flogging in the army.[8] The rural labouring population were apparently as sympathetic to his case as were workers in the towns, indicating the extent to which the countryside was politicised.[9] Major Wyndham received an official reprimand, authorised by the King. Somerville became the hero of the reform movement, used for political ends, in many cases against his inclinations. He was indeed embarrassed by the journalistic licence of some papers discussing the affair, which contributed to turn his name into a popular slogan with which he felt unable to identify. A public subscription was started for him, and he met and was befriended by William Cobbett, who also had considerable experience of the army, and who had made his voice heard against military flogging. Cobbett offered him advice on a future career as a writer. Somerville was able now, in August 1832, to purchase his release from the army, and he returned to Scotland, where he went back to work as a wood sawyer in Edinburgh. His efforts to start a paper and then a shop were unsuccessful. So he joined the so-called "British Legion," serving with it in Spain for two years, engaged in the very grim warfare of 1835–7 on behalf of Queen Isabella against her uncle, Don Carlos. He received special commendations and was promoted to lieutenant, before being invalided out in 1837 with a bullet in his arm which he carried with him to the grave.

His politics over this period were certainly not of the more radical kind, and it is evident that he became increasingly "conservative" during his life; although his "conservatism" was of an idiosyncratic, deeply humane and economically liberal sort, informed also by his Scottish covenanting background. In the 1830s he supported the Tolpuddle Martyrs, but berated trade union leaders for seizing on the Martyrs' cause in an opportunistic way, which did not adequately recognise the plight of the persecuted individuals involved. He condemned anti-combination laws, but criticised restrictions on entry practised by trade unions, via apprenticeship, and the unions' secrecy. In 1837 he published his *Narrative of the British Legion in Spain*, an account of his military experience of the Spanish Civil War of 1835–7.

This was followed two years later by his *Warnings to the People*

on Street Warfare, a series of penny pamphlets, attacking the
"instructions" issued by the revolutionary Colonel Francis Maceroni to the people regarding street warfare, in which Somerville
argued for the futility of using violence in England to achieve
political ends.[10] Somerville had returned in the autumn of 1837
with first-hand experience of the savagery of war in Spain; and he
was soon introduced to two members of a Chartist "Secret
Committee of War," as an experienced soldier "who could give a
practical opinion of the feasibility of their intended insurrection".
He told the secret committee that he had seen, besides the
horrors of bloodshed and death in battle, "fertile fields trodden
under the hoofs and wheels of the artillery . . . vines cut down . . .
the houses of rich and poor . . . of political and non-political
inhabitants, battered to atoms."[11] In particular, he attacked the
"absurd . . . dangerous, warlike notions" of the Chartist Peter
McDouall, pointing out that British troops were unlikely to go
over to the side of the crowds, unlike continental soldiers.[12] His
Warnings to the People on Street Warfare were felt by many to
have contributed to avert a rising in the summer of 1839.[13] He
spoke to similar effect, in his *Public and Personal Affairs*, of how
"the agitation in the manufacturing districts is high enough for
immediate action, and from a too well grounded discontent—
but that agitation is not yet national, nor from the mingled
indifference and opposition of the middle classes will it soon
become general—therefore an armed movement must be defeated."[14] He was solicited to join in the "Welsh insurrection of
1839," the Newport Rising, but refused to support it or become
involved.[15] He also wrote critically of the Chartist Land Plan in
the *Manchester Examiner*—so much so, in fact, that two historians have since referred to him as "the vitriolic anti-Land Plan
propagandist."[16]

It is for the part Somerville played in the troubles of these years
that he has been remembered, mainly by historians concerned
with the history of the Chartist movement, who have also found
his autobiographical account of Chartism valuable. In 1849
Cobden even suggested in a letter to Bright that Somerville would
be the ideal person to write a "temperate and truthful" history of
Chartism.[17] But it is arguable that his most enduring literary work
was to commence with the writing he thenceforth engaged in as a
rural commentator and journalist: devoting himself largely to
social and economic topics and their political ramifications,
writing for the *Morning Chronicle* and the *Manchester
Examiner*, with a particular sympathy for the issue of Corn Law
reform and the work of the Anti-Corn Law League. *The Whistler
at the Plough*, his *Letters from Ireland During the Famine of
1847*,[18] and his *Free Trade and the League* were written at this

time, when his public influence was undoubtedly at its height.

A meeting with Richard Cobden, following some letters he had published in the *Morning Chronicle* in 1842 on the corn laws, led to his being supported by the Anti-Corn Law League to travel in the country districts to report on rural sentiments, material standards, and all possible rural effects of corn law repeal.[19] Known to the League organisers as a rather difficult character they called "Reuben," whose occasional drinking bouts they tolerated because of his excellent writing,[20] he published his many letters on different regions under the authorship of "One who has Whistled at the Plough." His views were widely discussed at the time. His tours continued throughout 1842–7, and he also toured Ireland, reporting on conditions there in 1847, the worst year of the tragic famine. That famine, appearing in Ireland with the potato blight of 1845, was to have a decisive influence upon corn-law repeal. "For the attainment of the facts involved" in agriculture and the effects of protection laws, he tells us, "I travelled over many thousands of miles of the rural districts."[21] He sometimes seems to have taken his wife with him, although we know little of her. *The Whistler at the Plough* was his own selection from the total letters written. "My purpose is to present a kind of moving view of the country, at the same time that a record . . . will be made of that process of education which Mr. Cobden and his coadjutors applied to the 'agricultural mind.'"[22] His journeys discussed here began on 25 August, 1842, in Buckinghamshire.

Landlord and farmer sentiment in 1842 was very supportive of corn-law protectionism—they had lived with it for so long—and Somerville was aware that he would have a considerable task persuading these two rural classes (particularly the landlords) that free trade could be in their interests.[23] He would have much less difficulty with the rural labouring class—there was after all a long rural tradition of food "riots" against high prices,[24] labourers' diets were heavily bread-based, and it is clear that the labouring poor generally opposed the corn laws.[25] However, at this time they lacked the vote, and in that sense at least were politically irrelevant.[26] He tells us that "I resolved to write . . . in a manner that would not at first sight let the main purpose be seen. The design was to keep the 'ridiculous' doctrine [free trade] out of sight until I had got some hold upon the public; and, to get that hold, it seemed that the best style of writing would be one which eschewed the didactic and the still less welcome array of dry figures, which in newspapers had hitherto made agricultural politics an uninteresting subject, and to take up a style of narrative and description."[27] The result, while perhaps exaggerating the significance of the corn laws,[28] was a remarkable and often moving account of rural life and conditions, which remains highly readable today.

The obvious comparisons to Somerville are William Cobbett's *Rural Rides*, or the rural tours of Arthur Young. *The Whistler at the Plough* certainly deserves to rank alongside these, and it is remarkable that agricultural historians have overlooked it for so long.[29] Probably this is because Somerville's views were so sympathetic to the rural labouring classes and to many of the smaller farmers, and often critical of what he recognised as the manifest incompetence, greed or wastefulness of a largely parasitic landlord class.[30] Certainly, Somerville had a political stance and a set of economic proposals which he wished to communicate; but then so too had Cobbett and Young, like all other commentators on eighteenth- and nineteenth-century rural affairs. In Somerville's case, he took care to declare honestly his political position from the start; his journalistic skill, his literary and descriptive imagination, and his sympathy for rural subjects produced a book which is much more than a pastoral treatise for the Anti-Corn Law League, a book indeed which contains very many passages which have little to do with anti-corn law argument.[31] Although he went well beyond this, his main aim was to discuss all rural features of corn-law repeal: the effects of corn laws on agricultural profitability, manufactures, and commerce, and "their effect on morality and religion, or, in other words . . . their effect on the domestic comforts of the working classes, on which comforts a sound practical morality and a due respect for religion so much depend."[32] But, as he put it: "I am not burdened with the task of proving one thing or another in respect of the corn-law and the landowners."[33] He was far too independently minded (as his previous career had often indicated) to allow his writing to be narrowly circumscribed by an immediate political programme dictated by the economic interests of Manchester, despite his sympathy with that cause.[34]

Somerville valuably discusses so many different features of rural life that it is impossible to do justice to the range of his writing here. Perhaps one of the most instructive lessons of the book is his account of social relationships in the country. It was obvious to him that the countryside was a place divided by social tension, in some regions of a particularly bitter kind.[35] There were many reasons for this: enclosure, the decline of "living-in" farm service, the New Poor Law,[36] unemployment, low wages, the game laws, the corn laws themselves, restrictions on allotments, atrocious cottages, landlord "mismanagement of land,"[37] the types of farm leases insisted upon by landlords, the efforts of landlords politically to subjugate their tenants, the destruction of crops and general disruption caused by fox-hunting,[38] among many other such considerations. "The farmers", he wrote, "do not trust [the landlords] and they never will,"[39] a theme to which he returned many times, particularly in his arguments for better leases, and more independence and security for tenants.

Nor was there simply tension between landlord and farmer. At the level of the labouring poor themselves – the vast majority of village populations—the matter was much more serious, particularly in the southern and Midland counties of England:

"All the elements that make up the relationship, the mutual dependence of workman and master" have gone, he wrote. And so one has a "hand-to-mouth, turbulent, unmanageable, unserviceable population as that now swarming in the south of England" . . . "We have a population who would burn the houses, haystacks, and barns of any farmer who dared to erect a thrashing machine[40]—a population which, as it is, whether because they are ignorant, and irreligious, and immoral, or whether, in spite of being as intelligent, religious, and moral as the churches which crowd upon our eyes would indicate them to be, light the incendiary fires, taking awful vengeance on men of property, for wrongs real or fancied. We have those people always under-fed, even if always employed. We have many of them partly or wholly unemployed, seeking subsistence as paupers, or as poachers and thieves . . . they look on . . . the men who sentence them, the men of haystacks, and stables, and barns, the guardians and justices, as their natural enemies, on whose property they may make war, on whose haystacks, and stables, and barnfuls of grain, they do make war—fearful, savage, wasteful war."[41]

Somerville turns time and again to investigate why agriculture and its workers were in such a critical state. He interviewed at length farm labourers and the poor, and reported in depth their sentiments, trying to locate the reasons for class unrest in the more general underlying structural problems of English and Irish agriculture. In so doing he pointed his finger above all at the Corn Laws, and at what he saw as the corollaries of landlord political dominance and agricultural protectionism. These included laxity of cultivation; short, yearly farm tenancies which militated against improvements being made in agriculture or in cottage provision,[42] which stood in the way of steady employment and contentment for the labourers, and which had also contributed to undercut the earlier institution of yearly hiring contracts, so aggravating class tension;[43] prices that were artificially inflated, to the detriment of rural real wages and demand for rural products from the industrial sector,[44] in turn adversely affecting agricultural investment and production; a landlord class so accustomed to protection that they squandered their rents in idleness and destructive leisure pursuits, contrary to the more careful practice in industrial areas, and contrary to the economic needs of the nation. British landlords have received more than their fare share of praise from the conservative historians who have mainly been predisposed to appraise them, and Somerville's verdicts will enable a more balanced and less flattering assessment to be arrived at.[45]

In order to rebuff political attacks by many gentry on urban entrepreneurs, Somerville found it "necessary to shew that hunger and crime are not exclusively town-bred."[46] It was no coincidence that he started his tours by heading for Lord Shaftesbury's estate in Dorset, where he found even this famous factory reformer's land rife with social evils.[47] Landlords, he wrote, in discussing the enclosure movement, "have always proceeded on the principle of teaching our rural population to respect property by taking all property from them".[48] He complained frequently both in England and Ireland of "the political subjugation of the tenantry", and the effects this was having on agriculture. "Thus, because the miserable satisfaction of compelling a tenant to vote for a particular party is an object with landlords, sloth lies on the fair fields of England and hunger wails on her city streets", he wrote, with slight exaggeration.[49] And he was scathing in his discussion of some estates, like for example that of the Duke of Marlborough: "worse farming, poorer farmers, and poorer labourers are not to be found within the British shores than on the Duke's property. The estate is one vast wreck; and political thraldom has rendered more feeble those heads and hands that were always weak."[50] The Earl of Abingdon, like many other landlords, had done all he could to have the poor ejected from his estate.[51]

Landlords' carefully preserved game was badly spoiling crops grown by farmers, and to them this was more demoralising even than tithes.[52] "It is, in short, enough to break the heart of any man whose heart is not cast iron, to see his crops destroyed by vermin bred there, and preserved for the pleasure of some one who bears no part of the expense."[53] Unlike urban entrepreneurs, the rural aristocracy used their property for pleasure, to finance hunting, gambling and the like, and were readily inclined to spoil crops in pursuit of this pleasure—in pursuit of what Somerville calls the "great days of killing, wounding, and unwinging".[54] Somerville comments on how remarkable it would be if urban entrepreneurs and factory owners wasted their own profits and despoiled their own property in this way.[55] As to estate villages—that is, "some pet village near a nobleman's park or in the park itself"—the conditions appeared to be better, but cottages were often only planned with a view to outward ornamentation of the wealthy man's residence. "We very frequently find such ornamental

cottages and lodges at park gates as destitute of comfort as the
hovel on the farm; mere ornament being everything, the comfort
of the indwellers nothing."[56]

With regard to Protestant landlords in Ireland, Somerville was
particularly outspoken, and with good cause. The small tenantry
"have no security of tenure, and sad experience tells them that to
enrich the soil is to invite an ejectment. Many of them . . . have
leases, but even a lease in Ireland is no security. A landlord has
only to make a profession of a wish to exchange a Catholic
tenantry for Protestants, and, under cover of such a pretence, he
may commit, *and does in this very year*, 1843 *commit* the most
damnable and detestable robberies."[57] The tenants were very
suspicious of agricultural innovation, because "they have invari-
able seen, that such doctrines, and specimens, and injunctions to
improve, were only preparatory to their being sacrificed and their
land seized. And in a country almost devoid of trade and
manufactures, to be turned out of a holding of land is a calamity
on a family like a death stroke."[58]

The very adverse conditions of southern and Midland England,
let alone Ireland, were not found to the same extent in some other
areas. Despite the poverty his family had experienced, Somerville
compared his own childhood region of the East Lothians favourably with the situation found in so many English counties.[59] He
was always alive to regional differences, in the economic nature
and aesthetic features of the landscape, and in the way agriculture, working conditions and social relationships varied. One
receives a very clear sense of how country life in, say, Dorset, or
Berkshire, differed from that in the East Lothians, or around
Manchester, or in the varied parts of Ireland he described.

His book is invaluable for the comparisons it makes of Scottish
and English rural conditions. The East Lothian labourers, he tells
us, are generally yearly hired, more steady and dependable than
those in England. Their masters had long leases, and encouraged
them to remain with him. The "hind" (a married Scottish
ploughman) is "invariably a steady man, not very bright in
intellect it may be, not very well informed, not much interested in
the passing affairs of the day, unless on some topic of religious
controversy; but you will find him zealously devoted to his
master's interests, and always ready to work, that is, when his
hours of working arrive. He is ever ready when called on, *because
he is not called on but at stated and scrupulously observed
hours*. But look at the south of England labourer. Either he must
be starved to compel him to work, or be bribed by beer or some
temporary stimulant to induce him to work. *He is only ready for
his master when it suits himself, because his master deals with
him on the same principle. He is hired one day and paid off the*

next, or at most his term is for a week. Thus paid, with a little loose money, and much loose time, he meets others like himself, who spend their money, and, without work or food, betake themselves to poaching and thieving."[60] The reasons for this difference lay in the different agricultural systems of the two regions. Somerville believed that Scottish labourers in the south of England would act in the same way as the English, accustomed as the latter were to "the vice, the ignorance, the idleness, the hostility to the rich . . . with the addition of irritated prejudices, withering hunger—in many cases cruel persecution—to perpetuate their degradation; for these vices are monsters that generate and feed on each other. The landowner must amend his own system if he would amend the condition of the labouring poor."[61] The frequently more advanced condition of Scottish agriculture, despite the often comparatively adverse natural conditions, was he thought owing to the longer leases enjoyed by its farmers, the ease of bank loans, the absence of tithes and poor laws, the stimulus of recent poverty, and a considerable improvement in technology and implements which "have left England far behind."[62] And this is not just Somerville speaking with pride in his native Scotland—there is very little sign of that. He is quite ready to criticise much about his native country, like its education: "a meagre affair . . . greatly over-rated."[63] These are level-headed comparisons, borne out by other commentators, which can be taken very seriously as historical documentation.

Some of the most remarkable features of Somerville's literary style are his versatility, the way in which poetic vision and pastoral embellishment are juxtaposed against harsh realism to considerable effect, his imaginative use of different literary devices to persuade his readers, and the persistent humanity and empathy of his sentiments.[64] He had an excellent eye for symbolic example, and could turn folktales and moral stories to good purpose to make a point.[65] His variety of literary method is striking. Many of his chapters were written in quite different forms. His poetic sensibility is well illustrated in his description of winter and then the arrival of May, and passages of this sort remind one of Richard Jefferies.[66] Unlike Arthur Young, William Marshall, or the other agricultural "improving" writers of an earlier generation, his style was never simply unremittingly descriptive, economical and prescriptive, dealing just with the dry facts of farming practice, how it could be altered to enhance profit and rent, perhaps varied only by passing mention of the works of art accumulated by the landed aristocracy.[67] There are certainly many agriculturally descriptive passages in Somerville, as when he describes the way in which manure is applied in

Berkshire[68]—but his text goes far beyond such discussion, fascinating though it will be to some agricultural historians. No doubt it was partly owing to his Scottish background, to the influence of Robert Burns, to his being of the generation which read Sir Walter Scott and experienced the early nineteenth-century interest in folklore and antiquities, that he is so alive to local history and legends in each area, in a way one will seldom find in Young or Marshall, or for that matter Cobbett. There are many topographically descriptive passages here dwelling on the romantic and historical associations of places. Frequently one discovers that Somerville has read intensively about a region and its history before visiting it. He discusses the meaning of local names, like "Buckingham"; he knows the local aristocratic seats in the area and the politics associated with them;[69] he recalls local poets and writers; he brings his own apposite interpretation of poems like the "Castle of Indolence" to bear in his discussion.[70] And throughout, he is far more inclined to comment comparatively, at the European as well as British level, and to be imaginative and open-minded about the possibilities of alternative agricultural systems, than were most other rural commentators.[71]

For the social historian of the countryside, his lengthy and frequent use of verbatim oral evidence is especially remarkable and valuable. Again, perhaps it was the influence of novels like Scott's *Waverley*, combined with the influence of the verbatim question-answer form of the Parliamentary Blue Books, and the developing style of journalistic realism, which underlay Somerville's emphasis on oral testimony. As a source oral testimony has come to be increasingly appreciated by historians. Unlike many other commentators and some historians. Somerville is careful to allow the labouring poor and farmers to speak for themselves. One will not find in his writing the tendency to impose certain unlikely and stereotyped views onto the people being discussed. The bovine, comic and stupid figure of "Hodge," so hamfistedly depicted by many other rural writers, never appears in Somerville's pages. Instead, the poorer rural inhabitants, the large majority of country dwellers, emerge in their own words as sensitive individuals with views of their own, with strong feelings which deserve expression, as far as possible in their own dialect. Somerville's interviews with rural labourers are classic examples of this: highly detailed, localised, replete with colloquial expressions[72]—always alive to the social ill-feeling he encountered and the many reasons for it, and not pre-disposed to cover it with a pastoral gloss.[73] There are few counterparts in nineteenth-century rural literature to the close-to-the-earth vivid empathy of Somerville's accounts of the labourer, and (leaving aside the different genre of the agricultural autobiographies), none by farm (or ex-farm) workers themselves.

This empathy comes across most strongly in his discussion of the New Poor Law. I have argued elsewhere for the deleterious effect which this law had on the quality of rural class relations, between the labouring poor and the farmer and landlord classes, and one need only read Somerville for the point to be driven home.[74] Here, Somerville is sufficiently certain that his views stand for those of the poor to dispense with oral testimony:

"It has always seemed to me a grievous error in the national economy to shut people within workhouse walls because they sought employment and could not get it . . . a grievous error in moral economy[75] to think of making the idle industrious by shutting them up where they have no useful thing to do, and where they can learn, and feel, and understand nothing but how to hate their fellow-men . . . To me it has seemed cruel, terribly cruel, to take the aged and infirm from the cottages they have laboured to keep above their heads, and which they have sanctified with their affections, and shut them up in the work-house, drilling them in their old days under the discipline of a barrack-yard, conducted by some non-commissioned officer of the army, whose fitness for keeping the workhouse in order is estimated by his success on the drill-ground and in the barrack-yard over a long period of years . . . terribly cruel to break up 'the old house at home' of an old couple whose eyes see 'home' written in every corner of it, in every crevice of the walls, whose affections rest upon the old stools where their young babies sat, on the old table where many a scanty, yet many a happy frugal meal was eaten; to part them from all and from each other, and drill them in their old days into military habits, under military men, as if they were young recruits! The impolicy of shutting up the able-bodied who cannot get work outside, compelling them to do worthless, profitless, filthy work inside, merely to punish them, is only surpassed in enormity by this cruel treatment of the aged and infirm, whose helplessness only compels them to submit. All others leave the workhouse walls as soon as they can. *They* only leave to go to their graves. And to put the deeper shame on age and poverty, most workhouses present them with graves within the walls, as prisons do to the most felonious of criminals. All, save the aged and infirm, and the incapable of acting for themselves, can escape and do escape, from the stupid punishment of the workhouses. They escape to kill game, steal sheep, rob hen-roosts—to do anything, to take any chance, rather than be punished in the workhouse for seeking parish relief . . . But the old, the venerable fathers and mothers of the villages, cannot escape save into their graves; and, that even the hope of the grave

may not be too comfortable to them in the imprisonment of their
old age, they have the certainty placed before them that since they
are such vile creatures as to be old and poor, they will not be
buried in the old church-yard with their kindred, but will be
consigned to pauper's ground.

Say the best that can be said for the workhouse system, and
even then there is a frightful balance of ignorance of human
nature, irrational efforts to reform the idly disposed, and of cruel
irreverence for the holiest affections of mankind left in it . . .
Strange that in an age that boastfully calls itself the nineteenth
century . . . and in this country called England a systematic code
of punishment for the aged, the infirm, and the unfortunate
should for the first time in the world's history be adopted and
rigorously applied . . . Strange that men, foremost in civilizing,
and humanizing . . . should turn back to use cruelty and coercion
in the rear of their moral army, upon the aged, the infirm, and
unfortunate—upon the *helpless*, who in all ages and countries
the most ignorant and barbarous, have been spared and
protected."[76]

Given the rhetoric of so-called 'Victorian values' today, it is as
well to be reminded of some of the salient, inhumane and
autocratic forms these values took in their heyday. The evidence
is overwhelming that the poor themselves shared Somerville's
judgement on the New Poor Law.[77] And on many other issues too,
like enclosure,[78] the game laws, or the social sentiments of the
poor, the essentially moral views he adduced to the labouring
classes can be authenticated as evidentially correct by historical
evidence from labouring people of his class.[79] Despite his inci-
pient conservatism, his sympathy for them is always manifest.
But over this, as a Scotsman and itinerant outsider, he maintains
a detachment which can open up real insights into the people he
nevertheless associated himself with. Take for example his
account of "Engishness," which follows his description of the
labouring poor's hostile view of enclosure. The inhabitants on the
verge of village commons, he tells us, "are yet possessed largely of
those feelings which have been respected in other classes of
Englishmen. Even their vices, as inhabitants of an English
common, are virtues when seen in the whole people who
comprise the English nation. The love of native soil, the desire to
attain and determination to defend independence, the resolute
resistance to all encroachments on territory, the openly
expressed hatred of all persons who would dare, rightly or
wrongfully, to question the propriety of what they do; the
generosity of today in helping a distressed neighbour, and the
readiness of tomorrow in appropriating to themselves the property of some other neighbour; the regard for their own privileges

and disregard of the privileges of other people; all these are characteristic of the rustic idler in England and of the English nation. What is a vice in one case, may not be entitled to the name and esteem of a virtue in another, if morality be the rule of logic. But be the characteristics vicious or virtuous, they are the distinguishing features of the English over centuries of years, at home and abroad, and to their exercise we owe all our liberty, all our extended territory, all our power."[80] The emphasis on "we" at the end here reminds one of the ambivalence of his own situation: a travelling Scotsman in the south who spoke "broad Scotch,"[81] someone attenuating his own critical views so as not to give offence, indignant at what he saw while knowing that reform would depend on gaining his readers' sympathies and identification with him.

For more reasons than his discussion of Englishness, his concern for the poor, or his brand of conservatism, Somerville has become increasingly apposite today. No doubt this is partly because of the political swing towards free-market principles, the interest in early political economy and agricultural free trade in some current political circles, which harks back to the influence of Cobden and Bright, to many of the themes Somerville discussed. The associated ideas were to be considerably influential for the rest of the nineteenth century, after the corn laws were repealed in 1846. Somerville himself commented that "My political life has been spent in rescuing the Science of Political Economy from the soulless materialism which had made it . . . odious to the People . . . I assert man to be the primary element in national wealth"[82]: and the relevance of this today is inescapable. Of course, the conditions facing agriculture have changed considerably since the 1840s; there is now far less class tension in the countryside than during Somerville's time, and it is commonly of a different sort.[83] Putting such considerations aside, however, there is no doubt that *The Whistler at the Plough* has a rural as well as a political relevance now which is not just owing to growing interest in rural social history. As European Economic Community agricultural supports are eroded, and as concern develops in the western world with Third World poverty, indebtedness and the ways to amend it (which will no doubt include provision for securer markets in the West for comparatively cheap Third World agricultural produce), it may be that some of his arguments will reappear as issues of agricultural protectionism come to be resolved.[84]

And finally, what more can one say about this largely self-taught, stubborn, forthright, deeply moral, energetic, creative, poor and in some ways tragic man? It is certainly high time now to accord him the recognition he deserved, and which largely escaped him during his life. Had he written to support established interests, had he embellished his work with glowing accounts of the worth of the landed aristocracy, of their supposedly invaluable role in promoting agricultural improvement, of their "service" to some narrowly defined concept of the "community," his future would have been more secure. Sinecures of one sort or another would have been assured him. But, as was evident during his period in the army, this was never his inclination. As one account of his life put it: "Sympathetic and sensitive to a degree, he might have fared better in this world had he been less so."[85] He was outspoken to an extent that some found embarrassing. His concern for the more defenceless farmers, and his humane sympathy for the poor and their plight, completely overrode any temptation to self-serving pusillanimity within the corrupt aristocratic system of clientage. In this he is an example to all rural historians of his period. Like the rural painter George Morland, or like the ageing Arthur Young when he came to reassess the adverse effects of enclosure on the labouring poor, he was abused (and viciously flogged) for the social views he stated, and he gained little economic security because of them.[86] His literary output was to be considerable, and his career as a writer continued for many years, but largely in another country—Canada, to which he emigrated in 1859. Sadly, his wife died eleven months after his arrival there, although they left a number of children. Despite his many literary initiatives,[87] his own fortunes did not much improve. Late in life he listed his British publications, and remarked that "it will be seen that many of the subjects are, unfortunately, such as an author may become poor upon, rather than popular and well remunerated."[88] He died in 1885, aged seventy-four, in poverty in a squalid boarding house in Toronto. For some years he had been sleeping throughout the year in a woodshed outside, with the snow in winter seeping through the window—much as it had done, no doubt, around his father's moveable pane of glass, in the cottages of his childhood in the Lothians.

NOTES

1. Alexander Somerville, *The Autobiography of a Working Man* (1848, 1951 ed., to which reference will be made, also published in 1965). This autobiography provided the basis for the summary of the life of "a peasant, bred and nurtured under the most disadvantageous circumstances" in Scotland. See R.M.Garnier, *Annals of the British Peasantry* (1895), pp. 321–8.

2. Alexander Somerville, *History of the British Legion and War in Spain* (1839); and his *Free Trade and the League: a Biographical History* (1852), the latter originally published with *The Whistler at the Plough*.

3. *Autobiography*, p. 107.

4. For discussion of this rural unrest, see in particular E.J.Hobsbawm & G.Rudé, *Captain Swing* (1969).

5. A passage from the letter was published in the *Weekly Dispatch* on 27 May, 1832. For its contents, see Somerville's *Autobiography* (1951 ed.), pp. 159–60.

6. *Autobiography*, p. 189.

7. *Autobiography*, p. 190. As R.L.Gales put it: "It is odd to reflect that all through the agitation about the Oxford Tracts, the Gorham Judgement, the Papal Aggression, the thunders of Lord John Russell, the charges of the Bishops, the riots in defence of the black gown, British soldiers were being flogged, sometimes . . . literally to death. Flagellation, *usque ad mortem*, was part of the sacrifice demanded by the ruling classes from the populace for the sake of discipline, of patriotism, of the Union Jack, of the country under whose just and equal laws they enjoyed the inestimable benefits, unknown to foreigners, of the British Constitution . . ." See his *The Vanished Country Folk, and Other Studies in Arcady* (1914), pp. 57–8.

8. Following Somerville's ordeal on 29 May 1832, "Orator" Hunt agitated against military flogging in the House of Commons, and addressed a large rally against such flogging at Kennington Common in July 1832, organised by the N.U.W.C. See J.Belchem, *'Orator' Hunt: Henry Hunt and English Working-Class Radicalism* (Oxford, 1985), p. 262. In December 1833 Richard Carlile started the *Political Soldier*, subtitled *A Paper for the Army and the People*, a one and half pence unstamped weekly, with Somerville as editor, to inculcate a "rational sense of citizenship" among soldiers. It printed accounts of malpractice in the army, demanding an end to military flogging and other types of "military torture." Somerville resigned as editor of the *Political Soldier* after the first number, because he objected to Carlile's interference and dictation. In resigning, he wrote to Carlile that "I must have the sole management of [the paper]; my will must be uncontrolled." See J.H.Wiener, *Radicalism and Freethought in Nineteenth-Century Britain; the Life of Richard Carlile* (1983), pp. 204–5, 214 n.

9. See his *Autobiography*, p. 201.

10. *Narrative of the British Legion in Spain* (1837); *Warnings to the People on Street Warfare. A Series of Weekly Letters*

(1839). Francis Maceroni's instructions were issued in his *Defensive Instructions for the People in Street Warfare* (1832, 1834). Somerville also wrote *Public and Personal Affairs. Being an Enquiry into the Physical Strength of the People, in which the Value of their Pikes and Rifles is compared with that of the Grape Shot ... of the Woolwich Artillery* (1839). For brief discussions of Somerville's role in the controversy over Chartist physical force tactics, see W.T.Ward, *Chartism* (1973), p. 262; F.C.Mather (ed.), *Chartism and Society: an Anthology of Documents* (1980), pp. 37, 139, 246; M.Hovell, *The Chartist Movement* (Manchester, 1918, 1970 ed.); H.Weisser, *British Working-Class Movements and Europe, 1815–48* (Manchester, 1975), p. 100; A.Plummer, *Bronterre: A Political Biography of Bronterre O'Brien, 1804–1864* (1971), pp. 107–9, 137; and see Somerville's *Autobiography*.

11. A. Plummer, *Bronterre: A Political Biography of Bronterre O'Brien, 1804–1864* (1971), pp. 107–8.

12. H.Weisser, *British Working-Class Movements and Europe, 1815–48* (Manchester, 1975), p. 100. On McDouall, see for example J.Epstein, *The Lion of Freedom; Feargus O'Connor and the Chartist Movement, 1832–1842* (1982), eg. pp. 197, 221, 271–2, 295–7.

13. A.Plummer, *Bronterre*, p. 109.

14. A.Plummer, *Bronterre*, p. 109.

15. A.Plummer, *Bronterre*, p. 137.

16. See J.Epstein & D.Thompson (eds), *The Chartist Experience: Studies in Working-Class Radicalism and Culture, 1830–60)* (1982), p. 302. See also A.R.Schoyen, *The Chartist Challenge; a Portrait of George Julian Harney* (1958), p. 174; J.T.Ward, *Chartism* (1973), pp. 192, 199; A.Somerville, *Cobdenic Policy the Internal Enemy of England* (1854), ch. 5; and his *The Land Plan of Feargus O'Connor* (Manchester, 1847).

17. John Morley, *Life of Richard Cobden* (1881), vol. 2, pp. 54–5.

18. His *Letters From Ireland During the Famine of 1847*, originally issued with *The Whistler at the Plough*, will shortly be published by Merlin Press as a separate volume.

19. The League's organisers were much concerned with rural labourers. See for example, A.Briggs, *Victorian Cities* (1963, Harmondsworth 1975 ed.), p. 142; A.Bisset, *Notes on the Anti-Corn Law Struggle* (1884), p. 6, on Cobden in 1844 speaking of sending investigators into the south-western counties to investigate the condition of the agricultural population, and to see "particularly how much of the average

earnings of a peasant's family goes in purchasing clothing and articles paying excise or duty to Government."

20. N.McCord, *The Anti-Corn Law League* (1958. 1968 ed.), p. 144, 176; N.Longmate, *The Breadstealers, the Fight Against the Corn Laws, 1838–1846* (1984). p. 115. McCord, like Longmate, mentions his tendency to drink on occasion, in such a way as to eclipse his real achievements, although there is no sign that they read him. It is peculiar that they do not also mention the drunkenness of many members of higher social classes involved in the history they write. Perhaps this is because of the stereotypes of working-class (i.e. "drunken") and middle- or upper-class (i.e. "sober") behaviour which some historians unconsciously perpetuate.

21. *The Whistler at the Plough*, p. 7 (hereafter referred to as *Whistler*). Somerville warns us at one point that "The reader must not attempt to follow my course on a map, or, if he does, he will either lose the road or discover what I cannot find on any map I have seen." However, a map of the places he visited and discussed is presented here.

22. *Whistler*, p. 7.

23. At the end of the day, and with the spectre of famine in Ireland as the catalyst, landlords' votes in Parliament were split on the repeal of the corn laws. But this of course is not an adequate reflection of the views they had held over the previous decades. W.O.Aydelotte, "The country gentlemen and the repeal of the Corn Laws," *English Historical Review*, 82 (1967), 47–60.

24. On this, see E.P.Thompson, "The moral economy of the English crowd in the eighteenth century," *Past & Present*, 50 (1971); Roger Wells, "The revolt of the south-west, 1800–1801: a study of English popular protest," *Social History*, VI (1977); J.Stevenson, "Food riots in England, 1792–1818," in R.Quinault & J.Stevenson (eds), *Popular Protest and Public Order: Six Studies in British History, 1790–1920* (1974); A.Booth, "Food riots in the north-west of England, 1790–1801," *Past & Present*, 77 (1977); John Walter, "Grain riots and popular attitudes to the law: Maldon and the crisis of 1629," in J.Brewer & J.Styles (eds), *An Ungovernable People: the English and their Law in the Seventeenth and Eighteenth Centuries* (1980).

25. On rural labouring opposition to the corn laws, see for example the ex-farm worker John Buckmaster, *A Village Politician* (1897, Horsham, 1982 ed.), pp. 133ff, on "the injustice of the Corn Laws," on village Anti-Corn Law Associations being formed; A.Prentice, *History of the Anti-Corn Law League* (1853), vol. 2, pp. 381–2, on "the coercion

used by the protectionists to stifle the complaints of the labourers." One farm labourer, chairing a meeting being reported upon, said that: "It is the arbitrary Corn Law that has done all the mischief and we believe free trade will be beneficial to ourselves and families." It is evident that there was certainly no united "agricultural interest" supportive of the corn laws, when one considers the three main social classes of the countryside. The notion of a "whole agricultural interest" (of the sort stressed by A.Armstrong, *Farmworkers* (Frome, 1988)), is appropriately ridiculed by Andrew Bisset, *Notes on the Anti-Corn Law Struggle* (1884), pp. 153, 157–8.

26. Male rural workers were finally enfranchised by the Representation of the People Act, 1884, which extended the franchise on the same terms as existed in the boroughs.

27. *Whistler*, p. 4.

28. There were of course plenty of other considerations affecting rural living conditions besides the corn laws, many of which Somerville was aware of. For a fuller discussion of rural conditions during this period, see my *Annals of the Labouring Poor; Social Change and Agrarian England, 1660–1900* (Cambridge, 1985).

29. William Cobbett, *Rural Rides* (1830); Arthur Young, *A Six Weeks Tour Through the Southern Counties of England and Wales* (1768); his *A Six Months' Tour Through the North of England* (1770); and his *A Farmer's Tour Through the East of England* (1771).

30. His arguments on this are a much needed corrective to views like F.M.L.Thompson's, that "the landed aristocracy has done great service [sic] ... it continues to serve [sic] as the respected symbol of order and continuity in a changing world." See Thompson's *English Landed Society in the Nineteenth Century* (1963, 1971 ed.), p. 345, a book which contains many such questionable eulogies, as well as its delusive language of "service," rather than of usurpation, self-interest, power and privilege. See also Armstrong, *Farmworkers*, eg. p. 28, on the supposed role of the landlord as "the strategist of agrarian progress." *The Whistler at the Plough*, with its persuasive criticisms of rural landlord behaviour and inefficiency, and its appreciation of the extent of social conflict in the countryside, is a necessary remedy for the uncritical right-wing biases one encounters in some of the more old-fashioned historiography.

31. He could also be forthright in attacking poverty in Manchester, the headquarters of the "League." See for example pp. 207–8.

32. *Whistler*, p. 92.
33. *Whistler*, p. 88
34. In later years, he was to break with Cobden and Bright, making published criticisms of them.
35. Again, in this he is a helpful corrective to the views of the occasional historian who thinks otherwise. See Alan Armstrong, *Farmworkers* (Frome, 1988), eg. p. 15: "Never very far from the minds of many farmworkers at any time during the nineteenth ... century was a sense of identity with the interests of their employers"—a view which Armstrong is totally unable to substantiate with proper historical documentation from the class he discusses. On social tension and unrest in the countryside, there is an admirable and growing literature. See for example E.J.Hobsbawm & G.Rudé, *Captain Swing* (1969); A.J.Peacock, *Bread or Blood; A Study of the Agrarian Riots in East Anglia in 1816* (1965); J.P.D. Dunbabin, *Rural Discontent in Nineteenth-Century Britain* (1974); his "The 'Revolt of the Field': the agricultural labourers' movement in the 1870s," *Past & Present*, 26 (1963); E.P.Thompson, "The crime of anonymity" in D.Hay et al (eds), *Albion's Fatal Tree: Crime and Society in Eighteenth-century England* (1975); J.E.Archer, "'A fiendish outrage'? A study of animal maiming in East Anglia: 1830–1870," *Agricultural History Review*, 33 (1985); A. Charlesworth (ed.), *An Atlas of Rural Protest in Britain, 1548–1900* (1983); his (ed.), *Rural Social Change and Conflicts since 1500* (1982); Roger Wells, "Rural rebels in southern England in 1830," in C.Elmsley & J.Walvin (eds), *Artisans, Peasants and Proletarians, 1760–1860)* (1985); Roger Wells, "The revolt of the south-west, 1800–1801: a study in English popular protest," *Social History*, 6 (1977); Roger Wells, "Resistance to the New Poor Law in the rural south," in M.Chase (ed.), *The New Poor Law* (Middlesborough Centre Occasional Papers, no. 1, 1985); J.Lowerson, "The aftermath of Swing; anti-Poor Law movements and rural trade unions in the south-east of England," in A.Charlesworth (ed.), *Rural Social Change and Conflicts since 1500* (1982); J.Knott, *Popular Opposition to the 1834 Poor Law* (1986); H. Hopkins, *The Long Affray: the Poaching Wars, 1760–1914* (1985); Alun Howkins, *Poor Labouring Men: Rural Radicalism in Norfolk, 1870–1923* (1985); D.J.V.Jones, "The poacher: a study in Victorian crime and protest," *Historical Journal*, 22 (1979); David Jones. "Thomas Campbell Foster and the rural labourer: incendiarism in East Anglia in the 1840s," *Social History*, 1 (1976); P.Muskett, "The East Anglian riots of 1822," *Agricultural History*

Review, 32 (1984); B.Reaney, *The Class Struggle in Ninettenth-Century Oxfordshire: the Social and Communal Background to the Otmoor Disturbances of 1830 to 1835* (1971); R.C.Russell, *The "Revolt of the Field" in Lincolnshire* (1956); David Williams, *The Rebecca Riots; A Study in Agrarian Discontent* (Cardiff, 1955); Barry Reay, "The last rising of the agricultural labourers: the Battle in Bossenden Wood, 1838," *History Workshop*, 26 (1988); and his *The Last Rising of the Agricultural Labourers: Rural Life and Protest in Nineteenth-Century England* (forthcoming).

36. For discussion of these three factors, see Snell, *Annals of the Labouring Poor; Social Change and Agrarian England, 1660–1900* (Cambridge, 1985).

37. *Whistler*, p. 250.

38. *Whistler*, eg. p. 141.

39. *Whistler*, p. 35.

40. Threshing machines were particularly contentious because they took winter employment at hand threshing away from the poor.

41. *Whistler*, pp. 72, 128.

42. For a similar critique of short leases and their adverse effects upon agricultural improvement, see G.C.Brodrick, *English Land and English Landlords; an Enquiry into the Origin and Character of the English Land System, with Proposals for its Reform* (1881), pp. 198–210. Landlords, Brodrick argued, spent "much less money than tenants in agricultural improvements"; and he attacked the English yearly tenancies "under which Adam Smith declares that it would be absurd to expect an occupier to improve, and which Scotch farmers have long since declined" (pp. 203–5). He also made similar arguments to Somerville's on the self-interested political motives behind landlords maintaining precarious tenancies for their farmers. For a more favourable assessment of landlords "weeding their tenantry"—removing them frequently—see D.Spring, *The English Landed Estate in the Nineteenth Century: Its Administration* (Baltimore, 1963), p. 111. Compare Somerville's arguments also with the conservatively biased J.D.Chambers & G.E.Mingay, *The Agricultural Revolution, 1750–1880* (1966, 1978 ed.), pp. 46–8. Without any supportive documentation, they assert that occupiers under annual agreements "rarely felt insecure"; they also briefly try to discount landlord political pressure upon tenants, again without providing evidence on this.

43. See the extraordinary lease he transcribes on pp. 74–8. He returns many times to the way leases like this militated against capital being expended on farms. On the effects on

social relations of the decline of farm service, see my *Annals of the Labouring Poor; Social Change and Agrarian England, 1660–1900* (Cambridge, 1985, 1987), ch. 2. Contemporaries widely held that this change had adversely affected class relations; but Somerville was unusual in appreciating the way in which changes in leases may also have influenced the decline of farm service.

44. *Whistler*, eg. pp. 56–7.
45. One thinks for example of F.M.L.Thompson, *English Landed Society in the Nineteenth Century* (1963). Somerville was only one of the many contemporaries who gave a far less favourable account of the landlord class, and after reading him, it is hard to imagine panegyrics like Thompson's being written. It is symptomatic of Thompson's biases that he mentions neither Somerville, nor the vast majority of the many other works which were critical of the rural landlord class in the nineteenth century. One such was A.Bisset, *Notes on the Anti-Corn Law Struggle*, (1884), pp. 182–3, who claimed that the English aristocracy "were like the horse-leech which had swallowed more blood than was good for it," suggesting further that there might come a day of reckoning for it, as for the French aristocracy.
46. *Whistler*, p. 17.
47. In fairness to Shaftesbury, many of the problems on his estate had been due to his father. See J.L. & B.Hammond, *Lord Shaftesbury* (1923, Harmondsworth, 1939 ed.), pp. 88–91, 108–9, on the confrontation between the Anti-Corn Law League and Shaftesbury. Bright complained that Shaftesbury and his associates "looked at the evils of the manufacturing districts through one end of the telescope, and the evils of the villages through the other," *ibid.*, p. 89.
48. *Whistler*, p. 103. For a more extended discussion of this point, and the role of enclosure, see my *Annals of the Labouring Poor; Social Change and Agrarian England, 1660–1900* (Cambridge, 1985), ch. 4.
49. *Whistler*, pp. 126, 129, 215.
50. *Whistler*, p. 140.
51. *Whistler*, p. 141.
52. *Whistler*, p. 141. And see pp. 234–5 on the hunt trampling down corn, breaking fences, terrifying animals.
53. *Whistler*, p. 301.
54. *Whistler*, p. 351.
55. *Whistler*, pp. 347ff.
56. *Whistler*, p. 172.
57. *Whistler*, p. 187. (His italics.)
58. *Whistler*, pp. 187–8. For one of the many similar assessments,

see A.Bisset, *Notes on the Anti-Corn Law Struggle* (1884), pp. 194–6, who complains of "the disgrace of the frightful robbery committed on those poor Irish labourer-tenants," who after often considerably improving their properties "had the alternative given them of either having their rents at once raised to the full value of the improvements or of being turned adrift to wander about as vagabonds on the face of the earth, and carry with them to America an exile's sorrows and an outlaw's hate—for though it may be shown to be in accordance with the *form of law*, it was a robbery of the most cruel nature—a robbery that took advantage of the best qualities of the victims to make those very qualities the instruments of their destruction ... The inhabitants of Ireland have taken up a deep and murderous hatred towards the inhabitants of Great Britain." For such further discussion of Ireland and the shortcomings of Irish landlordism, see Somerville's *Letters from Ireland During the Famine of 1847* (forthcoming, Merlin Press).

9. For example, see *Whistler*, pp. 70, 153.

0. *Whistler*, pp. 70–1. (His italics.)

1. *Whistler*, p. 73.

2. *Whistler*, pp. 24–7.

3. *Whistler*, p. 24. Compare John Dent, "The present condition of the English agricultural labourer," *Journal of the Royal Agricultural Society*, VII (1871), 354, on Scottish children staying at school longer than those in the south of England. But see in particular the decisive intervention by Rab Houston, *Scottish Literacy and the Scottish Identity* (Cambridge, 1985). See also R.D.Anderson, *Education and Society in Victorian Scotland* (Edinburgh, 1983).

4. Richard Cobden wrote in another context of Somerville's style that "The difficulty with Somerville [is] to condense sufficiently his narrative—this would not be easy even with one who had a style less flowing and imaginative than he." See J.Morley, *The Life of Richard Carlile* (1881), vol. 2, pp. 54–5.

5. See for example, pp. 283ff.

6. *Whistler*, pp. 278–81.

7. As is the practice in Arthur Young's *Tours*—the works of art which he likes to mention presumably being added to indicate how successful certain aristocratic and gentry families have been in making tenant farmers pay more rent. The effects on labourers' wages are not spelt out.

8. *Whistler*, pp. 10–11.

9. He even discusses the politics of different public houses. *Whistler*, p. 55.

0. *Whistler*, pp. 12–15. See James Thomson, *The Castle of*

Indolence: An Allegorical Poem, Written in Imitation of Spenser (1748).

71. As for example is manifested in his discussion of the utopian community of Harmony Hall. *Whistler*, pp. 105–117, originally published in the *Morning Chronicle*, 13 December, 1842. This was independently published as *Notes from the Farming Districts. No. XVII. A Journey to Harmony Hall in Hampshire, with some Particulars of the Socialist Community, to which the Attention of the Nobility, Gentry, and Clergy, is Earnestly Requested* (1842). It is also reprinted in K.E.Carpenter (advisory ed.), *British Labour Struggles: Contemporary Pamphlets, 1727–1850. Cooperative Communities: Places and Descriptions, Eleven Pamphlets, 1825–1847* (Arno Press, New York, 1972).

72. For example, "he be's as long as a journey from here to London on a pig's back afore his memory be's good enough to raise wages at the time he promises when he takes 'em down." *Whistler*, p. 41.

73. See for example the interviews and meetings recorded on pp. 37ff, 118ff, 142ff, 261ff, 385ff, 425ff.

74. See my *Annals of the Labouring Poor*, ch. 3.

75. This term, "moral economy," has since become widely used by historians, following E.P.Thompson's famous article, "The moral economy of the English crowd in the eighteenth century," *Past and Present*, 50 (1971). Somerville was using it in a rather different sense here, and it would be instructive to examine the ways in which its use changed during the nineteenth century.

76. *Whistler*, pp. 257–9.

77. See for example my *Annals of the Labouring Poor*, ch. 3.

78. See in particular his discussion of enclosure in *Whistler*, p. 101.

79. For further light on the views of the labouring poor, see the sources and arguments in for example, E.P.Thompson, "The moral economy of the English crowd in the eighteenth century," *Past and Present*, 50 (1971); his "The crime of anonymity," in D.Hay et al (eds), *Albion's Fatal Tree* (1975); Roger Wells, "Rural rebels in southern England in the 1830s," in C.Elmsley & J.Walvin (eds), *Artisans, Peasants and Proletarians, 1760–1860; Essays Presented to Gwyn Williams*; my *Annals of the Labouring Poor* (Cambridge, 1985); N.Scotland, *Methodism and the Revolt of the Field* (Gloucester, 1981).

80. *Whistler*, p. 102. Needless to say, the subject is a topical one. See in particular R.Colls & P.Dodd (eds), *Englishness; Politics and Culture, 1880–1920* (1986); P.Corrigan & D.Sayer,

The Great Arch; English State Formation as Cultural Revolution (Oxford, 1985).

81. Somerville, *Autobiography*, p. 254.

82. Somerville, *Autobiography*, p. xix.

83. See H.Newby, *The Deferential Worker* (1977), for an interesting discussion of changes in the countryside (in an area of East Anglia) since 1945. He stresses the way in which an agricultural occupational interest has consolidated in the face of intrusions into village life of "outsiders," commuters, and the like—a very different picture to the agricultural class-based hostility of the Victorian era in the regions Somerville visited.

84. See for example R.Body, *Agriculture, the Triumph and the Shame* (1982), for a discussion of the current situation with some prescriptive similarities to Somerville.

85. W.M.Sandison, "Alexander Somerville," *Border Magazine*, XVIII, no. 207 (March, 1913), separately printed as a supplement, to which reference is made here, p. 6.

86. Modern historians have often overlooked him because his work has been difficult to come by. But see the appreciation of him and of *The Whistler at the Plough* by Raymond Williams, *The Country and the City* (1973), pp. 189–190, 281.

87. See the Bibliography of his writings for information on his considerable output in Canada. He also founded and for a while edited the *Canadian Illustrated News*, was editor of the *Church Herald*, and wrote on behalf of the Immigration Department of the Ontario Government.

88. W.M.Sandison, *Alexander Somerville, "The Whistler at the Plough"* (1913, reprinted from the *Border Magazine*, March, 1913), p. 8.

THE PRINCIPAL WORKS OF ALEXANDER SOMERVILLE.

(Place of publication is London unless otherwise stated.)

A Narrative of the British Auxiliary Legion, with Incidents, Anecdotes, and Sketches of all the Parties Connected with the War in Spain, from a Journal of Personal Recollection (Glasgow, 1838). 288 pp.

History of the British Legion and War in Spain, from Personal Observations and other Authentic Sources, Containing a Correct Detail of the Events of the Expedition under General Evans

... With an Appendix, Containing every Officer's Name, Rank, and Service that was in the Expedition and a Portrait of Lt. Gen. Sir G. De L. Evans (1839). 736 pp.

Public and Personal Affairs. Being an Inquiry into the Physical Strength of the People, in which the Value of their Pikes and Rifles is compared with that of the Grape-Shot, Shells, and Rockets, of the Woolwich Artillery. Also an Exposure of the Treacherous Patriots and Drunken Lawyers who have imposed upon the people, and are Connected with Alderman Harmer, and the Weekly Dispatch, the whole Comprising a Personal Narrative, by A. Somerville (1839). 90 pp.

Memoirs of Serjeant Paul Swanston, being a Narrative of a Soldier's Life in Barracks, Ships, Camps, Battles and Captivity on Sea and Land; with Notices of the most Adventurous of his Comrades, written by himself and now first published. (1839). [Anonymous] 434 pp.

Warnings to the People on Street Warfare. A Series of Weekly Letters (1839). [Originally published as a series of seven eight-page letters].

Jerry Queen the Toymaker (1840).

The Farthing Journal, A Pearl of Small Price, but a Great Literary Curiosity, by Jeremy Queen, of Lincoln's Inn (1841), 260 pp.

Eliza Grimwood, or a Legend of Waterloo Road (1841). 322 pp.

Notes from the Farming Districts, No. 17. A Journey to Harmony Hall, in Hampshire, with some Particulars of the Socialist Community, to which the Attention of the Nobility, Gentry, and Clergy is Earnestly Requested, by One Who has Whistled at the Plough (1842). 8 pp. [From the *Morning Chronicle,* 13 December, 1842]. Reprinted in K.E. Carpenter (advisory ed.), *British Labour Struggles: Contemporary Pamphlets, 1727–1850. Cooperative Communities: Plans and Descriptions, Eleven Pamphlets, 1825–1847* (New York, 1972).

A Letter to the Farmers of England, on the Relationship of Manufactures and Agriculture, by One Who has Whistled at the Plough (1843). 16 pp.

The O'Connor Land Scheme Examined and Described from its Formation to the Present Time. By One Who has Whistled at the Plough (Manchester, 1847). 64 pp.

The Autobiography of a Working Man, by "One Who Has Whistled at the Plough" (1848, 1854, 1951, 1967 eds). 1848 ed., 511 pp.

Somerville's Financial Reform Catechism (1849). 8 pp.

The Whistler at the Plough; Containing Travels, Statistics, and Descriptions of Scenery and Agricultural Customs in most parts of England: with Letters from Ireland: also "Free Trade and the League"; a Biographic History, 3 Volumes (Manchester, 1852–3). 654 pp.

Letters from Ireland in the Year of Famine.
[These are the letters contained in the 1852 edition of *The Whistler at the Plough*. They are forthcoming as a separate volume, edited by K.D.M.Snell and published by Merlin Press, under Somerville's original title, *Letters From Ireland During the Famine of 1847*].

The Life of Roger Mowbray, Merchant Prince of England and Member of Parliament (1853). 181 pp.

Free Trade and the League: a Biographic History of the Pioneers of Freedom of Opinion, Commercial Enterprise, and Civilisation, in Britain, from the Times of Serfdom to the Age of Free Trade in Manufactures, Food and Navigation (Manchester, 1853), 2 vols, 643 & 604 pp. [Sometimes cited as vols 1 and 2 of *The Whistler at the Plough*. Published in connection with his *The Whistler at the Plough*.]

Cobdenic Policy, the Internal Enemy of England. The Peace Society, its Combativeness. Mr. Cobden, his Secretiveness. Also a Narrative of Historical Incidents (1854). 104 pp.

The First Complete Account of Somerville's Diligent Life (1860) [Cited in W.Sandison (see below) as *Book of a Diligent Life.*]

Conservative Science of Nations, (Preliminary Installment,) Being the First Complete Narrative of Somerville's Diligent Life in the Service of Public Safety in Britain (Montreal, 1860). 320 pp.

Canada, a Battle Ground; About an Kingdom in America. Travels in Canada and the Frontier United States (Hamilton, Canada West, 1862). 64 pp.

Living for a Purpose; or, the Contrast (1865). 185 pp.

Narrative of the Fenian Invasion, of Canada ... with a Map of the Field of Combat, at Limestone Ridge (Hamilton, Canada West, 1866). 128 pp.

Memoir of and by "The Whistler" (T.Buncle, Arbroath, 1889), 28 pp. [Signed "One Who Whistles at the Plough."]

A fuller list (which is probably unreliable in some details) is printed in William M. Sandison *Alexander Somerville, "The Whistler at the Plough"* (1913, reprinted from the *Border Magazine*, March, 1913), p. 8. Sandison states that it was derived from Somerville's *Book of a Diligent Life* [sic], (Canada, 1860). It includes some further undated works which I have not been able to trace, some of which were published serially in periodicals and weeklies. For the sake of interest, and to give a further indication of the scope of his writing, these are listed below. Many further writings pertaining to his life in Canada will not be included among them, and an enormous pile of manuscripts he placed with a friend was lost at his death.

Somerville's School of Political Economy
Industrial Wonders of Manchester and Forty Miles Around
History and Romance of the Fiscal System and of the National Debt
Liverpool Financial Reform Tracts
National Wealth Tracts
Safeguards Against Commercial Panics
Popular Fallacies about the Aristocracy of the Army, the House of Commons Falling into the Occupation of Commercial Companies, the House of Lords Protecting the People— Recent Instances
"Free Sea": England on the Rock of Gibraltar Justified
Bowering, Cobden and China
"Comets and Earthquakes," an Inquiry
Eden Green, Garden of Dreams
The Whistler's Fairy Tales
Enchanted Children of the Sylvan Groves
Tom Robinson, the British Grenadier
Fallacies of Feargus O'Connor
Rural Life of England: Visits to Remarkable Farms
Legend of the London Penny-a-Liners
Memoir of William Pitt in Reference to Free Trade between England and Ireland
Memoir of William Huskisson
Poulett Thomson (Lord Sydenham): His Tariff Reforms in England and Union of the Canadas
Speculative Memoir of St. Dunstan, as an Eminent English Blacksmith
Apologues in Political Economy
Problems in Military Strategy
Operation of the Navigation Laws, in Reference ot the Revolt of the American Colonies, now in the United States
A Cry from Ireland in 1843
Temperance Tracts

PLACES MENTIONED IN 'THE WHISTLER AT THE PLOUGH'

Alexander Somerville

THE WHISTLER
AT THE
PLOUGH

AND FREE TRADE

BY
ALEXANDER SOMERVILLE,

ONE WHO HAS WHISTLED AT THE PLOUGH.

1852.

MANCHESTER.

JAMES AINSWORTH, 93, PICCADILLY.

THE

WHISTLER AT THE PLOUGH;

CONTAINING

TRAVELS, STATISTICS, AND
DESCRIPTIONS OF SCENERY & AGRICULTURAL CUSTOMS
IN MOST PARTS OF ENGLAND:

WITH

LETTERS FROM IRELAND:

ALSO

"FREE TRADE AND THE LEAGUE;"

A BIOGRAPHIC HISTORY.

BY ALEXANDER SOMERVILLE,

AUTHOR OF LETTERS

SIGNED

"ONE WHO HAS WHISTLED AT THE PLOUGH,"
"REUBEN," &c.

MANCHESTER:
JAMES AINSWORTH, 93, PICCADILLY.

DEDICATION.

TO THE

RIGHT HONOURABLE LORD JOHN RUSSELL.

MY LORD,

You were the first statesman who, as leader of a great party in the British Legislature, pronounced that "Protection has not been the support but the bane of Agriculture." Those who had, up to then, 1845, laboured to prove that truth, were filled with hope, which soon became a national joy, when they heard these words.

This Volume comprises a selection of Letters and Essays, written by me, and addressed to the demerits of Protection, from 1842 to 1847, inclusive. The two succeeding Volumes are a BIOGRAPHIC HISTORY OF FREE TRADE AND THE LEAGUE. They embrace Memoirs of Persons identified with the rise and progress of commerce and constitutional liberty, from earliest English History, to 1850.

In looking around, in 1846, when I first announced this work, to inquire which of her Majesty's subjects had a name, that, in a dedication would do such a book the greatest honour, the history of two centuries, and the legislation, expansive of constitutional liberty in my own time, (without which an Anti-Corn-Law League could not have existed) answered—Russell.

I am,

My Lord,

Your Lordship's obedient servant,

ALEXANDER SOMERVILLE.

" One who has Whistled at the Plough."

May, 1852.

INTRODUCTION.

In the early years of the Anti-Corn-Law League, free trade was viewed, alike by its advocates and opponents, as a question with manufactures and commerce on one side and agriculture on the other. But having been bred to agricultural employment, and accustomed to think though not to write much; having travelled some, and been observant in travelling, I was strongly impressed with a belief that, of all the interests to be promoted by free trade the agricultural interest would be most benefited, and of all persons interested in agriculture, living on or living by the land, the landowners were the parties who had most to gain. My reasons for so thinking will be found in various forms and places throughout this work. I saw and admired the sight of gigantic Manchester lifting up its head and crying, " No monopoly !" and I believed in the faith of that giant, that it, and those who were leagued with it, would some day overcome the mistaken monopolists, and compel them to yield. Yet how far distant did that time seem ; what unknown and unlooked-for elements of national unhappiness might be engendered in compelling the agriculturists to surrender their unserviceable, yet dearly cherished protection ! Nobody in this country has so large a stake in peace and order as the commercial classes, the owners of money and machinery. Nobody is more sensible of that than themselves. Nothing was more remote from their designs than the use of unconstitutional means to compel the agriculturists to yield. But how hopeless seemed the task of convincing two-thirds of the House of Commons, four-fifths of the House of Lords, and all the agricultural constituencies, that it was just to the other classes of the nation that they should yield, should submit to receive lower incomes and live at less expense. Yet so far as I had listened to anti-corn-law speeches or had read them, the advocates of free trade looked for success by these means, and these only. I speak of the time previous to 1842.

Wherefore, believing that the agriculturists would be gain-

1

ers by the surrender of their monopoly, I at last thought it might do good, and could do no harm, to give my opinions and the reasons for holding them to the public. But how was I, unknown as a writer, to get into print; or if into print, to get readers, to say nothing of believers? I tried, sent an article to an evening paper which was understood to be the London organ of the free traders, and waited a few days with some anxiety to see it published. It was not published. I then sent a note to the editor, calling his attention to it, and requesting that, if he did not intend to use it, to leave it out for me at the office, and I would call for it. I did call, and was told that it had been "thrown on the fire with other rubbish of the same kind."

This answer, coming from the paper which was generally understood then to be (which I now know to have then been) the paid organ of the League, led me to believe that there was no hope that such anti-corn-law opinions as mine could or would be admitted in support of corn-law repeal.

However, I tried again; re-wrote something of the same kind, and sent it to another paper. It was not inserted. The reason given was, that the publication of such opinions would do more harm than good to the cause of corn-law abolition; that they would only be ridiculed, for they were in fact ridiculous. And the editor added, that he regretted to say this of an article which " otherwise displayed a knowledge of the corn-law question and evinced some talent."

This last was rather more soothing than to have ones "rubbish" thrown into the fire. It was some small encouragement to try again; yet how to try again, when everybody seemed to think it " ridiculous" to advocate the abolition of protection to agriculture for the benefit of the land and the landowners, I did not so clearly see. I pondered on the subject for several weeks, and examined it on every side, to see if I was not labouring under some hallucination. No ; the more calculations made ; the more recollections of agriculture gathered from previous observation; the more reflection given to the capacity of the soil of England to produce and the capacity of the people of England to consume, the firmer was my conviction that free trade and large trade would be beneficial to the owners and cultivators of the English soil more than to any other classes or interests whatsoever. And though I did not dream that the apostle of free trade, the member for Stockport, would so soon and so successfully take this view of the question; and as little that the great constitutional states-man, Lord John Russell, would within three years of that time proclaim in parliament, and obtain political credit for that proclamation, that protection had not been the support but the bane of agriculture; far less that his great com-peer, the late Sir Robert Peel, would within four years confess the same conviction, and, in an illustrious self-sacrifice, risk his official exaltation and power, throw private friend-ships, political traditions, and party associations to the wind, regardless whether that wind was but a breath of enmity or a tornado of opposition, that he might minister to his country and to mankind in accordance with new truths, which were proved to be truths from new sources and by new circum-stances; still, though looking forward to none of those great changes in so short a time, the humble hand that now traces these words traced then the words of an undoubting faith, the faith of other prophets, that commerce would be emancipated, nation would be to nation as neighbour to neighbour; that monopolies, clouds of commercial night, would expire, each in succession, by the light which the pre-expiry of its associates permitted to fall upon it; that England, in the van of nations, would be the first to march upon this glorious millennium; that the downfall of England's greatest commercial monopoly, that which disordered her daily bread and her daily labour, would be the signal for the fall of all the rest; that this would fall when the owners of the land saw that they were not called upon to make a sacrifice, but to accept a benefit, in giving freedom to industrial enterprise; and that, until this was proved, the corn-law would not be repealed.

Such was then my belief; and though no single article of that faith was original to me, all having been expressed, and better expressed, by others, yet the last-mentioned article, which was the first to be practically adopted for the attainment of the rest, seemed to be only of fractional importance in the opinion of those who admitted it; while nobody had admitted it who at that time held possession of the public ear, or eye, or judgment.

So, to fix public attention on this; to bring it within the scope of proof and of belief, and to make every public finger and finger-post point to it as the only road to free trade, at least the shortest and safest road, I once more resolved to write, but to write in a manner that would not at first sight let the main purpose be seen. The design was to keep the "ridiculous" doctrine out of sight until I had got some hold upon the public; and, to get that hold, it seemed that the best style of writing would be one which eschewed the didactic and the still less welcome array of dry figures, which in newspapers had hitherto made agricultural politics an uninteresting subject, and to take up a style of narrative and description.

I sat down and wrote accordingly, (it was in February 1842;) and having finished the first article at a late hour, retired to rest without having decided what signature should be attached to it. The common A. B. C. or X. Y. Z. signatures did not seem suitable, and I fell asleep without having fixed on anything. My mind was at this time, and had been for weeks before, so full of the subject, that I dreamt of it in my sleep; and on this night, while sleeping, wrote, as I thought, the signature "One who has Whistled at the Plough," to the letter which was lying unsigned. When I awoke in the morning, I was so impressed with these words, and with the belief that I had seen them on paper, that I thought they must have been written in an hour of weariness on the previous night, and that what was like a dream was not a dream. The slips of written paper were turned to eagerly, but nothing was signed there, nor had anything been signed; so thinking this designation of myself, which was at least truthful, might do, I appended it.

After some doubt, I thought of trying the *Morning Chronicle* with the letter I had written. I sent it there, and found myself more fortunate than elsewhere. It appeared on the 22d of February 1842, and I was so pleased to see myself in print on a subject which now occupied all my thoughts, namely, the benefit which English agriculture would derive from free trade, that I wrote a second letter. This was also published, and I received an intimation that others in the same style would be accepted, and this intimation was accompanied with what gave me a favourable opinion of the liberality of the editor and proprietors of that paper. Owing to the pressure of parliamentary debates, or other causes which I might not have been made acquainted with, fewer of my articles appeared in the *Chronicle* than I had expected. From February to August there were only six.

In the early part of August I received a letter from the editor, Mr Black, requesting me to call on him at the office. I had not seen him before, having up to that time communicated with him by letters or messengers only. He received me in his editorial room with kindness, and proceeded to say that my letters had given great satisfaction; that he had heard them spoken well of in the highest quarters, as useful and ——. It is not for me to repeat all he said on this head, though I confess to have been rather pleasantly tickled with his expressions of approbation. I had never up to that time heard more than one single word for or against my humble productions, and that single word I supposed was against them. It was in a coffee-house one day, when two gentlemen were sitting over their coffee reading the morning papers, while I was sitting in an adjoining box. One of them had the *Chronicle* in his hand, and said to the other, " What do you think of this Whistler at the Plough?" To which the other replied, " Humbug!" that was the only word I had heard in praise or blame of what I had written, (and I suppose "humbug" meant blame,) until I now heard Mr Black speak of what had been said in " high places."

After these preliminary observations, he took a letter from the table before him, and, unfolding it, said, " Here is another gentleman who seems to have been pleased with what you have written. He wishes to know if he can see you, and I think it will be worth your while to make his acquaintance. It is Mr Cobden, the member for Stockport. He will be at the House of Commons this afternoon, and if you go there and inquire for him in the lobby, you will find him. If not, this is his address, where you will see him to-morrow morning any time before twelve. You should go down to the House at once; I think you might do worse than form an acquaintance with these Manchester men of the League."

I thought so too, and so I went, wondering as I went what kind of man Mr Cobden might be, and how I should know him. I found him, and was not many minutes in his presence until I felt his intellectual power, though in manners he was as simple and humble as a gentle child. His knowledge of the free trade question extended far beyond my knowledge of

it ; but he was pleased to say that I had afforded him some
information, and had opened a new channel of inquiry for
more. He said then, as he has said often since, that in the
process of instructing others the Leaguers had been themselves
instructed. But unless it were on the question of how far
the owners of land would be benefited by free trade, he
seemed to have the same opinions then as he continued to
have to the end of the controversy. On that point, and on
that only, was I enabled to make suggestions which had not
then occurred to him, but which he afterwards adopted.
Subsequently I have communicated new facts, and have suggested new applications of them for argument, but was always
too late ; my duller comprehension had never seen them so
soon as he had seen them himself. While, on the other hand,
he communicated new views to me which I had neither seen
before, nor comprehended clearly even when he introduced
them. But he always introduced new views as questions for
my consideration, not as positive certitudes. Of this kind was
the question of how far the farmers taxed each other for each
other's supposed protection? How far the wheat-growing farmer taxed the cheese-making farmer and the sheep farmer? the
oats and barley growers, the wheat growers? and so on. When
this subject was first opened to me, I doubted whether the free
traders had a case in it. Mr Cobden was sure they had. He
suggested the subject to Mr Morton of Whitefield Example
Farm, Gloucestershire, who confessed this view of the question
to be new to him ; but at the same time he said he thought
there was truth and force in it. He undertook the task of
examining it closely, and, in doing so, made a series of calculations, which were published, and did more, I believe, than any
single publication whatever, to convince thinking minds, not
before convinced, of the fallacies of protection. I was engaged
in similar calculations, and arrived ultimately at similar results.
But about that time (end of 1844 and spring of 1845) my
attention was directed more to the losses in live stock sustained
by farmers from the failure of the hay and turnip crops, comparing their positive losses with the certain advantages which
they would have gained had they given the money paid for
very dear hay—keeping the sheep and cattle barely alive—
for Indian corn, or beans, or oats, or barley of foreign growth,
to feed the sheep and cattle fat, such pulse and grain being

then obtainable at moderate prices, had not the law of *protection* prohibited their use, and condemned the live stock to hunger and the farmers to poverty. The loss of wool from the low condition of the flocks, and the inferiority of the lambs from the same causes in 1845; the loss of manure then, and at all times, from not feeding more cattle, cattle not being fed for the want of provender, and the consequent difficulty and increased expense in the production of wheat; these all formed subjects of inquiry for me, at the suggestion of Mr Cobden : and for the attainment of the facts involved in them I travelled over many thousands of miles of the rural districts.

In the following pages I have made a selection of letters and reports from various districts, without dwelling elaborately on any particular place or subject. My purpose is to present a kind of moving view of the country, at the same time that a record—imperfect I confess it to be—will be made of that process of education which Mr Cobden and his coadjutors applied to the " agricultural mind." If I knew all that was done by the many assistant teachers, most of them far abler than myself, I could not write all. So I have thought it best to confine my book to a selection of my own writings. But I cannot pass over this incidental allusion to others, without acknowledging the eminent services of such writers on the agricultural side of free trade as Mr Morton of Whitefield; Mr Lattimore of Whethamstead; Mr Hope of Fenton Barns; Mr Morse of Swaffham; Mr Hyde Greg; Mr Welford, who edited the agricultural department of the League paper; and others with whose printed opinions I am more familiar than with their names.

And, again, the acknowledgment must be made, that what they wrote and what I wrote would have had but little effect had there not been a master-mind, superior to all of us, who winnowed our grain from our chaff, and added to it from the riches of his own intellectual storehouse.

And saying this, I return to Mr Cobden, and will only farther remark in this Introduction, that at my first interview with him, he laid down for me as a rule to be observed, what he never failed to re-state at every interview I had with him during the four eventful years that succeeded, namely, Never to write a description of an estate or a farm so as to make any landlord or farmer feel aggrieved, though there should be much

to find just fault with, unless some important fact or principle
was at stake. Not to make enemies needlessly. Never to
write all the truth, but reserve some of it to fall back upon.
This reserve of facts to be brought up as a last resort should
those first produced be assailed and denied. Never to hazard
any statement on hearsay, no matter how credible the informant might seem to be; for there were often local and
private influences that prejudiced very good and well-meaning
men against landowners and their agents, and led them to
give a high colour to matters which, though facts, were
not facts of the shape and colour which they represented
them to be. And then he was pleased to say that he had
confidence in my discretion; that it was the absence of all
acrimonious feeling which he had observed in my letters
upon landlords and farmers that had led him to ask for
my assistance. He made some other observations about
what I had written, which it is not for me to repeat, and
then, taking me by the hand, bade me go upon the mighty
work which, with him and his fellow Leaguers, I had undertaken. Heaven, he said, only knew how much labour we had
before us, and how long we would have to work; but so
righteous did he believe the cause to be, so well founded in
justice and sound national policy, so all-important to our own
country and to the whole human race, that he felt confident
of ultimate success, and, further, he believed that every man
working to ensure that success, with zeal and honesty of purpose, would feel a consciousness of well-doing within his own
mind that would be a reward for any amount of labour,
though, at the same time, the League would defray all necessary expenses of such assistants as myself.

This interview occurred, I think, on the 24th of August
1842, and on the 25th I proceeded on a journey into Buckinghamshire, as related in No. I. of "*Notes from the Farming
Districts.*"

THE WHISTLER.

NOTES FROM THE FARMING DISTRICTS.

No. I.

Notices the Poet Gray and the " Elegy written in a Country Churchyard."—
Touches on the Ideal, and comes down to the Real.—Enters on the merits
and management of Farm-yard Manure, as seen at Stoke Poges, and as
written of by Mr James Jackson, an eminent agriculturist.

THE "country churchyard" of Stoke Poges, which has long
been the shrine of the Poet Gray, which in his lifetime drew
forth the language of his sweet fancy, and at his death received
into its earthly keeping all that part of him that had died or
could die—this doubly sanctified churchyard was to me the
principal object of attraction on entering the county of Buckingham. From the Slough station on the Great Western
Railway I proceeded along a pleasant road hedged on each
side by thorns, clean, neat, compact, and highly creditable to
the locality, when compared with the wide, unserviceable,
waste-spreading fences so commonly seen in other parts. All
that grew in the fields of crop-kind looked well, and all that
had been taken off to barn or market was well spoken of, so
far as brief conversations with farmers and work people elicited
information. The generous summer had done so much for the
perfection of an abundant harvest, that a passer by could not
help feeling happy with the happy farmers, whether the science
and industry of the latter rendered them deserving of the sympathy or not. Therefore I passed on, to reach, while the sun
still brightened the tree tops, the place of the " Elegy written
in a Country Churchyard."

I found the poet's grave by the tombstone erected to his
mother's memory; and the deep shade of the heavy broad
yew trees realized his description. The " frail memorials" of
which he speaks were also evident enough. Indeed their reality despoiled some of the poetry of the expression; for they
were not merely " frail," poetically speaking, as all monuments
are, but they were positively so, being in many cases made of
wood. However, a considerable majority of the " mute inglo-

1*

rious Miltons" and the "village Hampdens" were without any mark or monument save the grass rankly rising on their graves, to die when winter comes. But all of them had that deathless memorial around them which their poet had reared, and which obtains for their humble resting-places a more than common respect. The churchyard being completely imprisoned in a thicket of gigantic trees, and these being again surrounded by the formal neatness of a gentleman's park, a stranger would look in vain for the place where "the rude forefathers of the hamlet sleep," but for the white spire that shews itself among the trees, or for "some Cromwell, guiltless of his country's blood," who may be seen clipping a hedge or milking a cow in the adjoining meadows. The late Mr Penn of Stoke Park, a descendant of the family of the celebrated Quaker of Pennsylvania, erected a monument to Gray, on which is inscribed some of the poet's own lines. It stands at the bottom of the park, three or four hundred yards from the churchyard, and is altogether, in situation, style, and adornments, so out of keeping with the place where the body lies, (so I thought,) that I hastened away from it to find, or imagined to find, the "nodding beech," or some other of his favourite trees. I entered a grassy enclosure, from which many miles of country could be viewed. The woods and fields, reddened by the setting sun, stretched far away, and united Berkshire with the blue horizon of the south, while Windsor Castle sat in the centre of the scene, like a giant at rest, bathing his feet in the deep Thames and the gathering fog which rose upon the water's breast.

But though the ideal, rather than the real, had possession of the mind, I was constrained to hold companionship with the latter, and I found it associate itself with me in the shape of sundry cart-loads of cow and horse dung. I had pleased myself with the probability of Gray having stood on the same spot where I then stood, viewing the scene that I then viewed, sitting down to rest on the clean grass where I thought of sitting myself down to rest, when I perceived that all the grass was covered by a dry substance that had once been farm-yard manure. It had once been manure; and had it been taken to a field and ploughed into the soil, it might have continued to be manure until it was decomposed by the chemical influence of the matter composing that soil, after which its fertilizing power would have existed for a few years as a portion of the soil itself. But it had been carted out and spread upon the surface of a pasture-field, the bodily substance of it—that over which the sun and the gases of the air had no other power than to dry and leave to crumble—was there;

but as dead and incapable of quickening vegetable life as the
dry dust in the adjacent grave-yard was of renewing its own
animal existence. At the hamlet of Stoke I observed that
the manure was laid up in heaps in the yard, exposed to the
wasting power of the air, instead of being retained in a hollow or pit, or beneath a covering, where all its powers could be
preserved. And, unfortunately, this manner of wasting manure is common over all parts of England, unless, perhaps, in
Norfolk and Northumberland, or some parts of Suffolk. And
not only this manner of wasting it, by laying it up in dunghills instead of putting it into dungpits, but the absurd practice of spreading it on grass-lands to lie and wither is a universal practice, and a practice so wasteful that, in manure
alone, the farmer loses more than he would lose by the total
repeal of the corn-laws, were these laws repealed before he
brings his present crop to market. The loss by the manure
is a positive loss ; the loss by a repeal of the corn-laws is a
supposed one ; both of which, with some others, I shall estimate in the course of these letters. Meantime, for the good
of the farmers of the comparatively well cultivated district of
Stoke Poges, for the better economy of all cultivators, and
especially for the benefit of a bread-eating population, who
have a right to claim that the land and its fruits should not
be wasted, I shall give a few extracts from a practical farmer
and standard author on the value of that article which is so
universally wasted—farm-yard manure. The work from which
I quote is that of Mr Jackson of Pennycuik. He says—
"The situation of the dungpit should be near the stables
and cow-houses, and placed so low that all streams of urine
from them should flow at once into it, so that nothing be lost."
And he adds—"It should be covered by a roof, so as to prevent the action of the sun." He also says—"It is of the utmost importance, though too frequently neglected, to convey
to the pit the entire liquid refuse of the farm-yard, provided
the quantity be not so great as to make it advisable to have a
separate pit for its reception." And of dung-heaps carted to
the fields he says—"In every instance the dung-heap in the
fields should be placed in a hollow situation with a substratum
of earth, and should have a scattering of a few inches of earth
over it and around the sides, to keep in the volatile gases."
And again he says—"At whatever time the dung is applied,
it should in the first place be scattered evenly over the land,
and ploughed in as speedily as possible. Every instant in
which it is exposed to the air it is losing its value."
  To the foregoing, the editors of Jackson's work, the Messrs
Chambers of Edinburgh, add a note, which states—"We have

seen lands in Germany covered with stable dung which had
evidently been exposed on the surface for weeks, and was as
dry as a chip." If such is to be seen in Germany, it is also to
be seen in England, and in almost every part of it. But it is
not to be seen in Belgium nor in China, two countries where
manure is better cared for than in any other part of the world.

Jackson says—"There is no farmer but must have occasion
to keep up the fertility of his land by the application of lime,
bone-dust, rape-cake, and other ingredients, and a great part
of this expense may be saved by collecting and applying what
is absolutely wasting in his farm steading." And once more
he says, speaking of collecting the liquid manure—"To accomplish this object, proprietors of lands should, if required, assist
the tenantry in the erection of cisterns; for, as these are not
removable, few tenants having only a nineteen years' holding
would be willing to defray the expenses out of their own funds."

Now when the manure of the farm-yard is so wasted as we
see it; when it is so valuable as we find it proved to be; when
it is even doubtful if a tenant with a lease of nineteen years
(the common term of Jackson's locality) can venture the expense of the necessary apparatus for collecting manure, what
are we to expect of the English farmers whose landlords
leave them to flounder on as they did fifty years ago; who
give them yearly holdings of their farms, and employ lawyers
to collect rents at rent time, votes at voting time, petitions at
parliament time, and who, under a pretence of securing to
them a protection from foreign competition, keep them in an
unceasing fear of insecurity in respect of their own conduct?

But there is in many cases much to be said in defence of the
landlords, inasmuch as the tenures by which the land is held
are of such a nature as to mar all improvements and to render
leases inoperative. It is said that James Hogg, the Ettrick
Shepherd, declared, after his return from an agricultural project in England, that he found it more necessary to be an
acute lawyer than a skilful farmer.

No. II.

September 19, 1842.

It has been alleged that the name of Buckingham is derived
from the natural forests of beech-trees which grow in some
parts of the county, and which by the Saxons were called
Buccan; but this is an error, none of these forests have been
at any time in the vicinity of the town of Buckingham, the
point at which the name was first fixed. The word *boch* sig-

nified, in the Saxon tongue, a charter, and *boching*, a meadow charter, or meadow held by charter. *Ham* signified sometimes a hamlet or small village, as also a mansion. We have. therefore, Bochingham, (now written Buckingham,) the mansion. or villages, of the chartered meadow. On the other hand, a copyhold was called *foch*, and the land, with its village or mansion, Fochingham.

There are hills and dales, wood and water, in every variety in Buckinghamshire. In truth, it is a lovely section of lovely England; and many of its sweetest recesses and noblest eminences possess an interest from historical events, political and literary, which makes the foot unwilling to move, and the fancy linger long after the foot has moved away. In my last letter I spoke of Gray, and the Elegy, and Stoke Church. Now I have to speak of Taplow Hill, overlooking the Thames, and the broad meadows which wedge out the distant undulations of field and forest in Berkshire. Like the rich and titled residents whose dwellings crown his head, and who are but food for coming death, like their fellow-mortals labouring in the fields below, Taplow is, as his fellow-hills, a mass of crumbling chalk; but the infirmity of his nature is hidden, save on one side, where the untiring river gnaws into his breast as ceaselessly as restless time worms away the heart of human strength. On every other side, and on most points of this, Taplow wears the richest dress which the summers of England can afford him; and variously disposed in his leafy robes may be seen, diadem-like, the mansions and villas of rich men, in their several varieties of simplicity and grandeur.

We have Dropmore, the seat of the Grenvilles, where strangers may visit the gardens, rich in exotics—rich even to matchlessness in some departments. We have Hedsor, the seat of Lord Boston, high in situation, yet as nobly arrayed in its towering woods as its lord in his robe of state. We have other lords, with knights and baronets, and among the latter Sir Francis Burdett. But finest and most delightful of all their mansions is Clifden, centre-piece of the front group, the residence of Sir George Warrender. This has had several owners, among whom was Frederick Prince of Wales, great-grandfather of her present Majesty, who here congregated around him the most eminent men of all professions and ranks of life—men whose names and words will exist when the Thames has turned old Taplow and all his magnificence into meadows and mud. The mind swells even beyond the breadth of view, broad as that is, when the eye looks from this exalted paradise. We see the noble river in the vigour of its youth, uncontaminated as yet by the world's intercourse; and the

willing fancy winds with him a tortuous course, until he becomes
the parent of a commercial city vast beyond all rivals. We
follow him, and as he mingles with the eternal ocean, his
fleets, offspring of his strength, go forth to every sea-shore
of the world. Accompanying them in vagrant fancy, we
see them chief of all fleets in all seas, and at last, suddenly
recollecting our place of prospect, we find ourselves standing
on the identical spot where that most heart-swelling of national
melodies--*Rule Britannia*—was first sung. James Thomson,
its author, was one of those eminent visitors whom Frederick
drew around him ; and in this circumstance, as also in the
visits and poetry of Pope and others, we have the hallowed
light of genius and old days around us, in addition to a present
scene almost matchless in beauty.

Then, if we traverse the country towards the north, we find,
at the distance of a few miles, just as we are about to criticise
the agriculture of a great landlord—George Dupre, Esq.,
M.P. for the county—that we are once more on ground
otherwise remarkable than for its lovely situation. We are
in the pleasant town of Beaconsfield, and have around us the
estates which were the patrimony of a being rare in the world
—a rich poet. This was Edmund Waller. And when we
pass from his grave in the churchyard into the church itself,
treading lightly in the solemn stillness, we put our feet on the
silent dust of one who, at no distant time, commanded the
listening senate, and ministered with stupendous eloquence
to the admiration of the intellectual world : we are over the
grave of Edmund Burke.

Passing from thence, and advancing through a country
variegated with many of the beauties of nature, to wit, hills,
valleys, streams, and wild woods, with corn fields to match
the woods in their wildness, we shall find ourselves, in due
time, on a section of the Chiltern Hills. Here we find the
natural beeches growing to a goodly size, and extensive coppices of indigenous trees, including boxwood, stretching over
many miles. From lowest valley to highest woodland all is
luxuriant, if not checked by some superior agency ; but there,
as elsewhere, the strong checks the weak, with only this difference, that the weak are weaker there, and the strong
stronger than where we find humanity better schooled and land
better cultivated. We see there, in fullest contrast, the weak
bush and the strong tree, the weak corn and the strong weed,
the weak tenant and the strong landlord.

In our advance to the Chiltern Hills we may visit Hampden,
the seat of the Earl of Buckinghamshire, who, about twenty
years ago, succeeded to the property of the last of the descend-

ants of John Hampden the rebel-patriot. To the reader of history there are interesting associations at this place; to the curious in relics there are undoubted antiquities; to the lover of field sports there is sport; to the lover of the forest there are fine trees and forest scenery; to the student of geology there is ample instruction; to the lover of good mutton there are South Down sheep; to the lover of good farming there is bitter disappointment.

A portion of this district is known as the Chiltern Hundreds, the stewardship of which a member of Parliament nominally accepts from the crown when he wishes to resign his seat. When we advance to the front of these hills, we look down on the Vale of Aylesbury, an extensive tract of level land, remarkable alike for the richness of its soil and the indolence of its owners. I find that the writers of the Agricultural Survey of 1794 state that—" So rich and fertile is the soil about Aylesbury and Buckingham, that we are assured it is considered a disgrace to a farmer to suffer a heap of manure to be seen at the end of his field, to plough in straight lines, to disturb an ant-hill on his pasture, or to permit more water than falls from the heavens to pass over his meadow." And a topographical work, published twenty years subsequently, states—" In this district large tracts possess in such a degree the advantage of obtaining water, that the farmer can flow his grounds when and where he pleases, brooks and rivulets running through the greater part of these fine meadows, with few or no mills to interrupt or control him in the free application of their fructifying streams; yet, except in the neighbourhood of one or two of the paper-mills, there is scarcely an acre watered throughout the country."

The topographical writer says something in praise of the style of cultivation on and around the hills, where necessity has, in some degree, overcome the sloth of the valley; and adds—" *On the contrary, in the Vale of Aylesbury, and the more northern parts of the county, the richness and fertility of the soil has produced such a strong prejudice against any improvement among the farmers of these districts, that, contented with the natural fertility which nature has bestowed upon their lands, they neglect every artificial means by which they might be rendered more productive.*"

Reader, go over this *italic* passage again. It applies in a greater or lesser degree to much of England, and not alone to the vale of Aylesbury. Read it and recollect it. It is a text from which homilies must be preached. It is the key of the " Castle of Indolence," the key of the house of the bonded corn. One giant holdeth the doors of both. Let us knock

him on the head with his own key; awaken that which he
burieth in sleep; set at liberty that which he keepeth in
bondage.

No. III.

The Duke of Wellington having denied that there was a scarcity of corn in the country in 1841, the author questions the means by which the Duke formed his estimate.

With his camp on Torres Vedras, Portugal in front, Spain
in rear, the French occupying both, winter surrounding all,
and discontent at home ruling a feeble government, which
neither appreciated his talents nor dared support if they had
appreciated them, Wellington stood strong in his position,
but stronger in his own courage, protected in his deep
trenches, but better protected in his deep sagacity—and he
outreached all his enemies, whether armed with the sword in
the Peninsula, or, more formidably, with the envious calumny
in London. But great as was his defensive triumph—and it
was unquestionably one of the greatest achievements of his
great career—he had only to estimate and provide for con-
tingencies which his previous experience had prepared him
for. He might not know precisely how many French were in
Portugal nor how many in Spain. The quantity of powder,
and ball, and bread, in *their* stores he could only guess at, but he
knew to a day's consumption the amount of his own. How
much biscuit there was to each set of teeth he knew to an ounce
weight. How much duty could be done by each eater of biscuit
he knew to an hour's march. He could measure futurity, and
direct his foresight with certainty; he was able to measure to
each man his bread, and to the measure of the bread bind
each man's mouth to receive and be silent. Not so now. He
may compare for a nation a supposed supply with a supposed
consumption; but where are the items of his estimate—from
whence comes his knowledge of enough? Are there no empty
cupboards—no breadless tables—no weavers with potatoes and
gruel—no weavers with half potatoes and gruel—no weavers
and others without work and without gruel? Or is there not
a wide-spread necessity among the millions of working people
to cut with such caution at a loaf—to pinch with such self-
denial the meals of each day—that two loaves, and two meals
may suffice where three would be gladly eaten? On the
contrary, is it not known in every working man's family, and in
a majority of the families of all the shopkeepers, tradesmen,
clerks, and small gentry in the kingdom, that if bread and

flour and butchers' meat were cheaper, they could each day of the year consume more than they do ? And has the Duke of Wellington taken these deficiencies of consumption into account? He has not ; and this is our reply to the question of—" What is to be done with a supply from abroad and an increased production at home ?"

Yet this reply will not convince the owner and advocate of protected corn that the working population could eat more. Each will say there is distress in the factory districts, and that the masters have so mismanaged, that many people are unable to eat their fill of the " enough ;" and they will lament, through press and pulpit, that a virtuous, well-fed, rural population, should be seduced to the towns, first to earn high wages, next to starve, and, employed or unemployed, to become the most criminal of British subjects, the most sinful of God's creatures. But having arrived at this point of argument, it becomes necessary for us to shew that hunger and crime are not exclusively town-bred ; and, in doing so, I resume my observations on the condition of Buckinghamshire.

We are descending a valley with our faces southwards. Behind us is the town of High Wycombe, distant five miles. the intermediate space being farm fields, lovely in situation— lovely despite their weedy foulness and mismanagement. The Wyke rivulet, meandering through the meadows, is studded with flour and paper mills ; and the London and Oxford road, following the course of the stream, is studded with public houses. On each side the ground rises with gradual ascent. until, at the distance of two or more miles, and at the height of three or four hundred feet, it again declines, and forms the banks of other valleys. And here, where we now stand. we have these heights ploughed to the top on our right, while on our left are woods of goodly timber, stretching to the distance of several miles, interspotted by an occasional field of grass or corn, ultimately terminating with Taplow and its diadem-like display of villas and mansions. The orchards on each side of us, and the luxuriant hedge-rows bend their branches beneath the weight of their ripening fruit ; and wild flowers, offspring of the autumn, and plentiful as the fruit of the plants that flowered in summer, bloom as gaily as if summer and autumn contended for mastery and summer prevailed. In the shade of the orchards, cottages, clustered in groups and scattered singly, reveal themselves as we advance ; and tall poplars rise above cottage and orchard, many of them in rows, so gigantic in stature, so hedge-like in form, as to give the idea that we are in some enchanted paradise guarded by giants. The distant blue of Berkshire may be traced in their openings

2

and observed mingling with the blue of the heavens, while
nearer at hand the rich vegetation tells of the alluvial meadows deposited by the adjacent Thames.

Having noticed the wayside marks of parish boundaries as
we advanced, we are aware that Wooburn parish surrounds
us; and, arriving at a village, we are informed that it bears
the appropriate name of Wooburn Green. It is a sweet
place. A smooth level of green turf, several acres in extent.
is the centre-piece. Surrounding it are the houses, almost
forming a circle; orchards stretching behind the houses; the
tall poplars behind the orchards; and exalted woodlands towering above the poplars. The well-employed Wyke, almost
tired of turning water-wheels, floats calmly along, and, as if
conscious of having done its duty, prepares for the eternity
into which it is about to enter—the sweeping Thames. As
we linger, the loveliness grows upon us; and apples in tens of
thousands in single orchards suggest that if England can
produce an apple-pie we may hope for it here. Perhaps our
first observation to the first person we meet refers to apple-
pies, and, if so, the following will be the tone of the conversation—it is almost word for word that in which I engaged on
entering the village :—

"Pies!" said the person with whom I conversed, "we as
have apples and an income to afford flour may have pies and
puddings both, but every family—nor the half, nor the
quarter—have not fruit of their own, and, if they had, where
be the flour to come from and the sugar?"

This induced me to inquire at once into the question of
wages. The reply was that wages had been nine and ten
shillings a-week, but that many were employed only partially,
a few days at a time, while others were wholly without employment, and that in the heat of harvest! I proceeded to examine into the physical and moral condition of the people of this
district more minutely than I had at first designed ; for I was
surprised (a commissioner, if examining into the state of the
colliery or factory workers, would say *shocked*) at the extreme
depression under which each family, each principle of independence, each feeling of humanity struggled. Irregular
employment, family discomfort, female prostitution, drunkenness, idle habits, gambling, absolute ignorance, and, in many
cases, starvation almost absolute, were the prevailing characteristics of the working population.

No. IV.

The Letter by Robert Hyde Greg, Esq., on "Scotch Farming in the Lothians."

The subject of Mr Greg's letter is "*Scotch Farming in the Lothians;*" and he opens it by saying—"The Lothians comprise the counties of Edinburgh, Haddington, and Linlithgow, and have latterly become celebrated for the superior system of cultivation carried on, the flourishing condition of the farmers, and the high rate at which the land is leased." And after he has recorded his visits to the various farms which he saw in various parts of these counties, Mr Greg says—" I have thus endeavoured to give, in a somewhat unconnected way, the result of my observations on the Lothian farming, *where high rents, high profits, and a well-paid and contented peasantry, are all seen combined in a pleasing union.*"

It is, however, necessary to be more particular in describing the Lothians than Mr Greg has been, lest people at a distance may form an idea that these districts are *naturally* a broad paradise of peace and plenty.

The three counties stretch along the south side of an arm of the sea called the Frith of Forth, over a distance of between seventy and eighty miles. Linlithgowshire (called West Lothian) contains 71,680 acres, of which 50,000 are cultivated, but many of these are a poor cold soil; 10,000 uncultivated, yet capable of giving some profit to their owners; and 11,680 are altogether unprofitable;—Edinburghshire (or Mid-Lothian) contains 230,400 acres, of which 181,000 are cultivated, but much of that quantity is also a cold soil, and not one-half of it so good as the middling land of Buckinghamshire, very little of it, if any, so good as the Vale of Aylesbury ; 20,000 acres are uncultivated, and 29,400 are unprofitable ;—Haddingtonshire (or East Lothian) contains 160,000 acres, of which about 100,000 are cultivated, 30,000 uncultivated, and 30,000 unprofitable.

The uncultivated and unprofitable bears the highest proportion in the latter county, but the cultivated is, upon the whole, a better district naturally than that of Mid-Lothian, and much superior to West Lothian. Excepting some particular and very limited localities—limited when compared with poorer ones—such as the Merse of Berwickshire, the Carse of Gowrie, on the Tay, and small portions of some other counties, the cultivated land of East Lothian is greatly superior to any in Scotland, yet it is barely equal in its natural qualities to one-half—perhaps I would speak more correctly

if I said two-thirds—of the cultivated land in England. Of
the 100,000 acres under cultivation some idea of the difference
in its quality may be formed when I state that, with other
young men, I have been engaged ten or twelve days at harvest
work in the earliest parts of East Lothian; have then gone
to Dunse market, engaged with a Berwickshire farmer for his
entire harvest, only then beginning, his wages and work being
higher and harder than the wages and work of the Lothians.
We have been a month or five weeks with him, have seen every
straw cut down; have then penetrated into Northumberland,
reached Morpeth or the later districts of Durham, and had two
or three weeks more. Having finished off there, we have
returned to our own county, East Lothian, and engaged with
one of the upland farmers, then in the heat of his harvest, perhaps in the very parish where we began ten weeks before a harvest finished within a month. The parish of Innerwick is
one of those so varied in soil and climate. It comprises some
of the richest land in the county and some of the poorest in
the kingdom; is like a garden in some parts, a wilderness in
others. Such, then, is East Lothian; and I deem this explanation necessary to guard strangers from supposing that all
the county is a rich soil. Neither must it be supposed that such
good farms as Mr Greg saw could be seen in other parts of
Scotland, except in the limited districts already named; but it
must be recollected, and I crave pardon for again repeating
it, that one-half, if not two-thirds, of the land ploughable in
England, could be rendered as productive at as small an
expense as the best farms seen by Mr Greg, save, perhaps,
those adjoining Edinburgh, where advantages are found not
common to more rural districts.

What, then, did Mr Greg see? He enumerates the. farms
he visited; and of those beyond the influence of Edinburgh,
he says—"No. 7. 500 acres; rent, L.1750." This he states to
be a soil of stiff clay, which any practical person knows to be
the most difficult and expensive of all soils to farm profitably.
It is let at L.3, 10s. an acre; and Mr Greg states that the
farmer and his two brothers, who are in the neighbourhood,
pay the sum of L.4500 of annual rent. Such a farm as this,
of 500 acres, would be let in Bucks to three or four yearly
tenants, or perhaps more, who would with great difficulty pay,
including tithes and poor-rates, the sum of five and twenty or
at most thirty shillings an acre for it. Indeed, considering
the stiff quality of the soil, which with them would waste the
strength of six horses to a plough, they knowing little or
nothing of the art of ameliorating clay soils, such land would
more probably be let at fifteen or twenty shillings an acre.

Yet they would be whipped up to every election to vote for
the candidate who would vote for a protective corn duty; and
with the protection of that duty they would sit down with
their rosy cheeks and their long pipes over their ale, lament-
ing their hard bargains, fearing deeply for Peel, hoping highly
of the Duke of Buckingham.

"No. 9," says Mr Greg, "300 to 350 acres; 25 miles from
Edinburgh; *rent* about L.1200. Farmer absent; and being
the last year of the lease, the grieve (overseer) was not communicative, thinking we were looking at the farm for ourselves.
Seventy acres in wheat, about 5½ quarters to the acre, and
exactly equal over every inch of the field. The farm nearly
without a fence, and almost every yard in the highest state of
cultivation." To be without a fence is no merit, if fences are
necessary either for cattle or shelter to the crops, but in those
parts land is otherwise cared for than to put cattle on it to
graze; cattle are fed at the stall, and beef is made in half the
time, with no waste of food; manure is made, and good crops
are grown. What did I see in Buckinghamshire? the crops
struggling with weeds; in many fields they were suffocated,
in every field they were unequal. Scarcely a fence was capable
of keeping in cattle, and yet the fences were from twelve to
fifteen feet high, occupying, with ditches on each side from five
to fifteen yards of ground, and nursing in their warm shade
the most luxuriant and most varied crops of weeds which
vagrant nature could supply to her travelling emissaries—the
winds. "It being the last year of the lease," says Mr Greg,
"the grieve was not communicative, thinking we were looking at the farm for ourselves." It is always the last year of
the lease in Bucks; and that suspicion and taciturnity which
seize the Lothian farmer once in nineteen years keeps tyran-
nic hold of the Buckingham tenantry every year. Many of
them told me that I need not be too eager in putting questions
about their rent and produce, if I got the land I was looking
for I would not find it much of a bargain; and almost all
looked on me, as they look on every stranger, with suspicion.

"Considering the fate of the corn-laws to be sealed," writes
Mr Greg, "and all unequal protection to the landed interest
about to be withdrawn, I was anxious, both as a landlord and
a farmer, to prepare for the state of things which such a change
might introduce; more particularly, as a farmer, to prepare
myself, by increased skill and economy in the management of
my farm, for the keener competition and lower prices which
the free introduction of foreign agricultural produce must
establish." Accordingly he took his bailif with him, and

visited the Lothians.   He saw, as he says, that " there is as
wide a difference between the system existing there and in these
parts of England, as in that pursued in the small detached
spinning mills of thirty years ago and what is now practised
in the first-rate factories."

It is a singular coincidence that the finest farms visited
by Mr Greg were either the property of Sir George Warrender of Lochend, or very near the town of Dunbar, around
which is the Lochend estate; also that Mr Greg should have
been at the great agricultural show of the Highland Society
held at Edinburgh in a park belonging to Sir George Warrender, and that the best land which I saw in Bucks and
Berkshire—the best land and the foulest weeds—the finest
farms and the worst farming—should have been lying near,
stretched in front, and in view of, the splendid mansion of
Clifden, described in my letter No. II. the princely residence
of this same Sir George Warrender !   But beyond this remark
we must not go; the farms are not Sir George's, neither has
he any property there save the mansion and the wooded park
and garden adjoining.   His near neighbour, the Earl of
Orkney, has a farm, however, which I visited there, and found
depressed with the common disorder of the country.   The
barley absolutely wasted through the want of proper management; on the harvest field was, at least, double its amount
of seed, and the crops were not so luxuriant as to have much
to spare.   The dung-heaps were laid up to dry, with the liquid
running into a waste ditch, after the fashion of the most
ancient ignorance.

The land in the valley of the Thames, so rich by nature,
so valueless by cultivation, belongs in part, I was told, to a
Mr Lewis.   Close by, in another field, a man was paring off
the tops of the couch and other weeds with a hoe.   Beans
had been the crop; and so thickly and unopposedly had the
foulness grown, which, as the man told me, overtopped the
beans, that the ground which he had hoed looked like an old
pasture, or a piece of moor-land newly paired of its turf.   The
weeds were in seed also, and fully ripe, and he was mingling
them as effectually as he could with the soil for the ruin of the
ensuing crop.   A short distance from him there was another
bean field; and, to make the most of it, turnips had been
sown between the rows of beans.   The turnips were not much
inferior to some I saw in fields specially devoted to them, yet
they were so very feeble, so incapable of holding on against
the foulness that choked them, and the beans had been such
a meagre crop, at the same time the owner of them was so
full of complaints about hard times, that I turned from the

scene with shame. And I was within a few miles of the Great
Marlow Union Workhouse, crowded with the unemployed
poor; within a mile of Cookham and Maidenhead, in which
the half-employed, and less than half-fed labourers were crawling about, asking, in return to every question asked of them,
for " something to get a drop of beer," adding that " times be
so terrible bad that they couldn't get half enough of work to
do," that they couldn't get " bread enough no how."

Yet there is not in England's isle a county fairer in its
face than these two to which the Thames is here the beautiful
margin. Two days before I was in this neighbourhood her
Majesty the Queen had driven from Windsor to visit Dropmore and the fine scenery of Taplow. Doubtless she looked
down on this fine valley, and casting her thoughts to rugged
Scotland, which she was within a day or two of embarking for,
took one parting look of some of the loveliest scenery of lovely
England. Yet on that day week—exactly that day week—
the royal eyes saw the sun rise on Mid-Lothian, where farms
produce six quarters of wheat and pay L.6 per acre of rent.

" No. 3," writes Mr Greg, " 340 acres; old lease of 19
years recently expired—old rent L.1700, or L.5 per acre.
The farmer took off L.18,000 to L.20,000, and has just
bought a handsome estate in the neighbourhood, which he is
improving. The farm is re-let at a *rent of* L.2000, *or* L.6
per acre."

" No. 2. At two miles from town, with ample supply of
town manure, potatoes and turnips carried daily into Edinburgh—*rent* L.7 per acre."

These are samples of what her Majesty saw, or might have
seen, within a week of her visit to Taplow—these are the
farms on which Mr Greg says there are " *high rents, high
profits, and a well-paid and contented peasantry combined in a
pleasing union.*" In the lovely valley which her Majesty must
have looked on from Taplow, there are *low rents, low profits,
an ill-paid and a discontented peasantry.* The rents are thirty
shillings an acre, a railway to London is at hand, and barges
are passing and repassing on the Thames, ready to take away
produce and bring back manure.

Mr Greg, speaking of the Lothian rents and profits, says
—" It is an interesting question, but one I am not going to
enter upon, how this improved system of cultivation can be
introduced into England, particularly into our own and the
neighbouring counties. Where are the landlords ready to
grant a nineteen years' lease? Where the farmer of sufficient
intelligence and capital to manage successfully 500 acres and
lay out L.1000 to L.1800 on draining alone, during the two first

years of his lease?" And after these queries he gives an
opinion of the causes that have led to the great improvements
in Scotch farming. Of these I shall speak in my next letter.

No. V.

The " Scotch Farming in the Lothians," as described by Robert Hyde Greg,
Esq., is further noticed in this Letter, and the Causes of its Advancement
are spoken of.

" I am inclined to think," says Mr Greg, " the *superior and
more practical education* of the Scotch has been at the bottom
of the improved state of things. Education has given the
knowledge which has enabled them to apply their capital with
success, and to extract from the landowner the long lease
which enables them to invest their capital with *safety* as well
as success."

No; not education. The school education of the rural
population in Scotland is a meagre affair, and has been greatly
over-rated. *The long lease is one of the main causes of the
excellence in Scotch agriculture;* the facility of obtaining loans
from the banks is another; so is the absence of tithes and the
poor-laws—though there is much need of a properly regulated
poor-law—the Scotch paupers being wretchedly provided for;
*but the leading cause, which brought others into operation, and
which has promoted the culture of the Lothian farms to the present state of excellence, was the original poverty of the country,
which poverty impelled the owners of the soil to exertion, in order
to reach, in some degree, the opulence of the landlords in England.* Of this *cause* abundant evidence is furnished, even in
England itself. Scotland was once to England what the poor
soil of England is to the rich at this day. In Buckinghamshire, and other counties near it, we see the poorer soils cultivated with a science and industry comparatively eminent; the
richer soils lie in the profound sloth of two centuries. In Scotland, the husbandry of eighty or a hundred years ago was so
very bad, the crops, the cultivators, and the people all so very
poor, that the landowners were driven by *necessity* to do something for a reformation. The farmers being not only much
poorer than those of England, but the farms much smaller,
the landlords found it necessary to introduce a superior class
of farmers, and to break up the small holdings. This superior
class of farmers, being capitalists from the towns, or small tenants made great ones by favour of the landlord and assistance
of the banks, were forced by necessity to demand leases, and

the landlords were by necessity forced to grant them. The inferior implements of husbandry—at that time inferior to those of England—induced mechanics to study the construction of an improved class of implements, so that they have gone on improving until they have left England far behind. " Necessity is the mother of invention," says the proverb, and the proverb says truly.

Nothing could be a greater blessing to all interested in English agriculture, and that is the entire English nation, than the abolition of the corn-laws, if the abolition would withdraw that delusive prop which sustains indolence. Look to what age of the world we may, and to what country, we find individuals and nations falling into decay in exact proportion to the protection which obviates the use of exertion. Spain is an eminent instance. A nation once the most enterprising has become one of the poorest and most indolent, because an evil-working good fortune gave it mines of gold in other countries. There was no necessity to plough the rich soil of old Spain, and accordingly it is not ploughed, only scratched here and there. But Spain is now poor, and she must do something for self-redemption. She has some of the finest soil in the world, and lies within a short voyage of our shores ; she has no cotton factories, and her clothing is expensive and inadequately supplied ; her people are fonder of idle warfare than work ; but if work they must, they will rather be in the open fields than in close factories ; therefore, if they had a demand for their wheat, and a trial of our cheap clothing, we should see Spain improving. America excepted, we shall one day see her become our best customer for manufactures, and one of the best producers of wheat. Her people are extremely frugal in their diet. They could produce vast quantities beyond their consumption, and what they cannot eat they will learn to sell. When this and other competitors are seen in the corn market, there will be some *necessity* for our landlords to bestir themselves ; and, bestirring themselves, they will see the propriety of adopting the system which has improved the Lothians.

As to education, if Mr Greg means school education, which I presume he does, it is the birthright of every child ; and we, or the parents, or the government for us, rob that child of its birthright if we neglect its education. The parochial schools of the Lothians may have favoured the advancement of agriculture ; but it must not be forgotten that they were the same as now, or as they were recently, when Scotland had a hundred years of bad cultivation before her. Indeed it is a common complaint with old people in Scotland that education has retrograded—they meaning religious education, which, in fact,

must be the kind of education favouring agriculture, if anything from a school or church has favoured it. At all events,
a knowledge of the practical sciences, or of anything calculated
to expand the mind, formed no part of the education which I
received, and I got all that two schools could afford. These
schools were in East Lothian, and their teachers were equal
to any in the county, keeping off the town academies. The
course of instruction was the following:—

Lessons in a spelling book, and a flagellation with *the tawse*,
(a piece of saddlers' leather two feet long, two inches broad,
and split half the length into six tails.) When done with the
spelling book, the New Testament, and—the tawse. When
done with the New Testament, Barrie's Collection, (of select
pieces,) and—the tawse. Accompanying that, psalms on Mon-
days, and—the tawse; the catechism five days of the week,
and—the tawse; writing, and—the tawse; arithmetic, and
—the tawse, all of which lasted over a space of six years. I
was as seldom in mischief as any one; and, when I got any
encouragement, more zealous to learn than many others; yet
I hammered away, and was hammered on, for six dreary years
—the most dismal period of my life—and did not know as
much of arithmetic at the end of that time as I could now
learn in a day, or any child of ordinary capacity, properly
treated, could learn in six.

The education of the rural districts in Scotland has not
been what strangers suppose it is. If a clever boy could make
the discoveries which the schoolmaster is now supposed to teach
him, he of course learned something; but he dared not communicate what he knew to the one who had to sit a week over a
question in arithmetic, and then go home as ignorant of it as
at first. In fact, the range of knowledge to be acquired in the
school was so limited, and the necessity for each pupil acquiring all his knowledge without the aid of a superior deemed so
essential, that education, properly so called, did not exist.
And a flagellation being considered the natural accompani-
ment of each lesson by the schoolmaster, and all who abetted
him, our parents and neighbours, every one, young and old,
we, the pupils, believed it too; and, feeling the "tawse" to
be a punishment, we had no other idea of education than as
one of the evils of life which we could only hope to escape from
when we grew big enough to thrash the schoolmaster, or get
quit of him altogether by going to work in the fields. In short,
a mother had no readier method of frightening a refractory
child into obedience than by threatening it with the *school!*
An Englishman sees an occasional Scotchman pushing himself
forward in life, and therefore praises the Scotch school education; but, were I with any such Englishman in my native

parish, (and there the style of farming is of the most superior kind,) I could put my finger on at least a dozen individuals who would have been men of livelier mind and clearer intellect than they are, had they never been at school at all, so thoroughly benumbed were their faculties by hammering and thrashing, and attempting to force them to know that which was never explained to them. And in Lothian, and the neighbouring county of Berwick, I could point to four farmers, one of them paying L.2000 of rent, none of them less than L.1000, who were at the same school with myself, *and never at any other*, who were occasionally thrashed as I was, though not so frequently, their fathers being farmers, and mine only a farm labourer, and who, left to their own wits for education, are notwithstanding eminent farmers.

In short, it is not the schools that have advanced the agriculture of the Lothians; but it is now at that point where real education may assist. When chemistry and other sciences are practised by the farmers—and to such practice they must be educated—Lothian will advance beyond its present fruitfulness. Hitherto, all that has been done has been by sheer industry, protected by a lease, and a moderate attention to the common physiology of vegetation; but if the abolition of the corn-law brings competition, we shall not only see England equal the Lothians, but the Lothians stretch far ahead of what they have yet attained to.

No. VI.

Cranbourne in Dorsetshire is a village with an extensive parish, stretching towards Wiltshire on one side and Hampshire on the other. The parish contains 2444 inhabitants, chiefly farm labourers, but all dependent on agriculture. Wages are at present eight shillings a-week, the rate of recent years, but some have reduced that allowance, and all talk of a reduction. The village is a confused collection of houses, standing in all shapes and positions, from the respectable cottage of the tradesmen with its garden, to the crumbling hovel of clay and wood occupied by the labourer, at a rent of L.3 and L.3, 10s. a-year without a garden. It stands in a hollow, and is surrounded with land of excellent quality, farmed by tenants-at-will at a rent of about L.1 per acre.

Cranbourne has a redundancy of labourers. At the low wages of seven and eight shillings a-week there are those who cannot find employment. There is no part of England where the promoters of emigration could more efficiently plant an office and an agent. The following are a few of the conditions on which such an agent should act :—

1st. Ascertain if the labourer is without employment, or, if he is employed, ask if he wishes to improve his condition; in whichever way he is, the answer will be one favourable to the agent.

2d. Fit him out at once. His family need not all go with him at first; his wife can stay at home, and one of the children can follow with his dinner. There need be no passage-money paid, nor weeks and months of sea-sickness and danger incurred. The distance is only two or three miles to the nearest landing-place. Neither need the trouble of erecting a hut of clay or wood be incurred, previous to building the comfortable and permanent cottage; the labourer can return to the hovel of clay and wood which he left in the morning in the old country.

3d. The labourer will have no occasion, on his arrival in the new country, to hew and burn down the giants of the forest. The land is already cleared, and he may have his choice of any part of many miles of country. He may begin by paring and burning; and when he turns up the first spadeful, he will break a virgin earth, never moved before by human hand.

4th. Previous to a commencement of digging and sowing, the emigrant will require to form an arrangement with the native chiefs. This an agent might do for him through the British government. The chiefs are by no means hostile to those who merely walk over their uncultivated territories; if no game is killed, and no attempt at cultivation is made, a settler will not be interfered with; but there is a sharp jealousy ready to oppose all attempts at digging, and sowing, and reaping, if these are made by any but the chiefs themselves, or their servants.

5th, and lastly. The unimproved wastes are so extensive and variously situated, as already stated, that unlimited choice of situation may be made. The soil is all good. Some is of first-rate quality. It must be estimated not by acres but by miles. In some directions the stranger who does not know where the settlers are planted, may go five miles; in others, eight miles; and in some, from ten to twenty miles, over a country not producing sixpence an acre, which, in two or three years, might be made to produce, per acre, several quarters of grain. The settlements already made are not so productive as they might be, because of the uncertainty of the holders. This uncertainty, and the evils attendant on it, was well shewn by Lord Stanley, in the last session of parliament, as regarded New South Wales. In the uncultivated country now under observation, a security similar to that obtained in New Zealand and the Australian colonies must be obtained ere it would be safe to send out such as the labourers of Cranbourne. The chiefs to be applied to would be chosen according to the district in which the emigrant intended to settle. Suppose the labourer moved towards Salisbury, the Marquis of Salisbury, the Earl of Shaftesbury, and several landowners who are not enobled, would be the best to arrange with; while, if a movement was made in another direction, without intending to penetrate far into the interior, the Earl of Shaftesbury might alone be consulted.

However, all this is for the consideration of other parties, who will judge whether it is best to send labourers across an ocean of ten thousand miles at a great expense, or endeavour to employ them at a distance of two miles from their present homes.

No. VII.

Over a section of Salisbury Plain.—A Sunday in St Giles'.—A Notice of the Earl of Shaftesbury, Lord Ashley, &c.

Having visited Old Sarum, and the old tree where three old freeholders voted at the old elections, and having seen as much of New Sarum (so the city of Salisbury is fondly denominated by the inhabitants) as the worthy host of the —— inn and other kind friends thought fit to recommend to my attention, I set out on an inspection of what are seldom recommended to, and perhaps seldomer visited by, strangers— the dwellings of the agricultural labourers in the country. The first six miles of road brought me in contact with several shepherds, waggoners, and others returning from the great Weyhill Fair, which had been held during the week near Andover.

They were returning into various parts of Dorsetshire, and from them I learned the continuation of two important facts which had met me in every previous county, namely, that the harvest had been abundant, and that the labourers' wages were being reduced from one shilling to two shillings a-week in consequence of that abundance.

Around Salisbury I found the old wages to have been nine shillings for regular ploughmen and carters, and the reduced rate to be eight shillings, with a scarcity of employment. In those parts of Dorsetshire nearest to Wilts, the wages of the same description of men were, and had been, eight shillings, with some reductions to seven, and an expectation that such reduction would be general in a few weeks. A gentleman from the neighbourhood of Lord Portman's estate, near Shaftesbury, stated the wages in that district, and all the way down towards Devon, to be seven shillings, in some cases reduced to six.

One of my temporary companions was a dealer in geese. He bought them in the New Forest, in Hampshire, which stretches its bald downs and shaggy wildness into Dorset, and sold them to the farmers and millers near Salisbury. In the first instance, the breeders of them inhabiting an uncultivated country, which, though generally fertile, they were not allowed to cultivate, sold them at about eighteenpence, in order to raise money for the Michaelmas rents. He sold them at a small profit, and again purchased them at four or five shillings each at Christmas for the London market. Suppose the miserable dwellers on these vast commons were allowed to enclose, and compelled to cultivate well, a piece of land, the value to them may be at once seen as enormous even in the fattening of geese.

After producing eggs, and sustaining loss in breeding, they sell the ill-fed, yet full-grown bird, for eighteenpence, for the want of food to make it worth three times as much, which food is supplied by the farmers and millers in Wiltshire without almost any expense.

I had still six miles or more before me when this geese-dealer and the daylight parted, he taking the road to Blandford, the light following its westward career, both leaving me to loneliness, darkness, and the broad downs, the roads on which I was told could not be mistaken, they were so easily observed, but which I mistook from the easiness of perceiving so many of them.

Properly speaking, there was only one road, but it was such a jolly old-fashioned English road, that it branched into a hundred tracts the moment it escaped into the common. When the law of necessity came in force, as, for instance, at a declivity, or the crossing of a marsh or brook, these tracts re-united for common safety; but as soon as freed from the law, they were off again, each enjoying his liberty, each destroying the produce of more space, apparently for the love of destruction, than would have fed, and clothed, and lodged a state convict or a parish pauper.

My last travelling companion had told me to observe certain bushes and dark clumps of trees on the horizon, to keep one to the right and another to the left; and he accompanied his directions with anecdotes of robberies and murders committed in those parts in the olden times, hinting that at such a period as this, the great fair week, there might be people lurking about who might be tempted to mischief by a supposition that money was to be carried home, and that it was best to keep a sharp look out, and so on. With this injunction we parted.

I soon lost the way, and found on each side of me robbers enough—robbers of a nation's food; the most unjustifiable of all robbers, and filching more in one year than all the violent men have filched on Salisbury Plain since the Saxons first set foot on it.

These robbers were widely extending bushes of furze, and all manner of unprofitable rubbish, together with the open baldness of the downs, occupying many thousands of acres, which should have borne benevolent supplies of grain.

That the soil is capable of bearing grain profitably is abundantly testified by the patches of cultivation which, on my return some days after, in daylight, I saw interspersed amid the broken wildness. Other causes than a difference of soil had led to a cultivation of one part and a neglect of others.

A field of Swedish turnips, the best I have seen for a month, though journeying in search of them, was holding association with miles of furze, which occupied land of equally good quality, simply because of some difference in tenure. In at least a dozen places I saw young wheat, as fine as any I had seen a week before in Kent; and, in some cases, I inspected the crop of straw and grain which the recent harvest had yielded, and was told the quantity was four quarters an acre.

Furze, which was worth about a shilling an acre for fuel, or a bad material for a bad dead fence, was occupying the land which could produce four quarters of wheat, and this because the rich landowners will either have all the commons enclosed for themselves to the exclusion of the commonality, or they will not let them be enclosed at all.

Some of that down land might not be capable of bearing wheat in equal abundance, but all of it, more extensive than the largest landed estate in England, now almost worthless, might be rendered highly productive.

But, generally speaking, the districts which are reclaimed are so poorly attended to, and the population so ill paid and ill fed, that it matters little for their sakes whether these downs be ploughed or not. Each enclosure bill excludes the poor man from the common, and, upon the whole, it may be as well for them to live the mean life of breeders of geese, rather than be turned out to labour for wages less than the price of food. But the right of an individual is not the right of the nation; and the national right demands to know why there is to be a scarcity of food because of the caprice of the land-owners. All farmers are tenants-at-will in those parts, and incapable of using knowledge or capital on their farms with security, if they possessed either, which, in most cases, they do not in sufficient strength to advance in improvements.

However, this belongs to the daylight portion of my obser-vations, which I must at present omit, to continue my journey to Cranbourne.

Having been put in the right way by a labourer, who came out of his way for the purpose, and who told me that he laboured for eight shillings a-week; that he got up at four in the morning to his horses, and was then, at half-past seven in the evening, just quit of them in the stable; and further, that much of the rough country over which I had come was Lord Shaftesbury's, and that, should it be enclosed, much more of it would become his Lordship's private property; I proceeded until I again found it necessary to inquire which of two roads I was to take.

I entered a cottage where two men, who had just left work as the other had, were sitting down to a very small piece of boiled bacon and vegetables. I held parley with them long enough about the way I had come and the way I was to go, until they had finished their meal. They, too, were carters, rising at four in the morning and coming home to dinner and supper at seven in the evening. They had been receiving eight shillings a-week, but were now reduced to seven. I asked if they could afford bacon and vegetables to their dinner every day? and they said no, they could not when they had eight shillings, and they did not know how they would with seven.

I reached Cranbourne, and found a comfortable inn; talked with several people, who all agreed in stating that the labourers had a hard struggle to make a living.

All of them kept a pig or two; but they had to sell them to pay their rents.

There are cottage allotments of half an acre; but for various reasons, which I shall hereafter describe, these are by no means so profitable as they might be.

Next morning I walked out, intending to return to break-fast, not knowing there was any other village or inn within reach. But at two miles distance, while supposing I was only in the vicinity of St Giles' Park, the seat of the Earl of Shaftesbury, I found myself all at once in one of the sweetest little villages to be seen in England. It bears the name of St Giles', and has a pleasant little church nestling among the

lofty trees which overtop the entrance to Lord Shaftesbury's
residence. A clear stream comes calmly along a green meadow, and the green meadow is fringed with houses, which are
again surrounded with little gardens, these, in most cases,
having the last roses of summer still beautifying the walls and
the bright glass windows.

Her Majesty the Queen Dowager had visited at Lord
Shaftesbury's on the previous day, which visit having caused
the preparations of clearing away the fallen leaves and new
gravelling the walks, gave the whole place, pretty at any time,
a peculiarly pleasant appearance, particularly to one who had
come over the rough country I had crossed, and out of Cranbourne, for which, it seems, there are no special guardians of
cleanliness and comfort as at St Giles'.

At the latter, the Rev. Mr Moore, who holds the living,
and who is possessed of considerable private property, is the
chief promoter of the respectability which distinguishes it.
All the people residing there, and I conversed with many of
them, speak most respectfully of the Earl of Shaftesbury, of
Lord Ashley his son, and of the other members of the family;
but though they were admitted to be kind to those immediately about them, the words spoken in praise of Mr Moore
were the most frequently and zealously expressed.

There is a free school, principally supported by Lord
Shaftesbury, and the dwelling houses are let to the working
people at L.2 a-year, each having a little piece of garden
ground. His Lordship lets them have wood for fuel cheap,
and for those who are too poor to bring turf fuel from a common
some miles off, he sends his carts to fetch it. Mrs Moore
and some of the Shaftesbury family have established a savings'
bank, in which a penny a-week is deposited, to be drawn out
at Christmas, at which time they, the patronesses, double the
amount of each deposit, and bring a travelling haberdasher to
the village, who exchanges certain kinds of goods for the
money in the bank.

Mr Moore has given a field, his glebe I believe, to some of
the families in half-acre allotments, at the moderate rent of
twelve shillings each, which is, however, more by four or five
shillings the acre than the farmers pay. Lord Shaftesbury
has also given a few allotments, but several families are still
without them, because of the hostility which the farmers evince
to any such system; they will take no man as a regular
labourer who has an allotment.

On inquiring the reason for this, the answer was, that the
farmers were jealous of seeing the labourers in a thriving condition; but I was not satisfied with this supposition.

3

The real cause I believe to be the hand-to-mouth system in which the farmer carries on his work. He calls the men when he chooses in the morning, keeps them to any hour at night, detains them always late, but especially at those seasons of the year, spring and harvest, when the allotments would most require their attention.

The farm labourers are as badly provided on the St Giles' estate as elsewhere, save those resident in the village, where the clergyman's benevolence is largely diffused.

I can safely say that I never heard so much spoken in favour of any clergyman as was said in praise of the charities of Mr and Mrs Moore ; and I believe sincerity and justice dictated every word I heard. Yet, with all this charity, the people were no better provided than they ought to have provided for themselves without it. The comfort is not wholesome which is promoted by charity. For instance, the savings' bank in this village will give no proper idea of the value of savings. Should they remove to some place where there are no kind ladies to double the amount, he or she will have no inclination to deposit at all.

Moreover, this giving of charity causes the recipients to feel that they require it, and that they were not previously as well provided for as they should be. Those living within four hundred yards of Lord Shaftesbury's gate, which distance includes the village and living under the unusually benevolent superintendence of a clergyman, may not feel any very hard privations. His Lordship allows those who work in his park nine shillings a-week, which is a shilling more than the farmers give, and two shillings more than is given in other parts of the county; with this, and the perquisites, and the allotments, they may rub on pretty comfortably, being constantly employed ; but his Lordship's estates extend far beyond the village of St Giles, whereas the charity stops there. What the labourers require is real independence, not of wealth, to be above working, nor of relationship to a master, to be beyond obedience, but of agreement—an agreement which binds the master equally with the servant. Mr Hyde Greg saw in the Lothians, he says, that all the operations of the farm were carried on with the same regularity as in the great factories.

The time of working in the Lothians is observed scrupulously to a minute, ten hours a-day in some districts, nine in others—generally nine; but such is not the case in the country I am now describing.

Though there may be just landlords, and I do most sincerely believe Lord Shaftesbury to be one, at least in his motives, still all are not just, neither do all manage their own property; and if they were conscientious in their motives, they may be unjust indirectly. If they uphold a system such as the tenancy-at-will, marring improvements, lowering wages, and spreading poverty, they become unjust, however honest in the intention to let the farmer retain his farm until his capital is repaid. In no department of trade is money parted with without security; even if one borrows from another for a day only, he gives a written acknowledgment, which, in the event of his sudden death, will enable the other to recover what he has lent. But though landowners die, like other men, (and this Mr Moore exemplified in his sermon which I heard preached at St Giles',) they expect that a farmer should trust to them and their successors, whoever these last may be, for a return of expended capital. The farmers, however, do not trust, and they never will; and the result is, that we have foulness of soil and poverty of crop, and a population poor and uncultivated as either.

Having alluded to Mr Moore's sermon, I may state that, having heard so much said in praise of his good works by all with whom I conversed in the village, I had a desire to see so good a man, and to hear the sound of his voice. It being Sunday, I accordingly went to church, and found him engaged in a christening. He is a man of middle size, with a head that would fill a phrenologist with delight. The broad lofty brow, bald backwards, shewing forth benevolence in a very eminent degree, is a forcible argument in favour of phrenology when viewed in connection with what the people say of him. The Earl of Shaftesbury had been at church in the morning I was told; but at this time there were only four of his family there—Lord Ashley, Lady Ashley, and two others whom I did not know.

They paid devout attention to the worship, and the ladies, in the exceeding plainness of their dresses, shewed very humbly in contrast with the more expensively decorated wives of the upper servants. Perhaps ladies of title can afford to wear a coarse bonnet and a sixpenny ribbon—nobody suspects that they are really unable to get better; but poorer people's pride must not hazard a suspicion. The church is a handsome one, erected at Lord Shaftesbury's expense, and maintained by him. One of the parishioners, to a question I put, said, that though he had heard of church-rates, practically speaking he did not know what they were. All the people at church were neat and comfortable in appearance. I made a remark on the subject, and was answered by one who said—" Ah! you may travel far enough before you see such another place as this." The text was that passage in

the gospel of St John which relates that " a certain nobleman, whose son was sick at Capernaum, came to Jesus," &c.

I know not if this text were taken by design or rotation;
but knowing that the Shaftesbury family had only come to
St Giles' a few days previously, and hearing Mr Moore remark
on the uses of affliction in humbling the spirits of men, more
especially those of high rank, who were more likely to be
uplifted with the vanities of life than the poor, whose poverty
alone was often a great affliction; hearing such a sermon at
such a time, I could not help remarking it.

No. VIII.

The Country around Salisbury.—A Returned Convict.

Salisbury stands in a valley at the confluence of two streams,
which form a goodly river named *the Avon;* on each side of
which below, and for many miles on each side of its tributaries
above, are excellent meadows.　These are regularly irrigated
by sluices and trenches, which operation is called in the local
dialect " drowning the maids."　The level breadth of these
valleys may vary, perhaps, from half a mile to three times as
much, and then on all sides rises the land generally known as
Salisbury Plain.　Many excellent farms and several fair specimens of cultivation may be seen on each side of Salisbury;
but vast tracts of good land are lying waste, and much that is
under the plough seems imperfectly cultivated.　The general
aspect of the country is bare, there being few trees or fences
save in the valleys, and even there the fences are not well kept.
Standing on the high mound where once stood the citadel of
Old Sarum, a mile and a half north of Salisbury, the view on
all sides is very extensive.　Were the reader to fancy himself
the head of a pin, and Old Sarum a pincushion, left by some
playful kitten in the centre of a parlour floor carpetted with
drab cloth, and further, that the said kitten had amused itself
with a ball of white worsted, he, the reader, would see a
resemblance of the extensive downs and numerous lines of
chalky roads which stretch out and cross each other in every
direction, as viewed from the citadel of Old Sarum.　Moreover,
if he could imagine that a child had played on the drab carpet
in addition to the kitten, and with very small fragments of
ill-used toys had laid the outline of houses and gardens, and
enclosed fields, and, when tired of play, had scattered the whole,
and, with the kitten, had left the room to the reign of solitary
confusion, the said reader would see all that is to be seen in

shape of farms and enclosures in the wide country viewed from Old Sarum, including parts of Hampshire and Dorset, as well as Wilts.

Though the aspect of those parts of Wilts and Hampshire is so bare and unpleasing to the eye, there are fine woods at no great distance from Salisbury. There is the residence of the Earl of Pembroke at Wilton, three miles from Salisbury, up the valley of the Avon—a delightful place, rich in the adornments both of art and nature. There is in another direction Longford Castle, the property of the Earl of Radnor, with a park bearing excellent timber. Passing that, two or three miles eastward, I found Trafalgar Park, the property and residence of the successors of the famous Lord Nelson.

" What extensive woods are those ?" I asked of a man who was breaking flints for the public road on the side of the Avon opposite this park.

" Which be they you mean ?" said the man, raising himself up, and shewing his full height, which was about five feet four inches, with a firm breadth of body ; shewing also a weather-beaten face, apparently forty years old, and a smock-frock and hat which, judging from their condition, might have been even older. " Which be they you mean ?"

" Those opposite, with that very large mansion rising on the high ground behind."

" Ah, that ; that be Trafalgar. That be Lord Nelson's house ; but he be dead now, they say, and there be a young lord a-coming to live there."

" Indeed ! I was not aware that a property so very interesting as that of the famous Lord Nelson was here. Do you know if his Lordship, the great Nelson, ever resided here ?"

" There wur a Lord Nelson here, but he be dead, and there be a young 'un a-coming, I hear say, but I don't know nought of the other Lord Nelson, only I've heard people say he wur a terrible hand at fighting."

" Do you know whom he fought with, and where he fought?"

" No ; I suppose he fought with they as fought with he ; it was at sea, they say, but I don't know nought but what I've heard tell on."

" Then I suppose you have never read history ?"

" No ; I never learned to read nought—I never wur at no school."

" What wages can you earn ? Do you work by the day, or have you so much a load ?"

" I goes on by so much a-day. I work twelve hours a-day

in summer, and as long as I have light to see in winter. My wages be one shilling and fourpence a-day—eight shillings a-week. It be not much, be it?"

"No, it is not much. How do you manage to live?"

"Not well; and there be three more—wife and two children. We had another boy, but he died two weeks aback; as fine a boy as you could wish to see he wur, and as much thought on by his mother and I; but we ben't sorry he be gone. I hopes he be happy in heaven. He ate a smart deal; and many a time, like all on us, went with a hungry belly. Ah! we may love our children never so much, but they be better gone; one hungry belly makes a difference where there ben't enough to eat."

"Poor man! It is indeed a melancholy evidence of national distress to hear a hard-working man speak as you do. Have you got a piece of garden-ground with your cottage?"

"Ees, a small piece, about four log or so, it don't grow much for such as be so ready to eat everything as we. And it costs, with house rent, L.2, 10s. That ben't easy paid out o' eight shillings a-week, be it?"

"No; you must have a very hard struggle to keep your-selves alive?"

"Ees, hard enough. It makes one think on doing what one would never do, but for hunger."

"Did the late Earl Nelson employ many people on his estate?"

"No; I don't know that he employed many—not more than others here—not so many as some—not so many as Lord Radnor did at Longford; but he be gone from that now, and I hear say there ben't so many at work as wur."

"He, the late Lord Nelson I mean, was a clergyman—was he not?"

"I've heard he wur once, but don't know much of what he wur, 'cept that he transported me."

"Transported you! What for?"

"For poaching. I got seven year; and wur killed near almost. And they killed my brother dead at once—knocked his skull to pieces."

"Who—the gamekeepers, I suppose? Did you make much resistance?"

"No; I heard them fall on my brother, and I wur fifty yards from him. And when I wur hiding, they came and took hold on me, and beat in my skull. Here, you can feel with your hand; out of that part, and this, and this, eleven pieces of bone were taken. I never wur expected to live for a long time. No, I never made no resistance; for they had broken my head and killed my brother afore I knew they saw me."

This man went on to tell me, in answer to several questions, that he was at that time out of work ; that he and his brother went out to poach, leaving their father, mother, and two sisters, I think he said, at home ; that the result was, as already stated, that after lying long in the prison hospital he was tried ; that the Earl of Radnor, pitying the family for what had already befallen it, endeavoured to prove that the men were taken on his ground, and not on Earl Nelson's, but it was decided otherwise ; that he (the convict) was kept nineteen months at Portsmouth after trial, and then shipped off for Bermuda ; that he served the full term of his sentence there, at building the public docks and fortifications ; that about a thousand convicts were there during that time, who slept in barracks at night, and wrought by day under a military guard ; but who, apart from this unpleasantness, lived well. He wishes, he says, and prays to God, that he could now for himself and family at home have such an allowance of food as he had in the West Indies when a convict.

" We had *terrible good living*," this was his expression, " by as I ever had for working in England. Fresh beef three times a-week, pork and peas four times a-week. But the weather was so hot we *drowd* (threw) the soup away."

" Could you have remained there after your time was up ?"

" I don't know ; I wur tired of the confinement and the heat—it wur terrible hot, it wur, and we had no liberty. And then father and mother and sisters wur at home. But father died soon as I wur gone—one son killed, and me a'most, and then transported, wur too much for him to stand. Ah ! he wur broken hearted, he wur ; and as soon I was come home mother died."

" I suppose you had difficulty in finding employment when you came home ? People who wanted workmen would look on you as a bad character."

" Ees ; but some on 'em knew as I never would do no harm, and I got work some how, and got married. I be nine or ten year at home now."

" When you were in the West Indies serving your sentence, was any attempt made to instruct you ? Were there any attempts made to reform you, to give you instruction, teach you to read, and make you comprehend the duties of life, and prepare you to practise them when you would escape from bondage."

" Oh ees, we had a terrible sight of all that. We had prayers many times a-day, sometimes oftener, and sometimes fewer, but many times, and on Sundays nought but prayers. Oh ees, we had a terrible sight of that, too much many a time, we got tired on it."

"But had you any books to read? Or was any attempt made to teach you to read."

"No; nothing but prayers, and some preaching o' Sundays."

"No instruction was given on the moral duties of life, as, for instance, the relationship of one man to another as human beings, how to live comfortably, profitably, and honestly?"

"Oh ees; I wur told thousands o' times that poaching wur a terrible bad thing."

"However, you were not taught to read and write?"

"No, there wur none o' that."

"What is your name!"

"John Baillie—that be my name."

Having, after some other conversation about the present fall in wages, left this man, I entered a roadside inn at the distance of half a mile from where he was at work, and there, amongst other things, heard the landlady say—"The man you speak of must be John Baillie. He is a truthful man. Depend on it, whatever he told you was the truth, extraordinary as you may think his account of himself. There is no man, I believe, that is more honest and truthful than John Baillie, even though he has been transported."

Perhaps it will occur to some people that such a man as this might have been a better citizen, maintaining himself and family comfortably with a little expense in education, and early moral training; whereas he must, as it is, live a very unpleasant life, and have cost the country a great deal of money during his imprisonment. The public money expended on him alone would do a good deal for the reclamation of the waste land and the waste people in his native country.

Report on the Condition of the Agricultural Districts.

November 1842.

The following extract from a great quantity of matter collected by the author, and partly published in the *Anti-Bread-Tax Circular*, at this time, refers to the same locality as the last three letters. The precise place is outside the park walls of St Giles', the seat of the Earl of Shaftesbury. His Lordship is the nobleman spoken of; the farmer numbered as 21 is one of his tenants; and the labourer numbered as 22 was an eccentric subject met with at that time.

No. 22, A labourer putting flints on the highway, is spoken with shortly after leaving No. 21. He says he has eight shillings a-week, and has received notice that after next week he will only have seven. Says he saw me talking to old ——, and would like to know what *he* said about wages. I told him that we talked of many things, but I forgot to mention wages. The labourer asks what I did talk about to the " *old un.*" I reply that I talked to him about his manner of keeping accounts, whether he was particular in writing everything down. To which No. 22 says, " And what did *old un* say to thee?" " He said he did not keep any accounts, he trusted to his memory." " And," says No. 22, " what did thou say to he?" " I said it was not proper to trust everything to one's memory, that a man could not conduct his business properly unless he kept his accounts correctly." " And what did *old un* say to thee then?" " He said he never forgot anything." " Never forgot nothing!" exclaimed the labourer, as if highly amused with his examination and my replies; " Never forgot nothing!" he again repeated, " no, *old un* be not likely to forget nothing as will put a penny in his pocket and keep it out of another man's. *Old un* won't forget that he told his men last week he would take them down a shilling; but he be's as long as a journey from here to London on a pig's back afore his memory be's good enough to raise wages at the time he promises when he takes 'em down !" And having thus spoken, No. 22 applied himself with great vigour to his work. Observing at this moment a person at some distance, walking by himself, and supposing that he was some other farmer whom I had not seen, I called the man's attention to him, and inquired if he knew him, and if he was a farmer? After standing a minute, and scanning the person as narrowly as the trees would permit, the labourer said, " That be the *old un's* master; that be all our masters. The *old un* be as much afraid of that un as any of we." " Does he go out among the farmers much?" " I ben't no farmer myself; wish I wur." " Why do you wish you were?" " What do thee think I work for?" " For wages." " And how much do thee think I get?" " You told me you had only eight shilling, that you are to be reduced to seven?" " And how much do thee think I eat over a whole week out of that?" " I cannot say; I should like to know; perhaps you will tell me?" " Suppose, rather than I tell thee, that thou tries. Take thee to breaking flints and making roads at eight shillings a-week for a year, do thee think thou could tell what thee lived on?" " I don't know;

I think there would be no danger of having such an abundance as to forget." " Do thee think not? Well, an I wur a farmer I would always have as much to eat as to be able to know what it wur; I don't be able to tell it now at times, 'cause how I go with an empty belly so often that my grub ha'n't no name. Ah! you be a precious lot o' hard screws on a poor man, the whole lot of you be." " Which lot? You seem to include me, and yet you don't know who or what I am?" " Don't I though? I see you ha' got a good coat on your back, and a face that don't look like an empty belly; there be no hunger looking out atween your ribs I'll swear. You either be a farmer or somebody else that lives on somebody else. May be you be a lord for aught I know on; or a squire; or a parson, dang it—you be a parson perhaps! One thing I see, you ben't one of them as works fourteen hours a-day, to feed lords, and squires, and parsons, and farmers; dang the farmers, they be the worst of the lot of ye."

" Why do you think so? Why do you think the farmers are the worst?" " Why! what need of me to tell you why? You wouldn't believe me wur I to tell why; but I dare say you know without telling. I dare say you be one of them as has your daughter, an you ha' a daughter, playing on the piano on a Saturday night to drown the noise of them brutes of labouring men what come to get their wages through a hole in the wall; what cannot be allowed to set foot within a farmer's house now-a-days; what must be paid through an opening in the partition, lest they defile the house of a master what gets rich as they get poor; a master what must get his daughter to play music lest the voice of a hard-working man be heard through the hole in the wall! Ah! it be enough to drive men mad; it ha' made men think on things they never would ha' thought on."

" But," said I, " you are wrong in supposing every person to be your enemy who is not one of yourselves. Do you speak of a farmer in particular who pays his men through a hole in the wall while his daughter plays the piano inside, or do you say all the farmers do so?" " Oh, you know, master, what I mean; you be not such a stranger here as you would make me believe." " Did you ever see me before?" " I ha' seed enough o' thee, I dare say. I dare say you be about to go and tell all you heerd me say now. I dare say you be one of 'em as come from London to kill game, that a poor man, like I, must not look at. Ah! I don't care; we must just go on. We be all like to have justice sometime; there ben't no noblemen in heaven, they say." " Is there not? and will there be any *poor* men there?" " Not an the rich can help

it ; not an the rich can keep the poor out, I should think.
But I be told no rich be to get there neither." " Who says
so—the parson ?" " Oh, I ben't no friend of the parson's."
" Why are you no friend of the parson ?" " The parson be
no friend to me." " Why ?" " Because he ben't." " You
don't seem to be afraid to speak your mind ?" " Ah ! I ben't
like to be much longer here ; I be like to try my hand in
another part of the country. Seven shillings won't do ; eight
wur bad enough, but seven won't do."

No. IX.

*The Author having been criticised by Sir Charles Wolseley, and the Allotment
of Land to Labourers ridiculed by Sir Charles, while the Workhouse System
was denounced, this Letter, descriptive of the Town of Wilton, where the
Author happened to be at the time, and descriptive of the Unemployed there,
was written in reply to such critics as Sir Charles Wolseley.*

The town of Wilton, once the capital of Wiltshire, stands
in a valley, fertile and lovely, three miles from Salisbury. It
once sent two members to Parliament, and still sends one.
It once had a manufacturing trade in flannels and carpets,
now it has almost none. Its near neighbour, Salisbury,
robs it even of the value of its markets and fairs. I went
through and through, round and round, this poor remnant of
a town, and to a distance of some miles beyond it. Nothing
could be finer than its situation, with wood and water, hill
and valley, forming a sweet nest of nature, in which the
cottage streets reposed. Judging by the tower of a new
church, which was rearing its head above the trees, and holding
up to view several masons and their labourers, with hammers and
trowels, and mortar and scaffolding, as if to shew a stranger,
even when a mile out of the town, that he must not go away
with the belief that everybody in Wilton was unemployed ;
judging by this, when looking down from the elevated vicinity,
one would suppose that the little town was a young one just
peeping from the leafy nest for the first time ; and with such
a supposition to begin, the mind would soon stretch into the
probable future, and see the powerful stream that waters the
rich valley, and the rich valley itself, studded with buildings,
great as this great new church, for the manufacture of food
and clothing, (we shall say flour and flannels, the materials for
which are abundantly supplied by the surrounding country,) and
these buildings stocked with wheels and human hands, labouring
and giving birth to labour. Having the supposition of the

town being a young one, the first flight of the stranger's mind
is to form an opinion for the infant Wilton, and say what it
will be when it is full grown.

But descend from the elevated vicinity—enter the streets,
and all the beauty of the wood and water and green meadows
has vanished, so also the dream of youth and vision of future
greatness. You find, instead of a day to come, the day has
gone by. Wilton has had its day. If we might personify its
condition further, we would say there is an old man before us
stricken in years, yet not so feeble from age as from the accu-
mulation of other ills. He is time-worn and venerable, and
entitled to our respect; but he is hunger-bitten, and cold, and
friendless, and claims our pity. He can call to mind the
bygone days, and tell of what he did when making carpets
and flannels; how he ate bread and bacon and roast beef,
and brewed his beer, and was comfortable, because well
employed and well fed. But he is old and lonely now, he will
tell you, and his offspring with his trade have left him for
some place in the north called Yorkshire, where, by all accounts, they are not thriving so well as they should do.* They
are suffering hardships themselves, and cannot help him.
He moves on crutches, which, he says, are his only supports.
One of them, on which he depends most, is strong, but hard
and hurtful to his decayed frame; he grumbles at it, and
calls it the " New Poor-Law." The other is more pleasing
when he can lean on it, but it is too short, and were he to
trust to it, he would fall, and die where he fell; this he calls
" casual charity." Being old and ill provided for, he is fretful.
Of both his crutches he is constantly complaining. He speaks
of bad times and a hard-hearted world, and is not thankful
for either of his supports, because, as he says, if he had got
fair play he would have needed neither. He sees the splendid
new church building, at a cost of L.30,000, and he is told it
will be an ornament to his old age; but he says there is a
great cathedral three miles distant surrounded by parish
churches; that there are three more of the latter situate
between that cathedral and his own door; that he has another
at his own door, and that he thinks L.30,000 might have
been more rationally expended. Being argued with, he will
admit the possibility of a new church being required in place
of the old one, though he assures us the old one was large
enough; but he will not allow more than L.10,000 for a new
church, and maintains that the remaining twenty should have
been devoted to the improvement of the land or the renewal
of the manufacturing trade. In reply, he is told that the

* This was written in the year of Yorkshire distress 1842.

money expended on the new church is not his; that it is private money; that the Earl of Pembroke and members of his family have provided this money to build this church, and that no one has a right to question them on the subject. He says to this that he has no right, and he seeks no right; he knows the church will be an ornament to him, and a monument to those who are defraying its expense; but he says he wants the means of sustaining life; that he conceives the greatest monument which any rich family, such as that of Wilton House, could rear to their own honour, would be to renew his trade, recall his scattered offspring; rear around their domain a thriving population, who, being physically comfortable, might be trained in moral respectability.

But let us relieve ourselves from this metaphor; let us proceed to the bare "matter of fact." Come with us, Sir Charles Wolseley, and all who abominate the "Bastile Poor-Law," as you call it; come with us, and see the poor of Wilton, where there is little trade, where almost all are dependent on an agricultural neighbourhood; come, all who would deny an allotment of land to the poor, all who would keep the cultivation of land and the amount of human labour on that land at a *minimum*; come, all who drive the industrious people to the workhouse, and then seek public applause, by denouncing the workhouse as a "Poor-Law Bastile;" come, and tell us what you would do with the poor. Here we are, a landlord, Sir Charles Wolseley, a farmer, a guardian, a gamekeeper, and a ploughman. Let us speak to the first poor man we meet:—

Ploughman—"What is your name, my good man?"

"William Turner; some of them gentlemen know me well enough; I've lived long enough in Wilton to be known."

"You are an able-bodied labourer, I perceive; how old are you?"

"I be forty or thereabout."

"Are you married?"

"Yes; I have a wife and six children."

"What wages have you?"

"No wages; I be out of work, and can't get none."

"No wages and no work? What do you live on?"

"We don't be living; we be starved. I been to the guardians to get into the house, but can't get in afore next week. Don't know what we shall do till then. One-third the people in Wilton be without work, and t'other third don't have more nor three days a-week throughout the year. Them as be employed constant don't have more nor eight shillings a-week now; they had nine shillings; but now, since the markets came down, farmers be taking down wages. Ah! them be hard times; terrible hard times; a poor man don't know how to live no how."

" Well, gentlemen, what is to become of this man, his wife, and six children? I see many thousands of acres of waste land at no great distance from this, which should be taken into cultivation. I do not—mark me well—I do not mean the thin chakly down land, though doubtless the herbage of that might be improved by laying clay or some such substance on it; but I allude to the excellent corn land which may be found in every direction, forming part of those downs, and which, if broken up to grow corn and winter food for sheep, would enhance the value of the thinner soils left for summer pasturage. But, apart from these downs, there is the rich land around us, which is indifferently cultivated. Many parts of England are not so well cultivated as this district I admit, but this is bad enough—some of it disgraceful in respect of foulness, bad fences, and wasted manures. Why don't you, Mr Farmer, employ more people, and call into activity the neglected resources of your farm? By an expenditure of capital you might soon have a great profit out of that which is now comparatively unproductive; out of those meadows, for instance."

Farmer—" Why, sir, his honour my landlord knows I am only a tenant-at-will; and what with that, and what with politics and elections, and one thing and t'other, it would not be safe for me to lay out much money in employing people more than I can help. I don't say as how, by no means, that Lord Pembroke, or any one belonging to his family, would raise my rent when they saw me growing better crops by better cultivation, or that they would turn me out of my farm if I did not vote for their interest, I don't say that; but I say as how it would not be wise in me to lay out my money without the security of a lease."

Landlord—" Oh! a lease! you want a lease, do you? We would rather have tenants-at-will."

Sir Charles—" And so would I rather have a tenant-at-will; I never knew a farmer do any good with a lease. No tenant of mine, save one, ever asked for a lease."

Ploughman—" Well, gentlemen, the question is, what will you do with this man, his wife, and six children? They are starving. We have seen their wretched home. It is without any comfort, almost without furniture, and its rent is one shilling and sixpence a-week. Attached to it is about four log of garden ground. Two or three pecks of potatoes, and about eighty cabbage plants, is as much as this garden would bear in a season. Would it not be advisable to give such a family as this half an acre of land, at a rent of twenty shillings?"

Sir Charles—" Oh ! I see what you are for ; allotments of land to labourers ; no, no, we must have no allotments."

Ploughman—" Well then, gentlemen, what shall we do ? Perhaps, Mr Guardian, you will suggest something ?"

Guardian—" Why, the only thing the man can do is for him and his family to go into the workhouse. We would rather not have them in, rates are enormously high already, and the house full, but we must either admit them or let them starve to death outside ; if we do the latter the law will punish us, so we must do the former."

" What will such a family as this cost you in the workhouse ?"

" They will cost nearly at an average four shillings a-head per week ; a good bit of money, is it not?"

" What do you feed them on in the house ? You don't give them much pleasure in their pauper life, I presume ?"

" No, we have too many demands for admission as it is. We would have many more were we not to make the diet as low as will possibly sustain life. We give them bread and milk for breakfast—seven ounces of bread and half a pint of milk. We give them six ounces of bread, half an ounce of butter, and a pint of coffee for supper. This is throughout the week. For dinner they have, on Sunday, one pound of suet pudding; Monday, one quart of bullock's head soup ; Tuesday, one pound of potatoes and three ounces of bacon ; Wednesday, seven ounces of bread and two ounces of cheese ; Thursday, five ounces of beef and one pound of potatoes ; Friday, four ounces of bread and a portion of the liquor which boiled the previous day's beef; Saturday, one pound of potatoes and three ounces of bacon. Such is the diet of the workhouse. It is low, but, low as it is, one-half of the working population of Wilton and neighbourhood don't live better in their own houses—many of them not so well. How can they, with wages so low, and many of them without work ? In short, we are obliged to feed them meagrely, and give them hard task-work at breaking bones, or some such thing, lest they find the house too comfortable."

Sir Charles—" Abominable. This is an abominably cruel system this poor-law. The house is no better than a bastile."

Ploughman—" Well, Sir Charles, it is bad enough, Heaven and the poor know ; but what is to be done? You dislike agricultural improvements ; you deny security to your tenants. so that they cannot incur the risk of improvements, nor employ more labourers ; you will not give the labourers an allotment of land to keep them from idleness and starvation ;

you call the workhouse, to which they are driven by sheer hunger, a bastile, and yet you drive them thither. What is to be done?"

No. X.

From Wilton to Shaftesbury.—A Stage Coach Company.—A Somerset Farmer and a Gentleman from Paris.

Leaving Wilton to repose amid its fine woods on the banks of its clear streams, with its splendid mansion and its new church, the latter intended to be one of the finest parish churches in England, and already shewing an outside which fulfils the intention; leaving the natural and artificial beauties of Wilton to the companionship of a population ill-employed, ill-paid, and ill-fed, an unhappy mixture of paupers, poachers, and men not yet reduced to their condition, but fast approaching it, we shall proceed towards the borders of Dorset and Somerset. Let the reader give me his company, and he shall see and hear literally what I saw and heard.

We are on a four-horsed coach running between Southampton and some towns in the west. At Salisbury I tried to get on the box with the driver, to talk with him as we went along, but that seat was bespoke. I next tried to get a share of the seat behind him, but that was full. There was only room for one outside, and that was behind, on a seat which holds three facing forward to three others, who, with a pile of luggage at their backs, were seated on the roof of the coach, separated from those in front as the inhabitants of one side of a mountain are separated from the inhabitants of the other side.

Well, we are out of Salisbury, through Wilton, and on the Shaftesbury road, with some good farms on each side. We see the Honourable Sidney Herbert with his friends out shooting; and several Salisbury publicans and other burly, well-fed, and not very busy-at-home personages, who, having no privilege, or no gun, or no ability to shoot, are out looking at the sport, with the hope that the exercise will quicken their appetites for the dinner which is cooking at home. Having made the acquaintance of some of these gentlemen, we nod to each other, but the coachman, willing to let the Salisbury people see what he and his horses are, when out of Salisbury, is going at a canter, and there is no time to exchange words.

On we go; and I now suppose that the loss of a seat beside

the driver is not so much to be regretted. There is a guard to the coach, and a guard can give more of his time to talkative passengers than a coachman driving four in hand. But as yet it is impossible to say if he will be talked to. There is nothing seen of his face to tell the humour of his mind; yet he has a face as surely as the sky has a rising moon, when we see a streak of red light, with a cloud concealing her upper and the horizon cutting off her under limb. The guard has a face; but what with shawls of worsted, and cotton, and silk, piled up like wintry mountains, and an enormous breadth of brim lowered like the clouds, to which the mountains are near neighbours, there is almost a total eclipse. And although guards of coaches are a kind of common property, on which any one may intrude in virtue of the quit-rent of a glass of brandy when changing horses, and a shilling or two when leaving the coach; and though I am resolved to pick up what I may find this common property capable of affording, and have no doubt but there is life and something lively behind that red nose which is dipped into a fold of the uppermost whitybrown shawl, yet I hesitate. There is a gentleman from Paris between us. He is not *of* Paris; he is an Englishman returning to his native country *from* Paris, as I afterwards learn; and the newness of hat, exquisiteness of whisker, and dignified polish of manners, with my knowledge that he is an inside passenger sitting outside for his own pleasure, make me hesitate to send my words across him either before or behind.

Yet something must be done. I attempt to *draw* the Parisian Englishman ; but nothing with which I am acquainted will bring him out. There are hills of chalk on our left, forming the margin of the great tract which is in France, which comes across the channel, starts at Dorchester, and stretches to Whitby in Yorkshire. We are on the adjoining tract of clay and limestone, and the embrowned margin of chalk, which rises like a sloping grassy wall a hundred feet high, bounding us apparently in endless length, and the road on which we travel, taking all the windings of these chalky downs at the respectful and pleasant distance of half a mile, are prominently before us, and I start upon geology. Several polite " Yes, sirs," and nods of acquiescence are given by the travelled gentleman, but nothing more. Another passenger, who sits facing me, and whose knees are dividing the narrow space with mine, looks like one who may be spoken to, and he acknowledges that the sudden termination of the chalky ridge and the commencement of the clay on which our road is formed is very extraordinary. But he halts there. In vain I speak of the probable ages when these ridges and this valley took the place they now hold. This gentleman, who is encased in a

4

drab coat and several shawls, seems determined not to come
out, so I beg permission of the gentleman from Paris to say
a few words to the guard, which permission is most politely
granted, and I address myself to the two inches of red face
and the red nose which is reposing in the woolly shawl.

"How far are we from Shaftesbury? Where do you change
horses next? What do the farmers pay for land like that?
Do the railways affect you on a cross country road like this?
You have got a truss of hay strapped on behind—what is the
price of hay? Potatoes seem to be a fair crop in those fields
—do you know what the price of them is? Do the farmers
hereabout allow their labourers a portion of potato ground,
or must the labourers buy all their potatoes?" To these
questions I receive answers brief and indistinct. What little
I do hear is a "yes" and a "no;" the remainder is communicated by the Parisian traveller, who acts as agent. Seeing
that nothing is to be made of the guard, and fearing that the
polite gentleman who separates us on the seat, but who kindly
endeavours to unite us in conversation, may get tired of such
crude questions and barren replies, I desist, and leave the
red nose to undisturbed rest.

Potatoes; there are more potatoes being turned up on the
farms we pass, and I attempt to bring out the traveller in the
drab great-coat, whose knees divide space with my knees, on
the subject of potatoes. I find this gentleman has recently
travelled in Suffolk, and still more recently in Buckinghamshire. He thinks the potatoes are much better in Suffolk
than in Bucks. For his part, he never saw good potatoes in
Bucks. When by any chance they are good, the people of
that county call them bad. They dislike the floury potatoes
and prefer the waxy ones. I remark that when travelling in
Bucks I saw few good potatoes, and also observed the preference given to what I considered the bad ones. The Parisian traveller says potatoes are not much used in France; and
another traveller, in a dark pilot coat, who has not previously
spoken, and who sits with his face immediately in front of the
guard, says he likes, for his part, a floury potato; he likes
it hot, and never has a good dinner if he has not a nice smok-
ing-hot potato. The gentleman in the drab top-coat likes
mashed potatoes best, and prefers them done with butter or
new milk. There is now a likelihood of a general conversation, and, determined to bring the guard into it, I ask him
which he prefers, potatoes of the waxy kind or the floury kind?
The guard cares for none of them. "Give me," he says, "good
old English fare, and good old English times, and *dang* your
potatoes and railroads both!"

This is excellent. Potatoes and railroads! I attempt to take the guard back to the times, not yet very old, when no coaches travelled on the road—when our grandfathers, with their pack-horses, had all the trade, and the coaches did with them what the railroads are doing with the coaches now. But the guard is silent. We are about to descend a declivity. He alights on the road while the coachman is drawing up, and, having put the drag on the wheel, is up again to his seat with a nimbleness quite astonishing. We talk of the patent drag, but receive no information on its absence from this coach, save that the proprietors do not go to the expense of having one. At the bottom of the hill the guard again descends to the road, as a linnet descends from the upper spar to the bottom of its cage; the drag is removed, and, like the linnet, he is aloft again.

This nimble getting down and linnet-like getting up, by a being who but for these motions might be a mummy for aught we can see of his body, leads me to make a remark on the dangerous quantity of his clothes should these get entangled with his feet, for it is evident he does not wait for the coach stopping when he gets down, and as evidently the coachman does not wait for him getting up when he drives away. This suggests the fatal accident which befell the Duke of Orleans; and the Parisian gentleman relates the particulars of that melancholy event. He speaks highly of the deceased Duke, highly of the royal family, highly of Paris, highly of the French. highly of everything but his own health, which he says is not as he should like it to be.

Well, we are halted at a road-side inn. Determined to invade the taciturnity of the guard, I ask him to have a glass of something hot and strong. He has it. The coachman, a jolly, laughing-faced fellow, who neither conceals his face in a shawl nor his thoughts in himself, is in the hands of some other passenger, and is also drinking a stiff glass. In quick time we are on the coach again, seated and away. We are, at first, much the same as before, save the guard. who shews more of his face and somewhat less of his taciturnity.

But there is a short middle-aged gentleman not yet spoken of, the centre one of the three whose backs are to the mountain of luggage, whose faces are to us, and who sit on a narrow space saved for a seat by the piling of the luggage on the roof of the coach. This gentleman is in top-boots, and while other people's feet are resting where common feet on a coach are intended to rest, his are suspended from the seat, unable, however willing, to reach by several inches the resting-place allotted for them. He has spoken to nobody; nobody has spoken to him ; but the little top-boots dangling from his little body, and his little round face with a larger share of good nature shining in it than is to be seen in many longer faces, draws my attention. He is eating walnuts, and asks me to accept of a few. The Parisian gentleman is also asked, so is the guard, so are the passengers right and left of the little gentleman. All accept them, all are cracking and picking the nuts, and all are now disposed to talk. A whole stage has been wasted in vain efforts at conversation, merely because the right man was not spoken to, and because he did not choose to speak to those who did not speak to him. But here he is, just the man of all others to meet on a stage coach, if a stranger wants information about farming.

We are talking of the poor and the poor-rates. He tells us he pays L.70 a-year of poor-rate, for one of his farms, and about half as much more for other property. I ask him where his locality is, and he replies, "Somersetshire; down in the south of Somerset ; the farm that is assessed for L.70 of poor-rate must be no trifle;" and I inquire whether he is a grazier or a corn grower. He pauses until he cracks another nut, and then says, " I am both ; more's the pity." " Why ?" asked the gentleman from Paris ; " why do you say more's the pity ?" " Why ?" replies the other, " because between falls in the prices of corn and falls in the prices of cattle, buying dear and selling cheap, I don't know what to be at with myself." He skins another section of his nut, puts it in his mouth, and then replies to another question of the Parisian, by saying, " No, sir ; I don't say either corn or cattle be too cheap. Cheapness is a relative term. Provisions may not be too cheap for those who have to buy, but they too cheap for I who have to sell them to pay such rents and taxes as I have to pay."

This leads to a conversation on leaseholders and tenants-at-will. He is well aware, and smiles, and cracks another nut, as he replies, that he has good reason to know the value of a lease, if a rationally constructed lease, over a tenancy-at-will ; but he adds, " As times be now, and as leases commonly be made, no leases for me. No, no ; not even the most liberal lease that tenant ever had of landlord for me. Why, gentlemen, it be no farer gone than a fortnight since the proprietor of a large estate down our way sent for me to come to him. Well, I went. He know'd I farmed a good bit of land ; he know'd I had money to lay out ; he know'd I had laid out money on my land ; he know'd I grew the best corn, and turnips, and worzel in the country ; he know'd I was reckoned an improver of land. Gentlemen, I am one that tries to make the most of my land. This landlord know'd it. He said,

'Now tell me what you will give for *such* a farm, if I give you a lease, with liberty to improve it as you like?' Says I, 'Sir, I am much obliged ; *but tell me first what the price of my corn and cattle will be when I have improved your farm, and I will tell you the rent I can pay.*' To this the gentleman replied that the question of prices was now in a manner settled ; the co:n-law was settled, the tariff was settled, and prices would soon be settled. 'Corn-law settled ! tariff settled ! prices settled !' says I. 'Why, the whole three are unsettled ; we have had nothing but unsettled prices since we had a corn-law, and I suppose never will have. You won't let the corn-law alone, and you *can't* let it alone ; and it won't settle prices if it were let alone. No, no, sir,' says I ; 'no taking of leases with matters as they are now.' So to this the gentleman replied, 'Well, but it is your opinion that land cannot be properly farmed without a lease, is it not?' 'Oh yes, sir,' says I, 'that be my opinion, sure enough, and my experience too ; *but land must be badly farmed or go without farming afore I touch it on a lease in such times as they we now live in.*' That I did, gentlemen ; I told this landlord my mind ; I ben't afeared to speak to nobody ; I pay my rent and my taxes, and my debts, and care for nobody. So, as I said already, *cheapness* is a relative term. Things don't be too cheap for them as buy, mayhap ; but they be too cheap for me."

Hearing this, the gentleman in the drab top-coat says, "What would you do to settle the question of rents and prices?" "Ah," replies the other, "that be what I want to know. I want of all things, next to my heavenly salvation, to know what on earth we be to do ; nobody tells us—everybody inquires—and all that I can say is this, that if I am to be hanged, hang me as a dog should be hanged ; don't put a tin kettle to my tail, and hunt me about with a mob after me. in which I cannot know my friends from my foes. Why, dang it ! put un to death or save un at once ; don't torture and kill by slow degrees."

With this, and much more of the same kind, we are in Shaftesbury ; and here I shall take the reader from the coach and set him down at the Grosvenor Arms. This is the principal inn, and as its name indicates, is the property of the Grosvenor family, who have a residence and an estate in the neighbourhood, named Motcombe. I did not halt here myself at this time. The interesting conversation of the farmer on the coach, together with a promise I had made to visit, if I ever went into that part of the country, a gentleman living several miles farther down, caused me to retain my seat, and go onwards.

This farmer is, as I afterwards learned, all and more than what he said of himself. He is an extensive grazier and corn grower; has had great experience; is a man of considerable property, and seemed to me remarkable for the off-hand way in which he delivered his opinions, the chief of which opinions was that no confidence could be placed in the stability of the corn-law. The passenger who sat on his left hand, and who was immediately opposite me, turned out to be a commercial gentleman from London, connected, I think, with the glove trade. He expressed very decided opinions on the corn-law question, having no hope for himself, for commerce, or for the farmers, but in the total and immediate repeal of the corn-law. Wishing to hear the opinion of an intelligent farmer expressed decidedly on this subject, although understanding quite plainly, when he spoke of the dog hanging, that he was alluding to the protective duties, I asked our fellow-traveller what he would do in the event of another election, whether he would support the Repealers or their opponents? He replied, that so far as he knew at present he would support neither. He had lost all confidence in public men. He had formerly supported those who supported the corn-laws. He still believed that the total abolition of these laws would give a shock to English agriculture, although he would not go the length of saying that the shock would be more than temporary. "On that point," said he, "I cannot give an opinion—neither do I think any one else can; but I shall say this, that let the shock be what it may that we are to receive from a total repeal, it will be safety itself compared with the gradual abolition which we now see going on. I am losing my money fast; and, what is worse, I am losing it in the dark."

To this it may be added, that after I had been about ten days among the farmers of Dorset and Somerset, and had talked with them on their farms, in their houses, singly by themselves, and in company with their neighbours, I found that, with few exceptions, the subject on which they were most eager to converse was that of *protection*. Many of them seemed to have little knowledge of the complicated interests of this great country, especially on the importance of our manufactures and commerce; they knew there had been complaints of manufacturing distress, but their knowledge of that distress was indeed very limited, and their notions of its effect on themselves was absolutely a blank. They could not see how they were dependent on manufacturers, and when I say *they*, I include the great body of the farmers, excepting only a few of the more intelligent, who, when they read this, will easily see the exception, and pardon me for writing as I do of their brethren.

A class of more hospitable, hearty, joyous, uproariously free-hearted men than these farmers I cannot conceive. I am bound in honour to say that in Wilts, Dorset, and Somerset, I have invariably found them free and hospitable to an excess. I have dined with them, fifty at a time, and from two-thirds of that fifty, and other fifties and forties, and numbers downwards, I have had invitations to meet them at their own houses on their own farms. I told them plainly that my object was to inquire into and report on the condition of agriculture and agriculturists; that my reports would be published, with a view to advance the interests of both; that party politics formed no part of my purpose; that I carefully avoided all controversial questions, such as the corn-laws, the tariff, &c., and confined myself simply to the home operation on the farm.

It was thus I offered myself to their acquaintance, and thus I was received; but not in this neutral capacity was I able to remain. The sudden fall in the prices of corn and cattle had prepared every man to speak on the subject of prices, to the exclusion of almost everything else; and instead of being averse to talk about the corn-laws and the tariff, as they once were, they would talk about nothing else. Here is a specimen of a conversation. We have walked over part of a farm of 200 acres. I have been shewn the small proportion which is cultivated, the large proportion which is in grass. Have talked about lime and couch-grass, and twenty other things. The farmer allows me to have everything my own way; and as we are returning to the homestead, I observe the liquid manure being entirely wasted, and offer a suggestion for its conservation and application to the field. " Now, stop thee," says the farmer, who, by-the-by, is a tenant of a celebrated banker of London, " we have been over the farm, and, as should be, have only talked of the farm, and we shall have time afore you go to talk to the end of farm works—what I want to know now be's something about our prices. It is mighty fine to say do this, and do that, and do t'other—what about the tariff and the corn-law?"

Again, I was in a Tory inn at Shaftesbury; all the inns there are Tory or Whig inns, or rather, the customers are Tory or Whig customers—exclusive dealing being carried on to a most lamentable extent. I was in an exclusively Tory inn. I was invited to meet a farmer who is considered the best cultivator of green crops in that district. There were about half a dozen more, and we entered at once on the subject of turnip culture. I had seen this gentleman's turnips, and had been so pleased with them, had praised them so much to some of his neighbours, that he came designedly to

Shaftesbury to see me, and talk about them. About an hour was spent on this and similar subjects, when all at once one of the company, a farmer, who pays upwards of L.600 a year of rent, and who has been a leading man on the Conservative side, said, " Ah, that be all very well, but what about the tariff, eh? what about the tariff? Come, let us hear what landlords be to do with tariff and corn-laws? and then we'll talk of what we be to do with farms!" And the old gentleman, the grower of the good turnips, immediately added, " Aye, *they* be the questions for farmers now-a-days." Following which, a young gentleman, whose father is one of the Marquis of Westminster's tenants, said, "*I* should like to hear somewhat on the tariff."

The tariff and the corn-laws consequently became the subject of conversation there, as elsewhere, whether I was willing to touch on them or not; and I was compelled to know, what otherwise I might not have known, that, generally speaking, the farmers in those parts have but a feeble glimmering of knowledge on commercial subjects. For instance, the tariff was to most of them a kind of "Boo-man behind the bed;" a " Yahoo;" a " Will-o'-the-wisp;" a " Jack the giant killer;" an evil spirit ever present, and yet invisible; it was their terror, and ever-recurring subject of conversation. They spoke of it much the same as the Scotch used to speak of the *fairies* in days not yet far distant. The fairies were called the " good neighbours;" and when any household article was lost, they concluded and said, while their hairs stood on end, and drops of sweat fell from their faces, that " doubtless the *good neighbours* had come in and taken a *lend* of it." To speak ill of the " good neighbours" was the most fatal thing they could do, and therefore they spoke kindly of them, and trembled.

So did I find it with the Dorset farmers. They never, or very seldom, spoke ill of Sir Robert Peel, or their members, whom, to support the farming interests, they elected; but the tariff and the corn-law were invariably the chief topics of conversation, and the tone in which they were discussed was very like that of those who spoke forbearingly of the " good neighbours," the fairies.

On one of those occasions, when the tariff was blamed for all that it has done, and a hundred times more than it has the power of doing, I pointed out to them in figures that all the cattle, and sheep, and pigs, and geese, ducks, turkeys, &c. imported from the continent, with all the provisions from America and elsewhere, did not amount, since the passing of the tariff, to as much as the people of Bury and Bolton consumed in the same space of time when trade was prosperous, and which they do not now consume. This assertion startled them, and it may startle others ; but let others go into the calculation, and they will find it true. It is to the reduced consumption in our towns that the farmers must look for the cause of their dull markets. Those parts of Dorset and Somerset which I visited are dairy districts ; and when the fact just mentioned, together with that of the *cheap cheese*, which had not been touched by the tariff, was pointed out to them, they soon comprehended that some more powerful cause of dull markets than the tariff was at work.

Note.—It will be understood that the foregoing refers to the tariff of 1842, not to that of 1846.

No. XI.

Shaftesbury and the Country around it.—Fonthill Abbey.—John Benett, Esq. of Pyt House, M.P.

December 1, 1842.

Shaftesbury stands on a hill—that is, when you are yourself on the hill. When you descend into the low country on the Dorset side, by the winding road, which all the ingenuity of man can never make a good road, you find that fragments of the town have come down to meet you. A couple of churches, a score or two of houses, and as many gardens, singularly irregular in shape, size, and situation, have apparently toppled over from the town, and taken the shortest cut to the bottom. Here they are headlong as they came down, the door of one house higher than the chimney of another, and the garden of that higher than its chimney. Here is a church, an old respectable church, that one would never suspect of taking any mad pranks into its head, down at the bottom, while its grave-yard, with all the dead of its parish, is left on the high ground, a hundred feet higher than the steeple, the white tombstones looking down like parted spirits in the world above, unable to comprehend what the church is, now-a-days, doing in the world below.

If we recede, the singularity of the scene becomes more marked. If we have read of " Waterton the Wanderer," who, when hunting an alligator in South America, was suddenly left to the mercy of the ferocious beast by the affrighted Indians, and who, mounting on its back, bestrode it as he would a horse, seizing one of its feet in each hand, twisting them over its shoulders, and subduing it to a kind of riding-school exercise—if we picture to ourselves Waterton on his

alligator, we may see a representation of both when looking
at Shaftesbury on its hill—a hill that may be taken for a col-
lossal crocodile, whether as regards shape or beauty.

Approach the town by which road you will, you must toil,
and climb, and blow. If on foot, you must halt, and rest, and
begin again. If on horseback, and you love your horse, you
will dismount. If you are the horse itself, you will find no
difficulty in making your rider get off; you will never in your
life again rear more easily than on the road to Shaftesbury.
If you are her Majesty's mail-coach, you will certainly be
astonished, that in such a little town there should be people
with such government influence as those who cause you to be
dragged up one hill-side by four persecuted animals, while
your wheels are again dragged by chains, to keep you from
running over four other animals on the other side. If you are
a little boy, and your mother makes you carry all the water,
you will inquire of yourself, as for the dozenth time you halt
to rest on your way from the well, why the water must be carried up to the town rather than the town brought down to the
water. But if you are a reader of history, you will know that in
times gone by, when sword was drawn against sword, man's hand
lifted against man, when a place of strong defence was more
important than a place of good trade, Shaftesbury, or Shaston,
as it was anciently called, was built on this hill. And if you
are a commercial man, or philosophic man, or Christian man,
you will hope that such times may never return ; and to render their everlasting absence the more certain, you will do all
that in you lies to promote the extension of commerce, and
peace, and good will among fellow-men. When you surmount
the acclivity, and set your feet in the ancient borough, you will
regret to see so little of trade and hear so much of politics.

But trade, and politics, and the steep hill, and the bad roads,
and all other troubles, will dissolve and be forgotten in the
beauteous scene that lies deep below and far extended—opened
to the eye as if by enchantment. So lovely and so unexpected
is the vast breadth of country, that you cannot even praise it.
Deep silence is its praise—silence, lengthened and unbroken as
the distant blue into which it melts and dies away.

The fragmentary suburbs which we saw below are now
winking in the sun amid their little gardens, as comfortably as
cats that have nothing to do but bask and sleep. Beyond
these are fields skirted by hedge-rows, the hedge-rows dotted
with trees, and the trees, at the breadth of every two or three
fields, holding in their leafy shade some cottage, or farm-yard,
or village, as if these were too shy to be seen openly ; too
coy and full of rural simplicity to look town-bred Shaftesbury
in the face. We are looking southward upon the bosom of

Dorsetshire, and see nothing to wish away. Everything is beautiful; each tree, and meadow, and bushy hedge, and cottage, and village, and village church, mansion, and wooded park, is beautiful; yet none of them have individually the power of fascinating the eye. It is their whole, as seen from this commanding height, that compels our admiration; the broad country, undulating and varied—varied until its breadth subdues the variety and its distance melts the undulations into a pleasing uniformity; this it is that fascinates and seals you to the south, even though you are told that the west, the north, and the east are all as broad, lovely, varied, and uniform in their variety.

Move westward, and the horizon is still the boundary; north, and it is the same; east, move to the extremity of the alligator's tail eastward, and the beauty and extent of the view is undiminished. Here there are no mountains abruptly rising to exchange, for a broken prospect, their own hugeness, and force upon you the sensations of your own finity and littleness. Here there is no burning Etna nor thundering avalanche, nor Niagara Falls, to oppress you with awe, and compel the confession that you are a mere atom, tolerated to exist only because these devouring mouths of nature in wrath cannot get hold of you. Here the spectator is the monarch of the scene. Nothing appears greater than himself, while the subjugation in which all things lie before him, and around on all sides, exalts his greatness. Were he the vastest giant that can be pictured in the mind, his feet on the earth's highest surface and his eyes looking over the edges of the world upon space interminable and eternal, the prospect would be but an enlarged copy, the sensations but an increase of the intensity of what may be enjoyed here. Here you may dream yourself into a forgetfulness of your own humanity, and only return to a sense of mortal littleness when the blue beyond the boundaries of your prospect, like the eternity it represents, is felt to be too vast for your comprehension, too unfathomable for your penetration; or, perchance, when the Shaftesbury bell-ringers break in on you with all the clanging of their bell-metal, because it is the first of November, and because Somebody, the shopkeeper, has been elected town-councillor, while Somebody else, his next door neighbour, has been defeated; and because the shopkeeperites and the next door neighbourites have declared war against each other; open war, pamphleteering, exclusive-dealing, tar-barrel-burning, bell-ringing war.

Or, perhaps, the mind returns to the realities and details of the scene before the eye, by having loved it too well. It may be that the green meadows, hedge-rows, trees, cottages, farm-yards, villages, churches, mansions, parks, and all the other items that make up the united beauty of these dairy districts, are so potent as a whole, that they invite us from our eminence to come down and examine them one by one. Let us go. Let us descend into the low country and its details, even at the risk of discovering that a beautiful country may be, like some other beauties, not the better of being inspected too closely.

In the first place, the soil is clayey as we advance into Dorsetshire, and has a tendency to retain moisture when it should not. Never was there a district of country more in want of surface-draining than this. Never was there a district where draining is less attended to, and where the materials for tiles could be more cheaply and abundantly produced.

Next there is the road we walk on, the road between Shaftesbury and Stowr, between Stowr and Stalbridge, and all its branches. The bottom is clay. The water is not absorbed, neither is it drained off. The road is often higher at the sides than in the centre. But as the people tell us that it is much better now than it once was, we must be consoled, and hope that it will get a better allowance of better stones : the stones are soft, and not suited for road-making.

Next we have the hedge-rows, with their trees, which gave such beautiful variety to the landscape as viewed from Shaftesbury. These hedge-rows are not less varied now. They hold fellowship with all manner of vagrant vegetation, which some people would call wild-flowers, which others would call weeds, but which would be eradicated and for ever banished in districts where it is common to have a good fence to a farm field. And again, the variety is enlarged by the openings which violence or neglect has made ; there being, in some cases, good fences existing separately, but far oftener the good and bad bushes and gaps forming one row.

Next we have the farm-yards and houses that looked upon the landscape like so many spots of beauty. We did not then see that the manure is scattered about without much regard to propriety of taste, and much of it utterly wasted in regard of its fertilizing qualities—wasted in the sun, the air, and the ditch that drains away the richest substances.

Next we have the cottages which among their trees looked like so many dwelling-places of contentment, comfort, and peace. They, too, are best when seen at a distance, although they may be subjected to a closer outside examination, and the impression they gave at the first and distant view not altogether obliterated. But enter and see the interior, and hear of the pinched meals, the low wages, and the scarcity of employment, you will find they are anything but cottages of contentment or comfort, or even peace.

However, we shall leave these general remarks and proceed to some particulars. On the north side of the road to Shaftesbury from Salisbury is Wardour Castle, the seat of the Earl of Arundel. I did not see enough of this place and the estate attached to it to justify more than the mere remark that it is a lovely residence. But I visited the celebrated Fonthill Abbey, which is about seven miles from Shaftesbury, and lying, from the Salisbury road, two or three miles beyond Wardour Castle.

The money expended in the formation of this magnificent pile of modern ruins has been prodigious. To bring it to its present condition, the original owner, Mr Beckford, not only reared it on the vast scale of grandeur which no other house in the kingdom could match; not only did he furnish and decorate it until it became the envy of George IV., then Prince Regent, who sought to see it, but was not permitted; not only did Mr Beckford concentrate in it all that art and wealth, and voluptuous taste could furnish; but, as if ruin should be rendered more certain and complete when it came, he spent money on everything but the improvement of his land; and the stone which he piled on stone to more than monumental height, the luxury which he added to luxury, parted from him by the stroke of an auctioneer's hammer, and fell—not the lasting glory of the new purchaser—but into an irremediable heap of ruins. The great tower, 270 feet in height, fell among the minor turrets which stood around it, and crushed into wreck some of the richest specimens of grandeur and elegance that ever existed out of an oriental palace.

And now there is ruin and desolation at Fonthill Abbey. The night-bird, and the reptile, and the spider, inhabit there. Plants that were once the richest and rarest are now the associates of noxious weeds, or are themselves degenerated to the level of their companions. All is ruin, all is loss, all humiliation. The cultivation of the land has not retrograded, because it had never advanced. I was invited to visit some of the farms in that neighbourhood, on which I was promised specimens of some of the worst farming in England. Certainly, if crops of couch-grass and thistles, two-thirds of these to one-third of corn, are evidence of bad farming, I saw them. But I stumbled by chance on good farming in that neighbourhood, to see which gave me more pleasure then, to record a notice of which gives me high satisfaction now. I allude to the home farm on the estate of John Benett, Esq., M.P. for South

Wiltshire. This gentleman's residence is Pyt House, about two miles from Fonthill Abbey.

Mr Benett is a spirited agriculturist. I saw the finest turnips on his farm which are to be seen in any of the southern counties. In one of his plantations of oaks, where the trees stand at from ten to forty yards distance, and where a bottom of coarse brushwood had been growing, I saw as fine a crop of potatoes as any cultivator could reasonably desire. These potatoes were the property of the poor of Hindon and neighbourhood, who, with Mr Benett's permission, had grubbed up the brushwood and reclaimed the soil. I was told the wood which they took off the ground had paid the expense of the labour, so that they had this excellent crop of potatoes for nothing. Next year Mr Benett takes the land to himself, and gives the people another piece to break up. It may be remarked that this is the consequence of the Tithe Commutation Act.

I had no opportunity of seeing and talking to any person connected with Mr Benett's farm, therefore cannot say what the expenses were and what the profits of his improvements. One thing, however, was visible at a glance, that his crops were better than other crops, the land cleaner than other land, and the style of working different; also that, by *personally attending to his own estate, the poor were to some extent provided for, while his profits were augmented.*

The first information I received of him was to the effect that he was a high Tory. The last I heard said of him was a remark on his Toryism. All that I heard of Mr Benett, "John Benett," as he is familiarly called, from first to last, during my sojourn in and around Shaftesbury, had reference to his politics as member of Parliament. Never once did I hear those with whom I held conversation speak of his character as an agriculturist. It is of Mr Benett in this character that I speak. He may be a Conservative in Parliament, but he is an innovator at home; a radical reformer in agriculture, a true patriot and benefactor of his country. I shall leave anti-corn-law men and others to deal with him on the subject of his politics, and only remark that it would be a true and unspeakable blessing to England if all landowners would attend to their land like John Benett.

No. XII.

From Shaftesbury into Somersetshire.

It has been a dismal night—rain, hail, wind, chimney pots and tiles howling and cracking; doors and windows doing all they can to keep out the storm, and not able to keep it out, making more noise than if they would fly open and let it in at once. The " boots" was told, before he went to bed, to be up and stirring, and to have me up in time for the coach; every one charged him not to sleep too long, and during the night everything has been determined that he shall not sleep at all. In lying awake all night and thinking, for the want of something more comfortable to think on, that this storm *may* be the worst that ever blew over Shaftesbury, that it is possible that a town which has stood on the top of a hill for a thousand years *may* be blown away at last; I endeavoured to console myself with the reflection that, if it should not be blown away this night, I shall be away from it in the morning, and that the storm will render the good service of getting me up in time for the coach.

But even the brawling elements exhaust themselves, and towards morning fall asleep; and slumber is uppermost inside the house and out, on myself, " boots" and all. We are almost too late for the coach, when, in a moment, as if all the disembodied spirits of all the " boots" that this life ever saw were suddenly awakened in some other world, and came riding on clouds, whirlwinds, and chimney-pots, to knock up the sleepers of this; in a moment we are all awake, and the firmamental elements and the old houses of Shaftesbury are holding racket and warfare as before.

No time is to be lost. I am inside the coach, and the coach is outside the town. We are going down, down, and down. Every road from Shaftesbury is down. In the sky there is just as much moon left as renders the clouds visible, and the coach lamps give as many small streams of light as separate the two cubic yards of darkness, which with me fill the inside, from the measureless blackness which covers the world without.

A brief stoppage to take the drag from the wheels indicates that we are at the bottom of the hill, and that we are *not* drowned in the enormous well which stands open by the roadside on the declivity, with a mouth capacious enough to take in both coach and horses, without even doubling up the traces.

We are at Gillingham. The coach halts; horses are changed; a warm fire is blazing in the inn; buttered toast and a hot cup of coffee are on the table as if by magic; and both, on such a morning, have a most grateful odour.

We are off again. I am now outside, for the day is dawning, the wind and rain have abated, and I wish to see the surface of Somersetshire, into which we are soon to enter.

One of the first and most important features of the country which the dawn reveals is the want of drainage. On such a morning as this, the accumulated water is shewn in a way that tells fearful things for pasturage in a wet summer, and poor things for cultivation in any summer. We are on the estate of Sir Richard Hoare, the banker. I have already heard of the style of management, and have been prepared to see what I now see. Two-thirds or three-fourths of the whole is in old grass. The tenants are bound to plough only a certain number of acres, and to sow on these certain crops, and all are tenants-at-will, with the privilege and necessity of exercising the parliamentary franchise imposed on them. Thus they have neither inducement to be good farmers, through the want of security, nor permission, they being bound to do only certain things, and these things at variance with the practice and theory of good husbandry. It is singular that, of all people, a *banker* should impose on his tenants the duty of expending capital without *security* ; or, if he does not expect them to expend capital on his property, it is equally singular that he does not see in it a source of profit to himself. This estate is named Stourhead, from the river Stour, which rises on it. The estate is either all, or principally, in Wiltshire, for in this neighbourhood the counties of Wilts, Dorset, and Somerset join.

At a short distance in Wiltshire is the town of Mere, once a place with good manufacturing trade, now remarkable only for its enormous union workhouse. On the other hand, in Somerset, seven miles from Mere, is Wincanton. The common wages in these districts are seven shillings a-week for men; some have eight, and some only six. A few years ago the women were mostly all engaged in the shirt-button manufacture; but the pearl buttons being now used in preference to the covered wires, their employment has failed. Good land hereabout maintains one cow on three acres; what they call middling land has a cow to four or five acres; and indifferent soils are farmed at the rate of a cow to six acres! And it is asked if, with all our noise about improved cultivation, we mean to break up the old grass-lands? Break them up! Why not? Soused with water, or overrun with foulness, why should the grass-lands not be broken up and drained, and purified and fertilized ?

Leaving behind me Stourhead, I entered upon other property, the chief of which, for several miles, was the Maiden Bradley estate of the Duke of Somerset. We changed horses at the Somerset Arms, in Maiden Bradley, a small village inhabited chiefly by labourers. The country had still the same aspect; that is, three-fourths of grass-land to the remaining fourth of cultivation. Dairy farming was still prevalent; wages still as low; the necessity for draining and cleaning the fields still as great; labourers to effect that still as plentiful; and as few employers taking advantage of the cry for employment as in those parts of the country I had just left.

The reader must not attempt to follow my course on a map, or, if he does, he will either lose the road or discover what I cannot find on any map I have seen. The fact is, the coach I was on took some out-of-the-way roads to call at out-of-the-way places, and I am not able to name them all. But the next great estate we passed over was that of the Marquis of Bath. It is named Longleat. The morning sun was now shining brilliantly, and, though it was November, the country was beautifully variegated. The rain had swollen the rivulets, and had left on every bush a thousand drops glistening like diamonds. The park at Longleat is twelve miles in circumference, containing a vast quantity of fine timber, and exhibiting a splendid variety of forest and meadow. The mansion is very large, and is said to be the first well-built house in the kingdom. It was erected on the site of a suppressed priory, in the reign of Henry VIII., purchased from Sir John Horsey by Sir John Thynne, ancestor of the present Marquis of Bath. It must have been a sweet paradise for the monks in the days of their peace and prosperity. It is now a delightful retreat to the noble family who through so many generations have inherited it. It *will be* a rich inheritance to future generations when its abundant resources are called forth— resources teeming with agricultural richness, but now as utterly neglected, as profoundly asleep, as in the days of the monks.

We entered the town of Frome, and saw, what was new to me in the west of England, some fine stone buildings. One was an hospital and charity school, erected, as an inscription stated, and as the coachman told me, by a native of the town, who had left it when young and poor, who had journied to London, lived and made a fortune in *Prince's Street, Drury Lane*, rather an unlikely place now-a-days for fortune-making, and who had returned to Frome to do this and other works of munificent charity.

There are several beautiful churches and other buildings in Frome. All the houses are substantially built of hewn stone. The town stands on the front of a declivity facing south or south-east, and, when seen from the rising ground opposite, it appeared to me lovely beyond all other towns which I ever saw. All was brightened by the morning sun, each window winking in his face, each house and garden looking after the rain, like a child that had been in tears, but all the sweeter for being washed. But excepting beauty, there was little to admire in Frome. Stricken with poverty, as a strong man is, whose family, with little wages and less bread, pines around him, this town, notwithstanding its substantial edifices of stone, is sinking into decay.

In 1831 the number of inhabitants was 12,200 ; in 1841, 11,279, having decreased 921. Pauperism has increased as the population has fallen away ; the poor-rate in 1836 was L.5391 ; in 1840, L.6601. One-sixth of the houses are uninhabited, and the rents of those with tenants are lowered, I was told, fifty per cent. The staple trade is the broad-cloth manufacture. A few years ago there were twenty-eight mills fully employed ; now there are but twenty of these partially employed ; five are standing still, and the remaining three are converted into flour mills. This town sends one member to Parliament. His name is Shepherd. I saw his seat, on a lovely eminence, between Trowbridge and Chippenham, overlooking a low district of rich land. But, as there are several places to notice before I reach that, I shall at present halt where the coach halted, at the Commercial Inn, somewhere near the river which gives name to the town, which name the reader must pronounce as if spelt Froome, not, as it is written, Frome.

No. XIII.

From the Town of Frome in Somersetshire to Westbury in Wiltshire.—The Town, the Country, and the Country People.—Reflections on the Causes that obstruct English Agriculture.

Leaving Frome I journied several miles through a pleasant country to Westbury. Here I was once more in Wiltshire. Westbury has the appearance of a respectable, open, full-sized village, and, looked upon as a village, it is not to be found fault with. But a brief acquaintance with it, even drinking a glass of ale with the landlord of one of its inns, while the coach changes horses, informs the stranger that it is a borough sending a member to Parliament. Oh, bless you, yes! *a borough*. Why should it not be a borough? Its name is

Westbury; and Camden, the old and learned, says—" The name of Westbury is purely Saxon, derived, probably, from its being one of the considerable towns of the west, or from its situation west from a borough, or Roman station, as they call Selwood Forest in its neighbourhood the Western Wood by way of eminence." A borough! Yes; and it has a handsome town-hall, and a market on Friday, and three fairs, and a bank. There is the bank right opposite the inn; and there is, standing right in front of the bank, a young gentleman with moustachios and an imperial, a white beaver, kid gloves, and a superfine royal cigar, scented and scenting the morning air; that *he* belongs to the bank is as sure as the ornamental painting of the door. And the neighbourhood is honoured with the residence of several first-rate families too. There is the property of the Longs close by; one of them member for the northern division of the county, jointly with the great Sir Francis Burdett. And Sir Francis has property here and hereabouts as well; and there is Sir Ralph, member for the town—Sir Ralph Lopes—whose family have for a number of years done what they liked here—a rich family—made a fortune in the Indies at one time—bought land in Devonshire, married, and got land in Wiltshire! Great people! Oh, yes; a borough. Sir Ralph is member.

And Westbury has six hundred and seventy-six looms for weaving woollen cloth, and several steam mills for carding, spinning, and fulling. Of the looms three hundred and fifty-four are standing idle, while only three hundred and twenty-two have their shuttles moving. Some of the mills are working half time, and some are closed. The weavers are lounging about idle—idle as the banker (or the son, or clerk, or customer, or nuisance of the banker, I know not which) in front of the bank, but not so well fed as he, for they have expended their all for half meals of food; not so sweetly scented as he, for they live in poverty and filth, two qualities that adhere the more closely to each other when there is least ability to resist them; and not so well clothed as he, for their rags shew the truth of the evidence given by a dealer in ready-made clothes, who states that in Westbury, a few years ago, he sold to the amount of L.40 per month, while now he scarcely sells to the amount of L.2 per month, though his proportion of the clothes trade is as high, compared with other tradesmen, as ever.

Leaving this town on the road to Trowbridge, which is five miles distant, we have the land on each side of us much the same as before entering Westbury. The cultivation seems to become more general than beyond Frome, and the soil is decidedly of good quality. A chance field or two, may be a chance farm or two, shews good husbandry, which contrasts

forcibly with the sluggish neglect characteristic of the majority
of fields and farms surrounding them; and which supports
the truth of Mr Pusey's statement, when he said that the
improvement of agriculture, so common in Scotland, was not
new to England, that certain superior methods of tilling the
soil were common in some farms, but that farmers in the same
county—I think he said, or *might have said*, in the same parish
—do not know anything about them.

I heard a remark made recently by a gentleman* well
acquainted with every peculiarity in the English and Scottish
character, and as well acquainted with every circumstance
past and present, leading to, or resulting from, the character
of either people as any man living, that the English are more
inventive than the Scotch, but the Scotch are more ready and
discreet in the application of inventions—that they are, in
short, more applicative. Without halting to discuss the propriety of this remark as regards general matters, I shall only
say that, in regard of agriculture, the remark seems to be
decidedly just. Almost all the established methods of improved
cultivation now common in Scotland originated in England.
Mr Dawson of Frogden introduced the Rotherham plough
and the turnip culture to Roxburghshire from Norfolk. Mr
Small of Berwickshire, finding the district of that county called
the Merse too wet and tenacious for common cultivation, took
the Rotherham plough of Mr Dawson as a model, or rather as
a spur to his applicative genius, and effected, in its construction, such alterations as enabled the farmers of the Merse to
plough, with two horses, a soil remarkable for its adhesive
and stubborn qualities; a soil the same as in many parts of
England, where, at this day, the ploughs in use are constructed
as a hundred years before the Rotherham plough; where four
horses are required to draw an implement not adapted to
the soil; where four horses, by being so yoked, on such a soil,
do a serious injury to its fertility; where four horses treading
unnecessarily on soft clay, to the detriment of the crops, eat
up, in provender and other expenses, a considerable part of the
poor profits of the improperly cultivated clayey soils.

The question that arises from this is an important one.
What are the causes that obstruct the general use of agricultural improvements in England? We must not attempt to
answer this by saying the English are not so ready to apply
inventions as the Scotch, though this may to some extent be
true; because we have before us steam, and new, complicated,
wonderful inventions, applied to all branches of industry and
art throughout England save agriculture. We have new

* Mr Black, late Editor of the Morning Chronicle.

machinery making its appearance in one English town, and it
is instantly applied in another; the keenest master spinner,
or bleacher, or ship-owner in Glasgow—quick and applicative
though he may be—is not quick enough to have an English
invention many days, even if one day, sooner than his rivals of
Manchester and Liverpool. But we find the case very different in regard of cultivating the soil. Advances are made in
improvements so manifestly advantageous, that the fact is
visible as daylight, of men who adopt such improvements
becoming rich—rich in the very parish where men who do not
adopt them continue comparatively poor. We see the poorer
soils of Scotland producing crops, and the rich farmers paying rents, that stagger the southern agriculturists, even in
speaking of them—as witness the effect of Mr Hyde Greg's
account of the Lothians. Now there must be a cause for this
other than the genius of the people. Most agriculturists, writing or speaking of the superiority of Scotch cultivation, seek
to account for it by citing certain favouring causes, none of
which, in my opinion, have been superior to circumstances
everywhere ready to assist cultivation in England. Scotch
advancement has not been the artificial result of fostering
causes, it is the natural result of capital and industry having
free scope; at all events, a more free scope than in England.
But English agriculture has had, and *still has*, obstructions
retarding its advancement, which Scotland has not had, and
which have crippled the growth of English grain as effectually
as the bandages on a female foot in China restrict its growth,
and add to that which the *natives* call beauty. I have now
lying before me a copy of the annual leases granted by an
English nobleman to his farming tenantry. This nobleman is
one of the best men in England in respect of his good nature,
good intentions, and I may say good wishes to all men.* If he
is not the richest landowner in England, he is one of the few
who are the richest, and he would doubtless say, were he
asked, that he gives every encouragement to English agriculture in his power, and that he considers it should be protected
from foreign competition. I shall, in next letter, publish this
document—not to hold this nobleman up to invidious remark,
not to make his manner of entering upon agreements with his
tenantry a peg on which to hang remarks derogatory to the
whole of the landed aristocracy who do as he does, but to
shew them, in the face of the nation, what are the hindrances
to the advancement of English agriculture. Meantime, I shall
only say, *that were all the ingenuity of man taxed to the utter-*

---

* The late Marquis of Westminster.

most to produce a documentary tenure between landlord and tenant, which would have the design of destroying the energies of the tenant, if he ever had any ; of restricting the appliance of improvements, were he inclined to apply them ; of hastening land out of cultivation, were land in danger of being discultured —nothing, to wear a semblance of fair play to the farmer, could surpass this nobleman's leases.

As a branch of that subject which has led to so much discussion, namely, the superiority of Scotch over English agriculture, the question of labourers here presents itself. In several of my recent communications, mention has been made of the defectiveness of labour, of the inability of the English labourers to execute works, and to use improved implements, as in some parts of England and in most parts of Scotland. But this objection must be taken in a qualified degree. Give the labourers of the south-west of England a scythe, and a certain number of acres of hay or grain to mow, and the common men of them will surpass any picked men from Scotland. At many other kinds of work they will evince the same superiority, especially if promised *some beer* when done, or if aided with it while going on ; but they are not steady, they cannot be depended on, and they will starve or go to prison rather than work in any way but their own way. A farmer in the Lothians of Scotland, in Northumberland, in Norfolk, and in Lincolnshire, has his work performed thirty per cent. cheaper than in most of the English counties, even though he pays eleven shillings a-week to the labourer, while in these other counties nine shillings a-week is only paid. This may appear singular, but it is a fact which has been put to the proof ; and it depends entirely on the superior steadiness of the northern workmen, not, however, because they are northern. Look at the Scotch hind, whose master has a long lease of his farm, and who hires his hinds by the year, and encourages them to remain with him while he remains on the farm, or who, if they do not remain so long, still deals with them as men whose whole time and attention must be devoted to him ; look at one of those hinds, (this is the name of the married Scotch ploughmen,) and you will find him invariably a steady sober man, not very bright in intellect it may be, not very well informed, not very much interested in the passing affairs of the day, unless on some topic of religious controversy ; but you will find him zealously devoted to his master's interests, and always ready to work, that is, when his hours of working arrive. He is ever ready when called on, *because he is not called on but at stated and scrupulously observed hours.*

But look at the south of England labourer. Either he must

be starved to compel him to work, or bribed by beer or some temporary stimulant to induce him to work. *He is only ready for his master when it suits himself, because his master deals with him on the same principle. He is hired one day and paid off the next, or at most his term is for a week.* Thus paid, with a little loose money, and much loose time, he meets others like himself, who spend their money, and, without work or food, betake themselves to poaching and thieving. The old poor-law encouraged them in all these practices, and doubled, in many cases quadrupled, their numbers over what they would have been if left to their own industrial resources, which increase of numbers makes their employment still more uncertain, still more unlike that of the Scotch hind; which uncertainty, again, renders their domestic comfort, that should be the centre of all sound moral habits, the very reverse of what a man feels who, let him work ever so hard, has his regular meals to come home to at regular hours; which makes the English farm labourer so much inferior to the Scotch hind in regard of domestic comfort, moral habits, and steady application to his work and the interests of his master.

But follow the hind's brother, who, as we shall suppose, served an apprenticeship to the village blacksmith, penetrated as far as Glasgow when a journeymen, served a second apprenticeship to engine-making, perhaps with the Messrs Napier. In due time we find him in Manchester or Leeds, and we see, working alongside of him, the brother of the farm labourer of Wiltshire, who also learned to be a blacksmith in his native village, who went to Bristol when a journeyman, who there learned the art of engine-making, and who afterwards proceeded to Manchester or Leeds, where we now find him. What is the difference between him and the hind's brother from Scotland? Nothing, unless it be that the Scotchman is the most unsteady workman of the two. We may see a greater number of Scotchmen in a first-rate English factory than of Englishmen; that is, if we compare the extent of the population from which they are supplied; but I think much of this depends on the fact of Scotchmen and their parents through many generations being left to their own industrial resources and the freedom of their own inclinations, rather than on any inherent difference of organization. That different circumstances will in time produce a different organization is perhaps true; but if so, it only proves that the *feebler energies of the rural populace in the south of England are the result of unwholesome restrictions on industry and personal locomotion, such as have been effected by several laws,* the Curfew and the old poor-laws especially.

Take from England the causes that have corrupted the rural population and introduce them into Scotland, and the same results will follow. If this be doubted, let the supposition appear in another shape. Bring from Scotland 500 of the steadiest hinds to be found in the Lothians. Place them with their families in the little town of Hindon, in Wiltshire. Make them pot-wallopers; that is, give to each man who boils his pot twelve months previous to the election the right of voting. Introduce among them ambitious men of wealth to purchase, bribe, and bestialize them, that they, the ambitious men, may become M.P.s, and in the course of a few generations, if not in the course of the first, these new comers would be as debased in morals, as dependent on their own baseness for the means of existence, as the old pot-wallopers of Hindon. And take from them, by the same schedule A, the means by which they lived, and they would become the same thieves and poachers, starving, though they added crime to every other resource they could devise for a livelihood, as the wretched pot-wallopers of Hindon are at this moment. Or, take the same men, the Scotch hinds, and give them the old poor-law of England, with all the old enactments that kept the villagers to their villages all the days of their lives, in addition to the poor-law's inducements to remain in the village; take away by these means all the inducements to industry, all the elements that make up the relationship, the mutual dependence of workman and master, and put in the place of such absent virtues the positive elements of idleness and discord, and the offspring of the hinds, in a few generations, would be the same hand-to-mouth, turbulent, unmanageable, unserviceable population as that now swarming in the south of England. And bring from Scotland the best farmers with the best implements of husbandry, and set them down with their hinds upon any farm in England they might choose; but let all the complication of English tenures exist—all those quirks and cranks of the law which render it more necessary for an English farmer to be a skilful lawyer than a skilful cultivator; let the lease or the annual agreement be that which an English lawyer draws out and an English nobleman exacts adherence to from his tenant; let all these be the conditions for the Scotch farmer, and he would find himself reduced to the limited operations of his English neighbour.

In conclusion, I believe much, if not all, of the evil now afflicting the rural society of England can be removed by removing the causes that produce it. The amendment of the poor-law was a great step in the right direction, if it had been accompanied by a necessary movement on the part of the landowners to employ those whom it deprived of parish pay. It took away one cause of a great moral disease, but the landowners should not rest satisfied with removing the cause of a disease now existing ; the disease of a redundant population of loose moral habits, of vicious prejudices, of confirmed idleness, should also be removed, for it now exists independent of its original cause or causes.   Emigration to new countries would unquestionably assist ; but with so many prejudices to overcome this could only be applied to a partial extent under the best regulations.   And when we see before us the fact that L.100 of capital applied to ten acres of almost any of the arable soils of England, (keeping off two or three counties already well cultivated,) that this capital would bring in a return twenty times greater on ten acres in England than on ten acres in the back settlements of the colonies, for a period at least equal to one generation, we may well throw aside emigration as a secondary consideration.   The poor-law has been amended in so far as the false support of the ablebodied labourer has been removed ; but the landowner has not advanced to meet that labourer with a substitute.   The vice, the ignorance, the idleness, the hostility to the rich, are now the same among the labourers as under the old poor-law, with the addition of irritated prejudices, withering hunger—in many cases cruel persecution—to perpetuate their degradation ; for these vices are monsters that generate and feed on each other.   The landowner must amend his own system if he would amend the condition of the labouring poor.   Happily, in calling on him to do so, we call on him not for a sacrifice, but to add to his own wealth by improving his good land, which will, without any other effort of his, improve the condition of the labourers.   Give them work and wages, and they will have food and domestic comfort.   Let them have food and domestic comfort, and they may be educated and preached to ; but with the landowners neglecting their own property as they now neglect it, with the labourers looking to them for support and not receiving it as they now do, all the parsons and schoolmasters at home and abroad will not mend the morals of a people rapidly sinking, deteriorating every year in physical comforts.

No. XIV.

The Form of an Annual Agreement entered into by a Nobleman and his Tenants-at-will in the County of Chester.

Much may be said, and truly said, illustrative of errors in tenures, but so long as assertions are unaccompanied by documentary proof or precise specimens of error, it is not to be expected that much impression will be made on those who remain content with things as they are.

The first we shall examine is a form of lease, or annual agreement, with a tenant-at-will. The nobleman who issues this agreement is an extensive proprietor in several counties, and is, unquestionably, one of the most amiable men, whether in respect of public or private reputation, in England, (the late Marquis of Westminster.)

LEASE No. 1.—ISSUED IN Nov. 1842.

" *Conditions for the letting and holding a messuage, outbuildings, and farm, situate in the township of* ———, *in the county of Chester, the property of the* ——————— ; *containing* ——— *acres of land statute measure, or thereabouts.*

1st. " The premises to be held from year to year, commencing from the 2d of February 18—, at the clear annual rent of L.———, the said rent to become due by equal portions half-yearly, on the 2d of February and 2d of August in each year, always a half year in advance; the first payment to become due on the 2d of February 18—. Any subsequent change of the days for receiving the half-yearly payments of rent for the convenience of the landlord or tenant, not to alter or affect the times herein fixed for their becoming due, nor the power of the landlord then to demand or distrain for the same : SAVE AND EXCEPT to the landlord the mines, minerals, quarries, gravel, sand, stone, timber, and other trees, with the usual power to search for, get, stack, fell, and carry away the same. Also the game and fish on the said premises, with liberty for himself and his friends, gamekeepers, servants, and other attendants, to take, kill, or preserve the same: Also the power of taking and making use of such parts of the said lands as he may require for plantations, roads, or other improvements, or cottage allotments, making a reasonable abatement from the rent, according to the value of the land taken, and a compensation for any improvement the tenant may have made thereon ; the amount to be ascertained and fixed by the agent of the said ——— for the time being.

2d. " The tenant to pay and bear all rates, taxes, and impositions, (including the land-tax,) ———— the tithe rent charge payable in respect of the said premises; to maintain and keep in good repair the inside of the house and buildings; also all doors, gates, stiles, rails, and fences, ditches, drains, irrigation gutters, sewers, floodgates, paddles, and sluices, belonging to the said premises, being allowed bricks, lime, and timber; and to do all cartage required in repairs of, or in any additions to, the said house or buildings. To do for the landlord yearly —— days of labour with a cart or plough, and three horses and a man to attend them, when and where required by his agent. To keep a dog for the landlord. To consume on the premises all the hay, straw, fodder, turnips, potatoes, and food roots, which shall be produced on the said farm, except such turnips, potatoes, or other food roots as shall have been wholly raised with *purchased* manure; and to lay upon the meadow or pasture-land of the said farm all the manure which shall be made or arise upon the said farm, except what is used for the growth of potatoes, turnips, and other food roots *to be eaten on the premises.* At the time of quitting, to leave on the farm all the hay, straw, dung, or manure produced or made thereon. Not to plough, break up, or have in tillage any of the lands reserved for permanent meadow or pasture, *viz.,* the   *   *   *
(except such of the same fields as are now in tillage, and then only to lay them down for permanent pasture in manner hereinafter required.) Nor more than ———— statute acres of the said farm at one time, including summer and turnip fallows and green crops. Not to take more than two crops of corn during one course of tillage, unless the land have been at breaking up, or in such course of tillage, improved by a proper covering of lime or *purchased* manure or marl, and either a summer fallow made or a green crop taken; and in no case to take more than three crops of corn in one course of tillage; not to take more than one crop of wheat in a tillage; not to take more than two successive crops of corn without intervening summer fallow or green crops. To lay the land down at the end of each tillage in a clean state and neat form, with good seed, in the following proportions per statute acre; that is to say—Red clover, 9 lbs., white clover, 5 lbs., and fine perennial rye-grass, or other suitable grass seed, one peck; and not to break up the same again until all the other arable land shall have been tilled in rotation.

3d. " Not to mow any part of the land more than once in any one year, unless the same shall have been top-dressed

with *purchased* manure. After notice to quit, not to turn any
horses, pigs, or cattle into the meadow land later than the
20th day of November, and to give up possession of the said
tillage land on the first day of November after such notice.
Not to sow more than —— statute acres of the land with
wheat after such notice ; and, at the ensuing August, not to
claim or be entitled to a greater proportion of the crop of
wheat on the said —— statute acres than two-third parts on
summer fallowed land, and one-half on all other land ; and to
leave the straw from such proportion of the said crop upon the
premises ; being allowed, however, one-half of the market
price of all hay and straw left upon the premises. The landlord or succeeding tenant to be at liberty to sow clover or grass
seeds upon any crops sown the autumn or winter after notice.
Not to make marl-pits, except in such places as shall be
pointed out by the said agent ; and in every case in which a
new pit shall be made, one old pit of equal size shall be filled
up and made into land.

4th. " Not to fell, lop, top, or injure the timber, or any
other trees or saplings growing on the said premises, under a
penalty of L.10 for each offence, over and above the value of
the tree.

5th. " To pull up or mow, previously to the month of
August, all thistles and docks growing upon the said premises,
or on the roads and waste lands adjoining, and burn the same,
under a penalty of L.1 per acre, and so on in proportion.

6th. " To reside on the premises, and not to let, set, or
assign over the same, or any part thereof.

7th. " To use his best endeavours to preserve the game on
the said premises, and to warn all persons from sporting or
trespassing thereon ; and to permit his name to be used in
any action that may be brought against any person for sporting or trespassing thereon.

8th. " The tenant to pay an additional rent of L.10 a-year
for every acre on or in respect of which the foregoing rules,
restrictions, stipulations, and agreements, or any of them, shall
have been broke through or disregarded ; and the like additional rent of L.10 for every cart load of hay, straw, clover,
grass, muck, manure, potatoes, turnips, or other food roots,
sold or carried off the premises, (except such potatoes, turnips,
or other food roots as shall have been raised wholly with *purchased* manure.) Such additional rents and all penalties
hereby imposed to be respectively deemed an increase of the
said yearly rent, and to be recoverable accordingly, and to be
considered as fully due, and to be paid therewith on such of the
said rent-days as shall happen next after such penalties, or any

of them, shall have been incurred ; and to pay an additional rent of L.10 for and on every day of holding over the said premises, or any part thereof, after the said respective days of giving up possession after notice.

9th. " The said —— agrees to keep in repair the roofs and walls of the said messuages and buildings, and to find all bricks, lime, and timber necessary for the repairs of the inside thereof; and for making new gates; to find quick for planting new fences, and for filling up gaps in old ones; to find stones or tiles and timber for draining and irrigation; such repairs, drainings, and irrigation, gates and fences, to be done and made under the direction of the said —— or his agent; and of whatever shall be done without such directions the said tenant shall himself bear the whole expense, and not claim any allowance for the same on quitting the premises. That, whenever the said tenant shall have received notice to quit, and shall have quitted, the possession of the whole, or any part of the said premises, if it shall appear that he has, within the last three years, paid any expense of improvements made under the direction of the said ——, or his agent, of which a benefit equivalent to such expense has not been derived by him, and that the said premises have, in all other respects, been maintained and managed according to the true intent and meaning of this agreement, then such an allowance shall be made and paid to the said tenant as the said agent shall deem a reasonable and proper compensation ; also the prime cost of any good clover or grass-seeds which he may have sowed during the last year of his occupancy, and which shall have produced good and sufficient clover and grass roots, provided the same has not been grazed, but has been laid up and kept from trespass or injury, and provided the meadow land has not been eaten or trodden after the 20th of November. The tenant, on quitting pursuant to regular notice, to be allowed to occupy the house and outbuildings (except a lodging-room for workmen and a stable for horses) and an outlet or boozy pasture to be set out by the said agent until the 1st of May next following the day for quitting the land, and to stack his share of the corn upon some convenient part of the premises until the 1st day of August.

10th. " Provided always that, if the said yearly and penal rents, or any part thereof, shall be behind and unpaid for twenty days after the same shall have been demanded by the landlord or his agent, (although not demanded when and as the same shall have become due and payable as aforesaid,) or if the said tenant, his executors, or administrators shall break or omit any of the conditions or stipulations aforesaid, or shall underlet the said premises or any part thereof, or shall become bankrupt or insolvent, or assign over his or their effects for the benefit of creditors, or if the same shall be taken in execution for debt, it shall be lawful for the said ————, or his agent, either with or without any legal process, to re-enter upon the said premises, and to take and keep possession thereof, as if the same were unlet and unoccupied. In witness whereof the said parties to these presents have hereunto set their hands, the day and year first above written."

Such is the agreement which a landlord ratifies with his tenants, a landlord who, I am well convinced, would not injure any fellow creature knowingly, in the slightest degree; a landlord, however, who leaves his vast property, and the vast interests to himself and the public of that property, to the management of those who are either unacquainted with a better system, or who are so wedded to old usages as to maintain them at the expense of the estate.

Had I no other object in reprinting and remarking on this document than to ridicule the author of it, I would at once proceed to its ungrammatical and singularly confused composition. Were I disposed to be severe with the legal agent who either enforces, or may enforce or relax, its clauses, and from whose pen it doubtless emanated, I would proceed to point out that in several clauses there is not only mystery, but provisions which no human being could keep clear of infringing; and that the penal provisions are so worded as to catch the tenant at each error, and fine him more than once for the one offence, if the agent thinks fit; as also to prevent him from taking advantage of the compensatory provisions, if again the agent thinks fit, even though the penalties may have been paid. Were I disposed to open a sharpshooting fire on this nobleman and other landlords, all the errors of the agent might be easily charged on the principal, and in the skirmish something sharp might be said of the tenant keeping a dog for the landlord, of the tenant being required to preserve the game which eats up his own crops, and so on; but all this would be nothing more than a skirmish—a mere affair of outposts. The keeping of the dog is but a frivolous matter, viewed on whichever side we may view it; the destruction of crops by game is a great grievance, but it must be looked to as so much of a rent charge. So long as our gentry and nobility *are* gentry and nobility they will have their sports, therefore it is hopeless to say another word on this point.

I shall leave all these secondary matters to be considered afterwards, or by other persons, and shall, as soon as space permits, enter upon the main arguments; namely, that no tenant having such a tenure as this can expend capital on his farm ; that not only would he be restrained by a sense of insecurity, but he is positively bound down so stringently in regard of meadows, manures, croppings, and disposal of produce, that he cannot lay out money on improvements were he desirous so to do ; and, further, that those very farms, held by copies of this document, do not now return, and at no time have returned, to their noble owner a rental within one-third of what they would return if differently cultivated, even though prices of farm produce were considerably lower than at present.

Meanwhile the annual lease is here exhibited as it stands. By the time I resume my remarks, I shall, in all likelihood, have personally inspected the farms held by this tenure.

No. XV.

A chapter on the Men of the League ; being a Note from the Factory Districts, which must not be overlooked by those interested in Agriculture.

January 1843.

Having a day to spend in Manchester, previous to going into Cheshire to examine the practical working of the agreements between landlord and tenant, one of which was given at full length in my last communication, I determined to get a peep, if possible, at that extraordinary body the Anti-Corn-Law League. Being slightly acquainted with one of the members of the council, I inquired of him the conditions on which a stranger could visit the rooms, and was informed that any committee-man might introduce a stranger to his own committee, or a member of the council might take a stranger to the council-room ; and that I might be shewn over the whole establishment if I attended at ten the next morning.

Accordingly, at ten o'clock I was in Market Street, a principal thoroughfare in Manchester. A wide open stairway, with shops on each side of its entrance, rises from the level of the pavement, and lands on the first floor of a very extensive house called "Newall's Buildings." The house consists of four floors, all of which are occupied by the League, save the basement. We must, therefore, ascend the stair, which is wide enough to admit four or five persons walking abreast.

On reaching a spacious landing, or lobby, we turn to the left, and, entering by a door, see a counter somewhere between forty and fifty feet in length, behind which several men and boys are busily employed, some registering letters in books, some keeping accounts, some folding and addressing newspapers, others going out with messages and parcels. This is

the general office, and the number of persons here employed
is, at the present time, ten. Beyond this is the *Council Room*,
which, for the present, we shall leave behind and go up stairs
to the second floor.

Here we have a large room, probably forty feet by thirty,
with a table in the centre running lengthwise, with seats
around for a number of persons, who meet in the evenings,
and who are called the " Manchester Committee." On inquiring into the nature of their business, I was told they formed
a committee as distinct from the League as the committees of
any other town in England ; in other words, while the League
is *national* in its operations, this committee is *local*, and has
the charge of issuing subscription cards to, and collecting subscriptions in, Manchester. The members are all persons who
are engaged in their own business during the day. The
moment they are clear of their counting-houses or shops in
the evening, they hasten here, and find tea and bread and
butter on the table. They partake of this refreshment in preference to going each to his home, or coffee-house, or hotel,
and save time by so doing ; at least such was the observation
made to me by the person who introduced me to the room.

During the day this room is occupied by those who keep
the accounts of cards issued and returned to and from all
parts of the kingdom. A professional accountant is retained
for this department, and a committee of members of council
give him directions and inspect his books. These books are
said to be very ingeniously arranged, so as to shew at a glance
the value of the cards sent out, their value being represented
by certain alphabetical letters and numbers, the names and
residences of the parties to whom sent, the amounts or deficiencies of those returned, and so on.

Passing from this room we come to another, from which all
the correspondence is issued. From this office letters to the
amount of several thousands a-day go forth to all parts of the
kingdom. While here, I saw letters addressed to all the
foreign ambassadors, and all the mayors and provosts of corporate towns of the United Kingdom, inviting them to the
great banquet which is to be given in the last week of this
month. The amount of postage for letters going out during
the week ending 7th January was L.18 : 2 : 6 ; but the amount
of postage was frequently as much as this in one day—for a
single day it had been so high as L.38. In this office copies
of all the parliamentary registries of the kingdom are kept, so
that any elector's name and residence is at once found, and, if
necessary, such elector is communicated with by letter or parcel of tracts, irrespective of the committees in his own district.

Passing from this apartment, we see two or three small rooms, in which various committees of members of the council meet. Some of these committees are permanent, some temporary. Of those which are permanent I may name that for receiving all applications for lecturers and deputations to public meetings. The correspondence of each post having been opened, and read by the secretary and chairman of the council, the letters relative to lecturers and deputations are handed to this committee, who consider the merits thereof, and report to the council, at which a vote is taken decisive of the resolution of the committee. In like manner the letters relative to subscriptions are handed to the committee appointed to that department. Of the temporary committees may be named that which directs the arrangements for the forthcoming banquet. There are frequently as many as ten of these sitting at once.

Passing by the rooms in which the committees meet, we come to a large hall, lighted from the top by an expansive dome. This was formerly a picture gallery, and was fitted up by the League for public meetings; but of late the meetings have increased so much in importance, that a place called the Corn Exchange, in another street, has been taken, and there the public weekly meetings are now held.

In another large room on this floor is the packing department. Here several men are at work making up bales of tracts, each weighing upwards of a hundred weight, and despatching them to all parts of the kingdom for distribution among the electors. From sixty to seventy of these bales are sent off in a week, that is, from three to three and a-half tons of arguments against the corn-laws! The publications sent are twelve in number, a copy of each being put up in one cover for each elector and tenant farmer in the kingdom; one of them is the pamphlet containing the three prize essays. These single packages cost one shilling each for paper, printing, and preparation. They are put up into dozens or scores, I forget which, and these again into the bales of a hundred weight each.

Leaving this and going to the floor above, we find a great number of printers, presses, folders, stitchers, and others connected with printing, at work. But in addition to the printing and issuing of tracts here, the League has several other printers at work in this and other towns of the kingdom. Altogether they have twelve master-printers employed, one of whom, in Manchester, pays upwards of L.100 a-week in wages for League work alone. He sent in while I was there an account, which was shewn me as a specimen of the magnitude

6

of the League's operations, an account for paper alone of nearly
L.1000 ! all used within the brief period of a few weeks.
The amount of money paid for the carriage of parcels must be
high, but 1 did not find information on this point.

I shall now return down stairs to the " Council-room."
These words were seen in white letters, raised on a door
covered with crimson cloth. My friend pushed it open, and
bade me follow him. There were about twenty persons
present, chiefly seated around a long table covered with cloth,
the cloth covered in most part with books, newspapers, writing
materials, and elbows of members who leant thereon, and
listened to what the chairman was reading.

The chairman sat at the further end of the room, facing the
door by which we entered, his back turned to Market-street ;
on each side of him a window with crimson hangings looking
out upon the street, and in front of him the table which stood
lengthwise, and the members who, to him, sat sideways, except
when they turned their chairs to front him. The room seemed
to be about thirty feet in length. On one side was a fireplace
and a rack for sticks, umbrellas, hats, great-coats, and so on ;
on the opposite side were two or three windows looking out
upon a lane which turns at a right angle from Market-street ;
these windows had also crimson hangings. In one corner of
the room was a curious, yet simple instrument, representing
the sliding-scale, which had been presented to the League.

The chairman is George Wilson, a gentleman whose face
and forehead shew a promising fulness of intellect, while his
age—three or four years above thirty—his firm and full breadth
of body, together with his daily avocations, promise that he
will live longer than the corn-laws. On his left sits the secretary, who at first seems to be a copy, not excepting the nose,
of Lord Brougham, or rather the Henry Brougham of fifteen
or twenty years ago ; his name is Hicken.

I looked with much curiosity upon the councillors, to pick
from them the names which have become celebrated, or rather
the heads, which, according to my ideas, should belong to the
well-known names. Having seen the member for Stockport
when attending his parliamentary duties in London, 1 at once
recognised, in a gentleman who sat leaning on his left arm,
the arm on the top rail of his chair, listening to the letters the
chairman read, calm, reflective, and pale—I at once recognised
in him Richard Cobden ; and when he spoke, so mild was his
voice, so unassuming his style of giving an opinion, so clearly
was the opinion given, that I at once saw the source of much
of that importance he has acquired. I have never heard him
make a speech, and, therefore, cannot speak of his style, but

am told he is forcible, and often warm ; yet I could be sworn
that he is never in his warmth so forcible as when he makes
a calm statement.   Neither is it his wealth and position as
a great manufacturer that has given him his importance as a
public speaker.   At the council board of the League he has
around him other rich men who make little figure in public,
but whose wealth and mercantile operations are known for
their vastness throughout the whole civilized world.   I was
shewn a list of the names of the members of council, which
comprised men of all political parties, of all professions, resident in all parts of the country ; and every day, for a period
of two or three hours, from twelve to twenty of these men
attend the council, to see that all the operations are being
carried out in a business-like manner.   Several of them who
are there every day employ each from 500 to 2000 work-
people.

Alderman John Brooks is one of the most remarkable
members of the council.   He is said to be very wealthy.   He
keeps a carriage, and when he has it out, which, I am told, is
almost every night, he has it crammed with repealers.   It is
enough to Mr Brooks to know that the stranger in Manchester is a friend of the League ; knowing this, he will be invited to a seat in the carriage even after it is full ; nay, Mr
Brooks will get out himself that the stranger may get in, and
he will drive to any part of the town to set any one down.
He has several great establishments, on one of which, at Bolton, he has lost L.60,000, but jokes at the loss, and declares
that sooner or later it shall be made to pay.   He is an elderly
man, but full of vigour ; he shrinks at no fatigue.   To use his
own expression, his words " come rolling out like potatoes from
a sack, not in the most regular order, sometimes the one
rolling over the other, and getting before when it should be
behind, but always coming to the right point at last."   Others
who are acquainted with him say he turns a corner in his
speech so quickly, so unexpectedly, that for a minute he is
often lost sight of ; but he as quickly re-appears, with an increased comicality, which elicits a peal of laughter or a cheer
all the louder that he for a moment obscured himself.   He
goes off to distant towns after the earlier and more important
business of the day, attends public meetings, travels home
again all night, is attending to his leviathian establishment
early in the morning, at the League-rooms at ten or eleven,
at the Exchange till the close of business, and again doing
something for the League, all without repose.   And this is
done by a man of whom it is alleged, by those who know him,
that he would not take a seat in Parliament if the offer was
accompanied with a recompence of L.50,000.

Another remarkable member of the council is Mr Bright, "John Bright of Rochdale," as he is called. He is one of the Society of Friends, not quite thirty years of age, judging by appearance. But, though the Friends are proverbially modest and unassuming ; though John Bright is as a member of the society should be in demeanour ; though it is asserted that the League will dissolve, and its public men retire to private business or private life when its purpose is accomplished ; though the League may dissolve, and its men seek retirement ; and though the Friends should continue to be as unassuming as they have ever been, John Bright will, if he lives long enough, be a leading man in the British legislature. I am not aware that he ever whispered the possibility of his becoming a member, to say nothing of a leader ; but talents like his will take root too firmly in the public mind, long before the corn-law repeal is accomplished, to admit of his retirement, even were he desirous of repose. He is earnest, argumentative, eloquent ; clear in statement, apt in illustration, fluent in words, abundant in resources. John Bright is, in talent, a second Peel ; he was born in the same atmosphere. Let his career be observed—he has entered upon it.

To the other remarkable men of the League I shall devote a future chapter. Meantime, of the operations of that extraordinary body I may observe, that all the members being men habituated to business, they go to their work of agitation with the same precision in the minutest details as they do in their work of cotton spinning. The magnitude of their proceedings in printing, publishing, and distributing arguments against the corn-laws has been stated. The following is one of their circulars relative to details :—

" DIRECTIONS FOR DISTRIBUTING TRACTS TO ALL THE FARMERS AND COUNTY VOTERS IN THE KINGDOM.

" Procure copies of the last registration from the clerks of the peace of each county or division of county.

" Locate yourself in the most central town or city of the county or division wherein your operations are to be carried on. Get a small pocket map of the county or division, with all the parishes distinctly marked. Ascertain the number of polling places within the county or division, and the number and names of the parishes polling within each. Make each of the largest towns within such polling districts the central point from which the tracts are to be distributed throughout the parishes of that district.

" Having ascertained the number of parishes within the district you intend to cover with tracts, make out separate lists of parishes lying most conveniently together for the purpose of distribution. From three to four parishes will be found a good average day's work for a single distributor. For the purpose of saving time, let each list include a *double* line of parishes lying within a direct radius of about seven miles from the central town of the district. The first line of parishes to form the first day's work of the distributor, and the second line to be taken as a *returning* route on the *second* day. *Every* farm, house, and freeholder within each of the parishes must be visited, and a packet of tracts left at each by the distributor. Each distributor to be furnished with a sheet of paper, upon which the name and residence of every farmer *visited* within the parish must be written down. These *returned* lists of names to be compared with the list of registered county voters within each of the parishes, in order that your distributors may be kept in check, and security afforded that the work has been done. There will in each parish also be found many small freeholders, *who are not farmers*, but who have a little house and garden or orchard of their own, these should also be visited.

" The distributors should be men of some intelligence, and well acquainted with the districts in which they are employed. The best men for the purpose will be the carriers of county newspapers, wherever there is a *Liberal* county newspaper ; or such men as are usually employed in rural districts by lawyers or auctioneers. When all the parishes within any given district have been completed, move into the next district, and pursue the same plan.

" In order to facilitate his operations, and prevent delay or losing ground, the distributor will find it convenient to ascertain the number of farmers in each parish, together with the readiest route to each farm house. This information he will generally obtain readily at the blacksmith's or wheelwright's shops in each of the parishes."

In what age or country of the world was there ever anything like this ? By railways, penny postage, and printing presses, a mighty movement is in progress, which will achieve, *be it for good or evil*, what no other power or combination of powers ever achieved. By the railways some scores of men issue from and return to Manchester day after day over hundreds of miles of country to address public meetings. By the penny post several thousands of letters are daily sent and received, which, without it, would never have been written. By the printing press tracts are being distributed to each elector in the kingdom at the rate of *three tons and a-half weekly* ;—the whole forming an amount of moral power moving from one centre that never before existed in the world ; that was never before dreamt of as possible to exist. The *legality* of all this is an interesting question.

And look at the banquet. Their chairman has said to them, " If ten men come to any of our houses, what provision must we make ?" It was not difficult to calculate this, and when it was ascertained, the whole was multiplied by 1000, which produced 10,000, and they prepared for 10,000 accordingly. But as the banquet is to extend over several days, they resolved on entertaining 4000 a-day. For that purpose they have built a prodigious hall, forty-five yards by thirty-five in the interior. Rows of cast-iron pillars support the roof ; and, that there may be accommodation for the enormous quantity of stores, and attendants, *three adjoining streets* are to be roofed in as store-rooms and lobbies. For waiters, 150 men are being drilled for the occasion. In the Potteries 10,000 plates and 3000 other dishes are being made for the dinner and dessert. Sheffield is preparing for the same 12,000 forks and knives, and 800 salt and mustard spoons. Lancashire is making the glass, 4000 tumblers, 4000 wine-glasses, 400 salts, and 400 mustard-pots. On the first day there will be put on the table 200 dishes of tongue, 200 dishes of ham, 200 dishes of veal pies, 200 dishes of sandwiches, 200 dishes of sausages, 4000 small loaves, 4000 cabin biscuits, 200 canisters of wine biscuits, 3 lbs. each canister, 200 dishes of sponge and seed cakes, 4000 pies, 2400 Bath buns, 200 dishes of almonds and raisins, 400 lbs. of grapes, 2400 oranges, 2400 apples, 200 dishes of nuts, and wine as it may be ordered by the guests. The tickets of admission to be 7s. 6d. for gentlemen and 5s. for ladies. On the second day all the provisions will be increased by one half. I have not learned what the arrangements are for the third and fourth days, but the prices of admission are calculated so as to pay all expenses, and leave an overplus for the League fund.

I have stepped out of my usual rural walks to give these details of the League to the world ; for to all readers, and especially to agriculturists, they must be full of singular interest.

No. XVI.

A Ramble in Lancashire.—A Lecture in Cheshire by a Member of the League.

" Well, sir, what have you to say about rushes ?"

" Say ! I have to say that through the county of Stafford, through Cheshire, and from south to north of Lancashire, I have

seen very few fields of grass but which contained a bush
of rushes to every three or four square yards of space. The
farms are generally in grass, and, with few exceptions, they are
overrun with rushes."

" Well, sir, and you find fault with those rushes, I suppose ?"

"I do find fault with them ; rather, I should say, with the
farmers who allow them to usurp the place of a more respectable crop."

" Very good, sir ; but do you know that many of our farmers
think very differently from you ? Perhaps you are not aware,
sir, that cattle going out into a field, say on such a day as
this, when the snow is covering the shorter vegetation, may
pick up, and do pick up, a good piece of eating ?"

" Yes, sir, I believe that on a day such as this, when all
other vegetation is covered with snow, the tops of the rushes
may be nipped off and eaten by cattle, if you turn hungry
cattle out ; but the same cattle would prefer to eat hay or
straw, with turnips, under a roof, on such a day as this ; and
hay, and straw, and turnips, would grow on the land occupied
by rushes, would they not ?"

" Perhaps they would—I dare say they would—I have no
doubt they would ; but it is the cows giving milk that go out
among the rushes. The cows, sir, are much benefited by
them ; the butter, sir, the cheese, sir, and the milk, sir, are
better, and fetch a better price to the farmer, when the cows
taste the rushes ; oh, dear ! yes, all are better ; some of our
most experienced farmers, sir, give a decided opinion in favour
of rushes being preserved for the cows to pick at."

This is part of a conversation that I had with a gentleman
whom I met in Lancashire ; it is a singular conversation, and
it was attended with singular circumstances. We formed two
of the audience of a public meeting. We were entire strangers
to each other. Accident brought us into the same square
yard of sitting room, and, as it was an anti-corn-law meeting,
the gentleman asked me, during a pause in the addresses,
what I thought of the landlords' side of the case. " Here,"
said he, " we have heard about the master manufacturers,
about their workmen, about the farmers and their workmen ;
we have heard a deal of argument to shew that all of them
would be better off than now were the corn-law repealed ; but
what about the landowners? I am an owner of land, sir ; I
have an estate for which I paid twelve thousand pounds ; now
what am I to do? I am asked to subscribe to this league
affair : I come to listen to the arguments, and I grant you the
arguments have been very fair so far as they have gone ; but
while they have shewn a remedy for every one else, they leave

me to draw my own inferences, to fear my own fears : now what am I to do with my land ?"

In reply to this appeal, I said—" Since you have asked me what you, as a landlord, must do in the event of a totally abolished corn-law, I shall tell you one thing that should be done, whether the corn-law is repealed or not—you should make the most of your land by cultivation. Through more than a hundred miles of country, in fact from Birmingham to Lancaster, every third or fourth field, and every third or fourth yard of those fields are covered with rushes. I allow that you, as a landlord, have reason to be alarmed at the proceedings of this Anti-corn-law League : it is a formidable combination. You hear each speaker publicly avowing the determination of the League to wrest from the landowners the exclusive protection they now enjoy ; therefore, if you deem the corn-law to be a protection, you cannot help feeling a lively apprehension for your property. I am deeply interested myself in the prosperity of agriculture ; I am desirous to collect and publish to the world all facts relating to it which have hitherto been overlooked. I have come purposely into this part of the country to examine into the nature of tenures, and observe their practical operation. I am not burdened with the task of proving one thing or another in respect of the corn-law and the landowners, but I am glad to have it in my power to talk to an owner of land on the great question of cultivation, I should rather say on the question of *rushes*."

To which the gentleman replied, in the words with which this letter is commenced, " Well, sir, what have you to say about rushes ?"

As the business of the meeting was resumed, and our brief conversation was broken, I had no opportunity of discussing the matter of rushes with this rush-grower ; but I inquired of some other persons if they thought he could be sincere in speaking as he had spoken, and one of those persons seemed surprised that I should question his sincerity.

The rural districts of Cheshire and Lancashire present a melancholy sight at this time, not because winter is on the fields—winter is natural, and beyond it we see the coming seasons of leaf and blossom ; but beyond the darkness now gathered and gathering in the dairy districts of the north, there is no glimmer of coming brightness. I have seen farmers, in the towns and on their own farms, in and around Stockport, Bolton, Preston, and Lancaster, and all of them have the one complaint, namely, " We cannot sell half of what we sold in the towns—neither milk, butter, cheese, fruit, nor vegetables ; the factory people are not able to buy ; work is scarce and money scarcer." This depression in respect of the ready markets which daily and weekly furnished the dairy farmers and market gardeners with ready money for their produce, is deepened in gloom to a stranger's eye, by the poor, spiritless style of management, which again is aggravated by the absurd conditions on which the tenants hold their land. Near Preston there is a considerable extent of corporation property. I talked with some of the tenantry. One of them had been under an apprehension of leaving for several years, and had not, as any one would expect, laid out a single sixpence on his land, though Preston and its manure were within two miles. It is needless to say that his farm was a vile wilderness—it could be nothing else. I inquired about the other landowners in that neighbourhood, and found that the principal one was the Earl of Derby, and I am sorry to say his estate is no exception.

The lecturers of the League are busy among these farmers. Having seen a lecture advertised to be given on a certain evening, in a village a few miles from Stockport, by a gentleman from Manchester, who promised to address himself exclusively to the farmers, I made a point of being present, never having heard before any such address. The lecturer was Mr Prentice, editor of the *Manchester Times*. He was listened to with earnest attention. Of course he said all that he could say against the corn-law—all that its singular history and his own high talent enabled him to say; but he also touched on the questions of leases and improved cultivation. He pointed to the poverty of Stockport, contrasting the great quantities of all kinds of farm produce carried into it by the farmers, his auditors, a few years ago, with the small quantities carried in now. He told them of the markets for Manchester and Sheffield goods, which we could open in America and elsewhere, if we could take corn and sugar in return. He shewed them the protection they would still enjoy, by reason of the great distance and expense of the conveyance of American corn. He shewed that each corn-law had promised the farmers what it had never fulfilled ; and he asserted that all their engagements had been entered upon in accordance with the promises of this corn-law, and that on each failure in *its* intentions *they* had suffered. To which they responded with a tremendous outcry of " True ! too true ! We's be suffering noo !" and such like exclamations.

The lecturer, on the subject of leases, told them that, while they could not cultivate without a lease, they could not, and ought not, in the present condition of the protective duties, to take a farm on lease, if they had the choice; because, at no distant time, if not immediately, the corn-laws would be repealed; and that, even if not repealed, they would be the subject of continued alterations, and that therefore they could not estimate the rent which they would bind themselves to pay. In reference to some nobleman in the county who had opposed an application for a lease, on the grounds that a tenant should always depend on the honour and good will of his landlord, Mr Prentice related the following anecdote:—

A few years ago an English nobleman purchased an estate in Scotland. He found it was let to tenants on leases of nineteen years. Some of the leases were nearly expired, and his Lordship intimated his intention of restricting the future agreements to one year. The system of tenantey-at-will, he said, had worked well in England, and he did not see why it should not work well in Scotland. Accordingly, when the first tenant whose lease was expiring came to ask a renewal of it, this preliminary notice was duly given.

" But," said the tenant, " what can I do with a farm for only one year? Your Lordship surely doesna mean that we are to shift frae our farms every year?"

" Oh dear, no!" replied his Lordship, " not at all; you may retain your farm as long as you like. I am not desirous, by no means, of changing my tenants. I only wish to cultivate that good faith that should ever exist between us, that of mutually depending on each other."

" *That's* what you mean, is it, my Lord? Very weel, I'm glad o' that, my Lord. So, if I take the farm again I needna stop the draining, and the liming, and a' that kind o' thing, that I carried on heretofore?"

" Certainly not," replied his Lordship, " certainly not; you will go on as you did before."

" Oh, very weel; and, of course, your Lordship will never think of putting me out o' the farm till I am paid for my draining?"

" Certainly not."

" And I reckon your Lordship will let me stay to make the most of the lime that I put on the land?"

" Certainly."

" And the muck?"

" Certainly."

" And the compound?"

" Most assuredly; I have no intention but to let you remain and take advantage of all these."

" Very weel, my Lord; I'm glad to hear ye say sae; but

what for should na we just put that down *in black and white?* Ye ken it will be a' the same ?"

The force of this anecdote, and the humour of the lecturer in telling it, drew forth a hearty cheer from the Cheshire farmers ; they seemed to enjoy such anecdotal instructions exceedingly.

Mr Prentice gave them some others, and was warmly thanked for his lecture. One of his most effective points was on the question of " What are the farmers to do with their sons ?" He called their attention to the fact of the present competition for land ; asked if it was because farming was profitable, or because there was no outlet for young men as there had been in the neighbouring towns. " The farms," said he, " do not grow in number, but your families are annually increasing ; what are you to do with them ?" Then he pointed out, by special reference, that more than one-half of the shop-keepers in Stockport were the sons and daughters of farmers, which was confirmed by the responses of the meeting.

Mr Hyde Greg has land near Stockport let at L.2 per acre to tenants who cannot pay that rent, and the soil is not infe-rior, neither is the situation, in respect of manures and mar-kets, to farms near Edinburgh, which he himself saw paying L.6 per acre. His tenantry are pleading to be let down to thirty shillings per acre, so wretched is their style of farming, so depressed is the demand in Stockport and Manchester for the produce of their poor farms.

Wages, too, are miserably low. Near Preston, and about Lancaster, able-bodied men are working to farmers for nine-pence a-day. A shilling and fifteenpence a-day are the more common run of wages. The labourers in Lancashire are on a level with those of Dorset, Somerset, and Devon ; but, so far as I have yet seen, the farms of Lancashire and Cheshire are not so well managed as in these ill-cultivated counties of the west. The world never saw, it is but charitable to the world so to believe, such a contrast as Lancashire exhibits. The most perfect machinery, the highest excellence of manufactur-ing art, the most untiring enterprise, are seen in company with the most antiquated implements, wastefulness of agricul-tural resources, and undisturbed indolence.

No. XVII.

A Chapter on the Agricultural Operations of the League ; with some Words of Advice that may be worth the League's Notice.

About a month or five weeks ago, three sets of queries were issued by the League to all parts of the kingdom, requiring answers relative to the operation of the corn-laws. The first related to their effect on manufactures and commerce ; the second to their effect on morality and religion, or, in other words, to their effect on the domestic comforts of the working classes, on which comforts a sound practical morality and a due respect for religion so much depend. In seeking information on these subjects, the League was following up what it had already done, and done well. I am not aware that anything new was expected, nor do I believe that anything new was obtained. The most important fact elicited by these two sets of queries was, that no amendment had taken place ; that, on the contrary, manufactures, commerce, morality, and religion, were, this year as last, retrograding. Traders of all classes were still as a retreating army. Many who had struggled manfully and kept their places in the ranks so long as they could stagger on, had at last fallen out, and were in the enemy's hands. Forced sales without profits had been the order of the day, like forced marches without rations, to save those who, if they halted, would be overtaken by utter destruction, which, while they kept moving, there was a hope of escaping from. Commerce was still found to be kicking her heels in idle counting-houses, while her ships, that should have been full-fledged and cargo-crammed on every sea, were moulding in the docks, empty even as the rats that starved in them. And, as a natural consequence of this, the whole working population was in process of falling to the lowest level at which life can be sustained ; many, very many, had fallen beneath that level, and had perished, or were perishing. And thus, between human affections, that cling to the world most strongly when the world is least worth clinging to ; human passions, that live in the face of death, that grow strong with the strength of that which excites them ; between these and the laws of social civilization there was strife, which neither the maxims of morality could reduce to peace nor the rites of religion terrify. The animal and the moral nature of man were at war ; the animal was in rebellion against the moral.

In all this, lamentable, fearful as it is, there was to the

League nothing new; it was but a mournful confirmation of facts already known. Therefore, the first and second sets of queries, and their replies, and the digests of their replies, relating to manufactures and commerce, morality and religion, had only the effect of making the corn-law repealers determine to go on, and relax not in their work of repeal. They had before seen clearly, and as clearly saw now, the connection of the corn-law and limited commerce, of limited commerce and national poverty, of national poverty and moral degradation, and seeing this line of connection so clearly, they had no thought but to remove the first cause of the evil that its results might cease. It is a feature in the family likeness of all mankind, that persons thoroughly convinced of the truth and justice of a cause, in the promotion of which they are zealous, have not much tolerance for those who differ from them, nor much patience in watching the slow changes of those who are in process of being converted to that cause. " They who are not for us are against us," has been a maxim from the earliest times to the present. We find it in the oldest of histories, we see it in the most immediate of passing events; but it is not always true, and, as exemplified in the anti-corn-law movement, it is evidently erroneous. The most just argument and efficient that has been put forth by the manufacturers in favour of free trade is that wherein they point to their reduced profits, limited operations, obstructed markets, and, consequently, to the decreased wages which they are obliged to pay their working people. On the self-same ground, and justified by the same natural regard for their own property, the landowners who uphold the corn-law should be allowed to take their stand until the question is fairly discussed whether the protective duties have in reality increased the value of the land, or whether their abolition would tend to diminish it. The onus is upon the League to prove that the value of the land would be improved under a free trade, or, at least, not lessened; and until one or other, or both, is proved, the landowners should not be called on to surrender their posts of strength, far less be assailed with hard names and harder accusations of grasping avarice. If it is said that they should be acquainted with the merits of this question, and decide fairly on it of their own accord, and that they are blameable for their ignorance and unfair decisions, I would remind those who blame them that they, the free-trade party, should also be acquainted with the landowner's side of the question. Not only have they never discussed it with the landowners, but, with a few exceptions, they do not themselves understand it; and what, for the sake of free trade, is still more unfortunate, they are so well satisfied with what they know already, so zealous in the cause of repeal, so assured of being justified in their zeal, that they will not halt nor stoop to take up new arguments.

Now these observations bring me to the third set of queries. It was suggested to the League that, as the repeal is only to be, should only be, and can only be, effected by constitutional means, and that the constitutional means are the Houses of Parliament, wherein the believers in the virtue of a corn-law greatly preponderate ; further, that as Parliament could only be induced to abrogate the corn-law by a sense of fear, sometimes called " the pressure from without," which implies incessant, and perhaps long-continued agitation, or by a sense of propriety and justice, which implies a change of opinion from what is held at present, and which change can only be effected by shewing the landowners that their own interests would be promoted by the repeal, it was suggested that, to accomplish this last, great, and all-important end, a searching inquiry should be made into the value of various kinds of soils as at present variously cultivated. The queries, as drawn out for this purpose, or as proposed to be drawn out, (so I have been informed,) were considered by a distinguished member of the council as too comprehensive and elaborate, not as regarded the importance of the information to be gathered, but in regard of the possibility of getting replies previous to the great meetings at Manchester, which have recently taken place.

Accordingly, the queries were abbreviated, and sent to all parts of the kingdom, through the usual and most extensive corresponding machinery of the League. I have had an opportunity of perusing some of the documents returned in reply. Several of them are highly interesting, all are instructive. A letter accompanying one of them from Alnwick, in Northumberland, states that about the same time the queries from the League were received there, a similar paper, containing queries almost word for word, was received from a government office in London. It has been known for some time that Government had ordered an inquiry into the condition of the agricultural population, but it is rather a singular coincidence that the League and the Government, without collusion, (for it is not easy to suppose that they are in collusion, consequently they must be in competition,) should issue, each of them to the same parties, a document so similar in character at the same time. As regards Northumberland, however, the League had the start, its queries arrived there before those of the Government. The return

from Alnwick is very interesting, but it would suffer by
abridgment. I intend one of these days to give it at full
length, that is, if I succeed in borrowing it from the keeper
of the League records ; at present I do not know who he is.

The value of leases to farmers is also strikingly exemplified
in those returns. Whenever leases are common, and have
existed for a lengthened period, the agricultural labourers
are in a superior condition to those who inhabit the estates
farmed by tenants-at-will, and the primary cause of difference
is, that a farmer who has security in his farm, not only
employs more people on it, but hires them for lengthened
periods, and thereby renders them more steady and provident
than they are as day-labourers, occasionally employed and
occasionally idle, as is too common with those who labour for
tenants-at-will. A farmer in East Lothian (Mr Mackenzie
of Spott) fills up one of the papers, and to the question,
which is to this effect, " Does sheep-stealing and poaching
prevail more when bread is dear than when it is cheap ?" says,
" We have no sheep-stealing in this part of the country,
neither have we poachers, our people are better employed."
To the same query it is replied from Worcestershire, " We
have always sheep-stealers and poachers, but they are ready
made, and neither dear nor cheap bread has anything to do
with them." From a village in Yorkshire the answer to the
same query is, that nearly all the poaching and sheep-stealing
in the neighbourhood is traceable to necessity, and that when
work is plentiful the crimes are nearly unknown, while when
it is scarce they are common. This answer is the most
frequent from all parts of England.

These documents contain a body of evidence such as was
never before collected, and which, as regards the abolition
of the corn-laws, was never before equalled in importance. I
have been informed that in this session of Parliament Mr
Cobden intends taking the new ground of arguing that the
repeal would not injure the landed interest ; and certainly, if
he chooses to make use of these documents, he will have ample
grounds for such arguments. Though by no means so complete as they should be, and perhaps might have been, these
agricultural queries and their answers, together with practical
observations made in all parts of the kingdom by practical
men, give ample justification to those who assert that in
England there are vast resources for agriculture hitherto
undeveloped, and which have lain dormant because of various
obstructing causes, which causes must and will be removed
before land is suffered to go out of cultivation through
foreign competition. By these returns, and by other evidences,

it might be shewn, that one of the most remarkable fallacies that ever obtained credence and currency, relative to the value of land, is hugged, even by the members of the League, or a large majority of them, as a truth from which they cannot be parted ; from which it is not to be expected they should part, seeing that those manufacturers and merchants of them who have become rich and have bought land, adopt and practise most of the vices peculiar to English agriculture, save perhaps Mr Greg and one or two others, and even he seems to have faith in this enormous fallacy. The fallacy is, that it would be a sacrifice of property to break up the pasture lands, and that the natural tendency of land, when its produce is depressed in price, is to go out of cultivation, or, in other words, to be laid down in grass.

Believing that this is true, the greater number of the members of the League with whom I have had an opportunity of conversing while in Manchester, whether manufacturers or agriculturists, or persons whose lives and property combine both professions, have taken the position of assailants of the landowners. Accustomed to hear even from their agricultural friends, that *some* land will go out of cultivation if wheat falls to forty shillings, but that they, the agricultural friends, are willing to continue friends, notwithstanding this, deeming it incumbent on them to make a sacrifice for the common good of the country, hearing this, and seeing nothing throughout several counties surrounding their head-quarters but the feeblest efforts at cultivation—even at their very doors, between Manchester and Stockport, for instance, which should be one luxuriant garden for the supply of these towns with vegetables, there is a wilderness of sour grass and rushes, the manures of the towns unappropriated, the markets ill supplied, all kinds of vegetables scarce and dear; accustomed as the manufacturers are to hear their agricultural friends speak of surrendering something for the general good of the country, and to see palsied agriculture exhibited around themselves, and practised by themselves, they have adopted the notion that if the abolition of the corn-law would put land out of cultivation or reduce rents, the landowners *must* surrender ; for the abolition of the corn-law they, the manufacturers, *must* have.

This position of the League is not only calculated to render repeal all but impossible, and put it off, to say the least, for many years to come ; but it is positively erroneous, and there is, therefore, comfort for those who have free trade warmly at heart, and who are not holding such opinions ; comfort for those who are alarmed for their property by the advance

towards free trade and the menaces of the League, to both
and to all there is room for comfort in this, that those who
in the League speak most freely about the landowners know
least about the land.

At the late aggregate meetings there were anti-corn-law
deputies from all parts of the kingdom assembled in crowds,
morning, noon, and night. Morning, noon, and night, they
were repeating the details of their mission, and melancholy
enough the details were, yet there was not a sentence nor an
inference that was new. Morning, noon, and night, they were
provided with all manner of accommodation for repeating to
the world, and to each other, the oft-repeated grievances
attributable to the corn-laws. The clerical section of them
had, I am told, several apartments allotted as committee
rooms, so important were their statements deemed to be, and
yet, at best, they only spoke of corn-law consequences ;
whereas, to the agricultural consideration of the question, in
which *the means of getting rid of the corn-laws, the only possible
means, was entirely involved,* there was no attention given
whatever, not even a room provided in which those might
meet who wished to converse upon the subject.

I mention these matters thus publicly, not so much to shew
that this great question is, by many of the leading repealers,
dealt with in a partial manner, but to draw their attention,
and the attention of their friends in all parts of the kingdom,
to that side of the question which is now the most important.
Hitherto they have discussed the *operation* of the restrictive
duties, they must now direct themselves in the right direction
to their *removal.* If they set themselves up in hostility to the
landed interest, they put a rivet in the endurance of the corn-
law by every hard word they utter.

No. XVIII.

Remarks on the Undeveloped Agricultural Wealth of England.

In speaking of grass-lands that might and should be brought
into cultivation, it is necessary to except the chalky downs,
which, in many cases, would be positively injured by ploughing ; yet, in excepting them from the plough, they should not
be left entirely out of the question when speaking of deriving
an augmented produce from the soil of England. It is quite
within the truth to say that, on the downs of Wilts, Dorset,
and Hants, perhaps also in Sussex and other counties possessing such soils, the number of sheep fed now is four times

7

greater than the number fed forty years ago, and the downs
are not to the extent of a blade of grass more fruitful now
than then. The difference arises from the production of
winter food on portions of the same downs, in shape of turnips
and other roots. Therefore, if turnips have done so much in
forty years, what might they not do if cultivated in a proper
manner? If, instead of stupidly burning every piece of turf,
everything that can be raked together to burn, the farmers
would make lime, which they can always do in the chalky
districts, and form a compost with the lime and the stuff they
now burn, they would have a rich and (compared with the
pitiable handful of ashes now obtained for turnip culture) an
abundant manure. And if they would rationally use the
farm-yard manure they now have, instead of wasting its precious gasses in the sun and air ; and if they would appropriate
the liquid now wholly neglected, the winter food of stock upon
the downs might be greatly augmented. Also, if some attention were devoted to the herbage of the downs, there might
be stimulating substances applied to its increase ; and if landlords would encourage their tenants to make such efforts,
there can be little doubt that such improvements would be
effected. The most valuable manure on a stock-farm is the
liquid, to save which reservoirs are necessary ; but what
tenant can of himself, at his own risk, construct them ? No
leaseholder should be asked to do so ; far less should a tenant-
at-will be expected to do so.

But the grass-lands to which I would more especially direct
notice are those commonly called "meadows" in England,
composed in most part of what in Scotland is called "old ley."
These occupy extensive parts of the best counties of England.
I do not know on what authority M'Culloch and other statistical writers found their computations, when they allot a
certain number of acres to corn-growing and a certain other
number to grazing ; but, from personal observations, I have a
strong opinion that hitherto the corn-growing acres have been
greatly over-estimated, and the grazing or permanent pasture
acres greatly under-stated. It would certainly be a valuable
piece of information if the proportion of acres in grass to
those under cultivation, with particulars of the soils and subsoils, as also the tenures on which they are held, could be
obtained ; but without more knowledge than we already have,
I am fully justified in asserting that all the grass-lands in
England, dairy and beef-feeding, save portions of the downs
already excepted, should be broken up and put under a course
of cropping. Many people think otherwise, and I would give
them all credit for sincerity ; indeed, no man can be insincere

in an opinion which, to practise, lessens the amount of his own income ; but he may err in judgment, or he may never have had facts laid before him on which to form a judgment. The most remarkable feature in the agricultural condition of England which strikes an agricultural traveller from beyond the Tweed is, that the estates are mostly all under the control of lawyers or persons not practically acquainted with agriculture. The complication of tithes, tenures, political serfdom, and various causes obstructive of good farming, has led to this ; but most, if not all, of these obstructing causes must sooner or later be removed, and the land *must* be better cultivated.

In my last communication mention was made of a fallacy that has gained almost universal currency. It was stated that "the fallacy is, that it would be a sacrifice of property to break up the pasture-lands, and that the natural tendency of land, when its produce is depressed in price, is to go out of cultivation, or, in other words, to be laid down in grass." In this statement there are more fallacies involved than one. I shall direct attention to those that more immediately present themselves.

Before it can be called a sacrifice of property to break up the old pastures, we must be satisfied that it is better to let cattle roam at large in the fields, destroying much of the grass on the wet soils—and most of the meadows are wet—than economizing their food and their time of feeding at the stall ; better to let the fertilizing results of feeding be prodigally wasted in the open air than carefully collected in the farm-yard ; better to take forty shillings' worth of hay from a given space of land at a small expense of labour, giving five shillings of profit, than take two hundred shillings' worth of some other crop from the same space of land at a higher expense of labour, giving forty shillings of profit ; that it would be better to leave land at the annual value of twenty shillings an acre than raise it to the value of sixty shillings an acre ; in short, before the breaking up of the old grass-lands can be called a sacrifice of property, we must undo all that has been done, unsay all that has been said in England in favour of the best specimens of Scotch farming. I lately conversed with a Scotch member of Parliament on this subject, who doubted if such a profitable change could be effected in English landed property; "because," said he, "it is natural to suppose that the landowners, who are nearly all hard pressed for money, would readily adopt the means that would most quickly give them increased wealth." To this it was replied, that their pecuniary necessities operated against the improvement of their property in a twofold manner. First, they mortgaged their estates and committed their management to lawyers; and, second, their necessity compelled them to seek state appointments through political services, which to obtain caused them to subjugate their tenantry to a degree that left the latter no power to improve their farms.

On the same subject I lately talked with a Manchester manufacturer, a rich man, who had property in land. He said—" I do not see clearly that it would be proper to grow corn in our dairy districts. If all Cheshire, and Dorset, and Devon were ploughed, where would our supply of butter and cheese come from?" To this it was answered, that it might be wrong to plough up the meadows of those counties, if they were kept in grass from the merely benevolent desire of the landlords and farmers to supply the towns with butter and cheese; but as butter and cheese could be made whether the meadows lay in permanent grass or not, it would be as fair to expect a manufacturer to keep his looms going to weave muslins only, and not weave some other fabric on which there was double the profit, merely because muslins had been his staple trade hitherto, as to expect a landowner to keep his estate in grass at thirty shillings an acre when he might have it cultivated, and corn crops produced, at a rent of L.3 per acre.

But the manufacturer objected to the supposition that land could be so improved in value. " Look," said he, " to the expense of cultivation. Though the value of the produce be higher in amount when it is corn than when it is butter and cheese, we must not suppose it to be profit." " No," was the reply, " neither must we suppose that, because a piece of printed calico is dearer than a piece of the same quality that is white, that the excess of price is all profit. But you have extensive print works, in which capital is sunk, and from which profits are made, because you find the printed fabric produce a higher price than the unprinted."

This observation led me then, and it leads me now, to the second and principal fallacy, namely, that a depression in the price of produce has a tendency to throw land out of cultivation. The contrary is the fact, save in extreme cases, save in respect of land that never should have been cultivated, and of that there is very little in England. For each acre that would have been thrown out of cultivation through depressed prices there are five that would come into cultivation by the removal of the causes that obstruct successful agriculture, while, by the same process, nearly all the land now under the plough would be greatly increased in productive value. Before the assertion can be admitted that land will go out of cultivation through low prices, we must be satisfied that it cannot produce more than it now produces, that it cannot be worked more economically than it is now worked. And this would lead us to inquire what economy is.

Economy is not, in farming, the nominal reduction of expenditure; in most cases, among English farmers, it would imply an increase of expenditure. Sir John Sinclair has laid down as an axiom, which every good agriculturist has found to be true, that, supposing L.5 an acre to be the lowest sum, and L.10 the highest, which can be expended on the cultivation of a farm, the interest of the L.10 would be from ten to twenty per cent., while the interest of the L.5 would be from five to ten per cent. In my travels through England I have seen the truth of this exemplified on almost every estate.

No. XIX.

Through Berkshire to Strathfieldsaye, with some Remarks on the Division of Common Lands.

From Reading, the county town of Berkshire, to Strathfieldsaye, the Duke of Wellington's seat in Hampshire, the distance is about nine miles. There is much excellent land on each side of the road, with cottages and gardens, and orchards, and occasionally fifty or a hundred acres of common; the latter, in most cases, wet, sour, neglected, profitless, and hopeless of profit, unless we expect it to be enclosed and cultivated. Were those who have now a right of commonage to get a portion of the common, and compelled either to cultivate or resign their portion, much might be done, not only to improve their social condition, but to augment the general produce of the country. But it has, unfortunately, been the custom to exclude the poor from the advantages of the enclosure acts, and thus no one can speak or write in favour of the enclosure of the commons without incurring the odium of intending to oppress the poor. In my travels, wherever I find a common larger than what is requisite for a village play-ground, if it has the appearance of a good soil, I talk to the people living on and around it of the benefit they would derive from its enclosure and careful cultivation; and in all cases they reply with a bitterness expressive of no milder belief than that they think me an agent of some one about to rob them, about to invade their little privileges, and despoil them of an independence which, even if not worth a

penny, they would still cherish, merely because it was a soil
other than the bare highway, on which they could set the
soles of their feet in defiance of the rich man, their landed
neighbour.

Though there is a loose morality, consequent on a half idle
life and an irregularly provided table and fireside, to be
found on the verges of a common; though the mean condition
of such a population who starve, and steal because they starve,
and are not employed honestly, because they have been
known to steal, and who cannot live honestly, because they
are not employed, and who are of little use to employers,
because idleness, whether constrained or voluntary, is the
destroyer of industry; though such a population are the
natural enemies of men of property and magisterial authority,
and give to the world a species of criminals normally schooled
in crime, they are yet possessed largely of those feelings
which have been respected in other classes of Englishmen.
Even their vices, as inhabitants of an English common, are
virtues when seen in the whole people who comprise the
English nation. The love of native soil, the desire to attain
and determination to defend independence, the resolute resistance to all encroachments on territory, the openly expressed
hatred of all persons who would dare, rightfully or wrongfully,
to question the propriety of what they do; the generosity of
to-day in helping a distressed neighbour, and the readiness of
to-morrow in appropriating to themselves the property of
some other neighbour; the regard for their own privileges
and disregard for the privileges of other people; all these are
characteristic of the rustic idler in England and of the
English nation. What is a vice in one case, may not be
entitled to the name and esteem of a virtue in another, if
morality be the rule of logic. But be the characteristics vicious
or virtuous, they are the distinguishing features of the
English over centuries of years, at home and abroad, and
to their exercise we owe all our liberty, all our extended territory, all our power.

Even our commercial enterprise and manufacturing industry
as a nation, both of them positive virtues, are the offspring
of those individual energies which in the rustic idlers of
England produce vice; for, in fact, there are no people in
England who can live in real indolence. Many of them are
unprofitably energetic, as the fox-hunting, horse-racing, wager-
speculating, political-plotting, dinner-giving inhabitants of
palaces and mansions; or the hare-snaring, donkey-riding,
beerhouse-betting, trap-making, dinner-seeking inhabitants
of the cottages on the common; but all of them are consti-

tutionally enterprising, and all, with better management, might be made to turn their energies to national profit. The dwellers on the common have not degenerated. They are still what the forefathers of other classes were. Walled parks, hedged-in farms, commercial warehouses, and moneyed banks, have grown up with civilization, and from their interior we look out upon the rustic whom we have left behind and shut out, and we punish him for infringing on the property which we have placed in his way, a respect for which, and an interest in which, we have neither taught him nor permitted him to obtain for himself. We find it is dangerous to ourselves, and not advantageous to him, to have our enclosed property and his open common, our state of art and his state of nature, our respect for law and his lawlessness, coming in close contact. We are not insane enough to propose to go back to his condition, and live on equal terms with him. Even my Lord Stanhope, though he would fill up the commercial docks, disuse machinery, throw down the factories, despoil the towns, and fall back upon the land, says nothing about throwing down the park walls and returning all the land to a state of commonage. None of us are insane enough to propose this; but we are unjust enough to attempt the removal of a social evil, to wit, our unsafe neighbours on the common, by taking from beneath their feet the ground on which they stand, knowing that when it is divided amongst ourselves, they cannot longer exist as independent enemies; that they must either perish at once or live; that, if living, they must either be at once honest workmen or transported criminals. The attempt has never been made, save in a very few cases, and in those cases the attempt was made unfairly, to divide a common for the good of the commoners. Though we know from our own feelings that we respect the property of others most when we have some of our own, we have always proceeded on the principle of teaching our rural population to respect property by taking all property from them.

When, in talking to the people who live on the commons, I shew them, either by printed or written documents, or conversation, or by the arguments of all united, that in some parts of the kingdom three or four acres of land, middling in quality, maintain by good management a couple of cows, winter and summer, a few pigs and fowls, and give an ample supply of vegetables to a family for daily use, and occasionally for market, and for which land of middling quality the holders pay double as much rent per acre as is paid for the best soil in Berkshire, namely, from L.3 to L.4 an acre. When making such statements, and offering to prove them, I point to their common, and tell them that, if divided amongst them, they might each keep a dozen cows all the year, where at present they have bare pasture for one during the summer months; that they might breed and feed pigs—having six fat ones for each starvling that now runs on the common; that instead of sending out their children to gather the miserable particles of manure falling from starved animals, they would have an abundance of rich manure from their cows, and pigs, and fowls, not only for gardens much greater in extent than those they have now, but for their little fields, which would grow corn to give them bread they do not eat now, and straw, and turnips, and wurzel, and cabbages, for winter food to the cows, none of which, neither food nor cows, they have now. When I speak of such changes, the people stare in profound astonishment or laugh in scornful derision. In the first place, all husbandry by plough or spade, which they are accustomed to see, or have ever seen, (*read* of, they cannot, few of them can read,) is so different in its results from what it might be, that they very naturally believe their own eyes rather than the mere assertion of a stranger. But they will believe any prodigy of produce to be within their reach rather than believe they have the remotest chance of getting a share of the common if it is divided. " Touch the common with a plough and it is no longer the poor man's property," was the emphatic remark of an old man with whom I lately conversed, and who seemed to have an oppressive horror upon him at the bare mention of a division. I asked him why they did not at least make or obtain some rule for restricting the number of sheep, donkeys, and cattle that were sent out to graze, these animals being sent out in such numbers as to eat up the very roots of the herbage. The reply was, that it would be better to have fewer cattle and better grass; but if the grass were better the farmers and the lord of the manor would send their sheep and cattle, and eat it all up even in one day; whereas at present nobody who had better pasture for sheep or cattle sent them to the commons.

Though some of the common lands are not worth cultivation, and would not yield a quarter of grain per acre, in obedience to all the agricultural arts yet discovered, many of them of very considerable extent are to be found in every county of England, respectable and often rich in soil, but invariably neglected and profitless. To the improvement of these the attention of the Legislature is now, it seems, to be directed; but they had better remain as they are if the division is to be on the principle of all former precedents of injustice and impolicy.

Between Reading and Strathfieldsaye there are several commons, with the usual stock of old horses, lean cows, sheep, donkeys, geese, and ragged children. The soil of the whole country thereabout is heavy, and not easily worked. It is but justice to the soil, however, to say that it has had little inducement to change its character from any ameliorating treatment. Some of the fields I saw, the soil of which was a fine deep loam, capable of bearing any kind of crop under skilful management, were one entire mass of weeds and couch-grass. The young wheat is generally fine, in some cases splendidly rich, and dark beyond anything I remember to have seen at this season. Beans seem to be a prevalent crop in this part of Berkshire, and they look well where not over-run with weeds. The farmers seem to depend on the hand-hoe for cleaning the crop, instead of clearing the soil before the crop is sown. On some of the Duke's farms I found that more than usual care had been taken to clean and prepare the soil, but even there I saw farming at which I was astonished, considering that his Grace takes a personal interest in seeing that judicious improvements are made. For instance, four horses, and sometimes five, going a-head of each other in a plough is ridiculous. But more of this in a communication which I shall specially devote to a description of Strathfieldsaye and neighbourhood. I find I have not space for matter so lengthened and so interesting in this.

No. XX.

A Journey to Harmony Hall, in Hampshire; with some Particulars of the Socialist Community in 1842.

Having heard a remark made at the inn where I was staying for a few days in Salisbury, that two travellers, who had left behind them two cloaks and two walking-sticks while they attended to some business in the market, were supposed to belong to the Socialist community at Titherly, in Hampshire, from the circumstance of their walking-sticks having engraved on the heads the resemblance of a beehive, and the words, "The Working Bees," I was induced to make some inquiry about the distance to and situation of their *beehive*. The correct information to be gathered in Salisbury was extremely scanty, and accordingly, on being told that the distance was only twelve miles to the village of Broughton, and that the community were located near that village, I procured a conveyance, and, in company of another gentleman, set off for Hampshire.

This was two or three days after the visit of the two members of the Beehive to Salisbury. It was a lovely day. If a country with so good a soil and so poorly cultivated could have afforded pleasure to a traveller at any time it would have done so on such a day as this. But the road lay through a section of that bare country formerly described as visible from Old Sarum, and there was nothing to be satisfied with but the excellent roads, which, being of flint on a hard bottom, are maintained at little expense. Leaving Salisbury, we had the seat of W. Wyndham, Esq., one of the members of Parliament for the city, on our left; and, for the next twelve miles, the entire distance, I saw nothing worth mentioning, save that a field of good turnips, and another of beautiful young wheat, would be seen as spots on a wide uncultivated common, much of the soil of which was quite as good as that sending up the young wheat and the respectable turnips; which turnips again might have been of a much better quality, but for the neglect which characterized their cultivation. I have said nothing more was seen worth mentioning; but, at an inn called the Winterslow Hut, I received information that the wages of labouring men had been reduced to seven shillings a-week by the largest farmer in that district, and that the other farmers were expected to follow immediately with a similar reduction; and the common expression of those who were present, some of whom were tradesmen from Salisbury, and one, the landlady of the house, was to this effect:—" God above only knows how the poor creatures are to be fed! What matters it to them that flour and bread be cheaper this year than last? They could buy little of either last year, and they can buy as little this. They must buy potatoes, not bread, and potatoes are but a middling crop this year; they are good, but small."

This place, Winterslow Hut, was the scene of a singular incident six-and-twenty years ago. On the night of Sunday, the 20th of October 1816, the Exeter mail was changing horses at the door, when an attack was made on the leading horses by a lioness which had broken loose from a travelling menagerie. There is a coloured print of the scene hung up in the parlour, which purports to have been executed from the description given by Mr Joseph Pike, guard of the mail, the said Mr Joseph Pike being himself, next to the lioness, the most conspicuous figure of the group. The ferocious beast is worrying the offside leader, having seized it by the throat, and the courageous Joseph is standing on his seat, with a levelled carbine, as if about to fire. A dog, which, as the hostess informed me, was the most efficient assistant in getting the lioness secured, is shewn in the foreground, in very small dimensions, perhaps to set off the enraged assailant as larger and more formidable than she really was. At all events, the scene is a startling one ; what with the terrified faces at the upper windows of the inn and in the inside of the coach ; what with the blue, and the red, and the yellow which paints the faces and the waistcoats of the outside passengers ; what with each seizing his umbrella or luggage, as if determined not to die without a struggle ; and what with the likelihood of the whole being devoured by such tusks as have already destroyed a horse, the spectator, not of the reality, but of the coloured print, is excited to call, even at this day, to Joseph Pike and the carbine, " Why don't you fire ?" However, there is no sign of fire, nor is there any record. One horse was killed, and, by some means not fully explained, the lioness was secured in her caravan.

We arrived at the village of Broughton about one o'clock, and having put up our horse at the inn, we proceeded on foot to *Harmony Hall.* Broughton is but a poor-looking village, irregularly built, and surrounded by farms, which indicated that the Working Bee community would have no difficult task to compete with them. The soil all around is quite deep enough for common cultivation. It is deeper than many of those parts in the Lothians, or Roxburgh or Berwickshires, where a rent of from L.2 : 10s. to L.3 : 10s. an acre is paid for a middling soil. The subsoil is chalk, and I believe that wherever there is a sufficient depth of soil above chalk, that soil is, generally speaking, fertile. It might be shallow on some of the higher districts ; but all that I saw, and I examined it in several situations, varied from twelve to twenty-seven inches in depth. The chalk was a variety well adapted for lime, but, except by the Socialist community, little advantage was derived from it ; *their* lime-kiln was the only one I saw during the day's journey. The rent of the land about Broughton is from ten to fifteen shillings an acre. With other burdens, not borne by the Scotch farmers, it would amount to twenty shillings or twenty-five shillings an acre.

Leaving the village, we proceeded southward. For nearly a mile the lane in which we walked, hedged by coarse bushes, gradually ascended, and the soil on each side seemed wearing thinner and thinner. Having fortunately met a woman who directed us through a field towards the left, we followed a waggon's track, and in five minutes I was standing in a field of turnips which grew in drills, shewing a bulk of crop and robustness of health quite refreshing to the eye, after the poor

specimens of turnip culture I had seen in that and adjoining
counties. I observed to my companion that if these were
"Socialist turnips" they promised well.

But, before going further, I should remark that I knew
nothing of the Socialist property, nor of any individual connected with it. I had, like others, been reading wandering
paragraphs in the newspapers about this community, some of
which had not long before stated that the whole establishment
was broken up, that the members were dispersed, the property
seized by creditors, and so on. My companion knew nothing
of them but by hearsay. In fact, though living within twelve
miles, he knew as much of China as he did of Harmony Hall,
and that was not much. He was one of those jolly countrymen well to do in the world, who believe the British army and
navy can, and ought to, thrash all the world, if the world
needs a thrashing ; who grumble when the tax-gatherer comes
round ; who take in a paper which they seldom read, but who
still grumble at the government—no matter what party is in
power ; who think no times are so hard as the present times ;
but who forget all grievances when the next hot joint comes on
the table. Such was my companion. Little as I knew of the
Socialists, I had been able to inform him that they did not
wear claws, nor horns, nor wings, nor tails ; that though they
were human in shape they were not cannibals ; neither did
they steal little children and put them in boiling cauldrons just
for the love of the thing. But though able to tell him all
this, I was not able to obliterate the opinion which he had
imbibed from the hearsay common in Salisbury, that the
Socialists were an assemblage of the greatest vagabonds that
a too-lenient law had left upon the face of the earth. In
short, some of the stories I heard in Salisbury are too ridiculous, I might say criminally libellous, to be mentioned. Yet
by many they were believed. My companion had seldom read
for himself on any subject, and I was much amused with his
account of what he had heard of the Socialists. He had a
friend in Broughton on whom we called, and who gave us the
first information of their property and personal reputation :
it surprised both of us considerably. "Their property," said
he, "consists at present of one thousand acres of land, and
they are now in treaty for the purchase of another estate ;
they have paid down L.500 of a deposit on it, and it will be
theirs next year." To this I rejoined that I was completely
astonished, that I had never dreamed of their having such a
property, and begged to know how it was cultivated compared with the farms I had seen in the neighbourhood.
To this the gentleman replied (and I may state he is a man

of property and respectability in the village) that, so far as
he could judge, they were cultivating it very well. " But,"
inquired my companion, somewhat eagerly, "what sort of
people are they? We have heard such strange tales about
them, over our way, that I have been quite at a loss what to
think of such people being allowed to live among you."

" Why," replied the other, " all that I have seen of them, or
have heard, amounts only to this, that it would be a high
honour to this parish if one half of our inhabitants were as
decent in their behaviour as they are—it would indeed. And
more, it would be a credit to our gentry if they would employ
people in as great numbers and to as much advantage on the
land as they do."

" Lord bless me! you don't say so?" exclaimed my friend
from Salisbury, " and such stories as we have heard of them!
Do you say all this of them in sober earnest?"

" I do," replied the Broughton gentleman. " As for their
peculiar notions about property, I don't agree with them; but,
so far as saying they are well-behaved people, setting a good
example to this neighbourhood, I say it most sincerely."

" But," interrogated my companion, " are they not all *Deists*,
that believe there is neither a God nor a devil?"

" If I understand the term *Deist*," replied the other, " it
means a believer in God. As to their belief in religion, I suppose they are like other people, of different opinions. One
thing I know is, that they come to our church, and some to
the chapel. They sit and hear the sermons, and go away
again as others do. They never introduce religion nor politics into any conversation with us in the village, but I once
talked to two of them on the subject of religion of my own
accord, and they told me they had the same opinions of religion now as formerly; that there was no peculiar opinions
among the Socialists, save that each man might enjoy his
own opinion without molestation; that they, the two, being
believers in the Christian doctrine of salvation through Jesus
Christ, attended a place of worship, and that no attempt was
made by any member of the community to dissuade them from
going to church."

" Lord bless me!" exclaimed my companion, " you don't
say so in earnest, do you?"

" But," I inquired, for I had not been prepared to hear
this favourable account of their tolerance, " what do the
clergy say of them; *they* don't like them, I should suppose?"

" The Methodists and Baptists, and such like, make an outcry against them," replied the gentleman; " but our clergyman of the parish church says nothing about them. All of us

hereabouts were much alarmed when we heard of them coming at first, but we look on them now as very good neighbours; and as they set a good moral example to our population, and employ a good many of our poor; and as they never attempt to impose any opinion on us, we have no reason to dislike them. One of them married the daughter of a farmer in this neighbourhood a short while ago; the banns were put up in the parish church, and our parson married them. Oh, depend on it, they are doing good here in a moral point of view."

"Lord bless me!" exclaimed my Salisbury friend once more, on hearing this, "did the father of the young woman give his daughter to a Socialist?"

"Certainly," returned the other, "why should he not?"

"Because," said my companion, "they have a new wife whenever they tire of the old one."

"Nonsense!" returned the Broughton gentleman, "ridiculous nonsense. They have no such practices, and, so far as I ever heard, no such doctrines in theory. They propose, when they can get an act of Parliament for the purpose, to simplify the law of divorce, by allowing married persons to separate by mutual consent after several repeated notices, and repeated trials enjoined on them to try once more, and once more again, for certain periods of time, for some months each period, to agree; if after those trials they are still desirous of being parted, they may be divorced. As for any other laxity of principle, I know none. The most delicate and well-bred conduct characterizes them so far as I know; and nobody hereabout, however opposed to them, attempts to say a word against their moral character; *that*, as I said before, might be an example worthy of imitation to many in this parish. In short, the Socialists are very well but on one point, which concerns themselves more than anybody else; on that point I believe them to be fatally in error; and more, that sooner or later they will split and fall to pieces on it—I mean the community of property. There will always be idle men, willing to talk and to live at the expense of the industrious. Your talking men are not commonly the best workmen, and seldomer still are they willing workmen. In fact, those of them that are really the industrious men are pretty well tired of the numbers who come visiting and living idly from distant parts of the country. Besides that, if they were all willing alike, they are not able alike, nor used alike to such work as cultivating a farm; and I have heard that several of their carpenters, bricklayers, and such like, are but indifferent workmen when put to a job. In fact, the ignorance of most of those who came here at first of practical matters has led them into extravagant expenses. They have been imposed upon on every hand. Then, again, consider the folly of expending L.30,000, and upwards, on a building before improving their land. Instead of beginning like working bees they have done quite the reverse. The bees begin by making honey, using any place for a retreat that may fall most readily in their way. There we have the working bees and the drones living alike on the common store, building and building, and leaving the honey-making to the last."

Such was the account I received of the Socialist community in the village of Broughton, and it is given at full length, because of the opinions of others in the neighbourhood, who spoke to the same effect. When we reached the turnip field, as already said, I remarked to my friend that if these were "Socialist turnips" they promised well. They were Socialist turnips, and we soon after found seven hundred Socialist sheep, which made my friend exclaim, "Lord bless me! who would have thought it!"

Winding down a gentle declivity, we saw a red three-storied brick building near some large forest trees. These trees seemed the commencement of a wooded district, which contrasted pleasantly with the naked country we had travelled over from Salisbury. As we approached the red brick house we could observe that its outward form was tasteful and all its proportions substantial. It stood at about fifty yards to our right, while on the left was a farmyard, old and uncomfortable-looking, with some ricks of wheat, waggons, pigs, and cattle. Adjoining the farmyard was a new house, which might have been taken at first view for the respectable residence of a substantial farmer. This we found was built as a temporary residence for those members who arrived previous to the large house being built.

On every side of us we saw unfinished work; heaps of bricks, piles of mortar, logs of timber, half-built walls, and broken ground, as if in process of being laid out into gardens. No person being visible, we looked around us for some time; at last I saw three dogs approaching, which I proceeded to meet, supposing that, as it was Harmony Hall, there could be no harm in meeting the dogs. They did not deceive me; but one of them belied the reputation of the place by snarling at the other two. They growled in concert, and then departed on some errand of their own to a dust-heap, where one of them, finding a bone, produced a contention much in the same way as dogs do in the old world.

We advanced to the open door, which shewed a spacious lobby, from which stairs went down and stairs went up. I met a middle-aged female, who politely told me some one would speak with us presently. Following her were three younger women, plainly, but tidily and respectably, dressed. My eye was following them up stairs, when I perceived a man before me. He wore a cloth cap, and a respectable suit of clothes. After the preliminary courtesies, I told him that we had come to see the establishment, and any information he chose to give us would be received as a kindness. We were then conducted into an office, where two men were sitting, one as if posting a ledger, the other writing a letter. All the London daily papers, and several others, were on the table. A book lay open, in which we were requested to write our names, which done, our guide, whose name I afterwards understood to be Atkins, or Atkinson, told us to walk " this way."

We descended to the basement floor, which, on the other side of the house, looked out on a level with a lawn in process of formation. On this floor there were several large apartments; one of them a dining-room. Dinner was just over, and, as a finale to it, the members were singing in full chorus a beautiful piece of solemn music. We were not asked to go into their presence, but we went to the kitchen, after examining an excellent piece of machinery, which, through a tunnel, conveyed the dishes and the dinner from the kitchen to the door of the dining hall. A boy who was passing showed us how it worked, and presently several other boys appeared. All of them were so clean and neat in their clothes, so healthy in their appearance, and at the same time so respectful in their manners to us and to each other, that I could not help staying behind to talk with and look at them.

In the kitchen there were three or four women with a very large assortment of dishes to wash. I did not know what the dinner had been, but judging from the refuse of bits and scraps, which seemed to me to tell more of abundance than economy, I supposed they had all got enough of it. The women in the kitchen were, like all the others, tidy and respectable in appearance. The only thing that puzzled me was how they should be so well as they were, with such prodigious piles of plates washed and unwashed around them. I can say nothing adequately descriptive of the fittings of this kitchen. At Broughton I was told that the London architect who superintended the erection of the whole, said that there were very few kitchens so completely and expensively fitted up as it in London. I am sorry to say that such is, to all appearance and by all accounts, the case.

Outside the kitchen there were commodious washhouses,

cellarage, baths, and a well-arranged place for each member
to wash himself as he comes from his work, before going to
meals.

Ascending again to the next floor, we entered a ball-room,
and going up stairs we saw the sleeping rooms, all as conveniently arranged as can be under one roof. Upon the
whole, the house is commodious, but I was much disappointed
at seeing such a house. A village of cottages, each with a
garden, would have surely been more appropriate for a working community, and much cheaper. The sum expended on this
building, not yet half furnished, is said to exceed L.30,000.
Such extravagance previous to cultivating the land would
stagger most people on the question of the sagacity of the
working bees.

Mr Atkinson conducted us to the new garden, which contains twenty-seven acres. I was then introduced to a Mr
Scott, the chief gardener, whom I found to be an intelligent
and thoroughly practical man. His operations of trenching
and planting, and indeed gardening in every department, were
extensive. Brick-makers were making bricks ; builders were
building ; lime-burners were burning lime ; road-makers were
making roads ; the shepherds were with the sheep ; nine
ploughs were at work ; a hundred acres of wheat were already
sown, and more wheat land was being prepared ; a reservoir
was being constructed to save all the liquid manure ; and, in
short, everything was being done to improve the land which
industry and capital could accomplish and skill direct.

Mr Scott was having portions of some of the fields trenched
with the spade. He paid the labourers L.5 per acre for it,
and expected them to work so as to make two shillings a-day.
I remarked that this was more wages than common. He said
it was ; they only gave the ploughmen and other day-labourers
nine shillings a-week ; but as it was scarcely possible to get a
good workman in that part of the country, he allowed a higher
rate of wages to get them to work with some spirit. In
answer to a remark I made about proselytizing their workmen
to Socialism, he replied that they never made any attempt ;
but if they did attempt it, he believed anything might be
accomplished, any change might be effected, but a change in
the old slovenly style of working ; on that point he believed
the present generation of Hampshire labourers to be incurable.

It will be perceived by this that the members of the community do not themselves cultivate the land. Some of them
work in the garden, but few of them, I suspect, are fitted for
rough out-door work. Their number was at the time I was
there sixty, thirty more were expected soon after. The

8

quantity of land is 1000 acres, held on a lease of ninety-nine years, at a rent of fifteen shillings an acre. They have the power of purchasing it within that time at a certain price; and they have paid down a deposit on a neighbouring estate of 300 acres. Their landlord is Sir Isaac Lyon Goldsmid. There is some fine wood on the ground, and an avenue of fine old yews, which, for beauty and extent, is perhaps not equalled in any other part of England. The community intend converting a portion of that avenue into a summer ball-room. Adjoining are large numbers of full-grown trees, resembling the size and shape of the main-mast of a man-of-war.

I saw in several parts of the woodlands that the vegetable mould was gathered into heaps to be carried and used as manure. On almost every estate in the kingdom there is a rich soil of this kind, that might be collected and carried away without any injury to the trees. Mixed with lime it forms an excellent compost.

I did not see the agriculturist, but Mr Scott, the gardener, was conducting several experiments in the fields with the spade on alternate ridges with the plough. His manner of trenching was this:—The earth was lifted two spadefuls in width and to the depth of about a foot. This was taken in wheel-barrows to the place where trenching was to cease, there to fill up the last opening. A pick was taken, and the bottom of the trench loosened to the depth of eight or ten inches. This loosened subsoil was allowed to remain. The adjoining soil, two spadefuls in breadth, was then turned over, taking care to bury the weeds in the bottom. A second working with the spade, in the same trench, turned up a fresh soil to form the surface of the new seed soil. The bottom of this second trench was loosened with the pick as that of the first, and the next was begun by again burying the top mould. They had a subsoil plough on its way from Smith of Deanston's factory in Scotland. They were gradually introducing improved implements, but the greatest difficulty they found was to get the Hampshire labourers to work with them. They had thirty of these labourers at work.

I was told at Broughton that about one-half of the members ate no butcher meat, but lived entirely on vegetable diet. They at first brewed beer, but now they have curtailed that expense. One shilling a-week is allowed for pocket-money, but few of them are ever seen to spend even that in the neighbourhood.

To conclude, I may remark that I believe their land to be well worth L.2 per acre of rent, and they only pay fifteen shillings. They have an excellent bargain, if they manage it well ; and whatever may be said of their Social crotchets, it must be said of them that their style of farming is of a superior kind. Those noblemen, gentlemen, clergy, and others who dislike the Socialists, would do well to shew the working population that good farming is not necessarily an adjunct of Socialism, else, perhaps, the working population will think the doctrines of those who pay best, employ most, and produce the greatest abundance of crops, are the best doctrines. This is no light subject. Missionaries of all religions, in all parts of the world, in all ages, have succeeded in proselytizing more by introducing arts and sciences, by teaching new means of acquiring wealth, than by preaching abstract theories. We have an eminent instance of this in New Zealand at the present time ; and unless the landed gentry take a step in advance, or at least side by side in the same road with the Socialists, they will find the labourers of Hampshire voluntarily converted to the new doctrine. Again I say this is no light subject. Let the gentry and clergy look to it.

Notes on the Socialists.

The foregoing account of the Harmony Hall property attracted much attention at the time of its first publication. The Socialists reprinted and circulated 10,000 copies of it. Subsequent visits convinced me that I had not mistaken the good intentions and good moral behaviour of those persons. Indeed their effect upon the population around them, by their own example, in diffusing intellectual life, sober habits, and good manners ; and upon the farmers around them, by the example of their hired agriculturists, in moving them to dig down ditch banks and make compost, clear away foul accumulations, and use wasted treasures of earth and rubbish for manures, was apparent to all visitors, and admitted by all dispassionate neighbours ; yet neither had I mistaken the unsoundness of their scheme in its business principles. They were all intellectual men ; but they were not all industrious men ; while most of them, industriously inclined or otherwise, were unfit labourers in garden or in field. So long as money could be borrowed it was borrowed ; it was obtained when prudent men of business would have buttoned up their pockets, the delusion of the place becoming an Elysium still lingering in the minds of some monied men, and in the minds of many working men living at a distance. At last, in 1845,

as no profits arose, as L.30,000 had been contributed or lent
to sustain the scheme, the contributors and lenders would
not yield more. The resident members quarrelled, and split
themselves into sections, spoke evil of one another and to one
another, or became so inharmonious and unsocial as not to
speak to one another at all. They dropped away, the wisest
first, with such personal allowances as they could extract, such
personal effects as they could collect, or had preserved; the
most devoted and foolish at last, with nothing. Men and
their wives who had come from the manufacturing districts,
leaving behind them profitable work, at wages of thirty shillings, forty shillings, fifty shillings, and even sixty shillings
per week, to labour in Hampshire on the land in competition
with the Hampshire labourers, who were glad to work for
nine shillings per week, sought their way home again penny-
less, hopeless, and broken-spirited, empty in pocket, empty in
stomach, filled only with grudges and revilings towards one
another.

The governor, Mr Buxton, formerly a calico-printer's
engraver, after suffering much privation, the farm stock and
crops having been seized by creditors, and adhering to the
deserted Hall of Harmony against all commands to leave,
was, in the autumn of 1846, ejected by a creditor from Liverpool, aided by a number of Hampshire labourers. For some
weeks Mr Buxton lingered on the spot, having built himself
a hut by the wayside; but bad weather came on, and, hopeless and helpless, he too, with his wife and family, returned
to Lancashire, to seek the profitable employment which he
had been unwise enough to part from. Mr Bates, a creditor
to the amount of L.7000, had risked that sum, his all, in the
lucrative investment, and died broken-hearted. In vain the
creditors have tried to sell or sublet the property. It was held
by the Socialists on lease for ninety-nine years, and buildings
which cost above L.20,000 erected on it. Sir Isaac Lyon
Goldsmid, the landlord, is the only party likely to gain by
the adventure. When General Yates, who lives in the neighbourhood, saw Mr Owen, the originator of the Socialists,
walking with Sir Isaac at the time of bargaining for the
property, Mr Owen being in religion an unbeliever, and Sir
Isaac Goldsmid being a Jew, he called the attention of some
friends to them one day, and said—" There they are at their
bargain; the infidel trying to do the Jew; the Jew trying to
do the infidel; a thousand to one on the Jew!"

But Sir Isaac is far from deserving the imputation implied
in this sally of General Yates. He is simply a man of business, able to calculate per-centages, and not disposed to make

landed property an exception to sound principles of business. It would be well for agriculture if all landowners would do the same. It needed no deep sagacity in an observer like General Yates to foresee that a man of business-habits like Sir Isaac Lyon Goldsmid, opposed to a visionary dreamer like Robert Owen would get the best of a bargain.

The Socialists, in trying to sublet Harmony Hall, have advertised it several times, setting forth the purposes to which it may be adapted by new lessees, of which purposes one is a —————— *lunatic asylum.* Poor fellows! it was so from the beginning, and only ceased to be so when the lunatics, through low diet, came to their senses and left it.

No. XXI.

A Day's Ramble at Strathfieldsaye.

April 1843.

Strathfieldsaye Park is on the northern border of Hampshire, commencing at about seven miles from Reading, the county town of Berkshire. It is irregular in shape, but, measuring it from recollection, three miles from north west to south east, and half as much from north east to south west, may be about its extent, exclusive of irregularities.

Approaching it from Berkshire on the north, amid hedgerows and farm-fields, and pieces of common, and cottages, and farm-yards, with trees of all shapes and sizes, and varieties of kind, now thick enough to obscure farm, and, farmer, and all belonging to him, from view, and again thin and clear enough to expose them to the open world, with the addition of the common, and cottages, and geese, and goslings, and donkeys, and cows, and horses, the latter stunted as the over-eaten herbage they bite at. Approaching Strathfieldsaye through such a diversified country, so generally wooded, we cannot easily detect the commencement of the Duke's enclosures. But here is a man cutting a water furrow on the edge of a newly sown field. I shall let my two friends go on slowly in the phaeton which we have hired at Reading, while I get out and inquire where Strathfieldsaye is. I have inquired, and am told that all the country round here belongs to the Duke; that beyond the palings on the right is the beginning of the park; all those trees over yonder, down here, up there, all within view—if I do not look behind me—and the farms out-spread amid the trees, are the Duke's.

"The Duke must have a large estate here, if all that belongs to him?"

"Yes, he have a terrible sight of land. I ha' heerd how many thousand acres he be owner of, but forget now; it be a many thousand. He be a buying land and never done. Oh! the Duke be owner of a terrible sight o' land."

"Is his Grace supposed to be rich? Has he a large income?"

"Yes, he have a terrible sight o' money; nobody knows how much. They say he don't know himself. He can't count it, it be so much; he be terrible rich, the Duke be."

"Shall we get into the park? Are strangers allowed to go through it?"

"Yes; an' the Duke ben't there, you might drive all round, in at the one side and out at the other, or come back to where you went in. But I ben't sure an' you be let in at these times; for his Grace be here with company, and he be terrible particular they say. It be Easter now, and his Grace comes out of London to get some fresh air; and his rich friends, the great people, come out with him to keep him company. They say there be a great sight of rich people in London."

"Yes, there are many rich people in London, but there are also many poor; there are a hundred times more poor families than rich ones in London; many times more poor in proportion to the number of inhabitants in London than in this parish."

"Ah, that ben't true, we be all poor in this parish; and people in London ben't all poor."

"Why, you have the Duke in your parish, and you have other great people; and all the farmers, they are not poor, are they? and even the labourers, such as yourself—do you call yourself poor? You have always work enough I suppose?"

"Yes, I be always at work, but I be poor for all that. I han't but eight shillin' a-week—that ben't much to make six of a family rich, be it? And the farmers say they be coming down as poor as we, and can't afford no more wages. The gentry be the only rich people, and they go all to London to spend their money; they only come hereabout for their pleasure for a week or a month, or not much more—sometimes for a day only—to look at us, and they be off again to London. Ah! we be all poor as be working folks in these parts, and it be getting worse they say; we be like to be worse, not better."

"But wages are higher than eight shillings a-week, are they not?"

"Yes, some men have nine, and, for the matter of that, I

may say some have ten, and may be eleven; but they be not common men as I be, they be one or two ploughmen on each farm, or somebody particular. The Duke's men as work in the park have ten shillin', but there ben't many on 'em."

"Do any of your children get employment?"

"Yes, one be at work now, he be twelve years old, and gets two shillin' a-week, and my wife be gone to-day to hoe wheat on the farm over that side—you can see it, about a mile off, by looking through that opening—and we ha' had a loaf of bread from the parish for one young un; but I ben't sure an we shall get the loaf now when so many on us be at work, and I ben't sure how long so many can be at work. The hoeing will soon be done, and, were it to last, my wife might not be able to leave the house and the children every day. She have more nor enough to do at home to contrive how we be to get somewhat to put on us, and how we be to get somewhat to cover us. It ben't easy out of our income to get a bellyful for so many, be it?"

"No, I fear not, nor clothes either, when you need them."

"Clothes, bless you! we never have no clothes, not new— not to speak on as clothes. We thought to have something new as bread was getting cheaper, but wages came down, and we ben't better nor afore; it takes all we earn to get a bit of bread, and not enough of that. They say meat be wonderful cheap in Reading, but what of it being cheap to we who can't buy it at no price?"

"I should like to know what you do live on, if you have no objection to tell me? Do you go home to your dinner, or is it brought here to you?"

"I fetch it in the morning. I live two mile away. It be lying there now in my bag, aneath my smock. Here it be; here be the greater part of it. I eat this bit of bread and drink some of that water in the ditch, and when it be done I be done with dinner. What be'nt here I ha' ate on the way out for breakfast."

"Breakfast! and had you no other breakfast before coming out, nothing but dry bread?"

"No, I ha'nt every day a bit of bread for breakfast. I be many a day out in the fields without breaking my fast till mid-day, and then, an I have a bit of bread and a sup of water, I be better than them as have none. There be some working all day, at times when work be scarce only a day or two in a week, and they be glad to have something to go home to at night, let alone eating in the day. Ah! we ben't put past working by eating too much, and I be many a day here with a hungry belly; but, thank God, I ben't the worst either, for I ha' work and eight shillin' a-week, and

out o' that we get a bellyful once a day; if not sooner, we get
it in the evening."

"You do get a bellyful in the evening, do you ?"

"Yes, we pay a shillin' a-week of rent for house and little
bit of garden ; the garden grows some vegetables—not enough
—but still it is a help to us, and something can be got to help
that.   Nettles, when in season, be good vegetable eating.   We
have a bit of lard or butter an we can ; an cannot, why the
salt must do—that be cheap, thank God ; and if we have bread
to eat to such a dish, why it ben't to be complained on.   The
worst is that we be as ready for another bellyful next morning and ha'nt got none."

"But all the labourers are not so badly provided for as this
—some of them feed pigs, do they not ?"

"Yes, they feed pigs, but they don't eat much of them ;
they sell them to pay house rent and to help to get some
clothing.   Them as be paid the highest wages ben't so badly
off ; but the most on us have the smallest wages, and many
don't be always in work.   Work be scarce all the year round
in these parts, and in winter terrible scarce.   The Union-house
be full now."

"Is there any place forward here where we can put our
horse, any inn or public house with a stable ?"

"Yes ; there be a good place enough for that on the common before you, at the new inn—Rogers'.   They'll put up your
horse for you, and shew you where to get into the park ; that
is, if there be any allowance for you to get in when the Duke
is there.   Perhaps you may get in, I don't know.   You be some
of the well-dressed folks as come here, and they get in when
people not having such good clothes can't ; but even they be
not always admitted.   The Duke be a particular man, I hear
say terrible particular."

At the new inn, on the side of the common, we hastily
disburthened ourselves of all charge of horse and driving, and
things therewith connected, and, free for a pedestrian ramble,
we set out to walk round the outside of the park.   To me
the outside was more interesting than the interior, as my
object was to look at the farms and farming rather than the
silvan beauties of Strathfieldsaye.

To my accompanying friends the outside was more than
enough to fill them with all the joy that they were capable of
containing ; they were even filled to overflowing.   And beside
the happiness natural to myself amid such scenes—the glorious
sunshine all around, save when the leafy trees of a precocious
summer made a shade for flowers too bashful for the open
world, the rich earth blending in sunshine and in shade, the
green and the gold of grassy banks dotted with primroses, and

a hundred other wild flowers, all varied, but all lovely; besides the happiness natural to myself on such a day, in such a place, the overflowing joy of two younger minds, formed by nature for the enjoyment of the associated beauty amid which we rambled, was poured upon me, and I was overflowing also. All above and around us was brightness and beauty, all within a desire to be satisfied and a pleasing sense of satisfaction.

There were whistling larks, which we could see like motes in the blue sky, and others which we could hear revelling in the liquid sunshine upon which we could not look. On each side of the way, on the hedge-rows, and on the trees that mingled with the hedge-rows, sat the thrush, musical and uxorious, filling the time with rich melody which his mate must devote to the domestic duty of hatching eggs. There were around him the linnet, grey and green, the goldfinch, the robin, the wren, and fifty other varieties of birds—innumerable in each variety, all noisy and full of life, building nests, or singing with joy that their nests were built. The saucy blackbird, hopping from sprig to sprig, with nothing to do, yet too proud, as all professed singers are, to give us a snatch of melody, save when it pleases himself, and that is not in the open air in the open day—he was there; and the chattering magpie, that would neither sing nor let us hear others sing, fluttering about; and the solemn crow, black, discordant, and abounding in noise, the street preacher of the woods—he was there; and the cooing wood-pidgeon sounding everywhere, but making a monopoly of the more quiet retreats with his hurdy-gurdy notes—he, the Italian boy of the feathered race, was also there. And we had the cuckoo, the Monsieur Julien of the whole, whose signal notes had told that spring was come, and that the grand concert must begin; from his first solo the music had increased in variety and strength, and now we had one general chorus, a thousand voices singing to the million.

We came to a gate, through which there was a road into a park. A neat little cottage was at the side of the gate; and a woman was at the door of the cottage. I asked her if strangers were admitted into the park, and she replied that usually they were; but, his Grace being at present there with visitors, she did not know how far she might be safe in admitting us. I begged her not to think of it for a moment, if there was the least restraint upon her; hearing which, she said no orders had been given for the exclusion of strangers, but that she and others had a general understanding that his Grace liked the park to be kept private while he was there; that she was a widow, to whom his Grace had been indulgent and kind, in giving her a house and the means

of living ; that she could not do anything, on any account, to
give his Grace offence, but yet there could be no harm done,
she thought, if we wished to see the park, by our going in.

This somewhat qualified permission we declined ; and seeing before us a bushy waste on the exterior of the park palings,
we intimated our intention of rambling there ; for honey bees
and honey flowers, and birds nestled and preparing their
nests, were its sole inhabitants, so far as we could observe,
and our pleasure was to be among them ; but the old woman
said we must take care of the " vermin," by which she meant
snakes and adders. Those creatures are more abundant than
makes wandering in unfrequented places quite pleasant, so we
avoided them, and passed on.

For the space of two miles and a-half, or thereabout, we had
the park palings and its thickets of marginal timber on our
right. By the wayside we had cottages with ample gardens,
enriched with fruit-trees full of blooming promise. On our
left were farm fields bearing crops or undergoing preparation.
Leaving them behind, and passing on, we came to an inn of
some pretensions to gentility, called the " Wellington Arms."
There we found a person belonging to the Duke's household,
and who assured us there was not the slightest objection to
our walking in the park.

The main entrance being at this point, we took advantage
of it, and soon found that, lovely as the rich spring was outside the enclosure, she was richer within. A small river, which
comes through the adjoining meadows on the south, enters the
park, and, having a wide bed prepared, it exhibits a series of
lakes and waterfalls, forming on the whole a fine crescent of
water, reaching through the whole park.

From each bank the ground gradually ascends, shewing
like a gem on its green breast the mansion of Strathfieldsaye
on the south. The park is too fine in its form, and adornment,
and fulness of extent, to appear as an adjunct to the mansion.
The mansion is too trim and neat, and made up of littlenesses,
to appear the chief feature of the park.

The park would retain all its beauty and grandeur if the
mansion did not exist.

The mansion would have little beauty were it not in the
park.

But mansion and park, and all that is in and around either,
derive and give forth an element of interest beyond what is
inherently their own. They are Wellington's. The trout
that shot along the stream, and returned in playful gambols
to the pool beneath the bridge, holding revel in dozens and
scores, and fifties, delighting the eye, as such creatures of in-

stantaneous motion always do, these could not be regarded as
mere fish ! They were Wellington's; and yonder was the boat
in which the venerable hero sometimes puts off to catch them.
Even the butter-cups and daisies could not hide their little
heads in the meadow grass and conceal the fact that they
were Wellington's. There was not a tree, nor its tiniest leaf,
nor the softest breath of air, but seemed to me to say something of Wellington, and to demand that reverence should be
paid to the master-spirit of the scene. More than once my
hand took involuntary motion, as if it would lift from my head
the irreverent hat that did not uncover in approaching such
a place. More than once unbidden thoughts arose and depicted
Wellington as the opposer of the favourite men of the people.
More than once these thoughts were ordered to lie down
and rest, if ever they were to rise again, until a suitable place
and circumstance permitted them ; and at last they were
foregotten in the recollection of the twelve volumes of Indian
and Peninsular despatches.

If these twelve ponderous volumes were as easily read as a
newspaper report of a debate in the House of Lords, how
differently would the multitude think of Wellington ! When
he not only warred with, and overcame successively, the armies
of Junot, and Massena, and Marmont, and Jourdan, and
Soult, and Napoleon, weakened as he was by the indolence
and ill faith of his Spanish allies, but combatted the corrupt
and unfriendly practices of the British government at home,
listened to or read of the fiery-tongued orators who then ca-
lumniated him, and who now, though no better informed of his
abilities than they were then, or then might have been, think
fit, because he has been successful, to adulate him.

The general, who, in almost every letter expostulated with
the ministers of the day against their feeble policy, that made
the nation discontented at home and him weak abroad ;
who was weakened and crippled in power until he dared
scarcely to make a corporal; who wrote, in shape of despatches
to the government, essays on human character individually
and nationally considered, taking a view, not only sound and
sensible and new, but so accordant with the popular voice,
that the public would have then, and would now, give him one
of the highest positions as a popularly instructive writer, if
they knew what he had written.

This general and philosophical practicalist is at present
lost sight of in the political Wellington, and the great bulk
of mankind do not know where to find him. Next to the
Waverley Novels, I have read the twelve volumes of " Gurwood Despatches," with the highest interest, for pleasure

alone, to say nothing of instruction. The lives of Wellington, as so often published, are but feeble summaries of military events. The life of Wellington is in the twelve volumes, it cannot be extracted. Some publisher, who would aspire to sell 100,000 copies of a work in penny or twopenny numbers, should bring out a weekly issue, without abridgment, of these national, and as yet nationally unread, documents.

When we had wandered through pathless places, and along paths that seemed to have neither end nor relief to their intricacy and seclusion, and when we had made ourselves familiar with the forms of a thousand hoary oaks, the most gigantic and aged that I had ever seen within the British shores, and with vast numbers of pines, spruce, and larch, but chiefly spruce, ponderous in bulk beyond all my preconceived notions of the size of British pines ; when we had wandered amid these vast giants, and made acquaintance with the shrubs near them, and the flowery sward spread out among the shrubs, and the rabbits and other game that disported on the flowery sward ; when we had watched the frisky little lambs and their sober mothers, the lambs loitering to play while the mothers grazed, and moved away as they grazed, until the young ones knew not where to find each its mother ; when we had seen the temporary distress of the deserted innocent, and noted how quickly the mother came from a far distance when she heard its cries, and how eagerly it ran to her and drank her milk which with fondness she devoted to it, as a recompence for its recent grief ; when we had delighted for hours in looking on the beautiful foliage of the green hawthorn trees that dotted the parks, and wished we had been three weeks later, to see them all in full bloom ; when we had dwelt on the banks of the bright lake, with the snowy swans and shyer water-fowl for companions ; when we had said, how much better the mansion would have been situated if standing on the north side of the park facing to the south ; when we had noted that a great part of the park was newly tile drained, and had examined and found that the draining was done in the manner practised and recommended by his Grace's friend and relative, the Marquis of Tweeddale ; when we had said that it was a pity so many hundreds of the giant oaks should be decaying of old age, and had added that they would afford a fine supply of money to some younger and poorer Duke of Wellington than the present ; when we had seen and said all these things, and many more, and found that our faces were as red and glowing with the vehement sun as the sky in the red west, we bent our steps towards the new inn, on our way homeward, my companions asking, in a

tone of regret—Would they really have to go away without
seeing the old Duke ?

This last observation may give rise to some reflections curi-
ously illustrative of the natural history of mankind.   Here
were a brother and a sister, grown to maturity, or verging on
it, both fond of reading history, born and bred in London,
and yet they had never seen the Duke of Wellington.   They
had never thought of going to St James' Park, or to the
entrance of the House of Lords to see his Grace ; but now
that they were forty miles from home, it was painful to them
to have to move away and not see him.

Again, the fact of their being Londoners, would make some
people, and all authors, set them down, when visiting the
country, as ignorant of every bush, and tree, and leaf, and
flower, making them commit, most probably, the most ludicrous mistakes in regard of vegetable individuality, whereas
the cockney is, in nine cases out of ten, more learned in the
varieties of plants and flowers than the countryman.

If we would find a person in London who has seen all the
sights, and is familiar with the lions, with the features of
great personages, such as the Sovereign, the Prince, the Duke,
the Prime Minister, and Lord John Russell, go to a countryman who visits or occasionally resides in London, not to the
cockney.

On the other hand, if we would find a person familiar with
every plant and flower common to England, from butter-cups
and daisies upwards, we must go to the Londoner who visits
Hornsey Wood, Epping Forest, Greenwich Park, Norwood,
Richmond, and Hampton, and Highgate, and Kensal Green,
and the innumerable tea gardens, full of floral wealth, foreign
and domestic, we must go to the visitors of those places—
and what cockney does not visit them ?—and not to the
countryman.

Near to the southern verge of the park, four or five hundred yards from the Duke's mansion, and a few hundred
yards within the outside fence, we found a church, churchyard,
and a parsonage house.   On inquiring at a person that was
near, I found this was Strathfieldsaye parish church.   My
informant was able to say that the incumbent was the nephew
of the Duke, and that it was said to be an excellent living ;
but he could not tell which nephew, nor did he seem to know
that the Duke had brothers, or any other relative.   We
passed out of the park, sat down on the green bank that
skirted a field, where a man was ploughing with four horses
all in a line ; talked to him, and some others afterwards, about
farming matters, and learned from them that five horses were

sometimes used; that they had too many new fashions coming up amongst them already; that the good land varied from twenty to thirty shillings an acre of annual rent, and that, with other burdens, it was too dear.   To this I replied that, held as it was, without security, farmed as it was, without economy, I did not doubt but it was too dear; still it was land that, in some other parts of the kingdom, situated the same in respect of markets, would pay eighty shillings an acre of yearly rent, and yield a profit to the farmer.

Note upon the Duke of Wellington.

Certain parties with whom I was connected when the foregoing was published first, criticised it, and dissented from my observations about the Duke and his despatches.   Perhaps they never read and studied the Duke's despatches and letters. I did, and under the following circumstances:—About nine years ago several lives of his Grace were in course of publication ; all of them exalting the man as a military and moral wonder.   A London publisher thought it would be a good speculation to bring out a Life of Wellington which would place him in an unfavourable light.   My pen was idle at the time ; the task was offered to me, and I began to read for its execution.   I attended the reading-room of the National Museum, and read all the twelve volumes of despatches edited by Colonel Gurwood, and everything else on the subject which I could find there.   The result was, that I told the publisher that I could not touch Wellington with my pen, unless it was to try to exalt him higher than any writer had yet done.

No. XXII.

A Rambling Letter over much ground, and many Arguments touching on the Farmers who Dined at Wallingford, with Mr Blackstone, M.P., in the Chair.

April 1843.

The imperfection of the tenures on which land is held in England, partly for the political subjugation of the tenantry, and in all cases for the accomplishment of purposes equally short-sighted and pernicious, is so universally apparent, that, go into which county we may, the tenure is seen by its effects. That certain estates are to be exempted from this remark, and that their improved condition gives relief to the traveller's eye, and forbids him to charge all England with agricultural negligence, is true ; but these are so few, that the most to be said of and argued from them is, that they condemn the country which surrounds them ; and even if this is said, whole counties may rise up and protest against the condemnation, inasmuch as within their entire length and breadth neither an estate, nor farm, nor field, nor acre of land is held on a tenure admissible of good cultivation, nor under cultivation fit to be copied as an improvement.

A few weeks ago there was exhibited in one field, on a farm near Abingdon, four ploughs at work, with four-and-twenty horses drawing them, that is, six to each plough. Two weeks ago, the farmer who thus ploughed and still ploughs his land, was at Wallingford dinner cheering and joining in the cry of Lord Stanhope and Mr Blackstone for "protection to native industry!" All round Wallingford, and from that town to Abingdon, from Abingdon to Oxford, and from Oxford to Banbury, again from Oxford to Bicester, and across the county to Buckingham, where I have recently been, everything in agriculture, whether in respect of the style of farming, the wages of labour, the condition of the labourer, or the ability and hope of the farmer, all is meagre, has ever been meagre, and is at present more than ordinarily depressed. The land, naturally good, much of it excellent, exhibits a most pitiful appearance. The miserable rents of twenty shillings an acre for land that should be paying sixty shillings, of ten shillings an acre for what should be paying thirty shillings, are not paid ; the tenants cannot pay, and have no hope of being able to pay. On every acre of their land there is a demand for labour to drain, or clear weeds, or ameliorate by a mixture of soils ; but there is neither the capital nor the security for capital to employ such labour. Even where money is expended on labour, the low sum of seven and eight shillings a-week, the able-bodied man's price, is higher pay than fourteen shillings a-week would be in Norfolk, than eighteen shillings a-week would be in Northumberland, or Berwickshire, or Roxburgh, or the Lorthians ; and yet the labourer is employed a greater number of hours in Oxfordshire, and those parts of Berkshire around Wallingford and Abingdon, than in any of the counties named. The difference is seen in the economy of labour in the north, and its systemless waste in the south. We have here six horses yoked a-head of each other in a waggon, to carry manure, with three men *following* the waggon to fill and empty it, not carrying as much in a week as the same number of horses singly in carts, with three men to fill,

one to empty, and two boys to drive, would do in a day.
We have the same number of horses going with the waggon
to market, and not carrying more than three single-horsed
carts do in some parts, and should do everywhere. We have
oxen and horses yoked to the same plough, the inequality of
pace preventing the equality of draught. We have serpentine
ridges, shapeless and measureless, with furrows following their
prodigal eccentricity, until the four, or five, or six horses to
each plough, not only lose, by the bend of the furrow in which
they walk, a power additional to that which a line of horses
always lose on each other, but they and the plough travel over
an extra space of ground, such, in most cases, as if the field
contained eleven acres instead of ten. We have numberless
small enclosures, in which, by the turning of the plough, much
labour is unnecessarily lost. We have between those fields
masses of divisional fence, composed of ditch, mound, and
shaggy bush, occupying space that should be the centre of a
corn crop, or which, if necessary for a fence, is now useless,
save, perhaps, to birds that build a nest, lovers that sit by a
shady bush, or poets, who, not being farmers, can afford to
praise such a nursery of blooming wildness, and write sonnets
in praise of the wings of down that carry the seeds to new
soils when autumn breathes upon their ripeness. We have
streams abundant, and ready for water mills to thrash the
grain, and thus enable the farmer to take the labour, wasted
in his barns over the tedious flail, to his fields, to drain and
fructify. But we have a population who would burn the
houses, and haystacks, and barns of any farmer who dared to
erect a thrashing machine—a population which, as it is,
whether because they are ignorant, and irreligious, and immoral,
or whether, in spite of being as intelligent, religious, and
moral as the churches which crowd upon our eyes would indicate them to be, light the incendiary fires, taking awful
vengeance on men of property, for wrongs real or fancied.
We have those people always under-fed, even if always
employed. We have many of them partly or wholly unemployed, seeking subsistence as paupers, or as poachers and
thieves. We have the farmers paying rates, already heavy,
and still increasing in weight, to keep them in the workhouse
and county jail, in both of which they are punished—by the
test in the workhouse to prove them paupers, by hard labour
in the jail, because they are criminals. And they come out
of the jail and the " house" sensible that they have been
punished by men whom they look on as natural enemies—the
guardians in the one case, the justices in the other. They go
to work for a pittance which cannot secure comfort, or they

again starve for want of work, and return as paupers to the house, or steal and go back to prison. Perhaps, seeing that to starve or steal is the same ; that as paupers or criminals they are to be punished ; that they cannot avoid being one or the other, and therefore cannot avoid punishment ; they look upon the men who sentence them, the men of haystacks, and stables, and barns, the guardians and justices, as their natural enemies, on whose property they may make war, on whose haystacks, and stables, and barnfuls of grain, they do make war—fearful, savage, wasteful war. In London, though all the news of the kingdom concentrate, only a small portion of the rural fires are reported ; the directors of insurance companies have been taught practical philosophy, and know that publicity makes crime contagious. The provincial newspapers agree with them.

It cannot be doubted that the landowners are full of good intentions as respects the improvement of their land, but the first step towards that improvement is to them so full of newness, or alarm, or humility, or some other element of unpleasantness, as to prevent them from taking it? That step is the emancipation of their tenantry from political subjugation by the grant of leases free of stringent clauses, to secure the outlay of capital. Without a liberal outlay of capital improvements cannot be accomplished ; without improved agriculture, the general employment and fair remuneration of the labouring population cannot be secured ; without employment and fair wages, the labourers cannot live honestly nor be contented ; and if they are dishonest and discontented, they will either be punished or will punish ; so that we return at once to the point where capital must be expended in the improvement of the land ; but, before that can be done, there must be a security granted that the farmer shall have his fair return of profit.

In addition to a lease, free of the absurd conditions commonly imposed in the few leases that are granted in England, there must be a basis of rent agreed on, either on the principle of the tithe-rent charge, or something approaching to it.

Until the farmer is thus *protected*, it is vain, it is worse than vain, it is a heartless mockery, to lecture him at agricultural meetings about draining and manuring, and cleaning and ameliorating his soils. He might with advantage, even as a tenant-at-will, economize his horse and manual labour ; discard his cumbrous implements, and save the manures he now wastes; but to do so implies the renunciation of prejudices old as his grandfather, and strong because they are old. And prejudices are only seen by onlookers ; they are to their owners

9

honest opinions. To shew a man that he is prejudiced, we must make him think as we think; if a farmer, he must travel further than his own market town, he must be induced to examine in all parts of the country all kinds of systems; he must be taught how to appreciate them; but before this can be done, there must be a sufficient hope of interest excited. This last he can never have as a tenant-at-will. In that capacity his mind and his movements are subject to the restriction of others, and he confines himself to his parish, or, at most, his county.

But limited knowledge on agricultural science is not alone the property of the untravelled, unread, unreading tiller of the soil. Let us look into the advertisements of estates to sell in the newspapers, and we shall find the estate-agents acute men, well versed in most things, experienced in all smart methods of turning a penny—we shall find them ignorant, almost without an exception, of the first and simplest principles that should guide buyers and sellers of agricultural property; and why? because all things relating to agriculture have been considered so simple, the science of cultivating land has been so completely disregarded in education, that nobody, save a few old merchants or money-lenders, who buy bargains and hold their tongues, has given the mercantile value of land a consideration. In the advertisements of estates to sell, we see a strong point made of the assertion that " the land is in the highest state of cultivation." Now land in the highest state of cultivation is the most hazardous landed property that can be purchased, while land in the lowest state of cultivation is the safest and most profitable. If land is wanted with a view to profit, that will be preferred by the prudent purchaser which will return ten, or fifteen, or twenty per cent. in preference to that which will return three, or four, or five per cent. This is an observation so trite that nobody will deny it; each reader will think his time wasted in reading it, so careful will he be of a due amount of profit. But let us see whether highly cultivated Lothian or poorly cultivated Oxfordshire would be the most profitable investment for money.

In Lothian little more can be done by way of improving, unless some new discovery in science is made, which may never be made; so that the capital expended in raising the land to its present high annual rental has already returned its profit, and the farmer who expended it has become rich, and has made his landlord rich. This landlord, in selling his estate, will not sell for less than a price calculated from the present high rent, say eighty shillings an acre, and, as there is no room to improve, the purchaser must be content with a per centage, perhaps as low as the bank interest. But in Oxfordshire—indeed in four-fifths of all England, but in Oxfordshire especially—the improvements are yet to be made, and the purchaser of land would have the usual profit on a twenty-five years' purchase of the rental, or whatever else the computation of price might be, while he would have, in addition, the valuable return of money laid out in improving.

A notion seems to be abroad that money laid out in advancing the productive powers of land is sacrificed. Nothing can be further from the truth, that is, if the expenditure of the money is directed with prudence, as it must be in any other commercial speculation. Sir John Sinclair lays down an axiom which all practical men have proved to be true, namely, that supposing L.5 per acre to be the lowest sum, and L.10 the highest, that can be expended profitably on the improvement of an acre of land; and if the L.5 returns a profit varying from five to ten per cent., the L.10 will return a profit varying from ten to twenty per cent.

At the present time, most of those that may be called " spirited farmers" are either singularly unskilful, or have not the power to practise their skill. When visiting the Duke of Wellington's estate at Strathfieldsaye, I was told, and could perceive, that the Duke intended his property to undergo a process of improvement. I saw tile-draining going on in the Home Park—I saw new houses built for labourers, with ample gardens of a quarter of an acre each, the best cottages and gardens given to the poor at their rent (L.3 : 10s. a-year) that I have seen in any part of the kingdom. Besides, there was a school erected by the Duke, and in other directions were to be seen marks of improvement. The tenants, at least some of them, had been " spirited" enough to purchase the new-fangled manures from shops, while they were neglectful enough to allow the best fertilizing agencies in their own homesteads to go to waste. Even their farm-yard manure, carried out to the fields, was lying as if laid out to dry and bleach, the air filching away the gases in which consisted its chief value. If we saw a shopkeeper buying goods from a distance and at a high price, while he trampled under foot in his own shop, or threw into the common sewer, goods equally saleable and valuable, we would call him insane. And what shall we say of the farmer who does the same thing?

Yet again the farmer is not so blameable. The fact of his purchasing expensive manures shews how he struggles to do his best according to his knowledge. There is no excuse for him in carrying out and spreading his manures to lie and be wasted in the open air; but the want of proper cisterns for saving the valuable liquids of the farm-yard, and other scientific contrivances for concentrating the essences of all kinds of fermenting matter, is to be attributed to the want of security in his farm.

No. XXIII.

A Digression from Agriculture to Dr Pusey and the Church of England;* with a few remarks relating to the Town of Oxford.

Though the self-imposed task of writing descriptions of English agriculture leads me into the thinly peopled rather than the populous provinces—into the villages rather than the towns; and though I have in a manner precluded myself from deviating therefrom, by stating my communications to be from the farming districts, I cannot altogether withstand the temptation of occasionally touching on other topics. Some months ago, being in Manchester, and having heard much of the Anti-Corn-Law League, I paid a visit to the League's head-quarters in that town, and was so struck with the newness, the comprehensiveness, and the vast national importance of the proceedings of that body—foresaw, as I then thought and still think, in the League's proceedings the future destinies of the British empire—that I could not refrain from giving to the public a detailed account of what I there witnessed.

A few weeks previous to that, I went a dozen miles out of my way to visit the Socialist community at Titherly, in Hampshire, rather for the gratification of a not very respectable curiosity—principally with the view of seeing with my own eyes what I heard others say, that they were a sect of idle visionaries—than with the expectation of seeing anything which, according to my opinion, should be written of and held up to the world as an example; but in the management of their very large farm I saw what all England should copy as an example; what will be copied; what at no distant time will be the common practice in the agriculture of England, namely, the scientific working of the sub-soil as well as the surface soil; the chemical application of manures; the frequent use of spade husbandry; with a careful provision for the physical and intellectual advancement of the working population. And having seen those things, I published to the world what I saw, with my opinions thereon.

---

* This letter was the first newspaper notice of that remarkable sermon preached by Dr Pusey at Oxford, wherein he held forth the doctrine of the "Real Presence" of the body and blood of Christ in the sacrament of the Eucharist, and for which he was suspended from preaching for three years.

On Sunday, the 14th of May, being in Oxford, I was eye-witness and ear-witness to certain proceedings not less important as regards the future destinies of England than either of the foregoing. I saw the wedge which is now splitting the church receive a blow on the head, which will, with a few more such, send it home, and rive the establishment beyond the possibility of its ever being restored to what it has been, perhaps shiver it for ever. This symptom of church insanity, this evidence of her future suicide, shall be the subject of my present communication. And it is of such vast, in connection with other national movements, of such awful importance, that I need make no apology for making it my theme in preference to my ordinary remarks on agriculture. Perhaps agriculture, and commerce, and every national interest, are involved in this impending church commotion.

It was announced in the Oxford papers of Saturday that of the preachers for the ensuing day (14th May) "The Reverend the Regius Professor of Hebrew" would preach in the morning at Christ Church, (the cathedral.) This professor is the famous Dr Pusey. During the Saturday evening, in every shop, every house, at every corner of the streets where I happened to be, some one present, and frequently every one present, spoke of the excitement that would be to-morrow, because Dr Pusey was to preach. It was said that great numbers would crowd to the cathedral, and, hearing this, I resolved to be one of them.

About an hour before the time of service, students and others were moving in small parties of three and four, and five and six, towards Christ Church College. In fifteen minutes afterwards I passed through the magnificent quadrangle, and entered the cathedral, and found almost every seat occupied. A few forms in one of the side aisles were still empty, and on one of them I sat down. During the next fifteen minutes many people entered, and proceeded to reserved seats, or halted in the open spaces, there to stand. Among the latter were students in their gowns, several elegantly dressed ladies, (perhaps some of those who come from London and elsewhere, and esteem it a high privilege to tread on the same stones of the pavement on which they see the doctor tread, or are told he has trodden on; who gaze for hours upon the window of the room in which he is supposed to be sitting; and who crowd upon his steps, that they may even touch the hem of his garment;) these, with a mixture of ordinary town's people, filled up all standing room, and waited with seeming patience and resignation.

At last several venerable personages, one of them the Vice-

Chancellor, entered, and proceeded through the crowded passages, with some difficulty, to the seats reserved for them ; and soon after, at, I think, half-past ten o'clock, the organ broke the silence that had hitherto reigned, and indicated that the doctor was entering the cathedral.

I turned my eyes towards the door, as in that direction all other eyes and faces near me were turned, and saw one or two official persons opening a way of approach down the aisle by where I was sitting. Immediately following them came Dr Pusey, wearing a gown, or robe of some other name, half black and half red ; his head lowered until his chin rested on his breast, and his feet moving at a pace solemnly slow. He appeared to be of short stature, five feet four or five inches high, and somewhere between fifty and sixty years of age. Perhaps he is not so old. Perhaps the austere self-denial which he is said to exercise had fastened on him marks which, in other faces, are accepted as the indices of years. But whether so old or not, his thin features, seen through a shrivelled skin, bare and brown, contrasted forcibly with the full-fed, rosy faces of most of the other doctors of divinity present. I do not recollect to have ever seen a head, in the lower part of its fabric, so insubstantial, with a brow so full, so lofty, so dome-like as Dr Pusey's, save that of a hand-loom weaver, locally known in my native county as " Sandy Doughty of Pinkerton Hill," whose skin, and flesh, and grey hair, and family and friends, have been shrivelled and pinched by changeless poverty, while his capacious brain has been the intellectual store-room of all that is lofty in religion and poetry, all that is profound and speculative in true or problematic philosophy, and all that is useful and useless in general information ; save *his* head, or perhaps that of John Tait, of the Cowgate of Edinburgh, a wood-sawyer, whose head is as high and intellectual as Dr Pusey's, and whose cheeks and jaw-bones, by reason of sweating profusely and eating sparingly, are as thin—save those two, I do not recollect to have seen any one so full of brain and so extremely thin of flesh. Yet in these three there is much difference as I now see them before my mind's eye. The wood-sawyer is much younger than either, yet he most resembles the Regius Professor of Hebrew in his external form. The hand-loom weaver is the oldest and most shrivelled with age and poverty, and, therefore, in respect of thinness of face, joined to witheredness of skin, bears the closest comparison with the Oxford professor ; but then his head surpasses all other heads : though the world does not know him, the world has only one " Sandy Doughty of Pinkerton Hill."

When Dr Pusey had ascended to the pulpit, one of the audience, who was a stranger like myself, whispered to me if I recollected having seen Mr Cobden, the member for Stockport, and if I did not think Dr Pusey resembled him to some extent. I answered then with an unqualified *no*, that there was no resemblance ; but this was hastily said, perhaps because he was about to speak, and because I was eager, as the deathlike stillness of the thousands there shewed them all eager, to hear him speak, to hear what sound the voice of that man had of whom the world had recently heard so much. When he spoke there was a mildness, and earnestness, and ease, and clearness in his manner of speaking, that resembled Mr Cobden's style very much. Were the latter gentleman sixty years of age instead of forty, and were he over those twenty years which lie between this and 1863, by the same course that he is now pursuing, or is said to pursue—that is, by working hard intellectually, and starving himself on cold water and the merest fragments of substantial food, he might very probably present to us that withered appearance which the Regius Professor of Hebrew in Oxford University now presents. But even then, those enormous organs of intellect, as seen lying above Mr Cobden's eyebrows, would distinguish him under any circumstances, at any time of life, from the professor. Dr Pusey has no remarkable developement of the reflective faculties, as seen phrenologically, nor as heard in his discourse of yesterday, nor, so far as I can discover, as shewn in his literary productions. But phrenologically he is strong in the higher regions of the brain—in veneration, hope, wonder, ideality, and so on. The earnestness of his manner of preaching carries to his hearers the belief that his mind feels his doctrines to be truth, and the largely developed regions of wonder and veneration, so visible to the eye, will leave no one who sees him at liberty to doubt that he is under the influence of those sentiments.

The doctor's first proceeding when he ascended the pulpit was to close the door, and kneel down in prayer for the space of eight or ten minutes, during which the organ played, and a few boys, feeble in voice and vexatiously out of tune, sung a piece of music, to what words I could not ascertain, which is commonly sung, and very commonly better sung, in the churches and chapels of Scotland under the name of " Handel's Hundred."

When the doctor stood up, this sweet but ill-used piece of music was allowed to make its escape in the echoes of the roof as soon as the current verse was ended, and neither it nor any other piece was again disturbed; there was no more singing.

The doctor read a prayer. It *began* by invoking a blessing on "our Sovereign Lady Queen Victoria," on "his Royal Highness the Prince Albert," on "his Royal Highness Albert Edward Prince of Wales," on "her Royal Highness Victoria Princess Royal," on "her Majesty the Queen Dowager Adelaide," and on all the other members of the royal family. Having gone through these illustrious personages, it proceeded to "his Grace Arthur Duke of Wellington, Chancellor of the University of Oxford;" it included the Vice-Chancellor, all the heads of colleges, fellows, and scholars; it included the archbishops, the bishops, and all the clergy, their ranks duly specified; it included the ministers of state, the "great council of Parliament," and all magistrates; it invoked the blessing of "prosperity and peace to God's holy Catholic church, and especially this portion of it." It blessed God for giving unto them the founders and benefactors of the University, and particularized by name "King Henry the Eighth;" and having expressed a hope concerning them, much in the way that I have understood "prayers for the dead" to be uttered, (though, by the lowness of the doctor's voice at that passage, I am not certain as to each word,) the Lord's prayer was read, to which the people, or some of them, said "*Amen!*" and thus came to a brief end the only prayer of the day; and those were the only subjects included in it.

Dr Pusey next read his text. It was, *Matthew* xxvi. 28, "*For this is my blood of the new testament, which is shed for many, for the remission of sins.*" He opened his discourse by remarks on the "Divine love," much in the way as preachers usually preach on such a text. The first of his sentiments which I observed as in any way peculiar to himself, were not doctrinal but circumstantial. Speaking of the "holy joy" that the Christian feels in the contemplation of this divine love, he said—"Would that we could at all times live under its influence rather than hold vain disputations on the question of whether some of us have spoken too much of it or too little. Would that at all seasons of holy rejoicing, and especially at this season of Easter, we could rejoice under the divine love rather than question each other's knowledge of it, rather than seek to fathom that which is unfathomable !"

These sentiments were expressed in a subsequent part of the sermon, at a period when they did not seem to me to be so appropriate as at first; because the doctor proceeded to enlarge on the nature of the divine love, and the sacrament of the "Holy Eucharist," and very soon arrived at a point which,

I believe, has been the main subject of dispute ever since the Reformation between the Roman Catholic Church on one side and Protestants of all denominations on the other, namely, the doctrine of *transubstantiation*. He did not use that word ; well known as that word is, he used plainer words ; and plainly and repeatedly said that communicants, in partaking of the sacrament of the " Holy Eucharist," drank the blood and ate the flesh of the body of the Saviour. He spoke pointedly and somewhat bitterly of the negligent habits of the university men as regarded their due attendance on, and due preparation for, religious ordinances. He said that, though this was the university of Oxford, and though he was preaching in the cathedral church, they were not so well supplied with the conveniences for joining in the sacraments as in some village churches ; nor did they avail themselves of the opportunities they had of performing that bounden, indispensable duty of joining in the sacrament of the "Holy Eucharist" so frequently as they should do, which should, at the least, be once a-week. He referred to the opinions of " St Andrew" (did not say who St Andrew was) for the enforcement of the doctrine of the " Real Presence ;" and several times he quoted St Chrysostom and other saints. Only once, so far as I could hear, did he quote the Scripture. Having again and again reiterated his doctrine of the sacrament of the " Holy Eucharist," and deplored that divisions should exist in the church, he concluded, pronounced in a few words the benediction, and the people dispersed.

Now I hope that no believer in the doctrines of the Roman Catholic Church will think that an opportunity is here taken to say something against his faith. I do not write of this subject to say that Dr Pusey's doctrine of the " Real Presence" is untrue ; but to say that such doctrine is not that of the Church of England. As a matter of private opinion, it might be of little public importance ; but the assertion of the clergy being able to perform miracles, which this doctrine leads to, is of very great public importance ; and the inevitable schism which it will lead to is, in every respect, religiously and politically, of the most profound importance.

Three weeks ago the Oxford University paper quoted a passage, as worthy of approval, from the lecture of one of the professors. The passage stated that it would be well for us, now that we heard so much said in favour of education, " to be taught the value of ignorance ;" that, instead of the young being taught how to live for the " good of society," they should be taught how to " live for the good of their own souls." This antithesis may be admissible in a religious sense, but the

practical meaning of it is, that there should be no secular
education, no education but that of the church, which, now that
she is, by the voice of her most conspicuous and most potent
teacher, putting forth the pretence that she can work miracles,
must be guardedly observed.   That the English Church, with
her newly-adopted paraphernalia of candlesticks, crucifixes,
relics, and miracles, or the Scotch Church, with her arrogant
assumption of superiority to the civil power ; that both of
them, were they to *unite* the attributes of Papal Rome, which
they now *divide* between them, would ever succeed in turning
back the tide of progressive civilization, we have no reason to
fear ; there is not the remotest possibility of even their temporary success.   What we have to fear is the consequence of
their failure.   They are both insane.   Each day their mad-
ness becomes more manifest.   Each day there is a new symptom of impending suicide.   The danger to society will be seen
in the holding of the inquest when their dissolution comes,
if they should be mad enough to go on as they are going.

In the cathedral yesterday I observed several parties
holding conference together while the doctor was preaching,
particularly when he uttered some of the doctrines startling
and new to the Church of England ; and I observed that,
while some listened with reverent attention, of whom might
be those who are said to pay that homage to the doctor that
more sober Christians pay to Almighty God, others had, perhaps through disrespect to Dr Pusey, lost all reverence for
the ministers of religion who were there with him.   When
still in the cathedral, I heard some one near me naming certain of the learned and venerable doctors present, one of whom
was called " Potato Dick," a name affixed to the reverend
gentleman, I understand, in consequence of his having spoken
at some public meeting approvingly of five millions of the poor
" *rejoicing* on potatoes."

It is a fact that, in Oxford, which may be called a town
exclusively engaged in the manufacture of churchmen, there
is, perhaps, more practical infidelity than in any other town
of its population in the kingdom ; and its politics are either
the narrowest Toryism or the wildest Liberalism.   And it is
no less worthy of note that female prostitution and general
vice is there found to a degree not known in towns where
wealthy idlers are more rare and industrious employment for
rich and poor more common.   There is at present an attempt
made by the tradesmen not dependant on the university to
have the colleges rated for the relief of the poor.   This attempt is resisted by the trustees of the college funds.   But
the other party persist in the justice of their effort.   They

say they are legally and morally justified : legally, because the colleges are not exempted from assessment ; morally, because the town is heavily burdened with old servants of the university, for whom no provision is made, and illegitimate children with their mothers, girls from the rural districts, who come here and are seduced and deserted by the collegians.

I have not yet heard what the university men are saying of yesterday's sermon ; but I understand it contains doctrines which Dr Pusey has not heretofore ventured to utter in public.

No. XXIV.

Facts from the Banks of the Thames, about Abingdon and Oxford, and a few miles beyond.

I had lately the privilege of looking over some official documents of a very interesting kind—they were statistics relating to the condition of the rural population in various parts of the kingdom, from Cornwall to the Shetland Isles. I observed by them that certain districts of country had fewer crimes against property than others. For instance, in East Lothian, in Scotland, the crime of sheep-stealing was totally unknown to the most of the farmers who had filled up the documents sent to them for the purpose of collecting information ; while of poaching there was very little, and no professed poachers at all. In the same county the labourers were said to be hired by the year. They had *regularly* four meals a-day, and all of them had a stock of provisions laid in ; the tenants had leases of nineteen years' duration, and there were no unemployed poor.

Now these somewhat gratifying facts were not peculiar to East Lothian alone, nor to Scotland. In whatever part of England the system of letting farms on lease had been adopted, the labourers were seen to be in a superior state of physical comfort ; their engagements to masters were more lengthened and secure ; their employment more regular, and better paid ; their meals more regular, and of a better quality ; and the crimes of sheep-stealing and poaching least prevalent. But most of those who filled up the documents in England, wrote down the fearful truth of sheep-stealing, poaching, incendiary fires, want of employment, occasional hiring by the day, piece-work, and the words "no lease," as nothing extraordinary. The farthest they went in making remarks, was to compare the amount of crime in various years—never considering it possible that those crimes should have been unknown for one year ; and generally adding that the system of long leases had never been tried in their neighbourhood, and that, therefore, they could not give an opinion on their practicability.

But they gave evidence in favour of leases, or, in other words, *secure tenures*, by shewing what evils prevailed under the tenancies-at-will.

I have lately seen some remarkable instances of the mischievous effects of this strangely absurd yet common mismanagement of landed property in Oxfordshire. Indeed Oxfordshire is little else than one broad unvarying evidence of it. I saw one farm, however, the other day, 500 acres, purchased fourteen months ago by a manufacturer in Derby, which is let on lease to a tenant who entered upon it in April last year, and who has already done more to clean, fertilize, and generally improve these 500 acres, than all the tenants of the present Duke of Marlborough's vast estates have done since he became Duke, or ever will do, so long as they hold their farms under the bonds they now hold by. Indeed they are expressly bound down not to do some of the best things which this tenant of the Derby stocking-maker has done, namely, to cut their hedges and clear away the accumulated mould on ditch banks. I was sorry to observe that this farmer had got hold of the burning system ; for all his turf, and couch, and foul earth, instead of mixing them with hot lime, were burned ; but, excepting this, he was going on in the right direction with everything, and on the fair road, *while paying more rent than ever the same land paid before*, to carry away L.10,000 at the end of his lease. Is such a man as this, who raises five quarters of grain where three grew before, not a patriot and a blessing to his country? He has a beautiful stream of water, just enough for a thrashing mill, and he contemplates using it for that purpose ; but he is very uncertain about the result. Though he is employing, and will employ, one half more men than are employed on any other 500 acres, he apprehends, his friends apprehend, and it is extremely probable, that the ferocious population of the neighbourhood will burn down barns, corn-ricks, and all, if he erects a mill.

Having alluded to the Duke of Marlborough's estate, I may mention, in passing, that his princely domain of Blenheim is, palace and park, the most noble, regal-like, that I have seen in any part of the kingdom ; but worse farming, poorer farmers, and poorer labourers are not to be found within the British shores than on the Duke's property. The estate is one vast wreck ; and political thraldom has rendered more feeble those heads and hands that were always weak.

The Earl of Abingdon's estates are very extensive in this county, and particularly around Oxford. I was told the other day that the Earl had interfered to prevent the wages of labouring married men being reduced below nine shillings a-week on some part of his property; and the person who told me, added that his Lordship was not a man that could be called hard to the poor; that he did all he could to have all surplus poor removed from his estate, but that he liked to see those who remained have better wages than the farmers were willing to give.

If the Earl of Abingdon is justly entitled to this praise from a farm labourer, for it was a farm labourer who spoke to me, there is something ungracious in finding fault with him on any other topic. But I am afraid that on other topics, and even on this, his Lordship is not blameless. It may be an act of friendship to the labourer to prevent the reduction of his wages from nine shillings to eight shillings a-week; at all events, it cannot fail to make the labourer believe that his Lordship is the friend and the farmer who would reduce wages is the foe; but if we see, as I have seen on many of Lord Abingdon's farms, that half the work is not done that should be done; that more land is lying waste in huge ridges at the ends of fields, in undrained bogs, bearing on their surface rushes and stagnant water, and these only, than would employ all the poor of the union at a profit and higher wages than nine shillings a-week; we may very properly inquire if his Lordship is justified in making his tenants such slaves of uncertainty that they cannot employ labourers to the requisite extent of their farms, and yet, poor as they are, order them to pay a certain amount of wages.

Another evil which afflicts his Lordship's tenants most grievously is, the game with which the farmers are overrun. One of the farmers told me that last year, in one field only, he calculated a loss of ten quarters of grain by the vermin—pheasants, hares, rabbits, &c. He said, and said truly, that no compensation as a drawback from rent was an equivalent to a farmer for such a loss, (that is, if a drawback were allowed;) because a field of grain exposed to game, either at seed time or in the young blade, was as likely to be despoiled, if prepared at great expense, as if only the smallest expense had been devoted to it; that while tithes had formerly prevented the improved cultivation of land, this was still worse, the tithe having left the nine-tenths uninjured, while the game destroyed some and injured all.

But the fact of his Lordship having ordered his tenants to pay nine shillings a-week to married men, and the fact of

most other farmers in the county and on the Berkshire side
of the Thames, near Oxford, paying eight shillings a-week to
the same class of men, does not prove that the manual labour
of the farm costs eight or nine shillings a-week per man.   I
find that on the most of the farms in this district two out of
three ploughs, and two out of three waggons and horses, are
managed by young men under twenty years of age, whose
wages vary from three to five shillings a-week, never exceeding, and seldom reaching six, but sometimes for boys, who
are hired by the year, and who are at work sixteen hours
a-day, as low as two shillings a-week.

Two shillings a-week for lads twelve and fourteen years old.
From two and sixpence to three and sixpence a-week for lads
fourteen to sixteen years old.   Four shillings and five shillings
a-week for young men seventeen, eighteen, nineteen, and
twenty years old!   And by those youths and young men
two-thirds of all the ploughing and carting of the farm is done.
They are hired from a distance in almost all cases ; are hired
by the year ; provide themselves with food and clothing out
of their wages ; sleep in a stable-loft or barn, having no fireside to go to ; no hot dinners, but everlasting bread and lard,
bread and lard, bread and lard !

Here is a conversation with one of them on a large farm
near Abingdon :—

    " You hold the plough, you say ; how old are you?"

    " I bees sixteen a'most."

    " What wages have you ?"

    " Three shillin' a-week."

    " Three shillings !   Have you nothing else?   Don't you
get victuals, or part of them, from your master ?"

    " No, I buys them all."

    " All out of three shillings ?"

    " Ees, and buys my clothes out of that."

    " And what do you buy to eat ?"

    " Buy to eat !   Why, I buys bread and lard."

    " Do you eat bread and lard always ?   What have you
for breakfast ?"

    " What have I for breakfast ?   Why, bread and lard."

    " And what for dinner ?"

    " Bread and lard."

    " What for supper, the same ?"

    " Ees, the same for supper—bread and lard."

    " It seems to be always bread and lard ; have you no boiled
bacon and vegetables ?"

    " No, there be no place to boil 'em ; no time to boil 'em ;
none to boil."

" Have you never a hot dinner nor supper; don't you get potatoes ?"

" Ees, potatoes, an we pay for 'em. Master lets us boil 'em once a-week an we like."

" And what do you eat to them; bacon?"

" No."

" What then?"

" Lard; never has nothing but lard."

" Can't you boil potatoes or cook your victuals any day you choose ?"

" No ; has no fire."

" Have you no fire to warm you in cold weather ?"

" No, we never has fire."

" Where do you go in the winter evenings ?"

" To bed, when it be time ; an it ben't time, we goes to some of the housen as be round about."

" To the firesides of some of the cottagers, I suppose ?"

" Ees, an we can get."

" What if you cannot get ; do you go into the farm-house ?"

" No, mustn't ; never goes nowhere but to bed an it be very cold."

" Where is your bed ?"

" In the *tollit*," (stable loft.)

" How many of you sleep there ?"

" All on us as be hired."

" How many are hired ?"

" Four last year, five this."

" Does any one make your beds for you ?"

" No, we make 'em ourselves."

" Who washes your sheets ?"

" Who washes 'em?"

" Yes ; they *are* washed, I suppose ?"

" No, they ben't."

" What ! never washed ? Do you mean to say you don't have your sheets washed ?"

" No, never since I comed."

" When did you come ?"

" Last Michaelmas."

" Were your bedclothes clean then ?"

" I dare say they was."

" And don't you know how long they are to serve until they are changed again ?"

" To Michaelmas, I hear tell."

" So one change of bedclothes serves a year ! Don't you find your bed disagreeable ?"

" Do I ! I bees too sleepy. I never knows nought of it,

only that I has to get up afore I be awake, and never get into it afore I be a'most asleep. I be up at four, and ben't done work afore eight at night."

" You don't go so long at the plough as that?"

" No ; but master be always having summat for we to do as be hired ; we be always at summat."

Now, if the reader chooses to read on, I shall shew him the picture in which this young Englishman is a subordinate character—those who have been accustomed to read of, or look on, the rural beauty of England, must not, because of this, think that rural England is not beautiful.

Look at the distant hills—the Chiltern and the Cotswold— whose bare downs and beechy woods are veiling themselves in the cloudy blue, which, from this spot, forms the far margin of the landscape. See the forests, and meadows, and farm-fields, and farm-yards, and villages, and village-churches, how they emerge from the indistinct distance, and advance in fuller and fuller form upon the eye, until they stand before us there ; the forest, and meadows, and farm-fields, dipping their edges in the Thames, and the villages and village-churches bathing their shadows in the same bright element. And observe that noble stream, how he comes down from Oxford University ; prodigal of his youth and strength, how he rambles over the country, never halting, yet often turning, as if he preferred the scenes of his boyhood. As yet, he is not the hard-work-ing, toiling Thames of London barges and merchant ships ; he is taking his pleasure among the races of eight-oared cutters, gentleman wherries, and fancy yachts, bearing on his breast the young of England's aristocracy.

But now he leaves these, and in a valley meets, lonely and alone, the youthful Summer, at whose feet he loiters love-sick, and she gives him her hand, and they are wedded ; and the union of Summer with the lordliest river in England is attended as it should be. The tall limes, and the elms, the sturdy syca-more, and the beeches of plebeian race—not the less lovely that they are plebeian—she has arrayed in early and simple green ; the noble chesnut, like a field-marshal, comes out in a decorated uniform ; the laburnum, like a 10th Hussar, comes loaded with trappings ; and the tall pines have added to their winter livery shoulder knots of summer buds ; the ash tree, always late, is hastening to put on his narrow leaves ; and the oak, like other veterans, is ready when wanted—there he stands, trigged out as if he were young again. The bride's nearest and dearest relative in England, the hoary hawthorn, gives her away ; and troops of laughing flowers, blooming and about to bloom, come to see. There is the little white-headed daisy, straggling through the meadow, some of its kind far in the rear, and those in front so eager to see, yet so short that they must get upon the very edge of the grassy bank to look over, and the ground-ivy is elbowing them and disputing, while the lilies have lifted their heads to see the bridegroom, and, now that he offers to kiss them, they blush and turn away. The blue-bells are trooping along the old hedge-side, and the cowslips are running through the fields at the nearest, only avoiding the wet places; while the young forget-me-not, in the wood, is looking out and crying, "Stop and take me!" and all across the meadows, among the cows, the butter-cups are hastening, and in their haste saying, "Cow, do not eat me!" And there they are, in front of all others, laughing that their dimpled chins are reflected in the deep Thames, and that their more timid friends, the daisies, can see them look in without being afraid.

And in yonder thicket that hides the wedded pair when evening falls, and with them conceals the nightingale, there is at this moment music in all the riot of a thousand songsters. And yonder, by the lordly mansion in the woods, which miles can only measure, do the richest of England's melodists rejoice; and their joy is all the more that they love summer and summer loves England. Above there, by *that* church, and down here by *this*, and over by that other, and all around by the houses of the churchmen, which we here see embowered in trees, ten thousand choristers of nature's making pour out their happy noises. And in this very tree where we stand— this hawthorn, whose blossom loads the evening with sweet odours—the warblers have their nests, and are singing to their nestling young. Who would say that England is not lovely; that Englishmen should not be happy? On one side of that roof the hawthorn is resting his branches, as if the blossom and perfume thereof were too weighty for him to bear. On the other side are the lofty elms, leafy, and ready with their leaves to ward off wind and rain, or either, when they come here too roughly. On the elms, as on the hawthorns, the little robin, the blackbird, the thrush, and other birds cheerful as they, are singing the same notes as are sung in yonder woods around the lordly mansion. Surely no unhappy beings can have homes here? Let us inquire what house this is, and what this roof covers.

Well, we have looked into it, and have seen one of its inmates. We have talked with him, and he has told us— what we need not again tell the reader—we told it before. That roof covers the *tollit*, where sleep the young farming-men whose bedclothes are changed once a-year; who do two-thirds of all the work on the farm; and who have for break-fast " bread and lard"—for dinner " bread and lard"—for supper " bread and lard." Nothing but bread and lard, and not always enough of that !

If we look minutely around us here, we shall see as much liquid manure running to waste as would, after paying the expense of its own collection and application, produce an increased crop, sufficient to pay all the wages of labour, all the poor-rates, and all the other taxes paid on this farm. And if a similar advantage were taken of everything else that is now wasted by neglect or ignorance, or inability to sink capi-tal through insecurity of tenure, not only might the labourers be paid a reasonable day's wages for a reasonable day's work, but rates, taxes, and 50 per cent. of higher rent, leaving the tenant a handsome profit, might and *would* be paid.

This farm belongs to a Peer of Parliament. At the dis-tance of a few miles there is another as large as this, or larger, belonging to the Deputy Usher of the Black Rod, of which all may be repeated that has been said of this.

No. XXV.

On the Causes which determine the Value of Farm Labour.

June 7, 1843.

A Mr Bennet, of Bedfordshire, is represented to have said, at a recent public meeting, held at Hertford, on the subject of the corn-laws, " that a country in a high state of civiliza-tion, like England, paying so dear for labour, cannot possibly compete in growing corn with countries where the labourers eat rye bread and labour is comparatively cheap;" and this sentiment is echoed and re-echoed at every agricultural meet-ing throughout the country. I propose to question its cor-rectness. I propose to the reader to accompany me into other countries of the world and into several districts of England, and Scotland, and Ireland, and I shall shew him, if he does not already know, that wherever the wages of the labourer are highest, labour is cheapest; wherever wages are lowest, labour is dearest. We shall see that where the labourers are most skilful, tractable, moral, intelligent—in short, in the highest state of civilization—a higher amount of income is received by them than by those who, in other districts, are distinguished for the opposite qualities; and we shall see that the real value of the labour of the civilized population rises in a ratio far beyond the increase of their wages.

First, however, I take leave to deny—most emphatically deny—that Mr Bennet has truth on his side when, in calling England "highly civilized," he includes the English farm-labourers. There is refinement enough in England, we all know. In my travels through the country I find, by all my conversations, that the farm-houses and farmers' families are much finer than twenty, and thirty, and forty years ago; so much more refined, with richer furniture, and "accomplished" manners, that the unmarried labourers are no longer permitted to live within the farm-house, nor eat at the farmer's table, nor step within the farmer's door, but are committed to out-houses, at a small rate of wages per week, to furnish them-selves with food—to out-houses, where they have no meals cooked, no comforts of any kind, no cleanliness, no good man-ners set before them, no examples of good morals, and no influences whatever tending to instruct, restrain, and civilize; but are, on the contrary, left to themselves, as ignorant and uncivilized as any serfs of feudal Europe, with just this differ-ence, that they are not fed as the serfs, are not allowed to eat as much of the farm produce as they choose, as a first and fore-most condition of their labour. I have been on some of the best soils in England, within these last few weeks, in the dis-tricts watered by the Thames, where two-thirds of the farm work is done by persons who live in this deplorable condi-tion, and I, therefore, say that whatever may be the progress of refinement in England, among all classes above the labourer, the labourer has, during the present century, retrograded in condition in every respect.

In saying this I contradict Mr Bennet, and those who speak as he speaks, in one sense. I do not allow them to deceive us with the assertion that the progressive civilization of England carries with it the rural labourers; but I fortify them in this, that I admit the price of farm labour to be high in England, which they say it is. We, however, differ; we diametrically differ in respect of the reason of its being high priced. That we must now discuss. We shall take the border counties of Scotland, where the highest wages are paid to farm labourers which are paid in Great Britain, and where, as shall be seen, labour is cheaper than in any part of Britain. We shall take these agricultural counties and compare them with the regions of the Wolga and the Baltic Sea.

In those vast plains of Europe where the soil is tilled, and sown, and reaped by serfs, the frost comes early and lasts long. Even on the banks of the Vistula, where the best

European wheat is grown, and where the latitude is the same that encircles England and part of France, winter grasps the earth with a firmness, an annual regularity, an enduring obstinacy, unknown to us in this variable island of the sea. Attracted by the undrained marshes, and undisturbed by the oceanic and mountain tempests that vex and exhaust him elsewhere, the tyrant of the year spreads himself on the broad plains, seals up the earth, closes the rivers, the lakes, the roads, (such as they are,) and all labour, (such as it is,) that he may have four months of unbroken rest. During this time all field labour ceases, and almost all other labour. The bread which the serfs eat may be coarse, it may be black—it is sometimes made from rye, and no doubt it is black—but they have enough of it to eat, and during four months of the year they eat and do no work; the cattle are not fed for beef, they are only kept for working in the fields, and they, too, eat during this season at an expense which returns no profit. In short, the land belongs to the feudal lords, and the serfs and working cattle are the live stock upon the land. Live stock is never denied anywhere a sufficiency of " keep." The serfs, being the property of their masters, have at least the advantage of being fed and kept in working order. Indeed they have the feeding of themselves; they are entrusted with the whole produce of the soil, and being unable to use more than what they require to eat—there being no market within their reach at which they can sell anything and misappropriate the price—they eat what they require, and the agents of the chief collect the rest as revenue equivalent to rent.

Now, in the counties on the Scottish border there is never a working hour of any day of the six, of any week of the fifty-two, wasted. If there is frost, and the plough is frost-locked, the manure is taken out to the fields, or the thrashing-mill is put in use, and grain is carried to market, also drains are filled, coals carted, and many things else done ; at all events, every man and horse are kept at work. Such a thing as horses occasionally idle is never known. Men and horses have their set hours, and they adhere to those hours to a minute. The farmer hires his married men by the year, his unmarried by the half-year ; and if they were to go occasionally idle he would have to pay them their wages, as the feudal lords of the continent have to feed their serfs, for doing nothing. But the comparison must go further. There being few cattle kept as stock for feeding on the plains of the Vistula to produce manure, and the soil being in a frequent state of exhaustion, it is the custom to let the land lie fallow every second year, not to be enriched by manures as fallows are *supposed* to be

in this country, but merely to rest. Now this shews that
continental agriculture is in a very profitless state ; and how
can it be otherwise, unless those serfs were more than human ?
Aye, more than any human beings are or ever have been,
instead of being the debased, spiritless bondmen they are.
Without intelligence to direct, without capital and means
wherewith to work, and utterly without interest or necessity
to apply intelligence and capital to the culture of the land, if
they had both, they are now, and ever will be, so long as they
are the mere live stock of the feudal lords, the most profitless
cultivators of the soil in Europe.   In England, we find that,
whenever a farmer, or indeed any tradesman or merchant,
ceases to have an interest in a speculation, be it farm, or shop,
or ship's cargo, or if the interest is weakened and rendered
insecure, industry at once flags and becomes feeble.   Human
nature is the same everywhere ; and there is not the remotest
probability of the agriculture of the feudal estates of the continent being improved, even if we began at once to purchase
regularly a part of their surplus produce.   There are greater
obstacles in the wheat-growing districts of the continent to
improvements in agriculture than in England, where markets
are comparatively high priced, and where an incessant demand
for farm produce is continually urging to a larger supply.
Yet we see that in England the science of agriculture drags
far behind the spirit of the age, because it is not *protected*
from insecurity.

I hold, therefore, that the serfs of the feudal wheat-growers
will continue, for ages to come, to be what they are now, the
most expensive labourers in Europe ; and that not even their
enfranchisement as free citizens would enable them, in any
part of the present century, to compete with England in the
growth of corn ; because, even if we purchased 2,000,000 or
3,000,000 of quarters from the Baltic annually, (which, with
free trade and America ready to take and give, is barely
probable)—but suppose 3,000,000 quarters of wheat came
from the regions, shipping it by the Vistula—the increased
demand would not be as a loaf of bread to each acre, it would
be no inducement whatever to stimulate to better agriculture,
and without better agriculture, of which the value is not
known in those countries, the serf labour will continue to be,
as it is now, the dearest labour employed on any land in the
world.

What Mr Bennet should have said, and what those who are
daily declaring their fears for the English farmer should say,
is this :—" The land being so much more plentiful on the continent, and the population who consume its produce so much

less than in England, the continental supply, therefore, so far exceeds the continental demand, that there is danger to England, notwithstanding the extra expense of continental labour, in admitting the Baltic wheat into our markets." This, for such as fear the free introduction of foreign corn, would be the true statement; and it would be for those who combat them in argument to shew that their fears were groundless; in my opinion a task so easy, and already so often accomplished, that I shall leave it in the hands of those who make it their business to defend the propositions for free trade. For myself, I look chiefly to the advancement of English agriculture in writing these papers, I look forward to its ultimate excellence with the highest hopes, the most unwavering faith; yet for the present I feel much anxiety. Seeing the vast resources contained in the soil of England, to be yet developed by the joint application of capital, science, and industry, otherwise than now applied, I look with eagerness to see what advances agricultural men are making in agricultural knowledge. To hear a practical man, for I suppose Mr Bennet is a farmer, evincing such ignorance of the very alphabet of practical knowledge, is indeed melancholy. But remarks of this kind will be more appropriate when, in one or two other communications, I have shewn the cheapness of the higher-priced labour of the border counties, and compared it with the dearness of the lower-priced labour of the midland and southern counties.

No. XXVI.

Further Observations and Evidence on the Causes which determine the Value of Farm Labour.

We have seen what the *Quarterly Review* says, that "one Middlesex mower will mow as much grass as six Russian serfs;" that "the making and getting in of a certain quantity of hay will cost to an English farmer but one-sixth or one-eighth of what it costs a Russian proprietor." This is decisive of the question at issue, whether labour is cheaper in England, where the cultivators have *some* interest in the produce of the soil, or in feudal countries, where they are entirely without interest, consequently without energy, capital, and knowledge. We shall now compare the prices of labour in one part of Britain with another, and take the border counties, where the cultivators' interest in the soil, by security of tenure, is much stronger than in the southern counties of England, and we shall find that labour is cheaper there, though nominally higher priced, than in the south.

The right honourable the present speaker of the House of
Commons was, in 1836, chairman of a committee appointed by
the house to inquire into the state and prospects of British
agriculture. Prices had been low for several preceding years,
and in England agricultural distress was loudly complained of.
In some parts of Scotland, and by some farmers in all parts
of that country, complaints were made ; but most of the Scotch
farmers examined by the committee said that the only thing
they desired from Parliament was to be " let alone ;" that
legislation in any shape, promising them a benefit, would be a
delusion ; that it had hitherto been so, and that they verily
believed that human wisdom could make it nothing else.

The English farmers examined thought differently. They
not only believed that Parliament could help them, but
expected that Parliament would ; and from the fact of being
summoned to London to be examined, they formed the highest
hopes for future legislation. A voluminous report was published ; and subsequently Mr Shaw Lefevre gave to the world
the following facts, in his capacity of a landowner and private
gentleman, I presume, not as chairman of the committee ;
but, in whichever respect the statement was made, officially
or otherwise, it is enough to say that it was made by the
Right Honourable Charles Shaw Lefevre. The evidence of
three English farmers and three Scotch, whose land, judging
by its produce in wheat, was of nearly equal value, reduced to
a tabular statement, stood thus :—

Name of Witness.	Rent, tithe, and parochial burdens.			Annual average expense per acre.			Total.			Quality of land estimated by average produce per acre in wheat.
	£	s.	d.	£	s.	d.	£	s.	d.	
ENGLISH.										
Breckwell...	1	15	0	3	19	0	5	14	0	30
Rolfe	1	11	6	3	13	6	5	5	0	24
Cox...........	1	15	0	4	2	2	5	17	2	30
SCOTCH.										
Hope.........	2	3	9	2	12	0	4	15	9	29
Bell...........	1	8	8	2	0	7	3	9	3	28
Robertson...	1	19	0	2	16	0	4	5	0	30

This table does not shew all that should be shewn. For
instance, the value of the land is only to be judged by the
produce per acre, whereas the produce per acre depends on
the style of cultivation, as well as the intrinsic value of the
land. It so happens, however, that I have visited and closely
observed some of the farms held by the farmers here named,
both last year and this ; last year at harvest, this year at
seed time and subsequently ; and I can take upon myself to

supply information on the value of the soils, irrespective of cultivation, which the farmers themselves could not supply, being unacquainted with each other's farms, which some of them could not supply, because the comparative value of soils had never been to them a subject of study.

But as the table now stands, it shews that Mr Breckwell (near Buckingham) pays L.1 : 15s. in rent, tithe, and taxes, per acre, while Mr R. Hope (near Haddington, in East Lothian) pays L.2 : 3 : 9 in rent and taxes per acre. I have seen Mr Breckwell's farm and I have seen Mr Hope's. The former, compared with the latter, is not only easier worked, but is naturally a soil of a very rich quality. Mr Hope's is a wet clay, which, up to 1836, he could not with all his skill reduce to a state friable enough to grow turnips ; and without a course of turnips, to feed cattle and produce manure, the cultivation of land is additionally expensive. Mr Breckwell's farm is what is commonly called a deep loam, which, with proper management, can be made to grow the best and largest quantity of almost all crops. Now the annual cost of working Mr Breckwell's farm is L.3 : 19s. per acre, while the annual cost of working Mr Hope's is L.2 : 12s. per acre, yet Mr Hope pays higher wages to his labourers, and employs more of them, than Mr Breckwell.

Mr Breckwell says to the committee of 1836 :—" I have known the farm I cultivate eight-and-forty years. Some part of the farm was not in cultivation, but the part that was cultivated was as good as now." And again, he says of the neighbourhood—" The land is getting very foul and over-cropped."

Mr Hope says :—" I have done a good deal by *deep* draining within the last twenty years. Having got a new lease three years ago, I have, during the two last years, begun to furrow drain. The furrow draining costs me from L.4 to L.5 per acre. Almost the whole farm was done with lime at L.9 per acre, carriage included."

At this the committee seem to be surprised, and they ask Mr Hope if this has been done at his own expense. He replies, " Yes." He then adds, that during the two years of his new lease he had laid out L.120 in each year on furrow draining.

Mr Breckwell, in answer to questions, says of the Vale of Aylesbury :—" Has seen L.20 or L.30 laid out by farmers and deducted from the rent by the landlords." This was for draining the wet lands of the " vale." Of the farmers, he says, —" When the tenant cannot pay the rent out of the produce, he has been curtailing his expense in various ways ; in many cases not cultivating the land so well as he used, for want of means."

So far we can see that labour, though more money be paid for it, is cheaper on Mr Hope's farm in Haddingtonshire than on Mr Breckwell's in Buckinghamshire. But the population around Mr Hope is a constantly employed, regularly paid, and regularly fed population; they are neither poachers, sheep-stealers, machine-breakers, nor stack-yard incendiaries. Steam-engines of six, eight, and ten-horse power are used to thrash the grain in Haddingtonshire. A wheat stack, containing twenty or thirty quarters, is seen under its thatch in the morning, it is carried into the barn by "all hands," the sheaves are given to the mill, the grain is separated from straw, chaff, and all impurities, measured and bagged up, and might be, if necessary, in the market town the same evening. Thus Mr Hope can take advantage of any change of markets, or any other emergency.

Mr Breckwell can do nothing of this kind. He can neither take advantage of a favourable market nor a favourable day nor *week* for his seed sowing. He must pay dear for his thrashing, and await the tediousness of the flail; or if he attempt to erect a thrashing-mill, he has it broken by the unruly population amid which he dwells. Perhaps his barns are burned, and stables and rickyard, and all his stock, live and dead; or, if not actually burned, he dreads that they may be, and never reposes on his pillow, himself nor family, in peace. He insures his premises, but must pay a higher premium than Mr Hope, because he is not so secure from fire, even though Mr Hope has the furnace of his steam-engine blazing in his barns!

By all these disadvantages it is clear enough that the English farmer pays dear for his farm labour. But what is the cause of the dearness? Mr Bennet of Bedfordshire says it is because of the refinement and *civilization* of England!

No. XXVII.

Contains the Model, by the Earl of Stair, for a Landlord's Address at an Agricultural Meeting, with Remarks, and a quotation from Earl Fitzwilliam.

October 31, 1843.

During the last few weeks the agricultural meetings have been abundant, and the flattering speeches of wine-warmed landlords to the farmers have constituted the stock in trade of all country newspapers; but, so far as I have seen, not one of those landowning orators has uttered a single sentence shewing a real friendship for the tenant-farmer.

Presuming that some of them may not know what real friendship is, I shall here quote from a speech delivered by the Earl of Stair to 400 of his tenants on 8th September 1840.

His Lordship, better known as Sir John Dalrymple of Oxenford, a lieutenant-general of the army, and formerly member of Parliament for the county of Edinburgh, had, shortly before, succeeded, at an advanced age, to the Earldom of " Stair, and was there meeting and dining with the Stair tenantry." He had, therefore, in this initiatory discourse the advantage of lengthened experience to justify him in what he said.

Those portions of it which apply to the welfare of the tenantry with greatest force, and which should be adopted by those of the English landlords who are really in earnest when advocating a reform in agriculture, are printed in italics.

" I rejoice to find myself," said his Lordship—(but in saying this he was commencing as most others commence, the only difference, and a great one it is, between his speech and all other speeches of landlords is, that he does not leave off as they leave off)—" I rejoice to find myself in the midst of my tenants. The cordial reception I have met with amongst you, and your kindness in coming here this day, both tend to rivet the link that naturally unites us, and equally to an increase of that interest which I am disposed to take in you as part of my family and as my friends. I have said before, and I cannot say it too often, that no separate interest can subsist between landlord and tenant.

" If you thrive I thrive. On your well-doing will depend my comfort, my honour, and my character ; for I shall stand high or the reverse (and it is right that it should be so) as I act justly or unjustly by you.

" Entertaining such sentiments, my first duties will consist in an encouragement of moral and religious feelings among my tenants, and a gradual improvement of my estates. The most likely way to make them happy and good, is to teach them when young to know right from wrong, and that can only be effectually done by education. Whenever, therefore, I can encourage good and moral feeling, you will find me anxious to do so, as the best means of effecting it. I shall willingly contribute to the improvement or increase of schools, to be open to all, so that every child on my estate may be brought to know his God and the duty he owes him.

" The next object of my solicitude will consist in an encouragement of improved agriculture. The first of all improvements consists of draining and enclosing. My tenants will, therefore, find me willing to assist in both so far as my means will admit. In the best cultivated districts of Scotland, sheep stock is universally encouraged. I observe in the Stair leases the tenants are in general precluded from keeping such stock.

" I am willing, where it is advisable, to alter such clauses. I have my doubts too whether the growth of turnips is sufficiently attended to in this county." His Lordship was speaking of Galloway, (a district comprehending the county of Wigton and stewartry of Kirkcudbright,) on the south-west coast of Scotland, where farms are smaller, and the land inferior to the Lothians described by Mr Hyde Greg.

The English reader will, therefore, be pleased to bear the inferiority of the soil of Galloway in mind. But I may state that, even in Galloway, the turnip husbandry thus complained of by Lord Stair was then in a more advanced and profitable condition than it is even now in any part of the six counties which I have recently visited in the south and south-west of England. On some of the finest soils in Kent, Hampshire, Bucks, Berks. and even in Middlesex, where the unappropriated pollution of London should cover a hundred miles of country with the most luxuriant vegetation, the turnip husbandry is sadly neglected, the crops being mean and ill cultivated, even to a state deserving no better name than wretched. Lord Stair went on to state the amounts of the premiums which he intended giving for various improvements, the announcement of which drew forth hearty cheers from the tenantry ; but, as an ignorance of the locality to which they were applicable precludes the southern reader from judging of their value, I have omitted them.

" But," said his Lordship, " I will give no prize to any tenant who burns his wreck, (I mean the weeds gathered off the fallow-land,) which I observed was much done when I was here in the spring. Wreck, when carted and put into heaps, forms, when mixed with lime, the best of all composts ; or, when first gathered, if put at the bottom of a muck-hill, it will greatly increase the quantity of manure ; but to burn it is absolute waste ; and, for myself, I would as soon think of burning straw."

Had his Lordship travelled in the south-west of England, particularly in some parts of Bucks and Berkshire, near the Thames, he would have seen this wreck, the long roots of the couch-grass, in such quantities as to astonish him. On some of the finest soils of England, owned by landlords and farmed by tenants who say the repeal of the corn-laws would ruin them, he would have seen couch-grass overtopping the crops of beans, and robbing the wheat of strength and space, to the positive loss of from one to two quarters an acre, while the labouring poor, who should have hoed and eradicated such weeds for wages, were crammed into the Great Marlow Union Workhouse, ill fed and unprofitably employed, with hundreds more, literally unfed and unemployed outside. While, again, . if his Lordship had gone over those counties which I have traversed within these last two months, he would have seen this wreck or couch-grass, so prodigally allowed to exclude the grain and rob the soil, being raked together and unprofitably burned in every direction, that is, I should explain, in every direction where any trouble was being taken to get rid of it. Moreover, within a mile of Cranborne, in Dorsetshire, and almost within the same distance of the Earl of Shaftesbury's residence, Lord Stair, were he to be in that direction, would see, at the present time, a field which this year bore a crop of oats, which oats, to save the expense of harvest labour, was cut with the scythe, raked together without being bound in sheaves, the universally wasteful custom in that district, and which, in consequence of this saving of labourers' wages, were shilled out until more than the quantity of seed from which the crop grew is now growing up green and absolutely wasted. I say "more than the seed;" but a countryman, who was passing the field when I looked at it, gave it as his opinion that more than double the amount of seed was wasted. And this is where many people are unemployed, where all are ill fed and ill paid, and where many starve until sent off ten miles to the Union Workhouse. But the climax of Lord Stairs' address to his new tenantry is yet to come; hitherto what I have quoted of him has occasionally been said by others. What I am now about to quote has been said by none, so far as I have seen, save himself. It should be the golden rule of all other landlords; it is the first, and immeasurably the greatest, principle of all improvements. The evil which an opposition to it spreads and perpetuates in England, is such, that all the agricultural societies and all the familiarity of after-dinner speeches can never overcome. "I said," observed his Lordship in conclusion, "that I wish to see my tenants comfortable and happy. I hope I may be permitted further to say, that I shall have a pride in seeing them independent. *Whatever is due to me I will expect them to pay—whatever is not due I will never exact. Whenever, therefore, they are called on to exercise their political privileges, I wish them to do it honestly and manfully—not allowing themselves to be dictated to by me, were I disposed to attempt it, but only asking how their consciences bid them vote, being assured that he who obeys his conscience will never displease me.*

"*I should feel degraded myself were I compelled to vote one way while my known opinions were another ; and I shall never attempt to inflict upon you what would prove humbling to myself. I believe the poorest voter has his own notions of what is good and right as deeply implanted in him as I have ; and it is by allowing him to act up to his honest feelings that he is to be made a happier and a better, a more prosperous, and a more thriving man.*

" This is a subject on which I have thought much, and it is one on which I have had experience."

Lord Stair says of his tenantry—" Whatever is due to me I will expect them to pay ; whatever is not due, I will never exact." And when saying so he gives that true independence to the tenant which will enable him to pay. On this important point Earl Fitzwilliam has commented with great force and truth.

In his letter of 1831, addressed to the landowners, he says, speaking of the corn-laws—" Year after year the value of the farmers' produce had been diminishing, till it fell to little more than half the price at which Parliament considered he could be remunerated for his industry. Year after year he was deluded by fallacious hopes excited by the law itself ; his rent was paid out of his capital, and not out of his profits, till that capital became insufficient for the proper cultivation of the land, and then you yourselves began to feel the calamity by which many of your tenantry had been already overwhelmed.

" Compare, then, the situation of that tenantry under the protection of the corn-law of 1815, with what it probably would have been had the trade been avowedly free, or if you had been contented with the protection afforded by the law of 1804, under which it would have been practically free.

" Prices would indeed have lowered, but no such extravagant hopes would have been excited, no such erroneous calculations would have been made ; rents would have fallen to a level corresponding to the price of grain, the agricultural capital of the country would have been unimpaired, and the land would have remained in a better state of cultivation. Your nominal rentals might have been diminished, but your rents would have been collected with facility, and you would not have been driven, time after time, to the wretched expedient of returning a per centage to your tenants at each successive audit, in order to induce them to remain on their farms—an expedient that proclaims to your fellow-citizens that those who resort to it are in the habit of demanding from their tenants a larger rent than they are capable of paying. Nothing, I must confess, is more distressing to me than to witness these half-yearly annunciations of this miscalled liberality of certain portions of the landed interest. Has it never struck you, fellow-citizens, that this proceeding is no evidence of liberality, but rather of extortion. That the return of a part of the rent may be proper when called for by temporary calamity, by the effect of flood or storm, or by some accidental misfortune overwhelming a particular tenant or class of tenants I do not deny, but that, when resorted to habitually, is not to be justified ; that it convicts those who have recourse to it of continued attempts to extract from their tenantry a rent not warranted by the value of agricultural produce, and, so far from proving the liberality of the landlord, it affords evidence of a very different quality ?"

I have no knowledge of the Earl of Stair's opinion of the corn-law question.

He has been an actor rather than a speaker. I can recollect that, as Sir John Dalrymple and an officer of high rank in the army, he incurred the excessive displeasure of the anti-reformers, as the Tories were called, in 1832, for his attendance at, and active share in, one of those vast meetings which alarmed the Duke of Wellington, and forced the success of the Reform Bill. I can recollect the public demand for his name being erased from the army list, but have no further knowledge of him.

I have quoted his address to his new tenantry on succeeding to the Scotch peerage, and offer it to other landlords as a rare example worthy of general imitation, independent of any political views. Whatever his personal belief in politics may be, he is a noble instance of a noble landlord ; and although I have many rural details to communicate from the counties in which I have lately travelled, I deferred them to give place to this address, the republication of which must do good at a season of agricultural meetings.

NOTES FOR FUTURE HISTORIANS.

February 1843.

EACH reader of a newspaper is now for or against the League ; there is no neutral position, unless it be the painful one of hanging between two opinions. In whichever category the readers of this chapter may be, they cannot fail to have a lively interest in the League's proceedings. In whatever way this movement may end, whether in success or failure, it is at the present time pregnant with events on which will turn the future fortunes of mighty England.

Since writing a brief account of my visit to the League rooms, I have formed the design of collecting for the future historian as many particulars connected with this unparalleled combination as any single individual can gather together.

Finding, on my arrival in Manchester, that there would be no public meetings for some days, I was about to start for Cheshire, to pursue my examination into the practical results of the agreements between landlord and tenant, when, in the public room of the hotel where I was staying, I saw a paper announcing that a great tea-party would be held that evening at Bolton, in aid of the L.50,000 fund of the League. As the *waiter* in a Manchester hotel is not the person to put coals on your fire, (the same in Lancaster and Preston, by the bye,) he is not, it seems, the person to answer questions about railways, and trains, and fares, and hours of starting. Either he is too great to be so condescending, or it is not in his department to give such information. Perhaps the division-of-labour system, so common in the factories, is introduced into the inns of the factory towns ; if so, it may be worth the attention of the landlords and landladies to consider whether they promote their own profits by rendering it necessary for a waiter to go down stairs in search of an assistant to answer those questions which he might reply to while going outside to ring his bell for the more accommodating and seemingly better-informed personage named *Boots*.

But be the cause what it may, the waiter is *not* the man who knows everything about luggage, cabs, cars, coaches, trains, fares, and how many miles, but *Boots* is. Accordingly, on seeing the Bolton advertisement in Manchester, and putting some queries to the waiter, the ubiquitous, obliging, and obeisant Boots was summoned. He came.

" Boots, how far is Bolton from this ?"

" Twelve miles, sir."

" By what conveyance can I get there this evening ?"

" By rail, sir ; train goes at four, sir ; quarter to four now, sir; just in time, sir ; omnibus starts for the station directly, sir."

Accordingly I was at Bolton in due time. I had the offer of an introduction from two gentlemen who were with me in the railway carriage ; but being resolved to go to the tea-party alone, to see, and hear, and judge for myself, I left them at the inn to which we drove from the railway, and proceeded to the meeting alone. They followed soon after.

At the door of a large chapel-like building, called the " Temperance-Hall," I paid 1s. 6d. for a ticket, which I found marked with the letter E. and No. something, which I now forget. This letter E. and No. something on the ticket corresponded with a seat in an extreme corner of the house, to

which seat I might have gone, but only by walking over caps,
and combs, and curls, and lace, and ribbons, which seemed
to form a pavement resting on a substratum of human
heads ; or I might have got along the forms by making
every one who chose to have their seats and dresses marked
with my muddy boots rise ; or every couple who sat together, and they were equally distributed, husbands with
their wives, lovers with their loved ones, fathers and mothers,
little sisters and little brothers, I might have got along
by disjoining all these ; or by creeping beneath the tables,
at the risk of rising too soon, and, like an earthquake,
overthrowing a multitude of cups and other crockery, cakes,
sandwiches, dishes of oranges, dishes of grapes, and other
et-ceteras of teetotalism ; or I might have got myself into hot
water, and moved along the tables as that did which filled the
teapots and tea urns ; but I did none of those things.   I stood
still, and looked if there was any other corner into which I
could retreat.   While so standing, the company seemed to
consider me a part of the entertainment.   All were seated, to
the number of 1200 or 1300.   There was a dead silence.
Eyes which up to this had rested on eyes beside them, the
lovers and the loved ; eyes which, up to this, had been patiently
resting on nothing, the old and the companionless ; eyes
which, up to this, had devoured the cakes, and the grapes,
and the oranges, twenty times over, the little sisters and little
brothers, not excepting most of the fathers and mothers ; all
these eyes were suddenly and resolvedly turned upon me.
The great men of the deputation from the League had not
yet arrived ; the meeting was waiting for them, and seemed
willing to believe that any stranger was one of those they
were waiting for.

Anxious to escape the public gaze, I hurriedly penetrated,
by one of two intersecting thoroughfares, to the further side
of the house, and in my eagerness to get out of view went too
far.   I went behind the scenes, further than the public were
expected to go.   Some twenty or more waiters, male and
female, and twenty or more kettles, with two or three larger
boilers, kept up a buzz buzzing in this department, which prevented a stranger from being so quickly detected as in the
body of the house.   " Now it is positively wrong, James, to
do that."   " Pray, let me have my own way."   " We must
have some order."   " I seay, soome o' ye'll be scealded to deeth
an ye take nea better ceare."   " Oh, my cap ! oh, my new
ribbon ! to put boiling black kettle joost off feyre owre a body's
head !   How can I be seen now ?"   " Never mind, never mind ;
make way."   " Why don't 'em begin, I wouldn't wait not a
moment longer, I wouldn't."   " See ! who is that ?   Make him

go away and get a seat and keep it ; strangers must not come in here." " Pray, sir, allow me to shew you to a seat."

And I was shewn to a seat, and such were some of the expressions heard, where I should not have heard them, heard above the murmur of voices of stewards, and waiters, and kettles ; stewards and waiters directing and contending each with each ; kettles boiling and blubbering side by side, the steam contending with the lids and the lids with the steam.

Having seen what was not intended to be seen, I now directed my attention to what was intended for special observation—the most prominent of which were the flags and mottos exhibited in various parts of the house. Sometimes flags and mottos say a great deal ; sometimes they say what the boldest orators dare not say ; sometimes they are considered dangerous, sometimes highly criminal. At the Bolton meeting the mottos were exceedingly innocent.

The house had a lofty roof, having been built for public meetings. Facing the two entrances, and stretching between the two passages which ran the whole width of the house, and divided its sittings into three divisions, was raised a permanent stage eight or ten feet high, surmounted by a canopy, and hung round with two or three banners, of which I could not see the inscriptions. I was asked to a seat on this platform, and having no choice, the body of the house being completely filled, I accepted the offer.

While mounting the narrow steps, and stumbling over some baskets which had once contained the good things now displayed on the two platform tables, displayed there with all the artistic beauty which lady hands and lady tastes could devise, preparatory to filling the eloquent mouths of the deputation from the League and their friends—while stumbling over these baskets, I heard a voice read out two lines of a hymn, and commence singing it to the tune called the " Old Hundredth Psalm." Judging by the incompleteness of the singing, I suppose the audience were as much taken by surprise as I was, at this not very appropriate nor very harmonious attempt at religious worship. It was soon over : four lines, if I remember rightly, made a finish, and then there was—oh ! such a clatter of cups and saucers, spoons, and little plates ! and such a sudden falling to !—such an issue of boiling kettles and steam, and waiters trotting about like so many locomotive engines, in all directions ! Such a many compliments paid :—" If you please, sir, allow me to hand your cup !" " Pray, pass this to the young lady next you." " Do you take sugar, sir ? And you, ma'am ? And you ? And you, sir ?" " Out the way ! Out the way !" " Oh, my! some of you will run one another down with those jugs of boiling water; I am really surprised that you don't have more care." "Have more care yourself, sir—you are the only one I have seen in the way." "Now this is really———." "Huzza! Hurrah! Clap—clap—ap—ap!" The deputation coming in! "The who? Who are they?" "John Bright, of Rochdale, and R. R. R. Moore, of Dublin. Hurrah! hurrah—urah—rah—rah!" "Clap—ap—ap—ap!" "Now, pray be seated, gentlemen; pray be seated." "Ah! John, how d'ye do!" "Hope you're well, Mr Moore? Hope you have not got wet? Hope this cup will be to your taste? Oh! I forget, *you* don't drink tea! What *will* you take? Pray do take something. We know you don't use any article that pays duty to the excise or the customs, if you can help it; but after your journey, and with such a *task* before you, you must really take some refreshment." "Certainly." "Anne, get Mr Moore———get this gentleman a cupful of hot milk. And you never take anything to breakfast or supper but bread and milk? Is your tea to your taste, Mr Bright? I know you don't take sugar; you don't pay *that* tax to the government and the monopolists. You don't like green tea, I think? not any green? not even mixed? Oh! very good; we shall have some all black in this. Anne, let tea be made in this pot for Mr Bright, and all black, no green, nor mixed. Oh dear! I'm so sorry we had not thought of this sooner." "Now is *your* tea to your taste, sir?" "Ah! Mr Brooks, how d'ye do? Well? eh? glorious meeting this, is it not? splendid turn out for Bolton this, is it not? Ah! *that* is the point, the money—the subscription is the thing; well, I think we shall do something that way also—something good— something worth talking about." "Who is this sitting at the table behind us?" "Which one do you mean?" "He next to ———, close behind us?—speak low—the next but one to Dr Bowring." "Don't you know him?" "No; I never saw him before this evening. He came from Manchester by the train the deputation came by." "Did he? I shall inquire of Mr Moore if he knows him." "Well, does Mr Moore know who he is?" "No; he thinks he comes from London, but is not sure; but he is not one connected with the League. Nobody here seems to know him."

So he who was not one of the League, and whom nobody seemed to know, having heard all that is here related, drank three cups of tea, which were presented to him by the fair hands of a lady, who most kindly and politely did the honours of the table, and by the time his three cups were finished, everybody else was finishing.

In less than ten minutes after everybody was finished, the cups were entirely cleared away. In five minutes after that the mayor, a fifty-year-old pleasant looking but rather timid gentleman, was moved and voted by acclamation to the chair. Five minutes after that he was at the end of his speech; and in five minutes more Joseph Brotherton, Esq., M.P., was through the introductory sentences of his.

Joseph Brotherton is a mild looking man, five feet eight or nine inches high, apparently above fifty years of age, a little inclined to corpulency, with a round face and black whiskers neatly trimmed and pointed forward. He is, in Parliament, remarkable for his regular attendance and his opposition to midnight legislation. In the country he seems to be remarkable for his readiness to attend any meeting when called on for the promotion of free trade, also for his solid good sense, which never fails to instruct his hearers, though it seldom excites them to high applause. On the occasion under notice I did not hear him with the attention he deserves, and which I was disposed to pay to him, inasmuch as a gentleman sitting beside me undertook, on finding I was a stranger to every one present, to inform me of the names of those on the platform, as also of their professional and personal connections. The following are, as nearly as I can recollect, the words and manner of our conversation :—

" Well, sir, that is Joseph Brotherton, member for Salford, who is speaking. This is our mayor, Mr Walsh, who is in the chair. That gentleman sitting on his right, next but one, wearing spectacles, he with the high full forehead, that is one of our members for Bolton, Dr Bowring. Our other member, Peter Ainsworth, has cut our connection, and gone over to the enemy's camp; but we shall cut him at the next election."

" Will you ?"

" Oh, yes ; why should we not ? I have always supported him, but I shall not do so again ; we must have out and out free-traders, such men as the doctor and John Bright, for instance. Do you know John Bright ?"

" I think I do ; this is him, sitting on the back seat next the door, to our right, is it not ?"

" Yes, that is John—a clever man—extraordinary debater. On the subjects of wages and machinery he is one of the ablest men of the League. He carries on large works at Rochdale. All his family are repealers ; they give both their time and their money to the cause. No one acquainted with that man's movements could believe it possible for one individual to undergo the fatigue he does in this cause. Every day and night he is at some meeting or other. His sisters are as

zealous, and in the getting of money for the fund as successful.
They are all of the Society of Friends.   Excellent people all.
Highly esteemed by their factory hands.

"But, look here.   Do you see that lady sitting opposite;
the one that sat next to Moore when the tea was going on,
second from the corner ?—Yes, that is her, rather pale.
Why, as to her age—you know we never talk about ladies'
ages—yet her's may be talked of ; two or three and twenty,
I should say.   That is a most remarkable young lady ; her
name is Heyworth, Miss Heyworth, daughter of Lawrence
Heyworth, Esq., of Yew Tree, near Liverpool, a retired merchant, rich, and a most zealous member of the League.   Oh !
he is a determined worker in the cause.   And his daughter,
bless you ! she is not a whit behind him.   He makes speeches
—he is to speak to-night—excellent speeches he makes ; but
his daughter goes even beyond him in working for the cause.
She goes everywhere in Liverpool ; into the richest man's
mansion and the poorest man's cellar ; gives tracts, collects
money, reasons on the propriety and necessity of repeal.   Oh !
bless you, she deserves—I don't know what—she deserves at
the least our thanks and our prayers.

"This gentleman, with the round, good humoured face,
who wears a white neckcloth, is John Brooks, Alderman
Brooks, of Manchester.   He employs a great many people.
He has built a flax mill in Bolton, and lost L.60,000 on it.
We shall have a speech from him.   Always humorous, always
pleasant ; good man ; hits hard at the parsons sometimes ;
but full of the milk of human kindness ; either laughing,
either smiling with a face like a schoolboy, or——I tell you
what, I have seen that same John Brooks listening to some
of our pathetic speakers, who, in describing the distress of the
unemployed, have worked on his feelings until the tears fell
from his eyes.

"These are some of our Bolton friends next us : you will
hear the names of most of them when the subscriptions come
to be read.   Moore will undertake that part of the business.
A clever young man he is—clever, very clever ; you would
not think, merely to look at him, before hearing him speak,
that he could make such an impression on an audience ; but
he has a fine manly voice ; he is eloquent, is witty—a regular
Irishman at repartee.   He and John Bright will take a couple
of hundred pounds out of such a meeting as this more than
any other men of the League.   They do it in a way that
nobody ever thought of before.   They get up a complete piece
of auctioneering ; and, talk of George Robins ! George Robins
is a bagatelle in exciting an audience to competition compared

with Bright or Moore. Who *is* he? Who is Moore? He is an Irish barrister, a young gentleman of property; oh yes, a young man of respectable connexions. He will be called to the English bar next summer. He is clever, decidedly clever; and his natural eloquence and Irish banter tell splendidly on an audience. People that never thought of subscribing come out with their money, or down with their names, when they hear Moore at his auctioneering. Subscribers of L.10 put their names down for L.20, the twenty pounders increase their subscriptions to fifty, the fifties to a hundred, and so on. He gets hold of a particular trade, for instance, the tea-dealers, and he will make them subscribe in competition with one another; the shoemakers the same, and the tailors; he keeps at them, and puts the meeting into such good humour, such roars of laughter, and gets up such shouts of applause, administers to their love of approbation so vigorously, that they cannot help themselves; they are completely led off their feet as it were. Oh! he is just the man, he and Bright, for this kind of work. It is a great mistake to have so many speakers; the people get tired. What we want now in our towns is not arguments against the corn-laws, not lectures; we are all convinced of the justice of our proceedings on this question, and we want nothing but money, and men who can take it out of the pockets of those who have it, but who hang back. Bright and Moore are the men for that business. Cobden can do little at it, he is too diffident. You will hear them at their auction by-and-bye."

With this information of the men before me, and the manner of their proceedings, I now listened attentively to what was said. Mr Brotherton had finished; Mr Heyworth was just begun; John Brooks succeeded; and Dr Bowring followed him in a powerful oration, which drew down thunders of applause. I must certainly say that, so far as I can judge, it was a most eloquent harangue. Were it possible for Dr Bowring to use somewhat less of his violent gesticulation, he would, I think, be more effective. Being member for the borough, he was listened to with great interest, but not greater than the importance of his subject and his manner of treating it demanded.

Following him came John Bright, who read a letter from the other member of Parliament for the borough, Peter Ainsworth, Esq., excusing himself from attending the meeting, because, having voted for the tariff last session, which gave protection to certain manufactures, he was not now prepared to repeal the corn-law, which would be taking away all protection from the farmers. This letter afforded a text for a very effective speech, delicate in its satire, but all the keener that it was delicate.

Next came Mr R. R. R. Moore, whose initials being interpreted signify Robert Ross Rowan ; and with him came the subscriptions and the auction.*

NOTES UPON SCOTLAND.

Journey to the Farm of Mr Hope of Fenton Barns.

September 1843.

It will be recollected that the Anti-Corn-Law League advertised last year that they would give certain prizes for essays "demonstrating the injurious effects of the corn-laws on tenant-farmers and farm-labourers, and the advantages which those classes would derive from their total and immediate repeal." And it will be recollected also that the first prize was awarded to Mr Hope of Fenton Barns, near Haddington. The Hon. Fox Maule and some other landlords of high standing, formerly friends of protection, have publicly ascribed their conversion to total and immediate abolition to Mr Hope's essay. The essayist spoke of himself, his farm, and the corn-laws thus :—

"As a tenant-farmer in an exclusively arable district of Scotland, paying a rent depending on the price of grain, and averaging for several years past L.1500 a-year, for a farm possessing no peculiar advantages from vicinity to a market town or anything of the kind, and upon a lease originally of twenty-one years, of which there are a considerable number yet to run, and during which period repayment is confidently expected of large sums expended in thorough draining with tiles more than five hundred acres, and otherwise improving and enriching the farm ; thus situated, I should rejoice were the corn-laws to be abolished whenever Parliament meets."

Being in Haddington, and within five or six miles of Fenton Barns, I went one day to see that and some other farms in the same direction. I may state that the town of Haddington

---

* The "auction" was carried on by blank cards and pencils being handed round the assembly. As the cards were returned with the name of a subscriber and the amount which he intended to give when called upon at his own house, Mr Moore read the name and amount, commented on the individual and his profession ; if he were a shoemaker, shewing how he would be served by free-trade, and exciting other shoemakers to rival him ; so on with all the professions. A great deal of money was got in this way which never would have been got otherwise. This sketch may suffice as a specimen of all the League tea-parties in the provinces.

stands in a valley through which runs a small river called the
Tyne. With our faces southward we have a cultivated country
before us, gradually ascending for eight or ten miles, until it
merges with the heath of the Lammermoor Hills, which hills
run across the country from east to west, a distance of seventy
or eighty miles. We are now in view of the centre of the
range. At our back, rising abruptly on the north side of
Haddington, is a minor range of hills called the Garleton.
We must cross these to go to Fenton Barns. The road is
steep on each side, and by its steepness places a farm distant
from the market town six miles at as great a disadvantage as
if it were ten miles distant on an easy road.

Having gained the summit of the ridge, and parted with
the road for a brief period to pay a visit to a monumental
column, which stands on a rocky eminence, we scramble
through whins and over rocks, and arrive at the column, and
find it is, what we had been told when inquiring thirty miles
off, a monument to a late Earl of Hopetoun, (the Lieutenant-
General Sir John Hope of the wars of Wellington.) As this
is conspicuous from the sea and many distant places, so the
sea, that arm of it called the Frith of Forth, twenty or thirty
miles broad, and the county of Fife beyond, and many noticeable objects at greater and lesser distances, are public to the eye
from the hill on which stands this column. Far in the north-
west, beyond the shires of Fife, Kinross, and Clackmannan,
stand the Ochills, the advanced guard of the Highland
mountains. At a fourth part of the distance, hiding from us
the comparatively level country of the Forth and West
Lothian, rises the smoke of Edinburgh, and amid the smoke
the Calton Hill and the many monuments thereon; while
above all, above the Calton pillars, above the city and the
city's smoke, rises Arthur's Seat, as if keeping at bay the
more distant Pentlands, which we see scowling beyond him,
and the Lammermoors cold and bleak.

From that point in the west, where the Lammermoors are
lowest, we have them crossing on our south, as before said,
until they reach the sea at Fast Castle, forty miles to the
east of where we now stand. In that range they encircle
between them and the sea what is generally known as East
Lothian and a small part of Berwickshire; but the hills
themselves, the very bleakest and most profitless of them, form
a large portion of the shires of east Lothian and Berwick.
Fast Castle, on the very peak of a headland overhanging the
sea, where deep water vexes itself upon the perpendicular
rocks in its everlasting disquietude, because it has no beach
to play upon, and is unable to make one, is the farthest point

discernible in the east. It is the Wolf's Craig of the "Bride of Lammermoor," the nestling-place of Caleb Balderstone and old Mysie.

From that point many miles of the sea-shore and of the rich fields lying between the shore and the hills are hidden from our view by intervening heights, chief of which is Doon Hill, above Dunbar, both places, hill and town, of more importance in the days of war than in these times of trade and commerce, seeing that Dunbar is every day becoming less and less, and more feeble and poor. Following the line of sea-coast towards ourselves from Dunbar, we see the ruins of Tantallon Castle, once the stronghold of the Douglasses; as also the Bass Rock, two or three miles out at sea, once the state prison of Scotland. Nearer us is North Berwick Law, rising a hundred feet high from the level country on the sea-shore, between us and which lies a well-cultivated district, all in large farms, and on each farm a steam-mill, with a tall chimney rising up, as if it were one of the "factory districts," instead of being, as it is, "purely agricultural." Sir Thomas Hepburn, who is member for this county, may be as truly called the representative of tall chimneys as are the members for Stockport and Manchester.

Continuing our eyes along the coast, we run into the line already viewed, because the sea, west of Preston Pans, which is eight or ten miles north-west from us, forms a bay which bends inland between that place and Edinburgh. We shall therefore retreat; and we do so along the line on which Johnny Cope retreated from Preston Pans to Dunbar, and along which it is proposed to have the North British Railway,* which is to connect the North of England, and, through that, London and the South of England with Edinburgh and Glasgow.

Having returned to the road, I was told that, of the many tall chimneys I saw over the country, the one which was smoking at the distance of about four miles was Fenton Barns. We descended the hill, and in due time I approached it. Some English friends and others were with me, intending to go to the sea-side, but as there was one who had never seen a thrashing mill, we left the others at the distance of two hundred yards from the farm-yard, at which distance the public road passed on to the village of Dirleton. On our right hand were the extensive farm buildings and enormous stackyard; I did not go over the offices, as they were seemingly such as I saw in every other part of Lothian, commodious and compact, well arranged for the due economy of labour,

---

* This Railway is now made, and used as the thoroughfare to England.

and as unlike the farm offices of England as can well be, where we see a barn in one field, a stable in another field, a hay-rick here, and a corn-rick there, the houses, and produce, and implements scattered over the whole farm. The compactness of Mr Hope's farm-yard is common to Lothian, but I soon observed something about it not common to Lothian ; to the shame of that otherwise fine county and the owners of the land let the words be spoken. In front of me was a cottage, and on my left hand was a row of cottages, covered with roses and adorned with many other flowers and shrubs, the rarity of some of which told, as well as the inmates could tell, that their culture had been assiduously cared for. If a cottage is flowery outside, and the flowers carefully trained, we may be sure that inside there is neither a want of cleanliness nor a neglect of moral training. But Mr Hope has not only induced his workpeople to depicture that comfort outside which should be an indweller in every cottage ; he has, by building an extra room, and a small dairy behind each house, rendered comfort, neatness, healthfulness, and moral decency practicable, or at least he has made the want of them less excusable. I went into several of these houses, and the scrupulous cleanliness and the abundance of provisions and furniture in each were a pleasing contrast to what I have seen in most other parts of the kingdom. As the Lothian hinds have usually a year's provisions laid in at the beginning of winter, and as they have a cow giving milk and butter for market and for use all the summer, their houses are never the home of hunger ; but in nearly every case their houses are so small and ill-constructed, that social comfort and a due respect to decency are impracticable. Mr Hope has, at his own expense, as the people told me, done the great service of improving the physical and moral comforts of his workers, though he be only a tenant, and the houses are the property of the landlord.

We saw the thrashing mill at full work, but it was within ten minutes of stopping when we entered the barn. The time was between three and four in the afternoon, and already a large stack of wheat, of probably eighteen or twenty quarters, which had been standing in the yard in the morning, was nearly ready for market.

They do not build the stacks larger in Lothian than can be conveniently thrashed in a day ; and thus at any time they can take any advantage of a change of markets, if such be in the farmer's favour. Nor do they employ fewer people on the same breadth of land. The money saved by Mr Hope's mill is as so much more capital to him, and he pays it away in wages for some other description of farm work, which, without it, he could not perform. The more economy that is observed in a manufactory, the more people can the manufacturer employ ; and so it is with the farmer—the farmer is a manufacturer of food. If anything distinguishes him more than another from manufacturers of cotton and broadcloth, it is that he goes into business with too little capital, and depends on other chances than the certain calculation of what capital will produce for his profits.

Not having any personal knowledge of Mr Hope, I did not call on him ; moreover, he and his father—an aged gentleman, who, I believe, has been many years opposed to the corn-laws, seeing that their only effect was to mar good farming, by unsettling the prices of corn, and thus unsettling all the farmer's plans—had gone out on horseback to visit their shearers, who were at work in a field lying at some distance from our road. I found the people speak very highly of both the elder and the younger Mr Hope, as kind and attentive masters. Quarrels, reproofs, and disputes were unknown among them. Some of the ploughmen had been ten, twelve, and sixteen years there.

The Cottages of the Hinds—The Marquis of Tweeddale's Improved Land and Unimproved Cottages—Mrs Fergusson's Beautiful Village of Dirleton—The Neglect of the Cottages on other parts of the Estate.

Having mentioned the improved dwellings of the labourers on Mr Hope's farm of Fenton Barns, and stated that he had, at his own expense, added a small bed-room and a dairy to each, I may still remark that they are not even yet such houses as should be provided for labourers. Still they are, by Mr Hope's addition to them, and by his benevolent attention to the welfare of his workpeople, in advance of the ordinary dwelling-houses of the rural districts of Scotland. To have made them better than they are would have required new structures on new foundations, which, as a mere tenant himself, with a limited lease of the farm, he could not do, neither in point of law as regarded his lease, nor in point of propriety as regarded the expense to himself. But if the landlords, who must surely see that they have an interest in promoting a high tone of moral feeling in the working population, were to take notice of the cottages, they might soon do what such tenants as Mr Hope cannot do. As it is, I saw nothing in East Lothian or elsewhere, so far as the houses of the farm labourers were concerned, that indicated any improvement, not even where new cottages were in course of erection.

On the Marquis of Tweeddale's estate I saw a new farm-steading in course of erection. I noticed it the more particularly, as the Marquis has of late years devoted himself to the practical improvement of agriculture in a manner at once energetic, comprehensive, and successful. Previous to his departure for India, he, by his ceaseless attention to the practical details of draining, tile-making, and the amalgamation of soils on his own property, had given a stimulus to landlord agriculturists in all parts of the kingdom, but especially in Scotland. Doubtless the Marquis intended, as a primary object, to improve his rental—a most honourable intention; but, in producing turnips over many thousands of acres of cold wet land, where turnips never grew before, to feed cattle where cattle were never fed before, supplying markets with butcher's meat better than markets were ever supplied before, and on the same description of land producing wheat where wheat had never grown, and five bushels of oats where only three grew; in doing this on his own estate, by his own devices and superintendence, and on other estates by the example of his success, the Marquis was most truly a benefactor of his country, even though his own profit might have been the primary cause of action. Indeed, if he acted with a view to profit, he acted right, and would have done wrong with any other view. The severest losses to agriculture and to landowners have arisen from the fact that men of rank and wealth have either entirely neglected the management of their own property, or have attended to the beautifying of it without any regard to substantial and permanent profit. All parks, gardens, plantations, roads, lakes, bridges, and fancy farms, erected for the mere adornment of an estate, of which England presents such abundant specimens, preserved at great expense and no profit, might have been, and might yet be, kept up in all their beauty, while paying their own expenses. Even more; the face of England might be changed from what it is to an Eden-like beauty and fruitfulness, to the benefit of the whole nation, but more especially to the augmentation of the landed rent-rolls, if landowners would manage their own affairs. The Marquis of Tweeddale being, in my opinion, a rare instance of a nobleman managing his own affairs in a businesslike way, that is to say, as a manufacturer does, who, looking to ultimate profit, improves his machinery and makes a web-and-a-half instead of one web, thus giving more employment to mechanics and more cloth to the markets of the world, enabling millions of women and children to have two cheap dresses, who before could not appear but in one dress or in rags—the Marquis being a rare instance of one in his position endeavouring to enrich himself, while, by manufacturing food more plentifully, to be sold at a cheaper rate to the consumers of food, he enables them to save something from food to expend in clothing, thereby increasing the trade of the manufacturer, I looked to the result of his agricultural reform with much interest.

Fields, now enclosed with fences, substantial and beautiful, at the distance of only a few years, wet, cold, and worthless, smiled now in the face of heaven with crops alike abundant in quantity and excellent in kind. Others, which had been cultivated for ages, but which had been nothing better than "a cold hungry clay" up to a few years ago, and incapable of bearing that turnip crop which is so important to a farmer who would feed cattle, produce manure, and raise good corn crops, were now loaded with turnips that would turn off at the rate of twenty and thirty tons an acre. Yet, amid all the beautifying and enriching of that district of the country, the dwellings of the working population stood the same, small, uncomfortable, odious looking huts, that they have ever been. The new houses in process of erection were so far improved as to have the stone walls plastered inside, with a boarding over-head, instead of the bare roof, which is so common ; but in respect to size, of their utter incapability of allowing a decent distribution of a family, the new cottages seemed as faulty as the old. The wholesomeness of situation, to say nothing of that pleasantness of situation which should be attended to in order to make happiness of spirit attainable in the family of the cottager, happiness of spirit, having so much responsibility as a parent of morality, and morality in a working population so much to do with the peace and welfare of all society, up to the nobles of the land—wholesomeness of situation, to say nothing of pleasantness, was not attended to.

There are some cottages to be seen in Scotland, and some in all parts of England, which are an exception to the general rule ; but these are found only in some pet village near a nobleman's park, or in the park itself, and only there because they are ornamental to the rich man's residence. So truly is this the case, that we very frequently find such ornamental cottages and lodges at park gates as destitute of comfort as the hovel on the farm ; mere ornament being everything, the comfort of the indwellers nothing.

A few miles from Mr Hope's farm, in East Lothian, there is a village called Dirleton. I visited it on the same day I was at Fenton Barns. I had never seen it before, but had read of it, and often heard it spoken of. Its simple beauty had

been extolled as unmatched ; and now I must say that, in all
my travels, south and north, I have seen nothing so sweet, so
pleasing to the perceptive powers of the mind, so satisfactory
to the reflective.   The excellent and amiable Mrs Fergusson,
under whose patronage art has so liberally given its aid to
nature in beautifying Dirleton, must have a high satisfaction,
when she makes her occasional visits to the neighbouring
mansion, to see so much outward comfort, and hear that the
people, in the internal economy of their dwellings, and in the
moral rectitude of their lives, are so worthy of what she and
the late Robert Fergusson, Esq., M.P., her husband, have
done for them.   But Mrs Fergusson's rich property extends
far beyond this village.   Besides the Dirleton estate, there
is Biel, ten miles southward ; and where are there finer farms
than those encircling Biel?   Where a more independent and
wealthy set of tenants ?   Where a more industrious class of
workpeople ?   And yet the dwellings of the farm labourers are
really very wretched, as, for instance, in Peatcox, a place which
might be made equal to Dirleton, and which probably would
have been so made had it been as near a mansion and a park.

But as it is some years since I saw Peatcox, and as it is possible some of the wretched hovels have been replaced by better
houses, some of the filth drained away, and the people not so
continually suffering from fever as they were, (though, judging
by the want of cottage improvement on other parts of the
property, this is not probable,) I shall only speak distinctly of
the houses on the Biel estate which I have seen lately.

There are four enormous farms detached from the main
body of the property, lying twelve or fourteen miles east of
Biel, and about twenty miles from Dirleton.   Those farms are
Innerwick, Crowhill, Skateraw, and Thorntonloch.   The first
has six or seven ploughs, the second has seven, the third has
nine, and the fourth fifteen.   There is also a range of hill
pasture belonging to the first and fourth.   What the annual
rent may be I cannot say precisely ; but for the whole, it is
little if anything below L.7000, probably L.8000.   On each
farm powerful machinery has been erected for thrashing and
winnowing the grain.   The most ample barns, and stables, and
sheds have been erected.   Houses more fit to be called mansions than what are often so called have been built for the
farmers.   Each keeps a professional gardener and a groom.
One, when I knew them some years ago, used to have his butler as well, which butler had also his horse to ride on.   But
amid all this opulence, the hinds' houses continue the same as
ever.   I passed by Crowhill on my late visit, and remarked,
in a tone of satisfaction, to a friend resident in the neighbour-

hood, that the new farm-house had a noble appearance, and was quite an ornament to the place.

"Indeed it's no such thing," replied my friend, "it's rather a disgrace; it's far owre fine."

"Why so?" I asked.

"Because," said he, "look at its grandeur and look at the hinds' houses; look what shabby places they are, what pudges of places they are, hardly big enough for a swine's cruive, some o' them, to say nothing of a family of eight or nine bairns, and faither and mother."

"But," said I, "the fault is that the hinds' houses are too small, not that the farmer's house is too large." And I added, what I have before said in the *Morning Chronicle*, and shall again repeat, that I would like to see the farm labourers lifted up, not that I would like to see a farmer or a landlord brought down; that I would like to see, not only every castle, and hall, and mansion, with their parks and gardens, to remain the pride and ornament of the country as now, but that I would like to see the whole country as carefully beautified as the park or garden of the mansion, being persuaded that, while this would elevate the working population, it would add to the wealth of those who are already rich. To this my friend replied, with a shrug of his shoulders,

"Ah! there's no use talking about that; every improvement that takes place is for the rich, and not for the poor; the poor are aye hin'most, and, the farer the world goes, the poor seem to be left aye farer ahint."

"That sentiment," said I, "is unfortunately a common one; I find it prevailing south and north, in town and in country; but it only proves that the poor have been left behind, not that the gentry have advanced too far. The hinds of Crowhill might have three-roomed houses, with a better garden, with a dairy for their cow's produce, a good stye for their pigs, with roses and flowers of every kind embowering every house, instead of the miserable den of one small apartment which they now inhabit; and they might have all this, while their master retained his fine house and garden, and Mrs Fergusson, to whom all belongs, enjoyed her various mansions and parks, without her abating one pound of rent."

At the distance of half a mile from Crowhill is Thornton-loch, and there the houses are probably the meanest of any on the estate. They were old and dilapidated at the earliest period of my recollection, and they are the same now. Except two or three, they are all inhabited by people who work on the farm. There was a tailor lived in one of them once, and I remember having gone with my mother to his house on a visit. I was then only about seven years old, but was tall enough to stand outside and touch the roof of the house. It so happened that for seven or eight years afterwards, when new clothes were to be made in our family, and the tailor and his men had to be sent for to come and make them, it fell to me to go and "tell the tailors." As they made many appointments to come, and, if busy, did not keep them, which was quite usual, and very grievous to me when my new clothes were in question, I had to go again and again to "tell the tailors," and to urge on "Thamas," the father and master, how "Awfu' wearying I was, and how needfu' for my new claes." On each occasion I made it a point to ascertain how much I had grown from the last time, by going along the front of several of the houses, and touching the roofs with my hand. When there a few weeks ago, I had the curiosity to try once more, and found that, with many of them, my shoulder was now higher than the roofs.

These houses have steps downward at the door, so as to admit of a full-sized man standing up inside. There is no ceiling or lofting of any kind below the roof, save what mats, or canvas, or boards, the people may put up ; and outside, though the ground is so much higher than the interior floor, there is no drainage whatever. When the furniture is in the house there is but one apartment eight or nine feet square.

I hope the excellent lady—of whose property the gigantic farm of Thorntonloch is but a fraction—or her agents and friends, will receive these remarks in the spirit they are written. The late Mr Fergusson was the most popular landlord in the county ; of which fact the monument erected to his memory at Haddington is but one of the proofs. Mrs Fergusson is not less popular, and she has done much to deserve all the good that is said of her. But the very fact of her having done more than other proprietors, while so much remains undone, proves what a neglect of the comfort of the working people prevails in East Lothian.

A TALE FOR THE TIMES.

WHEN the progress of the National Anti-Corn-Law League became really national, and men of all ranks and of all politics, people numberless in multitude, and newspapers, magazines, reviews, and printer's devils of all degrees, rushed to lay hold of the League's traces, and drag its triumphal car to the final consummation of success, the lusty *Times*, bludgeon in hand, shirt sleeves tucked up, paper cap on head, and broad back

bent to the yoke, rushed with the multitude, and roared in the
national din to "Make way for the League !" Its services at the
last moment, so far as they swelled the multitude and gave
glory to the triumph, were not despised, though, if it had
then chosen to remain behind, or even to pull behind backward, or to jink round corners and throw dirt at the Leaguers,
picking up from choice the foulest handful which it could
select, throwing the filth always at the moment when it could
do most harm, and could do it with most safety to itself; if
it had still employed itself thus, the League would have just
had the same success at the same time without it as with it.
But when it could do no more harm, and might have received
damage itself had it continued to walk stealthily with the
crowd, and from behind a lamp-post throw a handful of something vile in the faces of the Leaguers, as it used to do when
League work was hard to perform, and League men were
not strong, and had no multitude to cheer them on and
rebuke the vile who attacked them from behind lamp-posts,
it came out vociferously, and laid hold of the triumphal car
with all its robust might, drowning the voices, kicking the
heels, and treading on the toes of those who had been working
at the task long and patiently.   This was its conduct in the
last month of the year 1845, and in the last months of the
League 1846. It was, as a free-trader, a strong bold man then.
In 1843, it was a large boy of ill-behaviour hanging behind,
pulling back, tripping up, and flinging filth.   Hoping that
better education might make it a better boy, the following
tale was written and published for its instruction in 1842 :—

THE HISTORY OF THE OLD WOMAN WHO LIVED IN A SHOE.

CHAPTER I.

Mrs Jenny Getapenny lived in a shoe.   It was a large shoe,
large enough to be a house to her, for it belonged to a giant.
One day, as she was going to market, she found a penny on
the road, and she said, " I will buy a sow and a pig with
this penny."   So she bought a sow and a pig with the penny,
and kept them in the giant's shoe.   And the big one grew fat
and the little one grew big ; and, in the course of time, the fat
one became bacon, and the big one, that had once been a little
pig, had little pigs of its own.

About this time the giant who owned the shoe said to the
dwarf who collected his rents, " I am going into far countries
to visit the kings and queens of the earth, and I must have
money."   And the dwarf rose, and straightway went to Mrs
Jenny Getapenny, and said, " I am come for the rent."   And

having got the rent, and paid it to the giant, he said, " Mrs Jenny Getapenny, the old woman who lives in a shoe, has more pigs than ever she had, and more bacon. She is increasing in wealth ; she can pay more rent." And the giant said. " Though I am a giant, and powerful over all other men, I am not a hard landlord ; but I am much among the great men of the earth, and my expenses are great ; I shall want all the money you can get." And, having said this, he departed on his journey. And the dwarf came to the shoe, and said, " Mrs Jenny Getapenny, his honour the giant has ordered me to get more rent." Whereupon the old woman who lived in a shoe looked out of her house with a long face, and said, " I cannot pay more than I pay." But the dwarf said, " You must, else the shoe will be let to another tenant." So Mrs Jenny Getapenny promised to pay the high rent, and resolved to do all she could with her bacon and pigs to get money. And fortunately there lived, outside the shoe, merchants who brought merchandize from far countries, and needed bacon, and pigs, and bread, and many things, for their working men, who ate so much as to increase the price of bacon and young pigs, as well as bread.

CHAPTER II.

Soon after this the old woman who lived in a shoe was going to the well, and she found another penny ; and when she had turned it over and over, and looked at it, and thought about it, she said, " The merchants are giving work to more men ; the men want more food ; the markets are rising. I will buy a cock and a hen, and hatch chickens." So she bought a cock and a hen, and hatched chickens ; and these brought her eggs and other chickens, and she was every day growing richer and richer.

And she was sitting one day counting how many she had hatched, when in came the dwarf for the rent ; and when he had got it, and paid it to the giant, who had returned from his journey in far countries, he said, " Mrs Jenny Getapenny, the old woman who lives in a shoe, is growing richer every day ; she has now cocks and hens, chickens and eggs, in great abundance, which she sells at market to the men who make cloth, and iron, and ships for the merchants ; these men are making money, they pay good prices, your honour must have higher rents." Whereupon the giant answered and said, " I am not desirous of wealth for its own sake, nor for my own pleasures ; but thou knowest my son, the young giant, spends all the money he can get of me, and runs in debt. To his brothers and sisters I must give a portion, and whether I pay that portion directly from my own purse, or procure them places of profit in the service of kings and queens, it must be

12

the same. I must spend my money to maintain the family influence that procures these places, just the same as if I paid it to the young giants, my younger sons, direct; therefore I must have money. The increased value of my estate is mine by right; let the rent be raised." Hearing which command, the dwarf went once more to the old woman who lived in the shoe, and told her once more that her rent must be raised; at which she once more put on a long face and said, "I cannot, and I will not." Whereupon the dwarf said, "Then I must seek another tenant." But he did not seek another tenant, for the old woman who lived in a shoe once more resolved to do her best, and the increasing wealth of the merchants, and the increasing mouths of the men who wrought in cloth, and iron, and ships, favoured her with increased prices and increased demands.

But soon after this the giant died, and was succeeded by his son, the young giant, who immediately called to the dwarf, "Get me money: my father hoarded it up; I shall spend it." Whereupon the dwarf said, "Nay, honourable sir, thy father hoarded up no money, it is all that a great giant can do to make ends meet; thy father was prudent, and tried to make the high expenses of the times meet the low rents of the land; he hoarded no wealth for the wealth's sake; pray thee be moderate." Hearing which, the young giant said, "Shall I have no pleasures in the days of my youth? Shall I have no money for my pleasures? Shall it be said of a giant that he is poor? And shall a dwarf tell him so? Nay, by the heads of a hundred ancestors, I will have money! Go, get me money."

And the dwarf came to the old woman who lived in the shoe, and said, "I must have the rent." To which Mrs Getapenny replied, "The markets are looking down, and I have not yet sold my fowls and my pigs; moreover, the rent is only due this day; surely you will give me time." But the dwarf said, "I cannot wait; his honour, the young giant, must have money; giants cannot live without money. You must sell at once, and pay." Whereupon Mrs Jenny Getapenny, the old woman who lived in a shoe, sold at once, and paid her rent; and, having sold at a low rate, she said, "The rents of cheap years must now be restored; I can no longer pay the high rents." But the dwarf shook his head, and said, "That is for his honour the giant to consider, not for me."

CHAPTER III.

Soon after this, as the old woman who lived in a shoe was going out for a holiday, she got a letter which told of the death of one of her rich relations in the West Indies, who had left her all his wealth, and that was a penny. So she considered what she would do with this penny; and when she got it, she hid it in the shoe, lest, if she increased her poultry or pigs, her rent might be again augmented, or, if the rent was not augmented, she might lose it in the fall and change of prices. So it lay in the shoe, tied up in a napkin, and, for a whole year and more, she did not know what to do with it, for prices were still changing, and the dwarf still kept to the high rent. But one day the giant, having summoned the dwarf to his presence, said, "Now it's no use all this humbug, I must have money." To which the dwarf said, "The rents are not yet due; and besides, your honour must know they cannot be paid; prices are falling, and rents must fall also; such is the theory of rent and prices." Whereupon the giant said, "Theories be blowed! what have I to do with theories? I must have money; let the rents be mortgaged. There are all my expenses for the last election to pay, and we are about to have another: I cannot show face until the old score is cleared." To which the dwarf, being loath to offend his master, answered nothing, save that it was not easy to collect rents now-a-days. "But they must be collected," said the giant. "Is it not a fact that my money is spent in maintaining my influence with government to pass laws for keeping up prices for the good of those who pay rents? Tell them it is for their own good they pay the high rents; tell them——but the short and the long of it is, I must have money; and as we shall be able to restore high prices by some means or other, we must draw on future chances; the rents must be mortgaged."

So the rents were mortgaged. And at the appointed day the mortgagee demanded his money of the dwarf, and the dwarf demanded the rent of Mrs Jenny Getapenny, the old woman who lived in the shoe, and she told the dwarf that the profits of all she had sold were not enough to pay him, and that in these bad times she could not pay the high rent; but the dwarf knew there was a penny in a napkin, and he knew the mortgage money must be paid, so he pressed for the rent, and would take no denial; seeing which, Mrs Jenny Getapenny went to the napkin and took out her last penny, even that which she had inherited from her Indian relation, and paid the rent.

CHAPTER IV.

And having nothing but fear before her for the next rent day, unless some great change should arise, she went to a wizard, a wise man, whose fame was great, and inquired of him if there would be any change for the better. And the wizard had a scythe, and a long beard, and three books,

marked "The *past*," " The *present*, "and " The *future :*" the first
and the last were shut, but the second was open, and on it
and over it were written those words—THE TIMES.   With a
look of great wisdom, the wizard heard the old woman who
lived in a shoe speak of her rent, and he said, " *Rent is that
which remains of the produce after remunerating the producer.*"
To which Mrs Getapenny, the old woman who lived in a shoe,
said, " But, sir, I am the producer ; I have had to pay my
rent as usual, though none of the produce was left, and though
I am not remunerated."   To which the wise man replied,
" This cannot be : how could you pay your rent if you had no
residue after being remunerated, or if you were not remunerated ?   This is quite contrary to the theory of the law of
rent, quite ; you must be mistaken, my good woman."   But
Mrs Jenny Getapenny replied and said, " I had pennies that
I need not tell how I came by, besides what my rich relation
left me, and I have paid these in rent ; and also all my profits
that were saved in the time of high prices.   What I want to
know, Mr Wizard, is—if you can tell me—how long we are
to have low prices, or if ever we are to have high ones again.
I care not what the learned men may say about the *theory* of
rent, as they call it.   You spoke of a residue of produce."
Whereupon the wizard again looked wise, and said, " *Any
diminution in the value of produce falls not proportionally on
all parties, but almost wholly on the residue ;* that is, after you,
the producer, are remunerated."   " But," said Mrs Getapenny,
the old woman who lived in a shoe, " I am not remunerated,
I tell thee once more.   My rent rose as prices rose, but now
when prices fall my rent does not fall, not so long as I have a
spare penny to pay it.   What am I to do with the low prices ?"
To which the wizard once more replied, " *It is almost a truism
to say that any improvement or deterioration in the value of
land or its produce must fall mainly on him who owns it, not
on him who hires it for what it is worth.*"—(*Times, 9th December*
1842.)   Whereupon Mrs Getapenny, the old woman who lived
in a shoe, said, " Ah ! I dare say them as be college-bred understand this; but it be too learned an explanation for one as has a
rent to pay.   Good day, Mr Wizard, I must go somewhere else."

CHAPTER V.

And Mrs Jenny Getapenny, the old woman who lived in a
shoe, went to another wizard who professed to know all manner
of secrets, even the secrets of other wise men, and when he saw
her he knew what she wanted, he was so wise, without inquiring.
He, too, like the other, had three books, the *past*, the *present*,
and the *future*.   He opened the past, and said, " Look here,

Mrs Jenny Getapenny—look here, and tell me what you see."

And the old woman who lived in a shoe put on her spectacles, and looked upon the *past*, and the wizard said, " Tell me, old woman, what do you see?" And she said, " I see bones bleaching in the air ; and I see banners lifted up and words of inscription on them. Some of these banners are ragged and worn, and by reason of the mist upon the hills where the battle has been and the bones are bleaching, I cannot read them distinctly. Pray, wizard, tell me the words of these inscriptions and the meaning thereof."

And the wizard answered and said, " I shall make all clear that you may see, and all plain that you may understand. The highest hill, now deserted, on which, and around which, the bare bones are bleaching, on which the mists of departed times are settled, and on which the foot of man shall never again be set, is an old stronghold of the giants ; it is called the ' Height of a Hundred and Twenty Shillings.' There is a deserted standard on it, with an inscription, which was erected when the giants lived upon the mountain and defended it against the assailing enemy, who carried the flags of ' National Distress' and ' Give us this day our daily bread'—the deserted standard, I say, has for an inscription the words ' A Hundred and Twenty Shillings, or no quarter,' which words gave name to the mountain.

" Now, look to the left and you will see a lesser mountain, to which the giants retreated, and on which they built castles and towers of great strength. It is not so far distant as the other ; look at it, old woman, and tell me what you see."

And Mrs Jenny Getapenny, the old woman who lived in a shoe, looked upon this lesser mountain, and saw on it also a deserted standard of the giants, on which standard she read the words, " Final Position of Eighty Shillings." On all sides of this mountain lay the bones of the slain in battle, who had fallen in the wars of the giants, the bones of those who perished in the assault, of those who perished in the defence, and of those who perished in the retreat ; for the giants had retreated from this mountain to another. And Mrs Jenny Getapenny was amazed at the numbers of the bones of those who had perished, and she said to the wizard, " Tell me the meaning of what I see." To which the wizard said, " Nay, old woman, look once more to the left and you will understand for yourself." And the old woman, Mrs Jenny Getapenny, who lived in a shoe, looked once more to the left, and she saw indistinctly a foggy mountain, with another deserted standard, with nothing left

but the word " Seventy," and she told the wizard what she
saw, but he bade her still look farther to the left, for the
mountain on which was the word " Seventy" was only a part
of that where the great battle on the ground called the " Final
Position of Eighty Shillings" had been fought. And she looked
still farther to the left, and said, " I see a lesser hill with many
walls, and battlements, and ditches, and drawbridges, all in
ruins. Here also are heaps of slain, some of the bones still
with the flesh on. What is the meaning of this?"

" The meaning of that, old woman," said the wizard, " is,
that the giants, driven from other mountains, intrenched themselves here ; and, professing to have a desire to live at peace
with the hosts of those who had driven them from a greater
to a lesser height, they had these drawbridges constructed on
the principle of a sliding scale. They called the place the
' Intrenched Camp of Sixty-four Shillings ;' and although the
fortifications were constructed under the approving observation of the immortal Wellington, they were singularly defective.
Battles took place as before ; the giants were again defeated ;
their standard was again deserted ; and thousands upon thousands were again among the wounded and slain. Many of
those bodies you see among the dead have no flesh on them,
though they seem to have. Those of them who fought under
the banner of ' National Distress' and ' Give us this day our
daily bread' are only skin and bone, not flesh and blood, as
you think ; but the bodies of those who fell defending the
positions of the giants have still flesh on them ; in fact, many
of them are still warm, having only recently died of their
wounds ; while others, though wounded, still live. You will
see the banners under which they fought prostrated beside
them ; the inscriptions and devices are various, but the principal of them are 'Farming Tenantry' and 'Labourers' Wages.'"

" But tell me," said Mrs Getapenny, the old woman who
lived in a shoe, " tell me how it is that amongst all the slain
there are no dead giants." To which the wizard said, " I will
shew you by setting before your eyes the warfare as it is now
conducted, and as it has ever been carried on. I will shew
you ; but, in doing so, I close the volume of the *past*, and open
that of the *present*.

" See here," he continued, " see here—you observe the giants
in the intrenched camp, with the flag of ' *Fifty-six*' hoisted.
Since they fell from the ' Height of a Hundred and Twenty Shillings' they have carried on the war as you see them now.
Hitherto you have only seen the remnants of the different battle-fields ; here you see the battle itself. There is no difference
in it from the former conflicts, as far as defence goes, but the

assailants are better equipped and drilled, and more firmly *leagued* together. Mark well the assault and the defence, and you will at once comprehend the whole mystery which you came here to have explained."

And the old woman who lived in a shoe looked steadfastly at the battle which was being fought around the intrenched camp of "Fifty-six Shillings." Whole battalions of men well armed marched against it, bearing flags with the words "Ships," "Colonies," "Wealth," "Foreign Customers," "Free Trade," "Peace and Commerce with all the World." And their trumpeters sounded a flourish, while the leaders proclaimed to the giants terms of peace, offering to live in friendly intercourse, giving to each a share of the profits of good trade. But the giants would not listen to the terms. A few of them proposed to surrender, but their voices were drowned in the strife. Others proposed new terms of a *fixed kind*, as they called them, to the assailants; but they only received a fillip on the nose from the other giants, and were turned to the right about by those who cried, "No surrender!"

And now Mrs Jenny Getapenny, the old woman who lived in a shoe, saw how it was that there were no bones nor bodies of giants seen on the former battle-fields. Whenever a heavy onset was made from the ranks of those bearing the banner of "National Distress," the dwarfs, one, and sometimes half-a-dozen of whom attended each giant, came behind several hundreds of the men, and also their wives and children, who carried the banners of "Farming Tenantry" and "Labourers' Wages," and thrust them into the front of the battle, so as to ward of the blows which otherwise would have prostrated the giants. These dwarfs possessed enormous strength for their size. A single man of them could do anything with any number of the battalions of the "Farming Tenantry" he chose. He possessed not only all the strength of the giant to whom he belonged, in addition to his own, but there was some power of enchantment which concentrated the entire strength of all the giants, and gave it to each and all of the dwarfs, without in any way diminishing the power of each individual giant. This, the wizard explained, was sometimes called "Class legislation."

And the old woman who lived in a shoe saw in the ranks of the assailants many of the men, workers in cloth, and iron, and timber, who had at one time purchased her pigs, and chickens, and eggs, and who now, with ghastly faces and skinny arms, carried the banners of "National Distress" and "Give us this day our daily bread." It was curious to observe, though deeply to be regretted, that certain dwarfs came into the ranks of these forces in disguise, persuading them that the giants were the friends of men who prayed for daily bread and got none—that the hungry men should fight for those who prevented them from eating bread. And it was still more to be regretted that many of these men in their desperation listened to and followed the disguised dwarfs, and were in consequence more plentifully and pitilessly slaughtered than ever.

And while Mrs Jenny Getapenny was grieving to see the success of the dwarfs in disguise, who thus deceived the men with the banner which said " Give us this day our daily bread," her own dwarf, who collected her own rent for her own giant, seized her in his arms and thrust her into the hottest of the battle ; and she was knocked down by those who aimed at the giants, and as often as she struggled to rise, she was knocked down again. Some giants cried, " Hold, enough ! let us give in." But the mortgagees came behind, nine out of each ten of them, and said, " Nay, fight it out ; stand to the last." Whereupon the battle became desperate, the men of the firm battalions drove back the "farming tenantry" who covered the breaches, which seeing, the main body of the giants retreated, as before, to new positions, leaving the bearers of the flags " Farming Tenantry" and " Labourers' Wages" once more behind, to cover their retreat. But they had no peace, not for a moment. And the wizard who had unfolded the *past* and the *present* was now on the battle-ground collecting the stragglers, and giving unto the new recruits the courage and perseverance of veterans. He opened to them the volume of the *future*, and shewed a vision of the world, which had on every sea, and lake, and river of the great globe, the national flag of England, inscribed with the words " Peace and Commerce with all the World." The luxuriant fields of England were more fruitful than ever. Necessity had stirred up energy ; energy had laid hold of science; agriculture and manufactures went hand in hand, and both were flourishing. The population and the demand for food were increased prodigiously, and the giants were now living in contentment with all around them.

And when this was seen, the people called to the wizard, " When shall those things be ?" To which he replied, " When the giants and the evil dwarfs, and those who join them in the warfare, surrender." Whereupon the multitudes, as with one voice, called out, " Let us go to the battle ; let us *league* ourselves together ; let us hasten the happy day for old England !"

And foot to foot, hand to hand, man to man, they waged war on the giants. Many of the latter proposed a surrender, and some retreated altogether, which weakened their ranks; yet still they were strong. The dwarfs, like spirits of mischief, rushed with the tenantry, as pioneers with sandbags, to fill up the breaches; and busy above all, sometimes openly, sometimes covertly, was the wizard who first expounded the mystery of rent. When the giants resolved to hold out, he whispered to them to capitulate; when they proposed to capitulate, he told them they would be put to death; that, whoever might be saved, *they* would be sacrificed; and when they paid him an enormous price to stay with them, and give his friendly advice, he stole away in disguise, and visited the camp of the enemy, offering to betray the giants for the same price that they had paid for his services. Men who saw this unblushing Iscariot, and who grieved for what they saw, exclaimed, " O the disgrace and baseness of the *Times* we live in !"

But, despite such treachery, the cause of the hungry against the giants prospered. The visions of the true wizard were realized. Agriculture and manufactures were joined hand in hand. Old England became young again, and grew in wealth. The giants waxed richer, though less proud; the dwarfs used their power to protect, and not to oppress; and many of those who carried the banners of " Farming Tenantry" and " Labourers' Wages," and who fell in the fight, got up again. Even Mrs Jenny Getapenny came out of the struggle, though more than once she had almost lost her shoe.

Anti-Bread-Tax Circular.

JOURNEY FROM NAVAN TO TRIM.—VISIT TO THE BIRTHPLACE OF THE DUKE OF WELLINGTON IN 1843.

We left Navan on the 16th of August, the day after the Tara meeting. Having hired a car to Trim, distant towards the south about nine English miles, we had a pleasant journey, on one of the loveliest days with which Heaven ever blessed a fruitful earth. My object in that direction was chiefly to visit Dangan Castle, the birthplace of the late Marquis Wellesley, eldest son, and of the Duke of Wellington, sixth son, of the Earl and Countess of Mornington; also the birthplace of another distinguished individual, Feargus O'Connor, chief of our English chartists. It is not a matter of undoubted certainty, but it is extremely probable, that the Wellesleys and the O'Connors were born in the same chamber; at all events, they were born in the same house.

We had a fine rich soil, wretchedly cultivated, on each side of us, journeying from Navan to Trim. I saw some dozens of able-bodied men in Navan standing idle in the streets, seeking employment, and no one asking their price. I saw others at Trim similarly situated, and was told at both places that had it not been fine weather, and the hay-harvest just at its height, I would have seen hundreds where I only saw dozens. I spoke to several of those men, and found them eager to be engaged at eightpence and ninepence a-day. In Kilkenny I had seen several hundreds of able-bodied men seeking work at sixpence a-day; but in Meath the wages were higher, many of those employed at haymaking having tenpence. Passing between Navan and Trim, those whom I saw at work near the road, and within reach of conversation, were receiving eightpence and ninepence, few as much as tenpence. Others, again, had threepence and fourpence a-day and their diet, which diet consisted of potatoes and butter-milk twice a-day; if oatmeal was used, once; if the latter was omitted the potatoes were used thrice; but many families could only afford one meal a-day. With a superabundance of labourers at such wages, a soil, equal to Northumberland, or the richest parts of Berwickshire, was lying with its crops overpowered by the rank ripening weeds; docks overtopping the corn; thistles contending with the docks in the cornfields, and literally subduing the hay and pastures; rushes displacing both thistles and grass, and proclaiming in the face of bountiful Heaven that they had the best right to a wet soil, when that soil, though rich, was too wet to grow anything else. Potato-fields, too, struggled with foulness, and they struggled feebly; for the ill-managed farms of Meath do not produce the necessary manures to make crops profitable. Waste ridges lay at each end of the fields, and frequently a piece of the enclosure, the very richest piece, lay worthless and idle, because ten men for a-week were not employed to make a cut through some rise to admit of this being drained, which, after being drained, would have been profitable to its owner for ever.

But however applicable these remarks may be to the country between Navan and Trim, they are still more so to the country lying between Trim and Dublin. I saw farms in that district which, in luxuriant foulness, exceeded anything seen elsewhere. The reader who has travelled by railway through Staffordshire and Cheshire to Manchester must have remarked the many miles of country in which every second or third field is yet in the state it was in on the landing of the first Roman on British soil; he must have noticed the stagnant mires and rushes, and all manner of *home-grown* aquatic weeds, on the low wet ground; and the thistles, and docks, and charlock, that occupy the drier soils on the higher ground. But no part of

Staffordshire is worse cultivated than many miles of the county of Meath lying south and east of Trim; while there is this to be said against the landowners of Meath, that their soil is richer, kindlier, far more fertile than Cheshire, Lancashire, or Stafford. The very rankness of the Meath weeds proclaims the richness of the soil. But there are occasionally fields of grain seen, which, happening to be cultivated by persons who dare to cultivate well, they being protected from ejectment, shew us what the soil can produce. Yet even such tenants as these go unskilfully to work; none of them that I have seen or heard of can produce a good crop of wheat without wasting an entire season in fallowing the soil.

Everywhere in Ireland, so far as I have yet seen, the land is comparatively profitless for the want of labour. And I find, in talking with the small tenantry, particularly about Kilkenny, that they are not ignorant of this fact; but even where they have this knowledge, and have in their own families a sufficiency of labourers, they choose to let their land assume an appearance of poverty which it should never wear. They have no security of tenure, and sad experience tells them that to enrich the soil is to invite an ejectment. Many of them in that county have leases, but even a lease in Ireland is no security. A landlord has only to make a profession of a wish to exchange a Catholic tenantry for Protestants, and, under cover of such a pretence, he may commit, *and does in this very year*, 1843, *commit* the most damnable and detestable robberies. He has only to assume the profession of political protestantism, and he becomes the defended and rewarded of the leaders of that party; all his sins are covered by the cloak of his political religion through the newspapers; and if aught be said against him on the other side—if he be only called a "notorious landlord," he prosecutes; and by moving the venue to some county where the dependant may not be known, he gets there—or, if he chooses, he may have the same in his own county—a jury of political Protestant landlords—men of his own station, of his own feelings, of his own character; he may have such a jury to try his cause, and give him a verdict.

Such is the present state of domestic affairs in Ireland. The landlord can do anything. The press of the dominant party protects and adopts him; and if the newspapers of the prostrate party expose him, or take but a step thereto—breathing but a whisper—he has the law and the jury of his own class ready to shield him.

I press these facts on the notice of the public, because the soil of Ireland is capable of producing crops far beyond anything yet common to agriculture, because her people are easily induced to adopt new theories and modes of working if their confidence in the experimenter or employer be first secured, and because, at the present time, in their own country, they regard with extreme jealousy any new doctrine in agriculture, any new specimen or lesson from a new comer, seeing, as they have invariably seen, that such doctrines, and specimens, and injunctions to improve, were only preparatory to their being sacrificed and their land seized. And in a country almost devoid of trade and manufactures, to be turned out of a holding of land is a calamity falling on a family like a death stroke. There are people in England who have insanely said—and they are only worth referring to because they are not yet shut up in madhouses—that England would be as rich and powerful a country as she is were all her factories and factory towns hurled into the sea, and the sites they occupy furrowed by the plough. These people also allege another untruth, though its fallacy is not generally so apparent, namely, that a fall in the price of agricultural produce, caused by an influx of foreign grain, would throw a large portion of the soils of England, Ireland, and Scotland, out of cultivation. They assume that if a certain quality of land, at a rent of L.2 per acre, each acre producing four quarters, does nothing more for the cultivator than pay its expenses, with wheat at 55s. a quarter, it will cease to afford any rent when wheat falls to 45s. a quarter; and they add, that when wheat falls below that, say to 40s., such land will go out of cultivation altogether.

Now, at first sight, this proposition seems plausible; but practically it is the reverse of true; and, startling as such a declaration may be to mathematical theorists writing pamphlets and leading articles, and making legislative speeches in London, or to well-meaning noblemen and other landowners, too rich or too busy with trifles to look after their own affairs and study their own interests, it is easily, though it cannot be briefly, substantiated. In this article I would be departing too far from my subject—a visit to Dangan Castle—were I to enter closely upon it. I will not, therefore, repeat the arguments and facts hitherto adduced in "*Notes from the Farming Districts*" of England, nor enter upon the still stronger facts tending to the same point which I see in Ireland; these I promise to use on an early occasion, when the proposition here asserted, in contradiction to the theorists, shall be fully proved. Meantime I give them the following truths to ponder over; they are not less at variance with the assumed facts of mathematical politics than the other proposition, and they do not require arguments and proof; they are visible to the eye.

Any one travelling through the rural districts of England, Scotland, and Ireland, as I have done, and am now doing, may see the facts to be as I state them; indeed the traveller cannot shut his eyes upon them, for they press upon the sight so unceasingly, stare him in the face so palpably, that he has no choice but to see and believe them. These facts are—

1. That wherever the supply of labour is most plentiful and cheap (and it is always cheapest where most plentiful) the land is worst cultivated.

2. Wherever the land is naturally richest it is worst cultivated and least profitable to the cultivators.

3. Wherever the expense of cultivation is greatest the comfort of the working people, the profit of the farmer, and the rent of the landowner are highest.

These truths will puzzle the rule-of-three writers as much as the denial of their other assertion; but they must see the world as the world is, before they presume to say it moves like clock-work. As seen through our agriculture, the world is a pig driven to market; it gets there by turning its head the other way, or it is like a crab, moving side-ways or back-ways, any way but the way right a-head.

The scenic appearance of the country I have been speaking of, the district of Trim, in Meath, where the soil is so rich, the agriculture so poor, the people so plentiful, wages so low, and so few labourers employed at wages—the scenic appearance of this district is soft, luxurious, and seductive. The country, on a far stretch of the eye, seems level, but it is gently diversified by undulations. The river Boyne winds through the rich green meadows, and the hedge-rows and dotted woods add to the beauty, until variety itself forms a broad unchanging sameness.

The farms are from twenty up to fifty acres; but more of them vary from fifty up to two hundred acres. I saw a fifty acre farm, held by a gentleman tenant, who did not work himself. He kept only two labourers in constant employment, and being in constant work at ninepence a-day—no other perquisites —they were considered well paid by the people who worked in the neighbourhood for less. There was not a good fence on the farm, the land was wet, foul, and most unsightly to an agricultural eye.

The cottages of the poor are poor indeed. They are mostly clay huts, thatched with straw. Some of them are very tidy, whitewashed outside, and, besides having good windows and doors, are ornamentally thatched and decorated. But for one of these there are ten that are neither pleasing outside nor comfortable within. In respect of darkness and dampness, being without windows, having clay floors, and being small and ricketty, they resemble what the dwellings of the farm labourers used to be in Berwickshire, and what on many estates in Northumberland, near Berwick, they are to this day. Coming out of Navan, on the Trim road, I passed between two long rows of miserable hovels; one of the rows so very long and so very miserable, that I at last stopped the car, and went into some of them to see the interior and talk with the people who, from strange choice or unfortunate doom, inhabited them. One of them was four paces wide and five long. I could touch the thatch with my hands. There was no light but what came in by the low doorway. A partition wall of clay, four feet high, parted off an apartment for a pig and a bed occupied by four children. The father and mother and two more children slept in the front apartment. There was no fixed bed; whatever the bed was, it was stowed away during the day. Some articles of crockery were arranged, not without regard to show, on shelves, and a couple of iron pots, a table, a wash-tub, two or three seats, some of which were large stones, completed all the furniture I saw. The father of the family was at work to a farmer; his wages were ninepence a-day. Last year he got tenpence, but this year he had, like others, been reduced. The mother complained of headache, and said her health had been bad for years. All the children had been in fever, and fever was never out of the row of houses. They were the property of the Rev. Mr Hamilton, the Protestant clergyman. The rent paid for that one now described was eightpence a-week. Since wages had been reduced, they tried to get house rent reduced, but had not succeeded. Some of the other huts were larger—as large as eight paces by five; but all were equally dark, dirty, and ill furnished. The rents were as high as a shilling a-week; the average being tenpence. The tenants were not suffered to run into arrear; the custom being, both in Navan and in Trim, to eject, by warrant of the magistrate, as soon as a fortnight's rent becomes due and is not paid. This Rev. Mr Hamilton is said to be rich—at least, he holds a good living, he has also landed property, which partakes of the management of other land in those parts.

Having visited some of the remarkable ruins around Trim, chief of which is a vast pile called John's Castle, we hired a car, and at six o'clock in the evening drove off to Dangan Castle, four miles south, or south-east. Arrived at the margin of the domain, we entered a narrow avenue by an iron gate, which was opened by a woman whose house was one of two or three low thatched huts. There were no trees shading the

avenue, but a high thorn hedge, bushy, wild, and lofty, skirted
it on either side.   When we had proceeded three or four hundred yards, the park, that had once been finely wooded, but
which, like a bald head, with a tree here and two or three
there, and a few more, stunted and denuded of their ornamental branches, beyond, this park, with its fine valleys and
finer eminences, once so magnificently wooded, now so shabbily
bare, opened upon our view.   The road went towards the left
and again wheeled to the right.   On the brow of a gentle
slope stood the castle, like a huge ill-shaped barn—grey, tree-
less, shelterless, and in most part roofless.   Broken cars, and
waggons, and ploughs that were idle, because it was summer,
and harrows idle as the ploughs, lay strewed about, and told
of people who were as idle as any of them, else they would
have had them put tidily out of the way.   Cows were lowing
in rear of the house to be milked, and calves were clamorous
for their allowance of what the cows were to give.   The gates
that crossed the road, at various places, keeping vagrant pigs
and cattle asunder, were kept to their posts by old ropes and
stones, which had to be rolled away ere they could be opened,
and rolled back again ere the pigs could be restrained from
accompanying the visitors to the front of the castle ; and even
then, a sharp admonition over the snout was requisite to make
them remember they were pigs.   The dogs, which were ready
to bite them on the ears, or to bark at the refractory cows
and calves, or at strangers like us, until told to be quiet, were
lying on the dunghills that lay on the roadside ; and those
who bade them be quiet were leaning idly on the hay waggon
or the stone wall, doing nothing more than trying to make us
think they were not looking at us.

On being spoken to, one came and opened a gate to allow
us entrance to the front of the castle, and another went the
back way to carry our compliments to the inmates and our
request to be admitted to the interior.   The front shewed us
the windows partly built up and the roof wholly carried away.
It may have been a pleasant house, it occupies a fine situation,
and is surrounded by ground which, if it has not been, might
be made, one of the finest pleasure parks in the world ; but at
all times the house must have been plain.   A red-painted
door, made to fit its place by a great portion of the doorway
being built up to fit it, being opened to us from the inside, we
entered and found the main portion of the building entirely
cleared of its partitions and party walls.   It was all open
above ; and what had once been the dining-room, parlour,
and library floors, was now a flower garden.   During the
time the house was occupied by the O'Connor family, who
rented it from the Marquis Wellesley, it was burned, save in

the wing towards the rear, where the present inhabitants now live. To this wing we proceeded; and the young lady who kindly led the way, on taking us to what is now a comfortably furnished parlour, told us that the common belief was, that in this room the Duke of Wellington and the other members of the Mornington family were born. There was a spacious bow window looking out upon the garden and farm-yard, which occupied ground sloping from this to a streamlet below, distant 100 or 200 yards. Inside the room was a large circular recess, now shelved round, the shelves filled with articles of ornament and use—glass, china, and such like. This recess is quite large enough to have held a large bed; and, as we were told, did hold the family couch of the Countess of Mornington, and subsequently that of the mother of Feargus O'Connor.

When about to leave Trim on this visit, I put a few questions to an old gentleman who stood by the doorway of the hotel, such as, "How far to Dangan Castle?" "Who lives there now?" and so on. He told me that he was a tailor, still carried on business in Trim, and had made clothes for the young Wellesleys when boys. He made clothes for the Hon. Arthur Wellesley, now Duke of Wellington, when a boy. He also did work for him when he was the Hon. Captain Wellesley, and came to Trim on the recruiting service. He remembered, "as distinctly as if it had been but yesterday," when the corporation of Trim elected this young officer to be one of their members in the Irish Parliament, when it was alleged that he had not attained his majority. On that occasion the nurse who attended at his birth was brought into the Court House at Trim, and he remembered seeing her, "as plainly as if it happened but yesterday," put on the witness's table and sworn, and she proved that that very day one-and-twenty years she saw the Hon. Arthur Wellesley born at Dangan Castle.

I found this venerable tradesman intelligent and instructive. His name is Sherlock. He and his brother still conduct a respectable business in Trim.

On leaving Dangan Castle we drove through the park, and returned by a road skirting its exterior. The sun had now gone down, and the marshy hollows wore a thin covering of white fog; which, as we came along, rose gradually thicker, until it seemed to be a sheet which the fields, tired with the heat and labour of the day, had drawn around them on going to bed. Where there was a height to which the fog had not reached, we had only to suppose that the world had gone to bed without a nightcap, and that this was its bare head.

NOTES FROM YORKSHIRE IN 1842.

"Jolly good fellows the Yorkshire farmers; always ready with open door, open countenance, open hand, and open heart. Fact! They are, indeed, the best of fellows. You have been over a great part of England—so have I; but I doubt if ever you saw such honest, industrious, hospitable, well-doing, well-deserving men as the farmers of this district, all the way down the Tees, between this and Northallerton. I never did. Fact! Never saw a better set of fellows. We shall pay some of them a visit to-morrow."

So spoke a gentleman connected with public business in the north of Yorkshire and south of Durham, about the time that Lord John Russell's eight-shilling motion first startled the country last year, 1841. He so spoke to me; and I replied that I needed no further proofs of the hospitality of the district; all I had witnessed then and heard of previously convinced me that the people were a generous people; that, in fact, hospitality to strangers was characteristic of all English farmers in all parts of England.

"But," continued I, "that circumstance would prevent me from accompanying you to their houses. A day, being all I have to spare, would be consumed in a visit to one farm, if I may judge from what I have already experienced and from what you tell me."

"No," replied my friend, "we should merely call at one for a few minutes, and be mounted and off again to another, so that you might see the country. It is a splendid country."

"Why not go to-day?" said I.

"I cannot to-day; cannot, indeed," was the reply.

There was some mystery in this reply. It had been intended to go the circuit proposed on this very day; and now, without any reason being adduced, my friend put the journey off, so far as I was concerned, until next day. Having accompanied him a couple of miles or so, and walked round a farmyard while he transacted some business with the farmer, he introduced me to the latter and departed, fixing the time of the grand tour for the day ensuing. I had heard of this farmer, and indeed had entertained a strong desire to see him, inasmuch as he was the reputed original of Boz's John Browdie, in "Nicholas Nickleby." Whether Mr Dickens copied this gentleman rustic, or ever saw him to copy, I cannot tell. But at no great distance the locality of Squeers, the Yorkshire schoolmaster was pointed out; and several other persons and circumstances depicted in the truthful fiction of Nickleby

13

which nobody could mistake. I had expected to see a hearty, jolly, well-fed, well-to-do farmer, when I heard of his being *the* John Browdie, and I was not disappointed. But I saw him under great disadvantages; John (for such I shall call him, though that is not his name) was in low spirits. He had heard bad news; bad news from London; so very bad, that, after many preliminary signs of alarm and vexation, he said— "Aw dunnot knaw what to think on't. Aw's never be yable to haud on ageanst it."

Having a fear that some family affliction had befallen the good man, and that my presence could only be painful, and, moreover, having particular business to attend to at the neighbouring post-office, three or four miles distant, I offered my early farewell. But John said he would be glad to accompany me. He would be glad, he said, to tell me anything I wanted to know, shew me anything I wanted to see, direct me in any way I wished to proceed, if I would just tell him downrightly what my candid opinion was " aboot fwok i' Lunnon."

" There are such multitudes in London," said I, as we walked along, " such varieties of people, varieties of interests, varieties of means by which interests are pursued, such worlds within worlds in London, that to tell of the people who live there is impossible. In fact there are few regions on the face of this great globe so seldom and inefficiently explored as London."

" There's a most terrible din on street, Aw knaw," responded John. " Aw've been at Lunnon. But it beant fwok on streets Aw's axin aboot. Aw want to knaw aboot Parliament fwok."

" Oh! the Parliament. I suppose you have heard about the proposed alteration of the import duties; the lowering of the duties for the purpose of making sugar, and timber, and corn more plentiful?"

" Aw dunnot knaw nowt aboot sugar and timber, and nowt as to coorn, seavin' this, 'at Squire's sent a peaper doon fra Lunnon with orders 'at we bud write oor neames to't, if we wouldn't be every yan o' us ootreeght ruined."

" A petition against the alteration of the corn-laws, I suppose?"

" Aw dunnot knaw as to that; bud Aw've heerd a bonny teale aboot what some o' gertfolk at Lunnon 'at dunnot knaw nowt aboot what they dea are scayin they *will* dea. Squire knaws all aboot it, an's sent peapers to steward; an' steward's gooin' gettin' oor neames, an' scays we mud as weel droon oorsens i' Tees as not pud oor neames doon."

"Drown yourself in the Tees! Surely not. You must have heard a wrong account of the danger you are in, it cannot be so bad as you imagine. What did the paper say, the paper you signed?"

"Aw dunnot knaw; but oor neames wor wanted to't. Squire sent it frae Lunnon, an' steward brooght it when thoo came, an' told me such a teale aboot coorn not needin' to be sown no more, that Aw scarcely knaw what gertfolk can be dean, that Aw dunnot."

It was not difficult to perceive, now, that my friend had other business to do with the farmers, over whose farms we had proposed to ride a circuit of ten miles, than that which a stranger could be a convenient witness to. I could see clearly enough that he had touched John Browdie on the quick; for John had no other idea, no other expectation from an alteration of the corn-laws, than absolute ruin. I spoke of the sugar and timber duties, which were a part of the same question at that time; but he had heard nothing of them. He admitted, however, that better timber and cheaper sugar would be great benefits; and so would cheaper bread, he ultimately admitted, *were it possible to get it.* I saw ample evidence around us to prove the possibility of getting cheaper bread.

There was within view the beautiful woods surrounding Rokeby Hall, the seat of Squire Morritt. Also the woods, and water, and rocks that alternately soften and embolden the scene in which the castle of the ancient Cliffords is hidden. Also the continuation of the same woods, and water, and rocks, which shelter and beautify, and give magnificence to the lordly seat of Archdeacon Headlem. Also the woods and preserves that shelter the pleasant retreat of Squire Craddock. Further off, and on higher ground, the woods and Hall of Barningham. Further still, in another direction, the princely domain of Raby Castle, the seat of the Clevelands. At a nearer distance, the towers of Barnard Castle, which have withstood the shock of many a siege; which are the remnants of feudal times, when lords held rule within and serfs did homage without; which now have no lords within, save the snail and the worm, and no serfs without, save creatures more miserable than they, the *unemployed*, unfed, ragged, barefooted carpet-weavers, crawling on the ledges of the rocks, and beneath the ancient walls, seeking from the dark surges of the Tees what the fair fields of the broad estates deny them; namely, *food.* However, to look at the hungry dyers and weavers, either fishing in the river or idling on the streets, or murmuring at hard times in their unfurnished houses, was not our object.

The situation of the town of Barnard Castle is perhaps too low to be seen from the spot on which I stood previous to this digression ; and the condition of its inhabitants is most certainly lower than I had intended to go in relating my conversations with the farmers. I had only intended to take a glance at the parks, and halls, and castles, and name a few of the landlords, which having done, we shall revert to John Browdie, and with this intermediate observation, that I need neither say whose tenant he is nor adhere to the very letter of his dialect.

"Those fields through which we have passed," said I, "and this now on our left hand are wet—they want draining. Those tufts of rushes, and that bent and sour grass, prove the soil to be wet. How much of the field is lost in this way do you think ?"

"Why," he replied, "you see the whole field is the same : in fact, the soil hereabouts has a tendency to run that way when it lies long in grass."

"Why let it lie long in grass ?" I asked. "Why not cultivate it ? And that immense meadow beneath, entirely overgrown with rushes, that must be excellent soil if drained and limed. And this next field, and the one beyond, seem much the same. Why not plough, and sow, and reap, and increase the supply of corn ?"

"Because that would require me to have more horses, and ploughs, and men, and I do not find the corn crops so beneficial as to induce me to plough oftener than I do ; at any rate, the place *pays* as it is."

"How much of the farm may there be in grass ?"

"Better than half ; or somewhere thereabout."

"And of this field fully one-third is rushes and foul grass."

"Yes, I should say there is ; but in winter time, in frosty weather, we find our cattle pick up some of that roughness, it is not all loss as you seem to think."

"But good straw, and hay, and turnips would be better for the cattle than anything they can get here ?"

"Very true ; but these are not grown without expense."

"No, not without expense ; but why not pay the expense —the expense of reclaiming this very field, for instance ?"

"*And who might reap the benefit ?*" asked John Browdie.

Thus the subject came to a point—the main point—at once. We were now led to talk of leases and a security for the repayment of the expense of improving land such as that around us. Having taken particular notice of the rocks which formed the barriers and beds of the Tees, the Greta, and other rivers and streams in that district, I was well assured that limestone was to be had in any quantity. I found, however, that no advantage was taken of its abundant presence. Instead of public limeworks issuing their fructifying agency to the soil, and drawing in wealth to some enterprising practical chemist, aye, a princely income, as I know some lime-burners to have reaped, (the late Earl of Elgin for instance,) there were at six or seven miles' distance a few wretched pits, and these only half in use. I stood aghast when I saw those miserable contrivances for burning lime, and asked the workmen if they had never seen a proper lime-kiln, at the same time describing one; but they knew of no other mode of burning lime than the primitive method they used. I cannot here enter on a description of proper lime-burning—for of itself it is a large subject; but these pits, with an inexhaustible supply of rock, were within half-a-mile of the great London-road, overlooking the great *coal* county of Durham; and the rock was easy of access, with no difficulty as regarded the clearance from water. All which conveniences I have known purchased at the price of L.12,000, with a continuance of machinery to continue those conveniences, which were here natural or ready-made.

Here, then, was one of the best agencies of fertilization utterly neglected; for John Browdie and his neighbours did not even patronize these works, easy as they were of access, the cause of which neglect was the want of security in their farms. At an average John's farm was worth twelve shillings an acre as it then stood—that was his rent—and I have not the slightest diffidence in comparing the soil to that of farms which I know (say portions of the Marchmont estate, belonging to the member for Berwickshire) situate at a distance of from twenty to thirty miles from lime, and which pay *two pounds an acre*, producing a proportionate quantity of grain over that of John Browdie. Has the nation, then, no right to demand that the soil of England shall be better cultivated?

As that part of Yorkshire and adjoining border of Durham which I have been speaking of is in such want of lime properly applied, and as lime might be so easily obtained, I proceed to give a few proofs of the great changes produced by this article in some parts of the kingdom where it has been judiciously used :—" When lime, whether freshly burned or slaked, is mixed with any moist, fibrous, vegetable matter, there is a strong action between the lime and the vegetable matter, and they form a kind of compost together, of which a part is usually soluble in water. By this kind of. operation, lime renders matter which was before comparatively inert nutritive."—*Sir H. Davy.*

" The application of lime occasionally has effected a complete change in the husbandry of Scotland. Since the first introduction of turnips and the sown grasses, the condition of the live stock has been greatly improved ; and, from applying lime in the cultivation of sheep, dairy, and tillage husbandry, which require to be administered to the above plants, an immense quantity of waste and hitherto unproductive land has been brought into active fertility."—*Jackson's Prize Essays.*

" By the aid of lime, immense tracts of land have been brought into cultivation in the southern parts of Scotland. Lime in unison with turnip husbandry has rendered fertile eminences on the banks of the Tweed which were formerly inaccessible to the plough."—*Highland Society's Reports.*

It is necessary, however, to have some chemical knowledge of the soil (an easy matter to acquire) to know when lime should be applied by itself or in connection with other materials. If the soil is not fibrous, like John Browdie's, the lime would require to be prepared with vegetable matter.

Latterly, lime has been applied with astonishing success to such rough fields as that of John Browdie without being ploughed. Accident prevented a farmer from ploughing a moorland field which he had spread lime on, and to his astonishment the following year brought a beautiful crop of white clover and sweet grasses, instead of heath, bent, rushes, and coarse grass. When this became known, other farmers tried the appliance—a " top-dressing," it is now called; and here are a few of their experiments, with their results:—" Mr Purdie's sheep-farm in Tweeddale was rented at two shillings an acre ; was moorish land, with rough bent and heath ; got a top-dressing of lime, and produced natural white clover and sweet grasses ; pays now a rent of L.1 an acre, and has done so for some years with a profit. The expense, including cartage, was L.5 per acre." " At Whim, fourteen miles south of Edinburgh, the top-dressing was applied at the rate of fifty bolls an acre," (four Winchester bushels is a boll.) " At the period of our inspection, May 1835, the grass was excellent, feeding a fine flock of sheep, and neither heath nor bent could be discovered, although the field was covered with these plants in its original state. The expense was about L.3 : 15s. per acre in dressing. The extent of drainage could not be ascertained. The field was enclosed and surrounded with plantations, which must have long since paid themselves, leaving the present stock of timber as profit; and it cannot be rating the whole reclamation too low at L.6 or L.7 per acre, and the ground is at present rented at L.2 per acre. There are few situations in Scotland or in England, where improvements could be undertaken with less prospect of success than at Whim."—*Jackson*.

"In the parish of Muirkirk, Admiral Stewart limed thirty acres of moss-land all covered with heath, and which per year was let for L.5 ; but, in a few years after the application, it rose to L.30 per annum."—*Farmer's Magazine*.

"Mr Maclean of Mark gives a statement of the top-dressing of his moorish soil. The original worth of the land he estimates at five shillings per acre, which, at twenty-five years' purchase, is L.6 : 5s. ; six bushels of lime at one shilling and sevenpence, carriage, &c., L.5 : 15s., making in all L.12. In two years it will be worth L.1 per acre at the most moderate calculation, and some of it is even worth L.1 : 10s. This, at twenty-five years' purchase, is L.25, giving a profit L.13 per acre."—*General Report of Scotland*.

These are a few instances of what lime will do on the *very worst of soils and worst of situations*. It renders land that would be absolutely worthless, if in the hands of a tenant without a lease, more profitable than the badly cultivated, yet naturally good, land of the district of Teesdale. In some grass fields, near the lime pits, I observed the moss plant in such abundance that grass was quite subdued by it.

"Who farms those fields?" asked I of a carpenter who accompanied me from the village of Bolderon to shew the lime pits.

"They belong," said he, "to a butter-merchant of Islington, near London. He got them some years ago, intending to make them assist his London business, but they have been a loss, and he is tired of them."

"And no wonder that he should," I replied ; "but if he does business in the butter and pork line in Islington, as you say, there is some excuse for him in not attending to a farm at 250 miles distance. Yet how easily might that pernicious moss be eradicated and the sweetest of grasses produced in its place, by an application of hot lime, by those means which surround the very fields requiring their agency."

"We have an opinion here," observed the carpenter, "that lime does not work the good effects near to where it is produced as it does at a distance."

"That depends entirely," I replied, "on how the lime is applied. If spread hot and powdery on this moss it would destroy everything for a season ; but the most luxuriant natural clover would rise the following year. If this was ploughed and lime applied, the effects might be otherwise; but a slight knowledge of practical chemistry would enable the farmer to know if those ingredients were in the soil which would act prejudicially with lime; and if they were, or rather, I should say, if those ingredients were not present which would act beneficially, the effect could be controlled by mingling the lime with vegetable matter. But the presumption is, that nothing is required save the lime itself; the abundance of that moss pleads strongly for lime."

To this my companion replied, as indeed did all others in those parts, that he never heard of such a thing as an application of lime producing an entire change of plants, without any other aid. It seemed strange, he said, that hot lime, applied to the surface of mossy or heathy lands should produce white clover. And so it is strange, all nature's works are strange, but it is true nevertheless.

But as it is the good land of England that more especially requires improvement, and as these instances of improvement, now adduced, refer chiefly to the worst of lands, I shall at another time take other instances in other situations. Meantime the following facts seem to be supported by the foregoing :—

1. That landlords, to maintain a political control over their tenants, sacrifice a large pecuniary interest.

2. That they do so, and the tenant submits thereto, through ignorance of what might enrich both.

3. That leases would give rise to energy, energy would improve the soil, and the improvement of the soil would add to the wealth of landowners, cultivators, and consumers.

4. That Teesdale, like Lancashire, Buckingham, Kent, and other districts described in former letters, is badly cultivated, and that fewer people are employed than might be.

5. That the means of improvement exist there as everywhere else, and only need to be taken advantage of in union with capital, skill, and industry, *to give us more bread at a less price.**

---

* About two years after the publication of this letter, a landowner in Teesdale wrote to me saying that he had acted on its suggestions with great success in his first efforts, and expected to do much more. I have not heard from him since.

TEESDALE.

"I should be sorry, gentlemen," I observed, in the conversation which still continued in the King's Arms, Barnard Castle, between A., the Tory farmer, B., the Tory farmer and innkeeper, C. the Whig farmer and cattle-dealer, John Browdie, and myself; "I should be sorry, gentlemen, to let you remain in the belief that I boast of the improved agriculture of Scotland, because I have been a ploughman on the other side of the Tweed. I admit at once that the Scottish farmers borrowed their first improvements from England. Previous to 1759 there was not an attempt made in Scotland towards the cultivation which now exists; and though Mr Dawson of Frogden, Roxburghshire, returned from Norfolk, and commenced operations in the Norfolk style in that year, it was not until many years after that his system took root. He had first a difficulty in getting Scotchmen, so wedded were they to old customs, to learn to plough the land as he sought to teach them. Ultimately ploughmen bred on his farm got situations elsewhere, at higher wages, and in preference to all others, still his system of ploughing, cropping, and manuring was not followed; nothing would excite the emulation of his neighbours but the fact of his becoming rich. They at last opened their eyes, and saw that he was rich; and what example, and reason, and argument had failed to do, *avarice* accomplished. Mr Dawson had become rich, while his neighbours, who spoke of his 'maggots,' and 'whims,' and 'new-fangled notions,' remained poor. They had no love for the 'new-fangled notions,' they had no ear for the arguments with which he defended them; but they had a desire for the wealth; and they arose and opened their eyes, and put on their strength, and became competitors in the race of improvements, until (without any original design) they completely changed the face of their once sterile country.

"If it is any comfort to those of the English farmers who have been standing still while the Scotch have been advancing, I will at once admit the meanness from which the latter took their start. A more wretched population, as regards industry and domestic comforts, than the Scotch of eighty years ago, is, perhaps, not now met with in the civilized world. But the system, which has so completely changed the face of a country and the condition of a people, is only the more remarkable, and worthy of being imitated. I am at this moment in possession of some documents from which I shall read you extracts. The 'New Statistical Account of Scotland,' drawn up by the clergyman of each parish, speaks thus :—

"Parish of Melrose, Roxburghshire.—'The displacing of the old small tenants was at first viewed with deep regret, but the introduction of a better and more spirited style of agriculture, which immediately followed the rapid improvement of the country, which in a limited period *has raised the rental* (mark this, and mark it well) *of this parish from* L.4000 *a-year to nearly* L.20,000 ! besides, the improved condition of the agricultural labourers seems to shew that it was a change for the better.'

"Parish of Moffat, Dumfriesshire.—'In the cultivation of the arable soils a very great improvement has been made ; and by removing obstructions, duly manuring and working the lands, observing a proper improved rotation, and keeping down or destroying noxious weeds—and further, by cultivating the most valuable crops—it is not too much to say that, within forty years, the returns of the arable soils have become far better, as well as more abundant. *Let any one now look into the cottages, and he will find them nearly, or fully, as comfortable as the farm houses were forty years ago ; and let him compare the dress of the cottagers and their mode of living with that of the farmers at the above distance of time, and he will find that at present they are not greatly inferior !*'

"Such, gentlemen, is the change in Scotland only since the beginning of the present century ; but you Teesdale farmers, save in improving the breed of your stock, which in itself is meritorious, so far as it goes, have been, comparatively speaking, standing still.　Here is another extract, which, from my personal knowledge, I know to be applicable to many parts of Scotland ; it is from the

"Parish of Udney, Aberdeenshire.—'There is an emulation in most cases between the proprietor and his tenants, whether the former shall be the more liberal or the latter the more industrious.　The result has been, that the rental of the parish, forty years ago little more than about L.2000, is now above L.7000, and the farmer's capital has increased more in proportion.　At the time of the former statistical account (1794) a great proportion of the parish was covered with broom, whins, (furze,) and bulrushes.　These are now extirpated, and the eye meets with nothing but cultivated and neatly enclosed fields.'　Here also is the

"Parish of Jedburgh.—'Since the period when the last statistical account was written, the state of the parish has been much improved.　Farms which were entirely pastoral, now bear luxuriant crops, the fields have been neatly enclosed with hedges, waste ground has been planted, the style of dwelling-houses is now vastly superior, the means of communication have been greatly enlarged, the population has been nearly doubled, and all classes seem to enjoy a large share of the comforts of civilized society.' To this may be added, (from the *Encyclopædia Britannica*,) 'The progress of a correct system of agriculture is generally allowed to have been more rapid in Scotland than in England ; the effects, at least, have been more conspicuous. Not only the rents paid in Scotland, but the actual produce per acre, *and, still more, the disposable produce*, seem to be greater than in England, wherever the comparison is made with land of similar quality, and with an allowance for the difference in climate and markets.' To these I shall make one other extract, and only one. It is from the excellent 'Treatise on Agriculture,' by Mr James Jackson, (published by Messrs Chambers, Edinburgh.) Within the last ten or fifteen years the improvements in Scottish husbandry have been conducted on a most extensive scale. Steam power has been introduced in many districts to move thrashing machinery, *and a stack of grain* (mark this, you who have no thrashing-mills of any kind) *may at any time be dressed and bagged for market in a few hours, and at an inconsiderable expense.* The use of the subsoil plough, by which fresh materials are constantly thrown into the mould available for vegetation, is another important improvement ; but both of these sink into insignificance when compared with the system of thorough draining by means of hollow tiles, which for the last ten years has been extending over the country, and everywhere immensely increasing the productiveness of the soil. The consequence of all these agricultural improvements, in combination with the progress of commercial wealth, is, that the Scotland of the present day is a very different thing from the Scotland of sixty or seventy years ago, when its poor and wretched condition excited the sarcasms of Churchill and Johnson.'

" Now, Mr John Browdie, those fields of yours, so much in want of draining, require the following outlay :—For an acre, your drains, two feet deep and fifteen feet apart, will cost L.7 : 7 : 9 ; eighteen feet apart, L.6 : 3 : 1¾ ; twenty-four feet apart, L.4 : 12 : 4 ; thirty feet apart, L.3 : 3 : 10. If three feet deep, and fifteen feet apart, they will cost L.9 : 8 : 0½. The other distances of eighteen, twenty-four, and thirty feet apart, being respectively L.7 : 16 : 8, L.5 : 17 : 6, and L.4 : 13 : 11¾. These sums include all expenses ; the cutting of the two feet drains being threepence per rood of six lineal yards ; and of the three feet drains, fivepence halfpenny. But it is necessary to remark that the acre thus calculated is a Scotch acre, and the wages Scotch wages. You would, therefore, accomplish it somewhat cheaper than at these sums, as four Scotch acres make five English, and your wages to work-people are not one-fifth more than those paid in Scotland. Sir James Graham, a spirited agriculturist, made an experiment on a field of eight acres of the wettest and poorest land on his Cumberland estate. It was in pasture of the coarsest description, (not worse, however, than some of yours, Mr John Browdie, although yours is naturally much better land,) overrun with rushes and other aquatic plants, and was rented at *four shillings and sixpence an acre*. The field was drained and ploughed by the subsoil plough (of which I have not yet spoken) and manured. Lime was not by any means attainable there as in Teesdale, and therefore common manure was used. The crop planted was potatoes, which that year turned out a failure all over Cumberland, but which were on this field above an average crop, yielding twelve tons per acre."

After adducing several more instances of profits reaped from draining by those who were either owners of the soil or leaseholders, I mentioned the virtues of saltpetre and nitrate of soda, as ascertained by several farmers, particularly by a gentleman in Kent, who communicated the astonishing result to the *Farmer's Magazine*. But John Browdie would not hear of such nonsense, as he termed it.

" Yan mud as weel believe 'at man o' muin meade coorn grow, as soda an' saltpetre. Nay, nay," said he, " thawt wunnot dea ; thawts beant nea better nor bean dust ; nonsense."

" And yet," said I, " bone dust has proved a powerful agent of fertilization."

Our conversation was now diverted to " ships, colonies, and commerce," by C., the free-trader, in course of which " steam-boats and railways" were spoken of.

" I'll tell you what it is," said B. the farmer and innkeeper, " if you would search the history of inventions through and through, you would find no two to equal in mischief steam-boats and railways. They've ruined parts of this country already, and they'll ruin it more, and that will be seen."

" Why did you, as a posting innkeeper, not protect yourself as the landlords do by the corn-laws ?" asked C.

" How could I ?" demanded the innkeeper.

" How could you ?" retorted C., " why, by passing a law forbidding the construction of steam-engines and the building of steamboats, and by refusing assent to all railway bills."

" But," objected the other, " how was that to be done ?"

" How was it to be done ?" said C. " By returning a majority of innkeepers as members of Parliament, to be sure."

" But," urged the other, " we were not powerful enough."

" No," said C., " you were not ; but you are monopolist enough to have done it if you could ; to have prohibited the making of all engines and railways, if you had had the power. And you would have done so, forgetting that our fathers set up the chaises, and mails, and turnpike gates, and posting-houses, to the deprivation of our grandfathers, who travelled with packhorses on bridle-roads, and were content with a journey to London which occupied a fortnight. There is a majority of landowners in Parliament, and hence the shackles on ships, manufactures, and commerce. Had there been a majority of post-boys or innkeepers, we would have had no railways nor steamboats ; and had our grandfathers returned a majority of packhorse carriers, there would have been no stage-coaches nor posting for you to lose ? Therefore, according to your own admission, the strongest protect themselves, and to enable them we are called on by the estate agents to sign petitions. As an innkeeper they left you to perish, but as a farmer they send intimation to you from London by express to sign petitions, else you will be ruined."

Such were the home-thrusts of C., the cattle-dealer, to which John Browdie responded,

" Ods maakins ! an they'd let us aleane we'd dea weel eneaff."

" With your rushes, and sour grass, and foul water?" said the cattle-dealer.

" Friend," responded John, " look at yersen ; look at yawm, afoore ye coom t' maw faults."

" And so I do," said the cattle-dealer ; " but I cannot improve land without a lease any more than you can ; and there is this difference between us—you would let things remain as they are, I would have a change for the better."

At this moment John Browdie heard some sound, or smelt some flavour, which in a moment unpoliticalized him. He started to his feet, and exclaimed,

" Dang politics ! Dang parliamenters ! Let's oop steairs an' topple into pleaces for guid dinner !"

HOW TO GET MORE BREAD AT A LOWER PRICE, WITH PRESENT RENTS TO THE LANDLORDS.

March 9, 1842.

MY LORD STANLEY,—Your duties as Colonial Secretary; your recent announcement of a new measure to regulate the sale of land in the colonies; your able exposition of the evils arising from the present system of land sales; the insecurity which the frequent changes in land sales have produced; the stoppage of improvements which insecurity has produced; the necessity for a new law whereon to found security ere the colonies can improve as your Lordship desires to see them improved; these circumstances, united to my recollection of the insecurity, waste land, and unmoving condition of your own tenantry in Lancashire, embolden me to address you, and crave the advantage of your great talents and high position to the better cultivation of England; to the production of *more bread at a lower price, with present rents to the landlords.* Surely there can be no objection to this plea? There is no objection to it, I believe, so long as it exists in mere words; but the moment we require a practical compliance, it is objected to. How many advantages the landlords may count on from the present tenant-at-will system beyond the political subjugation of the farmers, I know not; but I never heard one of the advantages named in any conversation, even with those who advocate the letting of old things alone; while on every hand, in every county of England, the disadvantages stand before the eye with a melancholy reality. There is no advantage gained politically, because tenants, even with twenty years' leases, will always have a tendency to coincide with their landlords. The Conservatives returned for such counties as Berwick and Haddington, where the great majority of the voters are farmers holding leases from Conservative landlords, prove this. If a farmer has a fair bargain—and it is always a landlord's interest to give him a fair bargain—he will have no desire to leave the farm when his lease expires. He will have a desire quite the reverse; because the interests and the personal associations of himself and family with the neighbourhood they have so long lived in, will always remind him that he must not stand in hostility to his landlord. On this point, therefore, you have no plea of advantage. But I do not advocate the granting of leases with any idea of the farmers becoming politically independent. The subject is a more important one than that of party strife; it is a national question, and points to benefits for all, with injury to none.

Presuming then, nay, claiming of your Lordship to admit that you have no advantages from the present system which lease-giving would not secure to you, I shall shew you a few of the many disadvantages accruing to all, to corn growers and corn eaters; and in doing so, shall take the liberty of conducting your Lordship to those vast estates which belong to your family.

We shall not at present go to Knowsley. We shall first go to that broad tract of land comprising the townships of Pilkington and Bury. As we emerge from smoky Manchester, we get a glimpse of the estates of Lord Wilton and others, but I must be understood to include all the landlords of your county, whether Whigs or Tories, or, like Trafford of Trafford, moving with five hundred tenantry in an entire lump from one party to the other, and *vice versa*, different at each election. There is no exception to be made in favour of a single landlord, and therefore they need not be named. Even the great mill-owners who have bought estates, and who might be supposed to have acquired some practical experience of the productive qualities of *capital, security, and energy*, sit down on them, too happy at having arrived at the rank of landowners to advance beyond the point at which the aristocracy are halting. Emerging from smoky Manchester, as I said, we see grounds belonging to various proprietors. If our ears have been open and our eyes, and if our minds have not been more insensible than ears deafened and eyes shut, we must have seen enough of poverty in Manchester. Enough of dirty mud, of dirty wretchedness, ill health, squalid hunger, and unanswered surprise at inquiring why those thousands of human beings so ill clothed, ill lodged, and ill fed, with bread so scarce and dear, do not die faster than they do! But what should we think when, once clear of all this, and breathing God's fresh air on Lord Wilton's and Lord Derby's estates, to see within a short distance some three hundred fields, which ought not to make more than forty moderate-sized enclosures? To observe that not only is the land wasted by seven times more fences than is necessary for either shelter or subdivision of property; but that each five hundred yards of fence occupies space enough for a quarter of wheat to grow? To observe that in most of those fields, in addition to the waste, by enormous double hedges, and open ditches, and ditch banks, in seven times greater number than requisite, there are waste ridges at the ends, neither ploughed, nor delved, nor sown, nor planted? To observe that in ploughing, the loss of time for men and horses must be, in turnings, seven times more than necessary; and that, supposing the waste ridges not to

exist, but to be ploughed up and sown, there must be in all
drilled crops, as potatoes and turnips, much waste by the
trampling of horses?   To observe that the land is generally
sour, and wet, and foul, undrained and unweeded; that the
waste ridges and ditch banks produce weeds, the seed of which
the wind sows in all directions; that the wide ditches contain
foul water, the malarious effects of which impregnate the air,
and the presence of which destroys even the natural drainage of
the soil?   To observe that these fields do not belong to small
cultivators, and that, therefore, there is no plea for not breaking the mup?   To observe that a man with a spade in his
hand could be employed in every corner of every field, letting
the water run off, and thereby saving often an acre of grain
in wet weather; but to observe that the man with the spade
is not employed at that or any other work of a like kind?
To observe that there is no thrashing-mill on the farm, and to
hear some of the farmers declare, as they are living men, that
though Lancashire has mills and machinery for almost all
kinds of work, *they never heard of machinery for thrashing
corn!*   To observe, in the last place, that every improvement
of the last fifty years (as introduced with such great advantage on well cultivated farms) is there awanting; and that
every evil, by good farmers discarded, is there present; and
that your tenants call out—" This Anti-Corn-Law League
will be the destruction of us! If we are not protected by the
corn-law, how are we to cultivate our land?"   To be observers
of such monstrous absurdities as we would see and hear on
those farms, my Lord Stanley, (and in all parts of Lancashire,)
would astonish us more than our Manchester surprise; namely,
why don't the hungry, ragged, diseased poor of Manchester
die faster than they do?

There is a green hill, a beautiful piece of ground, moderately
elevated, on one of your farms in Pilkington township, on
which I stood last year—a bright summer's day it was—and
had pointed out to me the various towns, and factories,
and landed estates within view of it.   It is not too much to
say that the globe's surface has no such other display of the
vastness of human enterprise.   The great manufacturing
towns of Lancashire, Manchester, Salford, Oldham, Rochdale,
Bury, Bolton, Blackburn, Wigan, Ashton, Leigh, Newton, and
the numerous factories which have arisen and given birth to
villages in the intermediate distances, stand distinct before the
eye, or are represented by their atmospheres of smoke.   Railways intersect the county on all sides, and heavy trains shoot
along in every direction.   Canals, too, despite the railways,
have their heavy traffic; and all manner of arts are in opera-

tion to increase manufacturing wealth. In all of those towns there is a bread-eating people, none of whom, judging by wages, have cheap bread, many of whom have not enough of bread, some of whom have no bread at all—aye, none at all, my Lord. While standing on that elevated spot, and thinking on the subjects which the view suggested, particularly the poverty of the working people in the towns, all the sides of free trade rose before me ; also over-populousness, over-speculation, unsound currency, expensive government, and unwholesome legislation ! all sides of those questions rose before the mind's eye with their difficulties, and, class interests considered, presented more reasons for despair than hope. But there was one remedy unconnected with legislation, and against which no class interest should be urged, one means by which the towns within view could be better supplied with corn, namely, by the land within view being better cultivated.

My Lord, a word about Knowsley Park. You could not fail to observe last summer the splendid crops of potatoes and Swedish turnips that grew on each side of the approach to the Hall from the Liverpool Road. You are aware, perhaps, that the preparing of the soil for the seed, with the summer clearing of the crops, was done in a different manner from the common style of working in Lancashire. You must, doubtless, know that the soil was previously sour, wet, and profitless, and that your noble father has allowed the Tweedside ploughmen, who within these last few years have been brought to Knowsley, to break up portions of the vast park that surrounds the ancient hall of your forefathers, for the purpose of improving the soil, to be again laid down in permanent grass. Perhaps you may have heard that your noble neighbour, Lord Sefton, has had one of those Tweedside men from Knowsley, whom he has elevated to the management of his own farm. Knowing those circumstances, the improvements made and still making in Knowsley Park, the splendid crops raised from a formerly unproductive soil, your Lordship must also well know that the Tweedside system of working is superior to the Lancashire system. But it can never be introduced to the Knowsley estate beyond the bounds of Knowsley Park, *unless the tenants obtain leases.* Within the park, Lord Derby's money pays the first expense of the improvements, and the improvements afterwards pay for themselves. Beyond the park, the farmers have either no money or no security to obtain it ; and if they have both, they are still without the security of reaping the profits derivable from the Tweedside style of working within.

You are aware, my Lord, that the cultivators of the soil of New South Wales must have security in their property.

Why then withhold it from the tenants of Knowsley? At least, why not use your influence with your noble father to obtain it? Were agricultural emigrants as unprotected, and, consequently, as void of enterprise and as wasteful of natural advantages as your tenants, our colonies would perish; your office would be the registry of famine and death.*

LETTER TO THE LANDOWNERS OF ENGLAND.

March 9, 1842.

My Lords and Gentlemen, owners of the soil of England,—My father had a kailyard. It was the same piece of ground through all my recollection; for he laboured many, very many, years on the same farm. He was poor. This kailyard (cottage garden) was small; about one hundred feet long by forty-five feet broad. We could not afford an inch of it to lie waste. We dug into the roots of the hedge, encroached on every thorn or holly-bush, above and below, until they were trained into respectable fences, seemly to look on, serviceable for their purpose, and unobtrusive on our little portion of the land of Britain. Five hundred square yards was not much. Yet though deaths, separations, and dispersions throughout the world, have severed us from that spot and the old thatched house for ever, it is a dear spot to me. Falsely do the owners of the soil estimate the feelings of the labouring poor who betake themselves to towns and trade, if they think that such become their enemies; and yet we hear such false things said. This world has not a holier place to me than our old kailyard! Save the grave in which my father lies, it was all of this great globe that was ours, though that only by sufferance. We had hard struggles, but from it we had some of the necessaries of life every day of the year, and occasionally the luxuries—aye, the luxuries; for we were not insensible to the melody of a thousand warblers on the surrounding bushes; to the hum of bees innumerable, busy as ourselves; nor to the beauty of summer Sabbath days, when, in addition to the furnishings for dinner, we could cull a nosegay; and we have had more substantial luxuries when winter came and these disappeared. Many is the time and oft, my Lords and Gentlemen, that I have taken a hare or a rabbit out of our kailyard, how I got hold of them I shall not tell you. They came there of their own accord. They could not live without eating. We were like them, and none of you were one whit the poorer, nor had one day's less sport.

---

* Since the date of this letter, the Knowsley tenants are assisted with advances of money to drain their land.

But why do I speak of this nook of earth? The next sentence will tell you. It was cultivated every inch; but not better than a farm might be, and as many around it were. Few farms in England, keeping off Northumberland, and *pet* patches in some other counties, are so well farmed as that district was; and yet I do not recollect one year in which some new improvement did not arise. The fact is, the farmers in that part (I speak of the sea-coast district of Haddington-shire) made profits. They paid rents of such an enormous amount as would make farmers in Kent sink into the earth, yet by their leases and capital they made profits. Improvements became a passion among them. The boisterous member for Knaresborough taunted the manufacturers the other day with having no other object in view when they built mills and employed cotton-spinners than the making of profits, which taunt is about as wisely conceived as the Rev. Mr Harris' celebrated prize-essay on *Mammon*, in which the sin of covetousness is most unmercifully belaboured. Wealth may be called Mammon, and profits covetousness; but where would arts and industry be developed without profits? What are our ships about on every sea, loaded with every nameable thing, from oysters to missionaries of the gospel; what are all intended for and intending, but profit? Did not Shakspeare write his prodigies of genius for a price, and amass wealth?

Did not the reverend essayist burrow in obscurity himself, until an advertisement proclaimed that L.200 would be given for the best essay on the greatest sin? And did he not then step forward, with a rare display of talent, denouncing the sin of covetousness, and win the prize of " filthy lucre?" And what does the member for Knaresborough wring his income from? An increase of wealth, a desire to possess, a desire to be something more than we are, to have something more than we have, is the very soul of all human energies. We should be sluggards, dying as wretchedly as we lived, had we not this principle, this motive to action, within us. It has been the dormancy of this principle in English agriculture, and the activity of it in trade, that has caused the present collision of those interests. Trade has arisen and struggled with a noble energy, because, without energy, it could have not only no profits but no existence. Agriculture has slept, because, sleeping, there was still a harvest to reap; the earth, and the air, and Heaven's goodness provide something, in spite of the sloth of the farmer and poverty of the farm. Trade has been going ahead, but agriculture, yoked to her by legal harness, has held her back; and because the one will not move, the other must stand still.

In East Lothian, Berwickshire, Roxburghshire, and Northumberland, the passion for profits has been as energetic, for many years past, as it has been in the manufacturing districts, and the production of wealth has been the same. The energy once awakened feeds itself. One improvement produces the necessity for another. If ever the saying that " every rood maintains its man" could be applied with justice to any country it could be applied to each rood in those countries just named. There is not a foot of land left untouched ; and though those who eat, *or should eat*, the corn grown there, do not delve the roods of land, and eat and sleep on them, they produce the clothing and comforts of those that do. That desire to possess, which necessity excites, and that desire to possess which a love of wealth excites, have been and ever will be the motives to exertion. The first desire always begets the other, and so invariably, that there is scarcely any improvement in our industrial arts but has had its origin in necessity. Many of the mechanical inventions now in use in factories are the results of " *strikes*," and a necessity to supply the place of workmen. Others are the result of local obstacles in regard of situation. In the county of Berwick, the beautiful plough now in use on all properly cultivated farms, which performs better work, and more of it, with one half of the horse labour formerly required, and still wanted in most parts of England—this improved plough was the result of necessity. The Merse of Berwickshire is an extensive tract of rich clay, now so fertile as to yield the finest crops of wheat that reaper ever reaped, but formerly so stiff as to be, in many seasons, incapable of tillage. The olden ploughs still used in England would not enter it in a dry season, and the number of horses required to draw them sunk in it in a wet season. A mechanic, named Small, observing this, applied all his skill to the scientific construction of a new plough, and produced the one which has wrought such wonderful changes in the value of land *and quantity of crop raised* wherever it has been used.

I shall relate another result of necessity ; and my reason for pressing those instances, truisms though they be, is, that I believe every foot of land in England will one day be cultivated in the best possible style, but not until sheer necessity has broken up the present wasteful and hunger-spreading system. I shall relate this instance of what necessity will do, and it will illustrate more doctrines than that which immediately suggests it. It is rather closely connected with personal affairs, but it may not be the less forcible because of that : the principle is a public one.

When Napoleon fell, prices fell : the war was done, and so were war prices. You, the landowners, protected yourselves

by the corn-law ; but the labourers, whose wages also fell, not
because corn was cheap and the farmers unable to pay them,
but because men had become plentiful, since war needed
neither fresh stores nor fresh blood.   Labourers, swarming in
over-abundance, offered themselves at wages far beneath
those of former years.   Corn, equally tending to abundance,
was prevented by your law from accommodating its supply to
their ability.   Well, there came the years 1816 and 1817.   I
was not old enough then to know the events which are now
history.   I must look into a book to find that in the first of
those years the average price of wheat was 75s. 1d., and in
the second 84s. 2d., with oats, and beans, and barley, the
only grain which we could get a smell of, when eating was the
question, at rates proportionably dear.   But though only in
my seventh year in 1817, I need no history to tell me what
that season was.   Oh Lord, that year ! never can the memory
of it perish in me but with myself.   The prices give no idea
of our difficulties.   The rain poured and poured all the summer.   The barley was maltened in the ear, the beans were
bitter and clammy, and the oats either heated or rotten ; all
had to be kiln-dried ere the miller could grind them, and when
the meal came home to us, any attempt to make it into the
common bread or porridge was defeated.   But even the supply
of it failed.   There were ten or eleven of us at l ome, all
inclined to eat good bread, all unable to get even enough of
bad.   The potatoes had been a failure, bad and few of them.
My father was at that time working for money wages, not as
some others did, for payment in corn.   What the wages
actually amounted to I do not now know ; but I know that
every farthing of all that each member of the family, who
could work, earned, went to buy the worst, and only grain
within our reach, and of that there was not enough.   As the
winter came on, it became scarcer and scarcer, worse and
worse, until, about that season of the new year when cares
are thrown partially aside, and joy mollifies the labourer's
heart for a day or two, the awful truth became known that
the potatoes were within a week of being done.   Those who
buy a daily or weekly supply can have no conception of the
dismay which this circumstance created in a family that never
bought any, and had nothing now to buy them, *though in full
employment*.   The pig had been killed to save the potatoes
before it was half grown.   The cow ceased to give milk long
before the usual time, in consequence of the unwholesome
fodder.   With two such years, there had been no money to
buy clothes ; and it sorely taxed a mother's toil and ingenuity
to mend the old ones, night after night, week after week,

while we lay in bed to allow of that operation, and cheat
hunger of its supper. This might not have been so bad, landlords, had you allowed prices to fall to the level of wages.
But we got over the winter in some way—God and my father
and mother only know how; but *we* got over it, and *you*
maintained your high prices and spent your high rents. And,
mind you, this was in a part of the country where farm
labourers are in a better condition than any part of Britain,
and in the family of a man who said then, and said to the
day of his death, that he had not spent " forty shillings on
drink for forty years." But this only brings me to the
instance of *necessity* already promised as an illustration. It
might puzzle most economists to know what such a man as my
father, with no ground of his own but the kailyard, could
devise to avert such another year of distress. He did this :—
During the spring and early months of summer, he devoted
an hour or two every night, three or four when there was
moonlight, all the time, in short, which he could steal from
the twenty-four hours, after devoting ten to his employers,
taking meals and rest, and performing family worship both
night and morning, which last I never knew him omit under
any circumstances. He devoted all the time spared from those
offices, or, I should rather say, wrung from the hours of rest,
to digging by the sides of the stone dykes that enclosed the
farm fields and planting potatoes. Had he planted the waste
ridges, the wide double embankments that skirt the fields of
English farms, he would have made a fortune. But our
ploughmen had ploughed to within eighteen inches or a foot
of every fence ; and there were no broad banks bordering the
ditches, and ditches on each side of double hedges, which
hedges between them, in England, contain another ridge of
waste ground ; our fences occupied the smallest possible space,
and being regularly pruned to compel them into economy,
they grew solid, and ornamental, and useful ; they became, in
reality, a fence.

However, it was at the narrow strips which skirted the
stone walls that my father obtained leave to labour. The
farmer was kind ; but he objected to the roots of the thorn
fences being disturbed. From these narrow sources we raised
an additional and valuable supply of potatoes. Ultimately
my father convinced the master that to plant them at the
roots of the thorn hedges would do good to the latter, and it
was done. In the course of a few years the neighbouring
farmers perceived that those hedges so associated with the
planting, weeding, hoeing, digging, and replanting of potatoes
at their roots, were in a more healthy condition than others ;

and the consequence is, that what was at first done by a poor man from necessity, is now universally done by the farmers from motives of prudence. They do not now tear the horses, the harness, the hedges, and the ploughman's hands, by ploughing so very close as they did before. They send men with spades to plant potatoes; and they have not only a crop on every inch of ground, but they have no weeds growing to seed, and spreading foulness over every field, as we see throughout the neglected farms of England.

Two years ago, when travelling over some of the best farms on the Duke of Buckingham's estate, I asked a farmer why he did not let some of his poor labourers (and there the labourers are certainly the poorest I have seen in any part of the kingdom) plant potatoes on the ample banks of waste ground by the hedge sides.

"Bless you," was the reply, "they would destroy all my hedges; they would break down everything; my fences are bad enough as they are."

"Yes," said I, "but I am pointing out an effectual way of restoring them. Give one of your men this bank (that on which we stood) to plant potatoes on for all the years intervening between this and next rotation of grass in this field, on condition that he keeps the fence in order; and by that time you will have a good hedge, depend on it you will."

"Ah!" asked he, "where might the man be before that time?"

"It would be an inducement to make him stop with you, if he were worth keeping," I replied; "while, if he went away, you would get another to take his bargain."

"But," objected the farmer, "where may I be myself?"

"Why," replied I, "you may stay here as long as you pay your rent and fulfil the conditions of your lease, I suppose?"

"Lease! Bless you, sir, I've got no lease: no, no, we don't have leases here; one year of a bad bargain is enough. The Duke can get rid of me, or me of him, when we tire of each other."

"And, therefore," said I, "it is not worth your while to mend your fences, level down those banks, cover in the ditches, drain your land, uproot those stumps and briars, and plant a neat hedge?"

"No," replied he, "it is not worth my while; the place as it is will do for me; it will do my time."

And thus, because the miserable satisfaction of compelling a tenant to vote for a particular party is an object with landlords, sloth lies on the fair fields of England and hunger wails on her city streets.

EMPLOYMENT FOR THE WINTER OF 1842-3 BY SPADE LABOUR.

BEING no advocate for spade husbandry where the same results can be obtained by the plough, as, *perhaps*, by Smith's subsoil plough; being no advocate for a system of working which would make employment plentiful for a short period of the year and leave an increased number of labourers unemployed during a large portion of the year, I ask no one to abandon the plough and adopt the spade. All I ask is, that those gentlemen who have land overstocked already with labourers, and who would rather see those labourers at work for wages than hear of their being idle, starving, poaching, and rick-burning during the present winter, would set them to work. Having said this to guard against objections about creating a pauper population, and such like, which would be urged against a universal system of spade cultivation, I shall state the benefits to be obtained from its partial use in districts already over-populated.

1. *Of mere Digging, without Trenching.*—The late Sir John Sinclair, in his "Code of Agriculture," speaking of the neighbourhood of Hamilton, in Lanarkshire, says:—"A field was taken, which was cropped with beans the preceding year and the previous year with oats. Two ridges were dug and two ploughed alternately, and the whole was sown on the same day. A part both of the ploughed and dug was drilled with the garden hoe. The whole was reaped the same day, and, being thrashed out, the result was, that the dug land, sown broad-cast, was to the ploughed sown broad-cast as fifty-five bushels to forty-two; while the dug and drilled was as twenty and a quarter bushels to twelve and a quarter upon the ploughed and drilled. The additional grain produced was not the only beneficial result gained by digging; for in this instance there was also a great deal more straw, and the land was much more free of weeds and more easily cultivated next year."

Two objections may be urged against the foregoing, as an example for this recommendation; first, that Sir John Sinclair has not recorded the difference of expense between digging and ploughing, and that this year is now too far advanced for using the spade on a soil to be sown with wheat. To both objections I say, first, that though the expense of digging is not recorded, the augmented crops prove a considerable profit to have been obtained, and that *trenching* with the spade, which is an operation distinct from common digging, may be carried on for spring crops during all the winter, save in very hard frost or very deep snow.

2. *Of Trenching with the Spade.*—Mr James Jackson, author of several valuable essays on agriculture, and of a work entitled "A Treatise on Agriculture and Dairy Husbandry," the latter published by the Messrs Chambers of Edinburgh, and which, for less money than a farmer pays for his dinner and glass at an ordinary on market-days, may be had of any bookseller in the kingdom; in this eminently practical treatise Mr Jackson says—"The most correct account which we possess of the comparative value of spade husbandry in professional farming is that given by Mr Archibald Scott of Southfield, near Addington, Great Lothian, in an essay which he wrote upon the subject, and for which he obtained a prize of L.100. The following extract from it is well worth the consideration of practical farmers:—

" ' I am quite convinced there is but one way of employing the surplus population of England and Ireland, and that is by a judicious introduction of spade husbandry. And I am also convinced that a system of management can be pointed out, whereby every labourer in Great Britain may be employed, with profit to his employer and advantage to the country.

" ' I should think it will hardly be denied, by any one at all versant in agricultural operations, that work done by the spade is superior to work done by the plough, and that the only drawback is the great additional expense. Now, if I can shew that at a particular period of the rotation spade husbandry is not only superior, but less expensive, 1 shall have got over this difficulty.

" ' To shew that I am not a mere theorist but a practical man, I may mention that I rent a farm from the Earl of Wemyss in East Lothian, consisting of 530 Scotch acres; that I have cultivated land to a considerable extent with the spade for the last three years, and that the result has exceeded my most sanguine expectations. As facts are stubborn things, I shall lay before you my system, crops, expenses, and profits.

" ' In 1831 I determined to ascertain the difference of the expense and produce between trenching land with the spade and summer fallowing with the plough, in the usual way. I therefore trenched thirteen acres of my summer fallow break in the months of June and July. I found the soil about fourteen inches deep, and I turned it completely over, thereby putting up a clean and fresh soil in the room of the foul and exhausted mould, which I was careful to put at the bottom of the trench. This operation I found cost about L.4 : 10s. the Scotch acre, paying my labourers one shilling and sixpence per day. The rest of the field, which consisted of nine acres,

I wrought with the plough in the usual way, giving it six furrows, with a suitable harrowing. I manured the field in August; the trenched got eight cart-loads per acre, the ploughed land sixteen. The field was sown in the middle of September. The whole turned out a bulky crop as to straw, particularly the trenched portion, which was very much lodged. On thrashing them out, I found them to stand as under :—

By trenched wheat per acre, fifty-two bushels, at 6s. 9d. a bushel, ...			L.17 11 0
To two years' rent, at L.2 : 10s. per acre, . . .	L.5	0	0
Expense of trenching, ...	4	10	0
Seed, three bushels, at 6s. 9d., ...	1	0	3
Eight cart-loads of manure, at 4s., ...	1	12	0
Expenses of cutting, thrashing, and marketing, . .	1	10	0
Profit, ...	3	18	9
			17 11 0
By ploughed wheat per acre, forty-two bushels, at 6s. 9d.,			14 3 6
To two years' rent, at L.2 : 10s. per acre, . . .	L.5	0	0
Six furrows and harrowing, at 10s., ...	3	0	0
Seed, three bushels, at 6s. 9d., ...	1	0	3
Sixteen cart-loads of manure, at 4s.	3	4	0
Expense of cutting, thrashing, and marketing, . .	1	10	0
Profit, ...	0	9	3
			L.14 3 6

" 'I now saw that though it might be difficult to trench over my fallow break during the summer months, it was by no means making the most of the system, as the operation was not only more expensive, owing to the land being hard and dry during the summer, but that *it was a useless waste of time to take a whole year to perform an operation that could be as well done in a few weeks, provided labourers could be had.* And, as in all agricultural operations losing time is losing money, as the rent must be paid whether the land is carrying a crop or not, so that in taking one year to fallow the land and another to grow the crop, two years' rent must be charged against the crop, or at least there must be a rent charged against the rotation of crops for the year the land was fallowed. As I felt satisfied that by trenching with the spade *the land would derive all the advantages of a summer fallowing, and avoid all the disadvantages attending it,* I determined on trenching thirty-four acres of my fallow break, immediately on the crops being removed from the ground, and had it sown with wheat by the middle of November 1832. I may here remark, that I did not apply any manure, as I thought the former crop was injured by being too bulky. As it is now thrashed out and disposed of, the crop per acre stands as follows :—

		L.		
By average of thirty-four bushels per acre, at 7s.,	. . . .	L.15	8	0
To rent of land per acre,	. . . .	L.2 10	0	
Expense of trenching,	. . . .	4 0	0	
Seed,	. . . .	1 1	0	
Cutting, thrashing, and marketing,	. . . . . .	1 10	0	
Profit,	. . . .	6 7	0	
		L.15	8	0

" 'The advantages of trenching over summer fallowing are, in my opinion, very decided, as it is not only cheaper, but, as far as I can judge, much more effectual. I am so satisfied of this, not only from the experiments above noticed, but from the apparent condition of the land after it has carried the crop, that I have this autumn cultivated about a hundred acres with the spade, and the crops are at present very promising. When I first commenced I was laughed at by my neighbours, but now, when they see me persevering in what they considered a very chimerical project, they are suspending their judgment, and several of them have made considerable experiments this year. I should think there are at least 250 acres under crop cultivated in this way this season in East Lothian. In 1831, the year I commenced, there was not a single acre. *I have, therefore, the satisfaction of knowing that I have been the means of causing L.1000 to be spent this year amongst the labouring classes in my immediate neighbourhood;* and I feel confident that, should the season turn out favourable for the wheat crop, and fair prices be obtained, their employers will be handsomely remunerated for their outlay. I do not say that this system will succeed on every description of soil, as it must necessarily be of some depth to admit of the operation; but there are few districts where such soils will not be found in sufficient abundance to give ample employment to the surplus population of the neighbourhood.' "

Mr Jackson's work, from which the foregoing is quoted, contains a note, stating—" We have been informed that the Earl of Wemyss put an early stop to trenching on his farms, under a belief that the system pursued was calculated to exhaust the soil." Observing this note, and being aware that trenching was still pursued in some parts of the Lothians, though prohibited on Lord Wemyss' farms; also, having seen the labourers of the West of England swarming in poverty and idleness; and having designed to call attention to a means by which many of them might be profitably employed, I addressed myself, by letter, to Mr Scott, the originator of the trenching system, and also to Mr Jackson, who quoted Mr Scott's essay on the subject. A few days ago I received a letter from each of those gentlemen, in reply to my inquiries. Mr Scott says of the essay :—

" It was widely circulated at the time it was written. Every newspaper in Great Britain and Ireland got a copy of it, though many of them, I dare say, did not think it worth inserting in their columns ; and every member of both houses of Parliament got a copy, besides almost every one else at all interested in the matter." This only shews how much trouble and expense may be incurred by individuals for the public benefit, and yet no benefit arise, because there happens to be no public excitement. Throughout all the south-western counties I did not, on my recent tour, meet a single farmer or agriculturist of any class, save the *Socialists* in Hampshire, who practised, or had ever heard of, trenching by the spade in lieu of ploughing or summer fallowing. Mr Scott, in the letter I have received, continues :—" You are quite right in supposing that I was prevented carrying out my system by my landlord, the Earl of Wemyss. I was also landed in a law suit with him, which cost me L.500, in consequence of my pursuing the system. The foundation of the suit was my infringing on the terms of my lease.   *   *   *   *
I was therefore compelled to abandon the system, thoroughly disgusted at the treatment I received."

Mr Scott goes on to answer some queries I put to him about subsoil ploughing, and states that, without thorough draining, the subsoil plough is worse than useless. His remarks are valuable, but they are not connected with the subject immediately before us, save that, by thorough draining, many labourers might be employed who are now idle and starving, or idly working and poorly fed in the workhouses. But draining is expensive to be worth anything, and a tenant must be something more than tenants are generally under the present system of tenures before he can expend a large sum of money on draining, which is only to be repaid in future years. But many tenants might employ people to trench with the spade during the winter, and by sowing spring wheat have a profitable return. Though Mr Scott has been compelled to abandon the system, he is still as sanguine in its favour as ever ; and Mr Jackson, in the letter which he has been kind enough to forward in reply to my queries on this subject, says—

" Trenching in the neighbourhood of Edinburgh has been practised in a different form than by Mr Scott. A strong furrow is first taken by the plough. This is followed by as many men as can keep the plough going, who dig spade deep, and throw the under mould on the top of the ploughed land as the plough proceeds ; and its effects in the improvement of the potato, the turnip, and the clover crops in particular, have been astonishing. This method is much cheaper than that of Mr Scott; it is equally effective, and must admit a more free percolation of rain, or other water, *than subsoil ploughing does*."

Now, then, if the farmers cannot, through some impediment in their tenures, betake themselves to this means of improving their crops, employing the pauper population, and lessening the poor-rates, surely some of the nobility and gentry will try the system on their own account. Unless it be on the barest soils, this trenching may be successfully tried. Surely there is now excitement enough to draw the attention of the land-owners to the necessity of employing the poachers, the fire-raisers, and the starving population, out of whose superabund-ant numbers these criminals steal forth to commit crime. And here is a safe mode of employing them. Next year's potatoes, or turnips, or clover, or spring wheat will give an abundant profit.

THE MARKET PLACES AND MARKET DINNERS OF ENGLAND.

READING, IN BERKSHIRE.

9th May 1843.

READING stands on both sides of that fine full-bodied river of third-rate magnitude, the Kennet, close by its junction with the Thames, thirty-seven miles west of London. The town consists of about thirty streets, besides lanes; has twenty thousand inhabitants, six parish churches, eight chapels, one theatre, sixteen principal inns, two places for public assemblies, three banking houses, one savings' bank, two newspapers, eight free schools, a county jail, a town hall, a county hospital, a medical dispensary, a public cemetery, several literary and scientific associations, two gas works, a water company, a railway station; two inspectors, two sergeants, and eighteen privates of police; a mayor, recorder, six aldermen, and eighteen councillors, two members of parliament; a good trade in flour and malt; a growing trade in farm implements, and all things for domestic use; a declining trade in the manufacture of silks, sacking, pins, ribbons, crape, umbrellas, floor cloth, and sail cloth; four annual fairs, and a corn and cattle market every Saturday.

The inhabitants are reputed to be religious, very sober, and very moral; but their town seems to have been dancing and not very soberly. Full-sized streets are thwarted in their

course by small; the short confuse the long; the genteel
mingle with the vulgar; and hard-working houses hold companionship with the idle; crooked lanes, narrow and unseemly,
are seen in the company of flowery gardens; and the gardens,
in their gaiety, have led away desert streets to places where
you would not expect to find them. All seem to have been
in confused motion at some time, and to have halted at that
moment when the market place was squeezed out of all shape
and just proportion. Like an Irishman's hat, it is bent in
and bent out; narrow above and wider below; is down on
one side, up on the other; looks round a corner; has its
widest openings where least required; and in its various
uses is the most unsuited for that use to which it is publicly
devoted.

The cattle, sheep, and pigs have each taken apartments in
other districts of the town; and latterly the greens and fruit
have moved to where they can be seen. Sacks of wheat, oats,
barley, beans, peas, tares, grass seeds, and ploughs, harrows,
waggons, and sowing machines, all for sale, with some butter
and some eggs, and some specifics in hawkers' trays, warranted
to cure corns, toothache, rheumatics, lumbago, and many
other troubles, internal and external, fill up the market place,
save and except the ground occupied by corn factors, farmers,
and farmers' men. Of these, in all, there are two or three
hundred—let us mark some of them.

This tall, dark-featured gentleman, so well dressed, so frequently spoken to by others, is the cultivator of his own land.
He feels the pressure of dull markets little himself, but he feels
for others who suffer by markets. Observe the group around
him. Two years ago they spurned him and his opinions, and
shouted and cried what they will not now repeat—what they
now most fervently curse, and wish they had never cheered and
cried for. Can we hear their conversation? Yes; snatches
of brief queries and briefer answers. "Parliament—Peel—
no—yes—fact—Canada—flour—ruin—petition—useless—
must—never—damn them—majority—Peel—betrayed—
impeachment—beheaded—no—damn—yes—Peel—what—
yield—curse—Peel—Conservative—no—damn—ruin—land—
church—sinking—Peel—pigs—Canada—smuggle—Peel—
Tories—League—Cobden—never—atrocious—Peel—cheat
—votes—majority—curse—damn—true—swear—never will
—trust—no—vote—no—Tories—no—damn—yes—condition
dreadful—hope for the best—League tracts—Peel—take in—
no hope—worse and worse—lower to-day—dinner—good bye
—Peel—good day—Peel—dinner—Peel—good morning."
Such are the fragmentary words heard over the shoulders of

this group standing around the tall dark gentleman who
farms his own land. All that he says is—and he says it with
a shake of his head—" You would listen to no arguments two
years ago ; experience has convinced you."

Who is this youngster with the boots of patent polish, the
wasp-like waist, the gold chain, the oily ringlets, and the under
lip pouting in supercilious scorn? He is one of the Mark Lane
gentry. He has come to buy, or to cheapen by not buying.
See with what a professional swagger of the arm he dives his
open hand among the wheat, shovelling it over the mouth of
the sack, purposely to spill some of it on the ground, and shew
by spilling it that he belongs to the profession. He shakes
his head ; and how remarkably unconcerned he looks ! But
his lips move ; he speaks ; he offers a price ; no, he asks a
question ; the farmer replies ; the buyer gives no rejoinder,
but walks away to another lot, having scattered some of this
on the ground, and having made the farmer feel that there
will be no rise this week.

And who is this farmer? He lives near Three-Mile-Cross,
" our village," the celebrated of Miss Mitford. It was but
three days ago that he came over to the village to pay his
poor-rate, and as he paid it he said to our friend who gives
the receipts, " This is paid ; thank God, this is paid ; but
where, or when, or how I shall pay the next, I know not.
Where my Michaelmas rent is to come from is more than I
know. I paid the winter half at Lady Day, but I shall have
nothing to pay with at Michaelmas. I paid at Lady Day,
thrashed out every bushel, sold all, all but five sacks, and they
must be sold on Saturday for money to pay my workers—
sold all but them five sacks to pay at Lady Day—not another
bushel left of last year's crop. What is to be done with
Michaelmas I know not. Peel, they tell me, is out of all possibility of helping us ; they say our members be as bad as him ;
the Lord help us at Michaelmas !" Such was the articulate
grief of this farmer when paying his last poor-rate with his
last shilling—his last shilling until he sold the last five
sacks of his crop, which he cannot now sell but at a reduced
price.

Who is that young gentleman on horseback? He is one of
the young Walters of Bearwood. What! He who lately
stood for Nottingham? No ; a younger brother. And who
are those in the carriage, those ladies? Those are his sisters,
Mr Walter's daughters. A fine family ! Oh, bless you, yes ;
a large family ; very good people all of them, very.

It is one o'clock. The various steeples proclaim the farmers'
dinner hour. Every inn has a public ordinary : which shall

we go to? The George is round here; the Angel is near at hand; here is the Broad Face; onward there is the Wheat Sheaf, the Wheel, the Elephant; and there is the White Hart, the Ship, the Black Horse, the Mitre, the Peacock, the Turk's Head, and several more to which we may go. This one round the corner will do; let us see, what is it called? Ah, never mind what its name is. Here we are in the public room, just in time. The clatter of knives and forks has just begun. Some of the guests are too busy filling themselves to speak; but the most are too full of the topics of the day to remain quiet. Let us open our ears.

"Roast beef, sir?—Robert Peel dare not—help you, Mr Jackson?—labourers' wages—potatoes?—Sir Robert Peel—salt?—waiter!—yes, sir—Robert Peel—potatoes—carve this pig—knife—cut off his head—Peel—roast pig?—roast—Peel—waiter! — Canada flour—fowl?—majority of votes—this way, gentlemen; seats disengaged here—turn them out—Conservative ministry—boiled mutton—church extension—over done—take in—glass of ale—no relief this year—coming, sir—waiter, remove—county members—help you to—parliamentary—greens—Peel—no more tongue, thank you—two thousand miles off—American wheat—cheated—petition—clear the table—thrown under and never read—petition—quite enough, thank you—Wallingford dinner, Mr Blackstone—powerless—nearly—false pretences—farmers—always suffering distress—Peel—so help me God—language in parliament—the League tracts—read—digest—old cheese—Cobden's speeches—relish—Wellington—1815—not the better of being too old—good port—porter with a head—ministers have, before now, lost their—Peel and Cobden—porter with a head—debate in the house—with a head—would have given something to have seen—porter with a head—in a passion, striking the table—the head—unseemly to be in a rage—Dublin stout—Conservative members in a tumult, applauding—Barclay's—the indignant manner of—porter with a head—retaliation—stout—gentlemen, silence please—silence—silence!"

And Silence having come when those who called for her held their tongues, and not before the chairman said, that as dinner was now over those who chose a pipe and a glass would adjourn to another room. Whereupon one half, or more, of the whole adjourned; the remainder, not choosing to smoke, nor to be smoked, remained where they were. They disjoined themselves and reunited into small parties.

AYLESBURY.

Monday, the 8th of May 1843, was a wet day in the Vale of Aylesbury. It was the day of one of the annual sheep and cattle fairs held in that little town, and perhaps never, since the town had a fair, was it filled with such an assemblage of hanging heads, of down-mouthed animals, quadruped and biped, as on that day.

Wet, weary, unsold, and unsaleable, stood the ox tribe, of all breeds, all ages, and all lengths of horn. The sheep, though not numerous, returned to whence they came. The horses, though inspirited by the cracking of the whips, the whooping of chanters, and the presence of little bits of ginger, kicked about, changing places in the market, but in only a few instances changing masters.

And the masters of all that were there, lean beasts, fat beasts, milk cows, and cows with calf; short horns, long horns, and oxen hornless; the masters of sheep shorn and sheep to shear; of pigs eager to eat and pigs ready to be eaten; of donkies few and horses many; the masters of all these, and of animals like these, not at the fair, hung down their heads, and (save and except the horses that had ginger to make them spicy) moved as slowly, as dispiritedly, as unhappily, and as hungrily as any poor brute in the market. They moved as slowly and as hungrily because they had nothing to do before dinner, and because the usual time of dinner had come, and still they could not dine. They were to go to the Town Hall to dinner, where the table was to be spread by the host of the fashionable inn, the White Hart, and where they were to sit down at the table with a lord! They were to dine with Lord Stanhope; and the dinner was to be, not a "commercial" nor a "King's-Head" dinner, but actually a "White Hart" dinner; and all for three shillings each.

It was painful to wait over the usual dinner hour on any day, and particularly on a day that was dull and wet, and at a time when markets were as dull as the murky weather, and falling, falling as the cloud upon the vale. But the inducements were great; and what with "snacks" and "crusts," and "least bits in the world," at the various inns; and what with glasses of "sherry and brandy mixed," "just to keep out the wet," the time passed on, and the Stanhope dinner-hour came.

Having mingled with various parties in the market place and in the inns, and talked with "town people" and "country people," I soon perceived that grumbling was the order of the day; and a little attention to the grumblers enabled me to record the following matters of public interest.

15

Messrs Cobden and Moore had been in the town on the previous Saturday, and the town's people who heard them were desirous of telling the farmers who did not hear them, (and few farmers did; for there were few farmers in Aylesbury on that Saturday, owing to the fairs in that and neighbouring counties, owing to the wetness of the day, and more especially owing to the orders they received not to attend;) the town's people were now desirous of telling the farmers what the deputation of the League had said; while, on the other hand, the farmers were desirous of venting their complaints. As usual, Peel and the tariff, and the false friends of the voting tenants, were complained of. Those farmers who came out of Bedfordshire or Hertford, or who belonged to the eastern parts of Bucks, adhered to the old topics of unhappiness and want, and went no farther than Peel and broken promises; but all those from the west of Aylesbury, from about Buckingham, and Brill, and Thanse in Oxfordshire, and Bicester, and Banbury, and Oxford, and Abingdon, were full of a new subject. Van Amburgh had been in those towns, or some of them, with his cream-coloured horses, driving eight in hand; and they had all been to see Van Amburgh.

" You didn't come to hear Cobden?" remarked a tradesman to a western farmer.

" No; went to see Van Amburg."

" Cobden seems to be an exceedingly plain and simple man, yet very clear and forcible," observed another inhabitant.

" Ah! that wur a grand turn out, wur it not? Eight on 'em all alike cream-coloured; eight on 'em all in hand, going like lambs. My precious eye! but it wur grand. What a fellow that Van Amburg must be, to be sure, to travel from town to town like that!" This was from another western agriculturist; and the conversational powers and propensities of all present were now heard in continuation thus:—

" And all the harness mounted with silver! Eh but that was a fine sight!"

" Cobden contends that the corn-law has never done good to the farmers, and never can; that it is only a pretence on the part of the landlords, that they may cajole the tenants."

" Van Amburg, I say, makes it all outside show. When you go to see his wild beasts, it ben't nothing after all. What say you—you saw him as well as I?"

" Nothing more than a take-in; a do. An elephant comes, with two or three or half a dozen codgers on its back, and goes round, and steps over a man what lies down in its way; and then it goes out again; and then we have Van and a lion and leopard, or something; and then the lion lifts his paw,

and Van orders him to lie down, and he lies down; and the
other beast puts up his paws on Van's shoulder; and then
they all growl; and then Van goes out of the cage, and says,
' Ladies and gentlemen, the performance is ower.' I say this
be only a *do* ; it ben't not half so fine as the outside show bes,
driving the eight creams all in hand in silver harness; had I
known I should never ha' gone inside."

" The farmers be always sacrificed. Let the promises be
what they may ; made by whom they will, the farmers are
cheated. I says landlords be all alike; governments and
prime ministers all alike, all tarred with one stick, as the
saying is ; all of 'em look to themselves, and only serve us with
pretences."

" Now, for my part, I don't think it be he as I seed at
Drury Lane Theatre at all. I'm a'most positive sure it ain't
Van Amburg; for *he* gave something for our money. This
chap do little more than shew us how he drives along the
road. I think he should be called Van *Humbug*, what do you
think ?"

" But what a sight of money he must have took. They say
he had more than three hundred pounds out of this here place,
and as good as two hundred pounds in Buckingham. He gets
a precious sight of money, that Van Amburg do."

" The League won't do much among the farmers, let 'em
say as they will. Farmers see too clearly what the object of
them Leaguers be to be caught with chaff; they ha'n't got
much money for their League Fund in them parts ; have they,
Mr Brown ?"

" No ; an they got no more money than I'd give 'em, they'd
leave off going about."

" And I say the same ; an they got no more than they
could get out of Buckingham they'd let Buckingham alone."

" Where be Van Amburg off to next?"

" He be to enter Oxford a Tuesday I hear say. They say
he won't have less than five or six hundred pounds during the
two days he bes to be there."

" Wilt thou go see him again? I thought o' going to Oxford to-morrow to see him go in, wilt thou ?"

" I don't mind much ; it be only ten mile to ride, and I
can be back to dinner. I think I shall go. Wilt thou, Mr
Smith ?"

And thus proceeded the conversation. A few complaints
about Peel and the tariff, a few fears about Cobden and the
League, and three times as many accounts of the sayings and
doings of Van Amburgh and his lions. There were some inti-
mations of displeasure from more than one landlady and land-

lord of more than one inn, that their regular customers, who
dined on market days, were holding off to keep themselves in
readiness for the Stanhope dinner. There were some other
detached grumblers; and, through the dull markets and dull
weather, the outside show of Van Amburgh's caravans and
the small doings within, the large promises of Peel and the
dissatisfaction with what he has done, the speeches of the
League and the hopes for better times, were the chief subjects
of plaintive dialogue; there were other topics brought forward
and despondingly discussed. Indeed, during several hours that
I listened, few matters escaped a sigh of regret, save one;
this was never touched on. Never was a word said of the
hundreds of thousands of our population who are daily pining
for want of food, because they are not employed and paid.
Not a word of the additional hundreds of thousands who may
have food of a certain kind, but who never taste butchers'
meat, because the demand for their labour is so small, and
their wages so very like the demand. There was never,
amongst all that I heard of Peel and the tariff, and Van Amburgh and his lions, and the League and Mr Cobden, and all
that was said of the unsold and unsaleable animals standing
in the market place on their tired limbs, with drooping heads,
because there they stood and nobody came to buy; amongst
all these topics not a word was said of the hungry people of
the town, who once ate beef and mutton, and now cannot;
who in hunger droop their heads because trade droops; and
who will never revive, and eat beef, until trade revives. Not
a word of complaint escaped a lip, in my hearing, on this
subject.

The dinner hour came. I presented my three shilling
ticket, and, entering the Town Hall, found one hundred and
thirty square yards of agriculturists at dinner, there being at
the rate of, to each square yard of floor, a knife and fork, a
plate, and a man.

Here the dissatisfaction that had filled the farmers with
complaints outside, which, while they were hungry, had fed
on every subject of discontent which they could possibly find,
always excepting that just now mentioned, and which should
have been their leading, if not sole subject of complaint,
namely, the non-consumption of the beef and mutton which
they fed and could not sell; here they found other matters
wherewith to be discontented.

The dinner, for the tickets to which they had paid three
shillings each, was a dinner, as the advertisement said, "to
Lord Stanhope." But as it is customary when a dinner is
given to a guest for the givers to partake with the guest, the

farmers in this case found the phrase, " a dinner to Lord Stanhope," rather too literally verified, and they did not like it. In short, they once more grumbled at those who call themselves " friends of the farmers." They had expected that in giving a dinner to Lord Stanhope they would get one to themselves ; and that the condescension of his Lordship in coming to dine with them would be a sufficient recompence for any inconvenience they might have incurred in coming to town in a wet day, and, wet or dry, in sitting down on rough deal boards and barrel heads, at rough deal tables, to pick their bones ; the condescension of a peer of the realm, the very Quixotte of "farmers' friends," to join them at a three-shilling-a-head dinner like this, was enough to reconcile them to many personal inconveniences, and most of them probably pronounced themselves to be reconciled and pleased.

But when they saw his Lordship evincing the very doubtful taste of eating with a select few at one end of the hall, *waited on by his own servants in livery*, the farmers, at least all near where I sat, grumbled rather indecorously, though not without excuse. They expected that a " friend" to dinner would have come as a friend, as a partaker of a plain dinner in a plain way ; but my Lord came with a retinue of servants, that he might not touch nor be touched by anything so common as what the farmers ate and drank and were served by. Besides two or three gentlemen whose rank as landholders entitled them to sit near the person of his Lordship, he had Dr Sleigh " of Brill House," and John Bell of the *Bucks Herald*, once of the " fierce democracy," who being to make speeches, were admitted into the circle from which were arranged to proceed, *and did proceed*, all the " hear, hears," the " yaw, yaws," and the " yees, yees."

A FOX HUNT IN DORSETSHIRE—1845.

THE following account of a fox hunt, at which I was present, is, as nearly as can be written, literally what I saw. The introductory dialogue, supposed to occur on the previous night, is also a sketch from fact.

" Bill ?"

" Well, Jack, what be it ?"

" The hounds be coming to draw Gorse-hill cover to-morrow."

" Be they ? Sha'n't I be after them ?"

" And sha'n't I ?"

" Bill ?"

" Well, Jack, what be it ?"

"Give up one of them tatoes thee be's a doing on in the ashes."

" Na ; they ben't for to-night, they be a doing on for break-fast. We ha'n't no bread, and father be to go out at five. He be gone to bed now ; and I be doing his tatoes for him. Mother be laid down as well, and all of them. Why ben't thou, Jack ?"

" Why ben't I a-bed ? I been with old Tom and young Harry a stopping the holes. Them foxes be all out at night seeing what they can get. We have stopped their holes for them ; and won't they find it queer when they go home and cannot get in, and have the pack come on them in the cover. I do so wish, Bill, to-morrow morning was come."

" I wishes, Jack, this precious cold night were over. We be a starved up in that topmost room, with no things a'most on us. There be such a lot on us in our house, we ha'n't got no money to get bread enough, let alone things to cover. See how us be obliged to stick them tatoes into our insides. It be a terrible cold night. I be afeard to go to bed for the cold."

" What I be most afeard on as to cold, Bill, be's this ; that it be frosty, and squire won't hunt. I wouldn't lose it for ever so much. Would thee, Bill?"

" Na, Jack, I shouldn't like to. Wilt thou go to cover first thing, or wilt thou go to work and chance the hounds coming down where thou be's a-doing that job on the road ? I sha'n't go to work myself. I would rather lose half a day than not have the sport. Half a day's pay ben't much to win, and it ben't much to lose. What says thee, Jack ?"

" I say this. I wouldn't think on it. Five shilling a week, for half a day be only fippence. And then the chance of a something to pick up. Morris got half-a-crown to open a gate the last time squire hunted over here ; and when young Lord What-do-ye-call-him fell off his horse that time, Court-ney, and Mason, and Jones, and What's-his-name, got two sovereigns for carrying him on a litter, and had such a blow out of drink and victuals on the head on't as thee never seed. Besides, there be the digging out of the fox, if he run to earth, and twenty more chances to get a trifle. But for my part I would go after the hounds for the sport. Split me if I wouldn't."

" So would I, Jack. And so would any one."

Such may never have been the precise words of any two men in Dorset. But these words are indicative of what may be seen or heard in every village of Dorset where hunting is known. And few counties are more remarkable than this for the spirit of the inhabitants, rich and poor, in running after a piece of diversion.

There are more people by half than get profitable employment in the county. So sporting is not much loss of time to them. It is sometimes a loss of shoes in the mud; but the shoes are always found again. Sometimes a loss of skin and clothes in scrambling and tearing through bushes; but skin grows on again, and clothes are tacked together somehow. The greatest advantage it does is, that while the mounted men who dined late last night ride to-day to find their appetites, the men on foot who did not dine at all are running to lose theirs, and for a while forget them.

Let us suppose the morning come. The meet is at some gate—I need not say what gate. From east, from west, from every side, horses and men, scarlet coats and green, jog along at a trot. What jolly happy-looking fellows they are, every one of them. Who could believe for a moment that, mounted on such nags, with such bright stirrups and shining boots; white leathers and well-fleshed limbs to swell them out; such broad chests and ruddy faces, the faces wearing a hue which may indicate either last night's wine or this morning's early rising and fresh air, just as you think fit to imagine—for theirs is a mixture of both; who could think that any of these are "farmers in distress?" But farmers they are, many of them.

This gentleman nearest us, on the bay mare, is not a farmer —not strictly speaking. He has land and he farms it, and he also complains at public meetings of agricultural distress and hard times; so he is doubtless an agriculturist. But he is also a clergyman. And that is the reason why young Sparks, the whipper-in, swears so. Sparks was once a lad in a smock-frock and round hat, and leggings just the same as those lads sitting on the style; but he was taken notice of and put into the stable, and in time mounted into office, and got up to where he is now. The fineness of his clothes and polish of his boots astonish those who recollect his old leggings and smock-frock. But his great card is to swear at the dogs, and at anything else, so close to the parson as to make them wonder that he is not afraid.

Here comes a farmer. One precisely after Squire Bankes' heart, the squire having declared a landlord's pride to be, "when he knows that his tenant is the best mounted in the troop of yeomanry, and that he now and then takes a good gallop with the squire's hounds."

Who better mounted than this tenant? Who oftener galloping? He even subscribes to another pack of hounds that hunt in another district. Yet this gentleman is one of Squire Bankes' own tenants, and he is not able to tell what the squire says—continuing the sentence already quoted as the greatest joy of a landlord—namely, "Proud, above all, if the farmers shall tell him 'there is not on my farm nor in my parish one single able-bodied man out of employ.'"

This well-mounted tenant may, I say, do the squire's heart good as far as horse flesh, horsemanship, and a good spurred, booted, and scarlet-coated turn out can go. I believe he has never been in arrear with his rent; that must be another matter of satisfaction. But in this parish there are rather more than the half of the able-bodied labourers out of work and out of wages; and the wages of those in work—in work to this farmer—are five shillings a-week to able-bodied men— young men, so able-bodied that they are five feet eight inches high, can carry a sack of wheat with any man in Dorset, and eat bread and bacon with any man in England if they could get it to eat. The wages of those in work who are married and have families are more. They are as high as six shillings and seven shillings, in two instances as high as eight shillings, and in one as high as nine shillings.

Are any of the children of these highest paid men here— here at the gate—at the meeting of the hunt? No; this is not in their locality. Here are young ones enough, and old ones too, but not from Mr Bankes'.

Here are two officers of the army, and three lords, two of them members of Parliament, but neither belonging to this county. All are well mounted. The master of the hounds, the squire himself, meets them.

Who would not be a farmer, even in hard times? One of the lords has nodded to one of these farmers, and the squire himself has introduced them. Is that nothing?

Here comes old Bob the shoemaker. The Gorse-hill cover has not been drawn once these twenty years but old Bob has been at it, he and all his apprentices for the time being. He had work to do to-day, shoes to make which were wanted; but who would work and the hounds out? Who, indeed, but some thrasher or ploughman that must?

And though old Bob is only on foot, he is somebody here. A farmer nods to him, just as a lord nodded to a farmer.

And here is a sporting draper mounted on the butcher's horse. And here is the butcher himself on the young horse that he thinks of buying. Here is the landlord of the inn where the magistrates hold their sittings. He is a high man, and mounted, of course. He is so high a man, permitted as he is to take the field with lords, and with squires richer even than the lords, that he looks upon all those foot people with the most thorough contempt. But on none more so than on that man who is a beershop keeper. "The impudence of

some persons! that a mere beershop keeper should pretend to
take an interest in fox-hunting! and, though on foot, to make
his appearance within the same palings with the landlord of
the head inn!

Here is a jolly good fellow on a jolly good horse. And one
of these bystanders says that he hasn't come away without his
breakfast this morning. Another adds, "No, nor without
knowing that everybody else had a good breakfast. He be a
trump to his men, he be."

Another parson comes up and joins the one already arrived.
Young Styles and Norman have been so fascinated with the
manly courage of young Sparks, the whipper-in, who swore in
the parson's face, that they swear also. They cannot help
feeling themselves to be more than mere eaters of dry bread
and cold tatoes warmed on the gridiron already. They
call one another B.'s and D.'s close to the clergymen's horses'
tails; and do not doubt but such courage may elevate them
into the stable some day, if not into a whip's saddle.

Here is little Josh Something, with his little smock-frock
all in tatters, and his toes, cold day as it is, bare and red,
through the old shoes he has on. He had no time to eat his
tatoes, hearing of the hounds, so he brought them with him,
and is eating one in each hand now; he calls one bread and
one cheese. He is an original in his way, that little Josh.

But the time is up, and the principal men have come. It is
considered the best field of the season. There have been more
numerous fields quite as well mounted; but there has been no
such brilliant company as this. The officers, the three lords,
two of them county members, one or two baronets, and not
less than half-a-dozen landed esquires. The farmers, butchers,
drapers, and innkeepers, who hunt in such company, are up in
the stirrup indeed, and they feel it.

"Get out, you young rascal; why ben't you at home, and
not come here to be rode down; get out with you!" This is
from the butcher to little Josh and his cold tatoes. It is
accompanied by a cut of a whip sharp enough to have made
Josh cry on ordinary occasions. But he only dives into a
bush and says, "Thee ben't no squire; thee be nought but a
butcher!"

There is an old fox in the cover who has known what a
hunt is before to-day. He is alleging to an inexperienced
companion that there is no danger; that, though the holes
were closed up when they came home from the pheasant preserves or the hen-roosts, or wherever they were this morning,
there is no danger. "Now they hear dogs and men, and the
young one cannot believe but there is danger. The old one

still denies its existence, if the young one will only take his advice. The young one knows not what to do. But the hounds come nearer, and he is surer than ever that there is danger. The old one admits now that there will be, if the young one does not get up and run. But if he runs at once he will be safe ; he, the old one, will keep between him and the hounds, if hounds there be. The young fox starts up and runs accordingly ; the hounds see him ; they seek no farther for another ; they open their mouths ; lay down their heads ; join in the cry and the pursuit ; and as the old fox hears them leaving the wood, and going off at a greater and greater distance, he says, or thinks the saying, which is all the same, " I wish you no harm, young friend ; but that was good policy of mine. Better you before the hounds than me."

There is no time here to moralize, and compare, and make suppositions ; yet it may be that this old fox, at some feast in the cover, had called himself the " foxes' friend," ever ready to *protect* the young ones, and ever regardless of himself.

But we are in haste. The young fox has discovered, as other creatures have to their cost, that the protection of his " friend" was simply to turn him out into the front of the danger ; and, now that he is in it, he tries to leave it as far behind as he can.

First of all, he tries to find how the wind blows, that he may run with it ; but he has no time to make experiments. Unluckily he is out on the wrong side. He is off at a great dash ; but he knows his course to be wrong. So does old Bob the shoemaker. He can tell already that this is a young fox ; and he can tell that, before long, he will turn ; he will wind by the upper heath, and come down upon the Stour by the common. And old Bob breaks away in a different direction from that taken by the fox, and hounds, and hunters, assured that he will meet them again. Save a few of the very rawest of the mob—the young foxes of it, who run the wrong way, because it is the way the hunters went—the whole follow Bob, who has had twenty years' experience.

And now for the chasing and racing. The racing first. The swiftest soon take the lead from even the most experienced in short cuts. Mr Hurst's meadow gate is opened in almost no time. If Mr Hurst were there he would give it to some of them, to run through among his sheep and cows, yelling that way, and then over the fence through his young tares and wheat. But he is not there ; he is with the hounds, and riding by this time through somebody else's fields. It would have been much worse for his sheep and cows in the meadow, and young tares and young wheat, if all the pack and fifty horsemen had gone over his fences and lands. But then it is an honour to have one's fences broken and one's farm trampled by the hunters, saving always such men as the sporting draper, butcher, innkeeper, and two or three more who have no land of their own to be trampled by others.

Then ensues the running to earth in a drain, the digging out, the new chase, new fields of wheat scoured over, ewe sheep great in lamb driven about in terror, and all the "farmers in distress," hallooing and rejoicing with voices loud and joyous as they in the company of the lords and squires, break down each others fences, cut each other's newly sprung wheat, and scare and drive in terror each other's breeding ewes, and cows, and fattening sheep.

A JOURNEY TO THE MEADOWS OF HERTFORDSHIRE.

Persons acquainted with the thoroughfares of London, know that they are sometimes choked, blocked, or locked with their traffic. It is as difficult to ascertain, when a lock occurs, which of the draymen shouting, cabmen whipping, or butchers' boys "chaffing," has been the cause of the stoppage, as it is to discover who have caused the lock in the political world. But there is a lock in the political world. Never was the line of street from St Paul's to Temple Bar more completely and inextricably choked, by its vehicles locking together, than is the Parliamentary thoroughfare at this moment, by which bills travel from the House of Commons to the House of Lords, and from the House of Lords to the House of Commons. And yet in the line of Fleet Street and Ludgate Hill, with the crossing at Farringdon Street, there are occasionally lockages in the traffic so inextricable that the most skilful of the police are baffled in making a clearance; and no clearance is made until some unlooked-for condescension on the part of a few drivers, who back out, leads to a general movement forward, as the unlooked-for perseverance of a few jolly waggoners, "all of a row," with their ponderous vehicles from the country—a "country party" in the street, formidable enough to obstruct the traffic, dogged enough to get into a fix and remain in it—led at first to the stoppage.

Being a passenger the other day for the country, to obtain a glimpse of the spring, the fresh green of grassy Hertfordshire, the new buttercups and daisies among the grass; the suckling lambs and their fleecy mothers among the buttercups and daisies; the farm fields, with new crops upon them; the farmers, with new notions in their heads about their fields and crops of corn ; and, perchance, the Lord of Essex, or his park and mansion, or his farms, who has become a kind of League lecturer, putting new notions into the heads of farmers about crops of corn, and corn-laws, and competition with foreigners ; being a passenger for the country on the outside of one of those busses which gather from the multitudes of the metropolis, one by one, the railway passengers, and transfer them by the score to the mouth of the iron giants, who swallow them by the hundred, I got fixed in one of those locks in the street which are unpleasant at any time, and particularly so when one's appointment is with a railway train. Still, it was not all lost time. Having nothing to do but to look and listen, to sit and see, I looked and listened, and sat and saw ; and the parallel between the street police and the political police in urging onward the loads which would not be urged onwards, seemed to be remarkable enough to justify me in drawing my pen on the subject, as some of them drew their batons, or as others have been drawing, or threatening to draw, their pistols.

There were several waggons loaded with grain or with flour. From their bulk, they were conspicuous among the other vehicles. They had come down the street, and were warned in their progress by others loaded with straw crossing from the bridge, and halted at the crossing. One or two butcher's boys in light carts, whether in joke or in earnest I did not know, demanded that the policeman should turn the corn-loaded waggons back, and allow them, the said boys in the carts, to get past, they being charged with the safe and early delivery of joints of meat for that day's dinners, to those rich enough to have prime joints of meat sent home in light spring carts. But though these impetuous youths, with all the volubility of tongue, all the forwardness, most of the impudence, and some of the "chaff" and the "slang" peculiar to them, insisted that the police should make the corn-loaded waggons go backward to let them and others in light vehicles get on, no such counter movement could be effected. I do not know that the street police said, but they might have said, as one of the political police did—one not unknown in Fleet Street and elsewhere, for his services in clearing a passage for obstructed traffic—"that as well might the corn resolutions of the House of Commons move backwards, or be turned aside, and left in the siding, as to think that those ponderous corn waggons, each with a tonnage of loading, should be backed up hill to let butchers' boys and the light fry of vehicles go by." I say, I do not know that the street police spoke thus ; nor am I sure that the political policeman, to whom I allude as celebrated for his services in clearing obstructed thoroughfares,

used the comparison as it is given here; I rather think it is
reversed from him; at all events, whether speaking of corn-
loaded waggons in the streets or corn-charged resolutions in
Parliament, he said it was impossible that they could remove
backwards, or even be set aside, to make room for butchers'
boys or the butchers themselves, who had come whip in hand
at an impetuous pace into the street, getting into a fix by their
impetuosity, and only stopped from running over some one
(some of those poor Irishmen with heavy loads on their backs)
by being stopped in their headlong career.

And speaking of Irishmen with loads on their backs, I am
reminded that in the street-stoppage the humblest carrier of
a load fares worst when he cannot get along. He has not
only to bear his burthen and make no progress, but very often,
and particularly if an Irishman, and known to be one, he has
to bear the "chaff" of the thoughtless, and even the back-
handed cuts of the impetuous boys, who have whips in their
hands, and who drive, or attempt to drive others that they
themselves may get along.

I cannot say that I observed any Irish gentleman with his
cab and his tiger, though gentlemen with cabs and tigers were
there, who at a moment when there was some hope of an early
extrication, drove into the confusion, to the locking up of himself and the hindrance of all who were about to move; and yet
there were cases not unlike this, of vehicles being driven in
which might have been kept out, for no purpose apparently
but the strange satisfaction of being locked up, to the great
annoyance of those seriously active in clearing the thoroughfare, and to the pleasure of their own drivers—if pleasure it
could be—of being in the midst of confusion, delay, angry words,
and personal accusations, of which there were enough to serve
all the streets of London, including Billingsgate Market, for
as long a time as the length of a session of Parliament.

Some brewers' drays, loaded with beer, had stopped the
countrymen loaded with straw; or, which amounted to the
same thing, the men of straw would not move, because they
said—and swore it as they said it—that the brewers stood in
their way, and that they had done nothing to be called on to
make way for the heavy waggons of the millers and the corn
merchants, which were coming down Fleet Street, and were
blocked there.

The police took hold of the reins and led horses, drivers,
and vehicles where they found an opening, whether the drivers
assented to it or not. They did so even against the loud pro-
tests of such drivers, that they were not to be led in that way
by the "Peelers," (a phrase more commonly applied to the

police in London than any other,) yet allowing themselves to be led notwithstanding.

Then one driver shouted to another that the lockage and confusion had been all that other driver's fault; and that other retorted the accusation; and cabmen shook their whips at one another, and gave significant hints of what each would do to each, if they had not happened to be where they were. And the drivers of such light vehicles as those we see in every street, with soda water and ginger beer, interfered with the stormy cabmen to quiet them, but made the confusion greater by adding new elements of discord. The tradesmen of the streets had their business suspended; customers could not approach the shops; or if they were in, they could not move out; and passengers who could move on some parts of the pavement were obstructed at others, and could not proceed on such business as they had intended to proceed upon. The very dogs of the street seemed to join in and add to the noise and confusion by their barking; and to the great hindrance and annoyance of those actively engaged in effecting a clearance, men, snarling more snappishly than the dogs, barked at and found fault with everything and every body that was engaged in doing something useful. Were it not a daring flight of imagination almost equal to that of the author of the "Revolutionary Epic," one might have thought that some snarling dogs had been bitten by some other dog labouring under Peelphobia, that sad looking dog for instance, which was unmuzzled at Shrewsbury in 1841, and became Peelphobious two years after, and bit the hand that he begged a bone from.

But a riddance was made at last, and the lighter carriages were obliged to give way to the heavier, and the heavier moved on and got out of the way; and we at last reached the railway station too late for the train.

A FARM-FIELD RAMBLE IN HERTFORDSHIRE.

In a farm-yard, with an orchard of cherry-trees and apple-trees clothed in blossom beyond it; and a field of green pasture with cows in the pasture beyond the orchard; and a field with ploughs, and horses, and men, and women, and boys, at work in it beyond the green pasture; and other pastures and meadows of grass for hay beyond the ploughed field; and white daisies, and yellow buttercups, and cowslips, in all of them; and hedgerows in green leaf and fragrant blossom surrounding the fields—large, rough, and rustic, though green

and blooming, like the men of the fields ; not free from vices,
but possessing virtues, and much to be pleased with ; the
woods of the lord of many acres rising above the fields, and
looking down upon them, as lofty above the humble shrubs of
the hedgerows, as the lord who dwelt within them in his noble
mansion was above the humble workers in the fields who dwelt
in tiled sheds. In that farm-yard, with pools of rain-water
large and foul in it, and wet dung which had been washed by
the rain-water ; and heaps of bean-straw and chaff upon the
wet dung ; and young pigs and old sows with their snouts
burrowed in the straw and chaff in search of cast-away beans,
as some legislators may be seen in search of cast-away arguments, gathering minute particles of fact with full mouthfuls of
fallacies, and swallowing all—digesting them, and existing on
that kind of provender scattered on the political dunghill by
men who have winnowed the grain from the chaff long ago,
only because it is their nature not to have a higher taste nor
a higher power of discrimination, in filling their mouths with
chaff and dirt for the sake of the one, or two grains of fact
which may be there. In that farm-yard, with the pigs in it,
some of which are grown up hogs, and are old enough to remember—if hogs have such memories or such knowledge—the time
when the lord of the land on which they were bred and fed,
was a monopolist, which he is not now ; when he was all for
the confining of hogs like them to the mere grains of " native
grown" corn among the chaff on the dunghill, and not as he
is now, in favour of hogs getting food good and clean, that
Englishmen may have enough of native fed bacon, even if that
bacon is fed on foreign grain. In that farm-yard, in the occupation of a tenant of that remarkable lord—the Earl of Essex
—I met that tenant, and had a conversation with him ; and
after talking on several topics, such as the making the most of
the manure which lay around, much of it wasted, and converting it into a productive element of new crops, and of the rearing of hogs and the conversion of hogs into good hams and
bacon, we talked of the conversion of the landlord from a
monopolist to a free trader, and the process by which it had
been done ; and of the effect which the conversion of a monopolist landlord was likely to have on a monopolist tenantry.

Farmer.—You know that I have always been in favour of
the corn-law. I cannot say I have changed my opinions as
Lord Essex has changed his. Probably I have not the capacity of judgment that he has ; perhaps I have not seen the
same arguments presented to me in the same way. He is a
landlord and I a tenant. A landlord may see things differently from a tenant. If I were a landlord I might have all

the high hopes for the future prosperity of agriculture which his Lordship has ; but I do not see what a tenant has to hope for. If he augments the produce of his land, by sinking capital in the land, he has his rent augmented upon him. If he does not improve his land, he loses by it. I see no hope for the tenant farmers.

Whistler.—It is to be fairly expected that Lord Essex will not stop in his own exertions to advance agriculture. He says there are some tenant farmers who never should have been farmers ; but there are landlords who never should have been landlords. As landed property has hitherto been managed, and must still for some time to come be managed, the landlord's services in promoting agricultural improvement are more necessary to it than the tenant's services. As tenures and conditions of agreement now exist between landlord and tenant, the power to improve the cultivation of the land is almost entirely in the hands of the landlord. But I think there is much to hope for from Lord Essex. On the question of free trade he adopted the opinions and prejudices of his class without inquiry, as he now confesses. May we not suppose that he has adopted the customs of his class in letting his farms on insecure tenures to his tenants, and loading those tenants with conditions as only asses are loaded—and they only so loaded by very thoughtless or very cruel boys—may we not suppose that his Lordship has as thoughtlessly adopted and acted on the tenurial customs of his class, as he confesses to have adopted and acted on the opinions and prejudices of his class about free trade? He says that, until the corn-law question came to a crisis, he had never given it any serious consideration, save on one side—his own side—that of protection. But when it came to a crisis, he was induced to inquire, and read, and study the arguments on the other side—the free trade side—to see what it was that had converted Sir Robert Peel ; by which inquiry, reading, and study, he found himself converted. And listen to what Sir Robert Peel confesses the other day, and not only confesses, but proclaims as a legislative fact. " I will not deny," he says, " that, during the debates on the question, my opinions have undergone a change—and it is this, that restrictions which I at first believed to be impolitic I now believe to be unjust."

Farmer.—But Sir Robert Peel is not a tenant farmer, with a rent to pay. He is a receiver of rents. Now, as I said before of Lord Essex, I might think as he thinks if I were a landlord, and had seen all the free trade arguments as he has seen them ; but as a tenant I see nothing to hope for. Explain to me, if you can, how improved agriculture is to do the tenants any good when his rent goes up with his produce and seldom falls with the price of his produce.

Whistler.—This is the very point at issue between landlord and tenant; but it is not the point at issue between the League and the tenant farmers, between free-trade and agriculture, between Sir Robert Peel, a prime minister, and you, a farmer. Sir Robert Peel as a statesman and Sir Robert Peel as a landlord is not the same. The conditions upon which you should hold your farm must be these:—That you will receive the profits of your improved agriculture for a term of years which no caprice or cupidity on the part of your landlord, and no accident to his life, can deprive you of. This is, and must be, the first principle in all agricultural improvement. Lord Essex will do nothing to achieve that success which he foretells to the agriculture of England, unless he adopts a system of leases liberal and long enough to secure practically to his tenants the profits of their capital and skill.

Farmer.—Do not you think that if tenants-at-will were to be legally entitled to compensation for all their improvements on quitting their farms, it would be a great benefit to them—as good as if they had leases?

Whistler.—A benefit, compared with their present state of helplessness as tenants-at-will, but not so good as a lease. I observe that farmers' clubs in different parts of the kingdom are discussing this question, and I regret exceedingly to see them wasting valuable time and a fair opportunity on such a worthless object as the improvement of tenancy-at-will. Under no form whatever, with no possible qualification, can tenancy-at-will be rendered fair and equitable to the tenant, or beneficial to the landlord and the progress of agriculture. I will say more, that no *honest* landlord, if not a weak-minded or ignorant man, will seek to have tenants-at-will upon his land, to expend capital, and skill, and health, and strength on that land. Many landlords who are honest men, let their farms on yearly tenancies, dismissing the tenants when they think fit; but if honest, they are ignorant, having never studied the subject, as Lord Essex says he never did until the corn-law came to a crisis; or they may be, unlike his Lordship, so weak-minded that they cannot study and understand such subjects; or, unlike his Lordship, they may be so inveterately prejudiced in favour of their territorial supremacy—the remnants of feudal power—that they will not yield independence and security to their tenantry, even when convinced that such independence and security would be to their own advantage. And it is possible that there are some, a good many perhaps, who have used their tenantry as political instruments in the polling booth, as mercantile men use their bills of exchange, bonds, and notes, and take them to the money-market to make profit of them, the profit being places of honour and emolument under Government, in the army, the navy, the church, the law courts, and the palace. But I believe the time has arrived, or it is not far off, when subserviency to a political party in Parliament, through the use of such men as you at the hustings, will be impracticable. We may therefore hope that you tenant farmers will be looked upon by your lords as farmers employed in the advancement of the national agriculture, and not as political beasts of burden, employed in the advancement of families to high prizes in the lottery of politics and plunder. And so I return to the point which I say is the one at issue between you and your landlord—that of security of tenure by a lease—and a liberal lease, untrammelled by game-law covenants, and all the other feudal covenants which you know well, but which are too numerous at present to mention.

Farmer.—Do you think we are, landlords and tenants, so near that age of prosperity and general well-doing foretold by Lord Essex, as to need nothing but a repeal of the corn-law and a system of leases? If you think so, I must say about you as I have said of my landlord, that I cannot see things as you see them.

Whistler.—But I must take the liberty of saying, my dear sir, that while you, like your landlord, did not read or listen to any arguments save those on your own side of the question, up to the coming of the corn-law crisis, you, unlike your landlord, have read nothing, or almost nothing since, on the free-trade side of the question; you told me that yesterday. You say that you have read the debates in Parliament during the present session, or so much of them as appears in the *County Herald;* and you complain that if the free-traders have good arguments in favour of the farmers seeking free-trade they do not state them. But, sir, the free-traders in Parliament are done with the argumentative part of the subject; that is taken out of their hands. Their business is now to vote, to consummate by enactment that which they have taught for years. When they were teaching, and you were not listening, that was not their fault; you should have listened to what concerned you so much. If you were to say to your clergyman, at the conclusion of the church service, " You must preach your sermon over again; I was not listening to you. I and my neighbours here were asleep, or we were playing and idling while you were praying and preaching; we must have it all over again, and the congregation must be halted here until we have it all over again." If you were to say that on Sunday, and every Sunday, to your parson, and go on sleeping at church, and idling, and never listening from week to week, from year to year, what would that large majority of the congregation who had been listening say to you?

Farmer.—I hardly see how this applies. But, admitting that it does apply, I want to know what we idle boys, the farmers, as I suppose you will call us, are to do now that we are woke up?

Whistler.—I do not call you idle boys. You are a most hard toiling and struggling class of men; but the best of your energies and the greatest of your struggles go for nothing. Some of them are mischievous. You must not only do new work, but you must undo some of the old. You are not "idle boys," but you are sometimes "mischievous boys," and you must undo some mischief by abstaining from a repetition of it. If you will let me, for a few minutes, compare you to school-boys, I will tell you what some of you have done in Hertfordshire. A boy who was far in advance of any of you, who sought to teach you and make you equal to himself—you, to please your master, (you do not do so now, when your master confesses that he was wrong and that boy was right,) you, though knowing that your neighbour was a better farmer than any of you, getting the best of crops out of indifferent land, and profit from cultivation when you were getting loss, you scouted that boy, fell on him, and abused him, and called him ill names in the market place. You must not do so again. Indeed you will not, for Lord Essex is now of opinion that this farmer was right, and he and you were wrong, and you only called that neighbour ill names in the market place, and hissed him and hooted him, because you knew Lord Essex was pleased at your doing so, and, like some other "bad boys," you had never been taught better. If I had nothing else to rejoice at in the conversion of your landlord to free-trade principles than the fact that his tenants will have no interest, or supposed interest, in ill-using their free-trade neighbours, I would rejoice, for that alone is a great gain in Hertfordshire.

Farmer.—Who do you speak of as the boy so far in advance of us, and whom we ill-used; the tenant who wrote against Lord Essex about the game, and whom his Lordship turned out of his farm?

Whistler.—No; I mean Mr Lattimore of Wheathamstead.

Farmer.—Because I was going to say, that it was not his

neighbours, the tenant farmers, that said anything against him who wrote against the game; quite the reverse. We were all too well pleased to say anything against him; and as for Mr Lattimore, I do not think he was ever opposed by us but in a fair way. We did not agree with him, and opposed him as we would have opposed you.

Whistler.—But you would not listen, and hissed, and shouted him down at public meetings. You now listen to him; you now listen to me. Two years ago, though you are still of the same opinion as then about the corn-law, so you say, you would not have permitted me to have stood here, not because this is your farm, but because the farm is Lord Essex's, to speak of free-trade as I have been doing. The truth is, you dared not have done so. Now my object with you farmers is, to get yourselves raised to independence as occupiers of the land; not that you may dare to differ in opinion with your landlord, but that you may be able to cultivate your land as it should be cultivated. I have spoken of leases, but a lease is not enough. It is absolutely requisite to secure you against the landlord, or his agents, or his successors, when he dies. But there are things which must be effected, through the united efforts of tenants and landlords, before agriculture can reach that healthy state predicted for it by the free-traders years ago, and now predicted for it by Lord Essex. The rights of lords of manors over copyholders must be qualified to allow copyholders to cut down hedgerow timber, divert springs, water-courses, or, in other words, to drain. The copyholders and their tenants being the parties interested in the improvement, and the lord of the manor, or other superior, as the case may be, having no direct interest in such improvements, the latter is a fatal obstacle in the way of progress.

Farmer.—What do you think of the Duke of Richmond's bill for charging the expense of permanent improvements, by drainage, on the heirs in-tail?

Whistler.—The object is good, and the machinery, so far as it goes, is good; but it reaches only a very short way. And so does Sir Robert Peel's proposal to pass an act, if the new corn-law scheme passes, to lend money from the treasury to assist in agricultural improvements. Sir Robert's intention to lend public money, as I view it, is not only useless but bad. Where proper security is offered for money, it can be got now to improve the cultivation of land to any amount, from private individuals or from banks. If the security offered is not good, the money ought not to be lent, not alone because public money should be as carefully parted with as private money, but because, to lend money to landlords or tenant farmers who do not give such security as a private lender would accept, is to offer a bounty on the continuance of the present loose system of tenures. Private individuals lend money fast enough to landowners, when it is notoriously for their private expenditure, when it is not for the improvement of their property, but when there can be no doubt it will involve them in debt for life, and their property in bondage and bad cultivation for many years. Why then should there be any difficulty in obtaining money to improve the property? Let a tenant be properly protected from mortgagees, from the landlord, and from the landlord's creditors, by a lease of twenty years' duration at least. Let him be the borrower of the money, and his lease the security, (I speak of estates where the landlords are already drowned in debt, and cannot borrow money.) Let the tenants in this and all cases pay their rents according to the prices of farm produce. Let the lawyers have as little to do with the land as possible; but, above all, let the tenant be efficiently protected from his landlord, and there is no fear but that the time will come, and come soon, of which Lord Essex speaks so hopefully, when he says he sees better times coming for landlords and tenants, and for all.

CORN AGAINST CATTLE—CATTLE AGAINST CORN.

HERE we are in 1845, past the middle of April, in a cold backward spring. This year has not yet given a leaf nor a blade of grass. Last year produced deficient hay and turnips, which makes the denial of early vegetation this year all the worse. "There is corn in Egypt;" beans, plenty of them, which would have brought our cattle over the winter, and sent them fat to market; but no, they must not come. And the manure must not be made to produce heavier crops of corn and heavier turnips for the ensuing season.

Instead of sending for beans to Egypt and for oats to Poland, the cattle must be sent to market only half fattened; and many farmers must sell, as perhaps one-half of all the renting tenants in England have done during the last autumn and winter, a large portion of their live stock at a dead loss to save a greater loss. And while doing this they must buy guano for manure. They may buy from one part of Africa the manure ready made to fertilize the land at home; but they must not bring from another part of Africa food for cattle to manufacture manure for themselves, and get the profits of it to themselves!

If they completed the fattening of their cattle on Egyptian beans, and paid thereby all expenses of purchase and labour, and had the manure for nothing, would it not, saying nothing of actual profit on the cattle and sheep, and the saving of the actual losses, be a great advantage over their present condition?

In the last number of the *Mark-Lane Express* the complaint —unfortunately too well founded—is reiterated of the heavy losses sustained from deficient winter food for cattle. And a correspondent of that paper, who joins in the cry of hard times for farmers, has the following passage :—

"Sir Robert asks the agriculturists what they want. He is a modern Isaac, who blesseth, not Jacob, but the manufacturers; and says, ' Yea, and they shall be blessed.' The agriculturists say unto him, ' Bless us also, O our father.' He answers, ' Thy brothers came with subtilty and stole away thy blessing.' "

Now, if Sir Robert Peel were to quote the words of Jacob when he himself was a patriarch and gave law unto his sons, and apply the words to the distressed farmers, viz.—

"Why do ye look one upon another? Behold, I have heard that there is corn in Egypt; get ye down thither and buy for us from thence, that we may live, and not die."

That our cattle and sheep may be fed, and that the millions of our population who do not now taste of their flesh may eat, and repay you abundantly. Such should be Sir Robert's addition to the admonition of Jacob.

What would the farmers who "stand and look one upon another" say to this? In all likelihood they would say, "It requires a large outlay of money to buy food for cattle. Though we might have more manure by so doing, we would have to be at the expense of more labour to prepare it. As it is, the money paid for guano gets it for us direct and ready for use." And they might add, most consistently and truthfully, "It would do us no good to produce manures ourselves; we lose the greater part, certainly all the best, of what we now produce."

Suppose a manufacturer of cottons took the same position with regard to his business that a farmer takes, who would rather have the ammonia of the excremental offal of the birds of Africa brought to his land than the ammonia of the excremental offal of his own bullocks fed on the beans of Africa, that manufacturer would say, " Cotton costs me money; it is bulky in ships; it takes carriage expenses from me; I must pay for coals for a steam-engine ; and for the engine and all that expensive machinery which is its offspring ; I must pay for many people to make all these things, and for many people to work them, and to spin and weave the cotton. No ; I will not send to Egypt (or America) for cotton. I will rather sell off such of my looms as are now standing, and such of my premises as are now empty."

The position of the farmer selling off his half-fattened cattle as he now does, and of this manufacturer as he would then be, is the same.

Let not the farmers deny it by putting forth the plea that manufacturers' profits from the use of an imported raw material to make cloth are larger than his would be from the use of an imported raw material to make beef. Were the question of profit or no profit on the importation of Egyptian beans and Polish oats raised, it would be easily demonstrated to be a real profit, and that too not a small one. Such food with grass cut in summer, and with turnips and straw in winter—for *hay* should then be sparingly made, the grass being more valuable as grass joined with corn-feeding than as hay—such food, I say, would produce an undoubted profit.

But our protectionists halt at an earlier stage than the question of profit. They deny the soundness and practicability of the principle of getting food from foreign shores even for cattle. Yet strangely enough they will let all their liquid manures run to waste, let the precious gases escape into the air from their manure heaps, and yet they will buy the same substances that they have themselves wasted from a foreign shore.

A WEEK IN THE WEST.

Remarks on the Hindrances of Agriculture.

27th December 1845.

I FOUND the following in an old parish record in the county of Hereford a few days ago :—" It hath been ye custom from time immemorial, now gone in part into disuse, to take ye boys in need of ye flogging to ye boundaries of ye parochial on perambulation day, Holy Thursday, and flog them as ye procession went round ye bounds, that it might so be in after-time to come, ye boys being men, would remember ye marches of ye parish."

It appears also, that in these perambulations certain mystic services were performed at the boundaries of farms and estates,

" for the good of the harvest." Probably this was the agricultural protection of those days; and doubtless the farmers paid for it as they do now. Now-a-days, the boys are emancipated from the infliction of the rod at the parish boundaries; and there is no reason to suppose that they forget or neglect to care for the good of the parish because they are emancipated. They live in an age that rejoices to call itself civilized, when, to carry staves in procession round the parish would not be deemed a protection to the harvest against "the enemy;" when a flogging, as the procession walked along, would not be necessary to make wayward boys mend their ways and be good parishioners.

But if the boys have been emancipated from such hard management, many of the men have not, civilized though this age is called. There are certain things to be done "for the good of the harvest" with as little reason to justify them, and as much hardship in them as there was in the old preambulations and the flogging of the boys.

In the same parish where I saw the old record, and to which it refers—namely, the parish of Ross, in the county of Hereford—the following case occurred within the last two years. It only needs to be put into words a little antiquated to make it appear a specimen of the times of the flogging of boys round the parish to make them in after-time remember the marches.

" There hath lived in this parish, in all grace and honesty, a worthy man, for many years, by name Joseph Cross; and he hath one farm of 200 acres and more, and payeth ye rent thereof to his landlord, the Lord Alexander Baring of Ashburton, who, being careful for the good of the harvest, doth perambulate ye acres, and mark out ye bounds which ye tenants must walk on, and no other; for if they walk not unto ye marks laid down to them by ye said Lord Alexander Baring of Ashburton, and other noble lords and gentlemen, they will be punished, and made to remember it in after-times to come. And it so fell out that Mr Joseph Cross did plant of potatoes one-half acre of land less in the year 1843 than he was in power to do by permission of ye said Lord Alexander Baring. And also it fell out that in the year 1844, ye said Joseph Cross did plant one-half acre of potatoes more than ye said Lord permitted to be done, thinking thereby to make even with ye time when he did not plant so much. But ye said Lord did hear thereof, and did say that his tenant must pay 800 shillings for not abiding within ye rules laid down at ye time of marking ye boundaries by which he was to walk; at which time also ye said Lord Alexander Baring did say all his care was for ye tenant-farmers, and all his services were for their protection. And ye said Mr Joseph Cross did take out of his pocket forty pounds, being 800 shillings, and did count it over to ye said Lord Alexander, who put it in his own breeches pocket, did button ye same, and walk away.

"And Mr Joseph Cross did suffer this punishment when ye parish was perambulated for protection to ye farmers, and for good of ye harvest, inasmuch as that he did first walk within and next without ye Lord's boundary."

It is not necessary to adduce new arguments in this paper to prove that wherever there is the worst cultivation, the poorest farmers, and the worst conditioned labourers, there we shall find the most stringent covenants existing between tenant and landlord.

I was lately on the estate of a gentleman not unknown to fame in the proceedings of agricultural protection societies— Sir Alexander Hood. This landowner is a great stickler for the corn-law for the sake of the tenant farmers, and especially the labourers. As to the labourers, it may be enough to say that their wages in full employment, including harvest, does not average over 7s. 6d. a-week; that 1s. and 1s. 6d. a-week is paid for house rent; and that for years past their daily diet is potatoes for breakfast, dinner, and supper, and potatoes only. This year they are not living on potatoes, because they have none. In the county of Somerset, everywhere, the potatoes are lost, with few left for seed. In the neighbourhood of Glastonbury, Sir Alexander Hood's country, they are utterly lost, seed and all; and the wretched farm workers are now existing on half diet, made of barley meal, turnips, cabbages, and such small allowance of bread as small wages will procure. No advance of wages has accompanied the advance in the price of bread. So much for Alexander Hood's labourers, and the benefit they derive from protection to agriculture. And it should be added also, that there is only wages paid at the rate of one man at 7s. 6d., and one boy at 3s., to each hundred acres of land. A great deal of the land lies in grass; it all wants draining.

And now for the tenant farmers. One of them, taking a lead among the rest, the rest intending to follow, or promising to follow, made an attempt to drain and cultivate a portion of his farm, only a few acres out of several hundreds, so that he might grow some more winter feeding for his cattle, employ two or three more men, and thus lessen the parish rates. But he was proceeded against for penalties, was forced into litigation, was sold up, expelled the farm, beggared, and made an example of, to deter others from daring to attempt to cultivate their land as they might think best.

Not long ago Sir Alexander Hood was at Wells. He was making a speech about protection being requisite to save the farmers from ruin. " Look at this man," cried some daring citizen of Wells, who, taking the ruined farmer by the hand, presented him in front of the platform. Sir Alexander had the virtue of being ashamed; he turned and addressed that part of the meeting on his right. But in a few minutes the remnant of his ruined tenant, led by the daring citizen, appeared there, and again the latter said, " Look at this man!" Sir Alexander turned to the left, and spoke with his face in that direction of his advocacy of protection for the benefit of labourers and tenant farmers; but again there came before him the same couple of tormentors, the one the picture of ruin staring him in the face, and the other calling, " Look at this man!" He drew his speech to an abrupt conclusion and retired.

The worst part of all this mismanagement of land by landlords is, that many good men do so conscientiously. There are many excellent men who cling to this illusory shadow of protection, believing that such cultivation as they have on their soils of middling quality (much of Somerset is of that character) would cease. The bugbear that inferior lands would go out of cultivation by the abolition of the corn-laws is constantly frightening them. I saw an excellent letter in the *Times* the other day, written by Lord Kinnaird, showing that the inferior soils now in cultivation would not be abandoned, but that free-trade would improve them. To this I add my humble but emphatic testimony of affirmation.

The first practical operation of free-trade on the middling and inferior qualities of soil now under cultivation would be to increase their fertility and productiveness. It is an expensive and profitless way to fertilize such soils by the purchase of guano and other manures not made on them; but it is a cheap way to fertilize them by purchasing low-priced oats, beans, lintseed, maize, and barley, to feed cattle and sheep, mingled with the straw and chaff, and the root produce, turnips, carrots, clover, &c., grown at home. The cattle and sheep will pay for their provender, and the best of all manures will be on the farms free of price. More acres must then be under turnips and other root crops than now on each farm, which increase will be practicable because of the increase of manure. This will augment labour. Fewer acres on each farm will be in wheat, but superior fertility will give a larger crop of wheat. The cost of its production will be less than now; the amount of its produce more than now.

The first principles of successful agriculture are security of tenure, regularity of price, and cheap fertility. The first of these might co-exist with a corn-law; it does not. The other two cannot exist with a corn-law, and never will come into operation until agriculture is free.

One other extract from the antiquities of Herefordshire will be pardoned; it is also from Lord Ashburton's parish, and is a continuation of the history of the perambulation day, when the boys were flogged to make them remember the parish boundaries, and when the people carried staves and crosses, and made use of mystic words, "for ye good of ye harvest." The records go on to say that after the perambulators returned, the backs of the boys still smarting, I suppose. "They did all of them go into ye church after dinner, and there being a figure of ye devil made of wood, it was placed upon ye altar. They did then, with a rope upon its neck, lift it up clean out of sight; wherefore they did let the rope slip, and ye devil made of wood fell down, and was broken in many pieces by ye boys falling upon it with shouting and joy and much loud noise."

It is not recorded of the boys whether they were so delighted with breaking this wooden devil to pieces "*after dinner*" as to forget the smarting of the forenoon floggings; nor is it quite clear whether the chastised tenantry of Sir Alexander Hood and the Lord Ashburton who, *after dinner*, at agricultural meetings, shout and knock to pieces the made-up images of the *evening*, forget their previous chastisements, or have no fear for the next perambulation day. But it may be assumed that the joy of demolishing a wooden devil would evaporate when the boys coolly reflected that the real devil was not dead, and felt the stripes of perambulation day upon their backs. So also, I presume, will those grown-up men, who in this age of civilisation are treated as the boys used to be in the half barbarous ages; they will feel their stripes, and have an unhappy certainty that the real enemy of agriculture is alive, even though they shouted and demolished some bogle made up for the purpose at a protection society's dinner.

WHAT IS RENT?

Sussex in the South ; Haddingtonshire in the North.   To the Farmers of both
Counties, and all whom it may concern.

Rent-Payers,—It is not a mere whim of mine to particularize the two counties named above on such a general subject, though at first sight it may seem so.

The county of Sussex contains some remarkable farms, so
does the county of Haddington.   Sussex contains some of the
best land and some of the worst in the kingdom, so does the
county of Haddington.   The one county skirts the sea, and
so does the other.   The one county contains the estates of
distinguished public men, and so does the other.

But it is for none of these parallels that I join the two in
the matter which I am about to introduce to you, to explain
practically what rent is and what rent is not.

Neither is it to make the contrast which these two counties
afford—one having, as a cultivator of its soil, Mr John
Ellman of Glynde, author of the Sliding Scale, and zealous
advocate of monopoly ; the other having, as a cultivator of its
soil, Mr George Hope of Fenton Barns, author of the
first of the League's Prize Essays, and the zealous advocate of free-trade.

It is neither for parallels nor contrasts that those two counties are particularized ; but it is, in the first place, because
the Presbytery of Haddington (the local ecclesiastical court
of the parish clergy) has appointed a day of " Solemn fast and
thanksgiving to be held in the several parishes, to return
thanks to Almighty God for the great blessing which He has
vouchsafed in giving us the *abundant harvest* ;" and because
Mr John Ellman of Glynde, published, in the *Brighton Gazette*,
while the northern harvest was still in the fields, a letter of
hope and cheerfulness to the Sussex farmers, congratulating
them on the continuance of wet weather, which for some
weeks threatened to damage the harvest in the north, while
the crops in Sussex were safe in the stackyard ; bidding them
keep back their corn from market, because the " muggy
weather" would damage the northern crops and raise the
prices of the southern.   It is, I repeat, *in the first place*,
because the greater portion, if not all, of the parish clergy in
Haddingtonshire are in favour of the corn-law ; that in
Sussex they are the same ; that Mr John Ellman, the mouth-
piece of the corn-law clergy of Sussex, professes to be a religious man, and in that character congratulates his fellow-
farmers in Sussex that the crops of the north will be damaged

by the providence of Almighty God, and the crops of the south will be enhanced in value through scarcity; while the clergy of Haddington Presbytery, all supporters of Mr John Ellman's sliding scale, return thanks to Almighty God that the harvest in the north was abundant, and was not damaged.

But, in *the second place*, I particularize these counties— Sussex especially—because a correspondent of the LEAGUE is publishing in this paper a detailed description of some of the Sussex estates and farms ; and I know that such descriptions will be read in that county ; the paper will be sought for ; it will be bought and borrowed, sold and lent, and one will ask another if they have seen it. So, while that letter is drawing your attention to the paper by describing your own farms, I will take advantage of that circumstance to turn your attention to the question of *rent*.

But, by all the sorrows that afflict humankind ! you need no writer to call your attention to the subject of *rent*. Michaelmas reminds you of that, or, if you should forget Michaelmas, the Browns of Cowdray and the Rusbridgers of Goodwood will put you in mind of it.

Forget ! You think of it all day, dream of it all night; and, sleeping or waking, you are planning, or sinking into despondency because you have no plan, how to get the rent paid. This wheat stack must be thrashed out and sold ; those young heifers must go to market; so must two score of wethers, that would be fitter for market when they have eaten the turnips and got fat ; but off they must go for ready cash to pay the rent. You would drain some wet soil, as they told you at last public dinner, and as you will be told again when you pay your rent, and listen to the speeches delivered on the day you pay; but how can you drain ? You must pay your rent, and you have no more money.

No more ! you have not enough ! you must get a bill discounted ; the bank will not do it with your name to it only ; you are a tenant-at-will, and are no security. Your uncles or brothers live in Chichester or Brighton. You have got them to join you in a bill before ; they did not like it. You know that, and rather than do so again, your wives must go ; and, under pretence of having come to the kinsman's house to have a cheerful cup of tea, the poor woman, with palpitating heart, manages, after much difficulty, to tell her real errand. She tries to make things look as well at home as she can. I dare say she makes the crop and stock worth more than their value. Mr John Ellman's letter in the *Brighton Gazette* is a good card for her, poor woman, if her kinsman is as blind a bat as John Ellman presumes the farmers to be. She says, " Corn is low now ; but the weather is muggy, and the northern

harvest is not yet saved ; it will be damaged ; prices will rise
in Sussex, and there will be no fear at all but we will be able
to meet the bill when it is due."

But no delusion of " muggy weather" or of corn-law—neither the *protection* to Sussex farmers of the one nor the other
—will set the mind of the farmer's wife at rest.   She spoke
confidently to her kinsman ; but she looks forward and fears
the worst.   Experience has taught her.   Year after year
everything has gone away in rent—year after year has she
been to have some new article of furniture, but as often has
the purchase been postponed until better times.

At last this dreadful rent-day is got over.   The sleepless
nights and the dreams of agents and no money to pay the
rent ; and of lawyers who come in the nightmare in the shape
of bulls and of cows which run after you where you cannot
escape, and where they get you down and gore you with their
horns.   O God! what horrid dreams are those dreams of a
farmer in September !   But Michaelmas past, all will be
pleasantness and repose—at least for another year.

Will it ?   The bill comes due at Christmas.   And a bill
dishonoured is even worse than a rent not paid to the very
day.   It is one continual round of vexation.   You know that
your farm would bear many improvements.   You know that
you would breed a better stock, if you could pay a high price
for rams and bulls.   You know that liquid manures might be
saved if you could lay out one or two hundred pounds on cisterns and the requisite accompaniments.   You know that in
many ways your crops might be increased if you could devote
the money to the labour and the science.   But you must pay
all the money in rent.   This dreadful rent-day, with corn
lower in price than you had calculated it to be when you took
your farm, is ever recurring ; and each, as it passes, leaves a
new train of difficulties to you.

But why should there be any trouble about the rent if Mr
John Ellman is a true teacher in all things concerning the
farmer ?   Mr Ellman tells you that *rent* is the surplus profit
after paying for labour, seed corn, keep of horses, rates, tithes,
tradesmen's bills, interest on capital, and for farmer's remuneration for his personal labour.   Why should rent be any
trouble to the farmer when this champion of the farmers lays
it down as an indisputable truth that rent is neither more nor
less than the surplus *after* paying all those charges ?

Brother rent-payers, you know well that, whatever this may
be in theory, it is a fiction in practice.   You know that you
must *first* pay rent, and then pay tradesmen's bills, and find
for draining, manuring, and ploughing, and sowing your farm.
You know that neither yourselves nor wives, nor sons and

daughters, must indulge in one bodily comfort or luxury, nor even necessary, until the rent is paid.

Moreover, you know that the landowners for whom Mr Ellman speaks and writes, and takes the chair at corn-law county meetings, have, sitting in Parliament legislating for themselves, made a law which secures the payment of rent before anything else is paid. Yet you are taught to believe in what Mr Ellman tells you! you are taught to *deny that the landlords have legislated for themselves, and themselves alone.* You are told to believe that they have legislated for the universal good—that the farmers and labourers have been their special care.

Why, their nearest neighbours, the farmers, and the creditors of farmers, are the first that are victimized. The law of distraint gives a direct contradiction to Mr Ellman's doctrine. Your kinsman who lent you money to pay last year's rent cannot be repaid this year should you fail until this year's rent be paid. No money can be set aside for interest on capital, nor for personal remuneration, nor for tradesmen's bills, until the rent be paid.

You know this every one of you. Yet Mr Ellman is your guide, who tells you that " *rent is the surplus after paying interest on capital, tradesmen's bills, wages of labour, keep of horses, and personal remuneration.*" He said so at the protection meetings last year, and he said so in his essay on agriculture nine years ago.

I shall not in this letter pursue the subject farther; but shall return to it and give you practical proofs, so plain that you cannot mistake them, that Mr John Ellman is just as wrong in respect of the theory of *corn-law protection* as he is in the theory of *rent.*

Meantime let those of you who can, refer to the first volume of the " History and Antiquities of Sussex," published in 1835. The section on agriculture is written by Mr Ellman; his name is at the top of it. And let these questions be asked :—Why is it that Mr Ellman complains of corn being at a ruinously low price in 1835, the same as he does in 1844 ? Why is it that he told us last year, and at the Steyning meeting this year, that the Anti-Corn-Law League was the cause of our low prices and difficulties, when the same low prices and difficulties existed, as he himself records, five years before the League was formed or even thought of ?

Ask the same question as regards the new tariff, which was only passed in 1842, *seven years* after the low prices of 1835, which Mr Ellman speaks of in the book. And then read what he says of *rent ;* and compare what he says of rent being the surplus with your own experience of what it really is.

The work is not easily purchased : it is expensive. But it may be borrowed from the libraries of the nobility, gentry, and most of the clergy in Sussex. The Duke of Richmond and Sir Charles Burrell are amongst the subscribers to it, I perceive. They will probably permit some of their tenants to borrow it. And Mr Ellman has doubtless a copy himself. Perhaps he will lend it to his neighbours, and explain to them how his theory of rent, when he is *writing for* the landlords, agrees with their experience of rent when they are *paying to* the landlords. At all events I shall explain the matter to them ; and, without leaving a shadow of doubt, I will shew them that he is as practically in error with protection as he is with rent.

LETTER FROM ANDOVER ABOUT PAUPERS AND CONVICTS.

11th October 1845.

ANDOVER ! The very name of this place must be to the public by this time like a well-picked bone, a bone which, falling to the daily newspapers at a season of scarcity and dearth of news, has been snapped up—*The Times* carrying it off for its own use, to gnaw it in its own corner, and growl over it as it gnaws—a bone which is now so bare, so old, so emptied of its marrow, a disagreeable bone of contention from the first, that even a pauper in the workhouse would hardly gnaw it.

Still, I think it possible that the " dailies," keen-scented as they are, eager and industrious as they have been here, may have overlooked some little morsels of fact, which a " weekly" may take up and turn to a useful purpose.

The name of Mr Hugh Munday of Down-farm has been frequently mentioned in connection with the poor-law inquiry at Andover. It was his petition to Parliament, praying for an inquiry into the allegation which he set forth, that the dietory was so low in the workhouse, as to starve down the paupers to the necessity of eating the rotten gristle off the bones which they got to break for manure, that led to the recent inquiry after much delay, much cavilling, and some attempts on the part of the Poor-law Commissioners to wriggle out of it. Personally, Mr Munday has taken no active share in promoting the charges against the late master of the union. These charges have been taken up as secondary thoughts, but promoted and proved so far as they have been proved as primary objects by other parties. Some of the parties may have been very honest, very pure, very humane in their motives; but if so, I must confess that, so far as I can see, the honesty, the purity, the humanity, seem sadly obscured by personal ill-feeling, political partisanship, (aye, even political hatred, strange as it may seem,) and by a rather large amount of that cowardice which affects the bravo to hound on the public indignation against one man's deeds, that it and its own misdeeds may escape. The honesty, purity, and humanity of the promoters of the charges against Macdougal, the late master of the workhouse, have been sadly clouded by such moral impurities as these; and also by the fact that some of the persons who gave evidence against him on the score of immoral character, and others who did not give evidence against him personally, but who worked hard behind the scenes to get up damnatory evidence, ransacking the memories of themselves and neighbours over a period of nine years, for everything that would tell against the man whom they once called friend; making friends of paupers, and of persons who had been paupers, and had always been odious to their new friends of to-day, and scornfully kept at a distance because they were paupers—prompting these persons, cramming them with stories which they were to remember the dates of, but which they could not remember the years of, when they came to be sworn—I say the fact of such opponents of Macdougal being now candidates for his vacant situation, throws an additional cloud over the alleged purity and humanity of their motives in getting him removed from his situation.

It has always seemed to me a grievous error in the national economy to shut people up within workhouse walls because they sought employment and could not get it, and that in a country whose soil has treasures buried and wasted in it for the want of labour—a grievous error in moral economy to think of making the idle industrious by shutting them up where they have no useful thing to do, and where they can learn, and feel, and understand nothing but how to hate their fellow-men. It has always seemed to me a grievous error to deny out-door relief to families in temporary distress, whereby they are compelled to undergo the most cruel privations, or submit to break up their little homes, sell off their furniture, (their houses and gardens it may be, as in the parish of Heyshot, in Sussex, and in numerous other parishes,) and become thorough, confirmed, irredeemable paupers. To me it has seemed cruel, terribly cruel, to take the aged and infirm from the cottages they have laboured to keep above their heads.

17

and which they have sanctified with their affections, and shut
them up in the workhouses, drilling them in their old days
under the discipline of a barrack-yard, conducted by some non-
commissioned officer of the army, whose fitness for keeping
the workhouse in order is estimated by his success on the
drill-ground and in the barrack-yard over a long period of
years, (Macdougal's service in the Royal Horse Artillery was
thirty years, twenty-seven of which he was a non-commissioned officer, and five of which regimental serjeant-major ;)
terribly cruel to break up " the old house at home" of an old
couple whose eyes see " home" written in every corner of it, in
every crevice of the walls, whose affections rest upon the old
stools where their young babies sat, on the old table where
many a scanty, yet many a happy frugal meal was eaten ; to
part them from all and from each other, and drill them in
their old days into military habits, under military men, as if
they were young recruits ! The impolicy of shutting up the
able-bodied who cannot get work outside, compelling them to
do worthless, profitless, filthy work inside, merely to punish
them, is only surpassed in enormity by this cruel treatment of
the aged and infirm, whose helplessness only compels them to
submit. All others leave the workhouse walls as soon as they
can. *They* only leave to go to their graves. And to put the
deeper shame on age and poverty, most workhouses present
them with graves within the walls, as prisons do to the most
felonious of criminals. All, save the aged and infirm, and the
incapable of acting for themselves, can escape, and do escape,
from the stupid punishment of the workhouses. They escape to
kill game, steal sheep, rob hen-roosts—to do anything, to take any
chance, rather than be punished in the workhouse for seeking
parish relief; they escape from the dietary of the unions to
the better fare of the prisons and the hulks, and the better
fed convict gangs of the Bermudas, Gibraltar, and New South
Wales ; but the old, the venerable fathers and mothers of
the villages, cannot escape save into their graves; and, that
even the hope of the grave may not be too comfortable to
them in the imprisonment of their old age, they have the
certainty placed before them that since they are such vile
creatures as to be old and poor, they will not be buried in the
old church-yard with their kindred, but will be consigned to
pauper's ground.

Say the best that can be said for the workhouse system,
and even then there is a frightful balance of ignorance of
human nature, irrational efforts to reform the idly disposed,
and of cruel irreverence for the holiest affections of mankind
left in it.

Strange that in an age that boastfully calls itself the nine-teenth century, and boasts of reforming its criminal code ; of banishing the criminal code ; of banishing the birch from its schools ; of working upon mind rather than upon matter ; on hopes rather than fears—an age in which even the cruelties of naval and military discipline are relaxed and amended ; and which promises at no distant period to abolish capital punishments in obedience to the progressive cry of charity and peace, and tolerant rationality instead of intolerant bar-barism : strange, that in this age called the nineteenth century, and in this country called England, a systematic code of punishment for the aged, the infirm, and the unfortunate should for the first time in the world's history be adopted and rigorously applied.

And the strangeness of the fact does not seem less when we call to mind that many of those public men who have been foremost—most sincerely and earnestly in the front, as I believe—in softening the rigours of the criminal code, for the better reformation of criminals, and in advocating a more comprehensive and rational system of education for the young, that they may be led and induced to imbibe education as a pleasure, ceasing to be treated as ill-used brute-beasts, and beginning to be treated as rational beings—that such moral reformers should at the same time be foremost in making industry compulsive, not by leading the idle to work, but by driving them in one common herd, idle, unfortunate, aged, infirm, and sick, as the worst-used of brute-beasts are driven, to compel them to work or die quickly at little expense. Strange that men, foremost in civilizing, and humanizing, and leading on the moral armies of the nineteenth century, con-quering old prejudices and old barbarities, should turn back to use cruelty and coercion in the rear of their moral army, upon the aged, the infirm, and unfortunate—upon the *helpless*, who in all ages and countries the most ignorant and barba-rous, have been spared and protected.

This is no idle sentimentalism ; it is but a feeble expression of what I have found during the last three years in my travels through almost every parish (two or three unions excepted) in the south and south-west of England.

I have said that Mr Hugh Munday originated this inquiry by a petition to Parliament. The inquiry had thus a respec-tability of birth which gave it a higher character throughout with those who know Mr Munday than it might otherwise have had. He is a practically liberal man. I paid a visit one day to Down Farm, and found nestled among some trees on the left-hand side of the Basingstoke Road, between two and three miles from Andover, Mr Munday's residence. He at one time, after succeeding his father, had 1800 acres of land in occupation. As his brothers grew to manhood, and got married, and needed farms, he parted the land with them. He occupies now, I think, about 500 acres, quite enough for one management, and has yielded up the parental house, with the best portions of the farm, to his brothers, he, being a bachelor, betaking himself to a smaller house ; also to the worst portion of the land. This is mentioned to shew that the gentleman whose genuine humanity led him to interfere in behalf of the famine-stricken paupers, has kindly feelings in him for other uses, and at other times, than to be exhibited for holiday show.

I found his work-people more comfortably provided for than is common on many other farms. But what pleased me still more, I found them greater in number, in proportion to the acres, than on most other farms ; and Mr Munday answered me that all the progress he had made towards this increase of employment on his farm had been attended with additional profit. He does not believe that his agriculture is by any means perfect ; he expects to advance ; but, as he now stands, he is far enough to say, that if all farmers employed as many hands as he does on the same number of acres, there would not be an idle hand in Hampshire, nor in rural England. And if every employer encouraged and assisted his work-people as he does, to feed pigs, keep bees, grow their vege-tables, and live regularly, soberly, and be industrious, there would be no need—at least less need—to ask relief from the poor-rates at times of sickness and temporary distress.

Walking in the garden and orchard behind his house, I observed a row of beehives, five-and-twenty in number I think, and made the remark to him that he had a goodly share of them. He said they were not his ; they belonged to two of his work-people, who had not a convenient place for so many elsewhere ; and he had invited them, as he kept no bees him-self, and had a good garden, to put them there. The bees belonging to these two persons produced L.12 last year, being L.6 each ; a small matter to people whose honey and money are always overflowing, but a great matter to agricultural labourers.

The current wages are 9s., 10s., and 11s. a-week ; but with such employers as Mr Munday, other advantages, some of them not to be estimated by money—I mean the moral advantages of being always cared for—are additional to the current rate of wages.

It being on a Friday when I was at Down Farm, I observed

that Mr Munday had established the good and convenient custom of paying his work-people on Fridays.

The readers of this paper know that it is an axiom with Mr Cobden to say, " Shew me a good farmer, a man cultivating better than his neighbours, and I will shew you a man not afraid to part with protection." Such a man is Mr Munday. He is not a political man ; and, I believe, neither an orator in practice nor in ambition ; but being at Winchester on the occasion of Mr Cobden and Mr Bright's well-known visit to that city, he was asked, as a tenant farmer of Hampshire, to take a part in the proceedings. He consented, and proposed and supported a resolution to the effect that the corn-laws had been of no benefit to the farmers, and that agriculture and the agricultural labourers would have been in a better condition than they ever have been in, had there been no corn-laws.

Being at Winchester the other day, I returned to Andover —the regular distance being about eleven miles—by way of Sutton Scotney, which made the distance four miles farther. Sutton Scotney is a goodly-sized village—a thousand people in it, or thereabout. It has the village of Newton, in which parish it stands, half-a-mile eastward, and Barton Stacey, a parochial village, a mile westward. It was in these villages conjointly that the Swing riots of 1830 first began. Several persons belonging to them were convicted and transported, and one hanged. One of those who had been sentenced to seven years' transportation, but got off with two years' imprisonment at Portsmouth, was mentioned to me, and I sent for him, and drew him into familiar conversation. His account was to the following effect :—

" My name? my name be's Joseph Carter. Ees, I had seven year on't for them mobs ; but they let me off with imprisonment at the hulks for two years and one day. That was the exact time. The way I got off was this—they found out when they put me to school there that I never could read none ; no reading nor writing. I never had a book put afore me never in my life, not as I minds on, till I went aboard ship a prisoner to serve my seven year at Portsmouth. I wish I had ha' served my seven year. They would ha' made me a scholard by this time. They learned me to read the Testament a bit ; but did not make me much of a scholard, 'cause, why you see, I wor only but two year and a-day there. But they finding out as how I had never been no scholard, they knew it could not have been I as old Barrowman called in to see if it wor a good ten-pound note. That old Barrowman was the father of young Barrowman as was hanged. The old one was transported. Both they were from Barton Stacey.

"Well, about the ten-pound note, it was in this here way. The mob goes up to Mr Callander—he is Sir Thomas Baring's steward—and they said they must have money, or they would do mischief. Well, he said, don't do mischief, come in with me and I will give you money. Old Barrowman went in to get the money; but he could not read a word of figures or writing, and he did not know if it wor a good note. So he comes out and gets another man to go in with him, to see if the note wor a good one. Mack was the man who went in. He be here now, and everybody knows he wor the man as went in. But he be a tall man like myself; and, i' faith, somebody swore it wor me; and they took me. But when they found I wor no scholard, they believed it might not be me.

"Oh, ees, ees, I wor with them. But then, everybody was forced like to go. There was no denying. I be an old man now. I was not young then. It was the young men as did it. They worked, you see, for little wages, as they do now. They suffers most. They get but 4s., and 4s. 6d., and 5s., and one or two may get 5s. 6d. a-week. At that time the married men got 9s. and 10s. a-week. But it was the young men as led the others and forced them into it. I was took afore Squire Wickham and the other gentlemen, for the squire to shew as how I had no business to be mobbing. I was a hurdle maker and thatcher, and jobbed at hedging. The squire shewed as how I got L.64 a-year from him for work of that kind for seven years. But then he did not shew that I had most times a man to help me, and two women besides at times. He did not shew that. I paid as much as L.20 some years for helpers. Oh, I did not say I paid the money away that way, because they would ha' thought I complained, and would ha' taken that as guilty of going out to mob. I said that I wor forced out agin my will. And so I wor.

"But you see, I wor at the meeting across the street there, in that corner house, the night as Joe Mason read the letter to us all, that came from Overton. There was no name to the letter. But Joe said he knowed who it came from. Joe was a good scholard. The letter, I know, came from old D——'s; he be dead; and it came out of Newton; never came from Overton. It said we was all to leave off work; and the Sutton men was to go out and stop the ploughs. They was to send home the horses for the farmers to look after them themselves, and was to take the men with them. And they was to go and turn the men out of the barns. And they was all to go and break the 'sheens' as the farmers had got to do the thrashing. That was what they was to do. They ha' got three sheens now in this place, now at this very time; and one farmer borrows one; and them four sheens does the work of eight men. They be a doin' of that at Sutton in this moment; and men be again doin' nothin'.

"Well; about the letter. Joe Mason read it. We did not then know who it came from. But we knows, all on us now in this here place, that old D——s had a hand in't. He was a great friend of Mr Cobbett. He used to write to Mr Cobbett. He never got into no trouble about it. He was too good a manager to get other people into trouble to get in himself. No; I do not blame this on Mr Cobbett. I mean old D——s, the shoemaker, Mr Cobbett was a good master. I ha' nothing to say agin he. I lived with him at Botley, and would never wish to serve a better master.

"About the letter; well, it was this: I was there at the reading on't, and that came all out, and you see that went agin me. And then some of them told as how that I carried the money; and, ecod, you see that was true. Joe Mason was by far the best scholard, but they would not trust Joe with the money; nor yet old Barrowman. They said I wor honest, and they gave it to me to carry. I had L.40 at one time—L.40 every shilling. Some people ha' told me since that I should ha' gone off with it. I did think of doing that once. The coach came by when we was up on the London Road, and it did come into my head to get on the coach, and get away from the whole business, with the L.40. But I thought about leaving my wife behind, and about what a vagabond they would all call me, and the coach was soon past. I never had another chance. But had I ha' knowed I was to be tried, and sentenced to be transported, I'd ha' got up on the coach.

"I needn't ha' been tried at all. They came to me times and times after I was in Winchester gaol, to get me to speak against the two Masons. They offered to let me clear, if I would only tell what I knowed agin them. Had I told what I knowed, they'd ha' been hung, as sure as Barrowman, and Cooke, and Cooper, was hung. I was took out with the other prisoners to see they hung. They tried to frighten us by it to tell all we knowed on one another. But I wouldn't split. So the Masons was only transported, and they transported me, too.

"Ees; the mob took me agin my will; but then that was

not enough to make me split, 'cause you see, I stayed with them. They took many a man agin his will. They took Harry Mills of Barton Stacey, and carried him a mile and a half. Harry Mills be alive now. He wor yesterday. I seed him in this here place. He have a pension of one shilling a-day, he have. He wor in the 63d regiment, and stood guard over Bonaparte at St Helena. The mob carried Harry Mills a mile and a half, and forced him to go with them. It wor the young fellows did it. The worst on them never got nothing done to them. Some of those as got most done to them, some as got hanged, never done half so much as some I knows on in this here parish."

" Were you ever in a workhouse?"

" Was I ever in a workhouse? No, thank God, I never did no harm to be put in a workhouse."

" But I do not mean a prison; you have been in a prison. I mean a union workhouse; were you ever an inmate of the union?"

" No; I never did nothing to be sent to the union."

" Do you mean by that answer that they send people to the union as a place of punishment?"

" I don't know, I ha'n't been in; but I hear tell it be a terrible place; and I knows this, that if a man does not please his master here with his work, the master says he'll be d—d but he'll send him to the union. An' if a man seeks more wages, and the master ben't willing to give more, and the man say he can't live on what he be getting, the master says, ' D—n ye; I'll send thee to the union; see how ye like that!' No, I never was in the union myself; hope I never shall be so bad as ha' to go."

" What kind of food had you on board the hulk at Portsmouth the two years and a day you were there?"

" Why, sir, not always good alike; and not always bad alike. The bread was mostly always bad, 'cause one man, who had great favour, had the contract all the time I was there. The butchers took the contract for six months; and there was a great deal of difference in one six months from another six months, according as to who might have the contract. The worst on't was better than I can get now in Sutton Scotney. I do not mean but there be's good meat to be got in Sutton by them as have money; but it ben't no working man like me as can get it. I wish I had as much meat now as I had in the hulk; and I wishes the same to every poor hard-working man in Hampshire.

" The allowance we had, sir, was this :—We had four ounces of biscuit a-day—the best of biscuit. The bread was one pound; it was black, and not good. We had oatmeal too, and pea soup; and we had garden vegetables that we bought with the money we worked for. We had fourteen ounces of meat each time, four times a-week; one six months the meat was beautiful. That man gave always good meat when he had the contract. We had plenty of victuals. The only thing was the bread. I wishes every poor, hard-working man in this here parish were as well fed with meat, and myself with them, as I wor in the hulk.

"Oh, sir, you are very kind. You need not say you are sorry to have troubled me. A man once came from Winchester and took down in writing, like you, all I had to say. He was a shoemaker somebody told me. I do not know his name, but he said he was going to make a history of the mobs. I never heard no more of him.

"Oh yes, sir, you are welcome to know all as I know; but to tell you the truth, I thought, at first, when you sent for me, it was about that old horse. You see I was to pay one shilling a-week, and that for twenty-six weeks, and it only lived a month. So they want to make me pay the whole price for it. I thought it was about that, and I was rather afeard. But I ben't the least afeard now."

So much for a Hampshire peasant in the year 1845.

THE HOP GROWERS AND THE HOP CULTIVATION.

THE hop is used in the brewing of beer. When the liquor is drawn off the malt it is sweet; hops being added to it produces an acidity. The longer beer is intended to be kept, the more liberally it is "hopped;" for instance, the directions to brew strong ale and strong beer are the following:—"Twelve bushels of malt to the hogshead for beer, (or fourteen, if you wish it of a very good body;) eight for ale. For either pour the whole quantity of water hot, but not boiling, on at once, and let it infuse three hours close covered; mash it in the first half hour, and let it stand the remainder of the time. *Run it on the hops* previously infused in water. For strong beer, *three quarters of a pound to a bushel* of malt, if for ale, *half a pound*. Boil them with the malt three hours from the time it begins to boil. Cool a paleful to add three quarts of yeast to, which will prepare it for putting to the rest when ready next day; but, if possible, put together the same night. Turn as usual. Cover the bung-hole with paper when the beer has done working; and when it is to be stopped, *have ready a pound and a-half of hops dried before the fire*, put them into the bung-hole, and fasten it up. Let it stand twelve months in cask, and twelve in bottle, before it be drank. It will keep five, eight, or ten years. It should be brewed the beginning of March."

Such are the uses to which the hop is put. The nature of the plant and the portion of it used will be seen presently.

The cultivation of the hop is a species of husbandry principally confined to that part of the island comprised in the counties of Kent, Surry, and Sussex. Each of these counties presents a great variety of external features when taken by itself; but when collected and compared together, they exhibit a remarkable uniformity and sameness. The great formations of the wealden, the sand, and the chalk, belong to each and to all. In the core of the district lies the wealden, comprising the wealds of Kent, Surry, and Sussex. This large and central tract of country is girt with a belt of chalk hills, which, rising from the sea about the Isle of Thanet, range in a westerly course over the north of Kent, and, passing through Surry, return in a circular sweep along the south of Sussex to the channel. A fringe of sand forms the union between the chalk and the wealden.

These three varieties of soil govern the kinds of agricultural occupation afforded at different seasons. The woodland is the great feature of the wealden. The sand, as it rises into the chalk, furnishes some of the most celebrated hop gardens and orchards. The most highly cultivated arable land is found upon the chalk of the Isle of Thanet.

There is perhaps no produce in the country that requires so much or such varied human labour as the hop at the different stages of its progress. The ground is at one time a field, at another a garden. Great outlay of force must be expended on the soil as on the corn-land; but the force is that of the human arm, not that of the beast of burden, which in some plantations, as those about Farnham, scarcely enters. Unlike corn, too, and other produce, which, when the soil has been prepared and the seed committed to the ground, is left in the main to the course of nature and the order of the seasons to bring to perfection, it must be trained and tended from its first shoot to its ripening. Then it is not gathered like corn, and stored upon the stalk, but is culled at once by the finger. It thus calls into play the energies of all ages and of either sex. The soil is handled and subdued by the man; the plant is trained and tended by the woman; in the gathering, are united all—man, woman, and child. The practice of taking taskwork, however, has in some places the effect of engaging both woman and boy, and sometimes the girl, in the more

laborious treatment of the land. The woman shares much of
the man's labour at taskwork—the boy all of it, even to the
digging, which is the most severe of any. It is, however, only
the lighter parts of the ground which boys usually turn up
with the spade; they dig what are called "the slips"—spaces
between the "hills," which the man leaves in digging the gravel
down, and which are left by the plough in order to drain the
surface-water off.

In describing the various processes through which the hop
passes before it reaches the market, I will begin at the beginning.

Digging is usually begun in the month of December, and
performed by the acre. The rate of payment is from
18s. to L.1 an acre. A man and a boy will dig about an
acre in the week. The next stage is *opening the hops*—that
is, levelling the hills which have been piled round the plants
in the preceding summer. Women and boys are occasionally
employed at this; but it is usually done by the men as task-
work. Sometimes they contract to do it by the acre, but it is
nice work, and therefore seldom done in this way. When the
woman is hired to do it by the day, she gets about tenpence
or one shilling. It lasts for about a week in the month of
March. It is hard work for a woman; the moving the ground
is heavy. When men contract, they are paid about fourpence
per hundred.

About the month of April, when the hop plants begin to
shoot, the poles are fixed in the ground. It is common for
men to contract to do this by the acre. It is called "*poling*
the hops." The wife often assists at this, generally by carrying the poles to the hills, where the man fixes them, and by
fastening them after he has done so by a "rammer," with
which she beats the ground into the hole. This commonly
lasts about a fortnight, but it depends on the weather, and
some farmers will only do it when the moon is new. 1200 hops
are planted on an acre, and when it is done by contract, it is
at the rate of about fourpence per 100. After the "poling,"
boys and women are employed at "choqclearing," or picking
up the chips and old pieces of poles from the ground; they are
hired to do this by the day. It lasts only for a day or two.
At the beginning of May, or latter end of April, the hops are
"tied." Neither boys nor men are ever employed at this
work. It is an "endless" job for a man; a man cannot get
on with it. Women generally contract with a farmer to "tie"
for the season, at nine shillings an acre. A woman will generally take two acres, or two acres and a-half. The trouble
depends on the weather. If it is boisterous, she has to bind

them over and over again, as the wind blows them from the pole, or blows them round in a wrong direction away from the sun. She can bind about two acres and a-half in about a week, and must visit them to rebind them every three or four days, till they grow out of her reach. This takes place on an average in five or six weeks.

The next process is that of "shimming," which is effected by an implement called the " shim ;" in other places it is called " breaking," " nidging," or " nidgetting," from the term " break," nidge, and nidget, being applied to the implement, which during the summer months is occasionally drawn by horse through the hop gardens and between the hills, to loosen the earth and remove the weeds. Boys of various ages are made use of to lead and direct the horse, which must, in the narrow spaces through which they are driven, be held in strict command. When the hops reach the top of the poles, it is a common occupation with the women to fasten the bines which may have been blown off again to their places ; this is called " horsing the hops," and is so named from a kind of ladder they mount for the purpose.

The hop is now prepared for the last out-door process, that of " picking." Few things are more beautiful than a hop-garden in this state. As the plant approaches to maturity, the numerous green and overarching alleys are brightened by the light-tinted flowers, which hang in clusters from the top to the bottom of the poles. The air is scented with the pleasant perfume they exhale to a considerable distance, and many who wander into foreign lands to look at the vine-clad hills of the sunny south, leave a much more beautiful sight unvisited at home, in the fertile and highly cultivated landscapes of Kent and Surry.

Hop-picking begins generally about the second week in September. All hands are employed at this—men, women, boys, and girls, down to the youngest that can work. The better the crop, the less money is given for picking the same quantity. In an average year, one shilling is given for picking seven bushels, and a good picker in the same year could pick fourteen bushels. Picking is usually continued for twelve hours in the day. A woman can pick rather more than a man. Immediately after the poles are gathered, the poles are stripped and stacked. Labourers commonly contract to do this at from five shillings and sixpence to seven shillings an acre. Their wives and children often assist them ; the refuse bine is their perquisite, in addition to their pay.

Rags are extensively used in manuring hops. The women are occasionally employed in cutting them ; but it is more generally done by the men on rainy days. The average price is about ninepence per cwt. In some parishes, where the population is large, the "beck and spud," which are used manually, do the work of the "shim," and horse-power is but little used. The work is very laborious, and the same observation applies to all the work on hop-grounds which men perform.

The "Report on the Employment of Women and Children in Agriculture," presented to Parliament in 1843, contains some interesting statements with reference to the physical, social, and moral condition of the population employed in the culture of the hop. It does not appear that any dangerous disease is generated by the occupation; on the contrary, it seems to be decidedly healthy. W. Newnham, Esq., surgeon, Farnham, says—"There is no work performed by women or children in the hop plantations calculated to produce disease, or to which these disorders can be fairly traceable, with the following exception :—If the hop-picking season proves a wet one, they are exposed frequently to become wet, and to stand for many hours upon the ground saturated with moisture; and when this happens to be the case, disorder of the digestive functions ensues, commonly shewing itself in the form of diarrhœa, and not usually of an obstinate or severe character. With regard to the imported population at this [hop-picking] season, they, of course, are exposed to the same causes of disorder, aggravated by their being lodged in very crowded and ill-ventilated apartments, and by their great want of cleanliness and generally imprudent and dissolute habits. Even here malady is not of a severe character ; and a death among the imported population is scarcely ever heard of. . . . . I have never been able to trace any endemic or epidemic malady, arising after the hop-picking season, which could fairly be attributed to it as a consequence."

Much evil results from the intermixture of the "imported population" here spoken of with the regularly employed inhabitants of the hop districts. As the season approaches, a new population of men, women, and children is poured into them. The crowd is motley, and differently composed in different districts. Mr Paine, a large grower, states that there resort to Farnham about 4000 or 5000 strangers, being an addition not far short of the whole stationary population, which is 7000 for the parish. These strangers "come chiefly from the towns and villages within twenty miles of Farnham, some few from a greater distance, and others are labourers who have no settled home : among these last are gipsies. Various means are provided for their reception ; part are admitted into barracks constructed for the purpose, others into spare rooms in cottages which are specially reserved from the tenants." This vast influx of strangers, in addition to the confusion which their very number produces in a small town or village, often bring with them habits and language calculated to degrade if not to pollute their companions. Farnham becomes thronged with a temporary population of country people, vagrants, and gipsies; the last of whom are in some few instances preferred to the others, from their wild and active habits, which speed the work during the day, and are content with any lair to rest in at night. The intercourse between them and the inhabitant work-people is more complete; because it is the custom for the mother of the family to take the very youngest into the hop-gardens, where the children pick, and the infants rest and play while the work goes forward; and at night many are crowded into the inhabitants' cottages by virtue of the reservation already mentioned. The Rev. R. Sankie, curate of Farnham, says—" I think the parish stands under considerable disadvantages from the peculiar nature of the labour which is employed at the hop-picking. I have seen the cottages crowded with strangers and their families at this season, who so much disturb the order of the household, that *provisions are bought for the day* instead of a longer period, lest in the confusion they should be lost or made away with. The crowded intercourse, both on the hop-ground and in the cottages, must be productive of mischief, especially to the young. There is little uproar until the close of the picking. The labours of the day, and, as is commonly alleged, a soporific influence from the hop itself, disposes them to be quiet. At the close of the labour in the grounds, when the workmen are being paid off, the scene changes. There is much drinking, fighting, and bad language."

The rector of the village of Brede, in the neighbourhood of Rye, speaks of the same influences in a different part of the country. " I am of opinion that the imported hop-pickers do much to demoralize the parish, as they are generally persons of the lowest character in both sexes, the very effect of whose manner of living while here is sufficient to produce the worst feelings and consequences. It is by no means uncommon to see from eight to ten, or more, sleeping under one shed, without any other partition between them than that which the darkness of the night may provide. It is a common practice for servant girls at this season to give their employers notice to quit their service, assigning no other reason than that they wish to go to hop-picking!"

Those who frequent the neighbourhood of Maidstone are stated to " come from all parts of England and Ireland, and amongst them may be found many unfortunate members of various classes. A great number of the English come from St Giles', Saffron Hill, White Chapel, and Kent Street, and they are the most vicious and refractory. The Irish, who are the most numerous, are extremely dirty, both in their persons and habits, and are very indelicate in their conduct and appearance. They frequently bring contagious disorders."

All the witnesses concur in representing female chastity as being at a very low ebb—and some go to the length of saying that in many instances the women are utterly devoid of the feeling. This, however, is not entirely attributable to the periodical influx of strangers into these districts. It has its root deeper, and is to be sought for in the disgraceful physical condition in which the labourers generally are permitted to rest by those who profit by their toil. The undivided state of the larger families acting upon the scantiness of house room and general poverty, or high rents, often crowds them together in their sleeping apartments, so as seriously to infringe on the decencies which guard female morals. Mr Hart, a professional gentleman of Reigate, says—" The great difficulty is to say *at what age brothers and sisters do not sleep together in one apartment*, but generally until they leave home, *be that at ever so late a period.*"

In the neighbourhood of Cuckfield, in Sussex, it is common for children of both sexes to use the same sleeping-room *and bed*, up to the age of twelve, and even fourteen. The Rev. W. Sankie of Farnham in Surry mentioned a case where two sisters and a brother, all above fourteen, habitually slept together. These are mere glimpses of the ordinary and every-day influences to which the labouring classes are subjected, and it can be no matter of wonder that they lose, or rather never acquire, that delicacy and purity of mind which is the origin and the safeguard of chastity.

Nor are the deteriorating effects of these vicious domestic arrangements counteracted by an education likely to promote the growth of principles of resistance or self-restraint. But upon this wide subject I have left myself no room to dilate, important as it is, and necessary to be fully understood, in order to form an accurate idea of the state of society in the hop-growing districts. It may briefly be said that education, in the ordinary sense of the term, is almost unknown. Superstition as a consequence lurks among the labouring classes of these counties to an extent of which the career of Mad Thom, *alias* Sir William Courtenay, at Canterbury, and its fatal termination, affords a melancholy illustration. The belief in charms for the healing of bodily hurts is not uncommon ; faith in the same means of fertilizing the ground and trees is said to exist; and that in witchcraft has not yet expired. A very substantial farmer in the north-east of Kent, within a few years, used to arrange scythes in a particular order around his stables to secure his horses from witchcraft.

RIDGLEY WOOD.
A TALE OF A PUNCH IN THE HEAD.
CHAPTER I.
The Poachers, and the Men whom the hard Winter makes Poachers.

In the village of Ridgley, which, measured by the down mail-train, is not four hours' journey from London, there were six men standing near the corner of a house where three roads meet. It was on the afternoon of a December day, a cold day; a day so cold that the very sun, afraid to come out, rolled himself up in folds of gray, and, like a miser, to save his light, went to bed while it was yet noon.

Three of the men, Rice, Reeves, and Russell, stood in the shelter of the house wall, their backs towards the wall and their faces to the road; their hands wrapped in the skirts of their smock-frocks, and so cold that they could not blow their noses with them, which were so red you could hardly have known them to be noses. Each stamped his heavy boots, with iron on them, on the frozen ground, hard as iron, to keep his feet from freezing like the ground.

True, they had some articles of wirework in their hands which had been hanging up in the chimney at home; and as these had never yet seen daylight, they might prefer to let the drops hang at their noses rather than take their hands from their smock-frocks to expose the wirework while they wiped the drops away.

Two others of the six, Mason and Masterton, caring less for the cutting of the sharp wind, or more eager to enjoy the coming adventure, or desirous to talk by themselves about what powder they had and what shot; what stocks, locks, and barrels certain other men were expected to bring under their clothes and in their pockets, and of the propriety or impropriety of having such associates as Rice, Reeves, and Russell, who put such long faces on the thing, and were not heartily in it—they stood in the middle of the road.

"I be as hard put to it to get a bit of bread for my young uns," said Mason, "as Rice be, or ever a man in Ridgley, and I be as ready to pick up a turnip as he; but may I never see

Ridgley Wood, or never come out of it alive this night, if I would pick up an old frozen Swede as he has done to carry with me all night to Ridgley preserves, and wherever us may go."

"He be a good fellow at work or at the fireside," rejoined Masterton; "but he ben't a good un for a job of this sort. I be as hard put to it as he—harder as I may say, for there ben't nothing doing in my way in the gardens in this here frost; still it ben't for that alone I go to Ridgley Wood. I likes it; likes to fetch down a bird as well as ever a squire this side of London. I'd be a rare un, I would, for my dog and gun, wor I lord of a manor! But Rice don't go with me because he like the sport, he go only for what he can pick up—a Swede for his supper, or a bit of paling to make a fire."

"Every man on us counts and makes a show against the keepers," said Mason. "The number frightens them more than the picking of the men. They'd engage three, or from that to six of the best on us; but they won't tackle twenty—not even twenty like Jem Rice."

"Still," rejoined Masterton, "I likes a chap as has his spirit in him. I likes to see it done for the sport, as well as for what us bags and brings away."

"Thee bes always for the sport of the thing, Bill; thee bes a rare un for sport."

"Ben't I? Was I in squire's place, would not I be a sportsman! I think I'd match him whenever he liked."

"But was thou in squire's place, squire would be in your'n mayhap; working for eight shilling a-week, and nothing for broken time; nothing in the wet, and nothing in the frost. Ben't this a terrible frost, Bill! What would squire do with a wife and six little uns, and only eight shilling a-week when at work, and no work in this here hard weather?"

"Do! why he'd go to Ridgley Wood to the preserves, and get a bird or take a hare in farmer Buncle's field, as we be going to do, to be sure! What else would he do, so fond of game as he bes? So fond of not going too long without a tuck into som'at to eat? So fond of his wife and little uns being well taken care on, and never worse nor he can help? What else *could* he do?"

While this conversation was in progress between Mason and Masterton, George Preston, the sixth of the men, kept himself in warmth and amusement by dancing, by singing, and by swearing how delightful it was to have such an adventure in prospect; but how terrible long it was that the time took to go by, and the other men took to come. But three hours past, and twenty-one men, seven guns, two nets, and wires

18

not numbered, are two miles from Ridgley, in two parties, in two of farmer Buncle's fields.

CHAPTER II.
The Snares and the Nets, and what was Caught in them.

(This chapter is omitted, as it is chiefly filled with an account of how snares are made and set in frosty weather. It contains also some account of why some of the poachers thought it no sin to break down the fences of one farmer, and why they thought it a sin and a shame to break down the fences of another farmer. After drawing the fields and taking up their wires and nets, they find they are twenty-men, all alive and well, with twenty-five hares and seven rabbits; and that Rice had got two more turnips, and Reeves and Russell, each one. They then draw lots to decide if they shall or shall not go that night to Ridgley Wood with their guns.)

CHAPTER III.
The Dark Wood—the Punches in the Head—the Pursuit—the Retreat—the Bloodhounds—the hard Winter worse than all.

To Ridgley Wood! the lots are drawn, and it is decided that the birds shall now be disturbed in their feathered rest. To Ridgley Wood. Silence, every men. Barrels are put in their stocks, and powder and shot in the barrels; seven of them. Silence, every man, till the wood is gained. If George Preston is to have that old Duke of Marlborough musket, whose barrel has been cut in half, let him look to the lock; it goes off at half-cock, and the pan spills the priming; he must keep his hand over it, and his thumb on the hammer above the flint. And he must mind that no tree-root trips him up, else the piece may go off and shoot somebody in front of him. This old blunderbuss belongs to one who neither likes it nor the use to which it is to be put. He is here, but would rather be anywhere else. There is a sympathy between him and Rice, and since the latter has got one hare, and three turnips, and a piece of paling, and knows where to get two pieces more on the way home, to make a fire, he would now like to see with his own eyes his own pot set a-boiling on his hearth. He does not like to see young Preston with that old gun; it is so very old, and he is so reckless. It may burst, and kill himself and all near him. He will keep as far from it as he can.

And now they descended into the darker thickets of the wood, and the silence deepened. Though they knew that their guns would ring and re-echo from the pine thickets over the meadow and across the river to the rocks beyond, and

again down the beech grove to the very confines of the squire's
mansion, yet they whispered, as if they thought the drawing
of a breath would awaken the solitude in which they moved.
The thick trunk of a forest oak, that had been alderman of the
ward in which he lived long before the pines which stood
around him were planted, stood up in the dim moonlight, as if
it had just heard strange footsteps, and had risen from rest
to see who intruded at that dreary hour. And it seemed to
listen to every whisper, and to stretch out its large naked arms
to push aside the pine branches and pry into the darkness to
see whose feet those were that made the fallen twigs crackle
among the frozen leaves.

And the pines looked black, and frowned upon the men who
were now where they had no business to be. They extended
their branches and bent them down, and now scratched a face,
as if to mark it to know it again, and then pushed off a hat, as
if to see whether the head that wore it was bald, or had black
or brown hair; and again they would turn a man round, as if
to look him in the face and shew him to their companion trees,
who were to bear witness that such a man was there that night.

And then the trees would whisper together as if a light wind
rustled through them, and they would gently stir their branches,
as if drawing the covering of the night more closely over the
endangered birds that slept in their bosom; tucking it into
their backs, and bidding them lie close, and not let themselves
be seen. And the moon, which had been watching the progress
of the long winter night behind a cloud, as a policeman watches
in a doorway round the corner, came out, and resolving to keep
awake, opened her eye and proceeded on her rounds, and looked
as wakeful as if she had never been winking.

Mason and Masterton spoke together in a low voice.

" There he sits !"

" Where ?"

" There !"

" Where ?"

" Don't thou see ?"

" No !"

" Right up agin the second branch, just under the edge of
the moon."

" I see him now; I've got him clear !
Has the three guns gone to the meadow to catch them flying
as gets out of this ?"

" Yes !"

" Then here goes !"

And Masterton fired, and a pheasant fell, and twenty more
fluttered, and some screeched and flew out above the trees to-

wards the meadow, and were shot there; and the repose of the night was broken. A moment before, and Ridgley Wood was in peaceful slumber. Now it was like a conscience with a crime upon it suddenly awakened. A pang shot through its darkness. A rebound went through the thick solitudes and tore the silence in pieces, and made perturbation of it and disorder.

The rebounding guns and the fire that flashed from them, and the screaming birds, and the echoing rocks that doubled all the din, gave to some of the men an excess of pleasure such as the mere shooting of pheasants in the preserves in daylight can never give to those who stand and slay without trouble, without exertion, and without danger. This had in it all the wild ecstasy of the excited senses, heightened by the presence of danger, and the daring that defied it. Daring and danger, which to invite, to go in quest of, which to delight in when found, whether for sport or for pain, at home or abroad, on land or on sea, now or heretofore, is often spoken of as one of the highest distinctions in the English national character.

Others there—waiters on the men with guns—who watched at different points, had more leisure and some of them more inclination to be alarmed. True, the consciousness of wrong-doing did not sit heavily on them. The question of trespassing where they had no right to be, of killing pheasants which they had no right to kill, they balanced in some way with a recollection of the squire having allowed the birds to go where they had no right to go, to feed where they had no right to feed; most of them on Mr Buncle's farm, who gave that as a reason for employing fewer men to work on the farm. And they recollected farther, that in the village of Ridgley it had been settled by the "best moralists," the parson only excepted, that to kill game was no sin. Else, said they, how should the payment of four pounds and tenpence for a license to kill it take away the sin?

Still there was a lively consciousness of being where they should not be in those who had time to think of it. Rice intimated to Reeves and Russell his inclination to retreat to the edge of the wood farthest from the keepers and nearest home; and they thought it would be best for all of them to keep in as dark a place out of sight as they could get into.

Rice said he wished he were not there; and with his hare and his three turnips, his piece of paling and his wires, he turned to retreat. But as he did so, he received such a "punch in the head," that he fell to the ground; the personal property just named rolling up hill and down hill and on each side of him. He attempted to rise, and got on his knees; but another punch in the head levelled him to where he was before.

Reeves was also punched, and lay alongside of him; so was Russell, twenty yards off, to which he had run in attempting to escape. There he was, like his two companions, undergoing the process of head-punching; and there could not be three more agreeable heads to practise upon. They were precisely of that kind which those inclined to break heads in such a situation as that like best to encounter: they took much, and gave little. Luckily they were hard heads: and after a short while, the prostrate bodies that owned them one by one lifted them from the ground; and, seeing no one near, they got on their feet, got each hold of his hare, and Rice his three turnips, and ran.

Hark! the firing of the guns has ceased, and the shouts of men calling upon men has filled its place in the echoing air.

The shouts cease too. Deep silence has taken hold of everything, and of every man. Has it seized them, and said they shall not fight? No: the silence is again broken. A voice breaks it, and an accompanying blow breaks a head. Another head is punched; a man falls, and a cry for mercy rises from where he fell. Another blow is struck, and a bludgeon is the weapon. Luckless weapon, and luckless hands that wield it!

They are the same that levelled Rice and Reeves; and, when these men rose to their knees, knocked them down again.

They are those of a strong man—a bold man; still he would attack six such as Rice and Reeves rather than him whose head he has last made a punch at, and whom again he strikes.

He gives the blow, but it is stopped, and he gets one in return. He receives another. He is before one who is his match.

He is the best man in the squire's service—the head game-keeper—no coward; but he falls—falls heavily; groans—struggles—groans again—stretches his limbs—contracts them—struggles no more—dies—and lies there until he grows cold and rigid as the frozen ground beneath him.

It was but yesterday that he told the squire for the tenth time that the man who is now his slayer should be made an under gamekeeper; that nothing would prevent his being a poacher but being shot dead, or hanged, or made a gamekeeper.

Had he known that this man was the one he struck at, he would have selected any one else to punch on the head, and would have avoided him; but in the heat of the strife he did not distinguish, and he has fallen by the hand of the man he has always feared, by the hand of William Masterton!

See!—a flash of fire!—a gun off! O George Preston! have you also killed a keeper? And to shoot him! it is dastardly to shoot him and he only armed with a stick—you with a gun! No; he is not mortally wounded. He struggled with you for that old Marlborough musket, and it went off in the struggle. But he will know it again. Away with it! carry it to an everlasting hiding-place! Sink it in the sea! the sea is not here; the river—the river is frozen! Then if you would save your neck and the neck of him it belongs to, home with you instantly and burn it, or bury it; bury it below the hearthstone, twenty feet down if you can. Yet stay; do not take it home. Kill the man dead that will be witness against you? No; do not—for Heaven's sake, do not! Hide the gun here; it will be found if taken home!

Ah, you cannot hide it here! You have not time! Every one runs, and you must run with them. Now you are upon the heath, among the furze; hide it among the furze! You have done so; that is so far well.

Listen! the bloodhounds! Your companion, who comes up breathless, tells you he heard them called for. They are on your track! Fly, every man!—fly for your lives! The hounds are in the leash, but they will be set loose the moment you are seen. They come unerringly forward. Here is a tree.

Hark to that voice!—it says, " Stand, men; stand round this tree!" The voice is Masterton's. "Stand firm, every one, or we shall be torn in pieces! Load your guns, stand back to back, faces outwards, guns in front, and be firm!"

"Who are they that have not come up?" " Rice and Reeves?" "No; Reeves is here, and there comes Rice." They have unleashed the bloodhounds. They come! Heavens, they are upon Rice! Run, man, run!" "He can run no faster; he is breathless!" " God have mercy on poor Jem Rice!" " The first bloodhound is on him!"

No; it is not. That was a good shot, Masterton. And so is that, Mason. Would to Heaven no other lives had been taken this night but the lives of these two bloodhounds! The keepers will not come nearer; their dogs are dead.

And they did not come nearer, the pursuers returned. And each of the pursued found his way home to his own house as soon as means had been taken to conceal everything effectually that might witness against them and tell of their being out that night. They had done more injury than they had received. They had given quite as many punches in the head as they had gotten. They admonished each other to be cautious about next day.

The next day came, and the next, and still no officer of the law was openly seen in Ridgley. It was known that this parish had furnished the poachers on that fatal night; but the parish had one hundred and fifty men in it, and the greater part of them were as likely to be poachers as those who had been

actually out.   Still there were suspicions, and some of them
well directed ; but these did not light on the men who had
received punches in the head and carried marks of the conflict
under their hats.   Nobody was apprehended.

Yet day after day did the stern unyielding winter hold in
his hand the spots of blood, and invite the world to look upon
them.   He had laid a white sheet of snow upon the earth and
taken impressions of guilty men's feet, and of the blood that
made them guilty.   He treasured up evidence against them ;
set his seal upon mother earth ; put her under lock and key ;
told her that though the criminals were her own sons, she
should not be permitted to soften and melt, to obliterate the
traces of their footsteps and of their crimes.   No.   So careful
was he to preserve the fearful evidence of blood, that he denied
even one additional particle of snow to obliterate it so long as
he could hold the earth in his hard bondage.

And while men were secretly searching, and asking who they
should suspect and accuse and punish, he, the stern winter, took
the law into his own hands, and punished the poachers unre-
lentingly.   He would not give them work, hard-hearted winter
that he was ! and he screwed the worm of gnawing hunger
into them.   They dared not go to the game, for he scared
them with the prints of their own feet, and the drops of blood
he would not wipe out.   He loaded them with heavy dread,
which they carried upon them all day, and made them afraid
to sleep at night.   And when weariness bore them down and
sunk them in slumber, he came and howled down their chimneys
and awoke them, and rattled at their windows, and whistled at
the keyholes, as if calling the constables to come and take
them to prison.   And in the daytime he would put out their
fires, and wring and pinch them with hunger and with cold,
until they almost wished themselves hanged and out of the
world.   And he would lay hold of the children, and make
holes in their shoes, and benumb their bare toes and make
them cry, and make their mothers weep and pray for summer
to come, and ask why it was that Heaven had ever permitted
poor people to be born.

And all this time he would sit with roast beef, and red-
faced jollity, and rich wine, at the squire's table, and with
toast and ale in the squire's hall ; and he would heap the fires
with coals and blazing logs, and roar up the chimneys that all
England was well-fed and happy, save the idle fellows about
Ridgley, who should be all hanged.

CHAPTER IV.

The end of Winter and the end of Rice.

But a change came, and winter ruled no longer; he was dethroned; and May, queen of the summer months, reigned in his stead. Where the imperious tyrant went to, none can tell. Some said that May had banished him to regions where human foot had never trodden, and that he had become king of the solitudes of the everlasting snow. And they said his palace was in the icy mountains, and that his vengeance was so cruel upon those who loved May better than him, that he came out upon the ocean to look for men and for ships that might have come from his old dominions. And they said, when he found the ships and living men in them, he hemmed them in, and went into them and put out every fire and every lamp, and nipped their noses off in the dark, and their toes and their fingers; and then took the life out of them. And then, they said, he would toss the ships about in their ragged sails and laugh at them; and, when he was tired of that, he would take two icebergs and crush the sides of the ships together, and grind them to atoms, and then go out upon the ocean to get more.

Others said that he was dead and buried in the deep caves. They said he must be dead, for more than once they had seen his ghost at dawn of day. They said they had seen little cherry blossoms with their eyes put out, and peaches smitten, and withered, and dying, all in the night—even in the gardens of May. And they had seen something white on the green meadows, which, the moment the daylight came, dissolved and disappeared, and was not seen until the next night, when it would once more appear and again dissolve, leaving the youngest flowers dead on the bosom of the leaves that nursed them. They said it must be his ghost, it was so like him. It could not be himself, it moved so silently, and was so timid.

But May, who had dispossessed him of his rule, knew it was himself, and feared him. And she rose early every morning; and with her attendants went out to look for him, and chase him away until he was gone altogether; and then she took leaves and flowers and clothed those whom he had stripped naked. And then she made every living thing happy that belonged to her; and she bloomed and sung in her gardens and in her fields; and thus it was that they called her "Merry May."

No longer did the river gather its waters and rush from old winter and his angry storms over the meadows and the farm-fields. It was all placid and clear now, and its little trouts disported themselves on its sunny bosom as if they had no fear.

And Ridgley meadow was no longer battered with broken ice and fragments of frozen earth, as if it had been the field of Winter's Waterloo. It was now all gaiety and greenness; with cows upon it, rich in milk as they were rich in grass; and maidens singing as they milked the cows; and laughing children trooping along with handfuls of buttercups, and cela-dine, and cowslips, and daisies, and violets; and the lark carolling in high air, as if earth was not large enough for all its joy, and had to send to heaven and borrow more room.

And Ridgley Heath, with its furze in bloom, had arrayed itself in green and gold, and it gave fragrance to the soft south wind, and loaded it with the hum of bees and the industry of ten thousand of the insect working classes. Thither came the laughing children with their happy voices, and their flowers, and the rushes they had pulled on Farmer Buncle's meadows, where there was more than enough of them; the flowers to make palaces for butterflies, and the rushes to plait into helmets, and swords, and whips for themselves; thither they came, the leaders and the led, those that were always in front, and those that were always behind.

There was young Jem Rice, that carried his little brother Bobby on his back, and led his sister Fanny by the hand, and lent his shoes to young Bill Masterton who had none, to go among the furze with Fred. Mason to look for nests. There were the Russell's three little girls with blue eyes, three buds from one stem; they tripped together hand in hand with little Mary Reeves between them, who had no mother; and she was always led by the hand because she had no mother. And when the house was made with rows of stones upon the grass, she was put inside to be mistress. And Bill Masterton's little baby sister was put with her, for he had promised to bring flowers to them from where nobody could go but himself, and also the magpie's eggs from the top of the lofty elm tree, if they would keep his little sister while he was away, and put her in their house. And they also put Jem Rice's little Bobby in the house, and called Jem "father," because he plaited the rushes for them and made helmets, and caps, and baskets, and made dishes upon which to serve out the buttercup feast.

In this did young Jem Rice delight rather than to go among the furze to rob bird's nests. But Mason and Mas-terton were keen nesters; and Mason looked into a cluster of bushes, and said he was sure he had seen a goldfinch fly out. And then he exclaimed, " By goom, if here ben't a gun !" upon which young Masterton looked in and said, " By goom, if it ben't !"

They had both been well taught by their fathers that no gun nor aught pertaining to a gun, nor any word relating thereto, must be seen or spoken at home. Would they then leave this here ? Some other boys might come and carry it away. Would it not be better to get Jem Rice to take it home to his house ? His father had never been suspected of having a gun, nor of using one ; he had only been suspected of going out with other men.

They accordingly told the finding of the gun to young Jem. And proudly happy was he, when, after much scheming to get it home unseen, (though it was not unseen,) he deposited it in the empty pig-stye ; for his father, so hard had the winter been and so late, was unable to buy a pig to put in the stye.

Secret and sweet was the pleasure he enjoyed when young Masterton brought some powder from the place where his own father had hid it, and in which only the son of such a father could have found it. Secret and sweet was Jem's delight when he found that he could purchase the whole right and title to this old Marlborough musket from the other two boys, as also some powder to flash in the pan, by giving Masterton his live rabbit that he got from his uncle, and Mason all the marbles he had, and the blade of a knife, and a bow and arrow which wanted only the string to be complete.

But he had possessed his bargain only a few days when he began to see what a dangerous purchase he had made. And the July assizes, when they came, revealed the awful fatality of it in the stark-naked horrible truth that his father was to be hanged for murder, the finding of this gun hidden in his pig-stye being a chief circumstance against him.

In what manner all the evidence was made to bear, it would be too tedious to relate. The Judge, in passing sentence, said he had never seen a clearer case of circumstantial evidence, and he could hold out no hope of mercy to him in this world.

And James Rice received no mercy. He was hanged by the neck until he was dead, and buried within the precincts of the prison.

And his wife, who, being a woman, had the heart of a woman—it broke ; and she received a pauper's funeral. And his children—young Jem, Nanny, and Fanny, and little Bobby, who was his mother's darling—where are they ? In the workhouse; and they are known by the designation of "The children of the man who was hanged for murder."

THE SHADOW AND THE PANIC.

A WITCH STORY FOR NEW YEAR 1846.

In my western travels through the grazing districts of Hereford, Brecon, and Monmouth, I heard complaints everywhere of the terrible disasters of the panic which followed the enactment of the tariff of 1842, that tariff admitting foreign cattle at L.1 per head of customhouse duty. The graziers thought they were to be ruined, and rushed to the markets to sell their cattle which, with the diminished consumption of butcher meat consequent on five years of depressed trade in the towns and factory districts of the kingdom, brought down the prices of cattle to a ruinous extent. The political landowners who supported protection and their newspapers made the case worse. They, in their efforts to make the farmers stand forth strong and bold to defend protection, never ceased to sound the alarm of agricultural ruin. The farmers and graziers, naturally inclined to timidity on policy which they did not understand, were urged into a state of desperation by those who professed to be their friends. One Mr Matthew White, an extensive grazier, was not only a loser by the panic himself, but, having some influence in Herefordshire, frightened many others, and made them run and sell. He is introduced in the following story. In Monmouthshire, to which it more immediately refers, some of the great landlords, foremost in frightening the farmers about the tariff, were not backward to distrain upon them for rent when the panic caused them to lose their farm profits. On this the story is founded.

CHAPTER I.

Some Account of where and under what circumstances.

How long it is ago can hardly yet be told. It may be known before we are done.

The time of the year was December. There were misletoe about and holly; there were carcases of prize cattle, which told of Christmas; but the weather did not belong to Christmas. It was not weather to rejoice the well-fed of the world. The butchers did not like it. It was not weather to rejoice the firesides of the very poor, for benevolent coal clubs did not open their hearts, because it was not a *hard* winter. It was foggy, muggy, muddy, chilly, shivery, drizzly, windy, cold, and wet weather; that is what it was.

It was like as if December had not taken his natural rest, and had not risen from his bed the sound-headed, hard-footed, Christmas-faced, dancing December which he used to be. It was as if he had turned his days, short as they were, into nights, and had been spending them with November in carousals of heavy-wettedness; coming home to the performance of his own business dosing and winking; bespattered from head to foot; refusing to be brushed and look respectable; storming and blustering; driving poor people about who were obliged to carry loads on their heads; wetting every body all over; tearing the soles from bad shoes, and the shoes from wayworn feet; spoiling the prize beef and mutton, and the geese and turkeys, and threatening to do the same with the mince-pies, and make Christmas, like himself, sour and unhappy. Such was that December in which occurred the events of our legend.

I do not know that our legend belongs exclusively to any one place. I have reason to believe it does not. We often find different towns in possession of the same legends. For instance, twenty villages in England, and nearly as many in Scotland, contend with half as many towns for the distinction of having buried a lady who was only in a trance, and of having had a sexton who opened the grave at night, and cut her fingers off to get her rings, who thus broke her trance, and enabled her to get up and tap at her own door for admittance, within which the bereaved husband was heard to declare that if his wife was not dead and buried he would say that she was at the door !

Some towns dispute as to which burned the last witch; some dispute as to which of them gave birth to the man who sold himself to ——, no matter whom; and others contend for the distinction of having had a ravine dug out, a bridge built, or a road made by that remarkable old " navvy" who bought the man who sold himself. It has even been disputed to which parish some ghost belonged, which made its appearance in several, as if it had been a parish ghost seeking a settlement.

There is no doubt but the events of our present story have occurred in more places than one. I believe there is scarcely a town distinguished enough to have a cattle market in it in which they have not occurred. But I adhere to a West of England version, as it happened in the county town of a shire which has the Bristol Channel on one side and South Wales on the other. This town stands on the banks of the river Wye, near to its confluence with the Mon, and they were both in high flood. It is a genteel river the Wye, but had then been getting in its first winter contributions, a kind of water rental from the plebeian working streams, and it looked familiar with them, and was not so genteel and reserved as it had been. It was of a fustian-jacket colour, but not so black as its vassal the Mon, which issued from the womb of the Welsh mountains, deep into which the human ants—worms, if you will—had penetrated for coal and iron to make wealth and strength for England. The Mon was a working river, embrowned with its coaly toil and with the iron rocks in the deep caves, and with the red earth which seemed to yield its very blood to give England treasure. A hundred humble streams of its own industrious order joined with it, and were swallowed up by the genteeler Wye, which, in its turn, was gobbled by the Severn, he rolling along like a tax-gatherer to the ocean to feed the great monopolist of all ; where the dyed waters from the Welsh hills bore no more evidence of having once been the water of working streams than do any three halfpence paid for a pennyworth of bread bear evidence of having been once a working-man's halfpence when they are in the treasury of a duke—the fractional part of an ocean of guineas.

The Mon rushed down in full flood, as if it could not spare a moment from business to linger anywhere. Its neighbours, larger and less, were all alike. The very springlets, by far too young as yet to do any work, imitated their elders, put their little feet in their father's shoes, put his hat on, which fell over their eyes, rambled about knowing not where they went, and raised their voices as if they bade all England bear witness that they had now grown big.

But it was a dreary day to such men and beasts as were obliged to be out in it. How the shepherd who had been twenty years in that one service, having his choice between the shelter of the hedge where the ground was wettest, or the windy side of the hedge where the ground was driest, longed to see ten other Decembers over his head, that he might then perchance get a " premium of a sovereign and a great-coat, with the society's buttons on it, for long service !" How strongly did he feel a conviction that stall and shed feeding for turnip eating sheep was the best ! and when he saw his flock knee-deep in earthy mortar, their food as deep in the mud as their feet ; and how the cattle in the wet meadows shivered, and felt what it was to be on farms which had not plenty of straw for them and winter food ; how they would have understood the operation of a corn-law, which their owners did not understand, had they been farmers as well as beasts ; how they would have said, bring oats and beans for us to eat and be fat with, and we will make the farm rich to grow wheat and plenty of warm straw to lie on, and much provender to be added by you to our oats and beans !

But shepherds, and sheep, and meadow cattle, shivered and were drenched, and nobody seemed to think they ought to be warm and dry. What between the ploughmen sinking in the undrained land when they ventured on it in the day time, and sinking in their potato burrows when they put their feet on them at night, unconscious that their stores of winter food had been transformed into heaps of rottenness ; what between their master seeing the wheat which was sown for next year's crop rotting in the ground, because the land was undrained and the weather so continuously wet ; what between his knowing that he had no money to drain it, and not much chance of getting the profit if he had money and did drain it ; what between having his hay spoiled in the summer by a month of rain, and the flooding of the rivers upon meadows where his rheumatic sheep now stood—rheumatic because they were in the wet, in the wet because they must pick up scanty grass, there being little hay, no corn to eat, and little straw to lie upon ; what between all these things, the continued gloom of the weather, and a gloomy foreboding of something which was once far off, but which was now coming near and nearer, and which such friends as they ever took pleasure in listening to, said was to be a terrible calamity ; what between all these things, they were every one, both masters and men, as low in spirits as the weather-glass in the parlour or as the cattle that hung their heads in the meadows.

But amid all this dreariness of man and beast, of earth and air, there was, at least in one place, a spot of joy, a focus of happiness, where the light spirits of youth, released from school for the Christmas holidays, had assembled. A young tradition says it was in the town which stands at the mouth of the Mon, or rather where the Wye snatches up the Mon in its mouth, that these light spirits, heroes and heroines of our tale, were assembled.

CHAPTER II.

An Account of the Giant Child and his Grandmother.

In that town indicated in the last chapter lived a fortune-teller, one Sally Morgan. It was often a subject of dispute with the townspeople whether old Sally really believed in her power of telling fortunes, or only professed to do so for the pence which the practice brought to her. If she did not believe, she simulated belief with wonderful fidelity. My own opinion is that she believed. The fact that out of hundreds of prophecies there was hardly one instance known of her being correct, only proves that her system of fortune-telling was false ; it does not prove that she did not believe in it.

She was grandmother to one Benjamin Morgan, a man of large stature and weak mind, who walked on crutches, and did not look straight with his eyes. He was old enough to be a man, but hardly wise enough to be a boy. He passed his time as a boy ; as a small boy ; as a boy petted and made much of—even unto spoiling.

There might be some excuse for this, inasmuch as he, being of weak mind and of feeble health, and being entirely under the charge of his grandmother, she had a tenderness of regard for him, increased by his helplessness. But this tenderness of regard led her to confine him entirely within doors, not suffering him to go out either for the increase of health or strength, or to assist in adding something to the family income. Indeed, on the last point, it was sometimes alleged that Old Sally made more money through the pretence of having a poor helpless, fatherless, and motherless " innocent" to look after, than she would have done had he worked for and looked after himself. And there is no question at all that her practice of fortune-telling was far more profitable to her than a more honest course of life would have been. And there was something in the appearance of the gigantic child in her house, always there and never out of doors, save when he peeped out at lonely hours, and instantly drew in again if he saw himself observed—there was something in this giant whom she " protected" that deepened the mystery of her own life, and thus added value to her prophecies ; for prophecies must be planted in deep mystery to take root and grow, and be rank, and rear themselves up with dark shadows, and look terrible. If there be no mystery at their roots, there is no life in them ; they are seen, and they perish. The world's eye withers them up.

The giant was not an unhappy creature ; though, by a kind of " whining"* noise he made whenever a stranger came within hearing, that stranger would have thought him greatly distressed. He begged halfpence from all who came to his grandmother to get their fortunes told, and it was her custom to foretell an indifferent fortune to those who in the least hesitated to give him halfpence. To those who refused, she prophesied disasters not much short of ending their days upon the gallows.

The gigantic Benjamin, by the halfpence thus obtained, and by other means to be explained presently, provided himself with toys for his amusement ; rather, it should be said, for his employment, for he had no employment but his amusements. He had a box of earth in the front window, and another in the back window, and in these he would plant a bean or two, and half a dozen grains of wheat. The hearthstone was his farm-yard ; and he had not only wheeled waggons and ploughs upon it, but horses on wheels. He had cows which lay down because they could not stand—not for fat, but for the want of feet to their wooden pegs. The floor was always in confusion. It was bestrewed with wooden hounds, foxes, and hunters, which stood still, save when he moved them ; and when he was tired of moving them, and tired of play, he grumbled to his grandmother, who comforted him with the assurance that somebody would soon be coming to get their fortunes told, of whom he could beg a few more halfpence to get a few more toys. And when they came, this he did accordingly.

It was a pitiable sight to see a creature, and that creature human, bearing the name, nature, stature, and years of a man, thus growing into mature life, year after year, with no higher enjoyment, and no higher purpose, than the play of a child. Pity suggests that we should hide such a helpless being, so humiliating to human nature, in obscurity for ever ; but duty says that he who could learn nothing himself must be made a lesson of instruction to others. The giant Ben had certain propensities and habits, and did certain acts which led some people to doubt if he was so harmless and weak-minded as he outwardly seemed to be. He was not altogether an innocent ; he was not free of guile ; but that I attribute to weakness of intellect and the teaching of his grandmother rather than to any inherent propensity to do mischief. He was taught to live by his helplessness, as has been already told ; how he acted up to that tuition we shall now in part discover.

It was in grandmother Morgan's house that the holiday children, who had escaped from school, were assembling to have sport with one another and with Ben. The old woman had this peculiarity about children coming to her house, that she did not hate them, else she would not have permitted them to come ; but she only loved them for what they brought with them. They brought their holiday halfpence ; and their fathers and mothers gave them liberty to take presents to her, that she might not cast an evil eye on them in after life. She also contrived to be friendly with the parents, and she was friendly with them because she foretold the good fortune that was to happen to the children, to such children at least as shared their cakes with her gigantic grandson, Big Ben. The children were also excellent listeners to her stories about witches, ghosts, fairies, and enchantments ; and as she loved to hear herself talk, she loved listeners. Thus far, and thus far only, did she love the children.

They, on the other hand, thought it such prime sport to see Big Ben, larger than any of their fathers, playing with toys, and they allowed to mingle their toys with his, that nearly every one, whose parents would permit, and who had a toy, or a box of toys to bring with them, were there in the play led on to the sport by the great man-child. And they put all the oddest looking toys and the most expensive together, and made a show of them. Their cows and bulls that ran upon wheels, and their pigs that had not a leg to carry them, they put them together, and clapped their hands and laughed ; Big Ben clapping his hands first, and laughing loudest. They called this their Christmas cattle show ; and then the little ones clapped their hands louder and louder, because Big Ben continued to clap his hands.

The world has many pleasant things in it ; things at once happy and beautiful. It has months called May and June, and they have fruit-trees and blossoms in them, and flower-gardens. The world has weddings. It has also first-born babies, and young mothers nursing them. Christmas belongs to the world, and boxing day, and so do many happy things that belong to Christmas and to boxing day. The assemblies of happy little children belong to both ; and the world has no lovelier sight than an assembly of little children, entertaining one another with their own cakes and fruit, with their own miniature table spread and surrounded by themselves, making their own mirth, singing their own songs, dancing their own dances, laughing their own laughter. They are fairies at such a time ; but, like the fairies of the summer groves, you must be good friends with them, and approach them discreetly, to be admitted into their society without spoiling it. They have come too recently from fairy-land, have advanced but too short a way into the mortal world, to have their joys fully understood or partaken of by mortals who cease to be mirthful as they grow into the world, and think they grow wiser as they cease to be mirthful.

There was not a happier assembly of young spirits within the regions of Christmas mirth than that which met at Sally Morgan's ; there might be a few, perhaps a good many, who had some distrust of both Sally and her grandson, but they got such a warm welcome, and were so caressed by the old lady, and so assured of friendship that would never vary by the very large and silly gentleman, Mr Benjamin, that they were speedily relieved of all distrust, and they proceeded with their show of toys, and their play as farmers and farmers' wives, led on by Big Ben himself, most gloriously and uproariously.

So long as the cakes and halfpence they brought with them lasted, and the apples, nuts, and oranges which the halfpence were sent out to purchase lasted, Big Ben was the best of friends. It has since been alleged that when he could get no more halfpence, cakes, apples, nuts, or oranges, from them, he began to help himself to their toys; and his avarice growing by what it fed on, as a prize pig does, he, in conjunction with his grandmother, who told them such ghost stories as nearly frightened them out of their senses, and who raised ghosts, or who made them shut their eyes that they might not see the ghosts which she said were there—his avarice growing by what it fed on, to wit, friendship for children's halfpence, and cakes, and toys, aided by his grandmother, who told him it was quite right that they should make dupes of those who would be duped, he proceeded to take from them things which they never intended to part with, and which they never knew how they lost.

But in saying this I am perhaps speaking too fast; too fast in respect of time and place, if not in respect of act and fact. We shall see.

CHAPTER III.

The Shadow, the Witch, and the Panic.

The gigantic child led on the play, by telling every one what they were to do. They were to play at farmers; and, as they were all in his house, he was to be landlord, and they were only to do what he bade them. And they all clapped their hands, and said they would only do what he bade them. And it was comical to see the large creature, with the body of a giant and the mind of a baby, directing their play; telling them how he would teach them to make nice pretty farms all over the floor and on the hearth; how he would tell them the best way to put out their toys to be like a real farm, while he had never seen a real farm in his life, and knew nothing of one but what his grandmother told him; and she, old woman, had been short-sighted, very, all her days.

His own eyes not serving him perfectly in estimating the number of children in the room, who contended for space to spread out their toys, and less perfectly in estimating the space of floor proper to each, according to the toys each had to put upon it, he gave some a great deal too much, and left none to others. Mat White was one who had not many toys, but who was to have all the room between the arm-chair at the fireside and the table at the front window. John Button, who had a great many toys, and no room to make a farm, seeing how much space Mat White had got, looked on in silence for a while, and at last said he did not care about playing at farms; he would make a shop. And others, who had been looking on, like him, and for the same reason, cried with delight at the discovery of this resource, that they would keep shops too.

"I won't have no shops," said Big Ben. "What do we want with shops? We be a playing at farmers. You are all farmers, and I am your landlord. I won't have no shops now, I tell you. And I tell you what it is, Button, if you don't do like the rest, you shan't play at all."

"But I can't do like the rest," replied Button. "There is Mat White making his meadows all under his grandmother's arm-chair, and over half the floor, just for his own few sheep and cows; and see how he is just getting anything, pieces of stick and cinder, and calling them bulls and cows! There is no room for me. I should keep a shop, and they as have farms should come to market and sell butter, and cheese, and corn, and buy things at my shop; and I should pay rent to you for my shop, as well as they do for their farms.

Upon which Mat White said pettishly, "Now, Button, you are always for something new, and spoiling the play, I'm sure Mr Benjamin knows better how we should play than you do, and he says we are to play at farms, and have no shops. What do we want with shops? Aint it genteeler to have farms than shops? (whispering) I'll let you have part of mine for one of your seed cakes."

And thus the first attempt was made at the middleman system and sub-letting. But in this case it was prevented. Big Ben had the merit of seeing his own interest in this instance. He saw the seed cakes in Button's pocket, and heard some jingling of halfpence, so he gave him and several others who had seed cakes and halfpence in their pockets leave to play at shops. He, however, impressed on them, or tried to do so, the fact that it was a great favour to let them play at shops; and though the space required was small, they must give him much more seed cake for that than any one gave for the same room who played at farms. Button said he did not mind giving one of his seed cakes and another halfpenny, only he did not think it was fair to make him pay for just half the top of the smallest stool in the house, while Mat White had all the room from the arm-chair to the table for a seed cake and two halfpence. He asked, in addition, how could they play at farms if there was not somebody to pay them for what they brought to market; and to sell that again, and to get the implements for them to work with, and the clothes for them to wear that played at farms?

At which Big Ben only laughed, and said, " Ah, Button, you don't know how to play; what has a farm to do with a shop? You mind your shop, that is all you have to do. Now all of you as have shops, put your things in them."

And the little shopkeepers clapped their hands, and said how nice it was to keep shops; and they called to Mat White, and all the little boys that had farms, and to the little maids that called themselves farmers' wives and dairywomen, to be quick, and make their butter and cheese, and fetch it to the shops; and to be quick and sow their corn, and get it reaped, and thrashed, and winnowed, and measured, and bagged, and carried to market. And all their little voices shouted, and called out, " Let us get butter, and cheese, and corn to carry to the market."

And so they went on as busy as little bees, and as noisy; and some never stopped, no, not for an instant, until long after they had seen Mat White stop and sit down on his farm, and let his cows fall down flat on their sides that had no feet to their wooden pegs. He was listening, and then they all listened, to a tale which Old Sally was telling of a witch that was to come across the Bristol Channel to the shores of Monmouth in a ship; and the witch was to take hold of all little children, and open their mouths, and put food down their throats until they bursted; and was also to fill all their fathers and mothers until they bursted; and all their big brothers and sisters until they bursted; and all the parsons, and doctors, and lawyers until they bursted; all the lords and ladies of the land until they bursted; and all the cats, and dogs, and pigs, and fowls, and horses, and cattle, farm-labourers, and all; paupers too, in the workhouses; every beast, and bird, and fish, and living thing was to be filled with food by the witch until everything bursted! And everything, with itself bursted, was to live and never eat another morsel of food, nor move from the spot upon which it was rent asunder by the fulness of the one great burst of food which the witch was to give it. All green things were to wither and die; nothing was to live to see the desolation but the creatures that had bursted with fulness of food. They were to live for punishment if they allowed the witch ever to set foot on dry land in Monmouthshire.

Mat White was so frightened that he was almost running away from his farm, but he was as near to Old Sally's arm-chair as he could get; so he held on where he was, and crept under her arm, and never looked over his shoulder to see if his toys were all safe. It was said that Big Ben took advantage of this diversion, and got hold of both cakes, and nuts, and pence, and toys. But, if it was true, it was only Button that saw it. There was such a panic among the little creatures, they could do nothing but hold on by one another, and cry in terror, "Oh, if the witch should come, and fill us all till we burst!" and look at Old Sally earnestly in the face to see if there was hope of her being able to save them from the witch.

And Old Sally understood their looks, and said there was only one way to be safe from the witch; they must each of them give Benjamin a halfpenny and a nut to crack, and not forget herself with something that was soft to her old teeth; if they did that, she and Benjamin would keep the witch away, and they would not be filled till they bursted.

Button murmured, though in a very low voice, "This is not playing at farms and shops, listening to a story about a witch. If you be all at work, as you should be, the witch will never catch you to fill you till you burst."

However, Button paid his halfpenny and his nut to Big Ben along with the rest, and gave a sugar plum to Ben's grand-mother; "For," said he, "if I don't, Ben will take more out of my shop." And then he called to Mat White and the rest, saying, "Come, now; get on and fetch your things to market, and let us buy them; and then you will get what you want out of our shops."

And Big Ben cried, "Yes, come; let every one come and be at the market selling their corn. Now you are all on the road to market. Now you are all in the market. Now you are to be all ready to sell your corn; but you are not to begin until I tell you; you are to do nothing until I tell you. Button, what are you about, buying and selling before I bid you begin? Grandmother, look at Button; he won't wait till I give the word; he *will* buy and sell; make him leave off, grandmother."

Whereupon old Mrs Morgan said something, and did something, and moved forward and then backward, and again said something, and once again did what she did before, and a black shadow was seen rising upon Button. And all of the little graziers and corn-growers, and the little maids that acted as if they were their wives, with butter and cheese to sell, saw the black shadow upon Button, and they started back and would not sell anything, nor exchange anything, nor do any-thing, neither with him nor with one another. They would not move; they could not. Their little hearts smote within them, and they trembled; for it was a real black shadow.

After it was gone, Button professed not to care for it, and said there was no use being frightened at shadows; and he told Mat White that he never would do anything on that part of the floor between Old Sally's arm-chair and the table, if he was to be frightened at shadows, for there were always shadows there—her shadow and Big Ben's. Indeed, he thought that when they were all frightened at the black shadow which Old Sally made, he had seen Ben's hand, his real hand, not a shadow of it, on more of the farms than Mat White's, and on that among the rest.

And so two or three of them suspected. Mat White found that some of the cows, which he had left lying for want of feet to their wooden pegs, were missing, and the remaining halfpence which he had been persuaded to deposit behind the arm-chair, on that part of the floor called his farm, and close to Big Ben's seat, were all gone.

He did not hide his loss. He grumbled loudly. At first, Ben and his grandmother frowned upon him for complaining. But when he blamed Button, or some of those who played at shops, for having taken his halfpence when the black shadow was in the room, they joined in the complaint, and said it was a shame to have taken Mat White's halfpence; and Button, or some one who was not friendly to Mat, must have done it.

Button denied that he had done it, and said that it was done when the shadow came, and when, as they all knew, he was trying to find out what the shadow was, for he did not believe it was anything but a trick; and perhaps it was not hard to guess who made the shadow and who stole the halfpence.

Whereupon Old Sally called him a little unbelieving cheating rogue, who would go to a bad place when he died. And all the children who believed Old Sally, and all who were afraid of her, though they did not believe her, called Button an unbelieving rogue, who would go to a bad place when he died.

But Button persevered in the truth, and asserted that it was not he that had robbed Mat White, nor was it any of the others who played at shops. He knew who it was, and he would tell plainly who it was. It was Big Ben. And he could prove to them all that more had been taken out of the shops when the witch story was told, and when the black shadow was in the room, even than from the farms.

Children as they were, and frightened as they were of Big Ben, lest he should be angry, they looked as if they believed Button rather than Ben and his grandmother. Seeing which, Old Sally told them she would let the witch come upon them

all and fill them till they bursted. "There is the witch at
the door!" she cried. "The witch will be here directly. Here
she comes!"

Whether it was a witch, or goblin, or ghost, or shadow, or
fancy, may not be told. But there, before the wild imagination and the disordered senses, stood a mysterious something,
with bags all hung around her, or his, or its body, and all the
bags stuffed with penny rolls; and the hands of the thing were
also full of cakes. And the thing advanced and laid hands on
Button, and opened his mouth, and held it open, and stuffed
cakes and penny rolls into him until he nearly bursted.

And as they saw this, and saw the thing putting out its
hands to stuff them and make them burst, they all ran, some
leaping out at the window and breaking, or nearly breaking their
limbs; some escaping by the door, and so getting away; but
the greater part running one another down in the dark passage.

Pen cannot write, tongue cannot tell, the height and depth,
length and breadth, the intensity, enormity, and disaster of
that panic raised by Ben Morgan's grandmother. One thing
only did not happen; not one child, not even Button, was
filled until he bursted. But the victims of it who survived
lost their toys. Some, alas, were never more seen. Mat
White was one of them. Whether Big Ben devoured him
up bodily, as some have said, or whether in his haste to escape
the flooded river swept him away, is not yet known. Some
were bruised and some broken, all were stripped. Button
asserts that Big Ben and his grandmother did it; and they
say that the children, waylaid and plundered, and misused by
the witch, got no evil treatment from them; that in their
house they received nothing but "protection." And, strange
to say, the children themselves believe it, or say they believe it.
Such is the influence of Big Ben and his grandmother. They
can bring together, alarm, disarm, and strip their little victims
with impunity. Button says he knows better, and one day
all the world will know better.

A VISIT TO THE BIRTH AND BURIAL PLACE OF WILLIAM COBBETT.

IF any person who has the convenience or the inclination
will look at a map of the county of Surry, it will be seen that,
on the right-hand corner at the top, there is the mark of
London. Proceed to the left hand, up the river Thames, and
come round by the border of Berkshire, then down the border
of Hampshire until the point is gained where the one county is

dovetailed into the other, and there will be found in the Surry dovetail the mark of a town called Farnham. That Farnham is the birth and burial place of the late William Cobbett, who said that, rather than see the working people of England reduced to live upon potatoes, he would see them all hanged, and be hanged with them, and would be satisfied to have written upon his grave, " Here lie the remains of William Cobbett, who was hanged because he would not hold his tongue without complaining while his labouring countrymen were reduced to live upon potatoes." I lately paid a visit to Farnham and its neighbourhood ; to the farm which Cobbett occupied at his death, to the house where he was born, and the grave where he is buried ; and believing that many readers would have willingly shared in such a journey, had all circumstances permitted, I shall endeavour to take them with me, by briefly describing to them how I went and what I saw.

On a lovely morning, the sun so bright that the fog which at first shewed itself durst shew itself no more, I was seated on a stage-coach, and bounding at a sound rate out of London over Putney Heath. We had just taken up the last of the passengers and the luggage, and the coachman said he hoped there were no more people waiting with luggage to be taken up, for he had no more room, and he was behind time. So away we went, competing with the railway, which has not swallowed up all the traffic down through Surry and Hampshire.

We had sometimes a heathy common, sometimes a mansion and a park, occasionally a village, and very frequently the enclosed fields of a farm, and the farmery itself on each side of us. We rattled over the heathy downs, through the lofty woods, and athwart the grassy meadows. We saw the churches and the beershops, had a glimpse now and then of a policeman sauntering along, saw occasionally a boy with six or eight, or ten or twelve pigs, which were eating the acorns that fell from the branches of the oaks that overhung the road, he at the same time shaking such branches with a long rod to force them to drop their fruit to his hogs ; all such things we saw, and many more.

We were in due time in the town of Guildford, thirty miles from London, and were dragging—oh ! such dragging—to keep the coach from taking a leap to the bottom ! down that most singular of streets, before we could see what a very curious old town Guildford is. Surely there is no other town in England nor in Scotland that has such a street. Berwick-on-Tweed has a street that very nearly stands on the crown of its head, but acts of Parliament do not allow Berwick to belong to either England or Scotland. Neither is the Berwick thoroughfare so long as that of Guildford.

Everybody and everything answerable for the safety of passengers is used to it, however, and the drags allowed us to come down safely enough. But where to go seemed the next puzzle. There was a river in the deep valley, the river Wey, and there seemed to be no room up nor down by its banks for coaches. But, by some quirk to the right and again to the left, our coachman managed to get his horses' heads turned up a road that might well make us congratulate ourselves on not being coach horses. Yet on they go; and up, up, never halting. On each side the land is cultivated, but the soil is whitefaced and ill-looking. If we look behind, there is a fine view of Guildford clinging to its hill-side, and looking over to us as if it laughed at rather than pitied our poor horses. Below, in the valley, is a railway making, to connect Guildford with a station upon the South Western seven or eight miles distant. Across the country, over two or three miles of farm fields, hedgerows, and thickets of forest timber, and beyond that, over two or three more miles of open heath, we can see a long earthy-coloured line intersecting the heath for several miles, which line, we are told, is the South Western Railway. We are with our faces to the west while thus looking to it; and far to the north-west, as far as the horizon, we can see some dots of white upon a dark ground, and these dots of white, we are told, are the stands and other erections upon Ascot race-course.

There is a twinkle in the eyes of some of our fellow-passengers, who have travelled this road often, who point out those places to us, and who agree that the view westward and round to the north is broad and fine. They seem to indicate that something is coming. What can it be? The railway goes almost in the same direction that we go, and keeps at that respectful distance; and they tell us that the country through which it goes continues to be the same brown heath which we now see it; what is it, then, that we are to see? We have been kept with our eyes turned to the west for some length of time looking to the right of the coach; let us wriggle ourselves round, and look to the south and the east; for surely we must now be at the top of that whitey-brown hill which stretched up to our left a while ago.

Great heavens! what sight, what scene, what enchantment is that? A new world—a fairy land—lies down below us. What is there elsewhere on the earth to compare it to? We are on a high narrow ridge. Our road is along the summit of this ridge—along its very back bone; and there, on either side, we might almost leap down into those woody countries which lie below. This narrow hill, so long, so thin, so bare-sided, is seven or eight miles in length. We might fancy it some enormous reptile ; if so, its huge head has been cut off, and Guildford has been disgorged. We got up somewhere about the shoulders ; and now we are travelling at the rate of ten miles an hour, until we shall get off at the tail, which tail ends imperceptibly in that low country between our vision and the smoke which issues from a hollow. That smoke comes out of the chimneys of Farnham, and Farnham is lying in that richly wooded valley, out of which this vast hill seems to have crept, before its head was cut off and it could go no farther.

But before we descend by the tail let us look upon that broad stretch of woody country. It is all below us, but it is not a level. It is a succession of hills and valleys of several sizes and many shapes. If we could imagine a garden twenty miles in breadth, all turned up by the snout of some monster which would do to twenty miles of country what a sow would do to a bed of onions, then we may have some idea of the shapelessness and brokenness of this mass of fantastic little hills below us.

Descending by the tail, I found myself, in the course of three or four miles, forty-one miles from London, in the town of Farnham. It consists principally of one street, from a half to three quarters of a mile long. It is stretched in a valley, or rather gentle hollow, by the side of a stream. Some green meadows with cows in them separate the main part of the town from the stream—I am not sure but it is called a river ; if so, I beg pardon—a river ; it is separated by the meadows from the main town ; and the meadows are somewhat broken and disjointed by gardens and hop grounds.

The cultivation of hops is the great staple of this neighbourhood ; and a good staple it is. The soil is exceedingly rich, and the hops are said to fetch in the market a price one-third over that obtained for hops grown elsewhere. One grower will sell L.10,000 worth of hops this year. Land is very high-rented, and much money is paid in wages for labour. As much as L.500 per acre has been paid of late for the purchase of prime hop ground ; and an annual rent of L.10 per acre is said to be common. The wages of labour is higher here than in the corn-growing districts. The work is all done by the piece ; but the men average 12s. a-week, besides which their children and female relatives work with them. At the present season the chief thing to be seen in connexion with hop-growing is the setting up of the poles upon which they grow singly in summer, in piles formed by a quadruple alliance.

Four pillars of poles of fifty or more each meet at top and form a mutual support ; and, as they are from twelve to twenty feet long, these piles, studded over some miles of country, look singular to a stranger.

There is a great fair for the sale of Farnham hops at Weyhill in the second week of October. All that I saw of the hops was when being packed into long bags called "pockets." This seems to be a serious piece of work for the men who pack. They must not put less than two hundred weight and a quarter in each ; to effect which, the empty bag is slung up and kept open by a hoop at the mouth. A man goes in naked, or nearly, with an iron weight, to which is attached a rope. This weight keeps the centre, and he tramps and dances all round it, pulling it up as the hops rise ; and these are let down upon his head in small quantities at a time by some of his children, or other young assistants. It is most suffocating work the packing of these bags.

Though I did not see, I was told of the other processes of hop-growing and gathering and preparing ; but I shall not at present say more on that head.

COBBETT'S GRAVE.

Having ascertained at the Bush Hotel, where I took up my quarters, what the various *sights* in the town and neighbourhood were, I walked out to see some of them. There was the Bishop of Winchester's residence ; the castle, standing aloft among old forest trees on the north-west or right-hand side of the town, our backs being towards London ; there was Waverley Abbey two miles off, and there was More-park not quite so far ; and in More-park there was Mother Ludlam's Cave, in which Swift wrote some of his works ; and there was the house close by in the town where Cobbett was born.

Nothing was said of where he was buried, but I knew he lay in that churchyard, and I had heard in London that there was a tombstone ; so, without any questions, I set out to the churchyard. It is rather spacious, is well filled, and has a great number of neat headstones of various shapes. As there are paths through it, I saw several people of whom I might have inquired for the particular stone I wanted to see, but I preferred reading my way to it. I was, after much reading and several journeys round the church, obliged, however, to inquire, and a person led me to it, almost close to the front door of the church. It is a flat stone, seven or eight feet long, and about three wide, laid upon some coarse brick-work, which raises it about twenty inches high. It occupies a triangular point of ground at the junction of two paths, and is most conveniently situated for a seat. And what between being used for a seat by the lazy and the tired, and as a platform for the boys to leap on to, and off from, it being a soft stone, is wearing rapidly away. Some carpenter or painter of ploughs and waggons has rested himself on it with his blue paint, and has amused himself while he sat by daubing his broad brush upon some parts of it. Others have chipped out part of some of the letters ; and one corner is chipped away two inches or more. The last time the roads had been muddy, some youngsters had been jumping on to it from a certain distance, for the mud from their nailed shoes stuck to the edges where they had got their feet to, but lost their balance from, preparatory to their falling backward.

I asked why it was not better protected, and was answered that it first had been the intention to put a railing round it ; but that for some reason it was not done. Perhaps this notice of its present condition will remind the relatives or political friends of the deceased of this unperformed duty. In the course of a very few years, if it remains exposed as it is to the ruthless feet of the young "chopsticks," the inscription will be illegible and the stone a wreck. The inscription is as follows :—

" Beneath this stone lie the remains of
WILLIAM COBBETT,
born in the parish of Farnham, 9th March 1762. Enlisted into the 54th Regiment of Foot 1784, of which he became Sergeant-Major in 1785, and obtained his discharge in 1791. In 1794 he became a political writer. In 1833 was returned to Parliament for the borough of Oldham, and represented it till his death, which took place at Normandy Farm, in the adjoining parish of Ash, on the 18th of June 1835."

Next to this stone and grave is an upright stone bearing the name of George Cobbett, who died at the age of 59, in the year 1760. I did not see the name on any other gravestones.

I found the house standing near the stream of water aforementioned, where report says Cobbett was born. It is at present a public-house, and bears the sign of " The Jolly Farmer." Across the stream, amid some houses which skirt the road leading up to and over the high ground between us and Waverley Abbey, I saw a mean-looking beerhouse, bearing the sign of " The Farmers' Retreat." I remarked that if the corn-law continued, the workhouse was more likely to be the farmers' retreat, as it had been to many of them and their labourers' during the last thirty years. The delusion practised upon the farming class by that most treacherous thing called corn-law *protection* has made the whole labouring population, but with a few local exceptions, paupers, or poorer than paupers, and it has brought the farmers to the verge of insolvency. Where was there, or when was there, in this country or in any other, a whole class, and so large a class, spread all over the kingdom, in such difficulties? Who ever saw master tailors or master shoemakers, or shopkeepers of any class, so universally and so very often, so almost continually, in distress as the farmers are? Can they have any doubt that something must be wrong? Yet many of them think they must not, not a few dare not, listen to any instruction which would explain to them why and by what means they are kept in distress; they must not listen to anything affecting their condition but what comes from the gatherer in of the rents.

Whether the little beershop has been the retreat of some broken farmer who has become its landlord, as is very often the case with beershops and broken farmers, or whether the sign indicates that any farmer, vexed with the world's cares, may hide his head in that little hole, and pour beer into his throat to kill care, as water is poured into rat-holes to drown rats, I cannot say; farmers, amid all their difficulties, generally find a better place to drink their beer in than that now referred to at the bottom of the hill. But from what I saw of the game, and from what I heard of its destroying practices to the farmers occupying land on the hill and over the hill, I should deem it the most natural of consequences if they, whose crops are so destroyed, were to rush down and hide themselves in this or any other hole, and never to go near the farm again. It is, in short, enough to break the heart of any man whose heart is not cast iron, to see his crops destroyed by vermin bred there, and preserved for the pleasure of some one who bears no part of the expense.

But of this hereafter. Bad as it seemed there, I have since seen it worse elsewhere.

WAVERLEY ABBEY.

Having come over this high ground, instead of coming round its elbow and down the valley, I descended by a steep road into this valley, and by a road overhung with lofty trees, the trees towering on the sides of the bold height on my right hand; a succession of green meadows lying to my left, with the river in the centre, or sometimes loitering in the shady places by the side; with deep, heavy woods rearing their heads beyond the meadows, I journeyed downward to the south, and at last found a gate, which I was told led into Waverley Abbey.

This was a famous settlement of Cistertian monks, who dispensed their hospitality to all comers and their bounty to the poor, previous to the spoliation by Henry VIII. Cobbett gives a glowing account of the monks' garden in his "English Gardener." It continued to exist in the time when he was a boy, and he says it was the first garden in which he "learned to work, or rather to eat the best kinds of garden fruit." It has since been, as he expresses it, all pulled to pieces. The old Abbey still remains; but a new house is built, and the old gardens made into a lawn. It has changed proprietors several times since the monks' garden was destroyed, one of whom was the late Poulett Thomson.

MOTHER LUDLAM'S CAVE.

Leaving Waverley on the right, I crossed the river, and turning into the dark shady woods on the east side, turned up by a path which I was told would lead back to Farnham by the bottom of the woods and the verge of the meadows. The greater part of this way was within the enclosures of More-park. The cave is in the bottom of a sandy hill overgrown with branchy trees, and a spring of water issues from it, and, crossing the path, falls down to the river.

Dean Swift used to visit Sir William Temple at More-park, and was fantastic enough to come (so tradition says) and study and write in this cave. I went into it as far as I could get, and drank of its water. As a cave it is nothing better than a sand-pit. It may be twelve feet high, and twenty feet wide at the mouth, and fifty or sixty feet lengthways into the hill. It was probably dug out to collect the various springs of pure water which ooze through the sand into one. Or probably it was dug out for the purpose of putting good Mother Ludlam's story into it. Being in the bosom of a forest, secluded from every human eye, it answered the purpose of those who had an interest in keeping up a belief in ghosts and witches exceedingly well.

Mother Ludlam was reputed to be a spirit of rather amiable temper, a kind of benevolent witch in *profession*. She was to the villagers of Farnham and people round Waverley in those olden days what the corn-law is to the farmers in our days. At great trouble to themselves, and at the cost of much dread and terror, they, when they wanted assistance—when, for instance, they wanted to borrow some utensil of domestic service, which their own want of skill or their poverty—poverty caused by those who deluded them—had prevented them from acquiring in a more direct and reasonable way—they went here at midnight to ask Mother Ludlam to help them, or to lend to them. It was of course absolutely requisite to profess not to be afraid of her. They were obliged to call upon her by saying, "*Good* Mother Ludlam, come and give me" so and so. If they had no faith in her *goodness*, or if they spoke evil of her, some *agent* of hers punished them. If they were not punctual to the very letter of time in repaying her for the assistance lent, she was very severe with them.

Her manner of lending was this :—They called upon her at midnight ; and, if they spoke her kindly enough, she put what they wanted at the mouth of the cave, which they found waiting for them in the morning. The whole was beyond question an imposture on the part of those who had an interest in keeping up a spiritual terror over the common people. To keep the *good* Mother Ludlam from doing any harm there was enough to be paid to the priesthood. And as those visiting the cave to borrow from her had to be prepared by faith and prayer with some priest, it was always known beforehand what they wanted to borrow ; consequently the article was procured and conveyed to the cave.

So much for Mother Ludlam, and so much for the delusion of the corn-law.

COBBETT'S FARM AT NORMANDY.

The name of Farnham is said to be derived from the abundance of *fern* that once grew there. I doubt not but the fine deep soils where the hops now grow were at one time covered with fern. That plant is to be seen yet in great quantities on some parts of the Surry and Hampshire heaths. I have observed that, in all parts of the kingdom, wherever the heath and the fern grow vigorously together, the soil, if broken up and planted with potatoes, brings forth first-rate crops.

Thus it is at Farnham. Notwithstanding all the prejudice of Cobbett against potatoes and potato eaters, the finest specimens of this year's crop which I have seen in any part of England I saw at FARNHAM. And in the country lying between that place and Normandy, where he had his farm, I saw some pieces of potato-ground bearing excellent crops ; pieces of ground newly reclaimed from the heaths which, in the natural state, did not produce one shilling for each twenty shillings produced now, besides not employing labour then as now. And there is such good land of that description still lying unreclaimed. Talk of emigration! of sending people to Canada or Australia, to get rid of a superabundant population! our superabundant people there have to make war upon primeval forests, and waste half a lifetime in making corn-land, wasting more than a whole lifetime in getting a good market for the corn, the good market at best being a low-priced market compared with the lowest in England! Talk of the backwoods in Canada when there is so much of Surry in England to cultivate; not the shallow heaths, but the good land!

But, unhappily, the parish of Ash, or a very considerable portion of it, cannot be cultivated as it should be because of law-suits arising out of mortgages, which mortgages and law-suits arose out of the corn-laws. But of this presently.

Having seen the birth-place and the burial-place of William Cobbett, and the place where he first learned to work in a garden and to eat garden fruit, I was desirous of seeing his farm. I knew it was a considerable distance from Farnham; but could not call to mind the name of it, although in the latter part of his lifetime every person that at any time glanced at his publications, or by any chance listened to one of his lectures, must have heard of *Normandy Farm*.

I had seen it in print and had heard of it many a time; yet could not recollect it now. So I was about to inquire, when, passing along Farnham Street, I read the following among other advertisements of farm property for sale:—

"*Normandy Farm, in the Parish of Ash, Surry.*—All the live and dead farming-stock, and part of the household furniture, comprising three useful cart horses; waggons, dung carts, and raved cart; three Guildford swing ploughs, and light and strike furrow ploughs; drags, harrows, rollers, ladders, corn lines, trace, thill, plough, and foot harness; Bennett's seed machine, corn screen, barley chomper, chaff box and knife, pair clasp drags, sieves, prongs, shovels, sheep bells, &c. The household furniture comprises fourpost and stump bedsteads, beds and bedding, chairs, glasses, card and other tables, fenders, fire-irons, butter tumbler, mash and tun tubs, barrels, copper, pots, tubs, kievers, stools, and a variety of very useful effects, which will be sold by auction, by Messrs Thomas Baker and Sons, on the premises, Normandy Farm, on Tuesday the 1st of Oct. 1844, at eleven o'clock precisely."

The tenant now selling off is the *second* since Mr Cobbett's decease in 1835; and he told me he was very glad to get out of it—he was losing money. He paid L.40 a-year more for the 160 acres, which is the extent of the farm, than Mr Cobbett paid. Cobbett's rent was L.160; this tenant's rent was L.200.

It was the evening before the sale that I saw the advertisement, so I resolved to go to it next day. Next day having come, I hired a conveyance, which bore the dignified name of a "fly," but which was rather a primitive machine of the fly kind, and jogged away at a rate which was by no means too fast for making inquiries about land, cultivation, tenures, lawsuits, mortgages, wages, potatoes, and so forth, as we went along.

THOMAS PAINE'S BONES.

When we arrived at the village of Ash, I stopped to make some inquiries of a general kind, or rather, to talk with anybody I met on any subject, to see what kind of topics might be introduced. Those to whom I spoke supposed at once that I was going to the sale at Normandy Farm, so that was the readiest subject of conversation. I inquired if the present tenant had been long in the farm, and also how long Mr Cobbett had been in it. To which it was replied, that no one had been long in that farm since Mr Weston left it; that he had been twenty-one years in it, and left it when Cobbett came. We then spoke of Mr Weston's present farm; and, on my saying I would like to see that gentleman, they told me that I had nothing to do but to drive on a mile and a half and stop as I came to his door, (I would know it by the new barn,) and I would not only see himself, but see "Tom Paine's bones" as well, if I chose.

It was, as every person old enough knows, a matter of public notoriety once, that Cobbett brought Paine's bones from America. I believe it was this that caused some public writer, in a fit of ill-nature, to call Cobbet the "bone grubber."

The bones were found in a chest at his death, and would have been sold at the public auction that followed, but the auctioneer would not offer them. They told me at Ash, that the auctioneer said "he had never sold any man's bones *as yet*, and he would not begin now with Tom Paine's." The chest and the bones, on everything else being cleared away from Normandy by the purchasers at the sale and by Mr Cobbett's family, were removed for a temporary deposit to Mr Weston's house, about half a mile off, and there, I was told, they still remained.

I proceeded to Mr Weston's accordingly. I would have done so for the sake of a conversation with him on farming

20

affairs, especially on his olden recollections of farming in Surry. But all these became secondary to my desire to see the chest and the bones, to see the skull of " Common Sense" and the " Rights of Man."

I knew Mr Weston's farm and residence when I saw it, as I had been told I would, by the *new barn*. There were a pair of sawyers sawing boards, and carpenters nailing up the boards, for all the barns are wooden ones ; and Mr Weston was in the barn also. On his being sent for to the house, I found him a most willing and intelligent informant on many matters ; but, by my not knowing precisely how to introduce the subject of Paine's bones, I felt myself in a difficulty. At last I became bold, and asked the question broadly, if it was true that he had such curious relics in his possession. At which he shook his head and said, " Not now." He had them up to about six months ago ; but at that time a gentleman came from London and got them away to bury them there. He seemed unwilling to say more ; and as I had no right to inquire, I did not pursue the subject ; but I was told elsewhere in the neighbourhood that this was correct. I heard names mentioned ; but as it seems some secrecy had been enjoined, I do not repeat the names. I think the parties performed a very proper duty if they really did take the bones to London *to bury them*.

NORMANDY FARM—RENTS AND MORTGAGES.

The fact of there being a *new barn* and other new wooden erections in progress on Mr Weston's farm, as also on some other farms which I had seen in the neighbourhood, led to conversations between myself and several parties on matters connected with the tenures and ownership of land.

An estate here had fallen into ruin through a mortgage which swallowed up its rents. The landlord, or a relative, his predecessor, had borrowed about L.30,000 on mortgage of the rental. The borrowing, as was too often the case in mortgages of the last thirty or forty years, was a corn-law speculation. The money-lenders, depending on the power of the Legislature to keep up prices of corn and rents of land, had lent more money than enough. The owner, depending also on legislative prices, borrowed more money than he could pay the interest of.

Normandy farm is on this estate, as is also Mr Weston's present farm next to Normandy. In the year 1811 Mr Weston commenced his occupation of Normandy at a yearly rent of L.210. At that time the war and the political fictions which accompany war had raised prices, and he got on pretty well. So he hoped to do when the corn-law of 1815 was passed to keep wheat up to eighty shillings a quarter *at least ;* but that corn-law, like all others, was a delusion, and up to 1822 Mr Weston had a continued struggle for bare life. Having paid everything in rent, and more than everything— for, owing to the depreciated currency of 1819, he paid in the three succeeding years a rent much higher than he contracted for in 1811, as all farmers did—he paid at least L.250 a-year instead of L.210, and he did this with low markets—with wheat down to forty shillings a quarter in one year, while he had contracted to pay a rent which the stupid and most treacherous delusion of the corn-law had caused him to calculate to pay, with wheat at from eighty shillings a quarter upwards—having, as all other farmers had at that time, paid away everything derived from the farm in rent, and more than he derived—having paid away all spare cash, the savings of the years of war prices—he could not keep on at such a rent. He got an abatement, and for the next nine years paid L.170 a-year.

Mr Cobbett came after him, and had the farm four years, at an annual rent of L.160. He must have entered upon it, I presume, in 1831, as he died in 1835. No person since 1811 has had a chance of doing much in it save Cobbett, not unless they had a good capital. It is a farm capable of great improvement. Had Cobbett been long enough in it to have done much, I would have been exceedingly surprised to see it as it is now, even nine years after his death ; but he had not time to do much. Yet Normandy farm, as it is now, and was when he took it, is a proof of his sagacity. It is an excellent piece of land, which, from the day that the dove went out of Noah's ark to the day that the Farnham " fly" conveyed me to it—namely, the 1st of October 1844—has never been treated in a manner deserving the name of good cultivation. Mr Weston had nothing but a continual struggle with difficulties, paying everything away in rent. Besides, I must take the liberty of doubting whether either he or the present generation of farmers in Surry are likely to do all they might do for themselves and their land, supposing them to have the money power.

Next to Cobbett came a Mr Thompson, or rather a company with Mr Thompson at its head. The rent was now L.200, a higher rent than that of the war prices of 1811, be it remembered, yet a rent which such land should easily afford where there is sufficient capital, good security of tenure, liberality of covenants, and *no game ;* that accursed game is the ruin of these counties.

BEETROOT SUGAR.

It is said that Mr Thompson began well, would have continued well, and would have found his rent of L.200 an easy rent, as his intention was to grow beetroot and manufacture sugar. Just, however, as the apparatus was got ready, and much expense incurred, the West India sugar interest took the alarm, and said to the government, It will never do to make sugar in Surry and refine it into loaf sugar to compete with us ; it must be taxed.

The owners of land naturally said, Why is beetroot sugar to be prohibited by this tax? Shall we not be allowed to produce what we choose from our own land, if we can make a profit from it? To which the sugar interest replied, You cannot make a much larger profit off your beetroot sugar than you can off your wheat. If you make sugar in competition with us, we will not help you to keep up the corn-law. Give up sugar-making to us, and we will help you to maintain your corn-law.

And accordingly Mr Thompson, who had no doubt but he could easily pay L.200 a-year for Normandy farm if allowed to make sugar, was prevented from making sugar, and left the farm ; and a Mr Wood, believing that the corn-law would be kept on, and that it would keep up the rising prices of 1837 and 1838, undertook to pay as much rent as Mr Thompson had undertaken to pay, namely, L.200 a-year.

Thus, taking this farm as a specimen, the landed interest seemed all right. The attempts to make sugar had increased the rent from twenty to twenty-five shillings per acre, while the alliance with the India sugar monopoly, which promised to maintain the corn-law inviolate, obtained for the land the continuance of twenty-five shillings an acre—the sugar price.

But the corn-law never did and never will keep up prices. So far as the sliding scale is concerned, it unsettles prices, and unsettles them to the farmer's disadvantage ; while the whole law tends to make the whole nation poorer and less able to buy and consume that which the farmer has to sell. The corn-law has cheated every farmer, and it cheated Mr Wood of Normandy like others. He found the corn-law did not keep up prices, and yet he had L.200 a-year to pay, with L.30 a-year of other burdens, tithes, rates, and taxes.

THE CORN-LAW INJURIOUS TO LANDOWNERS.

Moreover, he not only paid away all that he had in rent, but he suffered part of that evil which results to the owners of land from the corn-law. The estate had been mortgaged. A lawsuit ensued. It was for several years apprehended that the mortgagees would get possession of the estate, when, in order to take legal possession, they would eject the tenants who held from the landlord. This the mortgagees have at last done. And during the years of dispute, the tenants dared do nothing that required an outlay of capital. Barns and other buildings, and fences and gates, went to decay ; no draining was done ; no means taken to make the land fruitful to pay the rent. Yet the rent had to be paid. Receivers had been appointed by the courts of law, and to them the rent had to be paid with rigid punctuality.

And all this arose from the landlord and the mortgagees having expected that the corn-law would be able to keep prices and rents at an extravagant height. The landlord has lost his estate, the mortgagees saw it fall into dilapidation, and must now bear the expense of comprehensive repairs. The tenantry suffered for the want of suitable conveniences, and also because they had no security in laying out money in properly cultivating their land. All of them lived from hand to mouth by reason of the corn-law, hoping for something better, and all of them were cheated. Mr Wood had an agreement for fourteen years, and must have remained until that time was out, or until he became insolvent and was sold out, had not the success of the mortgagees given him the chance of escape, which, being cheated by the corn-law, he was but too glad to avail himself of. He was served with a notice of ejectment, and he took that opportunity of quitting so bad a bargain as he found Normandy farm to be at L.200 a-year.

A neighbouring gentleman named Warren has taken it at L.180 a-year from the mortgagees. But it is said the dispute is not yet settled, as the landlord is to make one more effort to regain possession.

But this is a rare instance of a farm being at present let for less than the old rent. I have been assured by several farmers, who are now offering for farms, that there is no chance of getting a new holding but at an advance on present rentals. This may not be so with the very large farms, for which there is not so great a competition ; but for small ones, or those of moderate size, for which the competition is great, an increase of rent is asked everywhere. Some landlords, Lord King for one, near Guildford, are reducing the size of their farms and getting a higher rent.

This reduction of the size of farms will become universal in the course of a few years. From the discoveries in chemical science, and other circumstances, tenants cannot cultivate farms of from 600 to 2000 acres properly : they have not

capital. A farm of from 150 to 300 acres is far more likely
to be profitable than one of 1000 acres, to a man of moderate
capital. The desire for the reduction of farms is extending
rapidly in the southern counties of Scotland at present, especially among the sons of farmers. The young men find they
cannot get farms at all, the parcels of land are so large and so
few. And they find that, to carry out the comprehensive new
system of tillage requisite in such a district as the Merse of
Berwickshire, they should not encounter more than 200 or 300
acres, even if they could get more. The sum of L.4000 laid
out in draining thoroughly; in subsoiling and in trenching
with the spade; in saving and applying every particle and
drop of home-made manure; in the raising of superior
green crops and in stall-feeding; they understand quite well
that L.4000 would bring a larger profit out of 400 acres than
that sum would out of 1000 acres. Yet 1000 acres is a me-
dium-sized farm in Berwickshire.

Not so in Surry, unless where there is a wide range of
heath, and not even there, so far as I have seen; but on some
estates there are large farms in Surry, and, as already said,
some landlords are reducing them, and, from the competition
that exists, are obtaining higher rents.

OUTWARD APPEARANCE OF NORMANDY FARM.

It is but a humble-looking place. The farm-house and
offices stand at the top of a common, removed from the farm
land, which to a good farmer is a great annoyance, and to any
farmer is a loss. A wide range of heath, variegated with
furze, gravel pits, and tracts of absolute sterility, extends for
many miles behind the farm-house; and on either side, right
and left, the heath extends for several miles, variegated only
with a few clumps of pine trees, chiefly Scotch firs.

In front lies a heathy common, in complete disorder, as commons usually are, and beyond it, to the front, looking eastward,
is the farm land, enclosed in small fields, with very badly kept
fences. There are trees in the hedgerows; and, in some parts,
more of them than should be upon a farm where there is a
tenant bound to pay rent.

The land is wet, and wants at least L.1000 expended on it,
to be repaid out of a lease of twenty years, before it can
develope fully its natural good qualities. At present it is
poisoned with weedy foulness and the sour wetness of its subsoil. Nothing has been done to cure this effectually, not even
by Cobbett; yet, had he lived longer, he would have, doubtless, had it in a much better condition than it is now in.

It is an excellent soil for potatoes. I never saw better potato-land in the kingdom than in this parish of Ash. In Farnham the land is more profitably employed in hop-growing, by far, than it could be in potato-growing. But were the farmers in those parishes who occupy that land which was originally heathy and ferny, and which is not used for hops, to turn their attention to the culture of *seed*-potatoes, they could make an excellent profit. The railway is near; the London growers of potatoes are always in want of changed seed; the soil in this part of Surry is that kind of soil which produces the best seed-potatoes. I mean by *seed* the potatoes that are to be planted again, not literally the seed of them from the apples.

VICTIMS OF PROTECTION—LETTERS TO INDIVIDUAL SUFFERERS.

No. I.

To my old Master, Mr W. T.—a particular Victim.

Sir,—Though you are not so rich as you once were, you are not dishonoured. Your money credit may be gone, but your moral credit remains. You struggled with a bad bargain, and only yielded in the struggle when you had paid away all your farming capital and private fortune in rent; capital derived by inheritance, and not accumulated by any former profits from the farm. Some persons have said you were foolish to do so; but, at the least, they must admit you were honest. In truth, you could not help yourself. With a large family to provide for, with no alternative if you left the farm; but without the power to leave it, you being bound by a lease, what could you do?

Some have said you were imprudent to have taken such a lease at such a rent; and, perhaps, you were so. But your imprudence was comprised in this, that you did not think it necessary to inquire into and understand that delusive corn-law which promised to do so much and which did so little, save to transfer your capital to the pocket of the Laird of ———, your landlord.

That you should have taken the farm upon a fixed money rental was, perhaps, indiscreet. You would not now do so. Nor would any of your friends. But when you took your lease corn-rents were not so common in your county as now; and, I believe, had not been then introduced upon the ——— estate at all. However, I am not perfectly informed on that point; but I do know this, that when B——— was sold out of your family, you were desirous to retain it even as a farm. You had a love for it; it was natural you should. You know nothing about the corn-law; it was natural you should not. The education of young gentlemen, such as you then were, did not comprise a knowledge of the causes which affect the value of property; which make corn dear at one time and cheap at another time; which shew that high prices are not always profitable, nor moderate prices always a loss.

The attempt to raise corn to an exorbitant price, and keep it up when it was up, had, through the failure of the East Lothian bank—that instrument by which wheat was never to be allowed to fall below ninety shillings a quarter in East Lothian—the attempt to secure such a price by such an instrument, resulted in the downfal of the projectors and shareholders of the bank, who included some of your nearest relations. This led to the farm of B——— going out of your family as an estate, and still it brought no instruction to you on that pernicious corn-law which first made you a tenant instead of a proprietor, and then ruined you as a tenant.

But even to this day the farmers, your late neighbours, are not taught by what they have seen and should have studied. I am told that many of them still cling to this agricultural "protection," as the corn-law is most absurdly called. Some of them may know better, yet fear to go against the landlords who uphold it, and the landlords' deputies—the factors. But I believe the greater part of the farmers do not know which is the right side and which the wrong of this question.

I have seen most parts of England since I left you, and have paid close attention to both sides of the corn-laws—the agricultural side and the commercial side—and I therefore place before myself the task of helping the farmers to a perfect knowledge of this all-important question. It is not so difficult to explain principles as it is to get those most concerned in them to listen to the explanations. It is not so difficult to bring facts together, and place them before a farmer's eyes, as it is to get him to open his eyes and look at them. "One man may take a horse to the water," we used to say, "but twenty men will not make him drink;" that is, if the horse is not inclined to drink. So, one man may put the whole history and mystery of the different corn-laws—their delusive promises and their disastrous effects—before a farmer, clear as the looking-glass in which he looks to see if he be clean shaved; and he may be shewn by that one man in that glass how the corn-law has shaved him; but twenty men will not make the farmer look into the glass if he be resolved not to look.

The only way I know of accomplishing this desirable end is to go to some of them singly, and tell them that they bleed —that in the dark they have been wounded ; and then, being addressed individually, they may open their eyes and behold each his own suffering and disfigurement, before any factor or agent can come and tell them not to look, not to read, not to understand.

To such as you, Mr T., I need not say you are hurt. You know that too well. But, if I am not much misinformed, you do not yet see clearly how you have been hurt. You will say by too high a rent ; but why did you contract to pay too high a rent ? It was not, as some say, that you were not a proper judge of the value of land—it is easy to say this after you have lost your all upon it—Job's comforters are always ready with their sayings ; but the real cause of your contracting to pay L.3 per acre for B——— was, that the corn-law promised you a price which would have got you a profit at that rent ; but the corn-law deceived you, it cheated you, and you have lost your capital, your patrimony, your farm, and your family's bread.

At one of the contested elections for the county, which occurred after you became a tenant of the Laird of T———, when much popular interest was excited in behalf of one of the candidates, you were asked by one of your workmen if you would not vote for that candidate. You replied—and your reply was, like all your actions, straightforward and honest—you said you knew no difference between the merits of the one candidate and the other ; that the one was a Whig and the other a Tory ; that both were alike to you, save that the Tory was your landlord's candidate, and that he would be yours ; that it was safest to keep on the landlord's side, "because," you continued, "what is for the landlord's interest must be for my interest, and the interest of all of us on his estate."

In this you spoke as it is common for a tenant to speak ; in this you voted as it is common for a tenant to vote. I blame you not for seeing no difference in the candidates. If Toryism be Conservatism—the principle of conserving the British nation as it now exists, and of extending and elevating its greatness and glory—then I am as much a Tory, though I do not like the name, as your landlord was who swayed your vote to the Tory side. If your landlord be a Conservative, so am I, though totally opposed to him on the subject of the corn-law. Indeed, the free-traders are the most thorough Conservatives of any party. Were the maintenance of the corn-law a part of Conservatism—Conservatism being the

preservation of the national power, prosperity, and integrity—
then it would be to uphold the national power, prosperity, and
integrity, that you were made to pay to the Laird of T———
every penny of the fortune you inherited out of B———
estate, and were at last driven from your farm with a helpless
family.

It is rank deceit to mix up the preservation of the corn-
law with the patriotic principle of Conservatism. The one
is personal, the other is national ; the one aims at the meanest
of objects, the other at the highest.

You have lived to prove, unhappily, that the interest of
your landlord was not your interest and that of your men.
By his parliamentary power you expected he would procure
you such a price for your corn as would enable you to pay him
L.3 per acre and provide for your family. You entered into
a bond that you would pay that rent every year, for a certain
term of years ; the landlord gave no bond that he would not
take all the money you promised him if you did not get all
the price he promised you. On whose side was the best of
the bargain ? You knew the best of the bargain was on his
side. Hence your reasons for the vote you gave.

But did that satisfy him ? Did he not exact his bond—his
"pound of flesh ?" He did ; and he got it too, and the blood
with it. After you had paid him all your profit, all your
capital, and every penny you possessed, and begged for time
to pay the rest, you were only saved from being sold out even
to the last wheel-barrow, even to the pillow upon which you
laid your head in that house which had once been your father's
mansion, and which had descended from that to be what it
now was to you and your helpless family, by the landlord and
the landlord's corn-law, and these alone—you were only
saved from losing the last stick and the last pillow, to satisfy
that landlord whose interest you said was your interest, by
the intervention of two friends—family friends—not " farmers'
friends."

I do not say that all landlords would have done as yours
did ; far from it. I do not say that yours would have done
the same to every other tenant ; and yet there is no reason
to suppose he was harder upon you than he would have been
upon others who might have had as bad a bargain as you.
But he proved in your case, against your own words, that a
landlord's interest may not be always a tenant's interest. So
long as the corn-law exists, or legislative protection to agriculture exists in any shape, the interests of landlords, tenants,
and labourers cannot be identical, unless a landlord acts

toward them in a spirit the very opposite of the spirit of the corn-law, which is personal and selfish, enacted for private ends by those who have had the power to enact it.

But here I may remark that the landlords have even injured themselves by it. See how many estates have passed away from their former owners by these owners speculating on excessive rents, indulging in expenses they could not support. See how many estates have been mortgaged, and all but the name of the property taken from the once independent owners. Extensive as the Laird of T———'s estate is, it is not clear of embarrassments. He has had an expensive family to provide for; and though he had the support of your votes and the votes of his numerous tenantry, to procure them admission where none are admitted without high influence, still that was not enough for them. To support his family he wrung from you the last penny which should have supported yours.

He is now no more; and I hope, for the credit of his memory, it was necessity on his part, and not greediness, that made him take your money from you which never belonged to the farm as such. But, whatever the actuating cause was, he took it. He never could have done so had not the delusion of high prices promised by the corn-law, which the corn-law could not fulfil, put you in his power.

I shall resume the subject in another letter. Meantime I am your old cowherd, stable-groom, plough-boy, &c. &c.

No. II.

To my old Master, a particular Victim of the Corn-Laws.

SIR,—The time that has elapsed since I was in your service has worked a great change in both of us. The change has been to your disadvantage, I grieve to say; but it has been rather favourable to me. Whether there be any person, situated as I am now, who could look back upon such a service and such a master, and not grieve for your misfortunes, I know not. I am not that person.

Neither am I one who, separated from the farm-fields where I once toiled in summer and harvest days with scythe and reaping-hook, with bended back and sweaty brow; in winter days clearing out the watery ditches with feet immersed, or picking the frozen turnips to the snow-bedded sheep—I am not one who looks back to despise those times and those employments. With much toil there was much satisfaction.

There were the merry days of spring, when we whistled along at harrow and at plough, committing the seed once more to the earth, and our hopes once more to God for a succeeding harvest. Then there was the annual winter supper when harvest was over, when every man, woman, and child gathered around you—the young with more joy than they could contain, the old joyous as if they were young again ; when my venerable father, being the oldest there, said grace, thanked Heaven for the harvest we had had, and prayed for another as good ; and then, old as he was, solemn as was the piety of his life, danced among the dancers, and sung some of the merriest songs, the songs of his young days, among the singers.

Then there were the long winter evenings around your kitchen fire, on which the piled up logs and the coals that made them fierce drove us back, as they blazed and reddened, into a wider and a wider circle, into the circle where one would mend his shoes or his horse harness; where another would stitch her new apron or knit her stocking ; where one would nod in the snoozy heat, where another would sing or tell a story ; where I would sit and listen for the sound of your horse's feet to meet you at the door with the stable lantern ready lighted ; where, on returning from the stable after grooming up your horse for the night, I would perchance find you, if it was market night, warming yourself for a brief period before you went to your parlour, asking the men what had been done while you were away, and telling them what was to be done to-morrow—whether the thrashing-mill was to be going or not, and whether the markets were in such a state as to make it desirable that the thrashing-mill should be set a-going. At this kitchen fireside I was a member of the circle ; and on such occasions have been referred to, to say whether there was straw enough to last the cattle in the close, the cows in the byre, and the horses in the different stables over Sunday ; and if there was, then perhaps you did not thrash until next week. And so the work which the men and horses were to go to next day was decided upon ; frost and thaw being the only doubtful questions.

And think you I have had no pride in sending you out in style to market or to a distant dinner ? If field work took me out, which it often did, before the stable work was completed, and some one came and called me, as often was the case, by the message, " The master wants his horse !" have I not been in the stable and stripped to the shirt before the echoes of the voice that called me had well died away ? And there have I brushed and wisped, and wiped down, and combed the mane, and sponged the hoofs and brightened them ; and have saddled and bridled, and have drawn the girths tighter, and have wiped the reins and the martingal once more, and the stirrups and the bit ; and have sent you away with a curb-chain shining. And when you have gone, and I have watched you through the trees cantering beyond the holly bushes, and have seen you fairly into the public road, with nothing but your hat visible bobbing above the hedge of the upper Butterlaw Park, I have shut the stable door, have thrown a fork over my shoulder, and my jacket over the fork, preparatory to going to another job, and have sung or whistled on my way to the other job from pure pleasure and satisfaction that there would be no stirrups, or bridle-bits, or curb-chains on the road to market that day brighter than yours were.

And you to have had at that period an independent fortune of several thousand pounds, besides all your working capital invested in farm stock ; and to have lost all—to have been deluded by the corn-law, to transfer all to the pocket of your laird in whom you reposed as in a "farmers' friend !" it is indeed, grievous.

There are those in the world, and there may be some of them concerned in the land on and around B——— now. who look upon an enemy of the corn-law as their enemy. There may be many farmers in that district of country who will read this, I know there will be some, and who will think that some lurking recollection of them, or fretful dislike to agriculture, prompts me to contend against the thing called *protection*, and thus bring the argument to their own doors by reference to the farm of B———.

If such there be they will do me wrong. I have paid close and widely-extended attention to this momentous subject, and am convinced, beyond the slightest possible doubt, that it is not more clear that commerce will be benefited by free-trade, than it is that agriculture has been wronged by monopoly, by the delusion of the corn-laws being a benefit to the farmers.

I have no dislike to agriculture : my interests and sympathies are with it. I have no disagreeable feelings towards any of those concerned in it whom I knew in my youth ; I have kindly recollections of every one of them. I have a constitutional veneration for agriculture, strengthened by my connection with it in early life, even though then I was not a master in it, but a servant, and one of the very humblest. But it does not follow that, loving agriculture, I should love the corn-law. On the contrary, every circumstance of past days which memory and history supply me with, and every observation of the present day which travel and business-transactions afford me the means of making, unite in dissociating the welfare of agri-

culture and the existence of the corn-law. In England the
pernicious influence of "protection" is more apparent than in
Scotland. Yet in Scotland protection has done its work of
mischief, as we see by your own case. Let me bring to your
recollection some facts.

The first harvests I have any distinct knowledge of were
those of 1816 and 1817; and I remember them more by
their results than their realities. I was then a child, and you
were a young man. It was one of those years I first saw you
to know you from your brothers. And a very trifling event
it was that made me distinguish and remember you—a trifling
event in itself, yet not to me, and destined to be fixed in my
mind until nails are fixed in my coffin. It was intimately
connected with the famine-stricken harvests of the two years
just named, and with that corn-law which has robbed you of
your farm and all your patrimony.

The crops of those years were great failures. In 1817,
which I remember most distinctly, the whole crop of the Horse
Hill, which was peas and beans—and which you know grows
as good wheat and beans as any on the farm—the whole crop
of that very good field was carted home for the cattle to
trample into manure—it never went to the stackyard; it was
absolute *muck*. Barley was that year growing in the large
field south of the Horse Hill. Though earliest ripe, much of
that barley was never even thrashed; it was lost by the continued dark wet weather. I have no recollection of where the
crops grew, though, in after years, I heard the crops of that
year often talked of; no recollection save of the potatoes,
which were at the west side of the Pond Park: they were
small, few in number, and bad in quality.

Yet corn was so excessively dear, this being a second bad
harvest, that my father's and brother's wages did not go far
enough to procure us half—not more than *half*—the usual
supply of oatmeal for porridge and barleymeal for bread; and,
moreover, what we did get was bad, very bad. The bread
was black, wet, and *clammy*. Foreseeing the failure of the
potato crop, my father kept no pig in the stye; we had, therefore, no pork. There were either nine or ten of us almost
dependent on what the wages of *two* could procure. So dear
was everything, we could not even afford salt herring at every
time we ate the miserable diet of small watery potatoes.
When brose was made of the oatmeal, we could neither afford
butter nor lard to our brose, but were only too happy to get
brose in any shape, made of water and oatmeal only.

As a matter of course, we could get no new clothing. The
previous year had been a famine year, and parents such as

mine hoped that the next (this of which I now write) would
enable them by its plenty and cheapness to restore the clothing of themselves and children. They were disappointed.
This year was worse than the last; two famine years were
worse than one. We decayed into rags, and almost to bare-
footedness, in the depth of winter. The nightly upsitting of
my mother (who is still a living witness of that dreadful time)
to mend and remend, to set patch on patch, contending
as she did for nine of us against the united attacks of
winter, nakedness, and famine—against all these, and the
corn-law, and the East Lothian bank—the corn-law being
to keep foreign grain out of the country, and the Lothian
bank to keep home-grown corn out of market until it had
reached the highest possible price at the longest possible
period to which the farmers could hold it and not sell—my
mother, I say, sitting up night after night during that dreary
winter to stitch and stitch, patch and patch our clothes when
we were in bed—she contending for nine of us—one woman
for nine of us, against the united hostility of winter, nakedness, famine, corn-law, and the farmers' combination bank—
one woman against all these—the task was unequal. She
could not mend as fast as our *duds* decayed. They went to
pieces, and she could not help them.

I am now at the point where I first saw you to know you.
At that time my chief garment was a pinafore. The famine
years had reduced me to one, and even that one was made up
of the best parts of several that had fallen to pieces. I had
only that single one, and it was ingeniously shaped and
extended in size to hide the poverty of the clothing beneath
it. When it was washed I had to stay within doors; and I
never went out without being charged to keep that garment
clean and untorn. I was careful of it; for, young as I was,
the unequal contest which my mother held with famine and
decaying clothes was bitterly felt by me. But I was out one
day playing on that green knoll where the whinbush grew in
front of the barnyard gate, and you and some other young
gentlemen came along with your greyhounds. The dogs were
playful. Perhaps they were kind; but, whatever their humour,
they leaped upon me, pulled me down, one behind and one
before, rolled me down the steep declivity, and did not leave
off until that best garment of mine was equal to the worst. I
ran home in the bitterest distress. I could not tell in the
fear of the moment how it had happened; but a neighbour,
who had seen the wreck and its cause, said it was done by
"Master William's dogs." My mother took the rags, one by
one, and looked at them; and knowing she could not go to a

draper's shop to buy calicoes to replace them, she mingled tears of despair with my tears of childish fear, and sat down and asked in anguish, " What *was* she to do ?"

Ay, what was she to do, indeed, with such a confederacy of famine-making seasons and famine-making men against her ? My father was in full work at full wages ; so was my eldest brother. One or two of the younger ones earned something ; and even my mother went out and worked at the thrashing-mill, and in the fields rooting and " shawing" turnips amid wet and snow in those winter days, the nights of which were partly spent in sleepless toil to mend our clothes which she could not replace. And all who worked at anything were working on the farm, and yet could not earn enough to get enough of mere food of the coarsest and meanest quality, to say nothing of clothing.

And what was the value of the exorbitant prices to those who received them ? They had less to sell, and, *therefore*, it will be argued it was proper they should have the highest possible price. Look at the result.

For nearly three years my mother did not go to the shop of Mr M'Intyre in Dunbar, which was the one and the only one she dealt at for cloth goods. You will remember M'Intyre's shop. And here I may remark, that at that very time, so I have been told, Mr Duncan M'Laren of Edinburgh, the highly talented enemy of corn-law famine, was an apprentice with Mr M'Intyre. See, therefore, how early the Edinburgh champion of free trade must have observed the evil influence of the corn-law !

We did not for nearly three years give custom to the draper's shop, and very, very little to the grocer's shop. The hinds of Lothian, who have a corn payment, would be in better circumstances. They have a similar advantage over fluctuat-ing markets that the farmers have who pay corn rents. But the hinds in receipt of corn payments are but the merest frac-tion to the whole working population of the kingdom. Even in Lothian one-half, at least, of working persons were at that time in receipt of money wages ; all in a similar state to our family.

And what was the consequence throughout the kingdom ? The shopkeepers could not sell, consequently they could not buy from the wholesale merchants. The merchants could not buy from the manufacturers. The latter stopped their works. Every one, from the shopkeeper upwards, dispensed with some of their domestic servants ; with clerks and workmen. These again could not buy grocery goods and clothes. Tailors and shoemakers, and every one employed in making and pro-viding the materials for things that should have been made, were wholly or partly stopped. Carriers inland had less to carry, and ships were laid up idly in the docks. Sailmakers, riggers, and shipbuilders were thrown out in their turn. So were sailors. In thickly peopled districts mobs met and rioted. Soldiers were called out to disperse them. Men were hungry and clamorous, and demanded political changes. Demagogues found them ready to listen to and act upon the wildest suggestions. They essayed to overturn the government, and blood was spilt. The Habeas Corpus was suspended, and the gibbets were loaded.

And while the mobs of unemployed working men were thus starving, and plotting, and threatening, because they were unemployed and did starve, mercantile men were cracking to pieces, their bills dishonoured, credit broken, and all enterprise stagnant—a panic sweeping them into a backward gulf, as a receding wave sweeps back the broken sea-weed.

And all these, comprising millions of individuals, had to retrench their family expenses. Millions had, like my father's family, to live on less than enough of the worst of food. The farmers got high prices for the little they had to sell; but the people were famine-struck, and the nation was shaken to its centre.

And what came of the farmers? The succeeding years brought better harvests. But the population was now too poor to *pay* for what the farmers had to sell, and markets fell far below what they would have been had the general population been fully employed. The farmers had thus to pay the high rents, calculated upon a continuance of dear years, out of low prices. In England they were worse off than in Scotland, and in some parts of Scotland they were worse off than in Lothian; but even in Lothian they were so badly off that they could not meet their engagements in 1818 and 1819. The combination bank broke, and it broke some of the most substantial men in the county with it.

No. III.
Mr W. T., of Branxton.

To glance over a table of prices for fifty years we see the "ups and downs" of corn to be very frequent and very abrupt. An eminent publisher of maps in London has given to the world a map of the prices of wheat from 1790 to 1840. The map also contains the fluctuations of the public funds, and the amount of bank notes issued in each year; the revenue and expenditure of the Government; the value of the goods exported out of, and imported into, the United Kingdom; together with remarks of peace or war, or other circumstances causing fluctuations. The map was not published for or against the corn-law; but it is nevertheless eminently useful as an assistant expositor of the national disasters arising from famine. I shall here endeavour to give you a view of it.

The lowest average of a year's prices of wheat between 1790 and 1840 is 40s. per quarter. This was the average of 1792 and of 1835. And that is taken as the base line divided into fifty parts; one part for each of the fifty years. From each year there rises a pyramid, or a small mound, or, as the case may be, a gigantic tower, shooting up abruptly from a deep valley, and the top of each elevation rises to the point to which the average prices of that year rose, the scale of ascent being by intervals of 5s. per quarter, each advance of 5s. measuring about the twelfth of an inch on paper.

All persons interested in securing equal prices and in putting agriculture on a sure foundation should study this map. The causes that affected prices before 1815 are not precisely the same as those after; but it was to perpetuate the high unequal prices that preceded 1815 that the corn-law of that year was enacted.

And first, you must admit that equable prices are of the greatest value to the farmer. To know in any given year what the price of his corn will be the next year, or that time five years, or that time ten or fifteen years, would be worth much more to him, as regards his rent, his plans for making a profit, and his plans of improving his land, than any chance, however sure, that at some time or other, yet not knowing when, some year of high prices will occur.

Move with me in imagination over an uneven space of ground, and let us compare it with the passage of the farmers over the space of time between 1790 and 1845.

Let us suppose ourselves at the cove just above the sea-beach, and that we have to journey westward to the sands at Thorntonloch. There is a good, smooth, hard, level road, if we choose to turn into it. Common sense would suggest to us that our comfort and convenience, and even the safety of our lives, would decide us in favour of the even road, instead of going down among the rocks and precipices which lie on the other side of us.

It is pointed out to us that everything comes to a level at last, that all nature adjusts itself to an even scale in course of time, however much men in their folly may disarrange it; but another "friend" advises us to go the other way. We stand, as it were, upon the ground of 50s., the price of 1790, and we are going to the point of 45s. in 1845. There is not much difference in altitude between the two; and we would never have known there was any difference at all had we come by the even road.

But we submit to the guidance of our very kind *friend*. Our first movement is down. The year '91 gives us 45s. the year '92 gives us but 40s. We next rise, and '93 gives us 45s. "Come on," says our friend, "the year '94 will give you more." And it does so; it gives us 50s. And now for a lift. All at once, in '95, we are up to 75s. How we love our friend, and shout for him and vote for him now! And the next year, '96, is the same. We may fancy ourselves secure, and sure for ever of 75s.; but we are only on one of those abutting precipices which lie in our road, as if some fairy had lifted us from the level and put us there. We are all at once dashed down to the level of the beach, and there we sprawl for two years, '97 and '98, at 50s. We sprawl only because we are bruised by the fall. Had we never been higher we would have known no fall, and had no bruises.

I have a shrewd suspicion our friend had his hand in our pockets while we were prostrated; but he befriends us again, and we rise in '99 to 65s. We begin to rejoice once more, and are so full of spirits that we rejoice to mount on the top of one of those fantastic pinnacles of rocks that have been erected on the line of our rough road in some great convulsion of nature. You have seen the pinnacles near Bilsdean shore. Well, we are on one of them in 1800, and its height is 110s. Five pounds ten shillings! How we shout now, and wave our hats, and dine, and drink, and dance, and hunt, and vote, and raise the price of corn. And next year, in 1801, we rise a step higher, and stand on the giddy pinnacle of 115s. The year 1802 is before us, and we cannot miss it. We got up; how are we to get down? The famine-stricken labourers—such as my father and his family—the hecatombs of famine victims gnash their teeth and cry in vain for bread. But, secure in our *guide*, we heed them not; when, all at once, we are in that gorge below, which is 50s. deep, though still 15s. above the point we first started from. Yet to leap from this wild turret of convulsed nature the whole depth of 50s. is a leap indeed. But down we must, and down we come. We plunge from 115s. to 65s.

Bruised and broken, we groan and cry of our distress. Our pockets are turned inside out while we lie there helpless. All our plans are frustrated. Our farms go to weeds and wreck; not because sixty-five shillings would not pay, but because we have been hurled from one hundred and fifteen shillings, upon which we reared our lofty heads.

And now our bruised bodies are rolled into a deeper gully of the broken rocks in 1803. Here we once more sink to 55s.

Every penny that we got in our glory we have lost in our humiliation. We crawl to our feet, still holding by our guide, and we move a step. In 1804 we reach 60s. Our guide tells us to cheer up, he is always our friend; and we do cheer up, and reach the point of 85s. in 1805. Once more we rejoice; but once more we are rolled down. The fall, however, is more moderate: 75s. in 1806; 70s. in 1807; and 75s. in 1808. In 1809, we take a flight to 95s.; and in the following year, 1810, we get five above the even hundred. Five pounds five shillings the quarter is again the price; and we hope to go higher, but go the other way. Not so far, however, as we fell from some other precipices. We are caught on a ledge of the rocky point. We have only fallen in 1811 to the distance of 95s.

But here stands 1812 before us, the pinnacle of the temple. And Buonaparte or the Devil, or both together, with our particular *friend*, our *guide*, take us to the pinnacle of our glory, one hundred and twenty-five shillings.

Now, thought the men of money, is the time to take farms and buy estates. Branxton was bought at this time. Consols, which were at 98 when wheat was 50s. in 1790, were now at 64; that is, the public debt or credit of the nation sunk to 64.

We fell, first to 105s. in 1813; and then, oh what a fall! to 70s. in 1814; and we writhed in our agony into 65s. in 1815.

It might have been supposed we had broken bones enough in this rough road, and that we would have been glad to get out of it. But no. Gambling has a mysterious charm in it, especially to those who have lost and have still something to lose. We got the corn-law of that year to perpetuate what we had suffered in the previous twenty-five years, and in 1816 we reached 75s. This was the first bad harvest in my recollection; and that of the year following, 1817, was still worse. Wheat now rose to 95s.; and that it so rose for *the last time*, let us pray to God and give thanks.

Then, *with* this corn-law we rolled down to 85s. in 1818; to 70s. in 1819; to 65s. in 1820; to 55s. in 1821; and to 45s. in 1822.

There we groaned and cried aloud; not complaining of the mad career we had pursued; but because we, having gone aloft in our journey, had to descend.

The year 1823 gives a slight rise, and things look up. The legislature promises a rise, and rents are calculated accordingly. You believe, and contract to pay L.3 per acre for Branxton, which is not worth more than L.2 per acre. In any county of England south of Yorkshire, such a farm as Branxton would not be taken at more than 30s. per acre, including tithe and poor-rates. Such is the difference between Scotch contracts and English; between the value of land where security of tenure and equality of rent and prices are comparatively good, as in Scotland, and where they are bad, as in England. Rents paid by the prices of corn protect the Lothian farmers from excessive loss by fluctuations; and leases secure them in the profit of their improvements, and give to them an improving spirit. They accordingly pay rents from 50 to 100 per cent. higher than the same quality of land pays in England.

But you made the mistake of contracting to pay a fixed money rental, without regard to the prices of corn. I know you put faith in the promise of future high prices. You were deceived: 1824 gave a price of 60s.; 1825 gave 65s. But 1826 gave only 55s.; and 1827 the same. 1828 and 1829 gave respectively 60s. and 65s.; 1830 and 1831 continued the last amount. But 1832 and 1833 gave only 55s. each. 1834 saw you running to the bank to draw out your money to pay the laird his rent, because wheat was only 45s.; and the following year, 1835, with wheat at 40s., saw you do the same.

Now, bear in mind, you *had* the old corn-law, which engaged that you should never have less than 64s. You *had* your guide, that farmers' friend, "protection." And it protected you in your rough road, by getting you down on your back and rifling your pockets, and by compelling you to go to the bank with your deposit receipts to draw out your money to pay the high rent which protection induced you to promise.

But the impossibility of investing money in the cultivation of the soil was the greatest disadvantage. From 1835 prices rose to 50s. in 1836; to 55s. in 1837; to 60s. in 1838; to 70s. in 1839; and fell to 65s. in 1840. With varying changes we have wheat now at 45s., or from that to 50s.

We have arrived at the point I bade you look to. Would it not have been better to have travelled by the even road, instead of coming over the precipices, so often raised up to be so often knocked down and robbed, and left with broken head and empty pockets?

The more extensive the space from which supplies to market are brought, the more equal will the supply of the market be.

And remember, the prices of food depend upon the ability

of the consumers of food to buy it and pay for it, as well as upon the quantity supplied to market.

Whenever corn has fallen to a moderate price, the national trade has flourished and wages have advanced. So also has the revenue of the country. When people have not to pay all their money away for bread, they buy butchers' meat, and sugar and tea, and the various other things that make commerce profitable and the government strong and rich.

The liberation and extension of commerce is the true conservatism of England, and the best protection to agriculture.

No. IV.

To the Rev. Thomas Skipworth, Rector of Pickwell, in the county of Leicester.

REVEREND SIR,—" Protection is the bane of agriculture," so says Lord John Russell; " Protection is a delusion," so says many an agriculturist who once believed in its truthfulness; " Protection is the Will-o'-the-wisp which is ever deluding the farmers, and leading them where they should not go, deterring them from following the lights they should follow—the light of agricultural science," so says your humble servant.

Sir, you are, it is exceedingly probable, a reader of the Church organ, the *Standard*, and of such papers only; you are probably a believer in the so-called " protection," and a believer in whatever the newspapers of your party say of the opponents of protection. I will, therefore, in sending you a copy of the LEAGUE paper which contains this letter, send you the previous number of it, containing the speech of the honourable member for Stockport, delivered in the House of Commons on the 13th inst., descriptive of the evil effects of protection; and I beg of you to read that speech. As a practical agriculturist myself, and acquainted with the state of agriculture and the condition of the farmers in almost every county of England, I agree with everything said in that speech. You will see from it, should you not have already learned the fact, that the free-traders are the best friends of agriculture. You will perceive that it proves that to be true of all England generally which you allege to be true of your own glebe particularly—that a larger expenditure of money in changing the culture of the soil would enlarge the profit of the cultivator. You will see that the doctrine taught by Mr Cobden, as regards the evil of restricting the enterprise of the cultivators of the soil, by making them entirely dependent on the will, and caprice, and ignorance of the men of law who manage most of the

English estates as agents under the landlords—you will see that this doctrine, laid down on Thursday night in the Commons' House of Parliament, was the same as you sought to establish next day, on the Friday morning, in the Rolls' Court, before Lord Langdale. The only difference between you and the honourable member is, that he attempted to do that for twenty millions of acres of land which you attempted to do for twenty acres. He attempted to liberate from the thrawl of insecurity and poverty, and bad cultivation, the major part of all England and Wales. You attempted to do the same for your own glebe.

It seems you were appointed to the living in 1814; that, subsequent to that period, the Duke of St Albans purchased the patronage of the living. It seems the glebe has been used as a pasture; but has become next to worthless, being overrun with moss and weedy foulness. You asked the advice of a skilful agriculturist, who very properly advised you to plough it up; to clear it of weeds; to crop it for some years; to manure it, and again lay it down in grass. It is quite possible, indeed I think . it very likely, that a different course of treatment might have been used more effectually, *seeing that your design was to restore the glebe to pasturage.* Being overgrown with moss it is very likely that an application of hot lime, applied as a top-dressing, would have eradicated the moss by destroying all vegetation for a-year; or it is possible that some other kind of top-dressing might have effected the same end. But this cannot be alleged positively unless one had a local knowledge of the soil, the subsoil, the rocks beneath, and such like matters. And here I may remark that the difficulty of determining what is right and what is wrong, in such cases, is one of the reasons why the occupiers of land should not be subjected, as they now are, to rules laid down by lawyers who have no practical knowledge of agriculture; to rules which apply to whole estates of great magnitude, the soils and subsoils and requirements of which are exceedingly various, and the treatment of which should be as various; rules which are the offspring of *law,* and not of agricultural science, even though administered by agents who are sometimes professed agriculturists.

Lord Langdale, in your case, seems more inclined to judge it by the rule of common sense than by any rule of the statutes. He inclines to follow Liebig, the chemist of agriculture, rather than Blackstone, the commentator of law. His Lordship is thus reported:—" He had (himself) had occasion to obtain agricultural advice; and he could say that, having followed it, he had found it most advantageous." That is, his

Lordship had used the science of agriculture instead of the science of law to his land, as you attempted to do to your glebe. This good sense is creditable to his Lordship as a lawyer. But Mr Parkinson, agent of the Duke of St Albans, being accustomed to rule the culture of the Duke's estate by *law*, and not by agricultural science; being accustomed to keep the tenantry in leading-strings *by protecting them* ; being accustomed to keep everything out of their reach that might lead to enterprise and experiment, by laying down the law to them as to what they shall do on their farms and what they shall not do; being accustomed to threaten them that they will not be *protected* if they dare to think or act as cultivators for themselves—being accustomed thus to treat the tenantry, he has proceeded thus to treat you, though you are a life freeholder of your glebe.

The law of the case as applied to the incumbent of a living I shall not inquire into. While I write, Lord Langdale has not given his judgment. But he has remarked that, though the case be of no great importance in itself, it is of great importance as regards the effects its decision will have on the occupiers of other glebe lands. He said—" If the law was as alleged, it would prevent the incumbent from making a potato ground or an orchard upon the glebe when he could not shew that at some former time the grass land had been broken up."

But this case opens other questions to our view of infinitely greater importance as regards the laws under which the farmers are bound and held down, powerless to do good for themselves, for the land they occupy, and for the multitudes who must be content with the small amount of food they produce.

Law is the primary subject for an English farmer to study. It is the Alpha and Omega of English agriculture. The late James Hogg, the " Ettrick Shepherd," left Scotland at one time to take charge of an agricultural project in England, but did not remain long. When asked why he had left it, he said he was not qualified to manage a farm in England. And when it was said that he had surely as good a knowledge of the best manner of breeding and feeding flocks as any man in either Scotland or England, and as good a knowledge of farming matters in general, he replied that such might be true, but the first thing required in England to make a successful farmer was *not* a practical knowledge of breeding, and rearing, and feeding sheep and cattle, of manuring and cropping land. Every qualification, he said, of an agricultural kind, was entirely subordinate to a knowledge of *law*. And he said the laws affecting the cultivator of the soil were so numerous, so completely interwoven into everything which a farmer could do ; and the lawyers were so keen-scented and so plentiful— the estates being almost entirely committed to the management of lawyers—that it was next to hopeless for a stranger to learn the laws which beset him and hindered him in all his actions, utterly hopeless, before a stranger, led by common sense and agricultural science, would break through them and incur ruinous penalties.

In this way you have been caught by the net-work of the law. Mr Parkinson, the Duke's agent, heard that your glebe, being overgrown with worthless moss and weeds, was about to be restored to fertility and usefulness ; full of that spirit of protection which controls the tenant-farmers, he stepped forward to protect your weeds and worthless moss ; to protect your glebe from being made fertile and profitable. He stood forward to *protect* it from having monied capital and manure applied to its cultivation. He stood forward to *protect* those labourers whom you would have employed in ploughing and digging and weeding, from being employed to plough and dig and weed. He stepped forward to *protect* the paupers, who, it may be, are now living on prison fare within the workhouse walls, from being liberated and elevated to the dignity of working for honourable bread by honourable and useful labour. He, full of protection, and in the full flow of protection, the everyday current of the protective spirit, arrested you, by an injunction of a court of law, from raising more human food from your acres than they now produced.

The advantage to the occupier of the land ; the advantage to the labourers who have not enough of work, and who, being more plentiful than their work, are obliged to submit to the lowest amount of pay and of food which will sustain life ; the advantage to the general consumers of agricultural produce, who augment their consumption as the supply and their ability to buy increase—all these, and also the advantage to agricultural science, were at once arrested by Mr Parkinson, the Duke's agent, who brought the law which binds the tenant-farmers to arrest, and bind, and tie you, and make you powerless and helpless, as the tenant-farmers are—miserable men !

He who is, at the Duke's instance, as other agents are at the instance of other duke's and of other landlords, the man who is first to lead the tenants to the hustings to vote for protection ; who is the first to bid them declare, in dolorous whine, that they cannot cultivate their land if they be not protected ; who bids them cry out that they are in distress, and who, to make them cry the louder, pinches them behind as the whining beggar pinches the alleged motherless baby whom he has stolen and professes to fondle, to impose on the public: this same Mr Parkinson, and those whose office is like his, are the first to prevent the farmers from cultivating their land to relieve themselves from distress.

It was laid down as an axiom by Sir John Sinclair in his "Code of Agriculture," and repeated by Brown of Markle, the first and long-continued editor of the "Farmer's Magazine," a thoroughly practical and successful tenant-farmer; repeated also by Jackson of Pennycuick in his excellent treatise; repeated and *acted upon* by the best experimentalists in England, and most successful practicalists in Scotland— the axiom is this :—

"Assuming always that the expenditure on a farm be *directed with judgment*, it will be found that the profit upon the outlay increases in more than a proportionate degree to its amount. Thus, suppose that L.5 be the lowest and L.10 the highest sum that can be employed in the common culture of the same acre of land, it is more than probable that, if the L.5 return at the rate of five per cent., the L.10 will yield twenty per cent., or any intermediate sum at the same progressive ratio. Now, admitting this to be true—and it is to be presumed that no experienced agriculturist will doubt it —it follows that L.1000, expended in the cultivation of 200 acres, will only yield a profit of L.100 ; while if applied to no more than 100 acres it would produce L.200. For this reason, although a farmer of limited capital may not be driven to the extremity we have already supposed, and although he may be able to carry on his business with a certain degree of advantage, it is quite evident that *his profit would be increased by diminishing the quantity of his land.*"

(See " Treatise on Agricultural and Dairy Husbandry," by James Jackson of Pennycuick ; the successful competitor for some of the Highland Society's prizes as a practical writer. This valuable treatise is published in the " People's Edition." by the Messrs Chambers, at the low figure of 2s. 3d. It should be carefully read wherever a spade or a plough penetrates the ground, or wherever a scythe or a cow crops the grass ; and particularly where the Mr Parkinsons of England interfere with their absurdities to keep monied capital out of agriculture and lay enterprise prostrate.)

But what is the use of either knowledge or money upon such estates as that of the Duke of St Albans? The tenants are not rich in knowledge and monied capital. They have had no means of obtaining either. But had they both, they could not use them. All their attention is turned to protection by act of Parliament. They are but puppets in the agent's hands. He leads them by the nose and squeezes them, and bids them whine and cry out for help.

If they would help themselves, they would break up some of their wet meadows to drain the wetness from them, to eradicate the rushes and make the soil sweet and fertile which is now sour and barren. But the agent steps up and says, "No, you mustn't. Let the wetness, and sourness, and rushes alone."

The tenants may see the huge banks between the double hedges, also the ditches and superfluous hedgerows; they may see that all of them are nurseries of stagnation, foulness, and vermin, and exceedingly wasteful in horse labour in ploughing, by the frequent turnings and unavoidable trampling of the ground: but if they offer to cut a branch of the hedge, or build and cover in a ditch, or dig down a useless bank, the agent comes and says, "No, you mustn't."

They see their old pastures overgrown as your glebe is with moss, and, like you, they may be told by skilful agriculturists to plough them up and clear them of weeds, and crop and manure them, and lay them down to grass again: but the agent says, "No, you mustn't." And if he found them offering to do it, he would not go to the expense of getting an injunction at law, as in your case; he would at once expel them from the land. Had your reverence been a *rector-at-will*, removable by the Duke, your case would never have come before Lord Langdale. You would have been at once turned out of your parish, a terrible warning to all rectors.

Should the tenantry see the trees standing round their fields and in their fields, as they very frequently do, injuring five acres out of twenty, defrauding the crops of the requisite sunshine and free air, and should they seek leave to cut some of them down, or to lop their branches, the agent says, "No, you mustn't."

Should they be persuaded of the truth of the established fact, that to feed cattle in the yard to produce manure is the foundation of all good husbandry, and that cattle should not waste their grass, their manure, and their fat by running at liberty in the fields—save milk cows and young cattle; and the latter may be more profitably reared on farms unsuited to the culture of corn; should the tenantry be convinced of these established truths, and offer to raise food for yard-feeding where they now have meadows, the agent says, "No, you mustn't."

Should the farmers say the liquid manures they can thus save from their cattle will be equal—over all England in one

year—to the whole of the guano of Ichaboo when the first
ship loaded at it; and further, that they require the erection
of cisterns or tanks to preserve the whole accumulations, or
some chemical apparatus to extract the ammonia; and that
they will apply one year's or two years' rent to such works, the
agent says, " No, you mustn't."

If they say that they are too poor to erect such works at
their own expense, or that, having the money, they cannot
venture to expend it on works of improvement without the
security of a lease; and that they must have leases to enable
those to obtain money who have it not to improve their land,
and to enable those to lay plans for future profit who have
money, the agent says, " No, you mustn't."

If the farmers urge that they could thus employ many more
labourers than they now employ; that they could give full
work and better wages to every labourer, had they leave to do
to their farms what they think best, the agent says, " No, you
mustn't."

If the farmers urge that all other persons engaged in trade
conduct their business as they think fit, adopting any improvements they may deem advantageous, trying any experiments
they may deem profitable; on the same principle that the
tailor makes a coat from whatever cloth he thinks best fitted
for a coat, and makes one in a new style when he chooses; or
on the same principle that a manufacturer works up his raw
material into whatever kind of goods there is most demand
for; if the farmers urge that the whole success of trade, and
of tradesmen of every degree, depends on their freedom of
enterprise, and the comparative security with which their
money is invested in business, and they, the farmers, ask to
be secured in the profits of their own business in a similar way,
the Duke's Mr Parkinson, or any other landlord's Mr Parkinson, says, " No, you mustn't."

It is " No, you mustn't" to everything asked or attempted.
" You are *protected*," say the Parkinsons. " You must get
more protection if you can; or at all events cry lustily about
your distress and keep what you have got." And, to say the
truth, the great bulk of the tenantry follow this advice, and
are exceedingly well contented to live without an effort to
make themselves independent and their farms fruitful and
profitable.

They might very well ask what protection has done for them;
they might point out the fact that the corn-law allows corn to
come in, if it comes at all, just at harvest, when prices are
highest, and the English farmer cannot take advantage of such
prices. They might shew that under the corn-law their losses

are greater by sudden fluctuations than they ever could be by steady prices, even though those prices stood at what they are now, 45s.; they might very well point to the ruinous price they pay the landlords, for their protection by being bound, as the now are, hand and foot, led by the nose by one agent, pinched behind their backs by another; obliged to pay high poor-rates to maintain a pauper population whom they cannot employ; compelled to endure game, and pay for the crimes and punishments arising from game, because they dare not complain; compelled to be put to all manner of mean uses in political prostitution; and, worst of all, while everybody else advances with the intellectual spirit of the age, they remain hopelessly and helplessly behind.

POSTSCRIPT.—LORD LANGDALE'S DECISION.

His Lordship decided the cause, " *The Duke of St Albans* v. *Skipworth*," and removed the injunction, affirming the right of an incumbent to break up his glebe, should it be in old grass, if he so chooses.

What a blessing to England if Cheshire and some ten or twelve other counties could be so broken up and put to profitable uses!

No. V.

To the Wife of Francis Horlock of ———, in Dorsetshire.

MRS HORLOCK,—You are the wife of an industrious man, who loses no time, wastes no money. You have kept an exact account of your incomings and outgoings for a year, and as you have allowed that excellent clergyman, the Honourable and Reverend Sidney Godolphin Osborne, to make the items public, I shall take the liberty of addressing you thus publicly, as the first of several mothers, in different parts of the kingdom, to whom I shall probably write a series of letters.

You live in a county remarkable for its production of butter —Dorset. The Vale of Blackmoor is said to produce the best butter in England. At all events, " Dorset butter" is well known.

Now, butter is what is called " protected;" that is, no foreign butter is allowed to come into England, lest it should reduce the price of English butter. It may be introduced, and is introduced, in large quantities; but before it leaves the docks where it is landed from the ships which bring it across the sea, it is mixed with tar, to prevent its being used as human food.

I perceive that, from the 1st of January to the 11th of December 1843, just forty-nine weeks, you paid the following sums for butter, for the use of yourself, husband, and four children. On the 15th of January you paid 8d.; 9th of February, 4d.; 13th of March, 4d.; April, nothing; 3d of May, 6d.; June, nothing; 5th of July, 6d.; August, nothing; September, nothing; 23d of October, 6d.; 13th of November 4½d; 3d of December, 6d. Total, 3s. 8½d.

Three shillings and eightpence halfpenny, Mrs Horlock, is the sum of what you contribute to the "butter interest" of Dorset. At 9d. per lb. this is very nearly five pounds weight; but you are well aware that, as a general rule in Dorset, you cannot buy butter at 9d. per lb. It costs you from 11d. to 13d., fully one penny per lb. more than the same butter is retailed for when it reaches London. This, to many people, seems a mystery; but it is accounted for in this way, that the dairy-farmers will not sell quarter pounds and half pounds of butter, such as you buy once a month, or once in two months. You must get it from the village shopkeeper, who, selling small quantities, and few of them, must charge a higher price, and must often give uncertain credit.

Your reason for buying so little butter is simply that all the family earnings are spent on something else which, with you, is more absolutely requisite than butter. Butter is an absolute necessary of life to everybody who can afford it. And in such a family as yours we need not doubt that it would be an indispensable necessary were you able to get it, and use it always.

Butter is what the lords and gentlemen who come out of Dorset to Parliament call *protected*. And it is *protected for* the sake of the labourers—so those lords and gentlemen say —that is, the tar is mixed with the butter which comes in ships to make it unfit to be eaten, and all for the sake of you and your family, and such as you.

The gentlemen of the Parliament were making a law on this subject on Wednesday last. One of them, Mr Bramston of Skreens, in Essex, was afraid that if grease was admitted free of duty, butter would come into this country in the disguise of grease. Sir George Clerk of Pennycuick, in Scotland, who is one of the Government members, said, to console Mr Bramston,

"That, so far from the agriculturists" (I am now giving his words as reported in the daily newspapers of Thursday morning) "being injured by the remission of this duty (on grease) they would be benefited, seeing that the uses to which it was put were agricultural. For instance, large quantities

of it were made use of by the sheep farmers of the north for
the purposes of smearing their sheep as a precaution against
the effects of cold. The honourable gentleman need not fear
that the article would be made use of as food—('Hear, hear,
hear,' from the Opposition benches)—the Custom-house officers took effectual means to prevent fraudulent traders selling
the article to the poor as food—(renewed cries of 'Hear, hear,'
from the Opposition benches.) He did not understand what
the gentlemen opposite were cheering; but he would repeat
that the Custom-house officers took care that the article
introduced as grease should not be sold as butter by mixing a
quantity of tar with it before it passed the Custom-house."

Sir George Clerk means that the butter which is to be
admitted duty free *as grease* has tar mingled with it in the
Custom-house, after which it is unfit for human food, and is
called grease.

Now, Mrs Horlock, you know well that 7s. a-week is the
full average of men's wages in Dorset; you know that unmarried men only get 4s. and 5s. a-week. You know that, at
this time, many men have no work at all. You know that
fully one-half of the whole are out of employment for several
months every year. Yet your husband, with 8s. a-week in
1843, and you, with your careful housekeeping, could only
spend 3s. 8½d. on butter during forty-nine weeks. In cheese
you expended 7s. 3d.; your total expenditure in butter and
cheese was 10s. 11½d. And your total for butchers' meat was
10d.! just *tenpence*. So that those great staple products of
your county, which are protected for the especial benefit of the
labourers, as Lord Ashley, Mr George Bankes, and Mr Sturt,
your county members say, were purchased and used by your
family of six persons to the amount of 11s. 9½d.

I know well that every other family were not in a condition
to buy so much; but assuming that they did, 48,000 men,
women, and children, which is the full amount of those
employed in agriculture, or unemployed, and calling themselves dependent on it, would annually support the beef,
mutton, butter, and cheese interests thus :—

Beef and mutton, . . . L.316 13 4
Butter and cheese, . . . 4383 6 8

Those familes who feed a pig sell it, more frequently to pay
for shoes and rent than they eat it. Thus, in a manner,
they may be said to be in competition with the farmers
rather than supporters of them by the consumption of their
farm produce. But in many parts of Dorset no pigs are
allowed to be kept by labourers. The dictum of the father

of Sir John Tyrrell, in Essex, is understood and acted on in Dorset—" No labourer can be *honest* and feed a pig !" But if every labourer's family did feed and eat, which they do not, a pig eight or nine score weight in a year, it would be no reason why they should not eat beef and mutton, butter and cheese, if they could afford them. A working man in London, or Liverpool, or Manchester, who has meat for dinner every day with his family, consumes more than a pig of nine score weight in the shape of bacon or ham for breakfast and supper, in addition to the beef or mutton from the butcher's shop for dinner ; so that we have it proved that consumption is only limited by the power to purchase, and consumption is the true protection to agricultural produce.

If we take fifteen journeymen printers in London, employed, say on the *Times* newspaper, whom we shall suppose to be all steady men and not drunkards—else they would not be employed there ; and suppose them to have each a wife and four children, as Francis Horlock, your husband, a steady agricultural labourer, has—those fifteen working men and their families, according to the London style of living and expenditure amongst people earning so much wages as theirs, will consume as much butcher's meat in fifty-two weeks as the whole 48,000 men, women, and children fed by protected agriculture in Dorset consume. A family man, like Francis Horlock, receiving from 30s. to L.2 a-week in London, will, for six of a family, give an average of about 8s. a-week for butcher's meat. At 8s. per week it will be found to amount to as much for ninety persons as the consumption for 48,000 in Dorset.

I may tell you, Mrs Horlock, that at the beginning of this session of Parliament, a great many lords, and squires, and farmers, all of them persons who live by selling cattle, some of them from your own county, came to London, and went before the Prime Minister and complained of distress—of being poor —of not getting such a good market for their produce as they once had. One of them dwelt especially on the fact that, in the great Smithfield market of London there were occasionally some foreign cattle, one hundred or so, to 2000 home-fed cattle, and to 18,000 or 20,000 sheep ; and that prices fell because of these occasional cattle. And it was urged that, as cattle were what the farmers so much depend upon—and especially the farmers in such districts as the Vale of Blackmoor —the foreign cattle should be prevented from coming to London.

Now, Mrs Horlock, there is a mode of doing business vulgarly called " Robbing Peter to pay Paul," or taking money out of one pocket to put it into another pocket. The system by which the lordly cattle-dealers of Dorset wish to make the nation prosperous is by robbing Peter to pay Paul; by taking money out of one person's pocket and putting it into another person's pocket; they representing Paul and somebody else representing Peter. They say if the Londoners pay dear for butcher's meat for the sake of making them, the landed gentry, rich, they go back to London to spend their money on the Londoners.

Now, according to this logic, they might with as much propriety, and certainly far more humanity and benevolence— and your Dorset lords and gentlemen are prodigiously humane and benevolent: you, of course, know your noble county member, Lord Ashley—they might with as much propriety and more humanity give their labourers the wages paid to printers per week to buy butter, and cheese, and butcher's meat. Fifteen journeymen printers in London, with their families, patronizing such farming interests as are involved in Smithfield market to as great an extent as the whole 48,000 men, women, and children, dependent on agriculture for their existence in Dorset, affords a wide scope for speculation. What would be the demand for cattle and sheep if, proceeding on the system of robbing Peter to pay Paul, the lords of Dorset should give the 48,000 men, women, and children money enough to buy and eat as much beef and mutton as the same number of journeymen printers with their wives and children buy and eat in London?

But you might as well put your husband's 8s. a-week first into one pocket and then into another, three times over, and say that he has 24s. a-week, as say that the robbery of Peter enriches Paul. Yet the lords of Dorset do say so when they ask people, and *compel* them, to pay high prices to them, that they may return the high prices in their lordly expenditure.

Wealth is only produced by giving a greater value to something by labour than it had before it was laboured at; or by exchanging something of which we have too much for something else of which we have too little.

And the only way to make the butter interests of Dorset richer, the Vale of Blackmoor more thriving, and its native population better customers for its native produce, is to direct money, and skill, and industry to its better cultivation.

All that is said in the letter immediately preceding this of mismanaged land, and the loss thereby to labourers, tenants, and landlords, applies most emphatically to the butter county of Dorset. All that Jackson declares to be absolutely requisite to profitable farming is absolutely wanting in Dorset. And it is certainly remarkable that Sir George Clerk of

22

Pennycuick, the political landlord, should be professing to *protect* the butter-makers by assuring them that foreign butter will be mixed with tar when it comes to this country to prevent its use as human food; while Mr James Jackson of Pennycuick, the practical agriculturist, is shewing that such farmers as the butter-makers of Dorset would be enriched by doing the reverse of most of that which they now do.

Mrs Horlock, your sugar-basins and tea-kettles want looking into. Meanwhile, I am a sympathizing friend, well acquainted with the struggles of poor mothers.

PASSAGES FROM THE LIFE OF AN ENGLISH FARMER.

PASSAGE I.—Indicating what kind of Man he was.

MR HURST took a hammer from his pocket and a nail; and when he had closed the gate of the Wellburn field, he drove the nail into the post above the latch. He then tried to lift the latch, and could not; and then he shook the gate with his arm outstretched, and it was firm. After that, he took the faggots of thorn which old Adam had cut from the hedge with his bill-hook, and warped them into the bars of the gate—the rough heads undermost, to keep out the pigs. When all was finished, he looked across the field, and said the second week of May was late to sow barley: still, if it pleased God, they might have a good crop even yet.

And old Adam said, "Ees, master, an it please God."

Mr Hurst then bade Adam go home with him to the farm-house. Whereat, when they arrived, the other men of the farm, who held the ploughs, and the lads who drove the ploughs, and the head carter, and the thrashers, and the shepherd, were all seated in the kitchen on the forms around the large table. And Mrs Hurst had put bread on the table and beer, and the round of beef, and the cold chine of pork, and the cheese; and Mr Hurst said he was glad to see it all ready, and bade the men begin. It had always been his custom, and the custom of his father and grandfather, in Berryhill farm, to give God thanks and the men their supper at the end of seed time and harvest; and he would not, he said, let the custom go down, if he could keep it up. Yet this might be the last seed-time they would all see in Berryhill together. The great event which had just happened, and which they were all to be engaged in, the last duties of to-morrow might bring about changes on the Berry estate which none there assembled would like to see.

All of them said they hoped nothing would happen to put

Mr Hurst out of Berryhill farm; or, if they did not all say so, they looked as if they would have all said so, had it been necessary for all to speak. Even the boys who drove the teams at plough, and scared the birds from the seed corn, seemed as if they would have said they hoped Mr Hurst would never go out of Berryhill, had not their mouths been so full of bread and meat that they could not speak. Old Adam said he remembered that time one-and-fifty years as if it had been but yesterday, when the last event of the kind happened, and that was the year before Mr Hurst was born, and he was not sure but there was barley in the Wellburn field that very year.

And then he reckoned how many times he had known barley in that field; how many times he had mown it, and how often it had been reaped; and how many bushels an acre he had known on it in the best years; and what was the price of barley in those years, and what the price of wheat; and when wheat was at a certain price, what bread was at a gallon. And Mr Hurst told what he had made per acre from that field, after paying the rent and all charges, in some years when it was barley and some years when it was wheat. And the shepherd told of the ewes with two lambs and the lambs which he had seen in that field when it was grass. And the ploughman said they had never turned up soil and harrowed in seed in better order than the soil was that day. And Mr Hurst said, that, to their credit, he must say the ridges had never been more neatly finished off, and the water furrows drawn more evenly and expeditiously in any field on Berryhill farm since he had known it, as had been done in the Wellburn that day. And the two young men who drew the water furrows in the ridges after they had been sown and harrowed, were so pleased to hear their master speak of their work in such a measure of praise, that, tired as they were, they would have gone out on that instant and furrowed up twenty fields if the work had been required, and never have felt the shadow of discontent upon them. They would have done anything to please Mr Hurst and one another—run a race, leaped the hurdles, danced a hornpipe, or sung a song; and they were so near the singing point of good fellowship, that Mr Hurst, perceiving it, said " No, not on this occasion. We have always had a song on such nights as this before, but the solemn and mournful duty we shall be all engaged in to-morrow must forbid singing and jollity to-night."

And then, speaking of what was to be done to-morrow, he said the horses not wanted to go in the procession would be turned into the meadow to grass. Diamond and Dick, the two black nags, would be taken to Crookley Down, to join the procession ; and as Adam was old, and not able to walk as he once could, he had better get the second riding saddle and put it on Rosy, and ride. But Adam said he would not ride. Mr Hurst pressed on him that for his own comfort he should do so. But Adam said no, it would trouble him too much to get on and off ; he was too old to ride. Besides, the nobles and the gentles would be all riding, on horses or in coaches ; no, he would not ride ; he would walk on foot. He had walked on foot on the last occasion of the kind, this time one-and-fifty years, and he would walk now.

Whereupon, Mr Hurst said they would, in that case, turn Rosy into the meadow with the other horses. And he soon after bade them all good night, and reminded them that to-morrow would soon be here. Upon which the men departed, and went to their own houses, and agreed as they went that the sky looked as if to-morrow would be a fine day.

Passage II.—Foreshadowing a Change.

The morning of to-morrow came, and it came early. It had no mountains of clouds to climb over to make it late ; no fogs to wade through, to make it ill-humoured and out of countenance. It came overflowing with the joy of the year's youthfulness. It came hand-in-hand with young summer ; not the full-grown, full-dressed, blooming June, but with May in her girlhood—fairy-footed, happy, romping young May. On her head were the first of the forest leaves, and sprigs of budding hawthorn from the hedgerows. Around her feet were the flowers that childhood loves—the field-daisies and the cowslips. She tripped along the copse-wood sides, where the cowslips grow, and stood on tiptoe and looked into birds' nests. She found the diligent thrush on her warm eggs, and dried the dew from her back, and bade her mate sit on the next bough and sing to her, and make her happy. She bade the bees, that had not been with her since last year, come with her, and she would shew them where blooming gardens were, and orchards. And the cherry blossoms that had slept all night in the darkness and the dew, awoke, and opened their eyes as infants do ; and she kissed away their tears ; and bade them, and the birds, and the bees, join all together, and bloom, and work, and sing. She found the young forget-me-not, infant of its race, and she embraced it, welcomed it to the world, and called it pretty. The primroses, then growing old, and the daisies, that are never old, she found on the grassy margin of the farm fields, where horses, and ploughs, and heavy-footed men had trampled and crushed them ; and she lifted their bruised heads and healed them, and made them look up and bloom as if they had never been trodden on.

Wherever she set her young foot and breathed her sweet breath, deadness came to life and age took upon itself a new youth. So frolicsome was she, that she would touch the log, felled last winter, that had neither root nor branch, but which lay at the carpenter's shop to be sawn into boards, and even it would put out buds and leaves. Not even the despised turnip from the farm-fields, which had fallen into the winter ditch, and was there abandoned as too worthless to be recovered, did she despise and think too mean. She touched it, and it felt the hand of life upon it, and put forth its feeble shoot to lay hold of that hand. And it grew in strength, and raised itself higher and higher every day, until it burst forth in bloom, as if in gratitude and praise to the Author of all life, whose summer angel had come upon the earth and had not overlooked even it, the lowliest and the lost.

Early as the morning came, Mr Hurst and his men came forth from bed as soon. The horses not to be used that day were turned out, for the first time for that year, to grass; and the very oldest of them, even old Captain, who could hardly reach a slow trot on other days, snorted and threw up his hind-heels, and lay down and tumbled, and got up again and cantered, so pleased was he with liberty and the first day of summer grass. As for the younger nags, they careered at the gallop to the farthest end of the meadow, below Berry turnpike and up again, and into the river itself. And the ass followed them routing with delight; and the cows, always sober and disposed to graze peacefully at that time of the morning, raised their tails and hobbled after the ass and the slowest of the horses. And the geese with their goslings, and the old drake, waddled to the meadow and cackled and ate grass, though it was ordered they were not to go there; and the sows and the young pigs went too, and gave much trouble to those who were sent to bring them back again.

And the boy Adam, grandson of old Adam, was out at the Wellburn field as early as any bird of the morning, to keep the rooks and the wood pigeons from the barley-seed sown yesterday. And never had rooks to contend with a more vigilant watcher of a newly-sown field; for this was young Adam's first day at working for wages. All the work he had done before had been voluntary, and paid for by a hunch of bread and cheese. Now he was hired, and this was his beginning. Not a rook alighted or came within sight of him, even on wing, but he shouted to it. And he not only walked round and round the field—he sometimes ran; and though he more than once asked himself what he was running for, he ran again, he was so light-spirited, and so pleased to be working for wages. He knew the squire was dead ; but if he had been made squire in his stead he could not have been more happy than he was at being advanced to earn fourpence-halfpenny a-day, and to have his dinner in a bag with him, to eat in the field, at whatever hour he chose. He knew all the people were going to meet the squire's funeral coming from London, at Crookley Down, or that those who did not go to Crookley Down to meet it would go to the top of Morton Hill to see it coming, and that Morton Hill was three miles away, and that nobody would be left within that space of three miles but himself. Still he was pleased even to be left alone, because he had been told that the care of everything on the farm had been left to him.

And by the hour before mid-day not a human being but himself was left on three miles of country between Berry Hill farm and Morton Hill—all had gone to meet the squire's funeral coming from London. But, long before that hour, the rooks had discovered that the watcher of the seed corn had nothing more formidable to keep them off than his loud voice and a stone thrown at them if they came near enough, and which stone they could avoid, and still pick up the seed.

And they did pick up the seed, and the solitary watcher could not prevent them ; but at last they flew away, one after the other, until only two were left, and everything round them was silent, and he almost wished that those two would not go away. But first one of them, and then the other, flapped its wings and rose into the air, and circled round him, and went away and left him alone. And the shining sun had also gone, and the south was black. Morton Hill had its darkly-wooded north side towards him, and it was black. Everything was still, not the chirrup of a bird was heard, and he thought he felt the shadow of the dark woodlands of Morton Hill, and of the black clouds above them, falling upon him, and going into him, and taking all the pleasant thoughts that were in his mind and turning them upside down, and making them horrid and fearful. One of these fearful thoughts was, that this might be the last day ; that everybody and everything was perhaps dying or dead, and nobody left in the world but himself ; that the whole world was putting on black to go to its own funeral.

There was a tree ; he would go up into that tree and look all round, and see if there was any living or moving thing within sight. And he did so, and almost fell from the tree with fear when he saw the white roads in the valley below him covered with a moving black line of people, and horses, and coaches, more than a mile in length.

It was the squire's funeral; and as it moved on, the darkness of the sky grew deeper, and the air became denser and hotter, and more silent and solemn, until about the time when the coffin was laid in the family vault of the old Abbey, at which time there was not an unweeping eye in or near the Abbey grounds—for he had been a good squire, and many mourned for his death, and those who did not weep for grief wept because others did so—they could not restrain tears upon a sorrowing day in sorrowing company.

The darkness of the sky grew deeper, the clouds came nearer, and pressed the hot thick air to the earth; and as the people turned from the death vault of the Abbey, and came out of the Abbey doors, the firmament seemed to have come down from its place in the heavens, and to stand upon the earth, and crowd into a heap the hearse and mourning coaches and black horses, and the horsemen and the foot people, as if it would suffocate them, and lay them all where they had been laying the squire's coffin.

Not one of them but expected to see every moment a flash of lightning followed by a burst of thunder. But there was no thunder. Drops of rain—slow, large, and uneven in their slow dropping—came down. Then they ceased. Then they began again, and once more ceased. And gusts of wind, that seemed to rise from the dead, came through the Abbey doors and made the plumes of the hearse flutter, and made weak women, and men weaker than women, think they saw ghosts upon the wing escaping among the trees by the chance of the Abbey vaults being open.

And the wind rose into conflict with the rain, and neither yielded to the other; both came on pouring and blowing, and the heat went as if it had never been a warm day, and left nothing but cold, and people shivering in the cold and the wet for the remainder of the day; or marvelling when they kindled good fires at home to warm and dry themselves, that the weather should have changed so unaccountably, or prophesying, when they tried to warm and dry themselves, and could not become comfortable, that "who could tell but this day was the forerunner of evil days to Berry estate?" The old told the young of such foreshadowing of changing fate, which they had heard of in their young days. And the young did not resist the prophecy.

The evil days to Berry estate did come, and to Berry Hill farm before long. But when we recount, as we may possibly do in a few other passages of Mr Hurst's life, the causes that brought about those evil days, we shall see that the state of the weather at the old squire's funeral was not one of them. though the death of the squire was.

PASSAGE III.—Giving some Account of his Landlord.

Mr Hurst's farm contained 490 acres, including roads, hedgerows, ditches on each side of the hedgerows, banks raised on the side of the ditches; marshes containing willows and wild ducks—the willows for himself, the wild ducks for the young squire; copses for game; a covert of furze (only in part on Berry Hill farm) for foxes; and the ground on which stood the farm buildings and some cottages forming the outskirts of Berry village. On the Berry Park estate there were from fifty to sixty farms as large as this, and upwards of one hundred smaller. Altogether, including 3000 acres in Berry Park, and 750 acres of copse and fox covert and common, outside the park walls, the estate contained nearly 47,000 acres.

And there was not an estate of land on the beautiful face of England more fair to look upon than that of Berry Park. There was not one less deceptive in its outward beauty; for below that beauty lay all the elements of excellent agriculture; and, as Mr Hurst has since said, they only wanted money and men's strength, and two or three other advantages which the young squire could have added to money and men's strength to have worked those elements into activity, to have made him a richer squire than his father was. And his father was rich enough to charge the estate only with £1000 of annuity to an elderly relation, and L.2000 a-year to his widow, the young squire's mother. All his other children, daughters as well as sons, and the widow, in part, were provided for out of his personal property.

No; there was not at that time a fairer inheritance of land in England than that which fell to this young squire by his father's death. Larger properties there are in England and in Scotland too. It would not have measured with the acres of the noble Cavendish of Chatsworth, Grosvenor of Eaton Hall, Percy of Alnwick Castle, nor with the acres of twenty or thirty other lords and commoners. Least of all with the regions of the grouse and the red deer of Atholo or Argyle, or the sheep-walks and the fields of oats and barley of Buccleuch. Yet it was a rich and a beautiful inheritance, large even amongst the lordly lands of England.

But fair, and fruitful, and exceeding lovely as were those 47,000 acres of woodland, rock, river, green meadow, and corn field, they lay not on the face of England more pleasant to the beholder than stood the young owner of them, generous and beloved, among those who enjoyed his personal friendship and favour. To have said to him who never heard the alms-seeker ask for a halfpenny without giving a shilling, who never

had an act of duty or generous service done to him, so far as he
knew it, without rewarding the duty with more than its payment and the generous service with five-fold generosity; to
have intimated to him that to sustain his dignity and provide
himself with the pleasures which he was educated to desire and
enjoy as necessaries of life, he would make poor men of men
not then poor, that men of honesty and industry would be by
him driven in old age to the workhouse—to have told him of
this, he would as soon have leaped from the tower of his college
at Oxford headlong, and broken his bones, every one of them,
as have believed it : nor, believing it, could he have continued
to ride his racers and steeple chasers across break and bar, ditch
deep and hedge high, and drive his mail coach to Woodstock
and Banbury and back again, loaded with young noblemen,
and the heir of a dukedom, in the uniform of a guard, blowing
the guard's bugle. No ; such was the native generosity of his
nature, that he would not, and could not, have made the pleasures and pastimes to which these college exercises were but
initiatory, the necessaries of his life, had he known to what
they would lead. But if he had been told to what they would
lead, or might lead—had he been told what as a certainty they
would prevent him from doing, namely, his duty to himself
and his country, as the owner of 47,000 acres of land, he
would not have believed those who so told him. His education
led him to form different opinions on the duties of a rich landowner.

Had it been intimated to him by some friend who sat near
his ear when he first went into Parliament, a young member
and a young man, two years before his father's death, that instead of being a protector of agriculture, as he was sent to
Parliament to be, and believed himself to be, he was its enemy though its owner, he would have deemed that friend unfit
for farther confidence, kind and forbearing as he naturally was.
Such had been the purport of every thought implanted in him
by others ; such the bent of every opinion which had grown
within him of his own conception ; for men's opinions, like
a plant's leaves, grow to the light by which they are cherished.

We need not now take time to recount in detail all the
elements of agricultural wealth which were then known to be
on the Berry estate, but though known, not applied to use ;
nor the greater store of unapplied resources on it, and not
then known—not known by reason of the traditions of agriculture having been for centuries deemed superior to new discoveries ; not then known, because it was left to the English
manufacturers to take science by the hand and say, " Come,

work for us," while English farmers turned their backs on science, and would not let it even touch their dunghills, saying, " We have always done as we do ; we will do well enough if let alone ;" the farmers speaking thus, because landowners had no higher knowledge of their duties and their interests than our young squire had. We shall not occupy time and fill space by putting into this narrative the details of the wasted wealth of the 47,000 acres of Berry Park, nor yet to put into form and shape, palpable to the understanding, that which is almost impalpable to human perception—the legal intricacies which are interwoven with all English tenures, and in such seemingly simple tenures as tenancies-at-will ; and which, unhappily for English agriculture, ensnare it, and mar its progress at every step. We may have yet time and space to give these in detail. At all events, we shall soon see in this little history what their effects are.

But at present let us proceed to say that the young Squire Thorncliffe—Francis Augustus de Aubrey Thorncliffe—at the age of 25, succeeded his father, Francis John de Aubrey Thorncliffe, who died at the age of 63. Let us proceed to review how the young rich man, now the possessor of property in land, the market value of which was about L.1,500,000 sterling, exclusive of timber, minerals, buildings, furniture, much valuable live stock, six church livings, the great tithes of several parishes, and the almost undisputed power to return two borough members to Parliament ; let us proceed to review how he, already two years a legislator, pledged to support the interests of agriculture in Parliament, and honestly inclined so to do according to his best ability, (his natural abilities were good,) and according to the political opinions which he had inherited with his high rank and great wealth ; let us see what he did to advance that great interest which he believed to be beyond comparison paramount to all others in this country—the agricultural interest. And as we write and read in this paper for instruction, and not for mere amusement, let us put the actions of his early life in that point of view where they will be most instructive, though at the risk of being less entertaining. And let us touch upon some of those facts of occurrence and traits of character which have sober truth in them, though little romance.

Squire Thorncliffe was not a frequent speaker in Parliament. He had little time and not much inclination to attend the House of Commons. His two packs of hounds, his horse-races, steeple-chases, yeomanry cavalry, game preservers, and grand battues among the game ; his coursing and breeding, and buying of hounds and horses for coursing, and hunting, and racing, his betting on all events and amusements, and paying of bets to gentlemen less wealthy, but sharper or more fortunate than himself; all these left him little time and less inclination to spend his evenings in the House of Commons. Still he was often there when a vote was required for the party to which he was attached by inheritance and education, and always there when a vote was required to support, as he honestly believed it was to support, that interest which was his interest, and to which he was voluntarily pledged.

He had spoken in Parliament before succeeding to his estate in deprecation of some motion for Parliamentary reform, and, in doing so, founded his objection to reform on the ground that it would weaken the agricultural interest, and transfer its political strength to the manufacturing and commercial towns. He spoke then slightingly of the men called cotton lords; and even seriously warned the legislature of the national danger involved in the increasing magnitude of English manufactures; and he has at times, when opportunities served, spoken similarily since. And when he has not spoken, his votes have conveyed to the public the fact that he has not altered his opinions.

Now it so happened that, in the year of his succession to the Berry estate, there died, at about the distance of 200 miles from London, a gentleman who was both a manufacturer and a merchant, and who left one son, the sole inheritor of his wealth, that wealth consisted of two coal-pits, with steam-engines and all the gear in working order; two large ships trading to the United States; shares in seven ships trading to the West Indies and South America; one steam-ship going between Liverpool and Dublin; shares in steamers working as pilots and ferry-boats on the Mersey; shares in several of the Midland Counties canals; one canal and the wharves on it all his own; a warehouse in Liverpool, and shares in a Marine Insurance office in the same place; also a cotton-mill, steam-engine, and machinery for spinning and weaving in the neighbourhood of Manchester; which last was leased at an annual rental of several thousand pounds to a manufacturer. Indeed, the greater part of all the property enumerated was under the management of second parties, who hired it and paid rent, or freightage, or dividends, as the case might be.

This young man of wealth, though not so rich as Squire Thorncliffe, was richer than most of the squires and many of the lords in England; and he might have used his property for pleasure, and pleasure only, as they used theirs, if he had been so inclined. Where he was educated, and what the maxims of his education were, cannot be now told with certainty.

But he did not stop the engine of the coal-pits and the pump, and go down into the pits for sport, and be hauled up again, and again let down for sport at break-neck speed, shewing courage and spirit on his part, yet hindering the work of the coal-master who rented the pits, and of the colliers who worked the seams of coal.

He did not, when the ships were loaded with cutlery, and crockery, and plate, and calicoes, and silks, for Boston, New York, and Baltimore, and Charleston, go and fill them with vermin, for the pleasure of hunting the vermin, and killing some of it, and holding some of it by the tail, and cutting off the tail; overturning bales of goods upon the deck in the pursuit; breaking the cutlery and the crockery; defacing the plate, and treading the calicoes and the silks under foot; ordering the merchants, whose goods these were, and who had freighted the ships, to leave the ships, if they complained, with their goods instantly, before the voyage was made, he still taking freight-age from them, by compulsion, because the goods were in his ships, and the law authorized him to take freightage whether the voyage was completed or not; he did not do all nor any of these things to the merchants his tenants.

He did not prevent those who held shares jointly with him-self in the ships trading to the West Indies and South America from making the most of any new merchandise or new mer-cantile project which the most sagacious of them deemed to be profitable.

He did not load his steam-ship, going between Liverpool and Dublin, with idle passengers, who paid no fares, merely because those idle passengers were agreeable companions, well-dressed, and pleasant to be seen in a steam-packet, even though that packet was entirely his own, and he might have got a premium for making such a shew.

He did not, for the sport of taking pleasure-trips every day for nine months of the year in the ferryboats on the Mersey, hinder the trade and the profit of those boats, and pay penal-ties to those who owned them jointly with himself; thus los-ing his own share of the profits, and making good their losses also.

He did not let the canal, which was all his own, flood the wharves and the warehouses, by defective drainage and broken flood-gates, nor keep that canal for the mere breeding of fish, with a force of armed men round it to preserve the fish, and keep away all fishers, and all boats and barges, and the navi-gators of them, who might attempt to use the canal for the common sense uses of its construction.

He did not, when he let his spinning and weaving factory to

the manufacturer, bind the latter to keep it all in repair, and yet allow him, the owner, to come into the mill with hot-headed associates, whose life was idleness, to get the steam up to a pressure which the safety-valve could not ease, that the machinery might be made to go at a rate which wheels, shafts, pulleys, cranks, spindles, and shuttles, never went at before—all to see which wheel could go fastest and longest without breaking down. Nor did he bind this manufacturer to spin only certain kinds of cotton, certain numbers of thread, and weave certain breadths and lengths of pieces of cloth, under penalty of being fined triple, quadruple, and quintuple, the value of the threads and pieces of cloth made against rule. Nor did he depute the power of doing all or any of those things, in his name, to lawyers who know nothing of ships and factories, and spinning and weaving, yet who like a job to do, and cannot live without a job to do.

He did not do all those things, and profess to be the especial friend, protector, and encourager of ships, canals, factories, and of the occupiers and workers of ships, canals, and factories. He offered his tenant, the manufacturer, no protection, but security that he would not interfere with him until the term of years for which the factory was leased had expired, save to draw the rent, and see that the machinery was not wilfully injured or destroyed. He gave the merchants who freighted his ships, and the captains and crews of the ships, no promise of protection—only liberty to sail with what tide they chose, and what wind, and to whatever port they chose, with whatever cargo—wisely judging that they knew better than he how to choose a cargo and take advantage of wind and tide. As for them seeking redress for his stocking of the ships with vermin, that he might hunt the vermin over the bales of goods, shouting and tally-hoing as he hunted, and hold the vermin up by the tail when it was caught, and cut off the tail, and each of the four nearest of his companions cut off a foot as a trophy; as for the merchants and the captains seeking redress for goods damaged, and time wasted thus, they never once thought of such a thing. In commerce, and also in the dealings of the manufacturers, such waste of property, and of the resources and energies which produce property, are not known.

Not so in agriculture. The young Squire Thorncliffe believed that he did only what it became a squire to do, and especially one so largely possessed of land as he was, in doing to his property, and to those who hired it and paid rent for it, all those things which the young merchant did not do to his mercantile property.

And yet he continued to marvel why this adventurer in

merchandise and manufactures became richer every year, and added to all his business that of a banker, and to all his ships and canals, and shares in these, more ships and shares in railways, and, before long, to all his wealth a landed estate; while he, the owner of land, born to it, and bred a landowner of the first-class, advanced not in wealth, but sank into debt. And farther, he and many more of his Parliamentary party, continued to marvel why the manufacturer, who only rented the factory, should become so rich as to build a new one for himself, and extend his business far beyond its former limits, while those who were tenants in land became no richer, and could not extend their manufacture of corn and cattle and human food without loss or complaints of loss.

'Yet did he continue to keep his two packs of hounds that he might hunt four days in the week, and also all the horses necessary for so much hunting, and many more than was required even for that. And his packs of hounds were the most complete in his county, and the hunts were the best attended. So was his mansion noted for its hospitality, as he was for generosity in all personal actions. Yet he was only a fair specimen of the richest of English landowners, and a specimen of what even the most moderately endowed of the squires attempted to be; for though they could not all spend thousands a-year on the mere items of hounds and horses, they all hunted and spent as far as their land, and those who lend money on land, would let them spend.

They rode with Squire Thorncliffe, and were proud of the honour and the privilege of hunting with his hounds four days of the week. And a hundred of them, and sometimes half as many more, would scour at the gallop across the farm fields, a fox first, hounds next, and the fleetest of them at the tails of the hounds. Some would halt not at hedge, or ditch, or high wall, but clear these, or any other obstacles, at a bound, plunging into another field of October sown wheat, it might be, or fold of fattening sheep, or meadow with cows in calf, striking terror into the sheep and cows, and making them run and stand appalled, as nothing else on earth can terrify them; others, and by far the greater number, did not clear at a bound every hedge, ditch, and high wall; they rode through gaps in the fences, if there were gaps; they pulled down palings to make gaps, if there were none, or they rode to the gates and forced a way through them, and rode on and left them broken and open. And even the richer of the tenant farmers rode over one another's land thus; and were proud of the permission to ride with their squire and the fifty other squires there. And they holloed and tally-hoed like the best of the squires, and called that farmer a "muff" and a "knave," whoever he might be, that grumbled to have his fields of new wheat, and his fences, and cattle, and sheep thus ridden upon, broken, and terror struck.

And least of all was it admissible for a tenant farmer to make deep drains, to draw the water from his fields to the great ditches, and cover in the drains and make conduits into which foxes could run for shelter in the hunt; nor was it pardonable to do anything, no matter what agricultural philosopher might recommend it, that would interfere with the pleasures of the chase, the breeding of foxes for the chase, and the preservation of game of all kinds for the dogs and guns, and great days of killing, wounding, and unwinging.

But, in sooth, there was little heard of the murmurs, if there were murmurs. It was in the conditions of their occupation of the farms for the tenants to submit to all those things, and to many more. The four-footed game, and the winged birds of the woodland coverts, and of the weedy wastes by the ponderous hedges and ditch banks, the farmers were bound not to injure, depredators though these were; but, on the contrary, to aid in preserving them until they were of numbers exceeding in multiplicity even the rooks, the sparrows, the mice, and the rats; yea, exceeding these, when added to all the fowls and chickens, ducks and ducklings, geese and goslings, hogs large and pigs little, on the broad estate.

Then, when the harvest had been gathered in, and the game could get no more of that, and the wheat seed and the winter vetches had been sown, and had sprung up, and they could not eat more of either than they had eaten, and longer life would have led to leanness, the birds and the beasts, which ten armed gamekeepers and assistants, with sticks in their hands, and as many Acts of Parliament as there were gamekeepers, and more magistrates than there were men with sticks—the birds and beasts which they had preserved to that time, by and with the assistance of the farmers on whose crops they were chiefly fed, were encompassed in the woodlands and in the weedy boundaries of the fields, and driven forth in the face of the squire and many lords and lesser squires.

And men, expert in loading guns, with powder and shot, loaded them and put caps to the locks, and handed them to the noble lords and the squire, and even to the lesser squires, who all of them fired at the shrieking birds as they rose above the copse one after another, and half dozens at a time, and brought them to the ground broken winged or killed outright, and never halted in their killing until they had brought many hundreds of pairs to the ground, and could tell of an excellent day's sport.

And then, when the shooting and hunting season was over, and birds were allowed to be at peace, and choose their mates, and hatch young birds for next year's battue, Squire Thorncliffe and the other squires and lords, who sat in Parliament, repaired thither, and sat on their legislative eggs and hatched them into new Acts of Parliament, still more to protect agriculture and preserve game.

And again was money lavished on London life, beyond the measure of income, on mere consumption without production. And again did the racing come round, and the betting and the cheating of those rich enough to be cheated. Again the hunting came, and the *battues*, and the steeple-chases, and again and again the Parliament.

At last Squire Thorncliffe had mortgaged Berry Park estate —even the whole of the 47,000 acres ; and what with the bonds of the mortgagees added to all the other disabilities of the tenants as agriculturists, and the breeding and feeding of game, which was not now lessened, though the squire went abroad and let the sporting out for hire ; and what with the inevitable consequence of augmented rents to pay the mortgagees their interest, and still allow the squire L.10,000 a-year, agriculture was marred and buffetted, and put back, and compelled to linger on the road a beggar for alms, while commerce and manufactures marched on, and gained strength, and wealth. and independence.

PASSAGE IV.—The Amended Poor-Law, when it was New.

It was a warm day in June—one of the days on which maidens who have butter to make, make it in the morning and go out to wash it at the springs, with dew on their feet ; a day when the mowers of the new hay rise with the birds, when birds are up before the sun ; a day when June hastens before the day is done to the wheat that's green, and looks for young ears, and gives them dew to drink ; and finds them again in the morning, and dries them and makes them strong enough for the hot sun, which, by God's command, must, for the sake of men and women and children hungry, be as hot as wheat can bear, to hasten on the harvest—it was a day when June gives her freshest greenness and her coolest breezes to those who deserve them best—the workers who go soonest out in the morning ; a day when the luxurious, idle, and indolent of all conditions, who lie late abed, come out to pant for breath, and to be broiled in a sun which is up high, and hot in the performance of other duties than that of caring for their comfort and their skin ; a day when, happy ordinance of Nature, even the mower in the fields is relieved by his violent exercise and his perspiration from the languor that afflicts the idle.

It was on such a day that Mr Hurst said to his men that they would all be required in the afternoon and the evening to wash sheep ; that they would begin sheep-shearing next day ; that all the flock would need washing, but those that grazed on the hill where the sand holes were would more particularly, as they had stained their wool by rubbing against the red sand. And he said two of the men and some of the boys must go at once and make a dam across the stream, stemming the water deep enough to take a man up to the middle, or nearly, but not deep enough to drown anybody standing on his feet.

It was on this same day that the venerable Adam, ten years older than when we saw him first, and now past all work but to rock the cradle of the fourth generation—a future Adam of the fields—was sitting on the bench within the honeysuckle porch of his cottage, winking his aged eyes as if he slept, yet not asleep. He said to Mr Hurst who was passing, and who stopped for a few minutes to speak with him, " Ees, master : it be God that gives the weather ; it be well for we that the hand of man does not hold the wind, and rain, and sunshine : it be well for we that we ha'nt to go to the parish for the showers and the shining sun, master, now that they have made that new law. I have been trying to understand the grounds of it ; but I ben't able to see through it. I have tried it with Scripture, but I can find no Scripture for it ; no, all Scripture be right against it. I have even tried to forget that I am the poor man, and have put myself in the place of the rich man ; yet I cannot see why this law should be as they have now made it. It be seven miles going and seven miles coming, and I have been twice, once this week and once the week before, at what they call the board of guardians ; all that way, ill able to go ; and I sat down on the door steps four hours until they called me in ; and then they said I must give up everything I am possessed of to them, and go into that great new house. Oh, master, what terrible things some of them as have been in and out again tell of that union house. They are put to their work and to their victuals like soldiers to drill. The unions, they say, are to have all masters out of the army and from the men-of-war ships as have been used to severity over other men ; and they say we be all to be drilled and punished if we do not obey the word of command. And I do not doubt it ; for him as they have got to this union came out and gave orders not to sit on the steps of the door, and orders for this one to come in, and that one to stand aside, just like as we used to hear the drill-sergeants speak in the time of the local

23

militia and the volunteers. It be a very hard case, master, for they as have worked a long life like I, and went, as you know, when I need not, for I was above age, and offered to be a volunteer at the time of all the fright about Boney. It be a hard thing when they would not drill me then because I was too old, though I was young enough to have the spirit to defend my country, that thirty years after, when I am old in spirit and body both, they are going to put me into the hands of a severe man, chosen because he has been a breaker in of men in a barrack-yard, to break me in now in my old days to what they call strict discipline ; to learn me and poor old Sarah, who have lived in this cottage, man and wife, nine-and-forty years come Michaelmas, and brought up a family in honesty and the fear of God—to 'sunder we whom God did join together, that we may live apart and meet death in our old age each alone, to deter, for they say that is it, to deter other poor creatures from coming on the parish. I never believed, Mr Hurst, it could have been true. When they spoke about mending the old law, they never said a word about this, as I heard on, never a word."

" No, Adam ; nor did I know what kind of new law it was to be when I complained like many other farmers of the old one. Here am I now leaving this farm where I and my fathers before me have been so long—obliged to leave it because I have not submitted quietly to imposition ; here am I with my last crop in the ground, with men working to me, all brought up to work by me and my father, all of them good workmen."

Adam.—" Good masters get good men."

Mr Hurst.—" It may be so. At any rate I have good men here, and I do not expect to find as good where I am going. Now one of the worst, if not the very worst, parts of the old poor-law is preserved in this new one, indeed the most mischievous part of the old law ; I mean that which prevents me from taking the people who work for me now, or any of them, or even you yourself, Adam, with me to another parish out of this union. This is a great hardship both to me as a farmer and to you all as workmen. I must submit to employ such as I find in my new parish, be they good or bad, and leave my best hands here to my successor in this farm, be he a good master or a bad. This is one of the evils which I see the agriculture of England suffering under ; and I must confess that since our young squire has run in debt as he has, and the management has got into the hands of the lawyers, I see many things more which I did not once think to be so detrimental to a farmer as I do now. Since the squire has mortgaged Berry estate, the game has been let with the mansion and park, as you know. New sets of game-keepers have been put over us, and that which was disagreeable before is now a pest. I have stood out against it, and here is the consequence—at six months' notice I am obliged to leave Berryhill. I begin to think that both farmers and their farm men need some different kind of laws than any we have now, or else not so much law as we have now. I am grieved, more than I can tell, that I had ever signed a petition against the old poor-law; but I had no thought of such a change being made as they have made. To deny an old worn-out man and woman, like you and Sarah, relief, until you give up and part with all your old furniture, and that you must even then go into a place ruled as the House of Correction is ruled, to deter others, is indeed grievous. I hope we may yet prevent this. It is that 'cold-hearted,' new-fangled doctrine, called political economy, that has led to this new law."

As old Adam had, perhaps, never heard of political economy, or, like many others who use its name, knew nothing about it even if he had heard of it, he could not make any remark upon it in response to Mr Hurst. We shall, however, take this opportunity to make a few remarks on this popular error, that of charging the oppressive clauses of the new poor-law on the principles of political economy.

In the first place, nobody supported those provisions of the poor-law which have severity in them, and which are intended to deter the poor from seeking relief, more zealously than the landed gentry and landed nobles, in Parliament, who make it their boast that political economy is neither believed in nor understood by them. They, as their ancestors, the feudal barons and knights of chivalry, who deemed it derogatory to acquire literary education of any kind, even the ability to write their names, boast now, in the same spirit, that the merest elements of political economy are a mystery to them. The time will come when their boast of being ignorant of political economy, at the very time they are sitting as political legislators, will be looked upon as evidence of intellectual barbarism, as truly as the declaration of the Norman knights, that they were not dishonoured by not having learned to write their names.

But even where persons professing to be political economists supported the cruel clauses of the poor-law, it is no more a proof against those principles which they professed to believe in, than was the cruelty of the inquisition by one party of believers in religion, and the enactment of penal laws against that party by another, a proof that religion justified the inquisition of Rome or the penal laws of England.

The principles of political economy are as true and unerring as the principles of gravitation, attraction, or repulsion in natural bodies, if political economy is freed from political superstition. There never has been any legislation unmixed with what we may call political superstition. The present free-trade measure is a step towards it, yet it is not more than a step upon the threshold.

Passage IV. continued.—The Sheep-washing.

Mr Hurst said again, that he hoped some plan might be devised to prevent Adam from incurring the terrible calamity of breaking up his old home and going with his aged wife into the union house, to be separated worse than by death and the grave—to be separated in life, in a grave alive. And he then asked if Adam would take his staff in his hand and walk up the dell, and sit down on the knoll by the green birches, and see the sheep-washing. He believed that Adam had never once been absent from a sheep-washing at Berryhill since the year he was born; and as this would be the last they would have in Berryhill while he was farmer, he would like to have it in all respects like the sheep-washings of days gone by.

And Adam took his staff in his hand and went up the dell above the pool to the knoll where the birches grew, and sat in the shade and looked down upon the sheep-washing, as did other old people and all the young children not engaged below. It made the old people young again; every one of them declared that, and they even rebuked some of the more timid of the young ones for not going to help; they, when they were young, never stood looking on. See how the young tegs, that had never been washed before, were breaking away.

At which all the youngsters—the very youngest that could toddle alone—ran to bring back the young sheep that were running away without being washed; the boys that were helping to swim the sheep along the pool to the men who stood in the deepest place got out and ran; the dogs barked and ran; the young women who came to look on, and be very timid in going near the edge of the pool, though they knew well they would be, before the evening was over, pursued and caught, and brought back and soused in the pool according to the custom of sheep-washings—they ran to bring back the fugitive sheep; and the shepherd called to them all to keep back, his dog would do more than the whole. But dogs, and children, and boys, and women, and sheep that would not be turned, went out of sight up the dell, each making their own noise, the sheep and the shepherd's oldest dog being the only parties to the uproar really in earnest; the rest in part or wholly in fun.

Meantime the more sober three-year-old wethers were brought forward from the corner beneath a crag where they were awaiting their turn. The shepherd, who knew best how to lay hold of them, introduced them to the water. He did it thus :—He got a wether by the long wool of the neck, and by the shoulder and fore feet. He lifted his fore feet from the ground, and stood astride over him, and made him walk on his hind legs to the water's edge. The wether did not like it, and did not go willingly in ; but when he really was in, and felt his hind part getting wet, he made a bold spring, such as would overturn a man that was not prepared for it into the water. Here two men stationed for the purpose caught him, and his only struggle was to get further into the pool, and further from the shepherd who put him in. But as soon as he was afloat and off his feet, he quietly resigned himself to be washed, which was done by a man standing beyond the two men, who held his head above water by the wool of the neck, and guiding him by the shoulders, which were below water, kept him thus on end for half a minute or more, rolling and plunging him to the left and to the right.

This man, the shepherd having another ready, turned his wether over in the water to another man who, like him, stood three and a half or four feet deep. This last held the sheep in the same way, and in his turn gave him to another man a yard or two farther in the pool. That man treated him in the same way, and gave him to a fourth, and perhaps a fifth, who at last pushed the drenched sheep to shore on the opposite side, where he climbed his way up the low bank, dripping and in silence, until he saw those that had gone before him dripping also. They greeted him and he greeted them, and then he turned round with them to watch the others, and salute them with the language and sympathy of sheep as they came out of the water in their turn.

Then the flock of tegs was brought back, and they were washed one by one the same way as the wethers. And beer and bread and cheese were handed across the water to the men who stood in the pool, for they declined to come out to get it. They said to stand in the water for a long while was not so bad as to come out and go in again ; and the old people who now came down to the side of the pool said that was true ; and some of the young ones said the best way to keep from cold was to be wet all over ; and they had no sooner said so than one of them was pushed in, and laid hold of by the men who had washed the sheep, and dipped deeper even than the sheep. And the young women threw water from the bank over the men in the pool to wet them ; and the men came out to catch the women, who in their turn ran, and screamed as they ran. And some of them were caught and carried back —the oldest matrons there, the grandmothers and great-grandmothers of the village telling the young men that it was well done, only to be gentle with it. And no on-looker thought wrong of it; save, perhaps, some very young child, whose eldest sister or aunt it was that struggled in arms which were too strong for her, and put her in the middle of the pool. And there was more cases than one where three women, or four or five, would pursue and get hold of one man, and carry him and throw him into the water, and some of them roll over on the top of him, where they might have been drowned but for the more grave of the old people, who drew them out again.

If anybody ever took cold at such a time the case was rare. Still rarer was it that such rough sport produced ill-humour. On this occasion so joyous was every one, they forgot even that this was Mr Hurst's last sheep-washing; and old Adam, after he had gone home and had his supper, and said family prayers, confessed that until he was on his knees beseeching Heaven for grace and mercy to himself and all men, he had forgot even the union workhouse, and the barrack-yard drill-sergeant who was set to be master of it. But at the solemn hour of family prayer solemn thoughts came back upon him, and he prayed fervently that he and his might be delivered from that great oppression in their age of helplessness—the oppression of the men who were possessed of riches, strength, and injustice.

Happy morning was it in Berryhill next day, when Mr Hurst mounted his horse and rode to the market town, six miles distant, to meet the agent of the estate and the solicitors of the mortgagees, who had written to him to meet them there, to see if they could not make a new arrangement to keep him as tenant of Berryhill. And when he returned and said the farm was again his, if he chose to take it at an advance of rent, the people were still happier, for Mr Hurst had said often before that he would rather pay a higher rent than leave it, provided only the game was kept within bounds. He had been told that day that prices, which had lately risen, would rise farther and be maintained; that the Conservative party was gaining strength in Parliament; confidence would not be shaken again as it had been in 1835, and prices would not fall as the Whigs had made prices fall. The only thing required now of the farmers was to support the efforts of the Tories to put down the Whigs.

Mr Hurst was not clear upon this doctrine, either for or

against it. But within a few days of giving in his new offer for Berryhill, news came that the king was dead, and a general election was pending, and Mr Hurst was called upon by all that was valuable to a farmer and to the labourers of the farms, to the landed estates and to the nation at large, to assist those who were now contending to rescue England and the young Queen from the counsels of " Whigs and destructives."

Mr Hurst's sheep-shearing was not yet done ; his ewes were still to shear when this political sheep-washing began— an immersion of one party by another far more uproarious and far from being so harmless as that at Mr Hurst's pool in the dell.

Passage V.

In which the political uses of the tenantry at an election are given. This is omitted.

Passage VI.

Which relates how Mr Hurst kept his old farm, and, not getting rid of his new one, how he, like many others, had more land than he could manage well, is also omitted.

Passage VII.

Which relates how the mortgagees caused Berry Park and mansion to be let to a sportsman who brought a new corps of gamekeepers on the estate, and preserved the game more than ever, is also omitted.

Passage VIII.

Containing an account of the movement (metaphorically) of heaven and earth, in 1841, to return Tory members of Parliament, who were to protect such men as Mr Hurst from the enemies of agriculture. This is likewise omitted.

Passage IX.

In which it is related how Mr Hurst, having followed the recommendations of the Royal Agricultural Society, in his efforts to make his farm more productive, was prosecuted for penalties, and made to pay them at the instance of members of that society for so doing. An instructive passage ; but also from necessity omitted.

Passage X.

Shewing how Mr Hurst examined closely for the first time, and found the conditions of agreement between him and his landlord to be such, that he was bound hand and foot not to improve the culture of his farm. This, too, must be omitted.

Passage XI.

In which Mr Hurst, being in London, is going up Fleet Street, and sees a notice on the house, No. 67, that a League meeting is to be held that evening in Covent Garden Theatre, and that seats will be reserved for tenant farmers who may wish to attend it, tickets to be had on application within. How he, always a believer in the virtue of the corn-law, went in, his political conscience smiting him at the same time, and got a ticket, and went to the theatre and heard Mr Cobden and Mr Bright; the first exposing the delusion practised on tenant farmers by the political landlords; the latter the wrongs to agriculture and to society by the feudal landlords in stocking the country with wild beasts, and preserving them by savage laws. This we must also omit.

Passage XII.

Setting forth how Mr Hurst thought he had heard the real farmers' friends speaking for the first time in respect of the feudal landlords and the game-laws; and how the corn-law was after all not such a sacred law as he had hitherto deemed it to be. How Mr Cobden's exposition of it took root in his mind as seed sown upon new soil, and how he applied for and obtained copies of all the League tracts, read them and believed them, and endeavoured to make his brother farmers believe them. This too is omitted.

Passage XIII.

Shewing how he had struggled to succeed, and had succeeded, in making his two farms pay the high rents that he had a few years before contracted to pay for them, notwithstanding the obstacles of unfriendly gamekeepers, swarms of game, and conditions of agreement which bound him not to improve his agriculture. How he employed more people per hundred acres than his brother farmers, and raised better crops; but how he had his character as a farmer decried because he had been to a League meeting, and now said that he believed the corn-laws had never been of any benefit to the farmers or to agriculture.

Passage XIV.

Tells how he went before the Parliamentary Committee on the game-laws, and gave evidence of the great injury done to himself and to the agricultural interests of his county by the excessive waste committed by the game; but owing to the parliamentary forms forbidding the publication of the evidence for the present, his statements are not inserted; and this passage of his life is also omitted.

PASSAGE XV.

Shewing how he was received by his brother farmers, whose interests he had served as well as his own in giving evidence against the game-laws, he being now an avowed opponent of the corn-law.

It was rent-day, the receiver of the rents was an elderly gentleman, a lawyer from the precincts of Lincoln's Inn. He came down to the Royal George Hotel in a glass coach; and when he alighted from it, there would have been no violence done to truth to have said, he looked as if he had come out of a glass case; so prim, so scrupulously perfect was this elderly little gentleman in his dress. From the gold spectacles on the wig of his head to the silver buckles on the shoes of his feet, there was no spot upon him.

And his professional conduct was as precise and formal, his moral character as spotless as his dress. Fiction will have it that lawyers living in the deep recesses of the temple and inns of court, in those caves of social life called chambers, are the spiders of human kind reposing in dust and cobwebs, sleeping with their eyes open to dart out upon any human flies that may go too near them. But this is only fiction, or if there be such lawyers, ours in the glass coach was not one of them; ours in the glass coach, if we may be so irreverent, was like a cockroach, or a black-beetle, to whose glossy exterior no impurity adheres, rather than a dusty spider. He had dealings with the world, and, as a lawyer, not unfrequently with those who bring upon it the appellation of "wicked world;" but he never touched wickedness, as we may say, with his bare hands. He read his law books through his glasses, and he knew mankind through his law books. He knew there were bad men and good men. He knew there were bad men, because laws had been made to hang them. He knew there were good men, because laws had been made to hang the bad ones. He knew the world must have more good men in it than bad, else the bad ones would have been strong enough to hang the good ones. He ranged himself on the side of the laws and of good men—thus, of mankind generally.

Individual men were revealed to him in a similar manner. He knew there were good farmers and bad farmers, because some were always ready with their rents on rent-day and others were not. He knew the relationship of landlord and tenant, because it was written on parchment. He knew the progress of agricultural science from the applications made to him by the tenants, when paying their rents, for authority to make and deduct the expense of making, next rent-day, new gates or repairs of old ones; repairs of floors and roofs of barns; construction of cesspools to save wasted manures; farm roads; drains to dry wet land; drains to keep the wasted manure of the yard from defiling the pond where the cattle had to drink; palings to protect young quickthorns; young quickthorns to supplant old ones; and other improvements akin to these. He knew that those who applied to have these things done had not done them. He knew their farms needed such improvements else such applications would not have been made; and he inferred that those who made no such applications for repairs and new works did not require them. Therefore it was logical to conclude that the tenants who, being content to have broken gates, dilapidated roofs and floors, wasted manures, poisoning the ponds and pools where cattle got drink, bad fences, who never made a new fence or repaired an old one, who never drained wet land nor cleared out a ditch that made land wet—it was a logical consequence to conclude that such tenants, who made no complaints and no demands, were the best farmers, and had their farms in the best condition, seeing agriculture, as he only saw it, through his gold spectacles on a map or on parchment, riding in a glass coach.

He was the very perfection of a legal land-agent. His integrity was as firm as the bank buildings; the cash committed to his keeping as safe as the bank cash. His rules of procedure were so squared off by a legal straight edge, that, as the clauses in the agreements between landlord and tenant were provisive of penalties for the landlord against the tenant, the latter never made a claim that was allowed to be good, so, as there were no good claims preferred by tenants, there were no decisions in their favour. He decided the claims made by the tenants according to the parchment. And, on the same authority, he decided the complaints preferred against the tenants. The complainants in such cases were the gamekeepers, for disturbance of the game, (some fields of hay being mown, when it was ready to be mown with pheasant's nests still in it—a grievous crime, if the farmer did not make friends with the gamekeeper,) or the woodman, the farmer having, perhaps, cut some overshadowing branches from a hedgerow tree; or the secret informer, never known precisely who, that had a farm on the estate, and kept his eyes open to see if all the crops were sown in the exact rotation written on the parchment, according to the rules of the agricultural science dwelling in the legal chambers of the Temple of Lincoln's Inn. The more numerous the informations laid by those servants of the estate, for disturbance of pheasants on their eggs, for the lopping of an overhanging tree, or for judging what crop would grow best by the quality of the soil rather than by the provision in the parchment, the more vigilant were they held to be, and the better claim did they feel themselves to have for augmented salaries and ultimate pensions.

Well, it was rent-day, or, as it is more genteelly termed, the audit. Those to whom it is the pleasantest day in the calendar call it by the pleasantest name. Those who see it coming on them long before it does come, coming as certainly and as sternly as an annual day of judgment, call it by the name which they know it best by—the rent day. It was the rent day at the Royal George Hotel, at the nearest market town for the Berry tenantry. They met there to pay their rents and to prefer their complaints. Let us look at some of them.

There sits in a private room of the hotel the little elderly gentleman with his clerk beside him. There stands before him Mr John Bull, with his hat in his hand. He has got his receipt—what more does he want? He might be as bold as any man that ever trod on English ground, yet he is timid. He has paid his rent, and owes no man anything. A little ago he was so bold in the public room as to tell Mr Hurst to his face that he and all like him who went to League meetings were "no good to their brother farmers," that all who minced matters now-a-days, and did not speak out for protection, would deserve to lose protection. Why does this Mr John Bull now hesitate in presence of this one man and his clerk to say his say? He has not a farm gate that will hold in a cow, or a horse, or a pig, and has not had for half a dozen years; they have been patched and patched, and again broken and broken, and at last thrown down by the fox hunters and by his own work-people, who found them more trouble than service, so often, that the wreck is fit for nothing else than firewood. He has no timber to mend gates and fences, and he is trying to ask for authority to have the old ones replaced by new, the expense to be paid out of his next rent. He has a mind, too, to ask for repairs to the old barns, which let rain through the roofs and the corn through the floors; but he has asked such favours before, and there is a feeling within him that those who have asked most earnestly and frequently to have their farm buildings repaired, have been least successful. Yet his have got into such a state of absolute wreck that he cannot help urging the request once again. He bears in mind the very eminent services rendered at the last election in getting in the candidate for whom the gentleman now before him was concerned, and he gives hints, imperfectly expressed, that he should not be overlooked in any *favours* which are to be conferred.

Here is Mr John Bull's error, the fatal error of farmers in submitting to ask for rights as for favours. The man who exacts rent for a farm of land which he does not provide with suitable buildings, and which he professes to provide, and at the same time lets the farm to the tenant on the condition that he shall quit at six months' notice, thus rendering it utterly impossible for him to supply the requisite buildings or fixtures himself—that man, be he agent or landlord, is no better than another Pharaoh, exacting the bricks from the bondmen without supplying the straw.

But look at the bondman, this John Bull, whose voice is as loud as a lion's—as a British lion's—so loud as to be called the British lion's voice, when he happens to roar on the same side of the table, or the same side of the subject, with the agent and the landlords. Listen to him, then, while now on the right side of a good cause—his own cause—in which the first principles of justice are involved, he dares hardly open his mouth to that one little old man.

But listen to the old gentleman. Mr Bull is to be *favoured*. Authority is to be given for the expenditure of L.100 in repairs. The tenant is pleased beyond expression. He bows low and is grateful, and retires. He should be grateful for a favour. He should be polite under any circumstances. But has he anything to be grateful for? Will this expenditure of L.100 in repairs be a favour? Will it not rather be a perpetuation of unfit buildings, make-shift gates, and fences? Will it not make it requisite for Mr John Bull to go again, next year or the next, begging once more to have some other part of his farm put in repair?

Then here is another tenant in the private room paying his rent. He has determined for the last nine months, and has sworn it a hundred times in his daily conversation, that he will not quietly submit to have his fields nearest the sand hills eaten up with rabbits any longer; again and again has he even this day formed in his mind what he would say to the agent when he paid his rent. But he cannot now say it. And why? because there is no door to his stable, and the stable itself is flooded whenever wet weather comes, and he has lost two horses by death, and the use of one or two more by disease, because the drainage cannot be made complete without leave to alter the water course and money to make another. If he begins to talk about rabbits, he will take the ground from under him to ask for a new stable ; for his ambition, or daring, does go as far as an entire new stable on a dryer piece of ground. So he talks of the stable, and omits the rabbits.

Then comes Mr Hurst. He also is in the private room, and has paid his rent. He has taken it into his head that all patchwork repairs are useless, and that no thorough improvements can be effected without he obtains a lease of twenty-one years. He thinks if a new set of farm-buildings were erected, and new fences also, at a cost of L.3000, on which he would pay five per cent. of additional rent, it would be of greater benefit to him and to the farm than if he received an annual drawback of ten per cent. from his present rental to repair the old buildings. He offers to prove this, and the old gentleman listens ; but at last stops him by saying he has no power to alter the present system of letting the farms—which is true.

Others of the John Bull family enter, and pay their rents, and tell how dilapidated their farms are, if they have any hope of an allowance for repairs. Some express a hope that they are not going to lose " protection to agriculture," to which the elderly lawyer says that is impossible ; it can never be taken away and never will ; and though he may grant them no drawback for repairs, no redress for rabbits, tell them he has no power to interfere with the game, doom them to their undrained bogs and sour cold clays, without an allowance for drain tiles, or for any one thing recommended by the Royal Agricultural Society as needful and indispensable to agriculture ; they retire comforted and happy in heart that they are not to lose " protection." They retire to their dining room, and in due time the dinner is on the table, and the elderly gentleman who came from Lincoln's Inn in a glass coach, and who reads his law books though his glasses, and mankind through his law books, is chairman of the dinner.

This was in the autumn of last year, 1845. The dinner might be worth description, and the speakers worth reporting, but they were the same as have often been given to the public in print. The " enemies of agriculture" were denounced, and the hints that there was only one " renegade " to the good cause of protection in the room, and on the estate, was cheered.

The only man who had dared to go before the parliamentary committee, to expose what they all suffered from—the overswarming game—and the only one who had the courage in the private room to speak of those requirements which alone would have been favours, if granted by the old lawyer, was Mr Hurst, who was roared at by the British lions around the dinner table as a " renegade to the cause."

I conclude this brief sketch. If the names are not real, the facts and the persons are ; and deeply do I regret to say that what is here written is too true, and too generally applicable all over England.

JOURNEY TO EARL SPENCER'S ESTATE.
THE FIRST DAY.

I was a passenger on the London and Birmingham Railway on the 31st day of May last, 1844, coming from the north ; and calling to mind that Earl Spencer's seat was in Northamptonshire, I bethought myself of going thither to see his Lordship's cattle and his celebrated breeding and feeding establishment. I was wrong in supposing this establishment to be at Althorp, in Northamptonshire ; it is in Nottinghamshire ; but of that hereafter.

Not knowing where Althorp was situated, save that it could be reached from Northampton, I came on to the Blisworth station, which is the nearest to Northampton, though, as I subsequently ascertained, I was nearer Althorp at the Daventry station, which I had passed.

Blisworth is between four and five miles from Northampton, westward, and Althorp Park is six, or perhaps seven miles northward from Northampton. It may be worth while to remark that the railway has its station at Blisworth so inconvenient to the principal town of the county, which should have been a principal station, because of the bitter, resolute, and expensively-continued hostility of the corporation of Northampton to the railway project when it was before Parliament. The corporation, and all the inhabitants who sided with it, have lived to repent their hostility to the railway, and that before they were much older than when the line was made. It is pleasant, however, to see that they gain in wisdom much faster than they grow in years. They are as eager advocates of railway intercourse now as they were hostile opponents to it before. The staple trade of Northampton, which is shoemaking, has been much improved by the railway, even though it did not come to the town. Thus it will be hereafter with many of those who are the bitterest enemies of the extension of trade and the facilities of intercourse between nation and nation. Freedom of intercourse will be carried on in spite of them;

they will reap their share of the general benefit ; and then they will be the most hearty approvers of it.

Thus it will be, that those who now suffer reproach and contumely for their labours in the liberation of commerce, will return to their enemies good for evil.

To be at Northampton, with one's face turned towards Althorp, and one's thoughts turned upon Earl Spencer, it is impossible to forget the question of the corn-laws. The simple honesty, the political integrity, and benevolent nature of Earl Spencer would excite at any time a high interest in the mind of a stranger visiting in his neighbourhood ; and all the more so, if that stranger listened to the repeated and never-ending testimonies of respect and love which the tenantry and their workpeople are ever paying to his Lordship when his name is mentioned by the stranger. And, in addition to that, the interest in the mind of the stranger is heightened, if it is remembered that this amiable nobleman is personally and untiringly engaged in advancing the increase of human comfort, by increasing the first element of comfort, human food ; but how much greater is the interest heightened, when we call to mind that this eminent agriculturist, who led when it was not fashionable to follow, but who is now followed because it is fashionable to be, or to seek to be, good breeders and feeders of cattle; how unspeakably more interesting is it to approach his estate with the recollection that he has declared it to be his decided and well-considered opinion that a free-trade between England and all other nations would not injure agriculture, but would, on the contrary, be for the good of agriculture, and the great good of all England.

I went out of Northampton on the road to Harleston, a village on Lord Spencer's estate, with all those things revolving in my mind. I knew no one in that part of the country, nor did I know if his Lordship was at Althorp. I had rather some reason to believe that he was in London ; but I had no doubt that I should push myself into a right channel by some means or other for seeing his estate.

The village of Harleston is pronounced as if written *Alston*. I had inquired at Northampton if it was a place which was likely to afford me a night's lodging, and, being told there was no doubt of that, I hired a gig, and a man to drive me there and take the gig back ; so I went in the evening, that I might have a walk in the early morning amid the fine old woods, which I was told covered the country about Harleston.

I entered the village by going down a rather steep road, midway by the side of which, facing upwards, stood the inn, or public-house of the village, as if it were looking out for customers, and waiting there to receive them.

Such was my impression while my face was to its face and
we had not yet met. But I was much disappointed to find that
its landlady was not disposed to admit me as a lodger for the
night. I inquired if there was no other house, and there was
none. I asked for the next village, and found that was some
miles off; and when the landlady said I could soon go there in
my gig, I suggested that they might be as unwilling to admit me
there as she was here; and again I pleaded to be allowed to
stay, for she had not said there was no room for me; she only
said that she did not think I could stay there. The man that
drove me knew, however, what string to touch. He intimated
that I was going to Lord Spencer's in the morning on business, and that it was necessary that I should stay in the neighbourhood all night.

The mention of his Lordship's name and residence, and of
business to do there, was enough. She had no objection now,
save a fear that I would not be satisfied with her accommodation; but such as it was I should be welcome to try it. I did
try it; and never was I accommodated with a bed chamber
more delightfully fresh, and fair, and comfortable. I might
have almost formed an opinion that it was too spotless and
perfect to be intended for use, had it not been that my experience in travelling has proved, long ago, that if the most
perfect cleanness, and freshness, and general comfort are to be
found in any bedchamber, that chamber is to be found in the
little village inns of rural England.

Nothing could be more delightful than this. Floral richness adorned the outside and fresh flowers were gathered and
brought within. In the lofty trees that overhung the roof,
blackbirds and throstles, and their musical companions of the
evening, sung to me almost at the very window; and for several hours after they were done, during the whole night indeed,
the nightingales kept up the sweet discourse. I had only to
sleep with their voices in my ears, and dream myself into Elysium. I had only to wake in the morning, and find that to
be in Elysium was no dream. The brilliant sun of four
o'clock in the morning of the 1st of June was out; and the
flowers of June were out with him; and thousands of vocal
birds, from the full-voiced thrushes—the Wilsons of the woods
—to the sparrows that were so happy as not to know what
key to sing in, nor which of them to make most noise; all
these, in such a place, make an awakening out of sleep glorious beyond my power of telling.

But I go too fast. On my arrival there, in the evening, I
walked out to see the village and its neighbourhood; the road
still descended until it came to a clear streamlet, which issued

from the deep shady woods on the left hand, and which, after watering the garden walls and hedges at bottom, went on its way, wandering farther than I could see into the country eastward.

I do not know how many houses the village contains; they can never be seen all at once. With but little stretch of the imagination, one might believe this village to have descended upon the earth from some place more blessed than the earth, and to have brought the beauty of blessedness with it. One might suppose that the more grave and aged houses were sitting quietly in their gardens, while the frolicsome and the young houses had run off into the woods and were hiding there, while others wandered out and scattered themselves to look for them. And if we could speak of smiling cottages as of smiling children, and speak of them peeping from beneath the lofty elms, decked in their roses and twining flowers, looking out to see if the pleased face of a mother was upon them, we might be at no loss to discover that mother—not only that a full-sized mansion looks down upon them from the gentle eminence upon which it sits, as if pleased to see their rosy faces through the trees, but that this mansion on the eminence is, in many respects, a parent to the little cottages below.

I did not, however, turn this way at first, which to have done, would have required me to turn to my left westward out of the public road. I kept on the public road and ascended, going northward, an acclivity upon which the road toiled, similar to that which brought me down to the village on the southern side. Gaining the top of this rise, I at the same time gained an unexpected view of a portion of the village which lay about three hundred yards to my left on the brow of an opposite height, separated from where I stood by a narrow deep valley, the height crowned with lofty towers of green branches, and the valley dotted with gardens and green enclosures, in each enclosure some of those remarkable cattle grazing, the breeding of which distinguishes the House of Spencer.

I say the House of Spencer, for these cattle did not belong to his Lordship, nor was I yet at Althorp Park. The mansion, of which I just now spoke, is that of the Honourable Captain Spencer, brother to his Lordship, and the cattle belonged to the captain.*

The scene before us, from that rise of the road on which I first caught a view of it, is most lovely; and it is most thoroughly English. The chiefest object on the opposite height is the village church, venerable and grey in its old graveyard. Next to it is the parsonage-house, with its bright

---

* The captain has succeeded his lamented brother, and is now Earl Spencer.

windows and slated roof, its shrubberies and its garden, and
its elaborate floweriness. Lower down are barns and stables
and a farmyard, all substantial and new. And all around are
those matchless beasts grazing in the dewy sunset, which help
to make up that most matchless of exhibitions, the London
Christmas Show. But, not being yet put up to be fed at the
stall for Christmas, they are not so loaded with fat as then,
and are consequently more comely and handsome to look upon.

I here turned direct to my left, went down a narrow road,
crossed the streamlet in the hollow, and went up to the churchyard and the church. As is always my custom in a strange
place, I went there to read the epitaphs and the ages of the
dead, and to pay my respects to the church. It may be
fantasy in the eyes of some and superstition in the eyes of
others ; but whichever it may be accounted, I must confess to
it, that I never feel that I have formed a full and fair acquaintance with a village until I have become acquainted with its
graves and its tombstones.

Leaving the church, and keeping on the footpath that led
towards Captain Spencer's mansion, I found myself in the park.
Here there were also cattle grazing ; and such splendid cows
some of them were ! But the cattle, fine as they were, did
not as far surpass the inferior and ordinary runts, such as we
may see in Galloway or Wales, than did the trees of this park
surpass all ordinary trees.

There they stood, each tree towering like a dome, and
spreading out its branches like the roof of a great cathedral.
And, looking along, they seemed in number and in breadth as
if all the cathedrals of Christendom had been collected and
formed into one ; their huge trunks, vast as if they had stood
there in the days of the giants, forming a succession of pillars,
each of a magnitude which would take three or four or more
men to encompass with their outstretched arms. And high
overhead among the millions of leaves there was a solemn
humming, that sounded as if the worship was just dying away
with the closing twilight. And it was a place which infused
into the soul thoughts of solemnity whether the soul desired
them or not.

There was so much of the greatness and the glory of the
Creator present, that the creature was overpowered thereby
with a sense of his own nothingness. And such thoughts
partook still more of devotion when the eye could see and the
mind could understand that all this majesty of nature was not
walled round and separated from the world to make one man
proud that it was all his own, and that nobody else could look
upon it. It was in this park, sheltered by the most magnificent of forest trees, and looking out upon the meadow-sward

that intersected their groups in many parts, that the houses
of the village lay scattered about ; and it was pleasing and
most grateful to the mind to reflect, after being told, that of
the industrious families who inhabited there, no hand was
unemployed, no mouth was unfed.

Finding the night coming on me fast, while I had to return
by paths of which I knew not the intricacies, I turned back,
and, in doing so, forgathered with a man who came down
another road. He was going towards that part of Harleston
where I was to lodge for the night, and offered to conduct me.
I remarked to him that this was a place of most singular
beauty ; and he replied that he had been, in his time, in nearly
every part of England, but he had seen nothing to equal this ;
" and more," said he, " I have seen few people to equal those
who are the owners of this place." Which remark of his led
us into farther conversation, and I found that he was a
mechanic employed in the building of new cottages, which on
all sides of Althorp Park, in several parishes, Earl Spencer was
at that time providing for the labouring population. His
Lordship was pulling down the old ones, not so much for their
inferiority or age, for they were equal and rather superior to
the ordinary class of labourers' houses ; but they were pulled
down, and new ones of a very superior kind were built in their
room, because the old ones did not come up to the class of
dwellings which his Lordship thought the families of working
men should inhabit. But I have here expressed myself errone-
ously. The old houses were not pulled down and new ones
built in their place. The new ones were built first, and then
the old ones were pulled down. But, as I saw these new cottages on various parts of the estate next day, I shall defer
a farther account of them until I describe my proceedings on
the next day.

THE SECOND DAY.

As stated before, the morning of the 1st of June was a
lovely morning. The weather had been long dry, and rain
was looked for, hoped for, and prayed for—prayed for by
those who never prayed for anything else. And in the absence of rain the copious dew was only the more delightful.

It was at that hour when dew is freshest and clearest and
most pleasing to look upon, when it is brilliant as diamonds
and far more precious, the hour of sunrise, that I went out of
the village towards Althorp Park. So far as I remember,
the distance might be a mile from the village to the park
gates. But I went out of the direct way into some fields
where people were beginning, or waiting to begin, to work,
and talked with them.

Here I saw a lad, thirteen or fourteen years old, who was plying himself well at a large hunch of bread. I said to him he would not get through it soon; and asked him how long he thought it would last. "Well," said he, "I cannot tell you how long it will last; all I know about it is, that it will be done too soon." He was sitting on the sunny side of a high thorn hedge, and some other lads of the same age were near him. One of these looked at me as if he saw an old acquaintance, and laughed; I looked at him, and laughed; yet I did not know him. Again he laughed and looked exceedingly familiar, so I laughed once more and looked familiar also. And then we both laughed together, and all the others, old and young, laughed. And we seemed to do so the more vigorously, that no one knew what the other was merry at. Eventually the youngster managed to say, "Don't you know I am one of the boys you gave the money to buy a new bat?" And again he lost himself in mirth, and winked his eyes in the bright sun, and screwed his face about most comically.

And then I called to mind that on the previous evening I had overheard a discourse amongst a number of boys who had been playing at cricket, or some game resembling it, and who, having broken their bat, were holding a little parliament under the hedge, and were discussing how to raise the ways and means to get a new one. They were rather astonished and somewhat pleased to find a mysterious stranger step out and relieve their difficulties.

I passed a space of two hours or more out of one field and into another, and off one farm upon another. And I had much satisfaction in talking with the persons whom I met. For the first time in all my travels I found, in society completely rural, on the estate of an extensive landowner, on the very verge of a nobleman's park, nay, almost in front of his gate, that I moved in a moral atmosphere of free-trade. The farmers spoke freely and unequivocally, and condemned the corn-laws without reserve. The labourers also seemed familiar with the question, and were not afraid to speak about it. Everybody knew Earl Spencer's sentiments on the subject, and everybody had discussed the question of corn-law delusion.

I subsequently discovered that much of this familiarity with the free-trade arguments here and all around the neighbourhood resulted from Lord Spencer's retirement from the Northamptonshire Agricultural Society. It may be remembered that certain of the members of that society intimated their intention to withdraw from it if Lord Spencer continued, he having declared that agriculture would thrive better without the delusive protection which is no protection; and that his Lordship, rather than have the society broken up, which he believed had conferred some benefit on the county, chose to withdraw from it himself. This generous sacrifice of himself for a supposed public good, together with the undoubted fact that he had been persecuted out of a society which he himself had founded and advanced to maturity, by those members of it who never, of their own accord, would have founded nor supported any society for any good public purpose whatever until led to it by such a leader as Lord Spencer; these various circumstances resulted in a general fire-side discussion on the merits of the corn-laws and free-trade. Because the population on the Althorp estate would not submit to see their venerated landlord come out of a society without discussing his merits and the cause of his retirement. They knew it must be a good cause of which he was the friend, and of which at least *some* of the other agriculturists in Northamptonshire should be seen as enemies.

Remarks on the merits of Earl Spencer led to the merits of the general question. His Lordship's tenants are, of course, at liberty to read what papers, or pamphlets, or printed circulars come in their way, without being reported and reproved at head quarters by the agents. They did read. They were enlightened, and they have enlightened others. Thus, though the ungenerous treatment of Lord Spencer is to be regretted for the sake of his Lordship's feelings, it has done great good to the progressive cause of free-trade. In no county in England has any single event done more to advance that cause than has the attempt of the Agricultural Society to persecute its founder and its chief patron, Earl Spencer, done in Northamptonshire.

As I said before, I moved in an atmosphere of free-trade in the vicinity of Althorp Park.

The park does not hold within its bounds such large old timber as I saw in Captain Spencer's mansion on the previous evening, yet the timber is generally large, and the park is picturesque. It seemed to be a mile or rather more across either way, and the house is in the centre, in a hollow. This house contains the most choice and comprehensive library (so I have been told) that belongs to any private individual in England. I saw the library; but, to me, books are not worth looking at if there be no time to read them. I was more interested in his Lordship's pictures, especially the family portraits. And of these, the most interesting were the portraits of Lord Spencer himself. I could conceive nothing more pleasing than to see the infant, the playful child, the youth, the young man from college, the young statesman in Parliament, the grave statesman a leading member of the Government—all following in succession; and then to see them all merged in the fine old English gentleman that had retired from public life, and now walks about at home enjoying the high luxury of doing good to his fellow-creatures in private.

I entered the park by a gate from the Harleston road, and walked by what seemed to be a carriage way. I soon saw cattle grazing; but there was nothing remarkable about any of them. As I subsequently found, they were nearly all bought in from different fairs and markets, and were only to be grazed for the season. There were, as nearly as I can recollect, between fifty and sixty of them. They were in two divisions. With those I saw first there was a boy who was keeping them in a certain part of the park, to allow the grass to get up in another part. The drought had kept the pasture very low, and they deemed it better to let the cattle eat one portion bare, so that another might get up for them to be eaten the week or fortnight following, rather than to have it all bare alike.

After going across the park, and out at the opposite side towards the west, I found that the morning was advancing; and having heard that Lord Spencer was at home, I thought it would be most appropriate to ask leave to go over the estate to look more minutely into things. This leave I intended to apply for from the head steward, Mr Elliot, but he had not then arrived. He lives at a farm about three miles from Althorp. But when I heard that Lord Spencer was at home, I thought it better to address a note to his Lordship.

It is not with every lord I would presume to take such a liberty. But I felt well assured that Earl Spencer would not take it amiss. And I was not mistaken. Yet his Lordship's personal condescension prevents me from writing as particularly here as some might wish me to do, and as otherwise I might have done. Suffice it to say, that though his Lordship was going to London that day, and though business extending over a year had to be transacted with the steward (it being a day of annual reckoning) I had his Lordship's attention for some time, and subsequently that of the steward, to whom his Lordship introduced me with orders that I was to see all the cattle, and everything else that might be of interest. It was now that I heard from Lord Spencer himself that his breeding establishment was not on this estate, but in another county. This was to me some disappointment, as the young cattle and calves were the chief of what I wanted to see.

However, as I have been describing, I may proceed with my progress here; for, being here, I felt an interest in looking over the estate, simply because it was Lord Spencer's.

When we parted from his Lordship, Mr Elliot took me to a district of the park where a number of cattle were grazing, of the most of which he gave me some account; such as saying how old they were, at what fair such a couple were bought, how long they had been grazing, and so forth, none of which particulars I noted down, nor, if I had, would they have been of sufficient interest for publication here.

We went westward, and, by a door in the park wall, which Mr Elliot opened with a key which he took from his pocket, we went out into an avenue of trees, near which we again saw cattle and sheep at grass; but they, I think he said, belonged to a tenant-farmer. Here we had a fine view of the adjacent country, west and north. It was what is called a fine fox-hunting country; that is, bold in its heights and hollows, with high fences, deep ditches, and covered with farmers' crops and farmers' interests. A good fox-hunt is rarely carried out without a very considerable loss to the farmers, on whose fields of wheat newly sown, or newly sprung through the ground, or among whose sheep it takes place; for it cannot be a *goou* fox-hunt if not in an enclosed and cultivated country.

Lord Spencer is too much of a kind neighbour both to poor and rich to deny the rich the privilege of the fox-chase on his estate. Consequently there are some great hunts there, and in the neighbourhood, as I was told.

On this western side of the park we soon came to a village called Brington; and, first of all, we came to its church. Into this we entered. There were workpeople cleaning and repairing it, who, when Lord Spencer's steward entered, came to him for orders, for he seemed to be chief man everywhere, even in the repairs and alterations of the church. When he had given his orders, he shewed me the different tombs and monuments of the Spencer family; for they had been buried here for many generations.

It was in the village of Brington where I saw the first of the new cottages in process of being built on different parts of the estate; they are generally formed so as to have four apartments, besides other conveniences. Some of them, at another village, were built so as one cottage with two or with three apartments should stand between two with more apartments; the outside architecture, a kind of Gothic, being particularly attended to. These were built in groups, and each group had a middle cottage, as it might be, for a widow or two poor women; while on each side dwelt the married people with families. In the largest houses there were two rooms up stairs and two below. The doors were of massive oak, pannelled and polished; the window frames were large and convenient. The people were encouraged to keep all clean inside,

and flowery and weedless without ; for they had flower gardens in front and potato gardens behind.   They had also to
each four houses a bakehouse and a washing-house. They had
pigstyes conveniently removed from the cottage, &c. &c.; and
the rents were to those who paid full rents £2 a-year, but
some poor people had them cheaper, and some had their dwellings altogether free.

They had allotments of land also at a moderate rent ; at
15s., and 20s., and 30s. per acre, according to quality.   The
quantity of ground was regulated in some cases according to
the number of persons in a family.   But these allotments were
mostly all at too great a distance from the cottages to be as
valuable as they should be.   Some of them were a mile, and
some more, and none that I saw were nearer than half a
mile, except at Brampton, (I think that is the name of another of Lord Spencer's villages which I saw,) where the allotments are close to the village.

In one of the new cottages at Brington which we entered I
discovered that the person who inhabited it, an elderly woman,
had only been in the village twelve months, and that she
came from London.   I had some curiosity to know why she
had come from the metropolis to live there, and was informed
she was a midwife.   The want of such a personage had been
felt in the neighbourhood ; so Lord Spencer provided the
people with her services, by giving her a house and garden,
and some portion of an income.   I was not told how much,
and did not inquire.   But this little circumstance is a pleasing instance of the kind respect of Lord Spencer for the poor.

When I had left Mr Elliot, and met another person belonging to the estate, I heard many more proofs of such kindness.
" In fact," said my informant, " Lord Spencer does harm
with his generosity.   When I came to this part of the country first, we had the old poor-law, and to get the labouring
men to work a day's work was beyond my power or the power
of any other employer.   The men just did as they liked, or
did nothing if they liked ; but, after the new poor-law came
into operation, things began to change.   It took some time ;
still they were growing better, and were obliged to work for
their wages.   But his Lordship came to live here, and, after
a while, he just began and spoiled them again.   They came
about him, some really poor and needy, but the greater part
impostors ; or, what is as bad, persons who fall out of work
because they will not work.   Well, on certain days of the
week, his Lordship gives them audience.   There he stands,
twenty, or thirty, or forty people about him.   Some have one
tale of distress, and some another—some true, and some a
parcel of lies.   He pretends to make particular inquiries into

their stories, and does do so, and learns that they have been trying to impose on him. But what of that? He puts his hand in his pocket to every one of them. It is not in his nature to refuse one of them—no, not one of them—who pleads poverty, no matter how undeserving they be. He says they must be needful, or they would not run the risk of telling him such lies! In fact, sir, Lord Spencer has virtually repealed the poor-law, so far as the people about him are concerned."

Some of the Lancashire readers of this paper will recognise a striking similarity in one point of his Lordship's benevolence to that of a late manufacturer remarkable alike for his generosity and his wealth. The gentleman whom I heard relate the anecdote illustrative of that one point says he was one day in company with the benevolent capitalist, when a man of very bad character, known to them both, but who had seen better days, came to beg. In his better days the man had done a deep injury to the manufacturer; he had libelled him and cheated him; but he was relieved with a liberal sum from the benevolent man whom he had injured so much. Observing which, the visitor said, " Mr G., you surely know what a vagabond that is? a libeller, a liar, a swindler, a common cheat, who never did good in his life, and will never try it; if I mistake not, you have suffered by him yourself?" to which Mr G. replied, with some uneasiness of manner, " Yes, yes; he is all that; but then what a dreadful state of poverty he must be in before he would come to beg from *me* ?" And Mr G. turned the conversation into another point as quickly as he could; for, in fact, his benevolence had been excited, and he was glad to get an excuse for his generosity, as if he had done something wrong in letting a third party know that he was benevolent.

That generous and in all respects good man and his brother were the originals of the *Brothers Cheeryble* of Dickens. Mr Dickens says, that for the honour of human nature he is glad to say, that, at least, two of his characters in " Nickleby" were not fictitious; and that these were the two brothers, who had done more good in real life than would be readily believed in fiction.

Having heard many anecdotes of the generous doings of these two brothers in their real characters, there appeared to me a most pleasing resemblance to their actions in those of Lord Spencer. His Lordship seemed to be under the necessity of getting excuses for himself even to his own servants for his benevolence to those who did not deserve it. And all this made me think the more highly of his Lordship, even though his generosity might have had the effect which my friend attributed to it, of virtually repealing the poor-law.

Having gone over different parts of the estate, first with one guide and then with another, I went to the farm at which Mr Elliot lived. Here were three fine animals put up to feed, each in a box, for the London Christmas Show. And, instead of so many beasts as his Lordship has been in the habit of sending to the show, these will be all he will send this year. Owing to the scarcity of grass at that time other cattle were to be put up to feed on oil-cake, corn, &c., but they were not of a class admissible at the show.

His Lordship has also begun the breeding of race-horses at Althorp; but I am not aware of anything connected therewith that deserves notice. I shall therefore proceed to another topic.

———

OF THE OCCUPANCY AND CULTIVATION OF THE FARMS.

Earl Spencer still keeps up the tenancy-at-will system on his estate. This is all but universal in Northamptonshire. I think it is much to be regretted that his Lordship does not break through this, for the sake of public example, if for nothing else. No doubt his tenants are safe enough. And, if all landlords were to be Spencers in this and every other generation, there would be no need of leases. Neither if all men were honest would there be any need of laws. But there is a need for laws, and there is a need for leases. His Lordship and some of his tenantry are first-rate breeders and feeders of stock; they are, in fact, eminent graziers. They stand much higher in that respect than as cultivators. Now it is in cultivating crops where the benefit of leases is most apparent. From what I heard, I can believe that great advances have been made there in cultivation within these few years; but there is, unquestionably, much to do yet; and the more so, as the culture of crops and the feeding of cattle must go hand in hand, if the highest rate of profit is to be extracted from the land.

There is a farm in that part of the country, but not on Lord Spencer's estate, which I shall here notice. It is the farm on which is situate the battle-field of Naseby. A Scotchman has found his way to it, and is now growing very fine wheat on the ground where Prince Rupert wheeled round to give Fairfax battle, and where Fairfax, and Cromwell, and Ireton overthrew the royal troops as a preliminary to the overthrow of the throne. This farmer has been draining and enclosing, and ploughing and sowing, and reaping on that ground, devoting it to better purposes than that of war. He has been increasing human happiness, not diminishing human life. Yet, from the day that the rebels and royalists slew each other on it up to a recent period, that ground, and much of North-amptonshire, has remained the same. Here is its description by a writer thirty years ago :—

"The open field is extensive, and in as backward a state as it could be in Charles I.'s time, when the fatal battle was fought. The lower parts are moist, rough grass, with furze, rushes, and fern abounding; the rest of the field a strong, brown, deep loam, in the usual bean and wheat culture; pasture enclosures near the village, and a good many cows kept. The parish is as much in a state of nature as anything I have seen in the country. The avenues across the field are zigzag, as chance has directed, with hollows and sloughs unfilled, except with mire. The village contains a good many dwelling-houses and other buildings, all of which I observed built with mud and covered with thatch, except the church and two dwellings. The walls of many of the houses were apparently shivering under the pressure, and seemed to indicate that a small weight or force additional would convert them and their contents into a ruinous heap. Yet neither the soil nor the aspect are by any means contemptible."

The appearance of this place is much altered now; but many parts of Northamptonshire have remained the same as in the days of Charles I., even unto this day. The soil is generally good; for grazing it is exceedingly good. But agriculturists have established the fact elsewhere, that even the best grazing land would be more profitable if cultivated. Of course the breeding of cattle and sheep requires grazing farms; but the feeding of them is most decidedly obtained with the largest profit by cultivating crops, by economizing food, and by saving all the manures that can be made while feeding the cattle.

On Lord Spencer's farm at Brampton this is partly attended to; and on some other farms a movement is made in this direction. Still, with excellent soil, the farmers of this county are very profitlessly employed, both for themselves and landlords; and I do not expect it will be much otherwise with them until a new spirit is infused by giving them leases of their farms.

I found the rent of good land to be from 20s. to 30s. an acre, if not used for garden ground nor nurseries in the immediate vicinity of a town. Wages 9s. and 10s. a-week, except at Lord Spencer's, where they generally ran about 2s. a-week higher. I should say, however, that 10s. a-week is fully the average of that part of the country.

Some people do not attach the same importance to the improvement of the dwellings of the poor that I do; but they have not, perhaps, attended so much to the subject. A good cottage, a good garden, and a tasteful adornment with flowers, is worth all the county police for making people stay at home and cultivate good behaviour. It was intimated to me that the expense of building Lord Spencer's cottages was too great for general imitation. I did not ascertain what the expense was; but I understood the steward to say that L.2 : 10s. of annual rent would not pay the expense. This I can well believe. But, in most counties, the meanest hovels are rented as high as that. In most of the wretched villages of Dorsetshire, for instance, where the traveller sees the worst of houses and the poorest of labourers, the cottage rents are L.3 and L.4 a-year, with not a yard of garden ground.

But I hold that, apart from the mere expense of building, there is another question of expense; that is, of keeping a demoralized population in the old hovels; the expense of shifting them alternately from their hovels to the prisons or to the workhouses. With good gardens and allotments for the labourers, according to the size of their families, that they may have an anchor, as I may say, to hold on by; with good cottages, that they may have pride and pleasure in their homes, we would soon see a saving of expense and of loss to both farmers and landlords in prisons and workhouses.

I just now spoke of Dorsetshire as containing the worst houses and the poorest population. The poorest population is correct enough; but on calling to mind that there is on the other extremity of England a county called Northumberland, where but a few years ago the houses were worse than ever they have been in Dorsetshire, I must retract the superlative degree of badness from Dorset, the more so as, on many estates, the Northumberland hinds' houses are not changed one whit, save to the worse, up to this very day of writing.

But even where they have been building new houses, both in Northumberland and in the neighbouring counties of Scotland, particularly Berwickshire, they have only built mere sheds. On the estates of the princely Duke of Buccleuch in Dumfriesshire, new houses for the farming men have been built recently, and they have neither ceiling nor lofting of any kind. Neither are they plastered inside; neither have they any partitions, nor inside doors, nor cupboards, nor conveniences for any purpose whatever. There is nothing but the bare walls, about twenty-four feet long and twelve feet wide, inside measure, and seven feet high; one door in front, and a little square window. The walls are built of stone and mortar, and, as said before, are not plastered. Into that shed, with the bare roof above their heads, the Scotch hind and his family are crammed, men and women, young and old. And these are the houses which are the *new* dwellings of the hinds on the Duke of Buccleuch's farms.

Though Lord Spencer should do nothing more than he has already done, agriculture is deeply indebted to him for his advances in the breeding of cattle ; and humanity is not less indebted to him for his advances in the moral science of advancing the comforts and the virtues of the labourers.

Let us hope that his Lordship will take the lead in his county in improving the condition of the farmers and their style of cultivation, by reforming the tenures of the farms. Landlords need his example.

LETTERS FROM WILTSHIRE IN THE SUMMER OF 1845.

LETTER I.

Meeting of Labourers at Upavon.

THE first who spoke was David Keele, an elderly man, who was chairman on the occasion. I did not arrive in time to hear him address the meeting. Mr Westell, a schoolmaster, from Marlborough, was speaking when I arrived ; and with him I afterwards found David Keele, and had some conversation with him. He seemed to be a sensible man of retiring manners. He is said to be a man of strict moral character, and a good labourer. He had once been at a labourers' meeting on the corn-law question in another village some months ago, and in consequence was discharged from his employment. He has been taken into work again. He was asked to come and be chairman at the Upavon meeting, as it was feared no labourer there would dare to make himself so prominent. And this was supposed, because twelve months ago the head agent of an estate there had said, in the name of himself and master, that no Anti-Corn-Law meeting should ever be held in Upavon ; and, further, because it was threatened that this very meeting should be prevented. A consultation among the farmers and gentry was held, however, on the previous Saturday, and it was then resolved to let this take its course, and not to interfere with it.

When I got there, I saw a temporary stage raised against the gable of a cottage, and facing to an open space of ground in the centre of the village. A very large tree—elm, if I remember rightly—prodigious in trunk and branches, overshadowed the space ; and underneath it, and from it up to the cottage gable, there were at least one thousand men, women, and children standing. The men constituted about two-thirds of the whole, and the greater part were in smock-frocks or fustian coats, just as they had come from their work. Two policemen stood in one part of the crowd, and two more stood singly. David Keele sat on the little stage, wearing a clean white smock ; but the crowd in front made it difficult for me to see him. The persons who had invited him to the meeting had undertaken to his wife that they would bring him safe home. She said she did not care how far he went out of her sight to do good, as she hoped the meeting was to do good ; but it would be the end of her if anything happened to him.

His opening address was as follows—a reporter from the *Wiltshire Independent* being present to report :—

" He said he was glad to see so many of his fellow-labourers assembled. He wished it to be understood that it was not their intention to break the laws of the country, for whatever laws were made by their legislators they were bound to obey, as far as they could according to the dictates of their consciences. Neither did he wish them to break the laws of their masters; it was their duty to follow their employment diligently, and if their masters did not give them sufficient wages to support their families, that was no reason why they should leave their employment. If John, or Thomas, or Harry steals my shirt, that is no reason why I should steal his. They were met to speak of those arbitrary laws called the corn-laws ;. and he would ask their opponents, or any reasonable man, if the legislature issued a law which did not work according to just expectation, whether they had not a right to petition for its repeal ? (Hear, hear.) It was the law of free-trade they were met to advocate—a law which would be every way beneficial to them, to their wives, and to their families. (Hear, hear.) It was very evident that distress existed among the labouring population ; he knew it by experience, and he doubted not many of them did also. (Cries of ' Yes, yes, we feel it.') There is many a man who goes out to work with a little bit of bread, and after working all day, returns home to potatoes and salt. (' We don't get half enough of that.') Was it not right, then, that they should seek out for something better ? The poor man had an equal right with the rich to attempt this, and to send his petitions to Parliament, to endeavour to get his grievances redressed. They would recollect the case of the four lepers, whom they read of in the Bible, that sat in the gate. They said, ' If we sit here we shall die, and if we go to the Assyrians perhaps they will save us alive ; and if they kill us, we shall but die.' You and I (said Keele) are in the case of starvation, (cries of ' Hear, hear,' and ' That's true enough',) and if we remain quiet much longer, starved we shall be. If we petition Parliament, it is more than a peradventure that we shall be heard ; and if we are not, we can but starve. (Cheers.) Our opponents, in my part of the country, serve the people like as the carters used to do the ploughboys when I was a boy. They would give the boys the whip, and threaten that they would give it them again if they told their parents ; and so it went on from day to day. The case is the same with the labourers. Your masters say, If you come forward to tell your case you shall be turned out of employment, (Hear, hear,) and thus they keep you in fear ; and you will never be better as long as you are kept down in this way. But if you come forward boldly and tell your case, you can't make it worse. (' That's true.') If the ploughboy had told his father of the carter, the carter would have been punished, and that is what he was afraid of. You are prevented coming forward by the arbitrary conduct of your opponents, (Hear, hear,) but fear not their frowns ; they are in the hands of the Lord, and can only go so far as he permits. Always remember, however, that whatever law is issued by the Legislature we are bound to obey ; whoever resists the powers that be resists the ordinances of God. It is the arbitrary corn-law that has done all the mischief ; and we believe free-trade will be beneficial to ourselves and families. (Loud cheers.)"

After this Mr Westell spoke, and then William Perry, a labourer from Charlton, a village distant about a mile and a half, offered to make a statement. Perry, as I have since ascertained, is a man of the best moral character, a steady good labourer, and deeply imbued with a sense of religion. He is, I think, a Baptist, but of that I am not sure, as I did not ask him. But having heard him speak reverentially of his hopes and trust being in God, I mentioned it to some of his neighbours, and they told me that he was a man of strict piety, who " never eat a mouthful of bread without asking a blessing on it ;" who " never went to bed at night without kneeling down by the bed of his children to pray." I had a lengthened conversation with him and some of his neighbours two days after the meeting, but I then confined the subject to their social condition.

Perry appeared to me to be about 35 years of age. He was of middling stature, wore a straw hat, red neckerchief, and a fustian coat. The following was his address, as reported ; and, having myself heard it, I think it is fairly reported, except, perhaps, that it does not convey to the reader that he was rather agitated at first, and hesitated so much as to make

some of his neighbours call, " Don't be afeared to speak,
William." It was to this that he alluded in saying that he
had no reason to be afraid to speak. The report proceeds
thus :—

"William Perry, a labourer, living at Charlton, then said he
was come forward to speak to his fellow labourers, and he had
no reason to be ashamed to speak before any man. He had five
children, the eldest ten years of age, the others of the age of
8, 6, 4, and 3. He had 7s. per week to maintain his family.
If any person present could tell him how to manage this for
all to have enough he should be glad. There were 21 meals
to be provided out of 1s., leaving no provision for clothes, firing, candles, and soap ! When he came home, two or three of
the children were generally going to bed, but when he came
in, they began crying, 'Father, bring me up a piece of bread.'
He had often heard this cry during the winter, and even within the last week. What could he do ?—he had no bread to
give them. Then there was rent and shoes to be paid for at
Michaelmas. How could he do this in an honest manner?
His desire was to live honestly, in a godly way, but he could
not do it. Perhaps he met a man to whom he owed money ;
of course he did not like to meet him ; these were not the
feelings of an honest man ; but what could he do ? If there
were not some good and charitable people in the country he
should be starved. (Voices—' The same here,' and ' 'Tis too
true.') He was thankful God had spared him and his family
to the present moment. This day he had walked three miles
and a half to his work. He took a bit of bread with him, and
had a drink of water ; and had a little when he got home.
(' We all know that's true.' A voice—' What makes you
tremble so ?') If, said Perry, I had been home to a good supper and a quart of good ale, I should not tremble. He wished
every labouring man to have three or four acres of land at the
same rent as the farmers gave. They would pay this, and
gladly. (Loud cheers, and cries of ' Yes, yes ; and we would
give a little more than that.') Yes, said Perry, we don't mind
10s. an acre more. (This speech was received with loud marks
of applause, and repeated confirmations of the truth of the
statements contained in it.)"

Next came a labourer, also of Charlton, named Ozias Seeley.
His address is not reported, nor was it easy to do so, as it was
rather long, and not very well connected. It took well with his
hearers, who understood the topics introduced. This man, it
seems, some years ago was a widower, with a family of children.
He then married a widow and children ; and now they had a
third family, in all seventeen children, eight of whom were, dur-

ing the winter dependent on his wages for support. His address was a mixture of the pathetic and ludicrous. He told of how he had one night in the previous week had only two potatoes in the house, and how eight children "scrambled" for them for supper over forms, stools, &c.

Here I may remark that, owing to the unmarried men receiving the inferior wages of 3s. a-week in winter and only 4s. and 5s. in summer; and, also, as they are most commonly sent to the workhouse to prevent men with families being sent there, they strive to get married as soon as they can; and, if a young man finds a widow with children willing to have him, he involves himself eagerly with a ready-made family, that he may not be compelled to go again to the workhouse. Moreover, the inferior payment of the young men renders a provision for marriage by economy and good conduct utterly out of the question. Hence they rush into marriage without furniture, or a lodging, or clothes, or without any hope but that of soon having a family, which will compel the farmers to give them employment.

All the worst features of the old poor-law are retained here and the best banished. At the meeting complaint was made of the parish-road system common here, of men getting relief from the parish by being sent to work at under wages.

Several little incidents attracted my attention. One of the speakers was telling the labourers that they must *tell* their masters this and they must *tell* their masters that. A labourer called out, "But how be we? Masters never gives us a chance to speak to them." This was subsequently explained to me to mean that some of the farmers always communicated through the bailiff with their men; never spoke to them themselves. Again, there was a point made by one of the speakers, which seemed to be well understood, about "pitting potatoes," to keep them until required. On inquiry I found this to refer to a farmer who had said that he did with his labourers as he did with his potatoes: he did not keep all the potatoes out for use every day; and he did not, like some farmers, try to find work for the men all the year round. When he did not need them he put them in the workhouse until they were needed.

All such topics as had bitterness in them against certain local ruling powers were warmly welcomed; and I could not help feeling, and also saying, that I thought such topics were most improperly dwelt upon by some of the speakers.

I was glad to hear that the bulk of the men assembled gave earnest and loud shouts of " No, no !" when they were asked

if they would ever again submit to be marched into Devizes
at an election to drown the voices of any of the candidates.
It seems that from this very place, at the last Devizes election, more than a thousand men, many of them those comprising the Upavon meeting, were paid a day's wages and
supplied with beer to go into Devizes to make such a noise
when the free-trade candidate or any of his friends offered to
speak as to completely prevent him or them from being heard.
They did this successfully, being marshalled and led on, and
signalled to when to make a noise and when not, by the very
agent and gentlemen near Upavon who threatened to prevent
them from holding this meeting, and from making their
grievances heard.

I saw a labourer the other day in the village of Charlton
eating a rhubarb pudding. He kindly offered me a piece of
it, which I declined. He again offered it, saying, " It be
made of good flour and good rhubarb; I grow the rhubarb
myself. The only thing as be against it is the want of sugar.
Rhubarb want a good bit of sugar to make it sweet; and
sugar be terrible hard to get by the like of we."

" You were one of the band of men," I said to him, " who
went last year to Devizes to prevent the free-traders from
being heard at the election; now, do you know that you
prevented those men from being heard who would have told
you how you might get sugar to your rhubarb puddings, and
you did all you could to prevent them from getting sugar
plentiful and cheap for you and such as you. Do you know
that ?"

" Why, you see," said the man, " it was not of our doing,
as you may say ; we was forced to it like. We had nobody
to tell us what was right. And they said Mr Sotheron was a
good sort of gentleman, and we was all to help him."

" Well," said I, " what would you have thought if a number
of men had been brought to the Upavon meeting last night,
paid a day's wages, and furnished with beer, to hollo and
make a noise to drown the voices of such honest men as
William Perry from being heard? Would you not have
thought that those who did so were afraid to hear the truth,
and afraid to let you who listened hear the truth ?"

" Ah !" said the man, " we been told many times since the
election that we did terribly bad to go there. They said we
made terrible fools of ourselves."

This man's remark relative to Mr Sotheron, one of the
county members, is, I believe, well founded. That gentleman
is highly spoken of as a kind-hearted, good man, and as such

he must surely disapprove of the means taken to stifle all discussion upon the momentous question which gave that election all its importance.

LETTER II.

It does not follow that every poor man down here is poor despite his efforts to the contrary. Some are quite willing to shift on any way rather than work. One of these spoke rather candidly to me. He said, "What we wants, master, is victuals and drink, and a little work—ever so little work." The listeners exclaimed, "That be just your fit."

The land about Charlton is the property of Lord Normanton, so remarkable for his game-preserves thirty miles further down the country. He has not had this estate long, and there is no game preserved on it. I asked some men if there was, and they said no, they wished there was. They said they would not be so hard run up for victuals then. "But the gaol," said I; "you might be caught and sent to gaol?"— "Well," they replied, "the gaol itself ben't so bad as the workhouse; and better do anything than starve."

Having ascertained that William Perry was a man of good character, I took occasion to see him and some others, to hear from their own lips an account of their income, expenditure, &c.

First I went to Perry's house. This was on the day after the meeting, at about twelve o'clock. Perry, being with other five men at a distant part of the farm mowing, did not come home to dinner. They had bread and cheese and a bottle of ale (small beer) with them. It must be always borne in mind that in Wiltshire and the west the liquors which in London are called strong ale are called beer; and the small beer or table beer of London is ale in Wiltshire. Thus Perry in his address, speaking of his desire to have a "quart of good ale" to his supper, meant a quart of good small beer.

I saw his wife and some of his children. She told me that Mr W. the farmer for whom Perry worked, had been to her in the morning, and complained that her husband should have gone to the meeting on the previous night. And then asked if she meant to say that she and her family were badly off? She told him yes; that there were seven of them—the eldest child only ten years old, and that a girl—who could not go out to do anything; and they had only 7s. a-week to pay house rent and get food and clothes.

Mr W. then reminded her that she herself might have been at out-field work when she did not go. The woman told me that she replied that she was, with so many young children, not always able to go out to work in the fields. Whereupon Mr W. told her that she must go out that afternoon; that he needed hands to the hay; and that, since they complained of poverty, she must go out and work or her husband must leave his employment. He then repeated what he had before said, that " he wished he could only find out which of his men it was that spoke first at the meeting; he would find means to make them regret it."

The woman told me this; and subsequently Perry himself. And both he and his neighbours said that, had any of them gone to the meeting prepared to tell their grievances, all might have done so, and more would have done so than did. They said it could do them no harm publishing what had occurred; they thought they were as bad as they could be.

Perry's wife was accordingly out at work in the afternoon. He and the five other men were mowing vetches—the clover of last year having failed for hay this year, Mr W. was making hay of the vetches. The men told me that when they asked how much an acre they were to have, he said 1s. 6d. They said they could not do it at that; and at last they went to work without any bargain. They said they would try to get 2s. per acre if they could, but perhaps he would only give them 1s. 6d.

This is one of Lord Normanton's farms. This tenant has not been long in occupation of it. He manages the land much better than some of the farmers near him. He may pay low wages—yet not lower than others; but he employs everybody he can get at this season of the year in keeping the farm clear and orderly. His crops look splendid. If anything is what it should not be, the wheat is too thick. It seems as if it would suffocat itself. Thick sowing, I understand, is common thereabout; but it is surely a great loss both of seed and of crop.

The chalky downs which rise above the village have rich crops of fine dark-bladed wheat upon them. Mr W.'s farm extends between three and four miles into Salisbury Plain. A portion of it on the plain was broken up two or three years ago, and has borne heavy crops every year since. Last year the crop was of the prodigious magnitude of fifteen and sixteen sacks of wheat to the acre, and the wheat, as also the straw, of superior quality.

Talking of this, the men who reaped it said they had to walk three and a half miles out to the downs in the morning, and the same back at night, and reaped that prodigiously heavy crop at 8s. per acre.

If any of these statements are incorrect I shall be glad to

publish a correction from Mr W. himself. But I believe them to be correct ; and, moreover, when he and his neighbours do all they can to prohibit inquiry and stifle complaints, and still ask the public for the thing called "protection" to themselves, they must allow us to publish such statements as we find presented to us.

One great grievance of the labourers is, that there being such large farms, and consequently so few farmers, two or three of the latter rule a whole parish. If a man gives the slightest offence to his master he is paid away, and a message is sent to the other farmers not to employ him ; and he is not employed save at hay time or harvest, when they cannot do without him.

If large farms are to continue and the corn-law also ; or rather, if the smaller farms are to be swallowed up by the larger ones, as is yearly the case now, what do the farmers expect to do with their families ? They cannot get farms to their sons, nor get farming husbands to all their daughters. Must they not go into trade? or follow some profession ? Whether has the farmer with 1000 acres and a large family most interest in the corn-law, which, in seasons like the last winter, and spring, starves his stock, or in a fine flourishing trade which will afford outlets for his family ?

Men of fewer years than forty have worked in the parish of Charlton when there were six farmers in it ; and a man still living there remembers when there were fifteen farmers. Now there are only two ; and now the labourers are worse off and fewer of them employed than at any former time.

LETTER III.

Diseased Meat sent to London—Causes thereof.

July 5, 1845.

In one of the many villages which occupy the fertile valleys beskirting the great range of sheepwalks known as Salisbury Plain, I met a person a few days ago, who, in the first three minutes of our conversation, told me that he was a general dealer in sheep, cows, pigs, and any other sort of animals that offered a fair chance of profit. And, as a return for this information, he at once demanded to know what I was, who I was, and where I came from. I told him I had come from London ; but had not time to say more, when he asked if I knew a certain salesman in London whom he named. I said no. Upon which he rejoined, " It be well you ben't known to he ; he'd a done ye as he have done me."

Starting upon this topic, he went on to tell how he had sent some lots of sheep to London for sale, and how this salesman had alleged that they did not fetch more money than paid the expense of transit and the commission for selling them. He did not, however, tell me all the facts of these transactions; and, as they seemed to me to be of public interest, I made further inquiries. The result of the inquiries shewed the case to be as follows:—

That all the sheep were diseased; that some of the lots were so bad that the salesman dared not expose them in Smithfield market; that they were not even taken into London as live animals; but were sold and killed somewhere in the suburbs, and taken into town in the carcase, and there sold at a low price in some of the low districts, where filth and fever and poverty associate with the meanest kinds of food.

I farther found that, though at all times the dealers in diseased meat in London can get supplies from dealers of the same stamp in the country to some extent, the supply of carrion has been this year very large, particularly from Dorset, Hants, Surry, and Sussex.

The dealer with whom I was first in conversation was by no means the only one in his district of six or eight miles; but even he had during this spring sent such large supplies of the famished, the diseased, and the dying—sometimes the dead—that his salesman at last found them unsaleable save as absolute carrion, and that therefore he could not return any payment for them.

Coming over the extensive sheepwalks, which extend from the farm-land in the valleys rearwards upon Salisbury Plain, I had ample demonstration that the flocks were in a pitiable state. I saw them in that district before some of them were clipped, and all the unclipped ones—the ewes more especially—wore ragged and ill-fleeced; while perhaps six out of every score had bare spots on them from which the wool had literally dropped off. And again the flocks that were clipped showed bare, scraggy carcases, painful to look upon.

And this was the case, though the downs were greener and in finer condition (so the shepherds told me) than they had been for some years. The starvation had been in the winter and spring, and its effect promised to last not only throughout the summer, but into succeeding years. First, because the condition of the breeding flocks, as breeders, was deteriorated. Secondly, because the cows and farm-yard stock had been robbed of their hay and straw to keep the flocks alive, by which means the cultivated fields were defrauded of manure which should have been made in the farm-yard. And, finally, because many farmers had been paying more cash for hay than was actually their own, to keep the flocks alive ; by which means they are crippled, and will be so for a considerable time to come, in all their movements—marred in many of their designs.

All of which are the results of that "protection to agriculture," which only intends to restrict the supply of human food, but which does so by restricting the supply of sheep, and cow, and swine, and horse food as well.

LETTER IV.

Fallacies about the Price of Hay.—The Isle of Wight.

In continuation of the foregoing subject I may draw notice to one of the reasons urged at a meeting in the Isle of Wight, the other day, why there should not be a railway in that island. As to the propriety or impropriety of an Isle of Wight railway I know nothing and care nothing. Were I resident there I might, if a despiser of trade and tradesmen, be one of the objectors to the intrusion of railways into that place of quiet retreat. I allude to the matter only because of the statement made by Colonel Harcourt to the farmers present at the meeting, urging them, for the sake of the high prices of hay and corn, not to favour the introduction of the railway. The colonel goes on the old fallacy that high prices and scarcity are the best for farmers. At the present time the Hampshire farmers will not believe that doctrine as regards hay. The colonel is thus reported :—

"He said that, for the last twelve months, he had paid L.6 and L.7 for a load of hay, and L.5 or L.6 for a load of straw, while the prices were only half that in the London market. Would the farmers wish to see their prices reduced so low as that ? If so, they should vote for the railway ?"

The colonel is not correct in saying "the prices were only half that in the London market." The prices, according to quality and kind, have ruled in London, from L.4 : 10s. to L.6. But the matter of fact can answer for itself ; it is the inference which the colonel draws from the alleged difference in the prices of hay in London and in the Isle of Wight that I write of. The Wight is a part of Hampshire, and partakes in almost all things of the fate of Hampshire. It has some rich meadows, producing, says a "Statistical Description," from "one to twelve tons of hay per acre." The other crops for cattle and sheep feeding are "clover, turnips, vetches, ryegrass, and trefoil." The same authority says, "The chief grains cultivated are wheat, barley, oats, peas, and beans. The wheat produced in the southern parts is about twenty-four bushels per acre, and in the northern about eighteen bushels. The

production of barley per acre is averaged at thirty bushels
and oats at thirty-five bushels." And then it is stated that
the island produces considerably more than its consumption.
" The downs," continues the statist, " stretching across the
island, furnish excellent pasturage for sheep, the number fed
thereon being computed at 47,000, sending 5000 lambs annually
to the London market."

In all these respects the Isle of Wight is much the same
as the rest of Hampshire. There may be a difference in the
size of the farms. In the middle and northern parts of Hampshire the farms are very large, running from 1000 to 2000 acres
of arable land. In the Isle of Wight they are from 100 to
500 acres, a few being 800. But the condition of the farmers,
their soils, products, and style of cultivation, are similar
throughout the whole of that great county. And, taking it
as a whole, its farmers have paid and are paying a fearful
penalty in the deteriorated condition of their flocks and cattle
for the fancied advantages of the price of hay being L.6 and
L.7 per load. Low as the condition of stock is in Wiltshire,
from farm-yard famine, and from that " protection" to the farmer which locks his gates against foreign provender, cheap and
profitable for his unfed sheep and pigs and cattle, the condition
of stock is still lower in parts of Hampshire. I went over some
farms the other day in Hampshire, where sheep and cattle have
died, and are still dying. One farmer, with a flock of 1200
sheep, assured me that his loss this year upon that flock—
to say nothing of the ultimate loss arising from the absence of
profit—but his absolute loss up to clipping time, inclusive of
deficient wool, was equal to one year's rent. His rent, I was
informed, was about L.800 per annum. Now this farmer did
not buy hay; he made his own last out as best he could. He
did not buy it, simply because it was L.6 per load.

So much for the statement addressed to the farmers in
opposition to the Isle of Wight railway, that those of them
who wanted hay reduced from L.6 and L.7 per load to " half
of that sum, the price in London," might vote for the railway.

Here, perhaps, I should drop this part of the subject ; but
it occurs to me that a few more remarks, suggested by Colonel
Harcourt's opposition to the railway, may not be misplaced.

He either meant that the railway would displace the use of
horses in the Wight, and so reduce the consumption and the
price of hay, or that hay was to be brought into the island
to make it more plentiful and cheap. This last the railway
could not by any possibility do, as it is confined to the island
itself. He must have meant that horses would be displaced.
But if this argument were sound, hay should have been cheap

all through Hampshire and Wilts, the South Western line being on one side and the Great Western on the other, instead of which, though many coaches have ceased to run through such towns as Andover, Basingstoke, Salisbury, and Winchester, hay has been as high-priced there as in the Isle of Wight.

What the inference to be drawn from that article being but half the price in London that it is in the Wight—supposing the assertion to have been true, which it is not—is by no means clear. If it is meant that there are fewer horses in London now than formerly, because of railways, to consume hay, and that therefore it is cheap, the colonel is in a deep delusion ; the number of horses in London is vastly increased every year. At the present time this number exceeds that of any former year. So in many other towns connected with railways.

But the question at issue between us and such gentlemen as Colonel Harcourt, who says it is good for the farmers to have hay at L.6 and L.7 per load, is simply whether it be good or not to have it at that price. The statements published in this paper last week and this week may be sufficient at present to prove that the scarcity and dearness of hay do service to nobody, but much mischief.

LETTER V.
Salisbury Plain.

It is far from being correct to call the extensive region of Salisbury Plain " waste land." All the dells and valleys which intersect it are cultivated. But even the higher levels which are not under cultivation are not waste. At this season of the year the beautiful herbage of these downs is most delightful. The wild thyme variegates the green grass, and both are kept down short and soft, as if ten or fifteen miles of country were covered with a soft carpet. The freshness of the herbage is alike sweet and nourishing to the native sheep and seductive to the loitering stranger. At no very distant time the " plain" extended from Winchester in the east to Salisbury, twenty-four miles ; from Salisbury to Dorchester and Weymouth, west and south-west, twenty-two and twenty-eight miles. The breadth from north to south was about thirty to thirty-five miles. But this great district was not a uniform plain. It is intersected in all directions by hollows, called " bournes," with streams in them, and several hollows that have no regular streams, but through which there sometimes come torrents of water. A village called Shrewton, situated in one of these waterless bournes, was visited with a sudden flood a few years ago, and almost all swept away. It stands in the hollow of a wide though shallow bason, into which the rain poured and the melting snow accumulated; and out of which the rain made egress by swelling up to the cottages of Shrewton, into the doors, into the windows, floating the furniture, drowning, or threatening to drown, people in their beds, if they would not get up to the lofts and upon the rafters; and then, when it got them there, undermining the walls and hurling them down into universal wreck, daring the outlookers on the high ground to bring in the heavy waggons and horses to the rescue. It was a terrible catastrophe; and maimed creatures who still survive are witnesses, yet they say they cannot tell—no, they shake their heads and say tongue cannot tell—how awful it was.

There is some fine rich land here under cultivation. The farmers are few, the hands employed few, wages low—seven shillings per week—and the farms very large: one person occupies 4000 acres.

Many people who never saw Salisbury Plain have heard of its dreariness to travellers; its cutting winds; its cold drizzling rain; its killing of the weary-footed and wrapping them in winding sheets of snow; its slaying man by the hands of man—the robbed by the robber—and leaving to solitary crows the unburied flesh for which it could not even afford burial. Travellers have told stories of Salisbury Plain until the listeners have shivered with thoughts of cold before the warmest fires, and crouched together for fear in the bravest companies.

And travellers, and those who tell their tales, may be right in all such dismal reminiscences; but it is not always gloomy on Salisbury Plain. I came over it from the direction of Devizes towards Salisbury, not by the public road, but on the untracked greenness, on the carpet of grassy velvet and wild thyme, nearly twenty miles in length, which, for its beauty and the fresh air upon it, and the odour that filled the air, one might imagine had been spread on that high ground —the level nearest heaven—for angels to tread upon. It was a warm day in June. Occasional divergencies to the brow of the high levels enabled me to look down upon the haymakers in the meadows and farm-fields below, and upon the corn-fields full of growth, and the villages in endless succession in the valleys, and the shady trees that obscured the villages; and the church steeples which at every mile or less reached, some of them could hardly reach, above the trees; and upon the little river which threaded its way through the clustering cottages and trees, and round the village churches, and behind the graveyards out of sight, as if it had found the dead there, and had gone with them to eternity. It was a day upon which the village bells were rung in honour of the Queen of England; in honour of that day when flowery June gave to England a young Queen.

Up came the tinkling sounds from the steeples among the trees, through the cawing rooks, across the meadows, and over the haymakers; not upon the breeze, for there was no breeze, June had no breath that day to come up the steep hill-sides; in the haymaking meadows below and in the gardens it was more than she could do to give breath to the hard workers and the idle loiterers; still the merry sound of bells came up and went over the broad downs, until they died away in shepherd's ears, telling them to sleep on in the warm sun. This was June, and this was England.

How easy to fancy and persuade one's self to believe that it is here that true happiness is to be found on earth, if earth has happiness at all! The clear blue sky above; the rich green fields below; the village churches with their bells.; the village cottages with their blowing roses clinging to the walls; wells of pure spring-water issuing from below the chalky hills, and the meandering rivulet in the meadows; the meadows with cows upon them, the cows giving the richest of milk, and the milk yielding the sweetest of butter. How easy, sitting on the cool elevation of the grassy downs, to be poetical about the new-mown hay, its odour scenting the breath of June; and the hedges encircling the fields bestudded and sweetened with honeysuckles and enlivened with the songs of birds!

But look at those mowers—William Perry is one of them. He is not in a worse condition than others; he is in a better condition than many, for he is a sober and industrious, hardworking man. He goes home to yonder cottage with the flowery front. He has but 7s. per week, pays a shilling for rent, a shilling for fuel, and has five children and their mother to supply with food and clothing, and with the requisites always wanted to mend clothing with the remainder. Having five children under ten years of age, he has, or fancies he has, a right by the poor law to relief for one of them. He applies for that relief, (he did so last winter,) and is told, after some demurring, that he may send one of them into the workhouse. He goes home—home to that cottage of which a poet would say, "If there's peace to be found in the world, a heart that is humble might hope for it here." He tells the children, and tells their mother, that one of them is to go to the workhouse, "there ben't enough of bread for them all at home." " One says," (I quote his own words to me,) " Oh, father, don't

send me ;" and another says, " Oh, father, don't send me ;" and
their mother says, " I be sure any one of them will break their
heart if they go." The father says, " But what be us to do ?
we be without enough of bread now, and tatoes be all gone,
or about ; what be us to do?" Then the oldest girl says,
" Oh, don't send me, I be willing to eat less bread not to go,
and Billy says he be the same ; father, we will not cry for
bread when we be hungry no more, so be's us ben't sent to
the union." " Then," said the father to me, " what could I do
with them ?" (Speaking in tears.) " I could only take up the
little dears in my arms one after t'other, and kiss them and
say, No, my loves, father be 'termined to go without bread
himself rather than part with you." And he continued, " If I
ben't going without bread every day, I goes most days, and
works hard without enough." Many are the cases similar to
this man's in every one of the villages.

Another of those men doing the " Poetical" among the
odoriferous hay would tell us—he told me—that, during last
winter, out of his 7s. per week he paid 50s. for potatoes, purchasing them at great disadvantage in small quantities. He
says, had he been allowed 50s. worth of land to grow potatoes,
he would have had, though paying 10s. per acre for it more
than the farmers pay, three times as many potatoes, " or double
as many potatoes, with some bread corn," as he could buy for
50s. last winter. " But," said he, and " But," said several who
heard him, " they has more land than they knows what to do
with, more, some of them says, than they can get profit out of,
and yet they be afeared to let me have a lug." (perch.) Surely
those " merry bells of England" would not ring less joyously,
nor the church stand less secure, nor the cornfields be less luxuriant, nor the scene before us be less English—not even less
poetical—if those labourers were somewhat better fed and
better clad and lodged ? They grow rhubarb in their little gardens, and gooseberries. They would make puddings and tarts,
but they are without sugar. Cuba, and Porto Rico, and Brazil
offer them sugar cheap and good. " No," says some Gladstone,
in ostentatious godliness, "the sugar of these countries is grown
by slaves ; we must not encourage slavery."

But what are those men and women in this Wiltshire valley?
If they obey not the master that owns them, he may doom
them to starvation or shut them up in the workhouse—man
and wife, children and mother separated ? Talk not of slaves
and slave labour, serfs and serf labour. It is not yet three
weeks since a Wiltshire newspaper, commenting on the recent
corn-law debate in Parliament, repeated the absurd untruth
—repeated it in the face of a thousand facts and proofs to the

contrary—that the object of the corn-law repealers was to lower wages by lowering the price of food ; that newspaper reported this in the face of the well-known fact that, with cheapness of provisions, wages have risen, wherever there is not a great superabundance of population, as in Wiltshire ; and though knowing that in Wiltshire young men, working at 5s. per week, have been offered within these last two months 14s., 16s., and 18s. per week to go into the county of Durham and parts of Yorkshire as farm labourers, the labourers there having gone to other employments. And speaking of serf labour and of serfs, the same paper, on the same occasion, said that the dearness of labour in England and the cheapness of serf labour on the continent of Europe would, under a system of free-trade, make cultivation of land in England impossible. Yet what says the "Quarterly Review?" One English labourer will mow an acre of grass in the same time which six Russian serfs would take to mow it. In the valley of the Avon in Wilts, into which, from the downs, we have now, by supposition, been looking, grass is mown at the following rates :—1s. 6d. per acre for light field grass ; 2s. per acre for heavy field grass ; 2s. 6d. per acre for good meadows ; and 3s. per acre for the very heaviest meadows. The hay mown at 2s. per acre is, in ordinary years, worth L.7—this year it is worth from L.12 to L.14. Therefore, in ordinary years, the Englishman whose labour is said to be so dear gets 2s. out of the grass that is worth L.7 ; and out of this he maintains himself and family. Whereas, out of the produce of the same breadth of land, six Russian or Polish serfs individually, and with their families, have to be maintained out of the land, at the expense of the lord who owns both them and the land. Taking the different counties of England and comparing them, we find the highest paid labour to be the cheapest labour ; and so also when comparing the different countries of the world.

A JOURNEY IN SUSSEX.

THE rent of land in the Midhurst district of Sussex has not advanced much during the last thirty or forty years. Perhaps it was quite as high forty years ago as now, but of this I could get no distinct information. If a stranger inquires of a farmer what he pays for his land, and what his predecessor paid, he will not readily get an answer, neither here nor elsewhere. The farmers are apt to suspect that you have some design upon them—some intention of bidding for their farms over their heads. The insecurity of their tenures and the great competition for farms—the increasing number of far-

mers and the decreased number of farms—render them naturally jealous of persons who put questions to them about the
produce of the land and the rent they pay for it.

But though rent may have remained the same as thirty or
forty years ago—though it be even something an acre less—it is
in reality higher, taking the prices of corn as the standard.
And it is a matter of regret that farmers should be so unwilling
to see that, while each successive corn-law has fixed upon a
lower and a lower price—first 80s., then 70s., then 64s., then
56s. as the prices at which the farmer might afford to sell his
corn—the makers of those laws never proposed an adjustment
of rent to such prices. This one fact, or series of facts, should
alone make farmers question if there is any real friendship
evinced towards them by those who say they are " farmers'
friends."

It struck me as worthy of remark, that in this hilly part of
Sussex, as well as on the richer soils lying level between
the downs and the sea, the farmers were laying out all their
manure to dry in the fields. It was dry weather, high winds,
without a shower of rain, for three weeks together, and all
that time I saw the farm-yard dung carted out, and laid in
little heaps ; and fields which were dotted with these heaps
when I went first into the county still retained them when I
left, excepting in some cases where the dung had been spread
out, as if to dry more effectually.

What a curious thing it is that the ammonia brought from
the coast of Africa in the guano should be so carefully preserved, so eagerly sought after, so dearly paid for, and that
the identical same substance, the ammonia of the stable-
yard, should be given to the withering winds and the scorching sun.

Mr Brown (Lord Egmont's steward) has said that nothing
will teach tenants but difficulties—nothing will stir them up
to good farming but distress. I do not believe Mr Brown.
A tenant will farm better if he can pay his rent easily than if
he has a hard struggle to pay it. But to me it would be
amazing if they farmed well when they are liable to be ordered
to leave their farms at any time a landlord bids them, liable
to be told what men they shall employ and what not, as is
the case now. ————

THE GAME AND THE GAMEKEEPERS.

I went through Cowdray Park one day, and walked to Petworth, six miles from Midhurst. Before I had gone many
hundred yards beyond the park, the bottoms of the fences on
each side of the road shewed that rabbits and hares were
frequent visitors to the fields within the hedges. Over a

space of road not quite two miles and a half I counted between
five and six hundred *runs* into and out of the different fields.
While counting them I met a farmer who owns some fields
and rents a farm close by. He told me that from the fields
he owned he had not this year got more barley than would
pay seed, labour, and poor-rates ; had he been obliged to pay
rent for that land he said he must have paid it entirely out of
his capital, or have been distrained upon. I remarked to him
that, the land being his own, he was surely at liberty to kill
the rabbits upon it. He replied that he was ; but it mattered
little what he did, when his neighbours on each side of him bred
the rabbits which came to him to be fed. " But," said he,
" they be getting pretty well sick on't." And he went on to
prove to me that rabbits and hares, though let at a good rent
to gentlemen who shoot them, or though sold in the market
by those who feed them, are not profitable : they eat a great
deal ; but they destroy—he thought he could prove it to any
one's satisfaction—twice as much as they eat. He told me,
and so did some other farmers, that Colonel Wyndham of
Petworth did not do them so much harm as a preserver of
game. He turned his attention more to foxes. They said
the colonel took most interest in breeding, and then hunting
and killing foxes ; and that where foxes were numerous the
rabbits and hares would be kept within bounds.

It was to the north of this road to Petworth, about three
miles from where I then stood, that some of the Cowdray tenants were obliged to kindle fires around their turnip-fields last
year to frighten off the hares. One of these tenants alleges
that he suffered damage from the game last year to the amount
of L.70. The size of his farm I could not ascertain precisely,
but it is not above 200 acres. This year he alleges a loss of
L.20 in one field. He has had it valued, and the valuers give
that sum as the amount of damage done. The gentleman who
rents the game on this part of the estate from Lord Egmont
has offered L.6 for the damage. The tenant had refused to
take it ; but he had no remedy save at great expense, and then
it was doubtful if he would succeed in recovering higher da-
mages. He was, however, leaving his farm. And I was informed of several others who had been told that they were at
liberty to go if they did not like their bargains. The renter
of the game, and not the landlord, employs the gamekeepers
in these outlying districts. It is the business of these gamekeepers to have as much game for their masters as they possibly can ; hence they and the farmers are not on the best of
terms.

On the road between Cowdray Park and Petworth, where

there were so many *runs* through the fences, I observed that
almost every field had a gate formed of upright spars of wood
nailed to the cross bars.   These spars were about two inches
apart, and were, when entire, a sufficient barrier to the rabits,
but every one of the gates had one or more of these spars
broken away at the bottom.   I asked the reason why, and was
told that the gamekeepers had broken them to let the rabbits
and hares get more freely into and out of the turnip fields.
There being so many patches of common, so many thickets of
furze, and so many coppices in the neighbourhood, the farmers
were obliged to resort to many schemes to defend themselves
from the game; but the keepers generally took the part of
the game and of its owners against the farmer.

WHAT IS MACHINERY?

Petworth is a small town, belonging to the Wyndham
estate, containing, with its parish, 3364 inhabitants. Its streets
are narrow, intricate, and indifferently paved, but its situation
is lovely, on the rising bosom of a beautiful country.   Close
behind it, and looking over its head, is the park and residence
of Colonel Wyndham, both of them extensive, pleasant, and
fit to be inhabited by the noblest of the land.

The only thing that struck me at Petworth as noticeable,
after looking at the handsome church, with a spire rarely
equalled in elegance, was the House of Correction, and not the
house itself so much as a board stuck up against the wall,
painted and lettered.   It set forth that a variety of articles
could be bought at the house, the work of the prisoners, such
as horse-clothes, girths, sacking, canvas, and other textile fabrics of a similar kind; and persons visiting Petworth were
recommended to buy these in preference to what could be
bought elsewhere, these being said to be *all woven by hand,
and superior to anything made by machinery*.   How long the
woodcutters and farming men, who get lodgings in the house
for poaching and pilfering, take to learn to make goods in this
superior style I could not ascertain; but they must get long
sentences if they learn to be such very superior weavers; and
must be very extraordinary criminals indeed if they can make
such articles without *machinery*, with bare teeth and nails.

Rents vary from 15s. to 30s. but 30s. including taxes, is a
common rent for the average quality of land. Upon this barley
is a more frequent crop than wheat; but there is fine wheat
land in the lower grounds lying between the sandy heaths behind
us and the chalky downs four miles in front of us.   Some of
that land is as high as L.2; and I have heard of some which,
including rates, was little short of L.3 per acre; but this is

an exception. Wages were commonly 9s. a-week on the farms ; for every man that got 10s. a-week there was a man only getting 8s., taking all the estate into estimate, and a great many men were not employed at all.

HEYSHOT PARISH—BIRTHPLACE OF RICHARD COBDEN.

I went one day out of Midhurst in another direction, namely, to the south, whereas Petworth lay in the direction of east or north-east.

The sand hills, covered with heath, and in parts planted with scrubby trees, were more frequent on this side, and extended almost to the very bottom of the downs, interrupting that range of clayey soils which elsewhere bordered the base of the chalky ridge ; and yet, amid these sandy heaths, there were spots of high fertility and great beauty. Here, again, I found the noble oak tree strong and healthy, enjoying himself on such soils as he would die upon in the north. Again I found the rabbit warrens and the game preserves on and under these sandy heaths ; and again, wherever there was a farm-field, devastating inroads were made upon it by the game. Wherever there was a cottager's garden, complaints of the same kind were made.

At the distance of about two miles from Midhurst I descended from the heath and entered a narrow green lane, in which was a waggon track, hedged on each side by thriving thorns overhung with brambles, the brambles loaded with berries black and ripe. I came to a gate where a footpath led over a stile into the inside of a field, still going the same direction as the waggon track upon which I stood, but keeping the bank above, while the waggon track went down a cutting between the high banks of soft sandy rock, getting deeper and deeper as it went.

I continued in this lower way ; found a little spring of clear water, which trickled in the wheel track, and went by its side until a level was reached, where it spread itself and made a mire across all the road knee-deep and more. From this it was necessary to climb to the bank, where the wisdom of the path that kept itself high and dry was demonstrated. But this soon descended to the level of the marshy road, only it did not wet itself. There was a brook, which at a short distance higher up drove a flour-mill, and over this brook the path crossed by a small wooden bridge ; then it left the ravine in which the brook ran, and went direct forward to the south, having high ground thickly wooded on the left, and ground not quite so high, yet quite as thickly wooded, on the right.

This wood on the right soon ceased ; and where it left off a

26

garden and orchard and house occupied its place, and beyond these one or more farm fields were indistinctly seen.

The path was still in the hollow, but the hollow widened, and there was an acre or two of a grassy green. In the centre of this green stood a waggon-shed, and at the waggon-shed I stood for some minutes, considering whether I would turn off and go up to the house. I knew nobody lived there but working people ; but, for some cause or other which I cannot account for, I feel always a diffidence, as if doing something wrong, when going to a working man's house unbidden and without business that particularly and immediately concerns him. I have heard it complained that those who are in the habit of visiting the houses of the poor do so with an air of freedom that is highly offensive ; and I believe there are some such people ; but, so far from everybody behaving in that way, I have often stood near a labourer's cottage, or have walked past it and back again, and past it once more, all the time as if looking at something else, before I could muster sufficient assurance to go in. When a man is met in a field at work or on the road breaking stones, it is easy to talk to him. The hardness of the stones he is breaking is an introduction immediately to all you want to know. You remark that they are either very hard, or rather too soft for road metal, and he, ten to one, answers that "they be too hard to make a living from ; too hard to get enough of bread out of for a family." The information of the wages he earns, the number of his children, and the kind of food he can afford to eat, follow this as naturally and as easily as you can desire.

So also, when in the cottage where there is a family of children, they retreat from a stranger and get behind their mother, or stand up in a corner. But a few pence and kind words never fail to bring them out and elicit their names, ages, and so forth. I never addressed them thus with any other design than to make them feel at ease, and to gratify a natural feeling of my own which takes delight in their friendship ; but I would advise those whose sole object is to obtain information from the mother not to overlook the children. In a great majority of cases the wives of farm-labourers introduce the subject of their incomings and outgoings, which I am unwilling to speak of first, because I am speaking to a child whose toes are out of its shoes, whose pinafore is torn, or whose clothing is otherwise scanty and much worn ; and, unhappily, we may go over many miles of country, and across some entire counties, and not alight on a family where this is not the condition of the children's clothes. In these cases the mother very commonly makes a remark on the difficulty of getting clothes for them. Seeing you notice the children, she says, " Ah, poor dears, I had intended all summer to get some new things for them after harvest ; but now winter is coming on, and I have not got them yet." Then she says she owed some rent, and that had to be paid out of her husband's harvest wages. It grieved her much to see her children going barefooted ; but it was all they could do, even by selling the pig, which they should have kept to eat themselves, to pay the shoemaker for her husband's shoes, for he *must* have them to work in ; and to pay for some other small things which they could not possibly do without, unless they went naked altogether.

I have almost always found a conversation of this kind arise out of an attempt to be friendly with the children. Two things ever ready to a mother's thoughts—the love of her offspring and the struggle she maintains with the world to fill their little mouths and clothe their little backs—are at once appealed to and excited by merely speaking to them, if they be any way ragged. But the pleasure of holding converse with innocence, with those whose souls came latest from Heaven—the mere pleasure of making them feel that the world does not contain such very bad men, as that every stranger should be one come to steal little children from their mothers and carry them away in bags, as even kind mothers will foolishly frighten them to a belief of—the mere pleasure of receiving and giving gratification has always secured to me a free and easy conversation with their parents, as soon as I got seated at their fireside.

But I have never been able to overcome the first difficulty of an introduction to a poor man's house with whom I had no business to transact and from whom I had no invitation. On the occasion now under narration, I stood a short while by the cart-shed on the green, gathering as I best could as much confidence as would introduce me to those who inhabited the old farmhouse, which, with a small garden before and a larger garden behind, stood about a hundred yards to my right.

I went up to it, and entering that part which had once been a scullery or back kitchen, and where a labourer and his family of wife and five children now lived, I inquired if this was Dunford, and was answered in the affirmative. A few observations about the transition of farmhouses into the dwellings of labourers, and the amalgamation of one farm with another— the making a few large farms out of many small ones—soon brought out the fact that the farm to which this house belonged was still of the same size, or nearly, as when " the late Mr Cobden occupied it." The farm itself was now occupied by a farmer who had a flour-mill, and who lived at the mill. The family in the kitchen paid L.3 a-year for their rent; and each of the others paid L.4. The garden was divided about equally among them; and was little more, if more at all, than a quarter of an acre. They got turf to burn, and some wood; but never had any coals. The wages were 9s. a-week; but the farmers of the parish had just had a meeting, and had given their men notice that they would be reduced to 8s. a-week. One reason for this reduction was, that they had all got allotments of land, and they could thus live cheaper.

W. A. told me, and on a subsequent day shewed me, that his allotment was at best of little value to him, and that this year it had been a loss. In the first place, it was a light sandy soil; next, it was three quarters of a mile from his house, and the nearest road by which he could convey manure to it was two miles; worst of all, it was part of a small field situated with plantations full of game on three sides of it, and a heath on which the game was also preserved on the fourth side of it. Everything which he sowed or planted upon it was eaten up by the game, save his potatoes, and they were also destroyed, less or more. I myself counted sixty and odd rabbit holes, mostly made by young rabbits learning to excavate, as young rabbits do, among the potatoes. He had sown peas, expecting a few dinners of green ones with a bit of bacon in the summer; but he only had in all about a gallon, where he should have had at least a bushel. This was entirely the result of the game. He had tried both last year and this to get some turnips and greens for the winter; every blade went to the rabbits. All his neighbours were in the same predicament, less or more. This land was rented from Colonel Wyndham of Petworth, and the game was his game.

But W. A. was rather worse conditioned this year than any of the others. The neighbouring farmer turned out his hogs into the wood to eat the acorns, and the hogs had got into the allotments; and W. A.'s quarter of an acre being the first met with, they had employed themselves a whole half day rooting up his potatoes with their snouts, and eating them.

He was not better situated with the hogs than with the game; there was no redress for the damage done by either of them. All he could do was to give up his allotment, and that he was about to do; for he said it was a hard thing that it should be no profit to him, and that wages should be falling a shilling a-week because it was said that the labourers could live cheaper having allotments.

The difficulty of getting manure to it operated in a twofold degree. It had been the custom for the farmers to cart home the turf for fuel to the labourers on condition of getting

the ashes and the dunghills in return. If W. A.'s dunghill
were taken to his allotment, it would not only cost the hire of
a cart to take it round two miles of road, but he would have
to pay for getting his turf carried home.

This turf is very inferior : the vegetable substance is exceedingly thin. The soil is nearly all sand, so that there is
only a blaze of dry heath, and then the fire is nothing but
black sand. Where there is a thick vegetable mould comprising the turf it is excellent fuel ; but this is not the case in
this part of Sussex.

W. A.'s wife told me that were it not for the potatoes they
would die in the winter. "But, sir," said she, "how it hurts
the constitution of a man to work hard on potatoes, and
nothing else but a bit of dry bread." And then she told
me that, on an average, there were four days of the week that
they had nothing more than potatoes and dry bread. They
said nothing evil of their master, far from it ; he was as good
as the best of them ; but this was to what they were reduced
in common with all other labourers whose families numbered
the same as theirs. W. A.'s mother lived with them, and she
had two shillings and sixpence a-week from the parish.

While I stayed in the house I observed what gave me great
pain. His wife was preparing some little articles of baby
linen ; her slender stock, of even the merest fragmentary
rags, was collected, from which to patch up one or two of
those indispensable articles required for new-born babies.
All that "over-production" of clothing, which ill-informed
politicians sometimes complain of as coming from the factories,
afforded nothing to her. Cheap as the fabrics of the loom
now are, the cheapest of them were too dear for her. Her
family could not get bread enough. The amount of her purchases in tea and sugar in a week was a penny for the one and
a penny for the other. They had often to sit in the dark for
want of a candle, because the money must first go for bread.
Now there was another mouth coming to be filled, another
back to be clothed ; and though the world teems with human
food, and though those who keep up the corn-law to keep up
the prices of food in England, *all for the good of the labourers*,
proclaim that the looms are making too much cloth, there was
neither food nor clothing in waiting for the expected little
stranger. At best, some of the veriest fragments of rags,
more than worn out, were all that awaited it ; and for food it
would have to compete with those who had not now enough.

A little boy in this family, twelve years old, sometimes got
a job to do. He got threepence a-day, and had been some
days picking potatoes, where he got fourpence a-day. He
sometimes drove the plough, for which he got threepence

a-day. The hours at plough were eight; but his real hours on the farm altogether being twelve each day, I mention this only to remark that the earnings of a boy at such work for such hours will not supply him with the bread he could eat. I have a lively recollection of my keen appetite when I used to be in the fields for so many hours at this age.

HOW ALLOTMENTS OF LAND BECOME NECESSARY.

Heyshot is the name of the parish in which this farm is situated, and I proceeded to the village of Heyshot. The most remarkable circumstance which came to my knowledge there was the reduction of a class of small copyholders to pauperism by the united working of the reform act and the poor-law. The labouring men, who had homes and gardens and orchards of their own in the village, were obliged to part with them—all, save one or two, who have as yet withstood the means which are brought to bear against them. The farmers refuse to give work to such owners of houses and gardens save in harvest time, or when there may be a great scarcity of hands, which seldom happens. These owners of houses and gardens thus find themselves without work; they cannot get parish relief until they have sold their houses and have spent the money; so, to get work, they have been obliged, one after another, to sell their houses. The money was not difficult to spend. Colonel Wyndham has bought the houses, and has managed to turn them into parliamentary franchises, over which he has the complete control.

THE DUKE OF RICHMOND'S COUNTRY—1844.

Going down to Chichester, and from that to Bognor, I found the farms getting larger and the soil richer. Three, four, and five hundred acres were but moderate-sized farms there. It is a fine wheat soil, which seems to be fallowed once in every rotation of crops. The want of labour upon this land is very striking to a stranger, such as I was, the more so as there is a large union workhouse close by the Duke's estate, full of people, most of whom are able and willing to work.

I was told between Chichester and Bognor what is the reason that the farmers in that part are making so many complaints. I do not give the reason as my own, but simply as that given by a gentleman resident there. "I shall tell you, sir, why it is. The farmers have been ruined because wheat was once L.40 a-load. Had it never been so dear, they would have been more prosperous now. They became gentlemen all at once; they paid high rents, and yet they could live like gentlemen; they got their blood-horses, their gigs,

their servants, and their greyhounds. Prices have come far
below L.40 a-load, but they cannot get down their rents.
And why? Because the present generation of them have
been bred to be gentlemen, and gentlemen they will be. And
what says the Duke of Richmond, who is landlord to so many
of them just here? Why, he says this:—'If my tenants can
cut such a dash as they do, with their gigs and silver-mounted
harness, and blood-horses to ride on, and greyhounds with
them when they ride, they cannot be in great distress; they
must be able to pay their rents. If I have a farm to let,
there are many of them all ready to offer for it. They offer a
high rent, why should I not take it?'"

This may be true. But the Duke should understand that
it is not the worth of the farm that makes them compete for
it: it is their own numbers; they must get farms or be
without the means of living. I am not one who would cavil
at their being gentlemen. Every man has the right to live the
life of a gentleman if he can do so honestly. The farmers
may not be able to live so well and so easily as they did when
wheat was L.40 a-load. But it is the rent-burden that wants
reduction. It is the delusion of the corn-law which wants
removal—the delusion that has led them to bid high rents in
the expectancy of high prices, which high prices cannot be
maintained but by the high prosperity of the consumers
of food.

The rents are about L.2 in this district; but the poor-rates
are heavy. The gentleman with whom I talked had no doubt
but one-half of the whole labouring population would have to
seek relief at the workhouse this winter. He remembered since
there used to be seven and eight men employed on each 100
acres, that was when farms were smaller. Now the highest
number was five to the 100 acres; and that number only on
a very few farms.

I may remark, however, that the coast of Sussex was a
great smuggling coast once, and the farm-labourers, over
many miles inland, used to be in the pay of the smugglers; so
that when a seizure was about to be made, in conveying con-
traband goods inwards, the labourers were ready on an alarm
to turn out, with pitchforks or more deadly weapons, and help
the smugglers. This was part of their employment.

I saw on the wall of a barn, which was near the road, two
miles from Chichester, a board nailed up with this warning on
it—" Man-traps and spring-guns set on every part of these
premises." On inquiring why this should be put up—
knowing, as I did, that no one was allowed to set " man-traps
and spring-guns"—I was answered that everybody did not

know that, and that there was no keeping corn from the labourers now-a-days, neither in the barns nor in the stacks. In reply to a question it was added that, in the first place, the morals of the population had not recovered the deterioration undergone in the days of smuggling; and, in the second place, there was neither work enough, nor wages to get food enough when there was work; and that hunger drove men to steal corn. One who had stolen some wheat at that place had been taken to prison, and had committed suicide, so desperate was his sense of misery.

On this farm of 300 acres the number of hands employed was five men and two boys. Some of the men were getting ten shillings a-week, but were afraid of a reduction. They had to pay two shillings a-week of cottage rent, and there was only a very small garden to the cottages.

I found it customary in some parishes to have the men who sought parish relief at work upon the roads. For instance, at Easebourne, near Midhurst, there were twenty of them working one week and lying out of work one week alternately, at the wages of nine shillings a fortnight. Most of these had large families; all of them were married. Some of them had allotments of land, and it was only by having these allotments that they could exist on four shillings and sixpence a-week. Thus the allotments, though good in themselves, if allied with full wages, are made instrumental to a depreciation of wages. In short, they are in this case made to reduce wages and to reduce the poor-rates at the same time. The number of persons who are in the workhouse at Easebourne is great for such a population, even though the married labourers be thus disposed of upon the roads.

It is certainly a curious question to inquire how such a population as this is to support that *home market* which the manufacturers are so often told is their best market, and the only one they should seek to sell in.

POOLE IN DORSETSHIRE IN 1843.

LEAVING Wimborne once more, I proceeded towards Poole, by a road which, for the first four or five miles, turned neither right nor left, but which, skirted on each side with rows of Scotch firs and miles of heath, joyless and hopeless as any Scotch waste, led dully on until a marshy fringe of the sea, stretching far inland, turned it aside. Another couple of miles brought me to Poole, which I found to be a town possessing the following characteristics :—

Between six and seven thousand inhabitants, with empty

houses for the accommodation of many more. Warehouses and workshops shut up, the unopened doors and shutters worn with weather, not with work. A spacious quay with water frontage deep and ample, and capable of being amplified to any extent. Ships of various tonnage, barques, brigs, schooners, smacks, sloops, and fishing boats laid up for want of trade ; the seamen idly lounging about, save those belonging to the only vessel that had a cargo on board, and they were raising from the hold and selling by retail half a ton of coals to a farmer, who, with his cart, was on the quay. The farmer had three or four bundles of straw for sale, and sought to have a customer in the landlady of the —— inn, close by, who said she could not afford to buy them at his price, and he said he would have his beer and bread and cheese in the house if she bought the straw ; if she did not, he must sell it somewhere else, and get his beer somewhere else, or take it home and go without beer, that he must, " for them be ticklish times."

Such was what I saw during half a day's wanderings in Poole, three or four hours of which time I spent upon that noble spacious quay, in which time I saw, and saw only, the shipmaster sell half a ton of coals, and this farmer, who told me he farmed 200 acres in Hampshire, try to sell his straw. I saw about a dozen ship-carpenters at work repairing an old vessel, and, on inquiry, learned that when that job was done they would probably be paid off; that, some years ago, there were several hundreds of them employed in Poole, and some of the finest vessels, of two and three, and four and five, hundred tons, launched there that ever navigated any sea. I found a cooper at work, doing a job at anything, as he said, to keep him in amusement, for he was not entirely dependent on work, though if he were he would not obtain it. He told me there were but five or six coopers in the town now half employed, while some years back there were above fifty with full employment.

The trade in Pool had once been the manufacture of sailcloth, rope, twine, nets, oilcloth, ship-building, wearing apparel, and the furnishing of all kinds of sea stores, as also extensive shipments of clay for potters' work. It was connected largely with the Newfoundland fisheries, and does yet a good deal of business, in the proper season, with the London fishmongers, chiefly in oysters ; but all these branches of trade have decayed, and, save the last named, are dead or dying. How long London may be able, as the head of this great empire, to open, and eat, and enjoy its oysters, when the outports, like palsied limbs, are decaying or decayed, is a question which time can only solve, though reason may conjecture ; but

already is Poole lying on the brink of its 20,000 acres of inland water helpless to relieve itself, hopeless of all relief unless
steps, speedy and well-directed, are taken to re-animate national commerce.   Unbroken stillness pervades it, and at first
sight, and upon first description, one might suppose it will have
the privilege of dying quietly; but if the ear is applied attentively, and for a time, the sounds of internal commotion will
be heard; uneasy sensations are following the days of ill-re-
gulated prosperity, as fevered dreams follow great excesses.
Men who were combined as a corporation to help each other
and each other's friends did so, regardless of all consequences
save immediate success.   Present enjoyment was succeeded by
ultimate adversity.   They quarrelled, and are now quarrelling,
about the spoil and the obligations to pay, and action at law
is succeeding action, and threats of disclosure have followed
threats, until all is disclosed, and the whole fabric of corporate
combination and confidence and mutual patronage is broken
up, with its secrets as openly revealed as is the vast breadth of
Poole harbour at high water; while the discordant members,
that were once bosom associates, are as unpleasantly fixed in
difficulties as are the unlucky pleasure parties who, abandoned
by the tide, make their way to shore through miles of Poole
harbour mud.

Save the bickerings of those defunct corporations, and the
unanimous grumble at the income tax, and the whisper which
occasionally conveys to the ear that Mr Such-a-one, so long
a Tory, and Mr Such-another, so long a Whig, are, now that
parties are not what they were, changing their opinions, and
are saying that nothing will save Poole but free-trade;" save
these sounds, nothing disturbs the repose of that trade-strick-
en town; and, save the last sound, nothing that the town
does for itself holds out a hope of redemption.

I received while there, from a gentleman who is a merchant
and magistrate, the following account of the shipments of potters' clay from the harbour:—

In the four years preceding the present, there were shipped 30,000 to 35,000 tons per annum, two-thirds of which went
to Liverpool for the Staffordshire potteries, employing about
350 vessels annually.   During the three months ending 28th
of February 1843, the amount shipped had been but half the
average of the three corresponding months of each preceding
year.   But not only had the quantity decreased; the freights
to Liverpool had decreased also from 13s. per ton in 1839 to
5s. 6d. and 5s. 9d. in 1843.   The decrease had been gradual;
12s. in 1840, 7s. 6d. in 1841, and 7s. in 1842.   One-half the
vessels only are now employed, and the wages paid to the

boatmen who bring the clay to the ships have been equal to L.1500 a-year; they are now reduced by one-half. The wages paid, and the demand for labour at the clay pits, were also much reduced, and the labourers were either in the workhouse swelling out the rates or were offering their labour to farmers at reduced wages.

About two days after receiving these statements I was in conversation with a labourer who worked for one of Mr Bankes' tenants near Studland. We talked of wages, the prices of food, the rent of cottages, the value of perquisites, and such like matters. The man told me that he had 7s. a-week, paid 1s. a-week for rent, and had no perquisite whatever, save the furze and turf that he might cut on the common, which, however, he could not cut himself, as he had not sufficient time, and which he could not have conveyed home when it was cut without paying for. He added that things were seeming every year to be getting worse and worse. He had once been employed at the clay pits, and received there 12s. and 14s. a-week, but now work could not be had at the pit for many of the men, no matter what wages they might offer to work for.

In a subsequent part of our conversation, he told me that some of the anti-corn-law tracts had been given to him to read. They had been sent from Swanage; but he was told it was all no good; that the tracts were not fit for Christians to read; that they were full of infidelity and treason; and could have no effect on the price of bread and the amount of wages, but to bring down both; and that he had been told so by those who knew more about those things than himself. On requesting him to say who were the parties that knew more about those things than himself, I found that they were a clergyman on one side and the farmer for whom the man worked on the other. The one had frightened him about infidelity and irreligion, and the eternal consequences of reading anything therewith connected; and the other had frightened him with a loss of employment, until, between both, the obnoxious tracts were resigned to be given to the flames, like the most, if not all, of those distributed in that parish. I called to the man's recollection what he had said about the clay pits, and told him that wages were reduced there and workmen thrown idle because there was so much less clay shipped from Poole than formerly, because there was a stagnation of trade in the potteries; that there was a stagnation of trade in the potteries because some of the countries to which we had sent our earthenware now refused to take it, because we did not take corn in return; that at home, owing to all branches of trade being so bad and people so poor, earthenware when broken was not replaced by new supplies, and thus the demand for the manufactures of Staffordshire had fallen off; and further, that if he had read the tracts which had been taken from him to be burned, he would have found that a demand for potters' ware would have made a demand for clay, a demand for clay would have made a demand for men to dig it, and wheel it, and boat it, and ship it; that a demand for these would have raised wages, that a rise in wages would have enabled him and his family to live more comfortably; while living more comfortably they could have devoted more time and attention to religion and all its duties. To which the man replied, that he, for his part, could not read; but if he had known that there was nothing against religion in the tracts, but so much good information about wages, he would have kept them, and would have got some one to read them to him; "some of the coastguard men, perhaps, for they could all read," he added.

The Newfoundland fisheries have been of great importance to Poole. I saw a curious specimen of free-trade while in that town. A trader had received from Newfoundland a consignment of salted cod. The payment was to be a shipment of goods, partly made of clothes and partly of grave-stones. The grave-stones were in process of manufacture, the letter of advice specified the length and breadth and thickness of the stones, and gave the names, ages, dates, and so on, of the parties to be commemorated; with the addition, that all of them must have four or more lines of religious verse at the bottom, the verses to be made in Poole. "You see," said the trader, "what we can give in exchange for human food, when we are allowed to bring it in. The Newfoundlanders would go without tomb-stones were we not to take their cod, for they have nothing else to give us; but as we are allowed to import their cod-fish, we can give our stone-cutters a job; perhaps if we were allowed to take corn in exchange, we would supply some other part of the world with grave-stones; at all events, we would supply some other portions of our workpeople with work."

Leaving Poole, I proceeded across a barren country, eleven miles westward, to Wareham. Several shabby farms were passed; but three-fourths of the country, or more, was covered with brown heath. I joined company with the relieving officer of the Poole Union, who was travelling outwards to dispense pecuniary relief to the infirm paupers who were not able to attend personally at Poole. He was also engaged part of each week in visiting the houses of those who applied for parish relief, to see if they were as poor as they represented themselves to be. His account of their distress, of the unqualified poverty of the entire rural population, was most appalling. The stagnation of trade in Poole had thrown outwards the country people, or prevented them from coming in as usual. They could buy no clothes, and few of the necessaries of life, as sold by shopkeepers ; consequently shoemakers, tailors, grocers, shipmasters, and all others, required no apprentices. The youngsters were at home starving like their parents, and the poor-rates were continually on the increase. In many of the cottages there was almost no furniture ; in some of them absolutely none. The people, he told me, were driven by sheer hunger to thieve.

When I left this gentleman and got within the parliamentary boundaries of Wareham, which extend seven miles outward, I found, on inquiry, that I was on the estate of Mr Drax, M. P. for that borough. The hopelessly barren brown heath still continued on each side of the road, unbroken, save by a few rows or clumps of firs and the wooden boxes, four feet square and six feet high, which are scattered over this moorland, to constitute L.10 borough votes. Wareham returns one member to parliament; and the majority, which has elected Mr Drax, is thus made up by fiction. It is only needful to put a trifling article, such as a spade, or shovel, or hatchet, into the wooden box, to constitute occupancy as a workshop, and the person registered for it can vote. Thus an elector of Salford, or Rochdale, or Dundee, or Greenock, or any large town returning one member, and who, from a connection with, and interest in, commerce, would vote for a candidate who in his turn would vote for free-trade and commercial redemption to the port of Poole, is neutralized by the fiction of one of these fictitious votes of the wooden boxes.

LETTER FROM HAMPSHIRE OF NOV. 8, 1845.

While the question of opening the ports for the admission of more food is occupying the attention of all who are learned on such a subject, or who should be so, in London, the disease in the potatoes, their actual dissolution into nothing but rottenness, is occupying the attention of those in Hampshire who know little about port opening and little of the potato disease, save that they are likely to have much hunger during the ensuing winter and very few potatoes.

It has appeared to me very extraordinary that so much should be written of the potato disease in Ireland, and so little said of it by the newspapers, or apparently known by them, or cared to be known, in England. I speak of the west and south of England more especially, as the districts with which I am best acquainted. If the state of the potato-crop in Ireland is to decide the opening of the ports, surely the English potatoes are not to be overlooked, nor the English labourers, whose chief article of diet potatoes are. With bread high in price, and likely to rise, even a large supply of potatoes would not be enough this year. How much greater must the suffering be when to dearness of bread there is the companionship of scarcity of potatoes ! Bacon is now 9d. per lb. in Hampshire. No labourer can buy it ; and, what is worse, those who have hitherto fed pigs to have some bacon to sell to pay the shoemaker and the tailor, cannot keep their pigs—they have no potatoes. Those who raised good crops, and stored them away apparently sound, find the mystery of rottenness upon them, and the heavy misfortune of want upon themselves.

Notwithstanding the advance in the prices of all kinds of food, and the repeated assertions of master agriculturists, that wages rise and fall with the prices of food, no rise whatever is taking place in many parishes ; and even where there is a rise, it is not in any degree commensurate with the asserted rule.

In the parish of Wallop, Mr Lewis, a farmer, with a good character for fair dealing, and who, like most others, settles with his men once a month, told his men last Saturday, at the monthly settlement, that he would advance their wages from 8s. a-week, at which figure they have been paid for a long while past, to 9s. The men begged hard to have the sum set at 10s. ; but Mr Lewis said he could not promise it until he saw how his neighbours would do, some of whom objected to give the 9s. Thus, though bread has risen between 40 and 50 per cent. since last year, wages are only now rising at the rate of about a fourth of that rise in bread. Yet almost every shilling of these wages is expended in food ; and this at a time when the potato mystery is emptying every cottage of its potatoes.

Already the village shopkeepers and tradesmen feel it, and complain that the labourers are neither paying what they owe for clothes and groceries, nor are they making new purchases. They are rapidly sinking by the high price of bread to that state in which they would live almost exclusively on potatoes ; and this while they have no potatoes, or soon will have none, to live on.

LABOURERS AND LANDLORDS.

On Monday (20th of October 1845) I was present at Stockbridge, in Hampshire, when premiums were awarded to about 80 farm labourers, ranging from boys up to old men, and also to some women ; the premiums, 101 in number, being given for long service, for cleverly-executed work, for careful attention to live farm stock, for the best cottage gardening, for the best managed allotments of a quarter of an acre each, for the virtue of foresight, and for generosity to suffering relatives. The premiums varied from L.5 to L.3 for each individual.

I shall not at present halt to inquire into the moral worth of these sums of money. Whether their amount and manner of distribution may effect all the good which is expected of them is one question, and the good intentions of the givers is another. Of the goodness of the intentions I have no doubt. But some of the sentiments delivered by the gentleman who presided for the day are worthy of special notice. I speak of Charles Baring Wall, Esq., M. P. for the borough of Guildford, in agricultural Surry, and the owner of a large landed property in agricultural Hampshire, a gentleman whose liberality is not that of sentiment alone.

In addressing the men and boys, and the women, who received the premiums at the Town Hall, he said, amongst other things :—

"The secretary had stated the pleasing fact that L.100 had been distributed that day ; but this was not mentioned because it was a large sum, nor as being adequate to the value of the labourers around him. They all knew their value as labourers. They all knew what they owed to them for giving them the sweat of their brow—the aid of their toil ; and it would, he believed, gratify those who thus honourably fulfilled the duties of their station to know that they were sympathized and co-operated with by their employers."

And, in addressing the clergy, gentry, and farmers, after dinner, at the Grosvenor Hotel, he said :—

"That they did their duty fully, he did not pretend to say ; few did ; but still they were on the way, and he hoped each successive year would find them approximating more nearly to it. Since he knew the county, great improvements had taken place in it, and especially during the last seven years, through the instrumentality of that society. They were all liable to ride their favourite hobby over-much, and though he highly estimated the value of such an institution, he did not think that it could cure all the evils of our present social state. It was merely one of many agencies which must be employed, and in its own way had its use ; and it was gratifying to state, that it had not only the support of a majority of the landlords, but also of the tenantry of the district, and under their auspices it was doing much good. They might not be able to go at railway speed, but he hoped they were steady and sure. The more happy they made the people, the more they would promote their individual interests. They must give education to improve the mind ; and, at least, they ought to secure to

the work-people good full bellies and well clad backs.—(Cheers.)
This would give them a better return than any speculation
whatever ; it would join them all in bonds of union, rich and
poor together, and soften down the asperities which were but
too apt to grow out of the want of friendly intercourse between the different classes of society."

Mr Twynam, a tenant farmer, having given utterance to
similar sentiments, a gentleman present, Mr Busigny, complained that much of what was done and said at these meetings
was idle show. The labourers wanted better wages, better food,
and better cottages ; and, if the landlords were sincere in their
friendship for the labourer they would all dine together on such
an occasion as this, instead of at different inns, at different
hours, on different kinds of fare.

Mr Wall, in reference to these remarks, spoke to this
effect :—

" With respect to the cottages round Stockbridge, he did
not personally know their condition—not thoroughly ; but
those on his own estate were very different from what they had
been.   In some districts much difficulty existed in improving
the cottages, because they were held on lives, and the landowners had no power over them whatever. Still, even with
such property, a change for the better was in progress.   He
did not like standing up to his own class, merely because he
belonged to it, but he had on several occasions when these life-
hold properties fell in, and he had an opportunity of "doing
what he liked with his own," taken advantage of that circumstance to improve the cottages upon them.   With respect to
the introduction of the labourers into the room, he was sure there
was among those present no more objection to sit with a smock-
frock on each side than a frock-coat—the class to which he
(Mr Wall) belonged. But he questioned whether there were
not practical difficulties in the way. If all had been admitted
the room would have been too full even for Mr Busingy, and
as the labourers could not themselves have afforded it, he did
not know whether Mr B. would have liked to pay for the wine,
&c., which the smock-frocks liked as well as the frock-coats.
—(Laughter.)   He had considered the subject, and had been
led to the conclusion that it was inadvisable. The workpeople
had dined at a more convenient hour, and had got away in
good time to their own homes. They enjoyed themselves more
among their own class ; they did not injure themselves by
spending above their means, and it would not be for the comfort or convenience of either one or the other class to drive
them forcibly together.   At the same time he repeated there
was no personal disinclination to dine with smock-frocks, and

if Mr Busigny would get up another society for the improvement of cottages, and a dinner at the Three Cups, he (Mr
Wall) would be happy, not to preside, but to take his seat at
the lower end of the table, and contribute to his utmost to aid
its objects."

I have given these quotations from Mr Wall's addresses for
two purposes. First, because they suggest some remarks on
a topic which has lately occupied some public attention. We
have read of the Messrs Chambers of Edinburgh holding
their annual soiree with their work-people, and enjoying—
masters, men, and invited guests—a social evening on perfect
equality. We have heard of the factory works of Oldham inviting their employers to a soiree; and, rising above mere social
equality, they (the workmen) have filled the position of hosts
to the masters. We have heard that the factory workers in
the employment of the Messrs Bright of Rochdale, stated
to be above 900 in number, were brought to Manchester in a special train the other day, as were also those of
Messrs Whittaker of Ashton-under-Lyne, 1200 in number, to
see the Free-Trade Bazaar, the day being given as a holiday,
and the expenses of transit to and from Manchester and the
admission to the Bazaar paid by the respective employers.
Other reports of holidays and kind approaches to occasional
equality of social life reach us from the regions of the factories.
We, who live at a distance, have heard the wings of the press
flapping over us, with poetry on them, mingled with the eloquent joy of Serjeant Talfourd at finding the hard-handed hard-
working men of Manchester taking boyhood's play, and boyhood's name to the play, of the " Saturday half-holiday." The
same press, on the same day, with the same wings; to
wit, supplements, double supplements, and additional supplements to the double, brought us from London—London having inhaled it as if by a breath from Manchester—Jerrold's
speech, with its simile, already illustrious, of the polar bear on
the polar ice, the bear and the ice drifting into lighter and
warmer latitudes; and the poor beast, used to darkness,
howling and roaring, *as if heaven and earth were coming together*
—fit type of the bears of human kind, who have loved darkness rather than light.

We have heard, too, of Leclair of Paris giving a hundred
workmen, and upwards, a share in the profits of his business,
on the principle and in the faith that he himself would have
higher profit because they would become better workers and
better men. All these things, indicating human progress, have
come upon us from the cities and from the marts of trade within a few weeks.

But in those few weeks we have also heard from Dorsetshire

27

that "an experiment" was made by George Bankes, Esq., M.P.
and his agricultural friends, to dine labourers and landowners
in the same room ; and farther, we have heard that the experiment was successful.   But again we have heard from other
quarters that it was a shabby thing to put the labourers at a
side table by themselves, and dismiss them as soon as they had
eaten their dinner and given "three cheers for the gentlemen."
Comparisons have been made between the sociality of the men
and masters of Dorset and the sociality of the men and masters
of Oldham in Lancashire.

Now I have never been inclined to admire the wisdom of
Mr George Bankes—but I think in this dinner experiment he
has not been fairly treated.   To compare the working men of
Oldham—who, many of them, in the experience of public meetings become public men, while in years they are little beyond
boys ; who all of them associate together through boyhood and
manhood in the direction of societies, assemblies, and delibera-
tive meetings—to compare them with the farm labourers, who
have no experience in public association (unless it be the experience of disaster, when Dorsetshire labourers associated, and
were dispersed by transportation,) to compare the factory
workers—who, being skilled in all the arts of managing their
masters by associative experience, and who at last, in friendship,
treat their masters to their hospitality—with the secluded and
excluded, the clodded and clayed, farming-men of Dorsetshire
is unfair.   But as you will see in my next letter, even landowners and land-labourers associate together, with a liberality and kindness on one side, and independence and enjoyment
on the other, not surpassed anywhere else by any other people.
I have, at least, seen one such assemblage ; and it is because I
have seen it that I have given the quotations in this letter from
Mr Wall's addresses at Stockbridge.

If any gentleman can contend at an agricultural dinner that
it is not desirable to mingle people together who do not desire
to be mingled, he can best *afford* to do so.   He asks to preserve the separate dinners, because he knows the parties on
each side prepared to dine are not prepared to meet.   But he
holds a festival with his own labourers and poorer neighbours,
because he and they are prepared to meet, and can enjoy the
meeting.

MR WALL'S FESTIVAL AT NORMAN COURT.

This occurred on Friday, the 17th of September.   I was at
that time attending the poor-law inquiry at the Andover workhouse.   Andover is eleven or twelve miles from Norman Court,
and ten miles from the village of Broughton.   That village is

four miles or thereabout from Norman Court. Hearing of the festival, I came across the country to see it. Not knowing anywhere else to go to, I took up my quarters at Broughton; and I wish I may never have worse; I should like to see all who can appreciate good accommodation as well quartered as I have been at the village inn there.

On the 16th, the day before the festival, the rain poured and the wind blew; cloud careered after cloud, and blast warred with blast. Still cooks cooked, carpenters hammered, tents were erected; and in the villages of Broughton on one side, and West Tytherley and West Dean on the other, preparations were going forward in boiling and roasting to supply the respective tents of the innkeepers in the park, only second in magnitude to the roasting and boiling at the squire's mansion in the park. But, large as they were, they were second to that; the cooking there was on a scale of great compass.

The reason why the innkeepers of the villages had tents in the park was, that more people were expected to come, and did come, than the mansion could hold; and because, on a former occasion, several thousands of strangers had been there more than provision had been made for, or were invited; and who, though admitted to the tables so long as anything remained on them, only displaced others who had been invited; all of them saying, if they had only been able to get something to buy to eat, the staying to see the sports and the grand fireworks at night would have been more agreeable.

This year Mr Wall issued tickets to all who had been invited to dine, amounting to about 1000, and better accommodation was therefore secured. The sports, consisting of a variety of healthful, pleasing, and harmless games, were open to every one who came, no matter of what rank, nor from whence.

The morning of the 17th dawned, and was fair and clear. For ten days and nights there had been rain and wind—sometimes more of the one than of the other, but always less or more of both. As already said, on the previous day was a storm. This morning was agreeably bright and fine. A few drops came on once or twice before the sun had risen high; but the sun himself, so pleasant upon the holiday-goers, seemed to say, as they said—

"What a shame! we ought to have no rain to-day." And then the rain said, "Well, then, I shall go somewhere else;" and it shrunk within its clouds, and they bundled themselves up, and mounted upon a high and dry wind, and rode away.

Having breakfasted at the Greyhound, or the Hare and Hound, or the Dogs—I am not sure which it is, but the traveller who likes a good breakfast, the freshest of watercresses, and eggs, and bread and butter, and coffee and cream, will not make any mistake, as it is " the house of the village." Having breakfasted, and read, while at breakfast, the printed rules of that day's vegetable, fruit, and flower-show, the competitors in which were all to be labourers living in cottages rented from Mr Wall, in Broughton, the two Tytherleys, (East and West,) for which show a liberal and comprehensive scale of premiums were awarded ; having breakfasted, and also read at breakfast the catalogue of the Norman Court Lending Library, which library consists of 500 or more volumes, provided at Mr Wall's expense, the only qualifications to obtain which is a desire to read and a request to be allowed to borrow a book, the books consisting of the best periodical and serial works of the day, and of the standard works in religious, moral, and scientific biographies, poetry, instructive tales, and so forth ; having also, when at breakfast, listened, as I have often done since, not only in Broughton, but in all the villages and districts around Norman Court, to the respectful, grateful, almost reverential remarks on Mr Wall, as a kind landlord and liberal helper of all who need a rich man's help—as an employer of many men, and a payer of good wages—as the protector, not only of the living, but of the dead—the restorer of gravestones of churchyards and of churches ; having breakfasted, read, and listened to all these things, I, with some other friends, drove off in a " trap" for Norman Court.

Up Broughton Hill, westward, we toiled, one or two getting out, that the horse might have less toil ; up Broughton Hill, a portion of the chalky ridge crossing the country, we went, and got to the top of it, and upon the old Roman road from Winchester to Salisbury, (Winton to Sarum,) locally called the " Devil's Walk," which road in part was altered and amended by the Socialists of Harmony Hall, who are now in difficulties with their property, difficulties which some venerable fathers and mothers of the villages say were to be expected to befall anybody who meddled with the " Devil's Walk ;" having surmounted Broughton Hill, and left the wide expanse of woodless farm fields behind, turning only round to look down upon Broughton in its nest of trees for a minute, and upon the three Wallops, in their bourne farther north, and upon " Lennard's Grave," (the cross roads which, so named, tell their own tale,) between us and the villages of the Wallops, we looked westward and southward into a country all different from that east and north of us. A succession of woodlands, now in hollows and now on heights ; now with open fields, and elsewhere with winding glades ; now humble and copse-like, and again lofty and majestic, lay before us and below us, over a distance of six miles, bounded by another bold range of chalky hills, resembling that which we had just come over.

By turns we went down and again up; to the left and to the right, and on forward, turning again and again. Elderly men and women were standing aside to let us pass in the narrow woodland roads, or setting down to rest themselves with their baskets of vegetables which they were carrying to the show. Boys with clean "smocks" on, or new jackets, were pushing on as fast as they had breath to Norman Court, and shouting as we passed; old and young, male and female, rich and poor—most of the rich, who had horses at home, walking as well as the poor, lest there might be no stabling for all the horses expected there; all these peopled the roads; and each gave the other joy of the fine day, as they journied onward.

To linger long enough to tell how the ripening filberts hung upon the bushes which bordered us in clusters; how the glittering wet in the morning sun gave freshness to the autumn leaves; how the dark woods towered aloft, and the stealthy rays of the sun, as if it crept into a solemn cathedral silently and softly to worship; to linger long enough to describe all these would be to leave neither space nor time for what is coming.

We arrived near the front of the mansion, commanding a magnificent view southward over woods, and meadows, and fields; dells, eminences, openings, thickets, and through noble park trees, amid which the carriage roads led off and lost themselves. On one side of the mansion next us, extending over a dozen acres or so backwards, and now on our right hand, was a green smooth sward embosomed in lofty lines of trees, these lines being but the front-rank men of deep tickets. Into this we turned, and drove to the tent of Mr Lane, from Broughton, which stood fronting downward and towards us.

On our right hand, at entering under the trees, was the sign of the Lion, Mr Beauchamp, from West Dean, and halfway up, in front of the trees, was the Black Horse, Mr Fowkes, from West Tytherley. Varieties of other smaller tents, with confectionary and exhibitions of natural curiosities, and such like, were in the intermediate spaces. But the grand attraction were two tents of Mr Wall's, on the left hand side, near the centre; one was for the show of vegetables, fruits, and flowers; and the other was a kind of store, at which Mr Wall himself presided, furnished with a variety of fancy and useful articles, to be given as prizes to those who might win them at such games as archery, for which there were six targets, with bows and arrows in abundance; such games also as cricket, and nearly all kinds of ball-playing, puff and dart, quoits, hurdle-racing, leaping, and so on.   There were generally such chances as twelve shots for a penny; the men attending to the targets, &c., receiving the pennies, and giving a ticket to the winners, who carried it to Mr Wall, and received prizes according to its amount.   If it was a two shillings and sixpence or three shillings ticket, there would be a silk handkerchief, and a knife perhaps, or a hat, or a waist-coat.   For the children there were swings and roundabouts; and ropes with seats on them were suspended between the venerable trees, that young people who wished to swing might swing there.

The vegetable and fruit show was exceedingly good, and would have done credit to many professional gardeners.   It certainly did credit to Mr Wall's cottagers, of whom about 100 were competitors.   The judges were Mr White, the gardener at Norman Court, and two other gentlemen, whose names I now forget.   The beautiful fuschias, and other flowering plants from the cottage windows, shewed favourably for the domestic neatness and taste.   So did the garden products tell for cottier industry.   But, if all dwellers in humble houses had as good dwellings and gardens, with as good a squire, and as good a steward between them and the squire, as they have, there would be more comfort and more industry exercised to obtain it throughout England than there now is.

As visitors arrived, some in carriages, some in vans, and some in holiday waggons, others in gigs and trap-carts, from distances varying from one to ten miles, those who were known had tickets given them by Mr Sergeant, the land-steward, to the dinner.   A yeoman cavalry band, in their uniform, mounted about and played music, which the woods re-echoed, or would have re-echoed, had there been less din of human voices and a lower breeze of wind.   There were several policemen of the county constabulary on the ground, but, as it was observed at the time, every man was his own constable; no mischief was done.

The chief dinner was spread in the court-yard of the mansion twice, from 250 to 300 hundred dining each time.   The great body of the people, however, dined in the tents on the green, having tickets which paid for their admission and their fare.   Each party dining in the court passed into the mansion, and went through the splendid suite of rooms on the ground-floor by way of exit.   On a former occasion, the house was left open to every person indiscriminately.   They did no wilful damage, but there being many thousands of them going in and out for a whole day, they did damage to elegant furni-

ture, whether intending it or not. On that occasion, a gentleman staying on a visit with Mr Wall had left his bedroom
door open, not expecting that any of the strangers would
penetrate there; also he left his money in sovereigns and his
jewellery lying open on his table. The staring wonderers,
who had never before been in such a house, went, hundred
after hundred, into that room, as well as into others; but
there was not there nor in the house a single act of theft
committed. Yet these people had the full complement of
poachers, petty thieves, and loose reputations among them;
persons who were honest against their inclination, because
they saw and felt they were trusted.

On the present occasion, Mr Wall sat down at one of the
tables, but did not preside; the presidency and several other
offices of honour devolved on some of the principal tenants
and the farm-steward. The domestic servants, from the
house-steward downward, waited on and served the visitors
with alacrity and kindness; as much so, indeed, as if the kind
spirit of their master was thoroughly infused into them.

On Mr Wall's health being given, he delivered a short
address, *thanking the people for coming to see him and dine
with him,* and hoping to see them again and again, and to see
a closer bond of friendship established between persons of all
ranks than there ever yet had been.

The sports upon the green went on. Every minute some
prize was won at one or other of the games. The floor of the
tent in which the vegetable show had been was boarded for
dancing, with a platform for the band. Accordingly there
was dancing. And, when night closed in, there were fire-
works; and these were on a scale of grandeur rarely excelled,
if ever excelled at all. Artists of first-rate ability were
brought from London to conduct their exhibition. Fire
balloons went off and away, and rockets went up and
shot off, and showered down brilliancies that illumined
the wondering country. While the multitudes gazed and
admired, devices in fire of all shades and colours, and of many
meanings, succeeded each other, rockets firing all the time,
with a magnificence that would have made Vauxhall clap
hands and shout. But there was little shouting here, and not
a hand was clapped. The excessive wonder at such prodigies done in fire constrained to silence. And the silence of
the human tongues was all the deeper, and the grandeur of
the fire-works all the greater, that the black shadows of the
trees started back, and struggled to be out of sight, each
behind his own tree, as if affrighted; while the lofty branches
showed themselves in the red glare and in the blue, as if the
giants of the forest stood with heads erect and hair on end.

A DAY AT TAMWORTH AND DRAYTON MANOR.

June 1844.

I SPENT a day lately in the neighbourhood of Drayton Manor, the seat of Sir Robert Peel, in Staffordshire. My visit related entirely to agriculture, as it did at Althorp Park, and had no reference to anything that might be seen and reported, and used for or against Sir Robert Peel as a member of the government or the head of a political party. I was one of those who hailed with pleasure the declaration which Sir Robert Peel made last year in favour of agricultural reformation ; and while some people professed to think that a Prime Minister might have been more appropriately employed than in talking to farmers about "leases," and "hares and rabbits," and "bulls," I thought otherwise. Believing, as I did, that much required to be done for agriculture—and in the soil of England lies a vast amount of undeveloped wealth—that much could be done if the owners of land would condescend to become men of business, and assist in the proper management of their own estates. I was filled with great hopes when I read Sir Robert Peel's speech to his tenantry, not only because it indicated his views as a landlord, but that he, being Prime Minister, and the most eminent man of many landlords, was likely to become an example to those who will follow but will not lead—to those who will not shrink from any task, however difficult, if the task be fashionable.

But if I had gone to Drayton loaded with prejudice against its distinguished owner, I could not have retained such prejudices many hours. For instance, after walking to the farm-yard and looking at two bulls—one of them a splendid animal, and I believe the same which Sir Robert promised to buy for the use of the tenantry—I went through the Park, passed the village of Drayton Basset, and got into conversation with the people whom I found at work on the farms belonging to the manor, beyond the immediate influence of the manorial steward, and I found almost all of these people speak readily and favourably of Sir Robert Peel, without any leading questions being put to them.

To one man, who was hoeing potatoes in his garden, beyond a thick lofty hedge that skirted the way-side, I spoke thus, after getting admittance by the little gate in front of the cottage :—

"You require rain, do you not? Do your potatoes grow at all in such scorching weather as this?"

"They hardly grow. Some do not grow at all, and them as do, wont grow much more if rain do not come. This is hard weather for the country; the pastures are gone everywhere, and the cattle and sheep have to be put in the meadows to keep them from starving; and then the meadows wont give no hay; and the potatoes, if rain should come, will strike down, those of them that have come any length, and potatoes never do no good that strike into the ground a second growth; yet, please God we have rain, things may come round yet. Wheat looks well, but barley don't; and cabbages make little way as yet; onions hardly shew themselves."

" You have a good garden here; how much is there of it, half an acre?"

" There or thereabout. I never heard it exactly said; but Sir Robert asked me just as you do if there was half an acre. That was when he came to take possession, after old Sir Robert died; and I said I thought there would be half an acre taking it all into account; taking in that corner where the hives stand, and that where the faggots are built on and the pigstye."

" The cottage and garden belong, then, to Sir Robert Peel?"

" Yes, I rent it of Sir Robert. I would not have such a garden from a farmer; at least not at the price I have it of Sir Robert; and, perhaps, not at any price. You see I am old now; I am turned seventy-one."

" You certainly don't look that age; I should not have supposed you were sixty."

" Every one says that. I have been very hearty, thank God, all my life, and until these rheumatics came on me I had nothing to hurt me; but I am crushed with the rheumatics that I cannot stand upright. I cannot put on or off my waistcoat without assistance, and I cannot lift my hand above my shoulders. But it is all the rheumatism. I do not know what I could have done, had it not been for this garden and the cheap rent. Sir Robert is very good to the like of me. He does not disturb us. The farmers would like to have the hedges stubbed up and the gardens thrown into the cornfields; but Sir Robert will not let that be done as long as we old people live, and he is very good in getting every family in Drayton a rood of land at a low rent. He does not do it as some gentlemen I hear of—he does not make the labourer's rood the dearest piece of land on the estate—he makes it the cheapest. You would see it down there beside the church, he lets them have good land at the price of worst land, and pays the rates; they have no rates to pay."

" Have you lived long here?"

" I lived here in Lord Weymouth's time, and then in

Squire Fisher's time, and then I saw old Sir Robert Peel get
the manor, and now I am under young Sir Robert. I have been
more than fifty years here : but I am not a native of this parish,
and they would have had me out of it only for Sir Robert, the
present Sir Robert, I mean."

" Who would have had you out ?"

" The principal men of the parish, the farmers and the born
natives, and I will tell you how. You see, when young Sir
Robert came and took possession of the estate, they had a
parish meeting at Drayton Basset, and Sir Robert Peel was
there, and it was proposed, because the rates were so high, that
every working man that was living in the parish and was not
born in it should be forced away. So after this had been
said, and was urged on Sir Robert, he said, ' Gentlemen, there
may be some justice in what you want me to do, if you have
nobody belonging to this parish living in other parishes. But
answer me that question first. Are all the natives of the
parish of Drayton Basset living in it ?' and they said no ;
there were many people living out of the parish who had been
born in it. ' Well,' says Sir Robert to them, 'you must lay your
account to have all them back again ; because if one parish
send all away but its own natives, another will do the same,
and those natives must come to their own parish. Do you not
see that in such a case you will have more people to provide
for than you have now ? Do you not see that all your natives
who have gone to settle at Tamworth, even it may be in Birmingham, or the Potteries, or London, will all be sent back to
you, besides your labourers who are working to farmers in other
parishes in this neighbourhood ? Before you ask me to assist
you in expelling every one from this parish not born in it, you
should tell me if you are ready to take all your own back.' But
never a word more did they say about it. They had never
looked at it in that way ; they only thought if they got the
like of me and my wife away, as we were growing old, that they
would save their rates. But Sir Robert Peel made them open
their eyes. He said every man that gets an honest living has
a right to get his living where he can."

" I think Sir Robert spoke good sense, but I would have
been surprised if he had spoken otherwise. I am surprised
that your natives of the parish should have been so silly as to
ask Sir Robert to do such a thing."

" It was well for me that Sir Robert spoke as he did, for
what could I have done to be sent away to my own parish
after being fifty years out of it ? He said to them, ' What does
it matter where a man goes to get his living if he gets it
honestly ?' and they had not a word to say after that. They

had tried before to get all the parish of one mind to press on Sir Robert to help them, but he said, ' What does it matter where a man gets a living if he gets it honestly ? ' "

" Sir Robert spoke good sense when he said that ; and I am glad to hear you and some other persons to whom I have spoken here speak so well of him as a considerate landlord."

" Aye, he said, ' What does it matter where a man gets his living if he gets it honestly ?' and they had not another word to say."

" What is your name ?"

" John Salt. I was seven years with one master, and all the rest of the time I have been here with another master. I never did no harm, so I don't care who knows my name. When I asked Sir Robert to let me have the house and the garden continued as it was in old Sir Robert's time, he said he did not know me, but if he found I was a man of good character he would not refuse me. I told him that I was not afraid of what any one could say of my character, and he asked them at the meeting at the church if I was a man of good character, and none of them had nothing to say against me. So he says, ' What does it matter where a man gets a living if he gets it honestly ? ' "

" But I think Sir Robert might have given you a better house ; it seems as if it would tumble to the ground ?"

" Stay now, stay, and I will tell you how that is. He said to me there was no objection to me continuing here, but there must be a new house built, and I said, I hope not, Sir Robert ; the old house, if it is repaired, will do all my time and my wife's time ; and he said, ' Are you really against having a new house built ?' and I said, ' Please you, Sir Robert, we have been so many years in the old one, and brought up all our family in it, we would just like you to let it stand !' ' Well,' he said, ' I will send the mason to look at it, and if he says it can be repaired it shall be done !' So, you see, that is the reason there is not a better house, and I did not want it ; because I saw that the time was coming when I would be too old to work ; and, though I dare say Sir Robert would not have looked ill upon me on that account, I thought that a fine new house and so good a garden might be taken from me if so be I could not pay for it, by some of them that have power at Drayton, and given to one that could pay for it. If Sir Robert were always here it might be different ; but it is not often we get a sight of him to make a complaint, if we have one to make."

" Do you make much honey ? You have several hives, I see."

" Only one of them has bees. When the rheumatics was

about to come on me, and keep me from working, the bees gave up, and went away we know not how."

" Do you mean that the bees left the hives because you were seized with the rheumatics ?"

" No, they left before the rheumatics came on. It was the year before last, and we noticed they were doing no good, and my wife said to me something will happen to us that is not good, for the bees is doing nothing this year, and, as sure as you are there and I am here, the rheumatics came on me and put me from working, and I well never work more. The bees have left us altogether, save that one hive, and it is not doing much ; it only does a little, to mean that I will be able, and nothing more, to do a little job, as you see, about the garden. I can only work for about an hour, and then I have to sit down and rest. I once thought this year that the hive would grow strong and come off, so as we would have two hives, and my wife said the rheumatics, if the bees did that, would perhaps abate, and let me do a light job in the summer months and earn something. But I said I doubted it would not mean more than we would get a load of faggots for firing from Sir Robert or the steward."

" Well, I hope the bees will not disappoint you even in that small expectation. How do you live at all ? Have you any parish relief ?"

"We have 2s. 6d. a piece, 5s. a-week for the two. I brought up a family and never asked a penny from the parish, and never got one, and was always against asking for it, and never did, so long as I could go to work. But I was obliged at last to go to the parish ; if it was not for the garden and the cheap rent, we could not do at all, we must go into the workhouse, and God keep us from that. We would not like to leave this house and our garden, after being fifty years in it and bringing up our family in it."

" I think you may keep your mind at ease on that point. Sir Robert will not interfere with you."

"No, I know he wont ; I understood from him that we would not be disturbed as long as we lived, and the old house, at the time when he prevented me from being sent out of the parish."

" Well, that was good of him ; and yet it was only the bare duty of a rich man towards the poor ; but it was more than some rich men think fit to do."

" Aye, he said, ' What does it matter where a man gets a living if he gets it honestly ?' "

I heard Sir Robert Peel complained of in respect of the high rents of the farms, but I take leave to say boldly, that the Drayton estate is not higher rented than might be paid comfortably. I have no doubt but the tenants have difficulties, especially with such a poor population as that of Fazley and Tamworth to buy their produce; but upon such good land the Drayton rents, to men of enterprise and capital, would not be heavy. What they want is capital and security. I no not mean security against Sir Robert Peel, because if he had a good tenant, I am sure he would not seek to part with him; but the security of a lease is a first requisite to the obtainment of capital. Who will give a tenant-at-will a loan of money to lay out on land which will not return it in less than from eight to twelve years? Some of Sir Robert's tenants are very persevering men, so far as tearing at the land and the dungheap, and sweating with their coats off go. I saw one, and was told by a neighbour that there never was a convict worked as that farmer worked himself. But I do not call that enterprise. It is well for a farmer to attend to his farm, but it is not his own personal labour that will enrich its soil and enlarge its crops. I do not know if any of them have availed themselves of Sir Robert's permission of last year, to apply for leases; but I am sure that they can never get over the present complaint of rents being too high until they have leases. Better trade at Fazley and Tamworth would be of very great importance to them; for wages are not only very low there, but a larger proportion of the population is at the present time unemployed. Hence everything the farmer has to sell goes at disadvantage, unless it goes to Birmingham, seventeen miles distant.

At a subsequent period, November 1846, business led me to the town of Tamworth, and inclination took me from Tamworth to the vicinity of Drayton Manor. I found an extensive system of farm drainage in operation, the capital being furnished by Sir Robert Peel and charged at the rate of four per cent. so I was told, upon the occupying tenants. This arrangement cannot fail to be beneficial to the estate and to the occupiers. If tanks for the reception of liquid manures are provided, and other appurtenances of scientific farming, and charged to the tenants at the same rate, they will find that augmentation of rent in reality a gift of capital and profit, while the future value of the estate will rise in a ratio bearing no calculable proportion to four per cent. In short, the soil of England offers the best investment for money, which is expected to bring in a profit, if there be security, and there cannot be better security for a landlord than his own estate.

At Tamworth I visited the reading-room, library, and

museum, instituted by Sir Robert Peel, and found about 2000 volumes, which had been well selected, and seemed to be well used. Those marked in the catalogue as presents from Sir Robert were chiefly works of instruction, and gave evidence of the inherent liberality and justice of the great politician; for several of them were written by authors who had been politically opposed to him.

EXTRACT FROM A LETTER WRITTEN IN NOVEMBER 1846.

Journeying into the country from Tamworth, I found the wages of farm labourers to be 12s. a-week, some only 10s. Sir Robert Peel pays 12s. and 14s.

Being desirous of seeing Drayton Manor, I returned to Fazley by the same way which I had travelled in the dusk with Jonathan. The sun was now shining in a sky of cloudless blue; which, reflected on the streams and waterfalls, and sheets of water which glimmered only in gaslight the night before, made everything gay and pleasing to the eye. The foliage of the woods, yellow, brown, red, and purple, seemed to linger against the law of nature, and suffer itself to be made more intensely yellow, and red, and purple, as if the law of nature had been applied with double force to get it off and it would not go. This foliage, dotted with the heavy green of the pines, and stretched in masses to be measured only by half-miles and miles, reflected the brilliant sun and the blue sky with a warmth of colour that glowed upon the eyes and entered the bodies at the eyes, in search of souls willing to be pleased, willing to be warmed and made joyous. You might have thought that the summer of the earth and the sun of the sky had parted as was their wont in November, but that he, as was not his wont, had returned and called her back for one other farewell, and that, from the chambers of her winter rest, she came forth to meet him, blushing red that he had called her only to embrace and part again.

With my face turned to the north I kept those beautiful woods on my left hand for the distance of a mile, but did not come to the end of them. On my right hand I passed Bonehill bleach-works, embowered in trees, with a lake in front— the bleaching and printing establishment originated by the elder Sir Robert Peel, now owned by one of the younger sons, and leased to Mr Buxton, a bleacher. Beneath my feet was a broad level roadway, with occasional cottages and cottage-gardens on its sides; overhead there were now and again beech trees, with the wind stealthily fingering, as it were, the leaves which the branches had retained so long, and, pulling them off quietly, dropping them one by one on the road. I came to a gate which was not barred, and which permitted my entrance by a waggon-track between two farm-fields. The field on the right had a crop of Swedish turnips of good quality on it, a woman cutting the tops and roots of some of them, and a man filling a cart with those she had topped and rooted while he was away with the last load. The field on the left had been recently sown with wheat; had pieces of faggot stuck up in different parts of it to keep poachers with nets from drawing it for pheasants; had in one corner, just over the hedge, a boy, in a smock-frock and rounded white hat, whose duty it was to keep rooks, pheasants, or any other natural enemies of seed-wheat out of the field. A girl, younger than himself, kept him company, and both were seated by a fire of tree-tops and tree-roots, which were easily found in the adjoining wood.

Going forward, my face being now west, I came suddenly upon a cock pheasant, and then another, and another, all of them proclaiming in their noisy flight my intrusion. I was not looking for them, but only wanted to see the farm-fields, if any, within the belt of woodland which I had been outside of for so long a distance. I saw the fields, and judged from them, as from the others, that more skill and good taste were devoted to the farming of that land, it being Sir Robert Peel's domestic farm, than is commonly exhibited in that part of Staffordshire. At half a mile's distance, on my left, standing south, or south-west from where I stood, was Drayton Manor-house, a mansion built within those fourteen years, and enlarged within the last three years. Its numerous chimneys and turrets, rising beyond detached pieces of young plantation, and seen between detached trees of venerable growth, the grassy pastures with cattle and sheep upon them intervening, looked as if the whole had been made for a picture as well a for a habitation.

Returning by the way I came, and entering by a road which Sir Robert Peel allows to be public, though it publishes to the traveller all the private places about the Manor, save perhaps the interior of the garden and of the mansion, I came up to a farm-yard near to which were some thatched ricks of corn and hay. The trimness of thatching and goodly shape of the ricks arrested my progress for a few minutes. Looking beyond them, I saw that all the buildings were disposed so as to look elegant as well as to be useful. I came to where two men were cutting trusses of hay from an old rick, not one of those already seen, and as a third person standing beside them seemed to be giving directions about that or other work, I addressed myself to him, thinking he was probably the farm bailiff. I was not mistaken. He answered my request to see the interior of the farm-yard by opening a gate and bidding me follow him. We paid our respects first to a very large sow too lazy to rise, and next to six or eight hogs of another breed twelve months old and very fat. As their troughs contained some of the meal and grains on which they were fed, and they did not deem it desirable to rise and eat more of it, there was no reason to expect that any invitation of ours would make them stir ; so Mr Wilson went in amongst them and stirred them up that I might see their fat bodies, small legs, and short snouts. They rose very unwillingly, and turned their faces to me, which faces had little holes in them, in which little holes eyes, lying deep down among fat, were supposed to be. They sat grunting on their hind quarters with the fat little eye-holes turned up in my face. What they thought of me I cannot say. I thought they would have been better porkers and more profitable if they had not been so fat.

Mr Wilson, in answer to a question which I put, and which was suggested by his dialect, said I was mistaken, he was not a Scotchman ; he was a native of Cumberland ; and came to Sir Robert Peel four years ago from the estate of Sir James Graham. I asked him some questions about the farm-yard manures, and he shewed me how all the liquids were collected in a cistern, and conveyed to a place where a cart could be put in, and the liquid run into the cart to be conveyed into the fields ; a plan which seemed to be a good one.

We next paid a visit to a very large bull, in a house by himself. He was rather thin of flesh, but otherwise a fine animal of his kind. He was very quiet, and took no notice of us. Leaving him, we looked in upon another bull ; but Mr Wilson said it was necessary to keep the door well in hand, and only opened a little, for he was sulky and mischievous. He was a younger animal, but of a different breed from the other ; was in higher condition, and looked as if he would make good his reputation for mischief.

Leaving this department of the farm-yard we came to a place where some implements stood, and my attention being fixed on a plough of a construction not commonly seen in Staffordshire, the bailiff said Sir Robert Peel had got all his ploughs of that kind now, and so had Sir James Graham. I told him that the same kind of plough had been in use at my native place from a period long before I was born ; and that it was as like as could be, save in one or two minor details, that which I used to hold in the furrow, long before I had written, or even expected to write myself,

ONE WHO HAS WHISTLED AT THE PLOUGH.

INDEX

TO

THE WHISTLER AT- THE PLOUGH.